The Essential Guide to User Interface Design

An Introduction to GUI Design Principles and Techniques

Wilbert O. Galitz

QA
76.9
.U83
G33
1997

WILEY COMPUTER PUBLISHING

John Wiley & Sons, Inc.
New York • Chichester • Weinheim
Toronto • Singapore • Brisbane

Executive Publisher: Katherine Schowalter
Senior Editor: Bob Elliott
Managing Editor: Robert S. Aronds
Text Design & Composition: Publishers' Design and Production Services, Inc.

Designations used by companies to distinguish their products are often claimed as trademarks. In all instances where John Wiley & Sons, Inc., is aware of a claim, the product names appear in initial capital or ALL CAPITAL LETTERS. Readers, however, should contact the appropriate companies for more complete information regarding trademarks and registration.

This publication is designed to provide accurate and authoritative information in regard to the subject matter covered. It is sold with the understanding that the publisher is not engaged in rendering legal, accounting, or other professional service. If legal advice or other expert assistance is required, the services of a competent professional person should be sought.

Library of Congress Cataloging-in-Publication Data:

Galitz, Wilbert O.
    The essential guide to user interface design : an introduction to GUI design principles and techniques / Wilbert O. Galitz.
       p.   cm.
    Includes index.
    ISBN 0–471–15755–4 (pbk. : alk. paper)
    1. Graphical user interfaces (Computer systems) I. Title.
  QA76.9.U83G33   1996
005.7—dc20
                                        96–22908
                                           CIP

Printed in the United States of America
10   9   8   7   6   5   4

To my wife and business partner, Sharon, for her many years of love and support in our home and in our office.

To our children, Kevin, Karin Roepel, and Kim Watters, and to our grandchildren, Mitchell, Barry, and Deirdra Galitz, and Lauren and Scott Roepel. And to my parents, Wilbert W. and Elvey. I deeply regret that my father was no longer here to see and read any of my published books.

Contents

Preface

This book is about designing clear, easy to understand and use screens for a graphical system. Is good design important? It certainly is! Ask the users whose productivity improved 25–40% as a result of well-designed screens, or the company that saved $20,000 in operational costs simply by redesigning one window. (These studies are described in Chapter 1.)

What comprises good design? To be truly effective, good screen design requires an understanding of many things. Included are the characteristics of people: how we see, understand, and think. It also includes how information must be visually presented to enhance human acceptance and comprehension, and how eye and hand movements must flow to minimize the potential for fatigue and injury. Good design must also consider the capabilities and limitations of the hardware and software of the human-computer interface.

Will graphics automatically assure good design? The style guides now available from many software providers are believed to solve many of the screen design problems that have existed for years, including much more user-centered design and application consistency. That they cannot solve such problems is evidenced by their lack of depth in good design principles and today's focus on prototypes and usability testing. In reality, because of much greater design complexity confronting the system developer, the opportunities for *poor* design are also greatly increased.

What does this book do? This book addresses screen design from the user's perspective, spelling out hundreds of principles of good design in a clear and concise manner. It blends the results of screen design research, knowledge concerning people, knowledge about the hardware and software capabilities of the interface, and my practical experience, which now spans 30 years in display-based systems.

Looking ahead, an example of what this book will accomplish for you is illustrated in Figures P.1 through P.4. Figure P.1 is an actual existing screen. It looks bad but you do not realize how really horrible it is until you look at Figure P.2, a redesigned version. The same goes for Figure

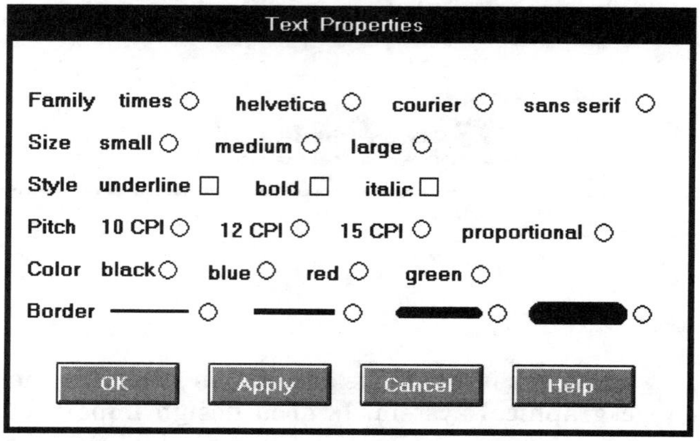

Figure P.1   An existing screen.

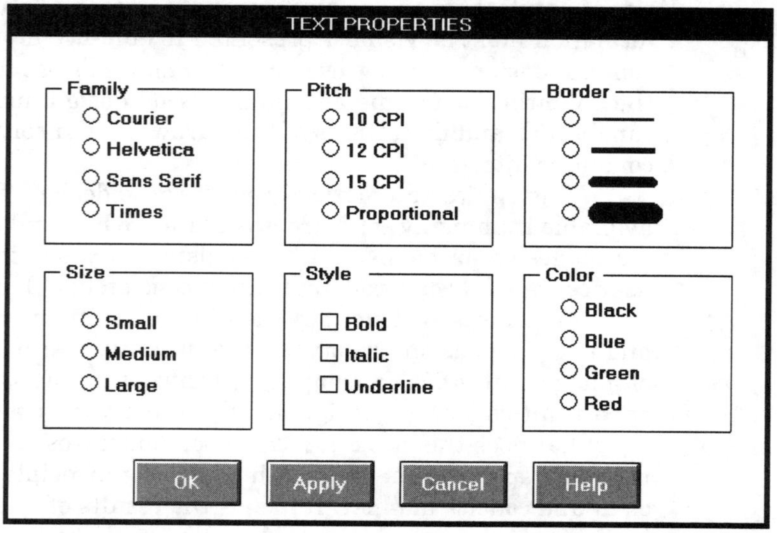

Figure P.2   A redesigned screen.

P.3, an original screen, and Figure P.4, a redesigned version. This book will present the rules for, and the rationale and reasoning why, the redesigned screens are much friendlier.

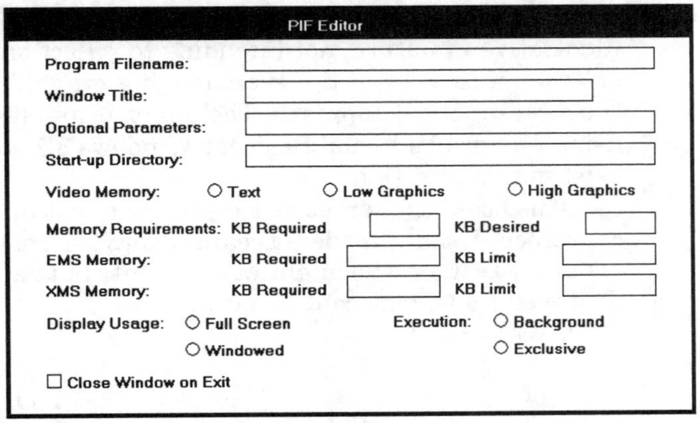

Figure P.3 An existing screen.

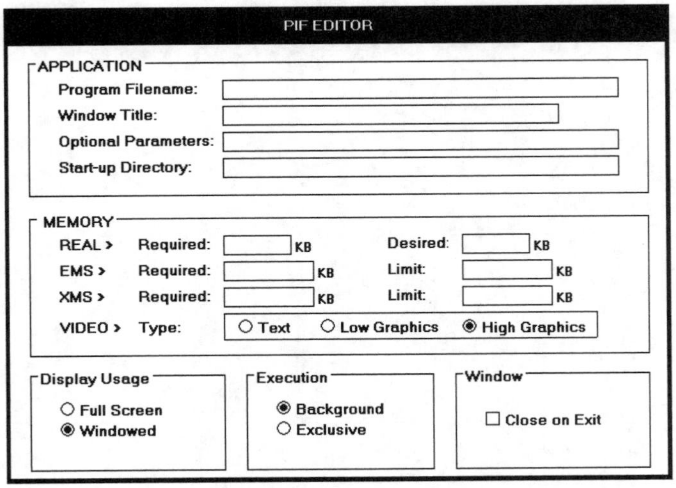

Figure P.4 A redesigned screen.

We'll fully analyze these screens later in this text. Sprinkled throughout the pages will also be many other examples of good and bad design.

How are the guidelines organized and presented? This book is both a reference book and a textbook. A set of related guidelines, many with illustrative examples, are first presented in checklist form. Each checklist is then followed by more detailed explanatory text providing necessary rationale and logic. Included screen examples are intended to be generic and illustrative in nature, not intending to reflect any one graphical product or system. In view of the everchanging graphical landscape, this seems the most practical approach. The screen examples, however, were created using Microsoft's Visual Basic for Windows 3.1 so an illustrative bias will exist in this direction.

This book also serves as a companion text to my workshop on graphical screen design. Readers seeking more information concerning materials in the text, or who might wish to contribute additional information for future editions, may contact me at:

Wilbert O. Galitz, Inc.
P.O. Box 310
St. Helena Island, SC 29920
(803) 525–0944

PART I

Introduction to Screen Design for the Graphical User Interface

CHAPTER 1

The Importance of Good Screen Design

In these times of metaphors, mice, widgets/controls, and usability, the user interface is being scrutinized, studied, written about, and talked about like never before. This welcome attention, along with the proliferation of usability laboratories and product testing, has significantly raised the usability of products we are presenting to our customers today. The voices of the users have finally been heard above the din. Their combined voices of frustration, fed up with complicated procedures and incomprehensible screens, have finally become overwhelming. "We're no longer going to peacefully accept products that mess up our lives and put everything we work on at risk," they are saying. They're also saying "That's just the way it is" as an answer to a problem that is no longer tolerable. Examples of good design, when they have occurred, have been presented as vivid proof that good design is possible.

We developers have listened. Greatly improved technology has eliminated many of the barriers to good interface design and unleashed a variety of new display and interaction techniques wrapped into a package called the Graphical User Interface, or, as it is commonly called, GUI or "gooey." The amount of programming code devoted to the user interface now exceeds 50 percent (Myers & Rosson, 1992). Almost every graphical platform now provides a style guide to assist in product design. Software to aid the design process proliferates. Looking backwards, we have made great strides in interface design. Looking around today, however, too many instances of poor design still abound. Looking ahead it seems much still remains to be done.

THE POPULARITY OF GRAPHICS

Graphics has indeed revolutionized design and the user interface. A graphical screen bears scant resemblance to its text-based colleagues. Whereas a traditional screen retains a one-dimensional, text-oriented, form-like quality, graphic screens assume a three-dimensional look. Information can float in windows, small rectangular boxes seeming to rise above the background plane. Windows can also float above other windows. Controls can rise above the screen and move when activated. Lines can appear to be etched into the screen. Information can appear, and disappear, as needed, and in some cases text can be replaced by icons representing objects or actions.

Screen navigation and commands can be executed through menu bars and pull-downs. Menus may "pop up." In the screen body, selection fields such as radio buttons, check boxes, list boxes, and palettes coexist with the reliable old text entry field. More sophisticated text entry fields with attached or drop-down menus of alternatives are also available. Screen objects and actions may be selected through use of pointing mechanisms such as the mouse or joystick instead of the traditional keyboard.

Increased computer power and the vast improvement in the display enable the user's actions to be reacted to quickly, dynamically, and meaningfully. This new interface is often characterized as representing one's "desktop" with scattered notes, papers, and objects such as files, trays, and trash cans arrayed around the screen.

Graphic presentation of information utilizes a person's information processing capabilities much more effectively than other presentation methods. Properly used, it reduces the requirement for perceptual and mental information recoding and reorganization, and also reduces the memory loads. It permits faster information transfer between computers and people by permitting more visual comparisons of amounts, trends, or relationships; more compact representation of information; and simplification of the perception of structure. Graphics can also add appeal or charm to the interface and permit greater customization to create a unique corporate style.

THE IMPORTANCE OF GOOD SCREEN DESIGN

With today's technology, today's tools, and our motivation to create really effective and usable interfaces and screens, why do we continue to produce so many that are inefficient and confusing or, at worst, just plain unusable? Is it because:

1. We don't care?
2. We don't possess common sense?

3. We don't have the time?
4. We still don't know what really makes good design?

I take the view that the root causes are number 4 with a good deal of number 3 thrown in. We *do* care. But we never seem to have time to find out what makes good design, nor to properly apply it. After all, most of us have other things to do in addition to designing screens. So we take our best shot given the workload and time constraints imposed upon us. The result, too often, is woefully inadequate for the importance of the task.

I discounted the "we don't possess common sense" alternative years ago. If, as I have heard thousands of times, screen design were really a matter of common sense, we developers would have been producing *almost identical* screens for similar applications and functions for many years. When was the last time you saw two designers create almost identical screen solutions, based on the same requirements, without the aid of design guidelines or standards (or with them as well)?

A well-designed screen is terribly important to our users. It is their window to view the capabilities of the system. To many, *it is* the system, being one of the few visible components of the product we developers create. It is also the vehicle through which many critical tasks are presented. These tasks often have a direct impact on an organization's relations with its customers, and its profitability.

A screen's layout and appearance affect a person in a variety of ways. If they are confusing and inefficient, people will have greater difficulty in doing their jobs and will make more mistakes. Poor design may even chase some people away from a system permanently. It can also lead to aggravation, frustration, and increased stress. I've heard of one user who relieved his frustrations with his computer with a couple of well-aimed bullets from a gun. I recently heard of another who, in a moment of extreme exasperation and anger, dropped his PC out of his upper-floor office window.

The Productivity Benefits of Good Design

Imagine the productivity benefits we could gain through proper design. Based on an actual system requiring processing of 4.8 million screens per year and illustrated in Table 1.1, an analysis established that if poor clarity forced screen users to spend one extra second per screen, almost one additional person-year would be required to process all screens. Twenty extra seconds in screen usage time adds an additional 14 person-years.

The benefits of a well-designed screen have also been under experimental scrutiny. Dunsmore (1982) attempted to improve screen clarity and readability by making screens less crowded. Separate items, which had been combined on the same display line to conserve space, were

Table 1.1   Impact of Inefficient Screen Design on Processing Time

Additional Seconds Required per Screen in Seconds	Additional Person-Years Required to Process 4.8 Million Screens per Year
1	.7
5	3.6
10	7.1
20	14.2

placed on separate lines instead. The result: screen users were about 20 percent more productive with the less-crowded version. Keister and Gallaway (1983) reformatted a series of screens following many of the same concepts to be described in this book. The result: screen users of the modified screens completed transactions in 25 percent less time and with 25 percent fewer errors than those who used the original screens.

Tullis (1981) has reported that reformatting inquiry screens following good design principles reduced decision-making time by about 40 percent, resulting in a savings of 79 person-years in the affected system. In a second study comparing 500 screens (Tullis, 1983), it was found that the time to extract information from displays of airline or lodging information was 128 percent faster for the best format than for the worst.

Other studies have also shown that the proper formatting of information on screens does have a significant positive effect on performance (Mann & Schnetzler, 1986; Pulat & Nwankwo, 1987). A recent study (Cope & Uliano, 1995) found that *one* graphical window redesigned to be more effective would save a company about $20,000 during its first year of operation.

How many screens are used each day in our technological world? How many screens are used each day in your organization? Thousands? Millions? Imagine the possible savings. Proper screen design might also, of course, lower the costs of replacing "broken" PCs.

THE PURPOSE OF THIS BOOK

This book's first objective is to present the important practical guidelines for good screen design. It is intended as a ready reference source for all graphical screen design. The guidelines reflect a mix of human behavior, science, and art, and are organized within the context of the GUI design process. The specific objectives are to enable the reader to do the following:

- Understand the many considerations that must be applied to the graphical screen design process.

- Understand the rationale and rules for an effective screen design methodology.
- Identify the components of graphical screens, including windows, menus, and controls.
- Design and organize graphical screens to encourage the fastest and most accurate comprehension and execution of screen features.
- Choose screen colors and design screen icons.
- Perform the Graphical User Interface design process, including interface development and testing.

The book's other objective is to provide materials that, when applied, will allow our users to become more productive—and more satisfied—using the screens we produce. A satisfied user also means, of course, a satisfied designer.

A BRIEF HISTORY OF THE HUMAN-COMPUTER INTERFACE

The need for people to communicate with each other has existed since we first walked upon this planet. The lowest and most common level of communication modes we share are movements and gestures. Movements and gestures are language-independent, that is, they permit people who do not speak the same language to deal with one another.

The next higher level, in terms of universality and complexity, is spoken language. Most people can speak one language, some two or more. A spoken language is a very efficient mode of communication if both parties to the communication understand it.

At the third highest level of complexity is written language. While most people speak, not all can write. But for those who can, writing is still nowhere near as efficient a means of communication as speaking.

In modern times, we have the typewriter, another step upward in communication complexity. Significantly fewer people type than write. (While a practiced typist can find typing faster and more efficient than handwriting, the unskilled may not find this the case.) Spoken language, however, is still more efficient than typing, regardless of typing skill level.

Through its first few decades, a computer's ability to deal with human communication was inversely related to what was easy for people to do. The computer demanded rigid, typed input through a keyboard; people responded slowly using this device and with varying degrees of skill. The human-computer dialog reflected the computer's preferences, consisting of one style or a combination of styles using keyboards commonly referred to as Command Language, Question and Answer, Menu Selection, Function Key Selection, and Form Fill-In. For more details on the screens associated with these dialogs see Galitz (1992).

Throughout the computer's history, designers have been developing, with varying degrees of success, other human-computer interaction methods that utilize a person's more general, widespread, and easier to learn capabilities: voice and handwriting. Systems that recognize human speech and handwriting now exist, although they still lack the universality and richness of typed input.

Introduction of the Graphical User Interface

Finally, in the 1970s, another dialog alternative surfaced. Research at Xerox's Palo Alto Research Center provided an alternative to the typewriter, an interface using a form of human gesturing, the most basic of all human communication methods. The Xerox systems, Altus and STAR, introduced the mouse and pointing and selecting as the primary human-computer communication method. The user simply pointed at the screen, using the mouse as an intermediary. These systems also introduced the graphical user interface as we know it today. Ivan Sutherland at the Massachusetts Institute of Technology is given credit for first introducing graphics with his Sketchpad program in 1962. Lines, circles, and points could be drawn on a screen using a light pen. Xerox worked on developing handheld pointing devices in the 1960s and patented a mouse with wheels in 1970. In 1974 Xerox patented today's ball mouse, after a researcher was suddenly inspired to turn a track ball upside down.

Xerox was never able to market the STAR successfully, but the concept was quickly picked up by Apple and Macintosh. Released in 1984, it was the first successful mass-market system. A new concept was born, revolutionizing the human-computer interface. A chronological history of GUIs through the 1980s and 1990s is found in Table 1.2. They are also briefly described in the next chapter.

A Brief History of Screen Design

While developers have been designing screens since a cathode ray tube display was first attached to a computer, more widespread interest in the application of good design principles to screens did not begin to emerge until the early 1970s, when IBM introduced its 3270 cathode ray tube text-based terminal. The 3270 was used in myriad ways in the office, and company-specific guidelines for good screen design occasionally began to surface (e.g., Galitz & DiMatteo, 1974). Typically, however, design in this time period had little to guide it, being driven by hardware and telephone line transmission issues. A 1970s screen often resembled the one pictured in Figure 1.1. It usually consisted of many fields (more than are illustrated here) with very cryptic and often unintelligible captions. It was visually cluttered, and often possessed a command field that challenged the user to remember what had to be keyed into it. Ambiguous messages

Table 1.2 Chronological History of Graphical User Interfaces

1980	• Pioneered at the Xerox Palo Alto Research Center.
	• First marketed as the Xerox STAR.
	— Introduced pointing, selection, and mouse.
1984	• Popularized by Apple.
	• Apple developed and marketed Lisa and Macintosh.
	— Macintosh first mass-marketed successful system.
1985	• Microsoft Windows 1.0 released.
1987	• X Window System becomes widely available.
	• IBM's System Application Architecture released.
	— Including Common User Access (CUA).
	• IBM's Presentation Manager released.
	— Intended as graphics operating system replacement for DOS.
1988	• NeXT's NeXTStep released.
	— First to simulate three-dimensional screen.
1989	• UNIX-based GUIs released.
	— Open Look, by AT&T and Sun Microsystems.
	— Innovative appearance to avoid legal challenges.
	— Motif, for the Open Software Foundation by DEC and Hewlett-Packard.
	— Appearance and behavior based on Presentation Manager.
	• Microsoft Windows 3.0 released.
1992	• OS/2 Workplace Shell released.
	• Microsoft Windows 3.1 released.
1995	• Microsoft Windows 95 released.

often required referral to a manual to interpret. Effectively using this kind of screen required a great deal of practice and patience.

At the turn of the decade guidelines for text-based screen design were finally made widely available (Galitz, 1980, 1981) and many screens began to take on a much less cluttered look through concepts like grouping and alignment of elements, as illustrated in Figure 1.2. User memory was supported by providing clear and meaningful field captions and by listing commands on the screen, and enabling them to be accomplished through function keys. Messages also became clearer. These screens were not entirely clutter-free, however. Instructions and reminders to the user had to be inscribed on the screen in the form of prompts or completion aids

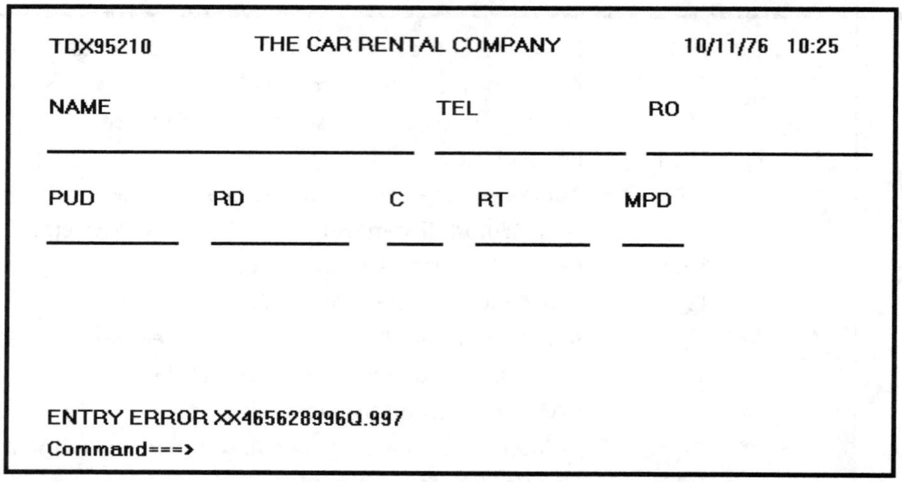

Figure 1.1 A 1970s screen.

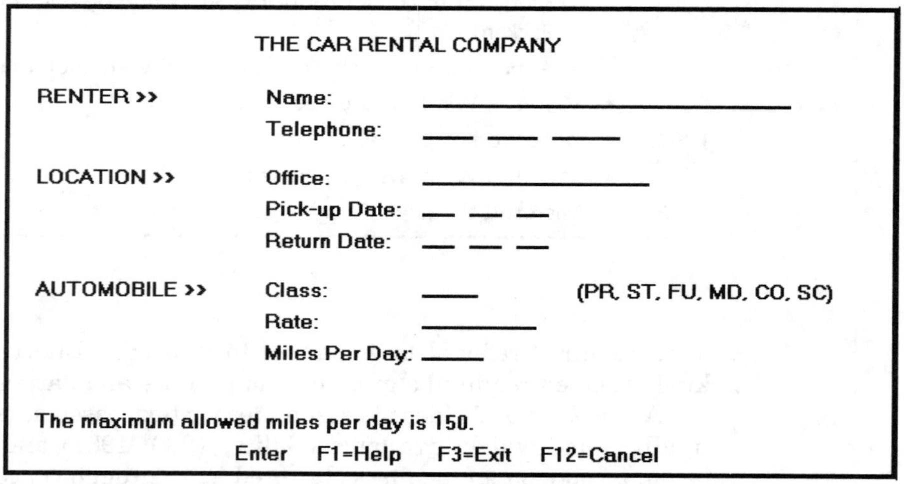

Figure 1.2 A 1980s screen.

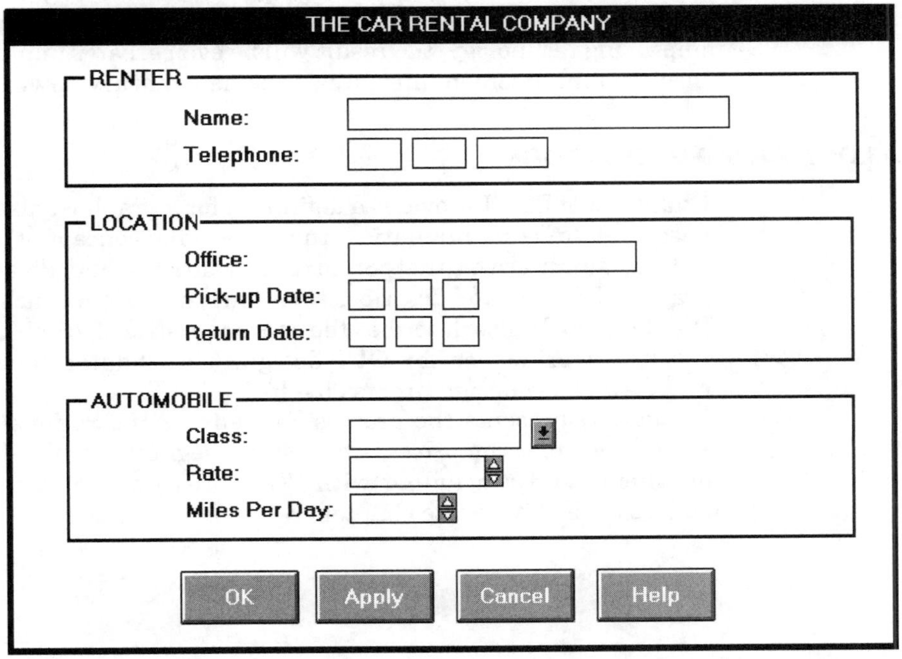

Figure 1.3   A 1990s screen.

such as the codes PR and SC. Not all 1980s screens looked like this, however. 1970s-type screens were still being designed in the 1980s and many still reside in systems today.

The advent of graphics yielded another milestone in the evolution of screen design, as illustrated in Figure 1.3. While some basic design principles did not change, groupings and alignment for example, borders were made available to visually enhance groupings, and buttons and menus for implementing commands replaced function keys. Multiple properties of elements were also provided, including many different font sizes and styles, line thicknesses, and colors. The entry field was supplemented by a multitude of other kinds of controls, including list boxes, drop-down combination boxes, spin boxes, and so forth. These new controls were much more effective in supporting a person's memory, now simply allowing for selection from a list instead of a remembered key entry. Completion aids disappeared from screens, replaced by one of the new listing controls. Screens could also be simplified, the much more powerful computer being able to quickly present a new screen.

As we pass through the late 1990s our knowledge concerning what makes effective screen design continues to expand. Coupled with ever-improving technology, the result will be even greater improvements in the user-computer screen interface as the new century dawns.

A LOOK AHEAD IN THIS BOOK

Chapter 2 of Part I provides a definition for a graphical user interface and describes direct manipulation, the underlying concept of a graphical system. It summarizes the potential advantages and disadvantages of a graphical system and describes some current systems, including Microsoft Windows 95. It also describes the characteristics of graphical systems and the broad principles for GUI design. The chapter concludes with an overview of the design process itself.

Part II presents the process, guidelines, and rationale for graphical screen design. It comprises twelve steps, beginning with "Know Your User or Client" and concluding with "Test, Test, and Retest." Each step is addressed in a separate chapter.

CHAPTER 2

Characteristics of a Graphical User Interface

DEFINITION OF A GRAPHICAL USER INTERFACE

In brief, a graphical user interface can be defined as follows. A *user interface* is a collection of techniques and mechanisms to interact with something. In a *graphical* interface, the primary interaction mechanism is a pointing device of some kind. This device is the electronic equivalent to the human hand. What the user interacts with is a collection of elements referred to as *objects*. Objects are always visible to the user and are used to perform tasks. They are interacted with as entities independent of all other objects. People perform operations, called *actions*, on objects. The operations include accessing and modifying by pointing, selecting, and manipulating.

THE CONCEPT OF DIRECT MANIPULATION

The term used to describe this style of interaction for graphical systems was first used by Shneiderman (1982). He called them "direct manipulation" systems, suggesting they possess the following characteristics:

The system is portrayed as an extension of the real world. It is assumed that a person is already familiar with the objects and actions in his or her environment of interest. The system simply replicates them and portrays them on a different medium, the screen. A person has the power to access and modify these objects, among which are windows. A person is allowed to work in a familiar environment and in a familiar way, focusing on the data, not the application and tools. The physical organization of the system, which most often is unfamiliar, is hidden from view and not a distraction.

Continuous visibility of objects and actions. Like one's desktop and office, objects are continuously visible. Reminders of actions to be performed are also obvious, labeled buttons replacing complex syntax and command names. Cursor action and motion occurs in physically obvious and intuitively natural ways. Nelson (1980) described this as "virtual reality," a representation of reality that can be manipulated. Hatfield (1981) is credited with calling it "WYSIWYG" (what you see is what you get). Rutkowski (1982) described it as "transparency," where one's intellect is applied to the task, not the tool. Hutchins, Hollan, & Norman (1986) considered it direct involvement with the world of objects rather than communicating with an intermediary.

One problem in direct manipulation, however, is that there is no direct analogy on the office desk on which we work for all necessary windowing operations. A piece of paper on one's desk maintains a constant size, never shrinking or growing. Windows can do both. Solving this problem required embedding a control panel, a familiar concept to most people, in a window's border. This control panel is manipulated, not the window itself.

Actions are rapid and incremental with visible display of results. Since tactile feedback is not yet possible (as would occur with one's hand when one touches something), the results of actions are immediately displayed visually on the screen in their new and current form. Auditory feedback may also be provided. The impact of a previous action is quickly seen and the evolution of tasks is effortless.

Incremental actions are easily reversible. Finally, actions, if discovered to be incorrect or not desired, can be easily undone.

Earlier Direct Manipulation Systems.

Using the above definition, the concept of direct manipulation actually preceded the first graphical system. The earliest full screen text editors possessed similar characteristics. Screens of text resembling a piece of paper on one's desk could be created (extension of real world) and then reviewed in their entirety (continuous visibility). Editing or restructuring could be easily accomplished (through rapid incremental actions) and the results immediately seen. Actions could be reversed when necessary. It took the advent of graphical systems to crystallize the concept, however.

Indirect Manipulation

In practice, direct manipulation of *all* screen objects and actions may not be feasible because of the following:

- The operation may be difficult to conceptualize in the graphical system.
- The graphics capability of the system may be limited.

- The amount of space available for placing manipulation controls in the window border may be limited.
- It may be difficult for people to learn and remember all the necessary operations and actions.

When this occurs, *indirect manipulation* is provided. Indirect manipulation substitutes words and text, such as pull-down or pop-up menus, for symbols, and substitutes typing for pointing. Most window systems are a combination of both direct and indirect manipulation. A menu may be accessed by pointing at a menu icon and selecting it (direct). The menu itself, however, is a textual list of operations (indirect). When an operation is selected from the list, by pointing or typing, the system executes it as a command.

Which style of interaction—direct manipulation, indirect manipulation, or a combination of both—is best, under what conditions and for whom, remains a question whose answer still eludes us.

GRAPHICAL SYSTEMS: ADVANTAGES AND DISADVANTAGES

Graphical systems burst upon the office with great promise. The simplified interface they present is thought to reduce the memory requirements imposed on the user, make more effective use of one's information processing capabilities, and dramatically reduce system learning requirements. Experience indicates that for many people they have done all these things.

Advantages

The success of graphical systems has been attributed to a host of factors. The following have been commonly referenced in literature and endorsed by their advocates as advantages of these systems.

Symbols Recognized Faster than Text Symbols have been found to be recognized faster and more accurately than text (Ells & Dewar, 1979). The graphical attributes of icons such as shape and color are very useful for quickly classifying objects, elements, or text by some common property (Gittens, 1986). An example of a good classification scheme that speeds up recognition are the icons developed for indicating the kind of message being presented to the user of the system. The text of an informational message is preceded by an "i" in a circle, a warning message by an exclamation point, and a critical message by another unique symbol. These icons allow speedy recognition of the type of message being presented.

Faster Learning A graphical, pictorial representation has been found to aid learning (Polya, 1957). Symbols can also be easily learned (Walker, Nicolay, & Stearns, 1965).

Faster Use and Problem Solving Visual or spatial representation of information has been found to be easier to retain and manipulate (Wertheimer, 1959) and leads to faster and more successful problem solving (Carroll, Thomas, & Malhotra, 1980). Symbols have also been found to be effective in conveying simple instructions (Dickey & Schneider, 1971).

Easier Remembering Because of greater simplicity, it is easier for casual users to retain operational concepts.

More Natural Graphic representations of objects are thought to be more natural and closer to innate human capabilities. In humans, actions and visual skills emerged before languages. Lodding (1983) suggests symbolic displays are more natural and advantageous because the human mind has a powerful image memory.

Exploits Visual/Spatial Cues Spatial relationships are usually found to be understood more quickly than verbal representations. Heckel (1984) suggests that thinking visually is better than thinking logically.

Fosters More Concrete Thinking Displayed objects are directly in the high-level task domain, or directly usable in their presented form. There is no need mentally to decompose tasks into multiple commands with complex syntactic form (Shneiderman, 1982). Abstract thinking is therefore minimized.

Provides Context Displayed objects are visible providing a picture of current context.

Fewer Errors More concrete thinking affords fewer opportunities for errors. Reversibility of actions reduces error rates because it is always possible to undo the last step. Error messages are less frequently needed.

Increased Feeling of Control The user initiates actions and feels in control. This increases user confidence and hastens system mastery.

Immediate Feedback The results of actions furthering user goals can be seen immediately. Learning is quickened. If response is not in the desired direction, the direction can be quickly changed.

Predictable System Responses Predictable system responses also speed learning.

Easily Reversible Actions The user has more control. This ability to reverse unwanted actions also increases user confidence and hastens system mastery.

Less Anxiety Concerning Use Hesitant or new users feel less anxiety when using the system because it is so easily comprehended, easy to control, and has predictable responses and reversible actions.

More Attractive Direct-manipulation systems are more entertaining, more clever, and more appealing. This is especially important for the cautious or skeptical user.

May Consume Less Space Icons may take up less space than the equivalent in words. More information can be packed in a given area of the screen. This, however, is not always the case.

Replaces National Languages Language-based systems are seldom universally applicable. Language translations frequently cause problems in a text-based system. Icons possess much more universality than text and are much more easily comprehended worldwide.

Easily Augmented with Text Displays Where graphical design limitations exist, direct-manipulation systems can easily be augmented with text displays. The reverse is not true.

Low Typing Requirements Pointing and selection controls such as the mouse or trackball eliminate the need for typing skills.

Smooth Transition from Command Language System Moving from a command language to direct-manipulation has been found to be easy. The reverse is not true (Tombaugh, Paynter, and Dillon, 1989).

Disadvantages

The body of positive research, hypotheses, and comment concerning graphical systems is being challenged by some studies, findings, and opinions that graphical representation and interaction may not necessarily always be better and, in some cases, may be poorer than pure textual or alphanumeric displays. Trying to force all system components into a graphical format may be doing a disservice to the user. Some also feel that as graphical systems become increasingly sophisticated and continue to expand, interfaces have become increasingly more complex, sometimes arcane, and even bizarre (Baecker, Small & Mander, 1991). Among the disadvantages put forth are these:

Greater Design Complexity The elements and techniques available to the graphical screen designer far outnumber those that have been at the disposal of the text-based screen designer. Controls must be selected from a huge pile of alternatives. This can easily be seen by comparing the typical but nonexhaustive listings in Table 2.1. This design potential may not

Table 2.1 A Representative Listing of Typical Textual and Graphical Screen Elements and Techniques

Textual Screens	Graphical Screens
Title	Title
Screen ID	Buttons
Headings	Menu Bars
Captions	Pull-Down Menus
Entry/Data Fields	Pop-Up Menus
Function Key Listings	Button Bars
Command Fields	Status Bars
Messages	Direct Manipulation
Blinking	Indirect Manipulation
Scrolling	Scrolling
High/Low Intensity	Headings
Upper/Mixed-Case Characters	Captions
Normal/Reverse Video	Text Boxes
Underlining	Radio Buttons
	Check Boxes
	Palettes
	List Boxes
	Spin Lists
	Attached Combination Boxes
	Drop-Down Combination Boxes
	Messages
	Sliders
	Icons
	Settings
	Primary Windows
	Secondary Windows
	Modal Dialog Boxes
	Modeless Dialog Boxes
	Upper/Mixed-Case Characters
	Underling
	Multiple-Character Styles
	Multiple-Character Sizes
	Thin/Thick/Double Rulings
	Multiple Foreground Colors
	Multiple Background Colors
	Proportion
	Oval Shapes
	Rectangular Shapes
	Scalloped Corners
	Beveled Edges
	Drop Shadows
	Shrinking/Growing
	Motion
	Etc.

necessarily result in better design, unless it is carefully, thoughtfully, consistently, and simply applied. Proper window types must also be chosen and colors selected from a seemingly unending rainbow of alternatives. With graphics, the skill of the designer is increasingly challenged. Poor design can undermine acceptance.

Learning Still Necessary The first time one encounters many graphical systems, what to do is not immediately obvious. Meanings of many words and icons may not be known. It is not often possible to guess their meanings, especially the more arbitrary symbols. How to use a pointing device may also have to be learned. A severe learning and remembering requirement is imposed on many users, and it will take a while to get up to speed. A text-based system can easily be structured to incorporate a set of clear instructions: (1) Do this, (2) Now do this, and so on.

Becoming accustomed to a graphical interface, the system providers estimate, should require about eight hours of training. Other experts say the learning time is closer to 20 or 30 hours.

Lack of Experimentally Derived Design Guidelines The graphical interface is burdened today by a lack of widely available experimentally derived design guidelines. Early on, more developer interest existed in solving technical rather than usability issues, so few studies to aid in making design decisions were performed. Today, studies being performed in usability laboratories are rarely published. This occurs because of a number of factors. First, builders of platforms and packages will not publish their study results to maintain a competitive advantage. If a better way is found to do something, or present something, why tell the competition. Let them make the same mistake, or find the answer themselves.

Second, the studies are often specific to a particular function or task. They may not be generally applicable. Third, it takes time and effort to publish something. The developer in today's office seldom has the time for the effort. Finally, it is also difficult to develop studies evaluating design alternatives because of increased GUI complexity. Too many variables that must be controlled make meaningful cause-and-effect relationships very difficult to uncover.

Consequently, there is little understanding of how most design aspects relate to productivity and satisfaction.

Inconsistencies in Technique and Terminology Many technique, terminology, and look-and-feel differences exist between various graphical system providers, and even successive versions of the same system. These inconsistencies occur because of both copyright and legal implications, product differentiation considerations, and our expanding knowledge about the interface. The result is that learning, and relearning, for both designers and users is much more difficult than it should be.

Working Domain is the Present Direct-manipulation systems, while providing context, also require the user to work in the "present." Hulteen (1989), in a parody of "WYSIWYG," suggests, "What you see is all you get." Walker (1989) argues that language takes you out of the here and now and the visually present. Language, she continues, makes it easier to find things.

Not Always Familiar Symbolic representations may not be as familiar as words or numbers. We have been exposed to words and numbers for a long time. Remington and Williams (1986) found that numeric symbols elicited faster responses than graphic symbols in a visual search task. Cairney and Sless (1982) and Zwaga and Boersema (1983) found some current or proposed symbols were not very effective. Hair (1991) had to modify a new system during testing by replacing iconic representations with a textual outline format. The users, lawyers, were unfamiliar with icons and demanded a more familiar format.

Human Comprehension Limitations Human limitations may also exist in terms of one's capability of dealing with the increased complexity of the graphical interface. The variety of visual displays may still challenge all but the most sophisticated users. The number of different icons that can also be introduced is restricted due to human comprehension limitations. Studies continually find that the number of different symbols a person can differentiate and deal with is much more limited than text. Gittens (1986) argues it will be difficult to find or develop and use icons dealing with the large number of computer system concepts and command parameters that exist. Kolers (1969) notes that claims for the easy understanding of pictograms are exaggerated, and that recognizing icons requires much perceptual learning, abstracting ability, and intelligence.

The motor skills required may also challenge all but the most sophisticated users. Correctly double-clicking a mouse, for example, is difficult for some people.

Window Manipulation Requirements Window handling and manipulation times are still excessive and repetitive. This wastes time and interrupts the decision-making needed to perform tasks and jobs.

Production Limitations The number of symbols that can be clearly produced using today's technology is limited. A body of recognizable symbols must be produced that are equally legible and equally recognizable using differing technologies. This is extremely difficult today.

Few Tested Icons Exist Icons, as with typefaces, must appear in different sizes, weights, and styles. As with text, an entire font of clearly recognizable symbols must be developed. It is not simply a question of developing an icon and simply enlarging or reducing it. Changed size can differentially affect symbol line widths, open areas, and so forth, dramatically affecting its recognizability. Typeface design is literally the product of 300 years of experimentation and studies. Icons must be researched, designed, tested, and then introduced into the marketplace. The consequences of poor, or improper, design will be confusion and lower productivity for users.

Inefficient for Touch Typists For an experienced touch typist, the keyboard is a very fast and powerful device. Moving a mouse or some other pointing mechanism may be slower.

Inefficient for Expert Users Inefficiencies develop when there are more objects and actions than can fit on the screen. Concatenation for a command language is impossible.

Not Always Preferred Style of Interaction Not all users prefer a pure iconic interface. Brems and Whitten (1987), in comparing commands illustrated by icons, icons with text, or text-only, found that users preferred alternatives with textual captions.

Not Always Fastest Style of Interaction Stern (1984) found that graphic instructions on an automated bank teller machine were inferior to textual instructions.

Increased Chances of Clutter and Confusion A graphical system does not guarantee elimination of clutter on a screen. Instead, the chance for clutter is increased, thereby increasing the possibility of confusion. How much screen clutter one can deal with is open to speculation. The possibility that clutter may exist is evidenced by the fact that many people, when working with a window, expand it to fill the entire display screen. This may be done to reduce visual screen clutter. Mori & Hayashi (1993) found that visible windows, not the focus of attention, degraded performance in the window being worked on.

The Futz and Fiddle Factor With the proliferation of computer games, computer usage can be wasteful of time. Stromoski (1993) estimates that five hours a week in the office are spent playing and tinkering. Experts say the most used program in Microsoft Windows 3.1 is solitaire! Tinkering includes activities such as creating garish documents reflecting almost every object property (font size, style, color, etc.) available.

Futzing and fiddling does have some benefits, however. It is a tool for learning how to use a mouse, for example, and it is a vehicle for exploring the system and becoming familiar with its capabilities. It is of value when done in moderation.

May Consume More Screen Space Not all applications will consume less screen space. A listing of names and telephone numbers in a textual format will be more efficient to scan than a card file.

Hardware Limitations Good design also requires hardware of adequate power, processing speed, screen resolution, and graphic capability. Insufficiencies in these areas often prevent a graphic system's full potential from being realized.

Some Studies and a Conclusion

Walker (1989) points out that many of the benefits of one interaction style versus another are anecdotal. This has often made the debate between advocates of graphical and other styles of interaction more emotional than scientific. This is certainly true for many of the arguments. In the last several years, however, there have been a handful of studies comparing alternative interaction styles. It is useful to summarize what they have found.

An early study undertaken by Whiteside, Jones, Levy, & Wixon (1985) compared the usability characteristics of seven systems, including direct-manipulation, menu, and command language styles of interaction. They found that user performance did not depend on the type of system. There were large differences in learnability and usability between all. How well the system was *designed* was the best indicator of success, not the style of interaction.

Brems and Whitten (1987) evaluated a family of seven commands for user preferences. The alternative design styles were commands described by icons only, icons with textual captions, and textual captions only. While the meanings of the icons were easily learned, textual captions were preferred to uncaptioned icons. Learning, they concluded, was not a good indicator of preference.

Frese, Schulte-Gocking, and Altmann (1987) compared learning and performance for direct-manipulation and command-based word processing systems. While no differences existed after the first experimental session, the direct-manipulation system user's performance became increasingly superior as the study progressed (and task complexity increased). It appeared that the direct-manipulation system facilitated the learning process as task complexity increased.

Shneiderman and Margono (1987) compared some simple file manipulation tasks using a graphical system (Macintosh) and a command language system (DOS). The graphical system was found best in learnability, performance time, and subjective ratings. Two other studies have also found graphical systems superior to command language styles for some kinds of tasks (Karat, 1987; Guastello, Traut, & Korienek, 1989).

Temple, Barker, and Sloane (1990) compared command line and graphical interfaces and reported that graphical interface users worked faster, were more productive, expressed lower frustration, perceived lower fatigue, were better able to self-teach and explore applications, and were better able to learn more of an application's capabilities. They did find inferior graphical system initial performance because of the systems learning requirement, but over the long term there was less training and higher productivity.

Other studies have found textual presentation of information (Shneiderman, 1982A; Stern, 1984) or tabular display of information (Tufte, 1983) superior to graphics. Another has found no difference between a graphical and textual format (Nugent and Broyles, 1992).

The conclusion, based upon what research and experience have shown, is that the different interface styles have different strengths and weaknesses. Some concepts and tasks are very hard to convey symbolically and do not seem to be suited for a pure graphical presentation. Other concepts and tasks, however, may be well suited. Which tasks are best suited for which styles still needs much study. Finally, all users may not like all aspects of a graphical system. The design should reflect this.

The following has also become clear:

- The design of an interface, and not its interaction style, is the best determinant of ease of use.
- User preferences must be considered in choosing an interaction style.
- The content of a graphic screen is critical to its usefulness. The wrong presentation or a cluttered presentation may actually lead to greater confusion, not less.
- The success of a graphical system depends on the skills of its designers in following established principles of usability.

CHARACTERISTICS OF THE GRAPHICAL USER INTERFACE

A graphical system possesses a set of defining concepts. Included are sophisticated visual presentation, pick-and-click interaction, a restricted set of interface options, visualization, object-orientation, extensive use of a person's recognition memory, and concurrent performance of functions.

Sophisticated Visual Presentation

Visual presentation is the visual aspect of the interface. It is what people see on the screen. The sophistication of a graphical system permits displaying lines, including drawings and icons. It also permits display of a variety of character fonts, including different sizes and styles. The display of 16 million or more colors is possible on some screens. Graphics also permits animation and the presentation of photographs and motion video.

The meaningful interface elements visually presented to the user in a graphical system include windows (primary, secondary, or dialog boxes), menus (menu bar, pull-down, pop-up, cascading), icons to represent objects such as programs or files, assorted screen-based controls (text boxes, list boxes, combination boxes, settings, scroll bars and buttons), and a mouse pointer and cursor. The objective is to reflect visually on the screen the real world of the user as realistically, meaningfully, simply, and clearly as possible.

Pick-and-Click Interaction

Elements of a graphical screen upon which some action is to be performed must first be identified. The motor activity required of a person to identify this element for a proposed action is commonly referred to as *pick*, the signal to perform an action as *click*. The primary mechanism for performing this pick-and-click is most often the mouse and its buttons. The mouse pointer is moved by the user to the relevant element (pick) and the action signaled (click). The secondary mechanism for performing these actions is the keyboard. Most systems permit pick-and-click to be performed using the keyboard as well.

Restricted Set of Interface Options

The array of alternatives available to the user is what is presented on the screen or what may be retrieved through what is presented on the screen, nothing less, nothing more. This concept fostered the acronym WYSIWYG.

Visualization

Visualization is a cognitive process that allows people to understand information that is difficult to perceive, because it is either too voluminous or too abstract. It involves changing an entity's representation to reveal gradually the structure and/or function of the underlying system or process. Visualization is facilitated by presenting specialized graphic portrayals. The best visualization method for an activity depends on what people are trying to learn from the data. The goal is not necessarily to reproduce a realistic graphical image, but one that conveys the most relevant information. Effective visualizations can facilitate mental insights, increase productivity, and foster faster and more accurate use of data.

Object Orientation

A graphical system consists of objects and actions. *Objects* are what people see on the screen. They are manipulated as a single unit. A well-designed system keeps users focused on objects, not on how to carry out actions. Objects can be composed of *subobjects*. For example, an object may be a document. The document's subobjects may be a paragraph, sentence, word, or letter.

IBM's System Application Architecture Common User Access Advanced Interface Design Reference (SAA CUA) (IBM ,1991) breaks objects into three meaningful classes: data, container, and device. *Data objects* present information. This information, either text or graphics, normally appears in the body of the screen. It is, essentially, the screen-based controls for information collection or presentation organized on the screen.

Container objects are objects to hold other objects. They are used to group two or more related objects for easy access and retrieval. There are three kinds of container objects: the workplace, folders, and workareas. The *workplace* is the desktop, the storage area for all objects. *Folders* are general purpose containers for long-term storage of objects. *Workareas* are temporary storage folders used for storing multiple objects currently being worked on.

Device objects represent a physical object in the real world, such as printers or trash baskets. These objects may contain others for acting upon. A file, for example, may be placed in a printer for printing of its contents.

Windows 95 specifies the characteristics of objects depending upon the relationships that exist between them. Objects can exist within the context of other objects, and one object may affect the way another object appears or behaves. These relationships are called collections, constraints, composites, and containers.

A *collection* is the simplest relationship, the objects sharing a common aspect. A collection might be the result of a query or a multiple selection of objects. Operations can be applied to a collection of objects.

A *constraint* is a stronger object relationship. Changing an object in a set affects some other object in the set. A document being organized into pages is an example of a constraint.

A *composite* exists where the relationship between objects becomes so significant that the aggregation itself can be identified as an object. Examples include a range of cells organized into a spreadsheet, or a collection of words organized into a paragraph.

A *container is* an object in which other objects exist. Examples include text in a document or documents in a folder. A container often influences the behavior of its content. It may add or suppress certain properties or operations of objects placed within it, control access to its content, or control access to kinds of objects it will accept.

These relationships help define an object's *type*. Similar traits and behaviors exist in objects of the same object type.

Another important object characteristic is *persistence*. Persistence is the maintenance of a state once it is established. An object's state (e.g., window size, cursor location, scroll position, etc.) should always be automatically preserved when it is changed by the user.

Properties or Attributes of Objects Objects also have properties or attributes. Properties are the unique characteristics of an object. Properties help to describe an object and can be changed by users. Examples of properties are text styles (such as normal or italics), font sizes (such as 10 or 12 points), or window background colors (such as black or blue).

Actions In addition to objects are actions. People take actions on objects. They manipulate objects in specific ways (commands) or modify the properties of objects (property or attribute specification).

Commands are actions that manipulate objects. They may be performed in a variety of ways, including direct manipulation or through a command button. They are executed immediately when selected. Once executed, they cease to be relevant. Examples of commands are opening a document, printing a document, closing a window, or quitting an application.

Property/attribute specification actions establish or modify the attributes or properties of objects. When selected, they remain in effect until deselected. Examples include selecting cascaded windows to be displayed, a particular font style, or a particular color.

The following is a typical *property/attribute specification sequence:*

1. The user selects an object, for example, several words of text.
2. The user then selects an action to apply to that object, such as the action BOLD.
3. The selected words are made bold and will remain bold until selected and changed again.

A series of actions may be performed on a selected object. Performing a series of actions on an object also permits and encourages system learning through exploration.

Application versus Object or Data Orientation Earlier graphical systems were usually application-oriented, a continuation of the philosophy that enveloped text-based systems. When a text-based system was developed, it was called an application. As graphical systems evolved, developers usually thought in terms of applications as well. When a real picture of the user began to emerge, it finally became evident that people thought in terms of tasks, not applications. They choose objects and then act upon them. Microsoft Windows 3.1 represents an application-oriented approach. IBM's SAA CUA and Microsoft Windows 95 now represent an object-oriented approach.

An application-oriented approach takes an action:object approach like this:

Action> **1.** An application is opened (e.g., word processing).
Object> **2.** A file or other object selected (e.g., a memo).

An object-oriented object:action approach does this.

Object> **1.** An object is chosen (a memo).
Action> **2.** An application is selected (word processing).

Many experienced users may experience difficulties in switching from one approach to another since an old interaction behavior must be unlearned and a new one learned. New users should not experience these problems, since it more accurately reflects a person's thinking. In any one interface, it is critical that a consistent orientation be maintained, either an object:action or an action:object approach.

Views Views are ways of looking at an object's information. IBM's SAA CUA describes four kinds: composed, contents, settings, and help.

Composed views present information and the objects contained within an object. They are typically associated with data objects and are specific to tasks and products being worked with. *Contents* views list the components of objects. *Settings* views permit seeing and changing object properties. *Help* views provide all the help functions.

Use of Recognition Memory

Continuous visibility of objects and actions encourages use of a person's more powerful recognition memory. The "out of sight, out of mind" problem is eliminated.

Concurrent Performance of Functions

Graphic systems may do two or more things at one time. Multiple programs may run simultaneously. When a system is not busy on a primary task, it may process background tasks (cooperative multitasking). When applications are running as truly separate tasks, the system may divide the processing power into time slices and allocate portions to each application (preemptive multitasking).

Data may also be transferred between programs. It may be temporarily stored on a "clipboard" for later transfer or be automatically swapped between programs.

SOME CURRENT GRAPHICAL SYSTEMS

In the last dozen years a number of graphic systems have been introduced and are available in the marketplace. Throughout the remaining pages of this book, an occasional reference will be made to some of them. These systems are briefly introduced in the following paragraphs. The reader in need of detailed information concerning their design and operation is referred to their design documentation. Another source of information is Marcus (1992), who provides a comparative evaluation of the operational characteristics of several of those listed.

Macintosh

Introduced in 1984 by Apple, it was the first mass-marketed, widely accepted graphic system providing the interaction style referred to as direct manipulation. Its success is attributed to its consistent and user-oriented interface. Its simplicity makes it easy to learn but limits the flexibility available to the expert user.

NeXTStep

Introduced in 1988 by NeXT, it was the first to present a simulated three-dimensional appearance for its components. Like the Macintosh, its simplicity and user-oriented interface is oriented toward inexperienced and nontechnical users. It provides a very good set of end-user customization tools.

OPEN LOOK

OPEN LOOK was developed as the standard operating environment for UNIX System V.4 by AT&T and Sun Microsystems. Providing more functionality than Macintosh or NeXTStep, it provided more power and flexibility for the expert user at the cost of increased learning requirements for the inexperienced user. It possesses many innovative appearance and behavioral characteristics in order to avoid potential legal challenges, and it also provides an excellent functional specification and style guide. OPEN LOOK is used by Sun Microsystems workstations.

DECwindows

An interface for workstation software, it was announced in 1987. One of its goals was to achieve a consistent interface across operating systems, including VMS and UNIX, and across different input and screen configurations. A resulting product for achieving consistency is the XUI (X User Interface) style guide and toolkit (Digital Equipment Corporation, 1988).

OSF/Motif

A window-manager and user interface toolkit, it was developed by Digital Equipment Corporation and Hewlett-Packard for the Open Software Foundation (OSF). Its appearance and behavior are based upon OS/2 Presentation Manager. Customization is encouraged, and some stylistic guidance is provided through a style guide (Open Software Foundation, 1991). Like NeXTStep, it presents a simulated three-dimensional appearance.

Microsoft Windows 3.1

Originally created in 1985 as a graphics-oriented alternative to MS-DOS, it opened the door to graphics-oriented software on the PC. Initially limited by the design characteristics of DOS, it has been enhanced over the years. The user interface is not as easy as desired for inexperienced users, and its extensive use of keyboard equivalents was intended to ease the transition for experienced DOS users.

OS/2 Presentation Manager

Developed jointly by Microsoft and IBM in 1987, it was intended as the graphics operating system replacement for MS-DOS.

OS/2 Workplace Shell

Developed by IBM when Microsoft and IBM dissolved their business relationship, OS/2 Workplace Shell is the GUI for OS/2 2.0 and beyond.

Microsoft Windows 95

The new mainstream version of Windows finally released in 1995, it incorporates a true operating system and networking features. It also possesses a data or object orientation. It is described in more detail below and in Table 2.2. With its many new features, Windows 95 was designed to eliminate a number of usability problems existing in Windows 3.1. Its general goals were to make it easier to learn for novices, more efficient and customizable for the experienced, and to reflect an object- or data-oriented approach.

Windows 3.1 problem areas Difficulties experienced by Windows 3.1 users differed depending upon one's experience (Microsoft, 1995). For

Table 2.2   Microsoft Windows 95 Components

Desktop	Description:	• The primary work area that fills the display.
	Purpose:	• Operational background and object storage location.
Taskbar	Description:	• Operational anchor or home base. • Normally located at bottom edge of desktop • Customizable by user. — Sizable / Repositionable / Removable
	Purpose:	• To switch between open windows. • To access global commands. • To access other frequently used objects.

	Elements:	**Start Button**
		
		• At left side of taskbar
		• Provides pull-up menu to:
		  — Start programs.
		  — Retrieve recent documents.
		  — View and modify settings.
		  — Find files.
		  — Access help.
		  — Provide enhanced command-line type functionality.
		  — Shutdown or exit.
		
		Window Buttons
		
		• A button for every open primary window.
		  — Remains when window minimized.
		  — Removed when window closed.
		• Size adjusted to accommodate as many as possible.
		• Can be used as drag-and-drop destinations.
		
		Status Area
		
		• Located at right side of the taskbar.
		• For status or notification indications.
		• Shared resource, for global information only, or what needs monitoring by working with other applications.

Icons	Description:	• Pictorial representations of objects. • May appear on desktop or in windows.
	Purpose:	• To represent objects.
	Kinds:	**My Computer** • Provides access to one's private, usually local, storage. **Network Neighborhood** • Provides access to objects stored on the network file system. **Folder** • Provides organization for files and folders.

Table 2.2   *(Continued)*

		Shortcut to My Favorite Folder • Provides access to other objects. **All Files** • Locates files or folders. **Window Explorer** • Allows browsing of the content of one's computer or network. **Recycle Bin** • A storage bin for deleted files. **Control Panel** • Provides access to properties of installed devices or resources.
Windows	Description:	• An object that displays information. • Opened from icons.
	Purpose:	• To view and edit information. • To view the content and properties of objects. • To display parameters to complete commands. • To display controls. • To display messages.

novice or casual users, mouse usage is difficult. Dragging and double-clicking are skills that take time to develop. Dragging requires continuous pressure on a mouse button and accurate destination targeting. Double-clicking is not discoverable by the user and difficulties in distinguishing timing differences between two clicks and double-clicks exist. That all actions require double-clicks is often erroneously assumed. Window management is confusing. That overlapping windows represent a three-dimensional space is not always realized and hidden windows are sometimes assumed to no longer exist. File management is also confusing. Only about one-half of all people ever used it. The organization of files and folders is difficult to understand because it is not as obvious as in the real world. Finally, task switching is not discoverable.

For people with an intermediate level of Windows 3.1 familiarity, difficulties with moving and copying files existed.

For the experienced, Windows 3.1 is not efficient as desired. There is too much middle management with confusing and overlapping functionality. The 8.3 filename structure was much too restrictive. And the interface is not as customizable as desired. Finally, network and connectivity integration is poor.

Windows 95 features The objective of Windows 95 is to make 95% of tasks easy to accomplish at all times. Among enhancements to achieve this objective are:

- A simpler main screen that can be customized by the user. Windows in 3.1 quickly got cluttered as more functions were added.
- To call up functions a Start button is used. In 3.1, icons in various windows were clicked. The Start button is three to nine times faster than 3.1, says Microsoft.
- Data-centered design. Data can be browsed and edited directly instead of the user first having to locate an appropriate editor or application. The relevant commands and tools become available automatically. The focus is on information or tasks, not the application. A *document* is the common unit of data used and exchanged.
- Switching between functions is easier. Items are selected from a task bar at the bottom.
- File management is simpler. The File Management function is gone, being replaced with a feature called Explorer.

Windows 95 components and features are summarized in Table 2.2 and illustrated in Figure 2.1.

What's Next?

Predicting the future is always difficult. Many have tried and few have succeeded. With that caveat, many experts predict that Windows 95 will probably be the last major new operating system built around the individual personal computer. Future software of this type will reside, at least partially, in electronic networks or the Internet. Its primary function will be to connect a PC to the network. The interface will be that of the server it connects to. It is also suggested that simple windows, boxes, and icons as user guides will disappear, being replaced by animation and the more fun approach that multimedia provides. Interfaces will also become more proactive, working with a person to find answers, instead of advising that "You made a mistake," or "It can't be done."

Windows 95 will also be the last all-inclusive operating system trying to solve all business and home needs. This extraordinarily wide focus has created too much complexity and many of the still-existing usability problems. Future operating systems will aim at niches, the home, the office, the backyard, the kitchen, the purse or wallet. A narrower focus will result in much less complexity. The new software will no longer arrive in a box, but will be selected, paid for, and downloaded through the Internet.

The point-and-click interaction method will be supplemented by voice commands to the computer. All those nasty words uttered in moments of

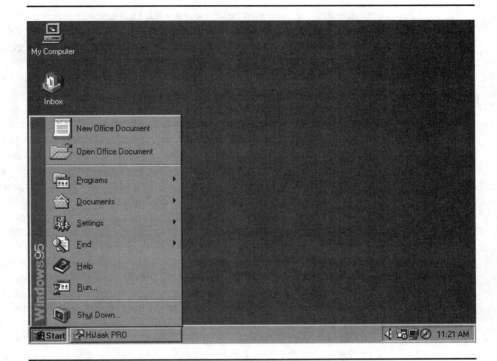

Figure 2.1   Microsoft Windows 95 components (with Start Button pull-up menu open).

frustration will now be understood by the computer. Hopefully, however, not all of these commands uttered in frustration will be implemented. Widespread use of voice commands will undoubtedly create waves of unrest through the offices of facility managers around the world. Everyone will be clamoring for their own private office to escape the resulting office din. Computer system developers may not control destiny when this issue "hits the fan." Imagine the chap sitting next to you on the airplane finishes his telephone call and then begins talking to his computer. All this while you're trying to read a book.

The full marriage of people and computers will not arrive, however, until the software recognizes facial expressions and gestures, a very important manner of human expression. A frown, a smile, or a wave of the hand all have meaning in human communication. The interface will never be complete until it possesses the ability to recognize, and react to, these forms of communication. (And it's noiseless, too.)

When will all this begin to happen? Most of it by the dawn of the new century, so the experts say. (You'll have to wait a little longer for gesture recognition.) When you're finished with this book, and don't need it for reference any longer, stick it on your library shelf and make a diary note to read this section again in the year 2001. You can then judge for yourself how right, or wrong, the experts were.

PRINCIPLES OF GRAPHICAL USER INTERFACE DESIGN

A graphical computer must really be just an extension of a person. This means the system and its software must reflect a person's capabilities and respond to his or her specific needs. It should be useful, accomplishing some business objectives faster and more efficiently than did the previously used method or tool. It must also be easy to learn, for people want to do, not learn to do. Finally, the system must be easy and fun to use, evoking a sense of pleasure and accomplishment, not tedium and frustration.

The graphical interface itself should serve as both a connector and a separator: a connector in that it ties the user to the power of the computer, and a separator in that it minimizes the possibility of the participants damaging one another. While the damage the user inflicts on the computer tends to be physical (a frustrated pounding of the keyboard), the damage caused by the computer is more psychological (a threat to one's self-esteem).

Throughout the history of the human-computer interface, various researchers and writers have attempted to define a set of general principles of interface design. As the popularity of the graphical user interface has escalated, the principles have been framed within its context.

What follows is a compilation of these principles. They reflect not only what we know today, but what we think we know today. Many are based on research, others on the collective thinking of behaviorists working with the graphical user interface. These principles will continue to evolve, expand, and be refined as our experience with GUI's increases. We will begin with the first set of published principles, those for the Xerox STAR.

Principles for the Xerox STAR

The design of the STAR was guided by a set of principles that evolved over its lengthy development process (Smith, Harslem, Irby, Kimball, & Verplank, 1982; Verplank, 1988). These principles established the foundation for graphical interfaces.

The Illusion of Manipulable Objects Displayed objects that are selectable and manipulable must be created. A design challenge is to invent a set of displayable objects that are represented meaningfully and appropriately for the intended application. It must be clear that these objects can be selected, and how to select them must be self-evident. When they are selected should also be obvious, as it should be clear that the selected object will be the focus of the next action. Verplank calls this "graphics with handles on it." Standalone icons easily fulfilled this requirement. The handles for windows were placed in the borders (window-specific commands, pop-up menus, scrolling, etc.).

Visual Order and Viewer Focus Attention must be drawn, at the proper time, to the important and relevant elements of the display. Effective visual contrast between various components of the screen is used to achieve this goal (STAR was monochromatic so color was not used). Animation is also used to draw attention, as is sound. Feedback must also be provided to the user. Since the pointer is usually the focus of viewer attention, it is a useful mechanism for providing this feedback (by changing shapes).

Revealed Structure The distance between one's intention and the effect must be minimized. Most often, the distance between intention and effect is lengthened as system power increases. The relationship between intention and effect must be tightened and made as apparent as possible to the user. The underlying structure is often revealed during the selection process.

Consistency Consistency aids learning. Consistency is provided in such areas as element location, grammar, font shapes, styles, and sizes, selection indicators, and contrast and emphasis techniques.

Appropriate Effect or Emotional Impact The interface must provide the appropriate emotional effect for the product and its market. Is it a corporate, professional, and secure business system? Should it reflect the fantasy, wizardry, and bad puns of computer games?

A Match with the Medium The interface must also reflect the capabilities of the device on which it will be displayed. Quality of screen images will be greatly impacted by a device's resolution and color-generation capabilities.

The General Principles

The design goals in creating a graphical user interface are described below. These principles are general characteristics of the interface, and they apply to all aspects. Specific guidelines on how to implement many of these goals will be presented in succeeding chapters. The compilation is presented alphabetically and the ordering is not intended to imply degree of importance. They are derived from the various principles described in Galitz (1992), IBM (1991), Mayhew (1992), Microsoft (1992, 1995), Open Software Foundation (1991), and Verplank (1988).

Aesthetically Pleasing

- Provide visual appeal by following these presentation and graphic design principles:
  - Provide meaningful contrast between screen elements.
  - Create groupings.
  - Align screen elements and groups.
  - Provide three-dimensional representation.
  - Use color effectively and simply.

A design aesthetic, or visually pleasing composition, is attractive to the eye. It draws attention subliminally, conveying a message clearly and quickly. Visual appeal makes a computer system accessible and inviting. A lack of visually pleasing composition is disorienting, obscures the intent and meaning, and slows down and confuses the user. Visual appeal is terribly important today because most human-computer communication occurs in the visual realm.

Visual appeal is provided by following the presentation and graphic design principles to be discussed, including providing meaningful contrast between screen elements, creating spatial groupings, aligning screen elements, providing three-dimensional representation, and using color effectively. Good design combines power, functionality, and simplicity with a pleasing appearance.

Clarity

- The interface should be visually, conceptually, and linguistically clear, including:
  - Visual elements.
  - Functions.
  - Metaphors.
  - Words and text.

The interface must be clear in visual appearance, concept, and wording. Visual elements should be understandable, relating to the user's real-world concepts and functions. Metaphors, or analogies, should be realistic and simple. Interface words and text should be simple, unambiguous, and free of computer jargon.

Compatibility

- Provide compatibility with the following:
  - The user.

- The task and job.
- The product.
- Adopt the user's perspective.

User compatibility. Design must be compatible with the needs of the user or client. Effective design starts with understanding the user's needs and adopting the user's point of view. One very common error among designers is to assume that users are all alike. A glance around the office should quickly put this assumption to rest. Another common error is to assume that all users think, feel, and behave exactly like the developer. Studies have proven otherwise. Users have quite different needs, aspirations, and attitudes than developers. A system reflecting only the knowledge and attitudes of its designers cannot be successful.

"Know the user" is *the* fundamental principle in interface design. User compatibility can only happen if understanding truly occurs.

Task and job compatibility. The organization of a system should match the tasks a person must do to perform the job. The structure and flow of functions should permit easy transition between tasks. The user must never be forced to navigate between applications to complete routine daily tasks.

Product compatibility. The intended user of a new system is often the user of other systems or earlier version of the new system. Habits, expectations, and a level of knowledge have been established and will be brought to bear when learning the new system. If these habits, expectations, and knowledge cannot be applied to the new system, confusion results and learning requirements are greatly increased. While compatibility across products must always be considered in relation to improving interfaces, making new systems compatible with existing systems will take advantage of what users already know and reduce the necessity for new learning.

Comprehensibility

- A system should be easily learned and understood. A user should know the following:
  - What to look at.
  - What to do.
  - When to do it.
  - Why to do it.
  - How to do it.
- The flow of actions, responses, visual presentations, and information should be in a sensible order that is easy to recollect and place in context.

A system should be intuitive and understandable, flowing in a comprehensible and meaningful order. The steps to complete a task should be obvious. Reading and digesting long explanations should never be necessary.

Configurability

- Permit easy configuration and reconfiguration of settings.
  - Enhance a sense of control.
  - Encourage an active role in understanding.
  - Allow for personal preferences.

Easy configuration and reconfiguration of a system enhances a sense of control, encourages an active role in understanding, and allows for personal preferences. Some people will prefer to reconfigure a system to better meet their preferences. Other people will not, accepting what is given. Still others will experiment with reconfiguration and then give up, running out of patience or time. For these latter groups of users a good default configuration must be provided. This default configuration must be easily established.

Consistency

- A system should look, act, and operate the same throughout. Similar components should:
  - Have a similar look.
  - Have similar uses.
  - Operate similarly.
  - The same action should always yield the same result.
  - The function of elements should not change.
  - The position of standard elements should not change.

Design consistency is the common thread that runs throughout these guidelines. It is the cardinal rule of all design activities. Consistency is important because it can reduce requirements for human learning by allowing skills learned in one situation to be transferred to another like it. While any new system must impose some learning requirements on its users, it should avoid encumbering productive learning with nonproductive, unnecessary activity.

In addition to increased learning requirements, inconsistency in design has a number of other prerequisites and by-products, including:

- More specialization by system users.
- Greater demand for higher skills.
- More preparation time and less production time.
- More frequent changes in procedures.
- More error-tolerant systems (because errors are more likely).
- More kinds of documentation.
- More time to find information in documents.
- More unlearning and learning when systems are changed.
- More demands on supervisors and managers.
- More things to do wrong.

Inconsistencies in design are caused by differences in people. Several designers might each design the same system differently. Inconsistencies also occur when design activities are pressured by time constraints. All too often the solutions in those cases are exceptions that the user must learn to handle. People, however, perceive a system as a single entity. To them, it should look, act, and feel similarly throughout. Excess learning requirements become a barrier to their achieving and maintaining high performance and can ultimately influence user acceptance of the system.

Can consistency make a big difference? One study found that user thinking time nearly doubled when the position of screen elements, such as titles and field captions, was varied on a series of menu screens (Teitelbaum & Granda, 1983).

Design consistency is achieved by developing and applying design standards or guidelines. In the late 1980s the computer industry and other organizations finally awakened to their need, and a flurry of guideline documents have recently been developed and are continuing to appear. These guidelines specify the appearance and behavior of the user interface. They describe the windows, menus, and various controls available, including what they look like and how they work. They also provide some guidance on when to use the various components.

Examples of industry-produced guidelines include Apple's *Macintosh Human Interface Guidelines* (1992b), Digital Equipment Corporation's *XUI Style Guide* (1988), IBM's *System Application Architecture Common User Access* (1987, 1989a, 1989b, 1991, 1992), Sun Microsystem's *OPEN LOOK Graphical User Interface Application Style Guidelines* (1990), Open Software Foundation's *OSF/MOTIF Style Guide* (1993), and Microsoft's *The Windows Interface* (1992), and *The Windows Interface Guidelines for Software Design* (1995).

Organizations working on guidelines or standards include the International Standards Organization (ISO), the American National Standards Institute (ANSI), and the Human Factors and Ergonomics Society (Billingsley, 1996).

Control

- The user *must* control the interaction.
  - Actions should result from explicit user requests.
  - Actions should be performed quickly.
  - Actions should be capable of interruption or termination.
  - The user should never be interrupted for errors.
- The context maintained must be from the perspective of the user.
- The means to achieve goals should be flexible and compatible with the user's skills, experiences, habits, and preferences.
- Avoid modes since they constrain the actions available to the user.
- Permit the user to customize aspects of the interface, while always providing a proper set of defaults.

Control is feeling in charge, feeling that the system is responding to your actions. Feeling that you are being controlled by a machine is demoralizing and frustrating. The interface should present a toollike appearance. Control is achieved when a person, working at his or her own pace, is able to determine what to do and how to do it. Simple, predictable, consistent, flexible, configurable, and passive interfaces provide control. Lack of control is signaled by unavailable systems, long delays in system responses, surprising system actions, tedious and long procedures that cannot be circumvented, difficulties in obtaining necessary information, and the inability to achieve the desired results.

In general, avoid modes since they restrict the actions available to the user at any given time. If modes must be used, they should be visually obvious (for example, a changed mouse pointer shape), easy to learn, and easy to remove.

The feeling of control has been found to be an excellent mitigator of the work stress associated with many automated systems

Directness

- Provide direct and intuitive ways to accomplish tasks.

Tasks should be performed directly and intuitively. Directness is provided by the object-action sequence of direct manipulation systems. Tasks are performed by directly selecting an object, then selecting an action to be performed, and then seeing the action being performed.

Efficiency

- Minimize eye, hand, and other control movements.
- Transitions between various system controls should flow easily and freely.

Eye and hand movements must not be wasted. One's attention must be captured by relevant elements of the screen when needed. Sequential eye movements between screen elements should be predictable, obvious, and short. Manual transitions between various system controls should also be as short as possible. Avoid frequent transitions between input devices such as the keyboard and mouse.

Familiarity

- Employ familiar concepts and use a language that is familiar to the user.
- Keep the interface natural, mimicking the user's behavior patterns.
- Use real-world metaphors.

Incorporate concepts, terminology, work flows, and spatial arrangements already familiar to the user into the interface. Operations should mimic one's behavior patterns; dialogs should mimic one's thought processes and vocabulary.

Flexibility

- A system must be sensitive to the differing needs of its users, enabling a level and type of performance based upon each user's:
  - Knowledge and skills.
  - Experience.
  - Personal preference.
  - Habits.
  - The conditions at that moment.

Flexibility is the system's capability to respond to individual differences in people. People should be able to interact with a system in terms of their own particular needs, including knowledge, experience, and personal preference. Flexibility is accomplished by providing multiple ways to access application functions and perform tasks. It is also accomplished through permitting configurability. Another benefit of flexibility is that it contributes to increased user control.

Flexibility is not without dangers. Highly flexible systems can confuse inexperienced people, causing them to make more errors. For this reason, flexibility appears desirable only for experienced expert users. The novice user should not be exposed to system flexibility at the start, but only as experience is gained. The concept of "progressive disclosure," to be discussed in the simplicity guideline to follow, is also applicable here.

Another problem with flexibility is that it may not always be used, people preferring to continue doing things in the way they first learned. A variety of factors may account for this, including an unwillingness to invest in additional learning, or, perhaps, new ways may not be obvious. The former problem may be addressed by making the new ways as easy and safe to learn as possible, the latter by including in training and reference materials not only information about how to do things, but when they are likely to be useful.

Forgiveness

- Tolerate and forgive common and unavoidable human errors.
- Prevent errors from occurring whenever possible.
- Protect against possible catastrophic errors.
- When an error does occur, provide constructive messages.

It is often said that "to err is human." The corollary to that statement, at least in computer systems, might be "to forgive is good design." People will make mistakes; a system should tolerate those that are common and unavoidable.

People like to explore and learn by trial and error. A system oversensitive to erroneous input will discourage users from exploring and trying new things. Learning will be inhibited, and people will be overcautious, working slowly and carefully to avoid mistakes. Productivity will then suffer. A fear of making a mistake and not being able to recover from it is a primary contributor to fear of dealing with computers.

Prevent errors from occurring by anticipating where mistakes may occur and designing to prevent them. Permit people to review, change, and undo actions whenever necessary. Make it very difficult to perform actions that can have tragic results. When errors do occur, present clear instructions on how to correct them.

Predictability

- The user should be able to anticipate the natural progression of each task.
  - Provide distinct and recognizable screen elements.

- Provide cues to the result of an action to be performed.
- All expectations should be fulfilled uniformly and completely.

Tasks, displays, and movement through a system should be anticipatable through the user's previous knowledge or experience. Screen elements should be distinct and recognizable. Current operations should provide clues as to what will come next. Anticipation, or predictability, reduces mistakes and enables tasks to be completed more quickly. All expectations possessed by the user should be fulfilled uniformly and completely. Predictability is greatly enhanced by design consistency.

Recovery

- A system should permit:
  - Commands or actions to be abolished or reversed.
  - Immediate return to a certain point if difficulties arise.

A person should be able to retract an action by issuing an *undo* command. Knowing that a command can be withdrawn reduces much of the distress of new users, who often worry about doing something wrong. The return point could be the previous action, previous screen, a recent closure point, or the beginning of some predetermined period, such as back 10 screens or some number of minutes. Reversing or abolishing an action is analogous to using an eraser to eliminate a pencil mark on a piece of paper.

The goal is stability, or returning easily to the right track when a wrong track has been taken. Recovery should be obvious, automatic, and easy and natural to perform. In short, it should be hard to get into deep water or go too far astray. Easy recovery from an action greatly facilitates learning by trial and error and exploration. If an action is not reversible, and its consequences are critical, it should be made difficult to accomplish.

Responsiveness

- The system must rapidly respond to the user's requests.
- Provide immediate acknowledgment for all user actions:
  - Visual.
  - Textual.
  - Auditory.

A user request must be responded to quickly. Knowledge of results, or feedback, is a necessary learning ingredient. It shapes human performance and instills confidence. All requests to the system must be acknowledged in some way. Feedback may be visual, the change in the shape of the mouse pointer, or textual, taking the form of a message. It may also be auditory, consisting of a unique sound or tone.

Never leave the screen blank for more than a moment, as the user may think the system has failed. If a request requires an unusually long processing time, or one that is longer than customary, provide an interim "in-progress" message. Also provide some unique form of communication if a user action results in a problem or possible problem.

Substantial or more informative feedback is most important for the casual or new system user. Expert users are often content to receive more modest feedback.

Simplicity

- Provide as simple an interface as possible.
- Five ways to provide simplicity:
  - Use progressive disclosure, hiding things until they are needed.
    - Present common and necessary functions first.
    - Prominently feature important functions.
    - Hide more sophisticated and less frequently used functions.
  - Provide defaults.
  - Minimize screen alignment points.
  - Make common actions simple at the expense of uncommon actions made harder.
  - Provide uniformity and consistency.

Simplicity is the opposite of complexity. Complexity is a measure of the number of choices available at any point in the human-computer interaction. A great deal of functionality and power is usually associated with high complexity. Complexity most often overwhelms and confuses new and casual users of systems. Complex systems are often not fully used, or used ineffectively, because a person may follow known but more cumbersome methods instead of easier but undiscovered or unfamiliar methods.

A system lacking complexity may have a different set of faults. It may be tedious to use or not accomplish much. It is better, however, to provide less functionality that will get effectively used than to provide too much functionality yielding an interface hopelessly complex and extremely difficult to use. Complexity, then, is a two-edged sword. To effectively solve problems it must be present without being apparent. The goal, then, is to provide a complex system while masking the complexity through a simple interface. There are several ways to minimize this complexity.

Progressive disclosure. Introduce system components gradually so the full complexity of the system is not visible at first encounter. Teach basic fundamentals first. Then, slowly introduce advanced or more sophisticated functions. This is called the layered, or spiral, approach to learning. Such an approach was first described by Carroll and Carrithers (1984) who called it the "Training-Wheels System." They found that by disabling portions of the system that were not needed and could lead to errors and confusion, improved system learning efficiency was achieved.

Provide defaults. Providing defaults is another form of system layering. When a system is first presented, provide a set of defaults for all system-configurable items. The new user will not be burdened with these decisions and can concentrate on the fundamentals first. Defaults can later be changed, if desired, as experience increases.

Minimize screen alignment points. A larger number of alignment points of elements displayed on a screen are associated with greater screen visual complexity. Minimizing these alignment points minimizes visual complexity. This concept will be discussed more fully later.

Make common actions simple. Make common actions within a system easier to accomplish than uncommon actions. Greater overall system efficiency results.

Provide uniformity and consistency. Inconsistency is a foolish form of complexity. It forces a person to learn that things that appear different are not really different.

Transparency

- Permit the user to focus on the task or job, without concern for the mechanics of the interface. Workings, and reminders of workings, inside the computer should be invisible to the user.

Never force the user to think about the technical details of the system. One's thoughts must be directed to the task, not the computer communication process. Reminders of the mechanics of the interface occur through use of technical jargon, heavy use of codes, and presentation of computer concepts and representations.

Trade-Offs

- Final design will be based on a series of trade-offs balancing often conflicting design principles.
- People's requirements always take precedence over technical requirements.

Design guidelines often cover a great deal of territory and often conflict with one another or with technical requirements. In such conflicts the designer must weigh the alternatives and reach a decision based on trade-offs concerning accuracy, time, cost, and ease of use. Making these trade-offs intelligently requires a thorough understanding of the user and all design considerations. The ultimate solution will be a blend of experimental data, good judgment, and the important user needs.

This leads to a second cardinal rule of graphical system development: *Human requirements always take precedence over technical requirements.* It may be easier for the designer to write a program or build a device that neglects user ease, but final system judgment will always come down to one simple fact: How well does the system meet the needs of the user?

THE DESIGN PROCESS

Designing a computer system is never easy. The development path is littered with obstacles and traps, many of them human in nature. Gould (1988) has made these general observations about design:

- Nobody ever gets it right the first time.
- Development is chock-full of surprises.
- Good design requires living in a sea of changes.
- Making contracts to ignore change will never eliminate the need for change.
- Even if you have made the best system humanly possible, people will still make mistakes using it.
- Designers need good tools.
- You must have behavioral design goals like performance design goals.

The sheer complexity of a graphical system will magnify any problems that do occur. While problems and poor design will never be completely eliminated, they can be significantly reduced if the following commandments are adhered to.

Designing for People: The Five Commandments

- Gain a complete understanding of users and their tasks.
- Solicit early and ongoing user involvement.
- Perform rapid prototyping and testing.
- Modify and iterate the design as much as necessary.
- Integrate the design of *all* the system components.

1. Understand the users The users are the customers. The product or system must be geared to their needs, not those of the developers. A wide gap in technical abilities, goals, and attitudes often exists between users and developers. A failure to understand the differences will doom a product or system to failure.

2. Involve the users Involving the users in design from the beginning provides a direct conduit to the knowledge they possess about jobs and tasks. Involvement also allows the developer to confront a person's resistance to change, a common human trait. People dislike change for a variety of reasons, among them fear of the unknown and lack of identification. Involvement in design removes the unknown and gives the user a stake in the system, or an identification with it. One caution, however: User involvement should be based on job or task knowledge, not status or position.

3. Perform rapid prototyping and testing Prototyping and testing the product will quickly identify problems and develop solutions. The design process is complex and human behavior is still not well understood. While the design guidelines that follow go a long way toward achieving ease of use, all problems cannot possibly be predicted. Prototyping and testing must be continually performed to uncover all potential defects.

If thorough testing is not performed before product release, the testing will occur in the user's office. Many problems will create a negative first impression in the customer's mind, and this may harden quickly, creating attitudes that may be difficult to change.

It is also much harder and costlier to fix a product after its release. In many instances, people may adapt to, or become dependent upon, a design, even if it is inefficient. This also makes future modifications much more difficult.

4. Modify and iterate the design as much as necessary Establish user performance and acceptance criteria and continue testing and modifying until all design goals are met.

5. Integrate the design of all system elements The software, the documentation, the help function, and training needs should all be developed concurrently. A system is being constructed, not simply software. Concurrent development of all pieces will point out possible problems early in the design process, allowing them to be more effectively addressed. Design trade-offs can be more carefully thought out.

The Design Team

- Provide a balanced design team, including specialists in:
  - Development.
  - Human factors.
  - Visual design.
  - Usability assessment.
  - Documentation.
  - Training.
- Select team members who can effectively work and communicate with one another.
- Locate the team in close proximity to one another.

Effective design and development requires the application of very diverse talents. No one person possesses all the skills to perform all the necessary tasks; the best that can be hoped for is that one person may possess a couple of skills. A balanced design team with very different talents must be established. Needed are specialists in development to define requirements and write the software, human factors specialists to define behavioral requirements and apply behavioral considerations, and people with good visual design skills. Also needed are people skilled in testing and usability assessment, documentation specialists, and training specialists.

Team members selected should be those who can effectively work and communicate with one another. To optimize communication, the team must be located in close proximity to one another.

The Design Steps: An Overview

Part II of this book is organized in the order of the design steps typically followed in creating a graphical system and screens. This organization enables all the screen design activities to be addressed easily, clearly, and sequentially. This organization into nonoverlapping linear tasks does not mean to imply, however, that the actual design process will fall into such neat categories, one step finishing and only then the next step starting. In reality, some steps will run concurrently or overlap one another, and design iterations will cause occasional movements backward as well as forward. If any of these steps are omitted, or carelessly performed, a product's foundation will be flawed. A flawed foundation is difficult to correct afterwards.

With these cautions in mind, following is an overview of the design steps to be addressed.

Step 1: Know Your User or Client To begin, an understanding of the most important system component, the user or client, must be obtained.

Understanding people and what they do is a critical and often difficult and undervalued process. Step 1 in the design process involves identifying user characteristics and understanding how they impact design.

Step 2: Understand the Business Function A system must achieve the business objectives for which it is designed. To do so requires an understanding of the functions and tasks performed. This is accomplished by determining basic business functions, describing user activities through task analysis, understanding the user's mental model, and developing a conceptual model of the system. The system's conceptual model must fit the user's view of the tasks to be performed. Step 2 also addresses establishing design standard or style guides, establishing usability design goals, and defining training and documentation needs.

Step 3: Understand the Principles of Good Screen Design A well-designed screen must reflect the needs and capabilities of its users, be developed within the physical constraints imposed by the hardware on which it is displayed, and effectively utilize the capabilities of its controlling software. Step 3 involves understanding the capabilities of, and limitations imposed, by people, hardware, and software in designing screens. It presents a very large number of general design principles for presenting information to people.

Step 4: Select the Proper Kinds of Windows Graphical screen design will consist of a series of windows. Step 4 involves understanding how windows are used and selecting the proper kinds for the tasks. The elements of windows are described, and the purpose and proper usage of various types of windows are detailed.

Step 5: Develop System Menus Graphical systems are heavily menu-oriented. Menus are used to designate commands, properties that apply to an object, documents, and windows. To accomplish these goals, a graphical system presents a variety of menu styles to choose from. Step 5 involves understanding how menus are used and selecting the proper kinds for the tasks. The principles of menu design are described, and the purpose and proper usage of various menu types are detailed.

Step 6: Select the Proper Device-Based Controls In addition to the keyboard, a graphical system might offer the user a mouse, trackball, joystick, graphic tablet, touch screen, light pen, or some other similar device. Step 6 consists of identifying the characteristics and capabilities of these various control mechanisms and providing the proper ones for users and their tasks.

Step 7: Choose the Proper Screen-Based Controls The screen designer is presented an array of screen-based controls to choose from. Selecting the right one for the user and the task is often difficult. But, as with device-based controls, making the right choice is critical to system success. A proper fit between user and control will lead to fast, accurate performance. A poor fit will result in lower productivity, more errors, and probably dissatisfaction. Step 7 consists of identifying the characteristics and capabilities of these various screen-based controls and providing the proper ones for users and their tasks.

Step 8: Organize and Lay Out Windows After determining what screen-based controls are needed, they must next be presented clearly and meaningfully in the work area of the window. Proper presentation and organization will encourage quick and accurate information comprehension and the fastest possible execution of display features. Step 8 involves identifying all necessary additional screen components and then laying out screen elements and controls in the most effective manner possible.

Step 9: Choose the Proper Colors Color, if used properly, can emphasize the logical organization of a screen, facilitate the discrimination of screen components, accentuate differences, and make displays more interesting. If used improperly, color can be distracting and cause visual fatigue, impairing a system's usability. Step 9 involves understanding color and how to use it effectively on textual and statistical graphics screens.

Step 10: Create Meaningful Icons Graphic screens often contain icons, which are pictures to represent displayed objects or actions. Step 10 involves understanding what kinds of icons exist, what influences their usability, and how to design them in a meaningful and recognizable way.

Step 11: Provide Effective Messages, Feedback, Guidance and Language Translation Effective messages, feedback, and guidance and assistance are also necessary elements of good design. For systems used by non-English speakers, proper translation is also a necessity. Step 11 addresses these aspects of screens.

Step 12: Test, Test, and Retest A host of factors must be considered in graphical design and numerous trade-offs made. Indeed, the design of some parts of the system may be based on skimpy data and reflect the most educated guess possible. Also, the implications for some design decisions may not be fully appreciated until the results can be seen. Waiting until after a system has been implemented to uncover any deficiencies and make any design changes can be aggravating, costly, and time-consuming. To minimize these kinds of problems screens must be continually tested and refined *before* they are implemented. Step 12 reviews testing, including creating, evaluating, and modifying prototypes in an iterative manner. It also reviews conducting a system test and an evaluation of the working system.

PART II

The GUI Screen Design Process

S T E P   1

Know Your User or Client

The journey into the world of graphical screen design and the screen design process must begin with an understanding of the system user, the most important part of any computer system, whose needs the systems are built to serve. Understanding users and what they do is a difficult and undervalued process but extremely important because of the gap in skills and attitudes existing between system users and developers.

- Understand how people interact with computers.
- Understand the human characteristics important in design.
- Identify the user's level of knowledge and experience.
- Identify the characteristics of the user's tasks and jobs.
- Identify the user's psychological characteristics.
- Identify the user's physical characteristics.
- Employ recommended methods for gaining understanding of users.

UNDERSTANDING HOW PEOPLE INTERACT WITH COMPUTERS

We will begin by looking at some characteristics of past computer systems that have caused people trouble and the effect they have.

Why People Have Trouble with Computers

Although system design and its behavioral implications have come under intense scrutiny in recent years, as we have seen, this has not always been the case. Historically, the design of computer systems has been the responsibility of programmers, systems analysts, and system designers, many of whom possess extensive technical knowledge but little behavioral training. Design decisions have thus rested mostly on the designers' intuition and wealth of specialized knowledge, and consequently, poorly designed interfaces often go unrecognized.

The intuition of designers or of anyone else, no matter how good or bad they may be at what they do, is error-prone. It is too shallow a foundation on which to base design decisions. Specialized knowledge lulls one into a false sense of security. It enables one to interpret and deal with complex or ambiguous situations on the basis of context cues not visible to users, as well as knowledge of the computer system they do not possess. The result is a perfectly usable system to its designers but one the office worker is unable or unwilling to face up to and master.

What has made a system complex in the eyes of its user? Listed below are several contributing factors.

Use of Jargon Systems often talk in a strange language. Words completely alien to the office environment or used in different contexts, such as *filespec*, *abend*, *segment*, and *boot* proliferate. Learning to use a system often requires learning a new language.

Nonobvious Design Complex or novel design elements are not obvious or intuitive, but they must nevertheless be mastered. Operations may have prerequisite conditions that must be satisfied before they can be accomplished, or outcomes may not always be immediate, obvious, or visible. The overall framework of the system may be invisible, with the effect that results cannot always be related to the actions that accomplish them.

Fine Distinctions Different actions may accomplish the same thing, depending upon when they are performed, or different things may result from the same action. Often these distinctions are minute and difficult to keep track of. Critical distinctions are not made at the appropriate time, or distinctions having no real consequence are made instead, as illustrated by the user who insisted that problems were caused by pressing the ENTER key "in the wrong way" (Carroll & Carrithers, 1984).

Disparity in Problem-Solving Strategies People learn best by doing. They have trouble following directions and do not always read instructions before taking an action. Human problem solving can best be characterized as "error-correcting" or "trial and error," whereby a tentative solution is formulated based on the available evidence and then tried. This tentative solution often has a low chance of success, but the results are used to modify one's next attempt and so increase the chances of success. Most early computers, however, have enforced an "error-preventing" strategy, which assumes that a person will not take an action until a high degree of confidence exists in its success. The result is that when people head down wrong one-way paths, they often get entangled in situations difficult, or impossible, to get out of. The last resort action? Turn off the computer and start again.

Design Inconsistency The same action may have different names: for example, "save" and "keep," "write" and "list." Or the same result may be described differently: for example, "not legal" and "not valid." The result is that system learning becomes an exercise in rote memorization. Meaningful or conceptual learning becomes very difficult.

Responses to Poor Design

Unfortunately, people remember the one thing that went wrong, not the many that go right, so problems achieve an abnormal level of importance. Errors are a symptom of problems. The magnitude of errors in a computer-based system has been found to be as high as 46 percent for commands, tasks, or transactions.

Errors, and other problems that befuddle, lead to a variety of psychological and physical user responses. Some psychological responses are listed below.

Confusion Detail overwhelms the perceived structure. Meaningful patterns are difficult to ascertain, and the conceptual model or underlying framework cannot be established.

Panic Panic may be introduced by unexpectedly long delays during times of severe or unusual pressure. The chief causes are unavailable systems and long response times.

Boredom Boredom results from improper computer pacing (slow response times) and overly simplistic jobs.

Frustration An inability to easily convey one's intentions to the computer causes frustration, which is heightened if an unexpected response cannot be undone or if what really took place cannot be determined. Inflexible and unforgiving systems are a major source of frustration.

These psychological responses diminish user effectiveness because they are severe blocks to concentration. Thoughts irrelevant to the task at hand are forced to attention and necessary concentration is impossible. The result, in addition to higher error rates, is poor performance, anxiety, and job dissatisfaction. Further, these psychological responses frequently lead to, or are accompanied by, the following physical responses.

Abandonment of the System The system is rejected and other information sources are relied upon. These sources must be available, and the user must have the discretion to perform the rejection. This is a common reaction of managerial and professional personnel.

Incomplete Use of the System Only a portion of the system's capabilities are used, usually those operations that are easiest to perform or that provide the most benefits. Historically, this has been the most common reaction to most systems.

Indirect Use of the System An intermediary is placed between the would-be user and the computer. Again, since this requires high status and discretion, it is another typical response of managers.

Modification of the Task The task is changed to match the capabilities of the system. This is a prevalent reaction when the tools are rigid and the problem is unstructured, as in scientific problem solving.

Compensatory Activity Additional actions are performed to compensate for system inadequacies. A common example is the manual reformatting of information to match the structure required by the computer. This is a reaction common to workers whose discretion is limited, such as clerical personnel.

Misuse of the System The rules are bent to shortcut operational difficulties. This requires significant knowledge of the system and may affect system integrity.

Direct Programming The system is reprogrammed by its user to meet specific needs. This is a typical response of the sophisticated worker.

People and Their Tasks

While we would like to think people sit idly at their desks anxiously awaiting the arrival of a computer system and the salvation it will afford, the truth is mostly the opposite. The user in today's office is usually overworked, fatigued, and continually interrupted. Documentation tends not to be read, problems are not well understood, and little is known about what information is available to meet one's needs. Moreover, the user's technical skills have often been greatly overestimated by the system designer, who is usually isolated psychologically and physically from the user's situation. Unlike the user, the designer is capable of resolving most system problems and ambiguities through application of experience and technical knowledge. Often the designer cannot really believe that anyone is incapable of using the system created.

The user, while being subjected to the everyday pressures of the office, is still technologically unsophisticated, sometimes computer illiterate, and possibly even antagonistic. He wants to spend time using a computer, not learning to use it. His or her objective is simply to get some work done. It is in this environment our system will be placed.

IMPORTANT HUMAN CHARACTERISTICS IN DESIGN

We are complex organisms with a variety of attributes that have an important influence on screen design. Of particular importance in design are perception, memory, visual acuity, foveal and peripheral vision, sensory storage, information processing, learning, skill, and individual differences.

Perception

Perception is our awareness and understanding of the elements and objects of our environment through the physical sensation of our various senses, including sight, sound, smell, and so forth. Perception is influenced, in part, by experience. We classify stimuli based on models stored in our memories and in this way achieve understanding. In essence, we tend to match objects or sensations perceived to things we already know. Comparing the accumulated knowledge of the child with that of an adult in interpreting the world is a vivid example of the role of experience in perception.

Other perceptual characteristics include the following:

Proximity Our eyes and mind see objects as belonging together if they are near each other in space.

Similarity Our eyes and mind see objects as belonging together if they share a common visual property, such as color, size, shape, brightness, or orientation.

Matching Patterns We respond similarly to the same shape in different sizes. The letters of the alphabet, for example, possess the same meaning, regardless of physical size.

Succinctness We see an object as having some perfect or simple shape because perfection or simplicity is easier to remember

Closure Our perception is synthetic; it establishes meaningful wholes. If something does not quite close itself, such as a circle, square, triangle, or word, we see it closed anyway.

Unity Objects that form closed shapes are perceived as a group.

Continuity Shortened lines may be automatically extended.

Balance We desire stabilization or equilibrium in our viewing environment. Vertical, horizontal, and right angles are the most visually satisfying and easiest to look at.

Expectancies Perception is also influenced by expectancies; sometimes we perceive not what is there but what we expect to be there. Missing a mistake in proofreading something we write is often an example of a perceptual expectancy error; we see not how a word *is* spelled, but how we *expect* to see it spelled.

Context, environment, and surroundings also influence individual perception. For example, two drawn lines of the same length may look the same length or a different length depending on the angle of adjacent lines or what other people have said about the size of the lines.

Signals vs. Noise Our sensing mechanisms are bombarded by many stimuli, some of which are important and some of which are not. Important stimuli are called *signals*; those that are not important or unwanted are called *noise*. Signals are more quickly comprehended if they are easily distinguishable from noise in our sensory environment. Noise interferes with the perception of signals to the extent that they are similar to one another. Noise can even mask a critical signal. For example, imagine a hidden word puzzle where meaningful words are buried in a large block matrix of alphabetic characters. The signals, alphabetic characters constituting meaningful words, are masked by the matrix of meaningless letters.

The elements of a screen assume the quality of signal or noise, depending on the actions and thought processes of the user. Once a screen is first presented and has to be identified as being the correct one, the screen's title may be the signal, the other elements it contains simply being noise. When the screen is being used, the data it contains becomes the signal and the title now reverts to noise. Other elements of the screen also assume the roles of either signals or noise, depending on the user's needs of the moment.

Memory

Memory is not one of the most developed of human attributes. Short-term memory is highly susceptible to the interference of such distracting tasks as thinking, reciting, or listening, which are constantly erasing and overwriting it. Remembering a telephone number long enough to complete the dialing operation taxes the memory of many people. The short-term memory limit is generally viewed as 7 ± 2 "chunks" of information (Miller, 1956), and knowledge, experience, and familiarity govern the size and complexity of chunks that can be recalled. To illustrate, most native English-speaking people would find recalling seven English words much easier than recalling seven Russian words. For a Russian it would be the opposite. Short-term memory is thought to last 15 to 30 seconds. Unlike short-term memory, with its distinct limitations, long-term memory is thought to be unlimited. An important memory consideration, with significant implications for screen design, is the difference in ability to recognize or recall words. The human active vocabulary (words that can be recalled) typically ranges between 2,000 and 3,000 words. Passive vocabulary (words that can be recognized) typically numbers about 100,000. Our power of recognition is much greater than our power of recall, and this phenomenon should be utilized in design.

Visual Acuity

The capacity of the eye to resolve details is called visual acuity. It is the phenomenon that results in an object becoming more distinct as we turn our eyes toward it and rapidly loses distinctness as we turn our eyes away— that is, as the visual angle from the point of fixation increases. It has been shown that relative visual acuity is approximately halved at a distance of 2.5 degrees from the point of eye fixation (Bouma, 1970). Therefore, a five-degree diameter circle centered around an eye fixation character on a display has been recommended as the area near that character (Tullis, 1983) or the maximum length for a displayed word (Danchak, 1976).

If one assumes that the average viewing distance of a display screen is 19 inches (475 mm), the size of the area on the screen of optimum visual acuity is 1.67 inches (41.8 mm). Assuming "average" character sizes and character and line spacings, the number of characters on a screen falling within this visual acuity circle is 88, with 15 characters being contained on the widest line, and seven rows being consumed, as illustrated below.

```
     3213123
   54321212345
  6543211123456
 765432101234567
  6543211123456
   54321212345
     3213123
```

The eye's sensitivity increases for those characters closest to the fixation point (the "0") and decreases for those characters at the extreme edges of the circle (a 50/50 chance exists for getting these characters correctly identified). This may be presumed to be a visual "chunk" of a screen and will have implications for screen grouping guidelines to be presented later.

The eye is also never perfectly steady as it sees, tremoring slightly. This tremor improves the detection of edges of objects being looked at, thus improving acuity. This tremor, however, can sometimes create problems. Patterns of closely spaced lines or dots are seen to shimmer. This movement can be distracting and disturbing. Patterns for fill-in areas of screens (bars, circles, etc.) must be carefully chosen to avoid this distraction.

Foveal and Peripheral Vision

Foveal vision is used to focus directly on something; peripheral vision senses anything in the area surrounding where we are looking, but what is there cannot be clearly resolved because of our visual acuity limitations just described. Foveal and peripheral vision maintain, at the same time, a cooperative and a competitive relationship. Peripheral vision can aid visual search, but can also be distracting.

In its cooperative nature, peripheral vision is thought to provide clues to where the eye should go next in the visual search of a screen. Patterns, shapes, and alignments peripherally visible can guide the eye in a systematic way through a screen.

In its competitive nature, peripheral vision can compete with foveal vision for attention. That sensed in the periphery is passed on to our information processing system along with what is actively being viewed foveally. It is, in a sense, visual noise. Mori & Hayashi (1993) experimentally evaluated the effect of windows in both a foveal and peripheral relationship and found that performance on a foveal window deteriorates when there are peripheral windows, and the performance degradation is even greater if the information in the peripheral is dynamic or moving. Care should be exercised in design to utilize peripheral vision in its positive nature, avoiding its negative aspects.

Sensory Storage

Sensory storage is a buffer where automatic processing of information collected from our senses takes place. It is an unconscious process, large, attentive to the environment, quick to detect changes, and constantly being replaced by newly gathered stimuli. In a sense, it acts like a radar, constantly scanning the environment for things important to pass on to higher memory.

Though seemingly overwhelmed at times, it can occasionally detect, proverbially, a tree through a forest. One good example is what is sometimes called the "cocktail party affect." Have you ever been at a party when, across the room, through the din of voices, someone mentions your name, and you hear it? In spite of the noise, your radar was functioning.

Repeated and excessive stimulation can fatigue sensory storage, making it less attentive and unable to distinguish what is important (called *habituation*). Avoid unnecessarily stressing it. Design the interface so that all aspects and elements serve a definite purpose. Important things will be less likely to be missed.

Information Processing

The information that our senses collect that is deemed important enough to do something about then has to be processed in some meaningful way. Recent thinking (Lind, Johnson, & Sandblad, 1992) is that there are two levels of information processing going on within us. One level, the highest level, is identified with consciousness and working memory. It is limited, slow, and sequential, and is used for reading and understanding. You are utilizing this higher level now reading this book.

In addition to this higher level, there exists a lower level of information processing whose capacity limit is unknown. This lower level processes familiar information rapidly, in parallel with the higher level, and without conscious effort. We look rather than see, perceive rather than read. Repetition and learning results in a shift of control from the higher level to the lower level.

Both levels function simultaneously, the higher level performing reasoning and problem solving, the lower level perceiving the physical form of information sensed. You've probably experienced this difference in working with screens. When a screen is displayed, you usually will want to verify it is the one you want. If you're new to a system, or a screen is new to you, you rely on its concrete elements to make that determination, its title, the controls and information it contains, and so forth. You consciously look at the screen and its components using this higher level processing. As you become experienced and familiar with screens, however, a newly presented screen can be identified very quickly with just a momentary glance. Just its shape and structure adequately communicate to you that it is the correct screen for the context in which you are working. Your reasoning and problem-solving continues unhindered; your lower-level information processing has assumed the screen identity task.

What assists this lower-level information processing? Visual distinctiveness of a screen is a strong contributor. If a screen is jammed with information and cluttered, it loses its uniqueness and can only be identified through the more time-consuming, and thought interrupting, reading process.

Mental Models

As a result of our experiences and culture we develop mental models of things and people we interact with. A mental model is simply an internal representation of a person's current understanding of something. Mental models are gradually developed in order to understand, explain, and do something. Mental models enable a person to predict the necessary actions to do things if the action has been forgotten or has not yet been encountered. People will bring their own expectations and preconceptions to a new computer system. Already being familiar with a certain kind of system will set up certain visual and usage expectations. The key to forming mental models is design consistency.

Learning

Our ability to learn is important—it clearly differentiates people from machines. A design developed to minimize human learning time can accelerate human performance. Given enough time, of course, people can improve their performance in almost any task. Most people can be taught to walk a tightrope, but a designer should not incorporate a tightrope into his design if a walkway is feasible.

Evidence derived from studies of computer system learning parallels that found in studies of learning in other areas. People prefer to be active, to explore, and to use a trial and error approach. There is also evidence that people are very sensitive to even minor changes in the user interface, and that such changes may lead to problems in transferring from one system to another. Moreover, just the "perception" of having to learn huge amounts of information is enough to keep some people from using a system. Learning can be enhanced if it:

- Allows skills acquired in one situation to be used in another somewhat like it. (Design consistency accomplishes this.)
- Provides complete and prompt feedback.
- Is phased, that is, it requires a person to know only the information needed at that stage of the learning process.

Skill

The goal of human performance is to perform skillfully. To do so requires linking inputs and outputs into a sequence of action. The essence of skill is performance of actions in the correct time sequence with adequate precision. It is characterized by consistency and economy of effort. Economy of effort is achieved by establishing a work pace that represents optimum efficiency. It is accomplished by increasing mastery of the system through such things as progressive learning of shortcuts, increased speed, and easier access to information or data.

Skills are hierarchical in nature, and many basic skills may be integrated to form increasingly complex ones. Lower-order skills tend to become routine and may drop out of consciousness. System and screen design must permit development of increasingly skillful performance.

Individual Differences

A complicating but very advantageous human characteristic is that we all differ—in looks, feelings, motor abilities, intellectual abilities, learning abilities and speeds, and so on. In a keyboard data entry task, for example, the best typists will probably be twice as fast as the poorest and make 10 times fewer errors. Individual differences complicate design because the design must permit people with widely varying characteristics to satisfactorily and comfortably learn the task or job. In the past this has usually resulted in bringing designs down to the level of lowest abilities or selecting people with the minimum skills necessary to perform a job. But office technology now offers the possibility of tailoring jobs to the specific needs of people with varying and changing learning or skill levels. Design must permit this to occur.

Table 1.1   Important User/Task Characteristics

Knowledge/Experience

Computer Literacy	Highly technical or experienced, moderate computer experience, or none
System Experience	High, moderate, or low knowledge of a particular system and its methods of interaction
Application Experience	High, moderate, or low knowledge of similar systems
Task Experience	Level of knowledge of job and job tasks
Other Systems Use	Frequent or infrequent use of other systems in doing job
Education	High school, college, or advanced degree
Reading Level	Less than 5th grade, 5th–12th, more than 12th grade
Typing Skill	Expert (135 WPM), skilled (90 WPM), good (55 WPM), average (40 WPM), or "hunt and peck" (10 WPM)
Native Language	English, another, or several

Job/Task

Type of System Use	Mandatory or discretionary use of the system
Frequency of Use	Continual, frequent, occasional, or once-in-a-lifetime use of system
Turnover Rate	High, moderate, or low turnover rate for job holders
Task Importance	High, moderate, or low importance of the task being performed
Task Structure	Repetitiveness or predictability of tasks being automated, high, moderate, or low
Primary Training	Extensive or formal training, self-training through manuals, or no training
Job Category	Executive, manager, professional, secretary, clerk

Psychological Characteristics

Attitude	Positive, neutral, or negative feeling toward job or system
Motivation	Low, moderate, or high due to interest or fear
Cognitive Style	Verbal or spatial, analytic or intuitive, concrete or abstract

Physical Characteristics

Age	Young, middle aged, or elderly
Gender	Male or female
Handedness	Left, right, or ambidextrous
Physical Handicaps	Blind, defective vision, deafness, motor handicap

Derived from Mayhew, 1992.

The above characteristics are general qualities we all possess. There are also a host of other human considerations by which people may vary greatly. These are important and must also be identified in the screen design process. The following listings of these characteristics are derived from Mayhew (1992) and are summarized in Table 1.1.

THE USER'S KNOWLEDGE AND EXPERIENCE

The knowledge possessed by a person, and experiences undergone, shape the design of the interface in many ways. The following kinds of knowledge and experiences should be identified.

Computer Literacy

Are the users highly technical such as programmers or experienced data entry clerks? Do they have moderate computer experience or none at all? Will they be familiar with computer concepts and terms, the keyboard and its keys, and a mouse or other input mechanisms?

System Experience

Are users already familiar with the interaction requirements of the new system? Have they worked on a system with the same interface? Have they been exposed to a similar interface or will it be new?

At one time or another, various schemes have been proposed to classify the different and sometimes changing characteristics of people as they become more experienced using a system. Words to describe the new, relatively new, or infrequent user have included *naive, casual, inexperienced,* or *novice.* At the other end of the experience continuum lie terms such as *experienced, full-time,* or *expert.* The words themselves are less important than the behavioral characteristics they imply. Experience to date is uncovering some basic differences in feelings of ease of use based upon proficiency level. What is easy for the new user is not perceived as easy for the "old hand," and vice versa.

For consistency in our discussion, the term *novice* will be used for the new user; the term *expert,* for the most proficient. Novice users have been found to:

- Depend on system features that assist recognition memory: menus, prompting information, and instructional and help screens.
- Need restricted vocabularies, simple tasks, small numbers of possibilities, and very informative feedback.
- View practice as an aid to moving up to expert status.

Whereas experts:

- Rely upon free recall.
- Expect rapid performance.
- Need less informative feedback.
- Seek efficiency by bypassing novice memory aids, reducing keystrokes, chunking and summarizing information, and introducing new vocabularies.

In actuality, the user population of most systems is spread out along the continuum anchored by these two extremes. And, equally important, the behavior of any one user at different times may be closer to one extreme or the other. A person may be very proficient—an expert—in one aspect of a system and ignorant—a novice—in other aspects at the same time.

Exactly how experts and novices actually differ from one another in terms of knowledge, problem-solving behavior, and other human characteristics has been the subject of some research in recent years. Summarizing some of the findings (Mayer, 1988; Ortega, 1989), experts possess the following traits:

- They possess an integrated conceptual model of a system.
- They possess knowledge that is ordered more abstractly and more procedurally.
- They organize information more meaningfully, orienting it toward their task.
- They structure information into more categories.
- They are better at making inferences and relating new knowledge to their objectives and goals.
- They pay less attention to low-level details.
- They pay less attention to surface features of a system.

Novices exhibit these characteristics:

- They possess a fragmented conceptual model of a system.
- They organize information less meaningfully, orienting it toward surface features of the system.
- They structure information into fewer categories.
- They have difficulty in generating inferences and relating new knowledge to their objectives and goals.
- They pay more attention to low-level details.
- They pay more attention to surface features of the system.

A well-designed system, therefore, must support at the same time novice and expert behavior, as well as all levels of behavior in between. In

Table 1.2   Microsoft Windows 95 Expert Aids

• The Windows Explorer	For easy file management and information browsing
• Shortcuts	For quickly accessing all objects
• Property Sheets	All objects carry context-sensitive properties that can be easily accessed and customized
• Pop-up Menus (Right-clicking)	Commands to perform common actions
• Quick Viewers	To review a file without opening the application that created it

general, the following graphical system aspects are seen as desirable expert shortcuts:

- Mouse double-clicks.
- Pop-up menus.
- Tear-off or detachable menus.
- Command lines.

Microsoft Windows 95 expert shortcuts are summarized in Table 1.2.

Application Experience

Have users worked with a similar application (e.g., word processing, airline reservation, etc.)? Are they familiar with the basic application terms? Or does little or no application experience exist?

Task Experience

Are users experienced with the task being automated? If it is an insurance claim system, do users have experience with paying claims? If it is a banking system, do users have experience in similar banking applications? Or do users possess little or no knowledge of the tasks the system will be performing?

Other System Use

Will the user be using other systems while using the new system? If so, they will bring certain habits and expectancies. The more compatibility between systems, the lower the learning requirements for the new system and the higher the productivity using all systems.

Education

What is the general educational level of users? Do they generally have high school degrees, college degrees, or advanced degrees? Are the degrees in specialized areas related to new system use?

Reading Level

If the interface is verbal, the vocabulary and grammatical structure must be at a level that is easily understood by the users. Reading level can often be inferred from one's education level.

Typing Skill

Is the user a competent typist or of the hunt-and-peck variety? Are they familiar with the standard keyboard layout or other newer layouts? A competent typist may prefer to interact with the system exclusively through the keyboard whereas the unskilled may prefer the mouse.

Native Language

Do the users speak English, another language, or several other languages? Will the screens have to be in English or in some other language? Other languages often impose different screen layout requirements. Will icons be meaningful for all the user cultures?

Most of these kinds of user knowledge and experience are independent of one another, so many different profiles are possible. It is also useful to look ahead, assessing whether future users will possess the same qualities.

THE USER'S TASKS AND JOBS

The user's job and the kinds and duration of tasks to be performed are also important in design. The following should be determined:

Mandatory or Discretionary Use

Users of the earliest computer systems were mandatory or nondiscretionary. That is, they required the computer to perform a task that, for all practical purposes, could be performed no other way. Characteristics of nondiscretionary use can be summarized as follows:

- The computer is used as part of employment.
- Time and effort in learning to use the computer are willingly invested.
- High motivation is often used to overcome low usability characteristics.
- The user may possess a technical background.
- The job may consist of a single task or function.

The nondiscretionary user must learn to live comfortably with a computer, for there is really no other choice. Examples of nondiscretionary use today include a flight reservations clerk booking seats, an insurance company employee entering data into the computer so a policy can be issued, and a programmer writing and debugging a program. The toll exacted by a poorly designed system in nondiscretionary use is measured primarily by productivity, for example, errors and poor customer satisfaction.

In recent years, as computers have become more common in the office, the discretionary user has become exposed to the benefits, and costs, of technology. He or she is much more self-directed than the nondiscretionary user, not being told how to work but being evaluated on the results of his or her efforts. For him or her, it is not the means but the results that are most important. In short, this user has never been told how to work in the past and refuses to be told so now. This newer kind of user is the office executive, manager, or other professional, whose computer use is completely discretionary. Common characteristics of the discretionary user are as follows:

- Use of the system is not necessary.
- Job can be performed without the system.
- Will not invest extra effort to use the system.
- Technical details are of no interest.
- Does not show high motivation to use the system.
- Is easily disenchanted.
- Voluntary use must be encouraged.
- Is a multifunction knowledge worker.
- Is from a heterogeneous culture.
- Did not expect to use system.
- Career path did not prepare him or her for system use.

Quite simply, this discretionary user often judges a system on the basis of expected effort versus results to be gained. If the benefits are seen to exceed the effort, the system will be used. If the effort is expected to exceed the benefits, it will not be used. Just the perception of a great effort to achieve minimal results is often enough to completely discourage system use, leading to system rejection, a common discretionary reaction.

Today, discretionary users also include the general population who are increasingly being asked to interact with a computer in their everyday lives. Examples of this kind of interaction include library information systems, bank automated teller machines (ATMs), and the Internet. This kind of user, or potential user, exhibits certain characteristics that vary. Citibank (1989), in studying users of ATMs, identified five categories. Each group was about equal in size, encompassing about 20 percent of the general population. The groups, and their characteristics, are the following:

- People who understand technology and like it. They will use it under any and all circumstances.
- People who understand technology and like it, but will only use it if the benefits are clear.
- People who understand technology but do not like it. They will use it only if the benefits are overwhelming.
- People who do not understand anything technical. They might use it if it is very easy.
- People who will never use technology of any kind.

Again, clear and obvious benefits and ease of learning to use dominate these usage categories.

Frequency of Use

Is system use a continual, frequent, occasional, or once-in-a-lifetime experience? Frequency of use affects both learning and memory. People who spend a lot of time using a system are usually willing to spend more time learning how to use it in seeking efficiency of operation. They will also more easily remember how to do things. Occasional or infrequent users prefer ease of learning and remembering, often at the expense of operational efficiency.

Task Importance

How important is the task to the user? People are usually willing to spend more time learning applications supporting important and key job tasks as efficiency in operation is again sought. For less important tasks, ease of learning and remembering are preferred, as extensive learning time and effort will not be tolerated.

Task Structure

How structured is the task being performed? Is it repetitive and predictable or not so? In general, the less structure, the more flexibility should exist in the interface. Highly structured tasks require highly structured interfaces.

Turnover Rate

Is the turnover rate for the job high, moderate, or low? Jobs with high turnover rates would not be good candidates for systems requiring a great deal of training and learning. With low turnover rates, a greater training expense can be justified. With jobs possessing high turnover rates, it is always useful to determine why. Perhaps the new system can restructure monotonous jobs, creating more challenge and thereby reducing the turnover rate.

Primary Training

Will the system training be extensive and formal, self-training from manuals, or will training be impossible? With less training, the requirement for system ease of use increases.

Job Category

Is the user an executive, manager, professional, secretary, or clerk? While job titles have no direct bearing on design per se, they do enable one to predict some job characteristics when little else is known about the user. For example, executives and managers are most often discretionary users while clerks are most often mandatory. Secretaries usually have typing skills and both secretaries and clerks usually have higher turnover rates than executives and managers.

THE USER'S PSYCHOLOGICAL CHARACTERISTICS

A person's psychological characteristics also affect one's performance of tasks requiring motor, cognitive, or perceptual skills.

Attitude and Motivation

Is the user's attitude toward the system positive, neutral, or negative? Is motivation high, moderate, or low? While all these feelings are not caused by, and cannot be controlled by, the designer, a positive attitude and motivation allows the user to concentrate on the productivity qualities of the system. Poor feelings, however, can be addressed by designing a system to provide more power, challenge, and interest for the user with the goal of increasing job satisfaction.

Cognitive Style

People differ in how they think about and solve problems. Some people are better at verbal thinking, working more effectively with words and equations. Others are better at spatial reasoning—manipulating symbols, pictures, and images. Some people are analytic thinkers, systematically analyzing the facets of a problem. Others are intuitive, relying on rules of thumb, hunches, and educated guesses. Some people are more concrete in their thinking, others more abstract. This is speculative, but the verbal, analytic, concrete thinker might prefer a textual style of interface. The spatial, intuitive, abstract thinker might feel more at home using a multimedia graphical interface.

THE USER'S PHYSICAL CHARACTERISTICS

The physical characteristics of people can also affect their performance with a system.

Age

Are the users young, middle-aged, or elderly? Older people may not have the manual dexterity to accurately operate many input devices. A double-click on a mouse, for example, is more difficult to perform as dexterity declines.

Gender

A user's sex may have an impact on both motor and cognitive performance. Women are not as strong as men, so moving heavy displays or controls may be more difficult. Women also have smaller hands than men, so controls designed for the hand size of one may not be used as effectively by the other. Significantly more men are color-blind than women, so women may perform better on tasks and screens using color coding.

Handedness

A user's handedness, left or right, can affect ease of use of an input mechanism depending on whether it has been optimized for one or the other hand.

Physical Handicaps

Blindness, defective vision, color-blindness, deafness, and motor handicaps can affect performance on a system not designed with these handicaps in mind.

METHODS FOR GAINING UNDERSTANDING OF USERS

- Visit customer locations, particularly if they are unfamiliar to you, to gain an understanding of the work environment.
- Talk with users about their problems, difficulties, wishes, and what works well now. Establish direct contact; avoid relying on intermediaries.
- Observe users working to see their tasks, difficulties, and problems.
- Videotape users working to illustrate and study problems and difficulties.
- Learn about the work organization where the system will be installed.
- Have users think aloud as they work to uncover details that may not otherwise be solicited.

- Try the job yourself. It may expose difficulties that are not known, or expressed, by users.
- Prepare surveys and questionnaires to obtain a larger sample of user opinions.
- Establish testable behavioral target goals to give management a measure for what progress has been made and what is still required.

Gould (1988) suggests using the above techniques to gain an understanding of users and their tasks. It is also very helpful to involve the user in the design process. Involving the user from the beginning provides a direct link to the extensive knowledge he or she possesses. It also allows the designer to confront the user's resistance to change. People dislike change for a variety of reasons, among them fear of the unknown and lack of identification. Involvement in design removes the unknown and gives the user a stake in the system, or an identification with it. One caution, however: User involvement in design should be based on job or task knowledge, not status or position.

Performance vs. Preference

Occasionally, when asked, people may prefer an interface design feature that actually yields poorer performance than another feature. Numerous instances of performance/preference differences have been reported in the literature (Andre & Wickens, 1995). Examples include pointing with either a mouse or cursor, alternative menu interaction techniques, use of color, two-dimensional vs. three-dimensional displays, and prototype fidelity.

Preferences are influenced by a number of things, including familiarity, aesthetics, novelty, and perceived effort in feature use. Rarely are people aware of the many human mechanisms responsible for the speed and accuracy of human-computer interaction. Ideally, in design, always augment preferences with performance measures and try to achieve an optimized solution. Where optimization is impossible, however, implement the feature that provides the best performance, and, very importantly, explain to the user why this is being done. In these cases the user may *not* always be right.

In conclusion, this chapter has addressed one of the most important principles in interface and screen design. Simply summarized, it is this: *Know your client or user.*

S T E P   2

Understand the Business Function

An understanding of the user has been obtained and the focus now shifts to the business function being addressed. Requirements must be determined and activities being performed must be described through task analysis. From these, a conceptual model of the system will be formulated. Design standards must also be created, usability goals established, and training and documentation needs to be determined.

A detailed discussion of all of these topics is beyond the scope of this book. The reader in need of more detail is referred to books exclusively addressing systems analysis, task analysis, usability, training, and documentation.

- Perform a business definition and requirements analysis.
- Determine basic business functions.
- Describe current activities through task analysis.
- Develop a conceptual model of the system.
- Establish design standards or style guides.
- Establish system usability design goals.
- Define training and documentation needs.

BUSINESS DEFINITION AND REQUIREMENTS ANALYSIS

The objective of this phase is to establish the need for a system. A product description is developed and refined, based on input from users or marketing. There are many methods for capturing information for determining requirements. Keil and Carmel (1995) and Popowicz (1995) have described a dozen or so as summarized in Table 2.1. Both have also pro-

Table 2.1   Some Methods for Determining Requirements

Direct Methods

Facilitated Team Workshop
- A facilitated, structured workshop is held with users to obtain information.

Requirements Prototyping
- A demo, or very early prototype, is presented to users for comments concerning functionality.

Personal Interview
- A one-on-one visit with the user takes place to obtain information. It may be structured or open-ended.

Observational Study
- Users are monitored for an extended period of time to learn what they do.

Focus Group
- A small group of users and a moderator are brought together to discuss the requirements. Discussion is loosely structured.

User-Interface Prototyping
- A demo, or early prototype, is presented to users to uncover user-interface issues and problems.

Usability Laboratory
- Users at work are observed, evaluated, and measured in a specially constructed laboratory.

Telephone Survey or Interview
- A structured interview is conducted via telephone.

Indirect Methods

MIS Intermediary
- A company representative defines the user's goals and needs to designers and developers.

Survey or Questionnaire
- A textual survey is administered to a sample of users to obtain their needs.

Marketing and Sales
- Suggestions or needs are obtained by company representatives who regularly meet customers (current and potential).

Support Line
- Information is collected by the unit that helps customers with day-to-day problems (Customer Support, Technical Support, Help Desk, etc.).

Table 2.1 *(Continued)*

E-mail or Bulletin Board

- Problems, questions, and suggestions by users posted to a bulletin board or through e-mail.

User Group

- Improvements suggested by customer groups who convene periodically to discuss software usage.

Trade Show

- Customers at a trade show are presented a mock-up or prototype and asked for comments.

System Testing

- New requirements and feedback are obtained from ongoing product testing.

vided insights into the advantages and disadvantages of many of these methods. The methods may be classified as direct and indirect.

Direct Methods

Direct methods consist of face-to-face meetings with, or viewing of, users to solicit requirements. Their significant advantage is the opportunity they provide to hear the user's comments in person and firsthand. Face-to-face meetings permit multiple channels of communication (body language, voice inflections, etc.) and the opportunity to immediately follow up on vague or incomplete data. Here are some recommended direct methods for getting input from users.

Facilitated Team Workshop A facilitated, but structured workshop is held with users. Structured workshops have the potential to provide a lot of good information, often too much being generated. They do require a great deal of time to develop the structure and set up and organize.

Requirements Prototyping A demonstration model, or very early prototype, is presented to users for their comments concerning functionality. Prototypes are discussed more fully in Step 12, "Test, Test, and Retest.

Personal Interview A one-on-one visit is held with the user. It may be structured or open-ended. The interview must have focus and topics must be planned, but a formal questionnaire should not be used. Time must be allowed for free conversation. Recording the session for playback to the entire design team provides all involved some insights into user needs. Interviews can be costly and time-consuming to conduct, and must be performed by someone skilled in interviewing techniques.

Observational Study Users are watched and followed for an extended period of time to learn what they actually do. Observation provides good insight into tasks being performed, the working environment and conditions, and working practices, and is an excellent method for obtaining needed requirements information. Observation, however, can be time-consuming and expensive.

Focus Group A small group of users and a moderator are brought together to discuss the requirements. Discussion is loosely structured. Their advantages and disadvantages are similar to that of the *facilitated team workshop*. Because they are less structured, however, they require the services of a skilled moderator.

User-Interface Prototyping A demonstration model, or early prototype, is presented to users to uncover user-interface issues and problems. Again, prototypes are discussed more fully in Step 12.

Usability Laboratory A special laboratory is constructed and users brought in to perform actual newly-designed tasks. They are observed, measured, and evaluated to establish the usability of the product at that point in time. Problems uncovered may result in modification of the requirements. Usability labs can generate much useful information but are expensive to create and operate. Usability labs are also discussed in Step 12.

Telephone Survey or Interview The interview is conducted via telephone, not face-to-face. It must have structure and be well planned. Arranging the interview in advance allows the user to prepare for it. Telephone interviews are less expensive and less invasive than personal interviews. They can be used much more frequently and are extremely effective for very specific information. Telephone interviews have some disadvantages. It is impossible to gather contextual information, such as a description of the working environment; replies may be easily influenced by the interviewer's comments; and body language cues are missing. Also, it may be difficult to contact the right person.

Indirect Methods

Indirect methods impose an intermediary, someone or something, between the users and the developers. Indirect methods can certainly provide useful information. Working through an intermediary, however, takes away the multichannel communication advantages of face-to-face user-developer contact. Imposition of a human intermediary can also create these additional problems. First, there may be a filtering or distortion of the message, either intentional or unintentional. Next, the intermediary may not possess a complete, or current, understanding of user's needs, passing on an incomplete or incorrect message. Finally, the intermediary may be a mechanism that discourages direct user-developer contact for political reasons. Indirect methods do exist and include the following.

MIS Intermediary A company representative who defines the user's goals and needs to designers and developers fulfills this intermediary role. This representative may come from the information services department itself, or he or she may be from the using department. While much useful information can be provided, all too often this person does not have the breadth of knowledge needed to satisfy all requirements.

Survey or Questionnaire A textual survey is administered to a sample of users to obtain their needs. Questionnaires have the potential for a large target audience and are much cheaper than customer visits. They generally, however, have a low return rate, often generating responses only from those "very happy" or "very unhappy." They may take a long time to collect and may be difficult to analyze. Questionnaires should be relatively short and created by someone experienced in their design.

Marketing and Sales Suggestions or needs can often be obtained by company representatives who regularly meet customers, both current and potential. This information is collected inexpensively, as the representative is going to visit the company anyway. Some dangers: The information may be collected from the wrong people, the representative may unintentionally bias questions, there may be many company "filters" between the representative's contact and the end user, and quantities may sometimes be exaggerated. ("Lots of people are complaining about . . ." may mean only one or two.) The interests and bias of the representatives should be known to the developers.

Support Line Information may be collected by the unit that helps customers with day-to-day problems (Customer Support, Technical Support, Help Desk, etc.). This is fairly inexpensive and the target user audience is correct. The focus of this method is only on problems, however.

E-Mail or Bulletin Board Problems, questions, and suggestions by users posted to a bulletin board or through e-mail can be gathered and evaluated. Again, the focus of this method is usually only on problems. The responsibility is on the user to generate the recommendations, and most often includes unhappy users. A fairly inexpensive method.

User Group Improvements suggested by customer groups who convene periodically to discuss software usage can be evaluated. They have the potential to provide a lot of good information, if organized properly. This requires careful planning and some effort.

Trade Show Customers at a trade show can be exposed to a mock-up or prototype and asked for comments. Dependent on the knowledge level of the customers, this method may provide only a superficial view of most prominent features.

System Testing New requirements and feedback stemming from ongoing system testing can be accumulated, evaluated, and implemented as necessary.

Requirements Collection Guidelines

- Establish four to six different developer-user links.
- Provide most reliance on direct links.

Keil & Carmel (1995) evaluated the suitability and effectiveness of the various requirements-gathering methods by collecting data on 28 projects in 17 different companies. Fourteen of the projects were rated as relatively successful, fourteen as relatively unsuccessful. Each requirements collection method was defined as a developer-user *link*. Their findings and conclusions:

Establish Four to Six Different Developer-User Links The more successful projects had utilized a greater number of developer-user links than the less successful projects. The mean number of links for the successful projects: 5.4; the less successful: 3.2. This difference was statistically significant. Few projects used more than 60 percent of all possible links. Keil and Carmel recommend, based upon their data, that, at minimum, four different developer-user links must be established in the requirements gathering process. They also concluded that the law of diminishing returns begins to set in after six links.

Effectiveness ratings of the most commonly used links were also obtained. On a 1–5 scale (1= ineffective, 5= very effective) the following methods had the highest ratings:

Custom projects (software developed for internal use and usually not for sale):

Facilitated Teams	5.0
User-Interface Prototype	4.0

Requirements Prototype   3.6
Interviews   3.5

Package projects (software developed for external use and usually for sale):

Support Line   4.3
Interviews   3.8
User-Interface Prototype   3.3
User Group   3.3

Provide the Most Reliance on Direct Links The problems associated with the less successful projects resulted, at least in part, from too much reliance on indirect links or using intermediaries. Ten of the 14 less successful projects had used none, or only one, *direct* link. The methods with the highest effectiveness ratings listed above were mostly direct links.

Keil and Carmel caution that *number* of links is only a partial measure of user participation. How well the link is employed in practice is also very important.

DETERMINING BASIC BUSINESS FUNCTIONS

A detailed description of what the product will do is prepared. Major system functions are listed and described, including critical system inputs and outputs. A flowchart of major functions is developed. The user interface activities described in Steps 1 and 3 are usually performed concurrently with these steps.

TASK ANALYSIS

The next step in interface design is to describe current user activities. This is accomplished through a task analysis. The task analysis may also be performed concurrently with the system functional specification.

Task analysis involves breaking down the user's activities to the individual task level. Work activities are studied and described by users. The goal is to obtain an understanding of why and how people currently do the things that will be automated. Knowing why establishes the major work goals; knowing how provides details of actions performed to accomplish these goals. Task analysis also provides information concerning work flows, the interrelationships between people, objects, and actions, and the user's conceptual frameworks. The output of a task analysis is a complete description of all user tasks and interactions.

Task analyses may be accomplished through direct observation, interviews, questionnaires, or obtaining measurements of actual current system usage. Measurements, for example, may be obtained for the frequency in which tasks are performed or the number of errors that are made.

A goal of task analysis, and a goal of understanding the user, is to gain a picture of the user's mental model. A mental model is an internal representation of a person's current conceptualization and understanding of something. Mental models are gradually developed in order to understand, explain, and do something. Mental models enable a person to predict the necessary actions to do things if the action has been forgotten or has not yet been encountered.

DEVELOPING CONCEPTUAL MODELS

The output of the task analysis is the creation of a conceptual model for the user interface. A conceptual model is the general conceptual framework through which the system's functions are presented. Such a model describes how the interface will present objects, the relationships between objects, the properties of objects, and the actions that will be performed. A conceptual model is based on the user's mental model.

The goal of the graphical system designer is to facilitate the development of a useful *mental model of the system* by presenting a meaningful *conceptual model of the interface*. Mental models in using a system are derived from the system's behavior, including factors such as the system inputs, actions, outputs (including screens and messages), and its feedback and guidance characteristics. Documentation and training also play a formative role.

Guidelines for Designing Conceptual Models

- Reflect the user's mental model, not the designer's.
- Draw physical analogies or present metaphors.
- Comply with expectancies, habits, routines, and stereotypes.
- Provide action-response compatibility.
- Make invisible parts and process of a system visible.
- Provide proper and correct feedback.
- Avoid anything unnecessary or irrelevant.
- Provide design consistency.
- Provide documentation and a help system that will reinforce the conceptual model.
- Promote the development of both novice and expert mental models.

Since the term mental model refers to a person's current level of knowledge about something, people will *always* have them. They will be developed regardless of the particular design of a system, and they will be modified with experience. The goal of the designer in design is to *facilitate the process of developing an effective mental model.*

Unfortunately, little research is available to assist the software designer in creating conceptual models. Development of a user's mental model can be aided, however, by following these general guidelines for conceptual model development.

Reflect the User's Mental Model, Not the Designer's A user will have different expectations and levels of knowledge than the designer. The mental models of the user and designer will be different. The user is concerned with the task to be performed, the business objectives that must be fulfilled. The designer's model is focused on the design of the interface, the kinds of objects, the interaction methods, and the visual representations on the screen. Objects must be defined, along with their relationships, behaviors, and properties. Interaction methods must also be defined, such as input mechanisms, interaction techniques, and the contents of menus. Screen visual representations must also be created, including functionality and appearance.

Draw Physical Analogies or Present Metaphors Replicate what is familiar and well known. Duplicate actions that are already well learned. The success of graphical systems can be attributed, in part, to its employing the desktop metaphor, a recreation of the desktop. A metaphor, to be effective, must be widely applicable within an interface. Metaphors that are only partially or occasionally applicable should not be used. In the event a metaphor cannot be explicitly employed in a new interface, structure the new interface in terms of familiar aspects from the manual world.

Comply with Expectancies, Habits, Routines, and Stereotypes Create a system that builds on knowledge, habits, routines, and expectancies that already exist. Use familiar associations, avoiding the new and unfamiliar. With color, for example, accepted meanings for red, yellow, and green are already well established. Use words and symbols in their customary ways. Replicate the language of the user, and create icons reflecting already known images.

Provide Action-Response Compatibility All system responses should be compatible with the actions that elicit them. Names of commands, for example, should reflect the actions that will occur. Organization of keys in documentation or help screens should reflect the ordering as they actually exist on the keyboard.

Make Invisible Parts of the System Visible Systems are comprised of parts and processes, many of which are invisible to the user. In creating a mental model, a person must make a hypothesis about what is invisible and how it relates to what is visible. New users of a system often make erroneous or incomplete assumptions about what is invisible and develop a faulty mental model. As more experience is gained, their mental models evolve to become more accurate and complete. Making invisible parts of a system visible will speed up the process of developing correct mental models.

An example of a process being made visible can be illustrated by moving a document between files. In a command language interface, the document must be moved through a series of typed commands. The file is moved invisibly and, the user assumes, correctly, unless an error message is received. In a graphical direct manipulation system, the entire process is visible, the user literally picking up the file in one folder by clicking on it, and dragging it to another folder.

Provide Proper and Correct Feedback Be generous in providing feedback. Keep a person informed of what is happening, and what has happened, at all times, including:

- *Provide a continuous indication of status.* Mental models are difficult to develop if things happen, or are completed, unknown to the user. During long processing sequences, for example, interim status messages such as loading, "opening . . ." or "searching . . ." reassure the user and enable him or her to understand internal processes and more accurately predict how long something will take. Such messages also permit pinpointing of problems if they occur.
- *Provide visible results of actions.* For example, highlight selected objects, display new locations of moved objects, and show files that are closed.
- *Display actions in progress.* For example, show a window being changed in size actually changing, not simply the window in its changed form. This will strengthen cause-and-effect relationships in the mental model.
- *Present as much context information as possible.* To promote contextual understanding, present as much background or historical information as possible. For example, on a menu screen, maintain a listing of the menu choices selected to get to the current point. On a query screen, show the query criteria when displaying the query results.
- *Provide clear, constructive, and correct error messages.* Incomplete or misleading error messages may cause false assumptions that violate and weaken the user's mental model. Error messages should always be structured to reinforce the mental model. For example, error messages addressing an incomplete action should specify *exactly* what is missing, not simply advise a person that something is incomplete.

Avoid the Unnecessary or Irrelevant Do not display irrelevant information on the screen. People may try to interpret it and integrate it into their mental models, thereby creating a false one. Irrelevant information might be unneeded data fields, screen controls, system status codes, or error message numbers. If potentially misleading information cannot be avoided, point this out to the user.

Also, do not overuse display techniques, or use them in meaningless ways. Too much color, for example, may distract people and cause them to make erroneous assumptions as they try to interpret the colors. The result will be a faulty and unclear mental model.

Provide Design Consistency Design consistency reduces the number of concepts to be learned. Inconsistency requires the mastery of multiple models. If an occasional inconsistency cannot be avoided, explain it to the user. For example, if an error is caused by a user action that is inconsistent with other similar actions, explain in the error message that this condition exists. This will prevent the user from falsely assuming that the model he or she has been operating under is incorrect.

Provide Documentation and a Help System that will Reinforce the Conceptual Model Consistencies and metaphors should be explicitly described in the user documentation. This will assist a person in learning the system. Do not rely on the people to uncover consistencies and metaphors themselves. The help system should offer advice aimed at improving mental models.

Promote the Development of Both Novice and Expert Mental Models Novices and experts are likely to bring to bear different mental models when using a system. It will be easier for novices to form an initial system mental model if they are protected from the full complexity of a system. Employ levels of functionality that can be revealed through progressive disclosure.

Defining Objects

- Determine all objects that have to be manipulated to get work done. Describe:
    - The objects used in tasks.
    - Object behavior and characteristics that differentiate each kind of object.
    - The relationship of objects to each other and the people using them.
    - The actions performed.

- The objects to which actions apply.
- State information or attributes that each object in the task must preserve, display, or allow to be edited.
  - Identify the objects and actions that appear most often in the workflow.
  - Make the several most important objects very obvious and easy to manipulate.

All objects that have to be manipulated to get work done must be clearly described. Their behavioral characteristics must be established and the attributes that differentiate each kind of object must be identified. Relationships of objects to each other and the people using them must be determined. The actions people take on objects must also be described. State information or attributes that each object in the task must preserve, display, or allow to be edited.

The most important objects must be made very obvious and easy to manipulate. Weinschenk (1995) suggests that if the most important objects are not obvious in the workflow, go through the workflow document highlighting all nouns and verbs associated with nouns. Frequently appearing nouns are possible major objects. Frequently appearing verbs are actions pointing to possible major objects.

Developing Metaphors

- Choose the analogy that works best for each object and its actions.
- Use real-world metaphors.
- Use simple metaphors.
- Use common metaphors.
- Multiple metaphors may co-exist.
- Use major metaphors, even if you can't exactly replicate them visually.
- Test the selected metaphors.

Select a metaphor or analogy for the defined objects. Choose the analogy that works best for the objects and their actions. Real-world metaphors are most often the best choice. Replicate what is familiar and well known. Duplicate actions that are already well learned. If a faster or better way exists to do something, however, use it. Use simple metaphors as they are almost always the most powerful. Use common metaphors; uniqueness adds complexity. Multiple metaphors may co-exist. Use major metaphors even if you can't exactly replicate them visually on the screen. Finally, test the selected metaphors. Do they match one's expectations and experiences? Are they easily understood, or quickly learned? Change them, if testing deems it necessary.

DESIGN STANDARDS OR STYLE GUIDES

A design standard or style guide describes the appearance and behavior of the interface and provides some guidance on the proper use of system components. It defines the interface standards, rules, guidelines, and conventions that must be followed in detailed design. It will be based on the characteristics of the system's hardware and software, the principles of good screen design, the needs of system users, and any unique company or organization requirements that may exist.

Value of Standards

Standards are valuable to users for the following reasons:

- Faster performance.
- Fewer errors.
- Reduced training time.
- Better system utilization.
- Better satisfaction.
- Better system acceptance.

They are valuable to designers for these reasons:

- Increased visibility to human-computer interface.
- Simplified design.
- More programming/design aids.
- Reduced redundant effort.
- Reduced training.

Unfortunately, past research on guideline utilization has hardly been encouraging. Mosier & Smith (1986) found that only 58 percent of the users of a large interface guidelines document found the information they were looking for, and an additional 36 percent only sometimes found it. De Souza & Bevan (1990) report that designers using a draft of the ISO menu interface standard violated 11 percent of the rules and had difficulties in interpreting 30 percent. Tetzlaff & Schwartz (1991) also report difficulties in interpreting guidelines from an interface style guide, although conformance with the guidelines was high. Thovtrup & Nielsen (1991) report designers were only able to achieve a 71 percent compliance with a two-page standard in a laboratory setting. In an evaluation of three real systems, they found that the mandatory rules of the company's screen design standard were violated 32 to 55 percent of the time.

Thovtrup and Nielsen, in analyzing why the rules in the screen design standard were broken, found a very positive designer attitude toward the standard, both in terms of its value and content. Rules were not adhered to, however, for the following reasons:

- An alternative design solution was better than that mandated by the standard.
- Available development tools did not allow compliance with the standard.
- Compliance with the standard was planned, but time was not yet available to implement it.
- The rule that was broken was not known or was overlooked.

Tetzlaff and Schwartz, in analyzing how their guidelines were used, found that designers depended heavily on the pictorial guideline examples, often ignoring the accompanying text. The implications of these studies for a design guide yield the guidelines described in the next section.

Document Design

- Include many concrete examples of correct design.
- Provide a rationale for why the particular guidelines should be used.
- Provide a rationale describing the conditions under which various design alternatives are appropriate.
- Design the document following recognized principles for good document design.
- Provide good access mechanisms such as a thorough index, a table of contents, glossaries, and checklists.

To be effective, a guideline must include many concrete examples of correct design. Learning by imitation is a much desired way to learn. Provide development tools that support implementation of the guidelines. If the tools cannot support the guideline, it cannot be adhered to. Provide a rationale for why the particular guidelines should be used. Understanding the reasoning will increase guideline acceptance. This is especially important if the guideline is a deviation from a previous design practice. Also, when two or more design alternatives exist, provide a rationale describing the conditions under which the alternatives are appropriate. The examples may illustrate alternatives and the toolkit may produce them, but when these various alternatives are appropriate may be difficult for designers to infer. Always design the document, be it paper or electronic, following recognized principles for good document design, and provide good access mechanisms such as a thorough index, a table of contents, glossaries, and checklists. An unattractive or hard to use document will not be used.

Design Support and Implementation

- Use all available reference sources in creating the guidelines.
- Use development and implementation tools that support the guidelines.
- Begin applying the guidelines immediately.

Available Reference Sources Use all the available reference design sources in creating your guidelines. References include this text, other books on user interface design, project-specific guidelines, and the style guides published by window system providers, such as IBM's SAA CUA, Microsoft, and Apple Computer.

Applying the Guidelines Two questions often asked are, "Is it too late to develop and implement standards?" and "What will be the impact on systems and screens now being used?" To address these questions, Burns & Warren (1986) reformatted several alphanumeric inquiry screens to improve their comprehensibility and readability. When these reformatted screens were presented to expert system users, decision-making time remained the same but errors were reduced. For novice system users, the reformatted screens brought large improvements in learning speed and accuracy. Therefore, it appears, changes enhancing screens will benefit novice as well as expert users already familiar with the current screens. It is never too late to begin to change.

Microsoft (1995) also suggests that evolving from Windows 3.1 to Windows 95 guidelines can begin immediately with 3.1. They suggest that the process need not be an immediate, complete overhaul, but that it begin by evolution. Start by adding contextual interfaces such as pop-up menus. Also, modify window title bars and add appropriate new icons. Continue to modify and build slowly.

USABILITY GOALS

A Definition of Usability

The term *usability* to describe effectiveness of human performance was first used by Bennett (1979). In the following years a more formal definition was proposed by Shackel (1981) and modified by Bennett (1984). Finally, Shackel (1991) simply defined usability as "the capability to be used by humans easily and effectively, where,

easily = to a specified level of subjective assessment,

effectively = to a specified level of human performance."

Usability Assessment in the Design Process

Usability assessment should begin in the early stages of the product development cycle and should be applied often. The assessment should include the user's entire experience, and all the product's important components. Usability assessment is discussed more fully in Step 12, "Test, Test, and Retest.".

Ten Common Usability Problems

Mandel (1994) lists the ten most common usability problems in graphical systems as reported by IBM usability specialists. They are:

1. Ambiguous menus and icons.
2. Languages that permit only single-direction movement.
3. Input and direct manipulation limits.
4. Highlighting and selection limitations.
5. Unclear step sequences.
6. More steps to manage interface than to do tasks.
7. Complex linkage between and within applications.
8. Inadequate feedback and confirmation.
9. Lack of system anticipation and intelligence.
10. Inadequate error messages, help, tutorials, and documentation.

Solving these problems will go a long way toward creating a usable system.

Some Practical Measures of Usability

Usability, or lack thereof, can often be sensed by a simple observation of, and talking to, people working. While these measures lack scientific rigor, they do provide an indication that there may be, or may not be, problems.

Are People Asking a Lot of Questions? Many questions are a sign that things are not as clear and intuitive as they should be. When in doubt, the first reaction of many people is to ask for assistance.

Are Frequent Exasperation Responses Heard? The "Oh damn!" reactions are usually used to express annoyance or frustration. Their frequency, and loudness, may foretell a strong rejection of a product. The absence of exasperation, however, may not represent acceptance. Some people are not as expressive in their language, or better able to smother their feelings.

Are There Many Irrelevant Actions Being Performed? Are there incidental actions required for, but not directly related to, doing a job? These include excessive mouse clicks or keyboard strokes to accomplish something, or going through many operations to find the right page in a manual or the right window on the display.

Are There Many Things to Ignore? Are there many elements on the screen that the user must disregard? Are there many "doesn't pertain to me" items? If so, remember, they still consume a portion of a person's visual or information processing capacities, detracting from the capacities a person could devote to relevant things.

Do a Number of People Want to Use a Product? None of us goes out of our way to make our own lives more difficult. (Unfortunately, other people may, however.) We tend to gravitate to things easy to work with or do. If a lot of people want to use it, it probably has a higher usability score. Attitudes may be a very powerful factor in a graphical system's acceptance.

Shackel (1991) presents the following more objective criteria for measuring usability.

Criteria for Measuring Usability

Effectiveness
- The required range of tasks must be accomplished at better than some required level of performance (e.g., in terms of speed and errors).
- By some required percentage of the specified target range of users.
- Within some required proportion of the range of usage environments.

Learnability
- Within some specified time from commissioning and start of user training.
- Based on some specified amount of training and user support.
- Within some specified relearning time each time for intermittent users.

Flexibility
- With flexibility allowing adaptation to some specified percentage variation in tasks and/or environments beyond those first specified.

Attitude
- Within acceptable levels of human cost in terms of tiredness, discomfort, frustration, and personal effort.
- So that satisfaction causes continued and enhanced usage of the system.

Human performance goals in graphical system use, like any other design goal, should be stated in quantitative and measurable ways. Without performance goals you will never know if you have achieved them, or how successful the system really is. Clear and concrete goals also provide objectives for usability testing and assure that a faulty or unsatisfactory product will not be released.

Values for the various criteria should be specified in absolute terms. An absolute goal might be "Task A must be performed by a first-time user in 12 minutes with no errors with 30 minutes of training and without referring to a manual." Goals may also be set in relative terms. For example, "Task B must be performed 50 percent faster than it was using the previous system."

The level of established goals will depend on the capabilities of the user, the capabilities of the system, and the objectives of the system. In addition to providing commitments to a certain level of quality, goals become the foundation for the system test plan.

TRAINING AND DOCUMENTATION NEEDS

System training and documentation needs will be based on user needs, system conceptual design, system learning goals, and system performance goals. It may include such tools as formal or video training, manuals, online tutorials, reference manuals, quick reference guides, and online help. Remember, documentation is a reference point, a form of communication, and a more concrete design, uncovering issues and revealing omissions. Therefore, it is a very important part of the system development process.

S T E P 3

Understand the Principles of Good Screen Design

A well-designed screen accomplishes the following:

- Reflects the needs and capabilities of its users.
- Is developed within the physical constraints imposed by the hardware on which it is displayed.
- Effectively utilizes the capabilities of its controlling software.
- Achieves the business objectives of the system for which it is designed.

To accomplish these goals, the designer must first identify the principles of good screen design.

- Human considerations.
  - Apply the test for good design.
  - Organize screen elements clearly and meaningfully.
  - Present information distinctively.
  - Present information simply and meaningfully.
- Hardware considerations.
  - Effect compatibility with the hardware capabilities of the system.
- Software considerations.
  - Utilize the toolkits and style guides provided by many graphical systems.
  - Effectively use the various display features.

What follows is a compilation of general screen design guidelines for the graphical user interface. It begins with an extensive series of considerations dealing with the user and concludes with those addressing hardware and software.

HUMAN CONSIDERATIONS IN SCREEN DESIGN

Use of a screen, and a system, is affected by a variety of factors. Included are: how much information is presented on a screen, how a screen is organized, the language used on the screen, the distinctiveness of the screen's components, and its aesthetics. First, let's look at what aspects of poor screen design can be distracting to the user, and what a user is looking for in good design. Then, we'll address the principles of good design.

How to Distract the Screen User

Barnett (1993) has compiled a list of factors that, when poorly designed, hinder the use of paper forms. These factors certainly apply for electronic forms, or screens, as well, and include:

- Unclear captions and badly worded questions. These cause hesitation, and rereading, in order to determine what is needed or must be provided. They may also be interpreted incorrectly, causing errors.
- Improper type and graphic emphasis. Important elements are hidden. Emphasis is drawn away from what is important to that which is not important.
- Misleading headings. These also create confusion and inhibit one's ability to see existing relationships.
- Information requests perceived to be irrelevant or unnecessary. The value of what one is doing is questioned, as is the value of the system.
- Information requests that require one to backtrack and rethink a previous answer, or look ahead to determine possible context. Inefficiency results, and mistakes increase.
- Cluttered, cramped layout. Poor layout creates a bad initial impact and leads to more errors. May easily cause system rejection.
- Poor quality of presentation, legibility, appearance, and arrangement. Again, degrades performance, slowing the user down and causing more errors.

Howlett (1995) based upon her experiences at Microsoft suggests the most common problems in visual interface design are:

- Visual inconsistency in screen detail presentation and with the operating system.
- Lack of restraint in the use of design features and elements.
- Overuse of three-dimensional presentations.
- Overuse of too many bright colors.
- Poorly designed icons.
- Bad typography
- Metaphors that are either overbearing or too cute, or too literal thereby restricting design options.

These kinds of problems, she concludes, lead to screens that can be chaotic, confusing, disorganized, distracting, or just plain ugly.

What Screen Users Want

What are people looking for in the design of screens? One organization asked a group of screen users and got the following responses:

- An orderly, clean, clutter-free appearance.
- An obvious indication of what is being shown and what should be done with it.
- Expected information located where it *should* be.
- A clear indication of what relates to what, including options, captions, data, and so forth.
- Plain, simple English.
- A simple way of finding out what is in a system and how to get it out.
- A clear indication of when an action can make a permanent change in the data or system.

The desired direction is toward simplicity, clarity, and understandability—qualities lacking in many of today's screens.

The Test for a Good Design

- Can all screen elements be identified by cues other than by reading the words that make them up?

A simple test for good screen design does exist. A screen that passes this test will have surmounted the first obstacle to effectiveness. The test is this: Can all screen elements (field captions, data, title, headings, types of controls, etc.) be identified without reading the words that identify or comprise them? That is, can a component of a screen be identified through cues independent of its content? If this is so, a person's attention can quickly be drawn to the part of the screen that is relevant at that moment. People look at a screen for a particular reason, perhaps to locate a piece of information such as a customer name, to identify the name of the screen, or to find an instructional or error message. The signal at that moment is that element of interest on the screen. The noise is everything else on the screen. Cues independent of context that differentiate the components of the screen will reduce visual search times and minimize confusion.

Try this test on the front page of your morning newspaper. Where is the headline? A story heading? The weather report? How did you find them? The headline was identified probably by its large and bold type size; story headings, again by a type size visually different than other page components; the weather report, probably by its location (bottom right? top left?). Imagine finding the headline on the front page of the newspaper if the same type size and style was used for all components and their positions changed from day to day.

Unfortunately, many of today's screens cannot pass this simple test and are unnecessarily difficult to use. Almost all the tools available to the creator of the newspaper's front page are now available to the screen designer. An effective solution can be achieved with the equipment at hand. It simply involves the thoughtful application of display techniques, consistent location of elements, and the proper use of "white space" and groupings.

Screen Meaning and Purpose

Each screen element . . .

- every control.
- every icon.
- each color.
- all emphasis.
- the screen organization.
- all screen animation.
- each message.
- all forms of feedback.

must . . .

- have meaning to screen users.
- serve a purpose in performing tasks.

All elements of a screen must have meaning to users and serve a purpose in performing tasks. If it does not, do not include it on the screen because it is *noise*. Noise is distracting and competes for the screen user's attention. That which is important will be more difficult to find.

Organizing Screen Elements Clearly and Meaningfully

Visual clarity is achieved when the display elements are organized and presented in meaningful and understandable ways. A clear and clean organization makes it easier to recognize screen's essential elements and to ignore its secondary information when appropriate. Clarity is influenced by a multitude of factors: consistency in design, a visually pleasing composition, a logical and sequential ordering, the presentation of the proper amount of information, groupings, and alignment of screen items. What must be avoided is visual clutter created by indistinct elements, random placement, and confusing patterns.

Consistency

- Provide real-world consistency. Reflect a person's experiences, work conventions, and cultural conventions.
- Provide internal consistency. Observe the same conventions and rules for all aspects of a GUI screen, including:
  - Operating procedures.
  - Component look and usage.
  - Component locations.
- Follow the same conventions and rules across all GUIs.
- Deviate only when there is a clear benefit for the user.

Quite simply, consistency greatly aids learning. It permits a person to employ conceptual learning and to transfer training. Inconsistency forces one to memorize, and remember, a variety of different ways to do something, or to interpret what is presented on the screen. Inconsistency makes it difficult for a coherent structure to emerge. It can also be distracting. Inconsistency creates a variation that makes it difficult to notice variation that may be important for a person's task.

So, be consistent with the real world in which a person already exists. This world will already have been well learned and generalization to the system will occur. Provide internal consistency so that learning may be focused on the task or job, not on irrelevancies. As far as consistent location of screen elements are concerned, people do tend to have good memories for locations of things. Take advantage of this phenomenon. The graphical system products and style guides have established consistent locations for most screen elements. Follow them. Also be consistent across graphical interfaces for all the reasons already mentioned. If an inconsistency will *benefit* the user, such as calling attention to something extremely critical, consider deviating from consistency. Be wary of too many deviations, though, as the impact of each will be diminished.

Upper-Left Starting Point

- Provide an obvious starting point in the screen's upper-left corner.

Eyeball fixation studies indicate that in looking at displays of information, usually one's eyes move first to the upper-left center of the display, then quickly move through the display in a clockwise direction. Streveler

& Wasserman (1984) found that visual targets located in the upper-left quadrant of a screen were found fastest and those located in the lower-right quadrant took longest to find.

Provide an obvious starting point in the upper-left corner of the screen. This is near where visual scanning begins and will permit a left-to-right, top-to-bottom reading as is common in Western cultures.

Navigation

- Assist in navigation through a screen by:
    - Alignment of elements.
    - Groupings of elements.
    - Line borders.
- Through focus and emphasis, sequentially, direct attention to items that are:
    - Important / secondary / peripheral.
- Tab through window in logical order of displayed information.
- Locate command buttons at end of the tabbing order sequence.

Screen navigation should be obvious and easy to accomplish. Navigation can be made obvious by grouping and aligning screen controls, and judiciously using line borders to guide the eye. Sequentially, direct a person's attention to elements in terms of their importance. Focus attention, using the various display techniques, on the most important parts of a screen. Always tab through a screen in the logical order of the information displayed, and locate command buttons at the end of the tab order sequence. Guidelines for accomplishing all of these general objectives will be found in subsequent pages.

Visually Pleasing Composition

- Provide visually pleasing composition with the following qualities:
    - Balance.
    - Symmetry.
    - Regularity.
    - Predictability.
    - Sequentiality.
    - Economy.
    - Unity.
    - Proportion.
    - Simplicity.
    - Groupings.

Eyeball fixation studies also indicate that during the scanning of a display in a clockwise direction, people are influenced by the symmetrical balance and weight of the titles, graphics, and text of the display. The human perceptual mechanism seeks order and meaning and tries to impose structure when confronted with uncertainty. Whether a screen has meaningful and evident form or is cluttered and unclear is, therefore, immediately discerned. A cluttered or unclear screen requires that some effort be expended in learning and understanding what is presented. The screen user who must deal with the display is forced to spend time to learn and understand. The user who has an option concerning whether the screen will or will not be used may reject it at this point if the perceived effort is greater than the perceived gain.

An entity's design composition communicates to a person nonverbally, but quite powerfully. It is an unconscious process that attracts, motivates, directs, or distracts. Meaningfulness and evident form are significantly enhanced by a display that is pleasing to one's eye. Visually pleasing composition draws attention subliminally, conveying a positive message clearly and quickly. A lack of visually pleasing composition is disorienting, obscures the intent and meaning, slows one down, and confuses.

The notion of what is artistic has evolved throughout history. Graphic design experts have, through perceptual research, derived a number of principles for what comprises a visually pleasing appearance. These include: balance, symmetry, regularity, predictability, economy, unity, sequentiality, proportion, simplicity, and groupings. Keep in mind that this discussion of visually pleasing composition does not focus on the words on the screen, but on the perception of structure created by such qualities as spacing, intensities, and color. It is as if the screen is viewed through "squinted eyes," causing the words themselves to become a blur.

Balance

- Create screen balance by providing an equal weight of screen elements, left and right, top and bottom.

Balance, illustrated in Figure 3.1, is a stabilization or equilibrium, a midway center of suspension. The design elements have an equal weight, left to right, top to bottom. The opposite of balance is instability, the design elements seemingly ready to topple over. Our discomfort with instability, or imbalance, is reflected every time we straighten a picture hanging askew on the wall.

Dark colors, unusual shapes, and larger objects are "heavier," whereas light colors, regular shapes, and small objects are "lighter." Bal-

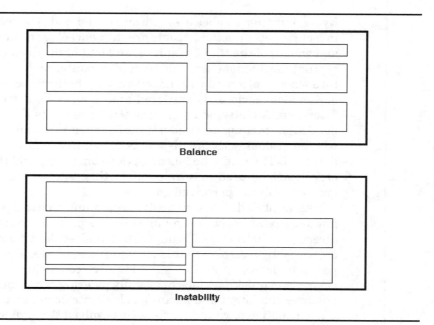

Balance

Instability

Figure 3.1   Balance (vs. instability).

ance on a screen is accomplished through centering the display itself, maintaining an equal weighting of components on each side of the horizontal and vertical axis, and centering titles and illustrations.

Symmetry

- Create symmetry by replicating elements left and right of the screen center line.

Symmetry, illustrated in Figure 3.2, is axial duplication: A unit on one side of the center line is exactly replicated on the other side. This exact replication also creates balance, but the difference is that balance can be achieved without symmetry. Symmetry's opposite is asymmetry.

Regularity

- Create screen regularity by establishing standard and consistently spaced horizontal and vertical alignment points.

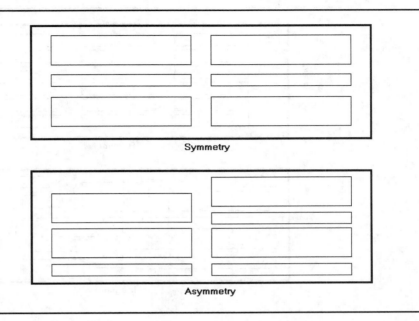

Symmetry

Asymmetry

Figure 3.2   Symmetry (vs. asymmetry).

Regularity, illustrated in Figure 3.3, is a uniformity of elements based on some principle or plan. Regularity in screen design is achieved by establishing standard and consistently spaced column and row starting points for screen elements. The opposite, irregularity, exists when no such plan or principle is apparent.

Predictability

- Create predictability by being consistent and following conventional orders or arrangements.

Predictability, illustrated in Figure 3.4, suggests a highly conventional order or plan. Viewing one screen enables one to predict how another will look. Viewing part of a screen enables one to predict how the rest of the screen will look. The opposite of predictability—spontaneity—suggests no plan and thus an inability to predict the structure of the remainder of a screen or the structure of other screens. In screen design predictability is also enhanced through design consistency.

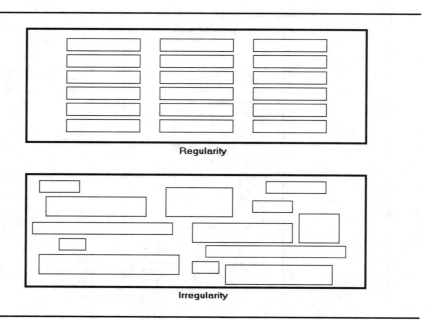

Regularity

Irregularity

Figure 3.3 Regularity.

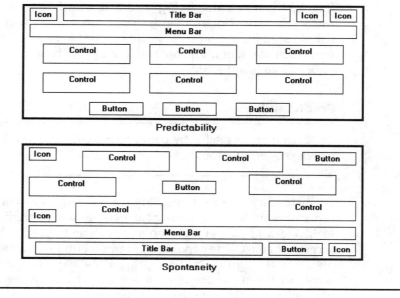

Predictability

Spontaneity

Figure 3.4 Predictability (vs. spontaneity).

Sequentiality

- Provide sequentiality by arranging elements to guide the eye through the screen in an obvious, logical, rhythmic, and efficient manner.
- The eye tends to be attracted to:
  - A brighter element before one less bright.
  - Isolated elements before elements in a group.
  - Graphics before text.
  - Color before black and white.
  - Highly saturated colors before those less saturated.
  - Dark areas before light areas.
  - A big element before a small one.
  - An unusual shape before a usual one.
  - Big objects before little objects.

Sequentiality, illustrated in Figure 3.5, is a plan of presentation to guide the eye through the screen in a logical, rhythmic order, with the most important information significantly placed. Sequentiality can be achieved by alignment, spacing, and grouping as illustrated. The opposite of sequen-

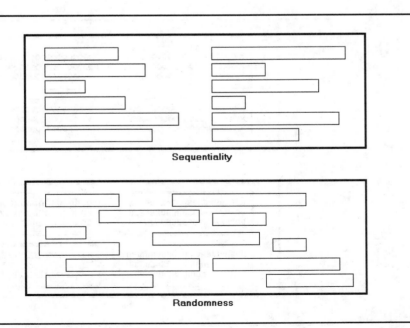

Figure 3.5   Sequentiality (vs. randomness).

tiality is randomness, where an arrangement and flow cannot be detected. The eye tends to move first to the elements listed above, and then from one to the other. For example, it moves from highly saturated colors to unsaturated colors, from dark to light areas, from big to little objects, and from unusual to usual shapes.

Economy

- Provide economy by using as few styles, display techniques, and colors as possible.

Economy, illustrated in Figure 3.6, is the frugal and judicious use of display elements to get the message across as simply as possible. The opposite is intricacy, the use of many elements just because they exist. The effect is ornamentation, which often detracts from clarity. Economy in screen design means mobilizing just enough display elements and techniques to communicate the desired message, and no more. In the past the use of color in screens often violated this principle, with screens sometimes taking on the appearance of Christmas trees.

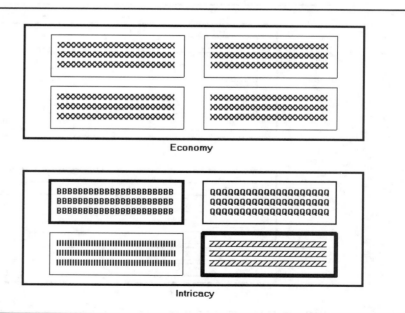

Figure 3.6   Economy (vs. intricacy).

Unity

- Create unity by:
  - Using similar sizes, shapes, or colors for related information.
  - Leaving less space between elements of a screen than the space left at the margins.

Unity, illustrated in Figure 3.7, is coherence, a totality of elements that is visually all one piece. With unity, the elements seem to belong together, to dovetail so completely that they are seen as one thing. The opposite of unity is fragmentation, each piece retaining its own character. In screen design similar sizes, shapes, and colors promote unity, as does *white space*—borders at the display boundary.

Proportion

- Create windows and groupings of data or text with aesthetically pleasing proportions.

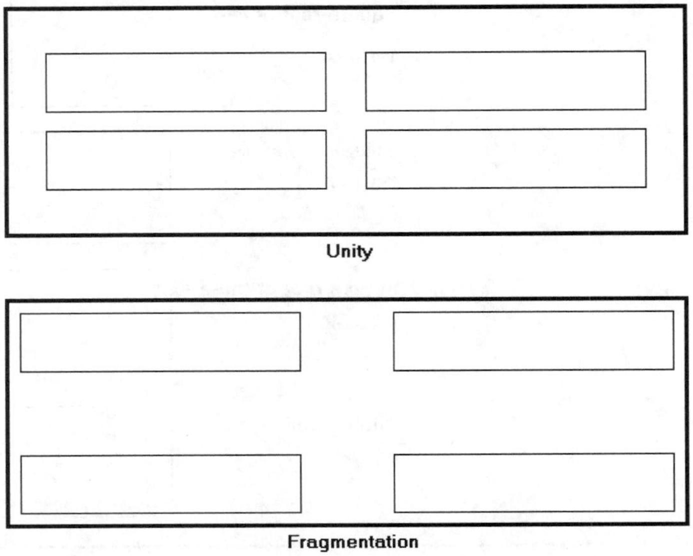

Unity

Fragmentation

Figure 3.7   Unity (vs. fragmentation).

Down through the ages, people and cultures have had preferred proportional relationships. What constitutes beauty in one culture is not necessarily considered the same by another culture, but some proportional shapes have stood the test of time and are found in abundance today.

Marcus (1992) describes the following shapes, illustrated in Figure 3.8, as aesthetically pleasing.

Square (1:1). The simplest of proportions, it has an attention-getting quality and suggests stability and permanence. When rotated it becomes a dynamic diamond, expressing movement and tension.

Square root of two (1:1.414). A divisible rectangle yielding two pleasing proportional shapes. When divided equally in two along its length, the two smaller shapes that result are also both square root of two rectangles. This property only occurs with this proportion and is often used in book design. An open book has the same outside proportion as the individual pages within it. The square root of two has been adopted as a standard paper size in many countries of the world (the United States excluded).

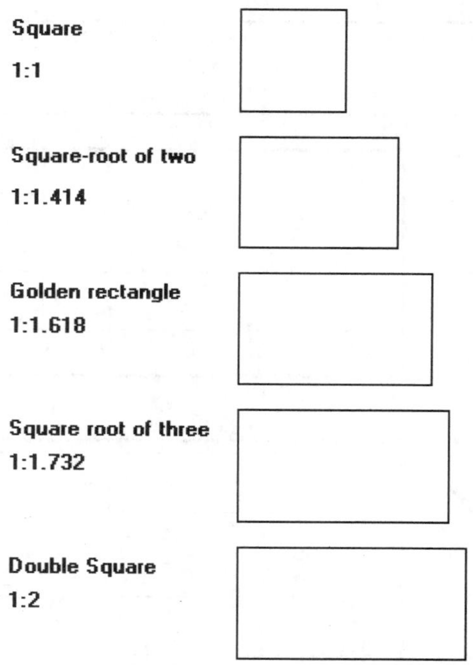

Square
1:1

Square-root of two
1:1.414

Golden rectangle
1:1.618

Square root of three
1:1.732

Double Square
1:2

Figure 3.8   Pleasing proportions.

Golden rectangle (1:1.618). An old (fifth century B.C.) proportion is the golden rectangle. Early Greek architecture used this proportion, and a mathematical relationship exists between this number and growth patterns in plant and animal life. This "divine division of a line" results when a line is divided such that the smaller part is to the greater part as the greater part is to the whole. The golden rectangle also has another unique property. A square created from part of the rectangle leaves a remaining area with sides also in the golden rectangle proportion.

Square root of three (1:1.732). Used less frequently than the other proportions, its narrowness gives it a distinctive shape.

Double square (1:2). In Japan, the tatami mat used for floor covering usually comes in this proportion. Rectangles more elongated than this one have shapes whose distinctiveness is more difficult to sense.

While these pleasing shapes have passed the test of time, not everything we encounter conforms to these principles. The American letter paper size has a ratio of 1:1.29, a typical American television screen a ratio of 1:1.33, and CRT screens typically have ratios in the range of about 1:1.33 to 1:1.50.

In screen design, aesthetically pleasing proportions should be considered for major components of the screen, including windows and groups of data or text.

Simplicity (Complexity)

- Optimize the number of elements on a screen, within limits of clarity.
- Minimize the alignment points, especially horizontal or columnar.
  - Provide standard grids of horizontal and vertical lines to position elements.

Simplicity, illustrated in Figure 3.9, is directness and singleness of form, a combination of elements that results in ease of comprehending the meaning of a pattern. The opposite pole on the continuum is complexity. The scale created may also be considered a scale of complexity, with extreme complexity at one end and minimal complexity (simplicity) at the other. While the graphics designer usually considers this concept as *simplicity,* we will address it as *complexity* since it has been addressed by this term in the screen design literature where an objective measure of it has been derived.

This measure of complexity was derived by Tullis (1983) based on the work of Bonsiepe (1968), who proposed a method of measuring the complexity of typographically designed pages through the application of infor-

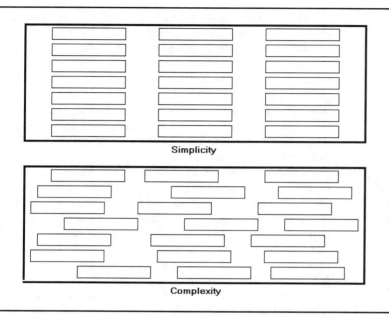

Simplicity

Complexity

Figure 3.9 Simplicity (vs. complexity).

mation theory (Shannon & Weaver, 1949). To illustrate, this measure involves the following steps:

1. Draw a rectangle around each element on a screen, including captions, controls, headings, data, title, and so on.
2. Count the number of elements and horizontal alignment points (the number of columns in which a field, inscribed by a rectangle, starts).
3. Count the number of elements and vertical alignment points (the number of rows in which an element, inscribed by a rectangle, starts).

This has been done for the text-based screens illustrated in Figures 3.10 and 3.11. These screens are examples from the earlier study by Tullis (1981) described in the introduction. They are an original read-only inquiry screen (Figure 3.10) from the screens whose mean search time was 8.3 seconds, and a redesigned screen (Figure 3.11) from the screens whose mean search time was 5.0 seconds. A complexity calculation using information theory for each screen is as follows:

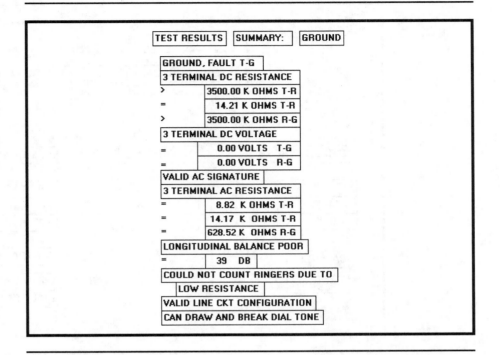

Figure 3.10   Original screen, from Tullis (1981), with title, captions, and data inscribed by rectangles.

- Figure 3.10 (original):
  22 fields with 6 horizontal (column) alignment points = 41 bits.
  22 fields with 20 vertical (row) alignment points = 93 bits.
  Overall complexity = 134 bits.
- Figure 3.11 (redesigned):
  18 fields with 7 horizontal (column) alignment points = 43 bits.
  18 fields with 8 vertical (row) alignment points = 53 bits.
  Overall complexity = 96 bits.

The redesigned screen is thus about 28 percent simpler, or less complex, than the original screen.

An easier method of calculation, however, yielding similar results, is to count the following: (1) the number of elements on the screen, (2) the number of horizontal (column) alignment points, and (3) the number of vertical (row) alignment points. The sums for the original and redesigned screens by this measure are:

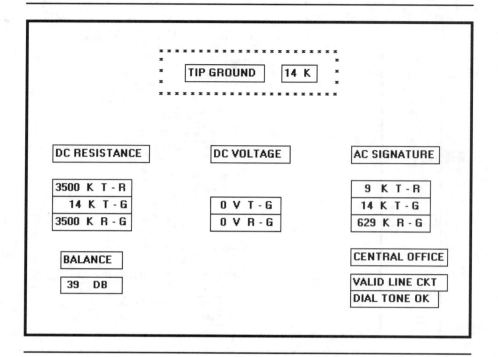

Figure 3.11   Redesigned screen, from Tullis (1981), with title, captions, and data inscribed by rectangles.

- Figure 3.10 (original):
    - 22 elements.
    - 6   horizontal (column) alignment points.
    - 20   vertical (row) alignment points.
    - 48   = complexity.
- Figure 3.11 (redesigned):
    - 18   elements.
    - 7   horizontal (column) alignment points.
    - 8   vertical (row) alignment points.
    - 33   = complexity.

By this calculation the redesigned screen is about 31 percent simpler, or less complex, than the original screen.

By both calculations the redesigned screen has a *lower* complexity measure than the original screen. In the Tullis (1981) study, the redesigned and faster-to-use screens had lower complexity measures. This leads to the following complexity guidelines:

- Optimize the number of elements on a screen, within limits of clarity.
- Minimize the alignment points, especially horizontal or columnar.

Obviously, the way to minimize screen complexity is to reduce the number of controls displayed. Fewer controls will yield lower complexity measures. This is unrealistic, however, since ultimate simplicity means nothing is there, which obviously does not accomplish very much. Indeed, Vitz (1966) has found that people have subjective preferences for the right amount of information, and too little is as bad as too much. The practical answer, then, is to optimize the amount of information displayed, within limits of clarity. What is optimum must be considered in light of guidelines to follow, so a final judgment must be postponed.

Alignment. What can be done, however, is to minimize alignment points, most importantly horizontal or columnar alignment points. Fewer alignment points will have a strong positive influence on the complexity calculation. Tullis (1983) has also found, in a follow-up study of some other screens, that fewer alignment points were among the strongest influences creating positive viewer feelings of visually pleasing composition.

Misalignments and uneven spacings, no matter how slight, can create bothersome unconscious disruptions to our perceptual systems. When things don't align, a sense of clutter and disorganization often results. In addition to reducing complexity, alignment helps create balance, regularity, sequentiality, and unity. Alignment also reduces variation on a screen. Common alignments are associated with a group identity of their own. Anything that breaks that alignment is quickly seen as an exception.

In laying out a screen, imagine a grid of horizontal and vertical lines beneath it. Use these grids to position elements and to achieve common alignment points.

Groupings

- Provide functional groupings of associated elements.
- Create spatial groupings as closely as possible to five degrees of visual angle (1.67 inches in diameter or about six to seven lines of text, 12 to 14 characters in width).
- Evenly space controls within a grouping, allowing 1/8 to 1/4 inch between each.

- Visually reinforce groupings:
  - Provide adequate separation between groupings through liberal use of white space.
  - Provide line borders around groups.

Grouping elements on a screen aids in establishing structure and meaningful form. In addition to providing aesthetic appeal, grouping has been found to aid recall (Card, 1982) and result in a faster screen search (Dodson & Shields, 1978; Haubner & Neumann, 1986; Treisman, 1982; Tullis, 1983.).

The perceptual principles of proximity, closure, similarity, and matching patterns foster visual groupings. But the search for a more objective definition of what constitutes a group has gone on for years. Tullis, in his 1981 study, described an objective method for establishing groups based on the work of Zahn (1971) using the Gestalt psychologists' law of proximity. For the Tullis (1981) screens shown in Figures 3.12 and 3.13:

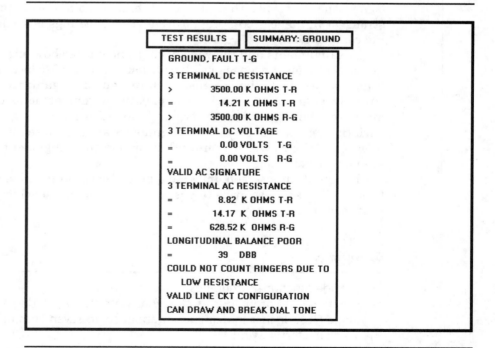

Figure 3.12   Original screen, from Tullis (1981), with grouping indicated by bold boxes.

1. Compute the mean distance between each character and its nearest neighbor. Use a character distance of 1 between characters adjacent horizontally and 2 between characters adjacent vertically (between rows).
2. Multiply the mean distance derived by 2.
3. Connect with a line any character pair that is closer than the distance established in step 2.

This has been done for these inquiry screens and the results illustrated in Figures 3.12 and 3.13. Boxes have been included around the derived groupings.

- Figure 3.12 (original):
  Mean distance between characters = 1.05.
  Twice the mean distance = 2.10.
  A line is drawn between characters 1 or 2 apart, not 3 or more.
  Resulting number of groups = 3.

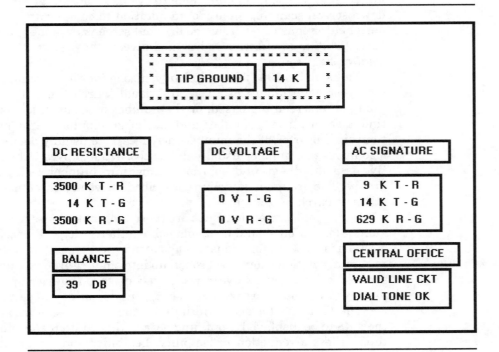

Figure 3.13   Redesigned screen, from Tullis (1981), with grouping indicated by bold boxes.

- Figure 3.13 (redesigned):
  Mean distance between characters = 1.09.
  Twice the mean distance = 2.18.
  A line is drawn between characters 1 or 2 apart, not 3 or more.
  Resulting number of groups = 13.

Tullis found that the redesigned screens had more groupings than the originals.

To perform a simplified version of this formula, connect with a line all characters on the screen separated by no more than one space horizontally and no blank lines vertically. Groupings will become immediately obvious.

Another grouping measure was also calculated by Tullis: the average size of each screen's group. The average size of the three groups in the original screen is 13.3 degrees in visual angle, whereas the 13 groups on the redesigned screen average 5.2 degrees visual angle. The redesigned screen group size, interestingly, closely matches the five-degree visual acuity screen chunk described in Step 1. It seems that groups five degrees or less in size can be scanned with one eye fixation per group. Therefore, screens with these size groupings can be searched faster. Groupings larger than five degrees require more eye fixations per grouping, slowing down screen scanning time. So, in addition to complexity, the Tullis redesigned screens differ from the original screens by some grouping measures. The more effective redesigned screens have a *greater number* of *smaller size* groups.

Tullis, in his 1983 follow-up study, also found that groupings were the strongest determinant of a screen's visual search time. If the size of a group on a screen increased, or the number of groups increased, search time also increased. Number and size of groups have an opposite relationship, however; if the number increases, size usually decreases. If the size increases, number usually decreases. What proves to be most effective is a middle-ground solution, a medium number of medium-sized groups. The grouping guidelines described above are based upon this and other research presented.

Functional, semantic groups are those that make sense to the user. Related information should be displayed together. A logical place to "break" a screen is between functional groups of information, but a massive grouping of information should be broken up into smaller groups. The most reasonable point is every five rows. A six- or seven-row grouping may be displayed without a break, if necessary, but do not exceed seven rows.

The 11- to 15-character width limitation must take into consideration the data to be displayed. Confining data to this width makes no sense if it thus suffers a reduction in legibility. Legibility and comprehension are most important.

To give unity to a display, the space between groups should be less than that of the margins. The most common and obvious way to achieve spacing is through white or blank space, but there are other ways. Alternatives include: contrasting display features such as differing intensity levels, image reversals (white characters on a black background versus black characters on a white background), borders, and color. Spacing, however, appears to be stronger than color. Two studies (Haubner & Benz, 1983; Haubner & Neumann, 1986) found that adequate spacing, not color, is a more important determinant of ease of use for uncluttered, highly structured inquiry screens.

Perceptual Principles and Functional Grouping

- Use visual organization to create functional groupings.
  - Proximity: 000   000   000
  - Similarity: AAABBBCCC
  - Closure: [ ]   [ ]   [ ]
  - Matching patterns: >>   < >

- Combine visual organization principles in logical ways.
  - Proximity and similarity: AAA   BBB   CCC
  - Proximity and closure: [ ]   [ ]   [ ]
  - Matching patterns and closure: ( )   < >   { }
  - Proximity and ordering: 1234   1   5
                                         2   6
                                  5678   3   7
                                         4   8

- Avoid visual organization principles that conflict.
  - Proximity opposing similarity: AAA   ABB   BBC   CCC
  - Proximity opposing closure:] [   ] [   ] [
  - Proximity opposing ordering: 1357 1   2
                                         3   4
                                   2468 5   6
                                         7   8

Perceptual principles can be used to aid screen functional groupings.

Use visual organization to create functional grouping. The most common perceptual principle used in screen design to aid visual groupings has been the proximity principle. The incorporation of adequate spacing between groups of related elements enhances the "togetherness" of each grouping. Space should always be considered a design component of a screen. The objective should never be to get rid of it. The similarity principle can be used to call attention to various groupings through displaying them in a different intensity, font style, or color. The closure and matching patterns principles involve using lines, borders, and unique symbols to identify and relate common information.

Combine visual organization principles in logical ways. Visual organization principles can be combined to enhance groupings. Proximity, being a very strong perceptual principle, can guide the eye through an array of information to be scanned in a particular direction. Scanning direction can also be made obvious through similarity (color, intensity, etc.) or matching patterns (lines or borders).

Avoid visual organization principles that conflict. Principles may not always be compatible, however. When incompatibilities are encountered by the viewer, confusion results. In the examples above, proximity destroys similarity, proximity overwhelms closure, and proximity overwhelms logical ordering.

Grouping Using White Space Today, the term white space is a misnomer, a carry over from the white paper of printed forms. It might more appropriately simply be called space, reflecting the variety of colors capable of being assumed by today's screens. Whatever we call it, space should be considered a screen element of equal importance to all others. It defines and separates screen elements, and gives a screen proportion and meaningful form, thus assisting in providing the distinctiveness that is so desired. Space is also used to direct attention to adjacent areas that do contain important information. Remember, if a screen is perceived as a homogeneous, cluttered mass, information will only be found through an exhaustive search of the entire screen.

Grouping Using Borders

- Incorporate line borders for:
  - Focusing attention on groupings or related information.
  - Guiding the eye through a screen.
- Do not exceed three line thicknesses or two line styles on a screen, however.
  - Use a standard hierarchy for line presentation.
- Create lines consistent in height and length.
- Use rules and borders sparingly.

Line borders. Line borders, or rules, can greatly enhance a screen. Thacker (1987) found that displayed information with a border around it was reported to be easier to read, better in appearance, and preferable. Figures 3.14 and 3.15 illustrate identical screens with and without borders around groupings. While many groupings are obvious without borders, borders certainly reinforce their existence.

Lines or rules assist in focusing attention on related information. They also aid in separating groupings of information from one another. Draw borders around elements to be grouped. Rules also serve to guide

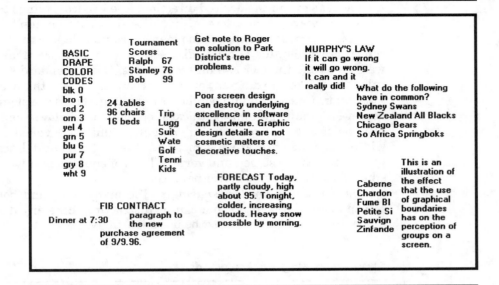

Figure 3.14   The effect of line or graphical borders. Groupings without borders.

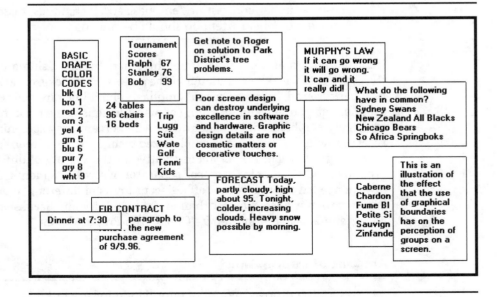

Figure 3.15   The effect of line or graphical borders. Groupings with borders.

the viewer's eye in the desired direction. Use vertical rulings to convey to the screen viewer that a screen should be scanned from top to bottom.

Line thickness variations. Too many variations in line thicknesses on a screen create clutter and are distracting. Use no more than three line weights at one time, or two different styles. Use a standard hierarchy for rules, the thickest to differentiate major components, the thinnest for minor separation. Consider a thin border for individual controls, a slightly thicker border for groupings, and the thickest borders for windows themselves.

Consistent line widths and heights. Similarly, variations in line widths and heights are distracting. Create horizontal lines of equal widths across the screen and vertical lines of equal height whenever possible. This will provide better balance.

Use lines and borders sparingly. Too many lines and borders on a screen also create clutter and can be distracting. Like any display technique, lines and borders must be used sparingly.

Grouping Using Backgrounds

- Consider incorporating a contrasting background for related information.
  - The background should not have the "emphasis" of the screen component that should be attended to. Consider about a 25 percent gray screening.
  - Reserve higher contrast or "emphasized" techniques for screen components to which attention should be drawn.

Information can also be visually tied together through using a background that contrasts with the remainder of the screen. The background should just be a background; however, visual emphasis should be directed toward foreground material. A common failing of many screens is the background being too highly emphasized. Consider about a 25 percent gray screening. Always reserve the higher contrast or emphasized techniques for screen components in need of attention. Be very conservative in the variety of different backgrounds used. Also, color is a poor separator of screen elements. A border is always needed to properly set off adjacent areas of different colors. Finally, less variation is always better than more. An additional discussion on screen backgrounds is found in Step 9, "Choose the Proper Colors."

Amount of Information

- Present the proper amount of information for the task.
  - Too little is inefficient.

- Too much is confusing.
- Present all information necessary for performing an action or making a decision on one screen, whenever possible.
  - People should not have to remember things from one screen to the next.
- Restrict screen or window density levels to no more than about 30 percent.

Presenting too much information on a screen is confusing; there will be greater competition among a screen's components for a person's attention. Visual search times will be longer and meaningful structure will be more difficult to perceive. Presenting too little information is inefficient and may tax a person's memory limitations.

In general, present all information necessary for performing an action or making a decision on one screen. This will require careful analysis of the user's tasks. One objective measure of "how much" should go on a screen has been developed: "density."

Density, by definition, is a calculation of the proportion of display character positions in the screen, or an area of the screen containing something. Density is clearly related to complexity since both measure "how much is there." Complexity looks at elements, density at characters, so they should rise and fall together.

In general, studies show that increasing the density of a display increases the time and errors in finding information (Callan, Curran, & Lane, 1977; Dodson & Shields, 1978; Treisman, 1982). There are two types of density to be calculated on a screen: overall and local.

Overall density is a measure of the percentage of character positions on the entire screen containing data. Danchak (1976) stated that density (loading, as he called it) should not exceed 25 percent. Reporting the results of a qualitative judgment of "good" screens, he found their density was on the order of 15 percent. Tullis, in his 1981 study, reported that the density of screens from an up and running successful system ranged from 0.9 to 27.9 percent, with a mean of 14.2 percent. Using this and other research data, he concluded that the common upper-density limit appears to be about 25 percent.

Thacker (1987) compared screens with densities of 14 percent, 29 percent, and 43 percent. Response time increased significantly as screen density increased. He found, however, that the time increase between 14 percent and 29 percent was much smaller than the time increase between 29 percent and 43 percent. He also found increased error rates with greater density, the 43 percent density screens showing significantly more errors.

Local density is a measure of how "tightly packed" the screen is. A measure of local density, derived by Tullis, is the percentage of characters

in the 88-character visual acuity circle described in Step 1, modified by
the weighting factors illustrated below.

```
       012222210
     0123445443210
    023456777654320
    1235679+9765321
    023456777654320
     0123445443210
       012222210
```

For every character on the screen, a local density is calculated using
the above weighting factors, and then an average for all characters on the
screen is established.

Figures 3.16 and 3.17 are the original and redesigned screens from
the 1981 Tullis study. Density measures for these screens are:

- Figure 3.16 (original):
  - Overall density = 17.9 percent.
  - Local density = 58.0 percent.

```
TEST RESULTS    SUMMARY:    GROUND

GROUND, FAULT T-G
3 TERMINAL DC RESISTANCE
>          3500.00 K OHMS T-R
=             14.21 K OHMS T-R
>          3500.00 K OHMS R-G
3 TERMINAL DC VOLTAGE
=              0.00 VOLTS   T-G
=              0.00 VOLTS   R-G
VALID AC SIGNATURE
3 TERMINAL AC RESISTANCE
=              8.82 K OHMS T-R
=             14.17 K OHMS T-R
=            628.52 K OHMS R-G
LONGITUDINAL BALANCE POOR
=               39  DBB
COULD NOT COUNT RINGERS DUE TO
    LOW RESISTANCE
VALID LINE CKT CONFIGURATION
CAN DRAW AND BREAK DIAL TONE
```

Figure 3.16   Original screen, from Tullis (1981).

- Figure 3.17 (redesigned):
  - Overall density = 10.8 percent.
  - Local density = 35.6 percent.

In both cases, the more effective redesigned screen had lower density measures. In his 1983 follow-up study, Tullis found a lower local density to be the most important characteristic, creating a positive "visually pleasing" feeling.

The research does suggest some density guidelines for screens. Maintain overall density levels no higher than about 30 percent. This upper overall density recommendation should be interpreted with extreme care. Density, by itself, does not affect whether or not what is displayed "makes sense." This is a completely different question. Density can always be reduced through substituting abbreviations for whole words. The cost of low density in this case may be illegibility and poorer comprehension. Indeed, poorly designed screens have been redesigned to achieve greater clarity and have actually ended up with higher density measures than the original versions. How it all "hangs together" can never be divorced from how much is there.

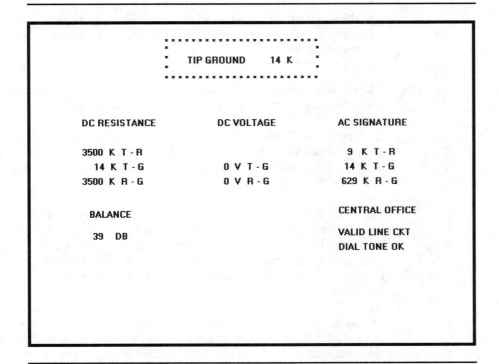

Figure 3.17   Redesigned screen, from Tullis (1981).

In conclusion, all this density research was performed using text-based screens. With many boxed or specialized controls found on graphical screens, like list boxes or sliders, it is much more difficult to calculate density as has just been illustrated. Is it necessary to do so on graphical screens? Not really. The research was described to show the value of reducing density in screen design. From a practical standpoint, if the guidelines for alignment and groupings are adhered to, screen density will usually be reduced to an acceptable level.

Meaningful Ordering

- Provide an ordering of elements that:
  - Is logical and sequential.
  - Is rhythmic, guiding a person's eye through the display.
  - Encourages natural movement sequences.
  - Minimizes cursor and eye movement distances.
- Locate the most important and most frequently used elements or controls to the top left.
- Maintain a top-to-bottom, left-to-right flow.
- When groups of related information must be broken and displayed on separate screens, provide breaks at logical or natural points in the information flow.

The arrangement of screen items should appear logical and sensible to the user. Common ordering schemes are the following:

Conventional Through convention and custom, some ordering schemes have evolved for certain elements. Examples are days of the week, months of the year, and one's name and address. These elements should be ordered in the customary way.

Sequence of Use Sequence of use grouping involves arranging information items in the order in which they are commonly received or transmitted, or in natural groups. An address, for example, is normally given by street, city, state, and zip code. Another example of natural grouping is the league standings of football teams, appearing in order of best to worst records.

Frequency of Use Frequency of use is a design technique based on the principle that information items used most frequently should be grouped at the beginning, the second most frequently used items grouped next, and so forth.

Function Function involves grouping information items according to their purpose. All items pertaining to insurance coverages, for example, may be placed in one location. Such grouping also allows convenient group identification for the user.

Importance Importance grouping is based on the information's importance to the task being performed. Important items are placed in the most prominent positions.

General to Specific If some data elements are more general than others, the general elements should precede the specific elements. This will usually occur when there is a hierarchical relationship among data elements.

Screen layout normally reflects a combination of these techniques. Information may be organized functionally but, within each function, individual items may be arranged by sequence or importance. Numerous permutations are possible.

The direction of movement between screen items should be obvious, consistent, and rhythmic. The eye, or pointer, should not be forced or caused to wander long distances about the display seeking the next item. The eye can be guided through the screen with lines formed through use of white space and display elements. More complex movements may require the aid of display contrasts. Sequence of use can be made more obvious through the incorporation of borders around groupings of related information or screen controls. Borders provide visual cues concerning the arrangement of screen elements as the eye will tend to stay within a border to complete a task. Aligning elements will also minimize screen scanning and navigation movements. In establishing eye movement through a screen, also consider that the eye tends to move sequentially, for example:

- From dark areas to light areas.
- From big objects to little objects.
- From unusual shapes to common shapes.
- From highly saturated colors to unsaturated colors.

These techniques can be used initially to focus a person's attention to one area of the screen and then direct it elsewhere.

Locate the most important or frequently used screen controls to the top left of the screen where initial attention is usually directed. This will also reduce the overall number of eye and manual control movements needed to work with a screen.

Maintain a top-to-bottom, left-to-right flow through the screen. This is contrary to the typical, text-based screen cursor movement direction that proceeds left to right, then top to bottom. This top-to-bottom orientation is recommended for information *entry* for the following reasons:

- Eye movements between items will be shorter.
- Control movements between items will be shorter.
- Groupings are more obvious perceptually.
- When one's eye moves away from the screen and then back, it returns to about the same place it left, even if it is seeking the next item in a sequence (a visual anchor point remains).

Unfortunately, a left-to-right orientation is recommended by most product style guides. This orientation is based upon the presumption that since people read left-to-right, a screen must be organized in this way. Many screens, however, do not present text but listings of small pieces of information that must be scanned. All the research on human scanning finds a top-to-bottom presentation of information is best.

Why do we persist in this left-to-right orientation for nontextual screens? A common screen metaphor applied in today's systems is that of the paper form. We often see a paper form exactly replicated on a screen. Unfortunately, the left-to-right orientation of the typical form is poorly suited to the needs and characteristics of its user. Its complexity is generally higher than it should be, and its sequentiality is often not as obvious and certainly not at all very efficient.

The left-to-right orientation of paper forms was not dictated by human needs but by mechanical considerations. The metaphor for earliest display screens four decades ago (although this term was not used then) was the typewriter. The left-to-right orientation of the typewriter was developed to permit one to type text on paper, a significant enhancement over handwriting as a medium of human communication. At some point early in the typewriter's life, however, its ability to be used to complete paper forms also became evident. So, we started designing forms to be completed by typewriter. They had to be filled out left-to-right because the design of the typewriter made any other completion method very difficult for a person to do.

Our earliest display screens reflected this left-to-right entry orientation and have done so for many years. Today, in our display-based world, the typewriter's mechanical limitations no longer exist. Let's shed the artificial constraints we have imposed upon ourselves and get rid of the left-to-right orientation for nontextual screens. A top-to-bottom orientation has many more advantages for the screen user.

Top-to-bottom orientation is also recommended for presenting displays of read-only information that must be scanned. This will be described shortly.

Distinctiveness

Elements of screen must be distinct, clearly distinguished from one another. Distinctiveness can be enhanced through separation and contrast.

- Individual screen controls, and groups of controls, must be perceptually distinct.
  - Screen controls:
    - Should not touch a window border.
    - Should not touch each other.
  - Field and group borders:
    - Should not touch a window border.
    - Should not touch each other.
  - Buttons:
    - Should not touch a window border.
    - Should not touch each other.
  - A button label should not touch the button border.
  - Adjacent screen elements must be displayed in colors or shades of sufficient contrast with one another.

All screen elements must be perceptually distinct. Distinctiveness is achieved by providing adequate separation between adjacent elements and screen boundaries and providing adequate separation between components of an element. Screen controls, field and group borders, and buttons should not touch window borders or each other. Colors or shades used for adjacent screen elements must also contrast well with one another. Guidelines for color and shading are described in Step 9.

Focus and Emphasis

- Visually emphasize the:
  - Most prominent element.
  - Most important elements.
  - Central idea or focal point.
- De-emphasize less important elements.
- Minimize clutter so important information is not hidden.

Apply a visual emphasis technique (brightness, size, etc.) to highlight the most important or prominent element, or elements, of a screen. Typically, the most important component of a screen will be its data or information. Minimization of clutter assists a user in focusing on the most crucial part of a screen.

Conveying Depth of Levels or a Three-Dimensional Appearance

- Use perspective, highlighting, shading and other techniques to achieve a three-dimensional appearance.
- Always assume a light source is in the upper-left corner of the screen.
- Display command buttons flat, or raised above the screen plane.
- Display screen-based controls on or etched or lowered below the screen plane.
- Do not overdo, and avoid:
  - Using perspective for non-interactive elements.
  - Providing too much detail.

The spatial composition of a graphics screen can also be communicated by using perspective, highlighting, shading, and other techniques to achieve a three-dimensional appearance. In creating shadows, always assume the light source is in the upper-left corner of the screen. To visually communicate function, consider displaying command buttons flat or raised above the screen. Conversely, display screen-based controls on or etched or lowered below the screen plane. Consistently follow this concept on all screens. One caution; Do not overdo or the effect will be lost and visual clutter will emerge. Avoid using perspective for noninteractive elements, and do not provide too much detail.

Techniques to achieve a three-dimensional appearance include overlapping, drop shadows, highlighting and lowlighting, growing and shrinking, and beveled edges (Marcus, 1992).

Overlapping Fully display the window or screen element of current relevance and partially hide beneath it other screen windows or elements, as illustrated in Figure 3.18. The completeness or continuity of outline of the relevant element will make it appear nearer than those partially covered.

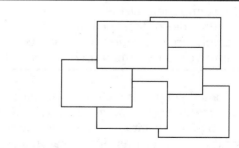

Figure 3.18   Overlapping screen elements.

Drop Shadows To further aid the impression of the placement of a pull-down above a screen, or a window above a screen or another window, locate a heavier line along the bottom and right edges of the pull-down or window. This creates the impression of a shadow caused by a light source in the upper-left corner of the screen, reinforcing the nearness of the important element. The light source should always appear to be upper left, the shadow lower right.

Highlighting and Lowlighting Highlighted or brighter screen elements appear to come forward while lowlighted or less bright elements recede. Attention will be directed to the highlighted element.

Shrinking and Growing Important elements can be made to grow in size while less important elements remain small or shrink. An icon, for example, should expand to a window when it is selected. The movement, as it expands, will focus attention upon it.

Beveled Edges A beveled edge (non-right-angle lines to the screen element borders) will also give the impression of depth. With beveled edges, windows, buttons, and menu bar choices will appear to arise from the screen. To strengthen the three-dimensional aspect of the screen element, give it a drop shadow by shading the bottom and right sides with either a tone of gray or a darker shade of the basic screen color.

Texture Change Increased density of an object implies a further distance. Increase the density of nonapplicable screen elements, and display currently relevant elements less densely. If textures are used as a code on screens, Shurtleff (1993) recommends using no more than six or seven. Also, a texture change should convey information that is not immediately apparent from name, shape, or other physical characteristic of an object. Finally, provide consistency; establish only one meaning for a texture.

Color Change Objects farther away appear hazy and less saturated. Increase haziness as screen element importance diminishes; display currently relevant elements more vividly.

Size change Objects farther away appear smaller. Decrease the size of nonapplicable screen elements; display currently relevant elements larger.

Clarity Change Objects not at the eye's focus distance appear fuzzy or blurred. Display nonapplicable elements blurred and currently relevant screen elements clear.

Vertical Location The horizon appears higher, objects up close lower. Present currently applicable screen elements at the bottom of the screen, nonapplicable elements at the screen's top.

Spacing Change Faraway objects appear more closely spaced, closer objects more widely spaced. Display nonapplicable elements more closely spaced, currently applicable screen elements more widely spaced.

Receding Lines Parallel lines receding to a vanishing point imply depth.

Motion Change Objects moving at uniform speeds appear to be moving more slowly the farther away they are.

Presenting Information Simply and Meaningfully

Following are guidelines for presenting information on screens. The fundamental goals are clarity and simplicity in form, comprehensibility in content, efficient information assimilation, and pleasantness in tone.

- Provide legibility.
  - Noticeable and distinguishable.
- Provide readability.
  - Identifiable, interpretable, and attractive.
- Present in usable form.
  - No translations, transpositions, and references to documentation required.
- Utilize contrasting display features.
  - Attracts and calls attention.
- Create visual lines.
  - Implicit and explicit.
- Be consistent.
  - In appearance and procedural usage.

Legibility. Legibility is distinguishableness. Is the type of adequate size and clarity for viewers of all ages? Is the contrast between text and its background adequate?

Readability. Is the information written at an understandable level? Is it direct, simple, and easy to comprehend? Is visual interference minimized?

Usability. Screen information should be presented in a directly usable form. Reference to documentation for interpretation should never be required.

Contrasting display. Use constrasting display features to call attention to different screen components, items being operated upon, or urgent items. Features chosen should provide perceptual cues, aiding in screen component identification so that attention may be quickly and accurately focused. Perceptual cues clarify structure and relationships, and give hints to the reader. Good readers make great use of the typographic and semantic cues found in well-presented text. Some recommended uses of display features are found in the following section on software considerations.

Visual lines. The eye should be guided vertically or horizontally implicitly through the screen through the use of white space and control alignments. In situations where a large amount of information must be presented on one screen, eye movement direction may also be communicated to the viewer explicitly, through the drawing of actual vertical or horizontal rules. Purposeless, unfettered wandering of the eye should be discouraged.

Consistency. Methods chosen should always be consistent in visual appearance and procedural usage.

Upper- and Mixed-Case Font

- Use mixed-case for:
  - Control captions.
  - Data.
  - Control choice descriptions.
  - Text.
  - Messages.
  - Instructional information.
  - Menu descriptions.
  - Button descriptions.
- Use upper-case or capitalization for:
  - Title.
  - Section headings.
  - Subsection headings.

The screen designer often has the choice of whether to display screen components in mixed-case or upper-case. Upper-case means all capital letters. Mixed-case usually implies a predominance of lower-case letters with occasional capitalization as needed (initial letter of first word, acronyms, abbreviations, proper nouns, etc.).

The research on textual material is clear. For example, Tinker (1955), in a study of reading from hard-copy materials, found that mixed-case text is read significantly faster than upper-case text. Rehe (1974) found a 13 percent advantage in reading speed for mixed-case text. Moskel, Erno, & Shneiderman (1984) found even larger advantages of mixed-case text compared to upper-case in comprehension and reading of screen materials. The advantage of mixed-case text is that it gives a word a more distinctive shape. Upper-case letters are all the same height; lower-case letters have different heights. These height differences aid comprehension.

The research on screen captions, however, leans in another direction. Vartabedian (1971) established that screens with captions containing upper-case characters are searched faster than those using mixed-case characters. Williams (1988) found identical results with menu choice descriptions.

Why this difference? The materials giving better results for mixed-case appear to be of a longer, textual-style nature. The caption materials appear to be single words or short phrases. It may be that the superiority of mixed-case does not exhibit itself until text of an extended nature is read. Why short upper-case captions were actually superior to mixed-case is unknown. In light of this research, the following is recommended.

Use mixed-case for text, messages, instructional information, menus, and pushbuttons. Text, messages, and instructions reflect the years of research on readability. The menu bar in mixed-case will provide contrast with the nearby upper-case title. Buttons in mixed-case will provide case compatibility with the component of similar function, menus. Also use mixed-case for control captions, data, and control choice descriptions. These mixed-case recommendations also reflect what is becoming a de facto standard, found in various product style guides.

Unfortunately, most style guides, such as IBM's *SAA CUA* and Microsoft's *Windows Interface Guidelines,* recommend presenting *everything* on a screen in mixed-case. That this is an extrapolation of the textual reading research to all written words can only be assumed.

Contrary to style guide recommendations, consider using upper-case for the screen title and, most importantly, all screen headings. For headings, capitalization will set them off from the many other screen components described above displayed in mixed-case. Headings on screens are a learning aid. They enable the user to become familiar with screen organization and relationships. With experience, the screen user finds headings less important. Capitalization will set them off from the remaining screen elements, making them easier to ignore when they are no longer needed. Screen design research does not discount using upper-case.

Typography A seemingly unending supply of typefaces, styles, and sizes are available to the graphical screen designer. As these guidelines are presented, note the limits in the number of variations permitted. Using too many techniques at one time only leads to screen clutter and the impression of confusion.

Typeface

- Use simple, readable fonts.
  - Any sans serif such as Helvetica.
  - Times Roman.
- Use no more than two families, compatible in terms of line thicknesses, capital letter height, and so on.
  - Assign a separate purpose to each family.
  - Allow one family to dominate.
- Use no more than:
  - Two styles of the same family.
    - Standard and italic.
  - Use no more than two weights.
    - Regular and bold.
- Use bold only when you want to call attention or create a hierarchy.

Size

- Use no more than three sizes.
  - Consider "X" height.
- Many systems use:
  - 12 point for menus.
  - 10 point for windows.
- Never change established type sizes to squeeze in more text.

Consistency

- Establish a consistent hierarchy and convention for using typefaces, styles, and sizes.
- Use standard system fonts to achieve consistency.

Other

- Always consider the visual capabilities of the user.

Typeface Visually simple, readable fonts are needed for clarity on screens. Ornate fonts should be avoided because they reduce legibility. Generally, sans serif typefaces are recommended (serifs are the small cross strokes that appear on the arms of some letters) if the type is 10 or less points in size or if the display environment is less than ideal. The serifs can wash out under these conditions. Types with serifs, it is felt, provide better links between letters in a word, provide a horizontal guideline for the eye, and help in distinguishing one letter from another. Helvetica is a sans serif typeface, while Times Roman is characterized by very small serifs.

All typefaces are named, some after their designers (for example, Garamond), some after locations where they originated (Helvetica after Switzerland), and other for the publications for which they were designed (Times). Within each typeface are style variations: regular, italics, boldface, outlines, and shadows. These groupings are called a *family*.

A family of styles is designed to complement one another, creating unity in design. An example of a family is that of Times illustrated in Figure 3.19.

Never use more than two styles at one time. A regular type and its italics is a good combination. Also, restrict a type to two weights, regular and bold for example. Only use bold when you want to call attention to something. Typically, screens will be used again and again and something bold often becomes too visually heavy.

Similar typefaces are grouped into what are called *races*. One kind of race is called *roman*, which contains the Times typeface illustrated as well as the Bookman, Schoolbook, and Palatino typefaces. A second race is *sans serif*, where the typefaces Helvetica and Avant Garde reside. Another race is named Old English. An effective design can almost always be achieved by staying within one typeface race. If it is necessary to mix typeface families on a screen, Lichty (1989) recommends the following:

- Never mix families within the same race. Typographic noise is created.
- Assign a separate purpose to each family. A sans serif typeface for the title and headings and a roman typeface for the body is a good combination.
- Allow one family to dominate.

For a much more detailed discussion of typefaces, see Lichty.

Times Roman

Times Italic

Times Bold

Times Bold Italic

Times Outline

Times Shadow

Figure 3.19   The Times family of type.

Size Type sizes are described by points, the distance between the top of a letter's ascender and the bottom of its descender. One point equals 1/12 inch. Variations in type sizes should also be minimized, no more than three being the maximum to be displayed at one time on a screen.

In selecting a typeface it may sometimes be important to consider its *x-height,* or the height of its lower-case x and other similar letters. Two typefaces may share the same point size but one may *appear* significantly larger because its x-height is larger, as illustrated in Figure 3.20. Legibility can be affected by x-height.

Many systems use a 12-point type for menus and 10-point for windows. Dropping below eight points significantly degrades legibility. For comparison purposes, recommended paper document type sizes and styles are as follows:

Chapter headings:	24-point bold
Section headings:	18-point bold
Subsection headings:	14-point bold
Paragraph headings:	12-point bold
Body text:	10-point
Annotations/footnotes:	8-point

Never change a selected type size for a screen component to squeeze something in to make it fit. The differences will be noticeable and very disturbing.

Consistency Apply typeface, style, and size conventions in a consistent manner to all screen components. This will aid screen learning and improve screen readability. To assure consistency, use the standard system fonts.

abcdefghijklmnopqrstuvwxyz

abcdefghijklmnopqrstuvwxyz

abcdefghijklmnopqrstuvwxyz

Figure 3.20　　Types with same point size and different x heights (from top to bottom, Gatsby, Times Roman, and Avant Garde).

Age Considerations Unfortunately, as we all know, the eye's capability begins to diminish as we age. The eye begins it aging process in our early 30s. At 40 the process accelerates and by age 50 most people need 50 per cent more light to read by than they did when they were in their 20s. Failing to be able to read a menu in a dimly lit restaurant is often the first time we become aware of this problem. Smaller type sizes will be more difficult for older people to work with. Type sizes and styles should always be chosen considering the ages of the screen users.

Comparing Paper to Screen Reading Printing technology has been evolving for several centuries. Factors such as type size and style, character and line spacings, and column and margin widths have been the focus of research for a good part of that time. The product of this research is highly readable and attractive printed materials. Conversely, CRT-based characters are a relatively new innovation, with many technical limitations. The result is a displayed character that often lacks the high quality a paper medium can provide. This disparity in quality has resulted in performance differences when paper and screen reading of materials have been compared. Various researchers over the years have found slower screen reading speeds, as much as 40 percent and more errors.

More recent research indicates that as display resolution improves, the reading speed differences can be reduced, if not entirely eliminated. For extended reading, hard-copy display of material still has significant advantages, however, and will probably continue to for some time.

Captions

- Identify controls with captions or labels.
- Fully spell out in a meaningful language to the user.
- Display in normal intensity.
- Use a mixed-case font.
- Capitalize the first letter of each significant word.
- End each caption with a colon (:).
- Choose distinct captions that can be easily distinguished from other captions. Minimal differences (one letter or word) cause confusion.

Identify Controls with Captions All screen controls should be identified by captions. The context in which information is found in the world at large provides cues to the information's meaning. A number on a telephone dial is readily identifiable as a telephone number; the number on a metal plate affixed to the back of an automobile is readily identified as a license number. The same information displayed on a screen, being out of context, may not be readily identifiable.

There are, however, some exceptions to this rule on read-only or inquiry screens. The structure of the data itself in some cases may be enough to identify its meaning. The most obvious example is name, street, city, state, and zip code. Date may be another possibility. Elimination of these common captions will serve further to clean up read-only screens. Before eliminating them, however, it should be determined that all screen users will be able to identify these fields all the time.

Structure and Size Captions on screens must clearly and concisely describe the information displayed. They are very important for inexperienced screen users. As one becomes more experienced, their importance diminishes. As such, they should be fully spelled out in the natural language of the user. In general, abbreviations and contractions should not be used. To achieve the alignment recommendations to be discussed shortly, an occasional abbreviation or contraction may be necessary, but choose those that are common in the everyday language of the application or those that are meaningful and easily learned. Also, display captions in a moderate brightness or intensity. Visual emphasis will be directed to the screen data or information.

Significant Word Capitalization With mixed-case field captions, capitalize the first letter of each significant word. This is commonly referred to as *headline* style. The opposing style, *sentence,* capitalizes only the first letter of the first caption word. A caption is not a sentence but the name for an area into which information will be keyed. This makes it a proper noun and should follow the headline style of presentation. In situations when a caption is phrased as a question, then it is a sentence, and only its initial letter should be capitalized. Never begin a caption or sentence with a lower-case letter. A capital letter makes it easier for the eye to identify the start of each caption.

Unfortunately, IBM's SAA CUA and Microsoft's Windows 95 style guides do not follow the significant word capitalization principle of only using a capital letter for the initial letter of the caption. They prefer the sentence style.

Designate with a Colon A caption should be ended with a colon (:) to clearly identify it as such. The colon is unobtrusive, does not physically resemble a letter or number, and is grammatically meaningful, as it is used chiefly to direct attention to matter that follows. Unfortunately, many graphical systems do not follow this convention and captions blend with other screen elements. The Windows 95 style guide *does* recommend using a colon after captions.

Since the recommended entry area for an entry control will be a box, adequately distinguishing the caption from the entry field itself, the inclusion of a colon may seem redundant. However, read-only/ display/inquiry screens are most effective if the data displayed is not presented in a box, making a colon to distinguish caption from data absolutely necessary. Including a colon after all captions, therefore, will provide consistency across all screens.

Distinctiveness Captions that are similar often repeat the same word or words over and over again. This directs a viewer's attention to the pattern created by the repetitive word, increases the potential for confusion, adds to density, and adds to screen clutter. A better solution is to incorporate the common words into headings, subheadings, or group identifiers, as illustrated in Figure 3.21.

Data Fields For the two kinds of data fields—entry or modifiable fields, and display or read-only fields—different considerations must be taken into account.

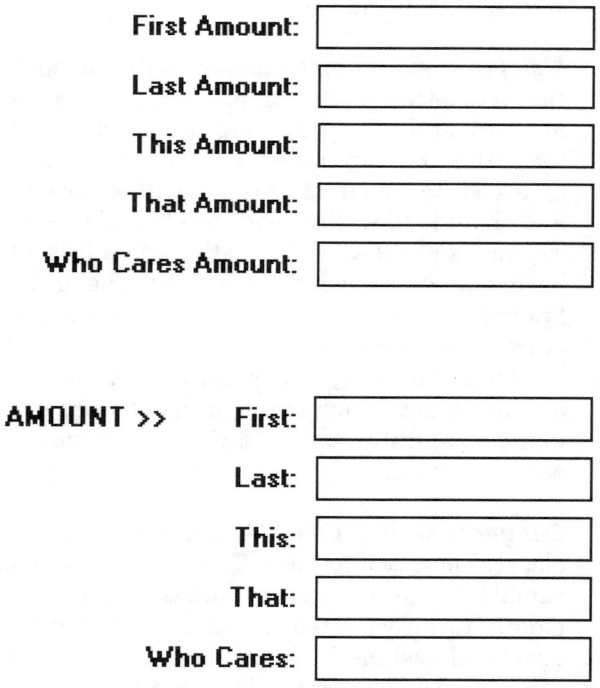

First Amount:

Last Amount:

This Amount:

That Amount:

Who Cares Amount:

AMOUNT >>   First:

Last:

This:

That:

Who Cares:

Figure 3.21   Providing better control caption discrimination. (The redundant word "amount" is incorporated into a heading.)

- For entry or modifiable data fields, display data within:
  - A line box.
  - A reverse polarity box.
- For inquiry or display/read-only screens, display data on the normal screen background.
- Visually emphasize the data fields.

Entry/Modifiable Fields An entry or modifiable field must possess the following qualities.

- Draw a person's attention to the fact that information must be keyed or selected in it.
- Not detract from the legibility of characters being keyed into it.
- Permit easy designation of the kind or structure of the entry required, such as incorporation of slashes (/) in a date field.
- Indicate the maximum size of the entry required.

In an early study using text-based screens, it was found that people overwhelmingly preferred something on a screen to indicate entry fields. In another study (Savage, Habinek, & Blackstad, 1982) it was found that the best alternatives for defining an entry field were a broken line underscore and a box. An underscore has been traditionally used on text-based screens; the box is now recommended for, and should be used on, graphical screens.

Display/Read-Only Screens For inquiry or display/ read-only screens, it is best for the data to be presented on the background of the screen. This permits easier scanning and information location; the reasoning will be discussed in the "Display/Read-Only screen section" following shortly.

Visual Emphasis Data or information is the most important part of any screen. It should be highlighted in some manner, either through higher intensity or a brighter color. Headings and captions are most important for the new or casual user. As people become familiar with a system and screens, their attention is immediately drawn to the data when a screen is presented. An experienced user will often work with a screen just perusing the data, ignoring captions and headings. Highlight the data and draw less attention to other screen elements.

Control Captions/Data Fields

- Differentiate captions from data fields by using:

- Contrasting features, such as different intensities, separating columns, boxes, and so forth.
- Consistent physical relationships:

Sex: | Female |

Relation: | Daughter |

- For single data fields:
  - Place the caption to left of the data field:

Relation: | Daughter |

  - Align the caption with the control's data.
  - Alternatively, place the caption above the data field.
  - Align justified upper-left to the data field.

Relation:
| Daughter |

  - Maintain consistent positional relations within a screen, or within related screens, whenever possible.
- For multiple listings of columnar-oriented data, place the caption above the columnized data fields:

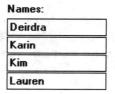

Captions must be complete, clear, easy to identify, easy to scan, and distinguishable from other captions and data fields.

Differentiating Captions from Data Captions and data should be visually distinguishable in some manner so that they do not have to be read in context to determine which is which. A common failing of many past screens is that the captions and data have the same appearance and blend into one another when the screen is filled. This makes differentiation difficult and increases caption and field data search time. Methods to accomplish differentiation in addition to designating them with a colon is using contrasting display features and consistent positional relationships.

Single Data Fields The recommended location is to position the caption to the left of the data field and to horizontally align the caption with the field data. Alternatively, the caption for a single data field may be positioned left-aligned above the data field. Maintain consistent positional relationships within a screen, and between multiple related screens whenever possible.

Columnar-Oriented Listings For multiple listings of columnar-oriented data, place the caption above the data fields. Left-justify the caption above the data fields. Use horizontal caption formats for single fields and a columnar caption orientation for repeating fields to provide better discrimination between single and repeating fields. The single-field caption will always precede the data, and captions for repeating columnar fields will always be above the top data field. Figures 3.22 through 3.38 illustrate common caption-data field discrimination problems and the recommended solutions for displaying both entry/modifiable fields and display/read-only/inquiry fields.

Control Caption/Data Field Justification

---

1. First Approach

- Left-justify both captions and data fields.
- Leave one space between the longest caption and the data field column.

Division:

Department:

Title:

2. Second Approach

- Left-justify data fields and right-justify captions to data fields.
- Leave one space between each.

Division:

Department:

Title:

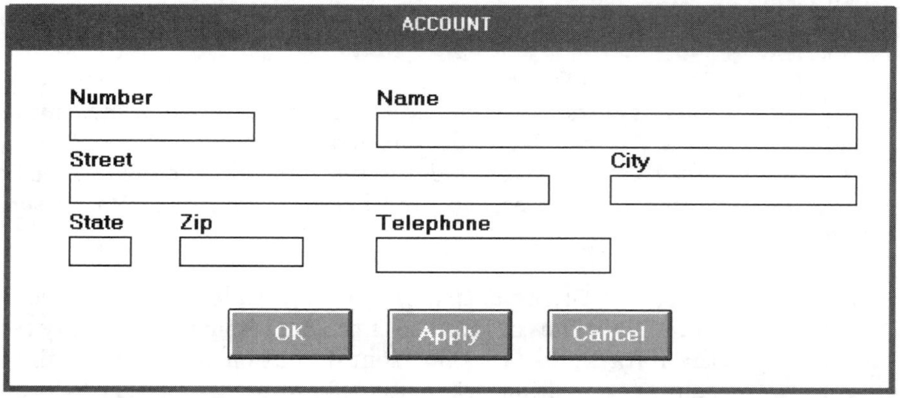

Figure 3.22   Figures 3.22 through 3.38 contain a series of screens in a variety of formats containing either entry/modification fields or display/read-only fields. The author's comments are found with each screen. What are your thoughts?

Entry screen with captions above single data fields. Captions distinctive from data but poor alignment and organization of fields. Left-to-right orientation and no groupings. Fair readability.

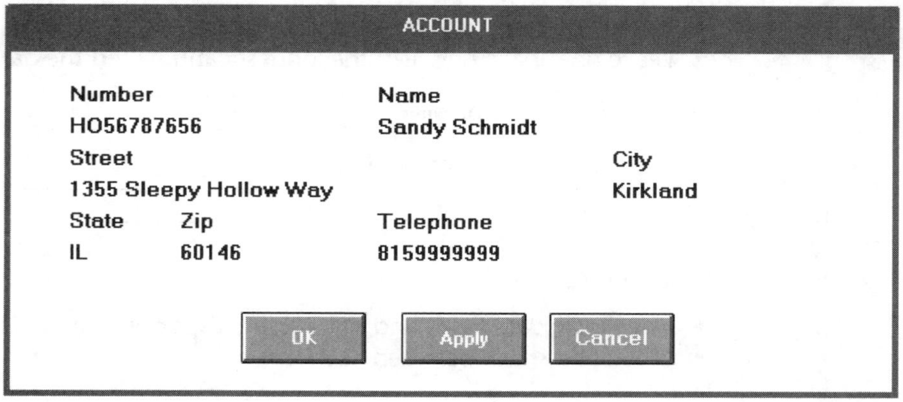

Figure 3.23   Display/read-only inquiry screen maintaining same structure as 3.22. Extremely poor differentiation of captions and data. Crowded look and extremely poor readability.

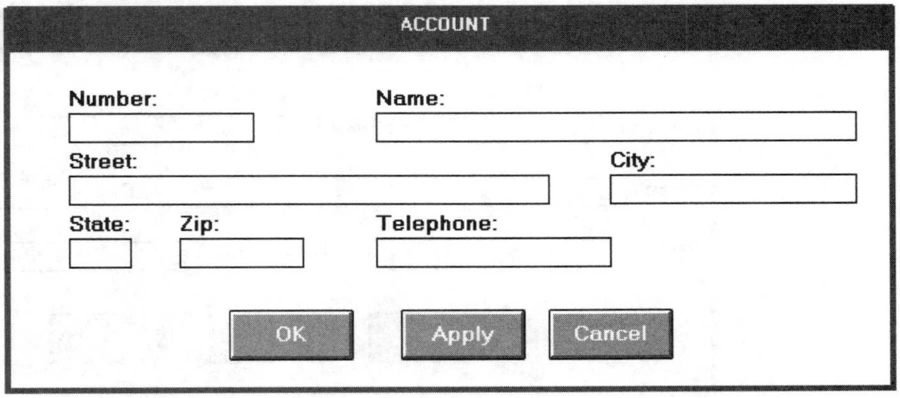

Figure 3.24   Entry screen in 3.22 with colons attached to captions. Captions somewhat more distinctive but still poor alignment and organization of fields, left-to-right orientation and no groupings. Fair readability.

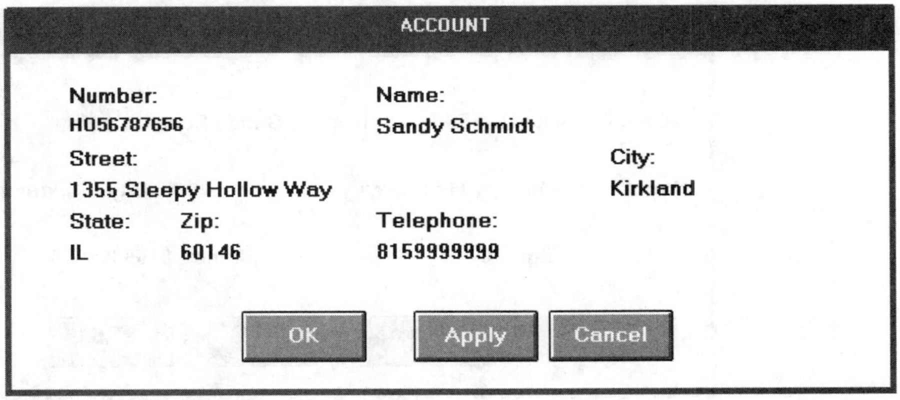

Figure 3.25   Display/read-only screen maintaining same structure as 3.24. Somewhat better differentiation of captions and data than 3.23 but still a crowded look and poor readability.

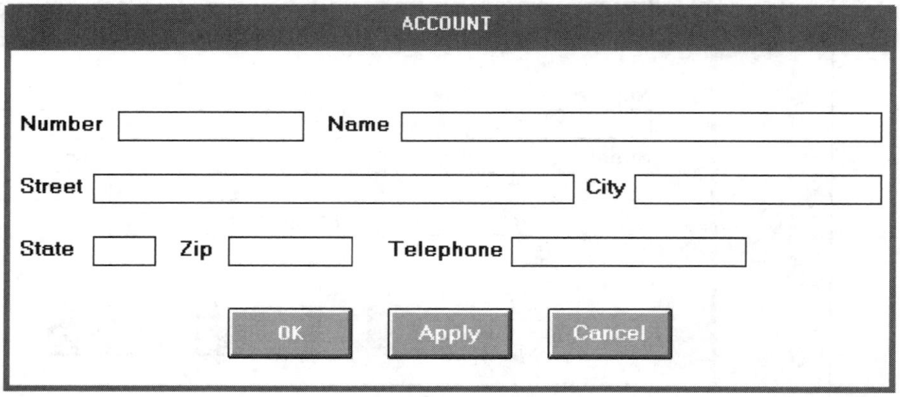

Figure 3.26   Entry/modification screen with captions to left of single data fields. Captions distinctive from data but poor alignment and organization of fields. Left-to-right orientation and no groupings. Fair readability.

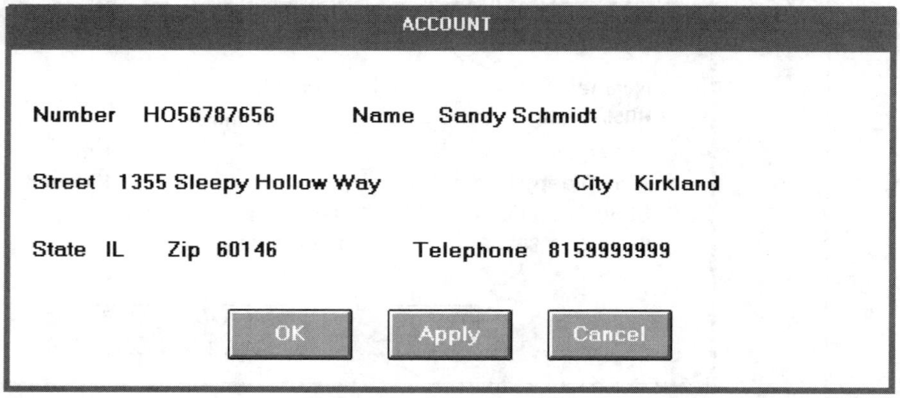

Figure 3.27   Display/read-only screen maintaining same structure as 3.26. Extremely poor differentiation of captions and data. Less crowded look than previous display/inquiry screens but still poor readability.

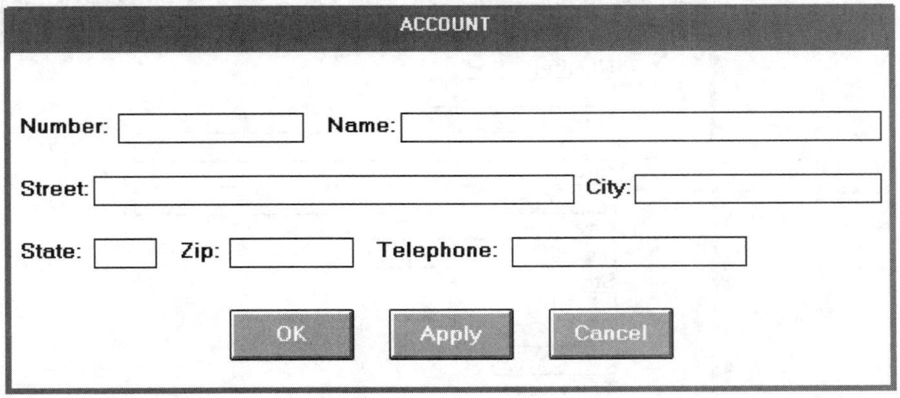

Figure 3.28 Entry/modification screen in 3.26 with colons attached to captions. Captions somewhat more distinctive but still poor alignment and organization of fields, left-to-right orientation and no groupings. Fair readability.

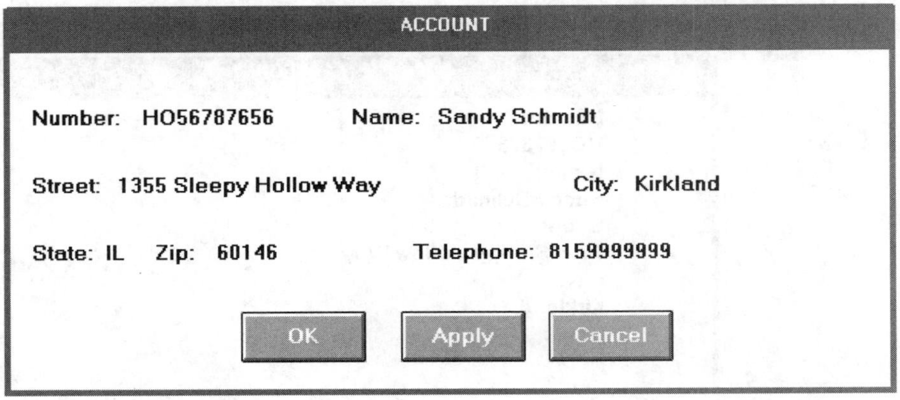

Figure 3.29 Display/read-only screen maintaining same structure as 3.28. Somewhat better differentiation of captions and data than 3.27 but still poor readability.

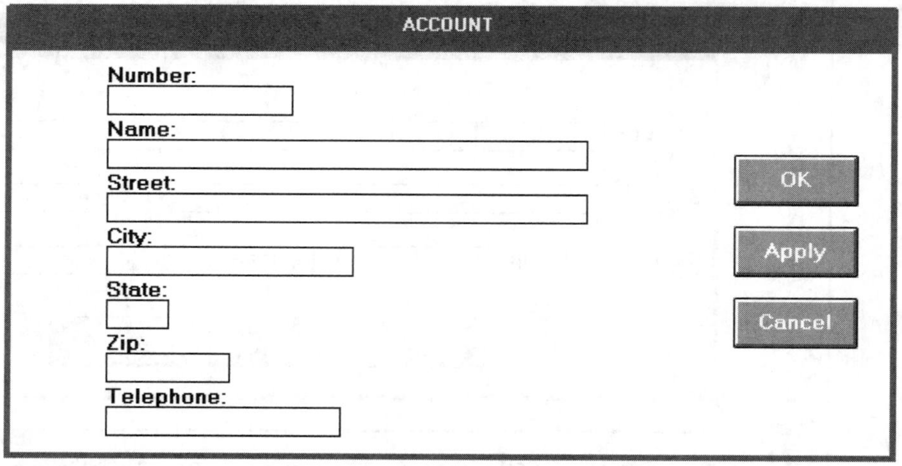

Figure 3.30 Entry/modification screen with much better alignment and readability than previous screens. Captions crowd data fields, however. Also, no groupings and does not maintain post office suggested format for City, State, and Zip.

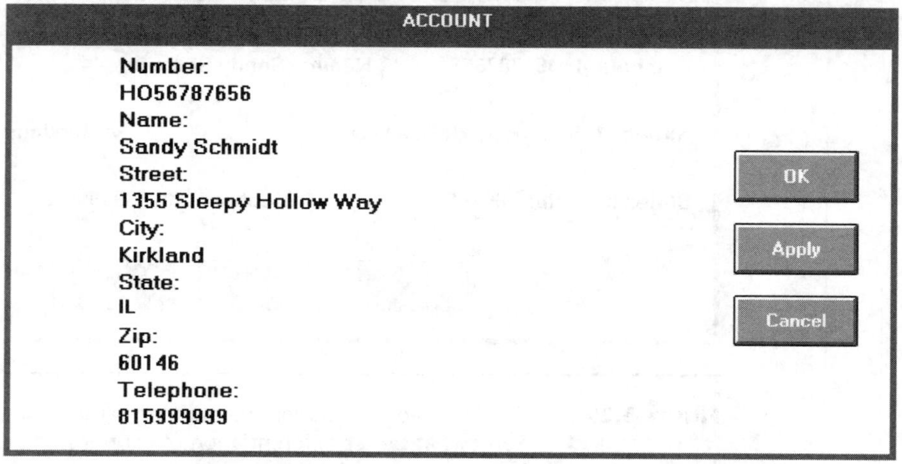

Figure 3.31 Display/read-only screen maintaining same aligned structure as 3.30. Captions not very distinctive and poor readability. Again, it looks very dense and crowded.

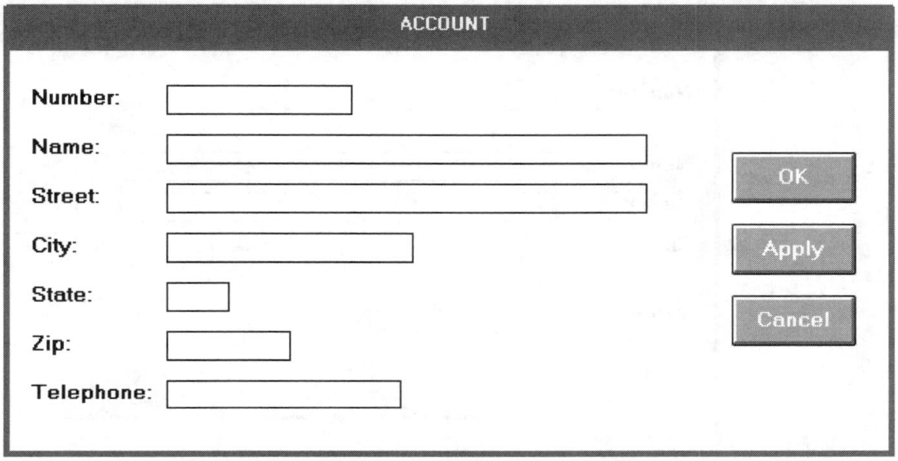

Figure 3.32   Entry/modification screen with the better alignment and readability of 3.30. Caption positioned to left, however, resulting in more distinctive data fields. Still no groupings, though, and does not maintain post office suggested format for City, State, and Zip.

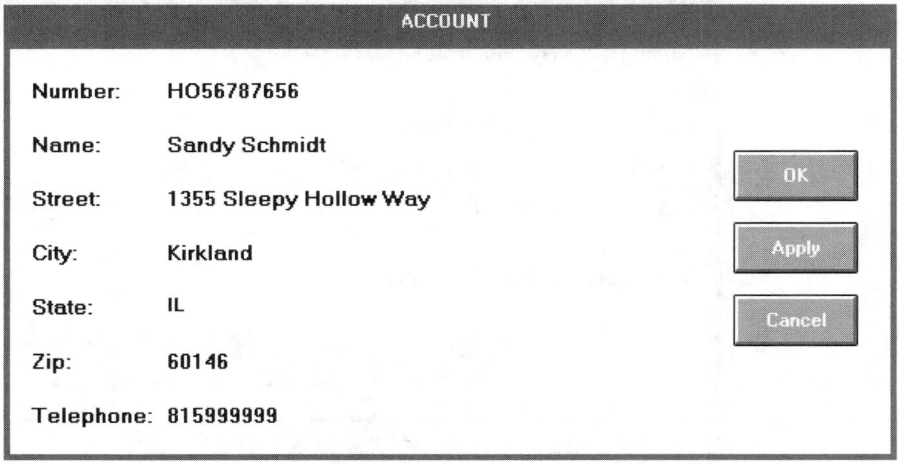

Figure 3.33   Display/read-only screen maintaining same alignment and positioning of captions of 3.32. Captions and data much more distinctive. Still no groupings, though, and does not maintain post office suggested format for City, State, and Zip.

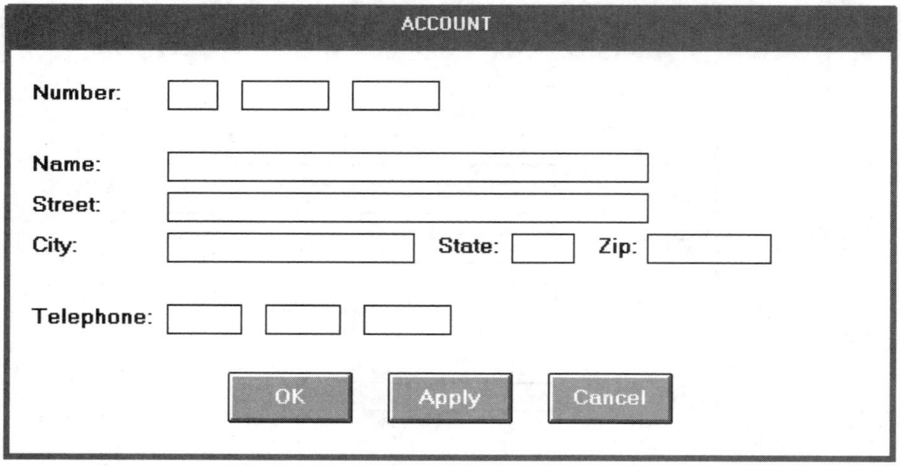

Figure 3.34   Entry/modification screen providing alignment, groupings, and the suggested and familiar post office address format. Data fields also segmented to enhance readability (Number and Telephone).

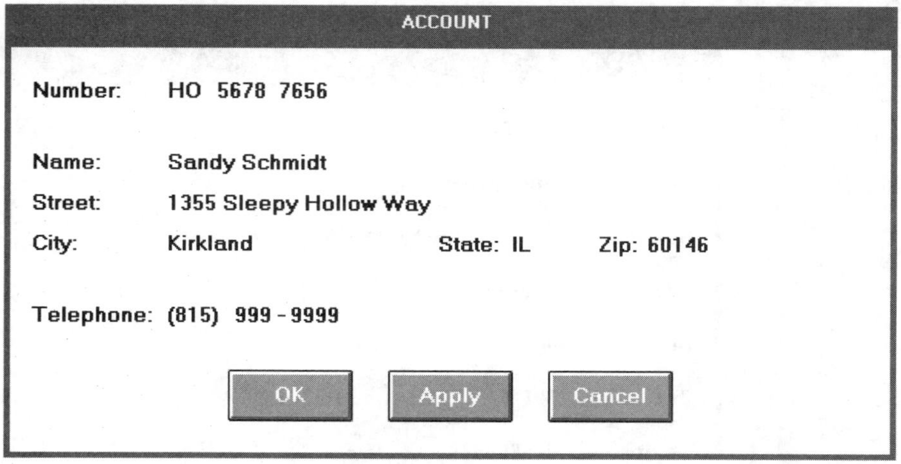

Figure 3.35   Display/read-only screen maintaining same item alignment and positioning, and data field segmentation of 3.34. Some data distinctiveness lost, and minor crowding occurs, however, because of the location of the captions for State and Zip between data fields.

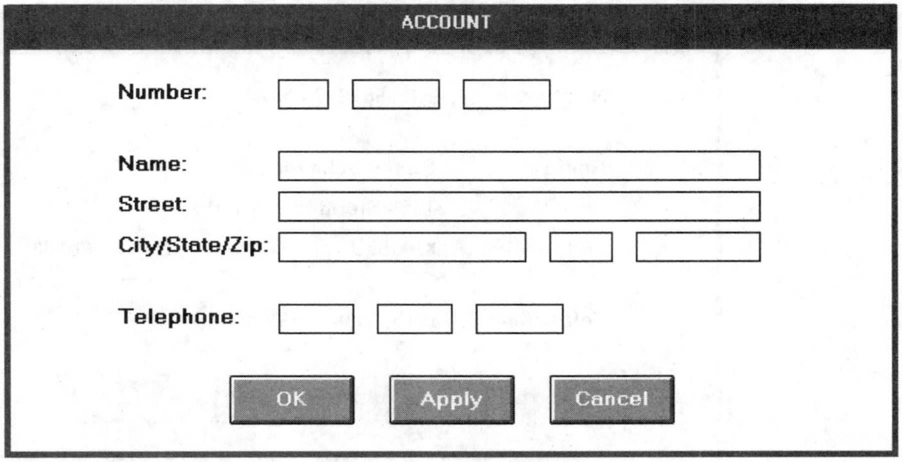

Figure 3.36 Entry/modification screen identical to 3.34 except that captions for State and Zip are stacked with City, enhancing distinctiveness and readability of the data fields. The screen also achieves a more compact and balanced look. The recommended style for this kind of entry screen.

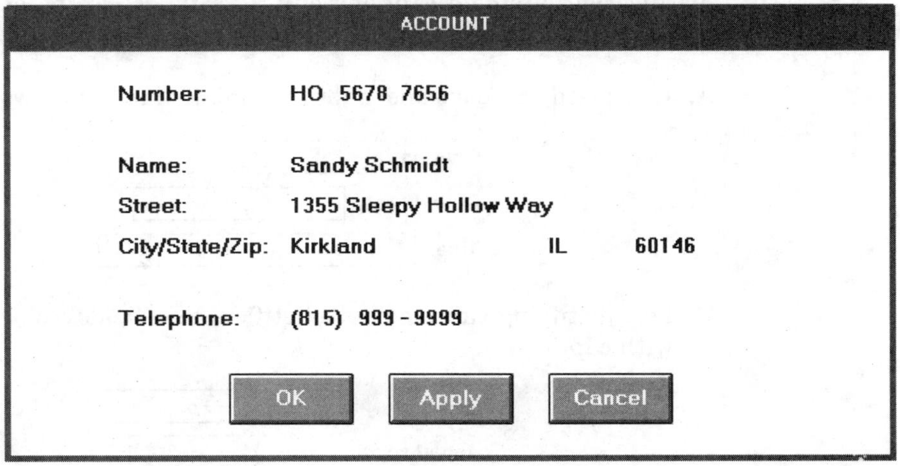

Figure 3.37 Display/read-only screen maintaining same alignment, item positioning, and data segmentation as 3.36. Good readability but the lengthy caption City/State/Zip does impinge upon the distinctiveness for the data.

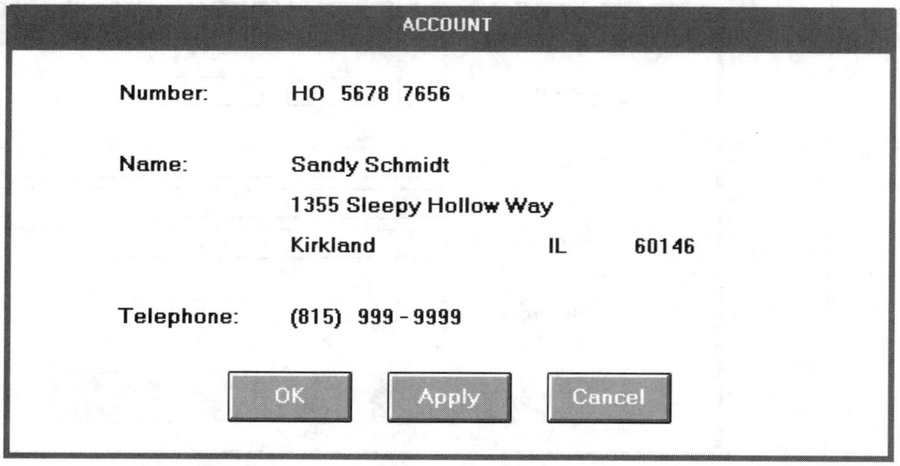

Figure 3.38   Display/read-only screen identical to 3.37 except the caption Street, and City/State/Zip have been eliminated to improve data field distinctiveness. The content of the data should make the identity of these fields obvious. The recommended style for this kind of display/read-only screen.

Justification of single captions and data fields can be accomplished in several ways. These include:

A. Left-justifying captions; data field immediately follows caption.

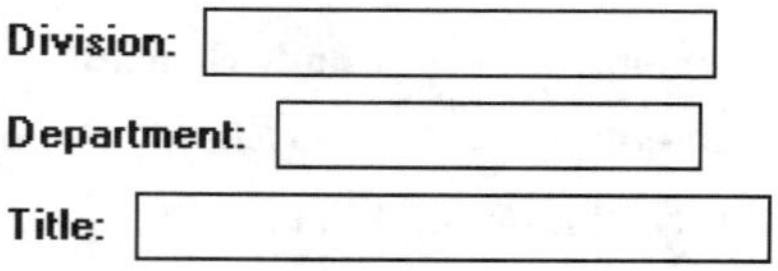

B. Left-justifying captions; left-justified data fields; colon (:) associated with captions.

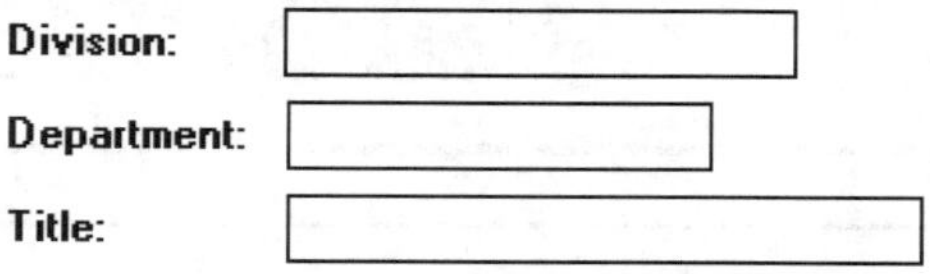

C. Left-justifying captions; left-justifying data fields; colon (:) associated with data field.

Division :

Department :

Title :

D. Right-justifying captions; left-justifying data fields.

Division:

Department:

Title:

Alternatives A and C are not recommended. Alternative A, left-justified aligned captions with data fields immediately following, results in poor alignment of data fields and increases the screen's complexity. It is more difficult to find data when searching data fields. Alternative C, while structurally sound, associates the colon primarily with the data field. The strongest association of the colon should be with the caption.

The two most desirable alternatives are B and D. Alternative B, left-justified captions and data fields, is the first approach illustrated in these guidelines. Alternative D, right-justified captions and left-justified data fields, is the second approach illustrated in these guidelines.

Left-Justified Captions and Data (B) A disadvantage to this approach is that the caption beginning point is usually farther from the entry field than the right-justified caption approach. A mix of caption sizes can cause some captions to be far removed from their corresponding data field, greatly increasing eye movements between the two and possibly making it difficult to accurately tie caption to data field. Tying the caption to the data field by a line of dots (. . . . .) solves the association problem but adds a great deal of noise to the screen. This does not solve the eye movement problem. Eye movement inefficiencies can be addressed by abbreviating the longer captions. The cost is reduced caption clarity.

An advantage to this approach is that section headings using location positioning as the key element in their identification do stand out nicely from the crisp left-justified captions.

Right-Justified Captions and Left-Justified Entry Fields (D) A disadvantage here is that section headings using location positioning as the identification element do not stand out as well. They tend to get lost in the ragged left edge of the captions.

Advantages are that captions are always positioned close to their related data fields, thereby minimizing eye movements between the two, and that the screen takes on a more balanced look.

There is no universal agreement as to which is the better approach. Experimental studies have not provided any answers, although most style guides recommend, and illustrate, the left-aligned caption approach. IBM's SAA CUA does discuss and permit both alignment styles.

Examples to follow in this and succeeding chapters reflect both styles. This is done to enable the reader to see and evaluate each. Whichever method is chosen, however, should be consistently followed, through a series of related screens.

Special Symbols

- Consider special symbols for emphasis.
- Separate symbols from words by a space.

DELEGATES >>

Special symbols should be considered to emphasize or call attention to elements on a screen. An error message, for example, can be preceded by an icon, or the "greater than" sign can be used to direct attention (DELEGATES >>). Symbols should be separated from words by one space.

Headings

Headings are used to give related controls a common identity. In addition to providing meaning, they foster the concept of grouping and aid screen learning. Three kinds of headings may be incorporated on graphic screens: section, subsection or row, and field group.

Section Headings

- Locate section headings above their related screen controls, separated by one space line.

PERSONNEL

Manager: _____

Employees: _____

Payroll: _____

- Alternatively, headings may be located within a border surrounding a grouping, justified to the upper-left corner.

PERSONNEL

Manager:

Employees:

Payroll:

- Indent the control captions to the right of the start of the heading.
- Fully spell out in an upper-case font.
- Display in normal intensity.

Sections headings should be visually distinguishable through a combination of location and font style. They should not be overly emphasized, however. Displaying in upper case and positioning to the left will provide the moderate emphasis needed. Many products display headings in the same type size and style as control captions. This provides very poor differentiation between captions and headings, each equally competing for the viewer's attention. This should be avoided. IBM's SAA CUA gives visual emphasis to section headings through higher intensity in a mixed-case font. This is not recommended. Higher intensity should be reserved for the more important screen data.

If right-aligned or justified captions are used, an indention greater than five spaces may be necessary to set off the heading from the captions properly. Section headings may also be positioned to the right of a group of controls, as is illustrated in the following section, "Subsection or Row Headings."

Other techniques than positional cues may be used to set off section headings. Choices may include different style characters, underlining, and so on. The method chosen should always permit easy, but subtle, discrimination of the section headings from other components of the screen. It should also be visually compatible with other screen components. Whatever styles are chosen, they should be consistently followed throughout a family of screens or a system.

Subsection or Row Headings

- Locate to the left of the:
  - Row of associated fields.
  - Topmost row of a group of associated fields.
- Fully spell out in an upper-case font.
- Separate from the adjacent caption through the use of a unique symbol, such as one or two "greater than" signs or a filled-in arrow.
- Separate the symbol from the heading by one space and from the caption by a minimum of three spaces.
- Display in normal intensity.
- Subsection or row headings may be left- or right-aligned.

AUTO >   Make: [   ]   Model: [   ]   Year: [   ]

Row or subsection headings may be positioned to the left of a group of related controls. A meaningful convention to designate subsection or row headings is a filled-in arrow or "greater than" sign. It directs the viewer's attention to the right and indicates that everything that follows refers to this category. Subsections should be broken by space lines. They may also be right-aligned instead of left-aligned, as follows:

AUTO >   AUTO >

REGISTRATION >   REGISTRATION >

DRIVER >   DRIVER >

Field Group Headings

- Center field group headings above the captions to which they apply.
- Relate to those captions by a solid line.
- Spell out fully in an upper-case font.
- Display in normal intensity.

———————————————— AUTOMOBILE ————————————————

Driver   License Number

[   ]   [   ]

[   ]   [   ]

[   ]   [   ]

Occasionally a group heading above a series of multiple-occurring captions may be needed. It should be centered above the captions to which it applies and related to them through a solid line extending to each end of the grouping. This will provide closure to the grouping.

Keying Procedures

For large volume data entry applications substantial keying may still be required. The following must be considered in establishing keying procedures.

Keystrokes

- Do not focus on minimizing keystrokes without considering other factors such as:
  - keying rhythm.
  - the goals of the system.

A sought-after goal in many past data entry applications has always been to minimize keystrokes. Fewer keystrokes have been synonymous with faster keying speeds and greater productivity in the minds of many practitioners. But this is not always true. Fewer keystrokes may actually decrease keying speeds and reduce productivity in many cases.

One example is found in Galitz (1972), who compared manual tabbing with auto skip in a data entry application. Auto skip, while requiring fewer keystrokes, was found to result in longer keying times and more errors than manual tabbing because it disrupted the keying rhythm. This study is described in more detail in the following section.

Another example is the study by Springer & Sorce (1984), who, in an information retrieval task, compared input keystrokes to the time needed to evaluate the system output. They found that more keystrokes yielded more meaningful inputs. This yielded more precise and informative outputs, which resulted in faster problem-solving.

So the number of keystrokes, and selections, must be considered in light of keying rhythms and the objectives of the system. Fewer is not necessarily always better.

Manual Tab versus Auto Skip

- Define fields to permit manual tabbing.

Auto skip is a feature that causes a cursor to automatically move to the beginning of the next text entry field once the previous field is completely filled. Auto skip obviates manual tabbing and requires fewer keystrokes to complete a screen. Theoretically, keying speeds should increase with auto skip. In practice, they do not always do so.

Rarely are many entry screen fields completely filled to their maximum length with data. When an entry field is not full, the user must still press the tab key to move the cursor to the next entry field. Figure 3.39 illustrates auto skip functioning.

Auto skip, therefore, imposes decision-making and learning requirements. After keying text into each field, one must determine where the cursor is and whether to press the tab key, or not, to go to the next field. Only then can the next keying action be performed. As illustrated in Figure 3.40, manual tabbing requires extra keystrokes but no decisions must be made. The keying task is rhythmic. Galitz (1972) summarizes user performance data from a study comparing auto skip and manual tabbing. In this study manual tabbing resulted in faster performance and fewer keying errors.

Auto skip can delay detection of one particular kind of error. If an extra character is inadvertently keyed into a field, the cursor will automatically move to the next field while keying continues. The error may not be immediately detected, and spacing in subsequent fields may also be one position off, at least until the tab key is pressed. Were this situation

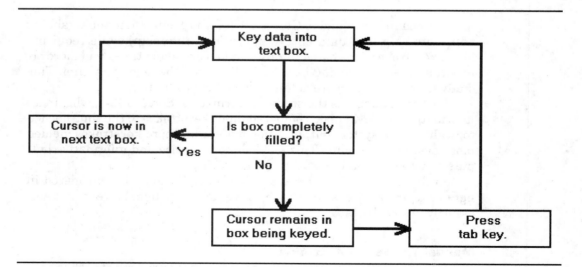

Figure 3.39   Text entry using auto skip.

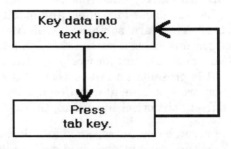

Figure 3.40   Text entry using manual tabbing.

to occur while using manual tabbing, the keyboard would lock as soon as the entry field was full. The error would be immediately detected.

Auto skip, despite its limitations, can be useful if a system's screens are easily learned or if all screen fields are always completely filled. Nevertheless, most large-volume data entry applications would not appear to meet this criterion.

Keying Rules

- Do not require recoding, changing, omitting, or including data based on special rules or logical transformations.

In large-volume entry applications, decisions that must be made during the keying process impose learning requirements and greatly slow down the entry process. The fewer rules and decisions involved in keying, the faster and more accurate entry will be. Coding, omitting, changing, and including data by special rules or transformations as a group represent probably the greatest single decrement to data entry speed.

Organization and Structure Guidelines

What follows is a series of organization and structure guidelines for specific kinds of screens. They are: Information Entry and Modification (Conversational), Entry from a Dedicated Source Document, and Display/Read-Only screens.

Information Entry and Modification (Conversational) Screens This kind of screen is used to collect and modify information, either by entry or selection. They are sometimes referred to as conversational screens. These screens guide a person through a task or process. The screen itself is the user's focal point for working with information. The viewer is driven by what is presented on the screen in the information collection and designation process. The information needed to complete a screen may be collected from, but is not limited to, these kinds of sources:

- A person being interviewed at a desk.
- A person being interviewed over a telephone.
- A collection of notes and written materials.
- An unstructured form.
- The mind of the user.

Organization

- Logical and clear.
- Most frequently-used information:
  - on earliest windows.
  - at the top of windows.
- Required information:
  - on earliest windows.
  - at the top of windows.

Captions

- Meaningful
- Consistently positioned in relation to data fields.
- Left- or right-aligned.

Text Boxes/Selection Controls

- Designate by boxes.

Spacing and Groupings

- Create logical groupings.
- Make them medium in size, about 5-7 lines.

Headings

- Capitalize and set off.

Control Arrangement

- Align into columns.
- Organize for top-to-bottom completion.

Prompting

- Include as necessary.

Most of the guidelines presented earlier in this chapter are directly applicable to this kind of screen. They are summarized below.

Organization Organize these screens logically and clearly, reflecting the exact information needs of the user for the task being performed. In general, place the most frequently used information, or required information, on the earliest windows and at the top of windows.

Captions Provide meaningful captions clearly identifying the information to be entered or selected. Use the headline style to display them (all significant words capitalized). Spatially, consistently position all captions in relation to their associated controls. They may be left- or right-aligned.

Text / Selection Fields Designate by boxes, either a line border or polarity reversal.

Control Arrangement Align controls into columns. Maintain a top-to-bottom, then left-to-right arrangement.

Prompting Include prompting messages on screens as necessary. See Step 11 for complete guidelines.

Text Entry from a Source Document Occasionally, it may still be necessary to key information directly from a source document into a screen. The document may take the form of an application for insurance, an application for a bank loan, a request for service, and so forth. The key issue for this function is that the document should be *dedicated* to the screen, and permit "head down" entry of data from the document to the screen, with the screen seldom being the point of the user's attention. An entire screen should be capable of being completed *without* the keyer ever looking at the screen. The design guidelines are based upon this assumption. Ideally, the document and screen should be created together so that an image relationship can be easily achieved. Creating them together permits trade-offs against *either* the form or screen to achieve this fit.

Occasionally, but not often, an existing form will allow the creation of a screen in its exact image. When this happens this form can also be considered as dedicated and will follow these rules. Most forms, however, because they were not designed with a screen in mind, cannot be easily matched to a screen. Their corresponding screens should be considered as entry / modification (conversational) screens and should be designed accordingly. The screen will drive the keying process, not the form, because the required screen information on the form must be searched for and found.

If an existing form is being converted to a screen format, and the existing form will no longer be used, its screens should also be designed following the entry / modification (conversational) guidelines. This is a much more effective approach for information collection, as discussed earlier in this chapter.

Following is a summary of the guidelines for dedicated source document screens. For more detailed information concerning their design, see Galitz (1992).

Organization

- Image of associated source document.

Captions

- Abbreviations and contractions.
- Consistently positioned in relation to data fields.
- Right-aligned.

Text Fields

- Designate by boxes.

Spacing and Grouping

- Logical groupings found on source document.

Headings

- Include if on source document.
- Capitalize and set off.

Control Arrangement

- As on source document.
- Left-to-right completion.

Keying Procedure

- Use manual tabbing.

Prompting Messages

- None needed.

Organization The screen must be an exact image of its associated source document. Skipping around a source document to locate information adds a significant amount of time to the keying process. It also imposes a learning requirement on people, since the order and location of screen fields must be mastered. Having the source document and screen in the same image eliminates these problems. Cursor position on the screen is always known because it corresponds with a person's eye position on the source document.

Captions To allow the screen to be in the image of a form, screen captions usually must consist of abbreviations and contractions. The form will always be available to assist in identifying unclear captions. Because text boxes fit fairly tightly on these kinds of screens, captions must be right-aligned so they are associated with the proper box.

Text / Selection Fields These are designated by boxes, either a line border or polarity reversal.

Spacing and Grouping Create the same groupings as exist on the document. Set off groupings like it is done on the form, through use of either white space and/or borders.

Headings Include the same headings as are found on the source document. Capitalize to set them off from the remainder of the screen.

Control Arrangement Control positioning and alignment on the screen will match that of the source document. Position in the same manner, or as close to the same manner as possible to facilitate eye movements between the document and screen. (A well-designed form should have aligned elements, too. If not, still follow the form alignment.) Maintain a left-to-right entry arrangement, if the form is organized for completion in this direction. If, per chance, the form is organized top-to-bottom, then follow this top-to-bottom scheme.

Keying Procedure Use manual tabbing, not auto skip, to permit a rhythmic keying process. Keying will be faster and less error prone.

Prompting Prompting messages are not necessary. Completion instructions will be on the document.

Display/Read-Only Screens Display/Read-Only screens are used to display the results of an inquiry request or the contents of computer files. Their design objective is human ease in locating data or information. Thus, they should be developed to optimize human scanning. Scanning is made easier if eye movements are minimized, required eye movement direction is obvious, and a consistent pattern is established. Next is a summary of display/read-only screen guidelines.

Organization

- Logical and clear.
- Limit to what is necessary.
- Most frequently-used information:
  - on earliest windows.
  - at the top of windows.

Captions

- Meaningful
- Consistently positioned in relation to data fields.
- Left- or right-aligned.

Text Boxes

- Do not include a surrounding border or box.

Spacing and Grouping

- Create logical groupings
- Make them medium size, about 5-7 lines.

Headings

- Capitalize and set off.

Data Presentation

- Visually emphasize the data.
- Give the data a meaningful structure.

Data Arrangement

- Align into columns.
- Organize for top-to-bottom scanning.

Data Justification

- For text and alphanumeric data - left-justify.
- For numeric data - right-justify.
- Create a data "ladder."

Data Display

- Consider not displaying "no" or "null" data.
- Consider "data statements."

Organization

- Only display information necessary to perform actions, make decisions, or answer questions.
- Group information in a logical or orderly manner, with the most frequently requested information in the upper left corner.
- For multi-window functions, locate the most frequently requested information on the earliest windows.
- Do not pack the screen. Use spaces and lines to balance the screen perceptually.

Information contained on a display/read-only screen should only be what is relevant. Forcing a person to wade through volumes of data is time consuming, costly, and error-prone. Unfortunately, relevance is most often situation-specific. A relevant item one moment a screen is displayed may be irrelevant another time it is recalled.

Organization should be logical, orderly, and meaningful. When information is structured in a manner that is consistent with a person's organizational view of a topic, more information is comprehended.

Finding information on a display/read-only screen can be speeded by a number of factors. First, if information is never used, do not display it. Limit a screen to only what is necessary to perform actions, make decisions, or answer questions. Second, for multiple window functions, locate the most frequently sought information on the earliest screens and the most frequently sought information on a screen in the upper left-hand corner. Never pack a display/read-only screen with information.

Captions Provide meaningful captions clearly identifying the information displayed, unless the identity of data is obvious by its shape or structure (e.g., an address). Use the headline style (all significant words capitalized) and consistently position all captions in relation to their associated data. Captions may be left- or right-aligned.

Text Boxes Do not place a border around display/read-only information; inscribe the data so that it appears on the normal window background. It will be much more readable presented in this manner.

Spacing and Grouping Provide easily scanned and identifiable logical groupings of information. Create groupings of a medium size (five to seven lines) and set them off through liberal use of white space and conservative use of line borders.

Headings Provide headings to identify groupings. Capitalize to set them off from the remainder of the screen elements.

Data Presentation

- Provide visual emphasis to the data.
- Give the data a meaningful structure.
  - Spell out any codes in full.
  - Include natural splits or predefined breaks in displaying data.

~~338302345~~   ~~072179~~   ~~162152~~

338-30-2245   07/21/79   16:21:52

- For data strings of five or more numbers or alphanumeric characters with no natural breaks, display in groups of three or four characters with a blank between each group.

~~K349612094~~   K349 612 094

Data should be visually emphasized to attract attention. This will enable the viewer to quickly isolate the data and begin scanning the display for the needed information. A higher intensity or brighter color is recommended to accomplish this. Also, fully spell out any codes and include natural splits or predefined breaks in displaying common pieces of data like telephone numbers and dates.

A data display should also reinforce the human tendency to break things into groups. People handle information more easily when it is presented in chunks. Display data strings of five or more alphanumeric characters with no natural breaks in groups of three or four, with a blank space between each group.

Data Arrangement

- Align data into columns.
- Organize for top-to-bottom scanning.

To aid scanning, align data into columns with a top-to-bottom, left-to-right orientation. This means permitting the eye to move down a column from top to bottom, then move to another column located to the right, and again move from top to bottom. This also means, if the situation warrants it, permitting the eye to move easily left to right across the top of columns to the proper column, before beginning the vertical scanning movement.

Top-to-bottom scanning will minimize eye movements through the screen and enable human perceptual powers to be utilized to their fullest. Display/read-only screens are often visually scanned not through the captions but through the data fields themselves. A search for a customer name in a display of information frequently involves looking for a combination of characters that resembles the picture of a name that we have stored in our memory. The search task is to find a long string of alphabetic characters with one or two gaps (first name, middle initial, last name, perhaps). A date search might have the viewer seeking a numeric code broken up by slashes. Other kinds of information also have recognizable patterns and shapes. Control captions usually play a minor role in the process, being necessary only to differentiate similar looking data fields, or for new screen users.

Vertical scanning has led to two key requirements in the design of display/read-only screens: call attention to data fields, and make the structural differences between data fields as obvious as possible. Differences are most noticeable in a columnar field structure, since it is easier to compare data when one piece is above the other.

Data Justification

- Left-justify text and alphanumeric formats.

| Name: | ~~Bill Watters~~ | Name: | Bill Watters |
| Street: | ~~612 Hidden Valley~~ | Street: | 612 Hidden Valley |

- Right-justify lists of numeric data.

Charge:	~~645,194.88~~	Charge:	645,194.88
Federal Tax:	~~19,235.16~~	Federal Tax:	19,235.16
State Tax:	~~5,204.03~~	State Tax:	5,204.03
Local Tax:	~~1.24~~	Local Tax:	1.24
Total Cost:	~~669,635.31~~	Total Cost:	669,635.31

- Create a data "ladder."

Tree:	~~Pine~~	Tree:	Pine
Age:	~~14~~	Age:	14
Number:	~~422,598~~	Number:	422,598
Class:	~~C~~	Class:	C
Location:	~~NW~~	Location:	NW

In general, columnized text and alphanumeric data should be left-justified, and numeric data should be right-justified. In aligning data fields, keep in mind how the pieces of data will look in relation to one another when they contain typical information. The visual scan should flow relatively straight from top to bottom. This may require that some data fields be right-justified in the column that is created, not left-justified, or vice versa. The objective is to create what looks like a ladder of data down the screen.

Data Display

- Consider not displaying data whose values are "none," "zero," or blank.

Elephants:	612		Elephants:	612
Lions:	123		Lions:	123
~~Hippos:~~	~~0~~		Giraffes:	361
Giraffes:	361			
~~Kudus:~~	~~0~~			

- Consider creating "data statements" where the caption and data are combined.

Elephants:	612		612 Elephants
Lions:	123		123 Lions
Giraffes:	361		361 Giraffes

Consider not displaying fields containing no data. When displayed on a display/read-only screen, some data fields may be blank or contain a value such as zero or none. In many situations it may not be important to the screen viewer to know that the field contains no data. In these cases consider not displaying these screen elements at all. Present on the screen only the fields containing data, thereby creating less cluttered screens.

If this alternative is chosen, space on the screen must be left for situations in which all fields contain data. In order to avoid large blank screen areas, a useful rule of thumb is to allow enough space to display clearly all data for about 90 percent of all possible screens. For situations where screens must contain more data than this, going to an additional screen or window will be necessary.

This nondisplay alternative should only be considered if it is not important that the viewer know something is "not there." If it is important that the viewer know that the values in a field are zero or none, or that the field is blank, then the fields must be displayed on the screen.

You may also want to consider displaying data statements. The traditional way to display data on an inquiry screen is the caption: data format, for example, "Autos: 61." Another alternative is to create data statements where the caption and data are combined: "61 Autos." This format improves screen readability and slightly reduces a screen's density. If this data statement format is followed, consider the statement as data and highlight it entirely.

Statistical Graphics

A well-designed statistical graphic, also referred to as a *chart* or *graph*, consists of complex ideas communicated with clarity, precision, and efficiency. It gives its viewer the greatest number of ideas, in the shortest time, and in the smallest space, and with least possible clutter. It will also induce the viewer to think of substance, not techniques or methodology. It will provide coherence to large amounts of information by tying them together in a meaningful way, and it will encourage data comparisons of its different pieces by the eye. A well-designed display also avoids distortions by telling the truth about the data. Much of this material on statistical graphics is based upon Tufte (1983), Smith and Mosier (1986), and Fowler and Stanwick (1995).

Use of Statistical Graphics

- Reserve for material that is rich, complex, or difficult.

Graphics should be reserved for large sets of data with real variability. The power of graphics should not be wasted on simple linear changes or situations where one or two numbers would summarize the result better. Tufte (1983) says that tables usually outperform graphics on small data sets of 20 or fewer numbers, or when data sets are noncomparative or highly labeled. Tables are also better if the data must be studied or very specific information must be retrieved (Coll, Coll, & Thakur, 1994).

Components of a Statistical Graphic Most statistical graphics have at least two axes, two scales, an area to present the data, a title, and sometimes a legend or key, as illustrated in Figure 3.41. Pie charts are the exception to this general rule. Guidelines for chart components include the following.

Data Presentation

- Emphasize the data.
- Minimize the nondata.

- Minimize redundant data.
- Show data variation, not design variation.
- Provide the proper context for data interpretation.
- Restrict the number of information-carrying dimensions depicted to the number of data dimensions being illustrated.
- Employ data in multiple ways, whenever possible.
- Maximize data density.
- Employ simple data coding schemes.
- Avoid unnecessary embellishment of:
  - Grids.
  - Vibration.
  - Ornamentation.
- Fill the graph's available area with data.

The most important part of a graphics display, as with an alphanumeric display, is the data itself.

Emphasize the data, minimize the nondata. A person's attention should be drawn to the measured quantities. The largest share of the graphic's "ink" should present data. Nondata—such as elaborate grid lines, gratuitous decoration, and extensive, detailed, and wordy labels—draws attention to itself and masks the data. So, nondata should be minimized, or eliminated entirely.

Redundant data, information that depicts the same value over and over, should also be minimized or eliminated. Redundancy, on occasion, can be useful, however. It may aid in providing context and order, facilitating comparisons, and creating an aesthetic balance. Use redundancy only if necessary.

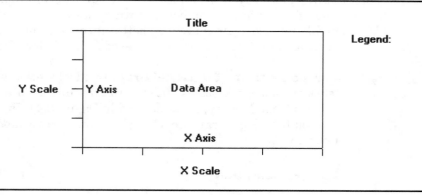

Figure 3.41   Components of a statistical graphic.

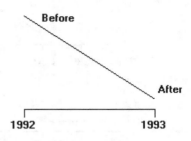

Figure 3.42   A change between 1992 and 1993 without proper context for interpretation.

Show data variation, not design variation. Each part of a graphic generates visual expectations about its other parts. The expectancies created in one part should be fulfilled in other parts so the viewer does not confuse changes in design with changes in data. Scales should move in regular intervals; proportions should be consistent for all design elements. If the viewer confuses changes in design with changes in data, ambiguity and deception result.

Provide the proper context for data interpretation. Graphics often lie by omission. Data for making comparisons or establishing trends must always be included to provide a proper reference point. "Thin" data must be viewed with suspicion. The graphic in Figure 3.42, for example, might have a number of possible interpretations as illustrated in Figure 3.43. All important questions must be foreseen and answered by the graphic.

Restrict the number of information-carrying dimensions depicted to the number of data dimensions being illustrated. Displaying one-dimensional data in a multidimensional format is perceptually ambiguous. With multidimensional data, changes in the physical area of the surface of the graphic do not produce an appropriate proportional change in the perceived area. Examples of multidimensional formats to display one-dimensional data would be different-sized human bodies to indicate populations or different-sized automobiles to indicate number of cars. Often the impression on the viewer is that the change is actually much greater than it really is. This problem can be avoided if the number of information-carrying dimensions on the graphic is restricted to the number of data dimensions being illustrated.

Employ data in multiple ways, whenever possible. Parts of a graph can be designed to serve more than one purpose. A piece of data may at

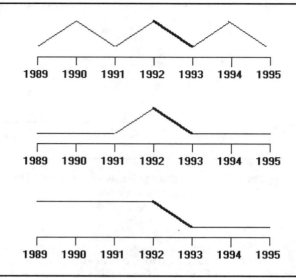

Figure 3.43   Changes between 1992 and 1993 with proper contexts for interpretation.

the same time convey information and also perform a design function usually left to nondata. Some examples are:

- A grid to aid readability of a bar chart, instead of being inscribed on the graphic background, may be positioned within the bars themselves, as illustrated in Figure 3.44.

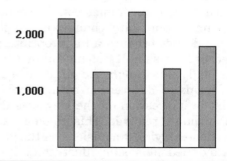

Figure 3.44   A piece of data (line in the bars) performing a nondata function.

- The size of what is being measured can be conveyed through the size of the graphical element, the intensity through color or level of shading.

Graphics can be designed to have multiple viewing depths. The top level provides an overall view, each succeeding level an ever-increasing closer view. They may be also designed to have different viewing angles or lines of sight.

The danger in employing data in multiple ways is that it can generate a graphical puzzle. A sign of a puzzle is that the graphic, instead of being interpreted visually, must be interpreted verbally. Symptoms of a puzzle are frequent references to a legend to interpret what is presented and extensive memorization of design rules before one can comprehend what is presented. By contrast, a well-designed multiple-function graphic permits a quick and implicit transition of the visual to the verbal.

Maximize data density. In graphics more is better than less—the greater amount of information displayed, the larger the number of visual comparisons that can be made, improving comprehension. This is so because the eye can detect large amounts of information in a small space. Simple things belong in a table or in the text.

Data density of a graphic can be maximized in two ways: enlarging the data matrix or shrinking the graphic. Enlarging the data matrix involves displaying as much information as possible. If the graphic becomes overcrowded, techniques such as averaging, clustering, smoothing, or providing summaries can reduce the number to be displayed. Shrinking the graphic means reducing it in size, but screen resolution may impose limitations on how much shrinking can be performed.

If visual differentiation in the types of data being displayed is necessary, use simple coding methods in the areas being depicted. Elaborate schemes or patterns can be eye-straining and can actually impede the flow of information from the graphic to the viewer. Some possible coding alternatives include:

- Varying shades or densities.
- Labeling with words.
- Varying colors.

Avoid unnecessary embellishment. All pieces of a graphic must tell the viewer something new. An unnecessary embellishment is "chartjunk." It does not add anything new to the graphic's meaning. It is decoration or noise that hinders assimilation of the message being communicated. Nondata and redundant data are forms of chartjunk. Three other kinds are vibration, heavy grids, and ornamentation.

A grid carries no information, contributes noise, and focuses attention away from the data. An excessively heavy grid can even mask the data. Grids should be suppressed or eliminated so they do not compete with the data. When a grid serves as an aid in reading or extrapolating, it should, of course, be included. Its tendency to overwhelm can be reduced by constructing it with delicate lines or muted colors and placing it behind the data.

The eye is never absolutely still; it produces continuous slight tremors that aid visual acuity. The result is that, when small patterns lines, boxes, or dots are viewed, they shimmer or vibrate. This vibration can be distracting; examples are illustrated in Figure 3.45. While eye-catching, vi-

Figure 3.45   Examples of patterns creating vibrations.

brations can also strain the eye. Simple data coding schemes like shades of colors are much more effective.

When the graphic is overwhelmed by decoration, it is very ineffective. Ornamentation can take many forms: extensive use of color when it is not necessary; creating multidimensional graphics when single dimensional will do; pointless use of vibrating patterns, or forcing data into a graphic when a table would work much better. Ornamentation is more effective as a piece of art hanging on a wall. It is a symptom of "See what I can do with my computer" rather than an effort to provide the user with the data in the most comprehensible way possible. The best graphic display is the simplest graphic display.

For ease of interpretation and efficiency, the graphic's data should fill up the entire display area within the axes. If it does not, the scale or the graphic is too large.

Axes

- Values on an axis should increase as they move away from the origin.
- Use the horizontal axis (X) to show time or cause of an event (the independent variable).
- Use the vertical axis (Y) to show a caused effect (the dependent variable).

Values on an axis should increase as they move away from the origin. If the numeric values displayed are positive, the origin point will be the lower left point of the graphic. If the data includes negative values and the axes must extend in both directions from the zero point, position the origin in the center of the graph.

Use the horizontal axis (X) to show time or cause of an event (the independent variable). Use the vertical axis (Y) to show a caused effect (the dependent variable). When the X axis plots time intervals, the labeled points should represent the end of each time interval. The X axis may also be called *abscissa* or *category* axis, the Y axis the *ordinal* or *value* axis. If the graphic possesses three dimensions, the third axis is called the Z axis, reflecting the graph's plane.

Scales and Scaling

- Place ticks to marks scales on the outside edge of each axis.
- Employ a linear scale.
- Mark scales at standard or customary intervals.
- Start a numeric scale at zero (0).
- Keep the number of digits in a scale to a minimum.

- Display only a single scale on each axis.
- For large data matrices, consider displaying duplicate axes.
- Provide aids for scale interpretation.
- Provide scaling consistency across two or more related graphics.
- Clearly label each axis in a left-to-right reading orientation.

A scale is a set of measurement points or markers. Scaling is the positioning of data in relation to these points or markers. Standard practices are these:

Place ticks to mark scales on the outside edge of each axis. Placing outside will prevent the tick from interfering with data located near the axis.

Employ a linear scale. Most people are more familiar with linear scales than with logarithmic or other nonlinear scales. These latter kinds are often interpreted inaccurately.

Mark scales at standard or customary intervals for they aid comprehension. Familiar standard intervals are 1, 2, 5, 10, and multiples of 10. Familiar customary intervals include the days of the week and the months of the year. Construct scales with tick marks at these intervals. To aid visual comprehension, it may be necessary to provide intermediate marks as well. Intermediate marks should be consistent with the scale intervals shown.

Start a numeric scale at zero. Using zero as the starting point on a scale aids visual comparisons since zero is an expected starting point. If a zero point is omitted because of the nature of the data, this omission should be clearly indicated in the graphic.

Keep the number of digits in a scale to a minimum. Smaller numbers aid understanding. Round off all numbers to two digits or less. However, place zeros in front of decimal numbers so the decimal point is not missed.

Display only a single scale on each axis. Avoid multiple scales associated with a single axis. For all but the most experienced people, multiple scales can be confusing and can lead to interpretation errors. Meanings can also be greatly distorted. If multiscale graphs must be used, permit the user to select any data curve individually and have the computer highlight its corresponding scale.

For large data matrices, consider displaying duplicate axes. The readability of large data matrices is improved if the X-axis scale appears at the top as well as the bottom of the graph, and the Y-axis scale at the right as well as the left side.

Provide aids for scale interpretation. When reading accuracy is extremely critical, provide computer aids for interpretation, such as the following:

- Displaying a fine grid upon request.
- Vertical and horizontal rules that the user can move to the intersection point.

- Letting the user point at a data item and the computer then providing the exact values.

Provide scaling consistency across two or more related graphics. If comparisons must be made between multiple graphs or charts, use the same scale for each. Data sets scaled differently lead to interpretation errors.

Each scale axis should be clearly labeled in a conventional left-to-right reading orientation. A complete description of the values with measurement units should be provided.

Proportion

- Provide accurate proportion of the displayed surfaces to the data they represent.
- Provide proper proportion by:
  - Conforming to the shape of the data.
  - Making the width greater than the height.

The displayed surfaces on graphics should be directly proportional to the numeric qualities they represent. Failure to display the correct proportions can create false impressions of magnitudes of differences in sizes or changes. This kind of graphical distortion can be eliminated through clear, detailed, and thorough labeling, a topic to be addressed shortly.

Provide proper proportion. When the relative proportions of a graphic are in balance, it looks better. Graphics should tend toward the horizontal, assuming a greater length than height. There are a number of reasons for this recommendation. First, people prefer this shape. Second, it is easier to read words arrayed left-to-right. Third, many graphics plot cause and effect relationships, with effect on the vertical axis and cause on the horizontal. An elongated horizontal axis helps describe the causal variable in more detail. If, however, the data being displayed suggests a shape either square or higher than wide, conform to the shape suggested by the data.

Lines

- Data lines should be the heaviest.
- Axes lines should be of medium weight.
  - Extend the lines entirely around the graphic.
- Grid lines should be very thin or absent.

The most important part of the graphic is the data. Emphasize the data by making the data lines the heaviest. Of secondary importance are the axes lines. Display them in a medium thickness. Axes lines should be extended entirely around the graphic to create a rectangle (or box). This will define the graphic area and help focus attention on the data itself. Grid lines should be avoided if at all possible, unless absolutely needed for accurate data interpretation.

Labeling

- Employ clear, detailed and thorough labeling.
- Maintain a left-to-right reading orientation.
- Integrate the labeling with the drawing.
  - Do not curve letters to match the shape of curved lines.
- Use only one typeface, font, and weight.
  - For emphasis, use different type sizes.
- Do not separate labeling from the data through ruled lines.
- Provide information about the source of the data.

The labeling principles for graphical screens should follow the general principles outlined earlier in this chapter.

Employ clear, detailed, and thorough labeling. Words should be fully spelled out. Follow standard capitalization schemes, using both upper- and lower-case, with lower-case for textual information. Use the simplest and shortest word forms possible.

Maintain a left-to-right reading orientation. Display all labels horizontally. Avoid words that are organized vertically or words that run in different directions. Whereas nonhorizontal words on hard copy graphics can easily be read by turning the paper, this screen capability is not available, or not yet easy to accomplish.

Integrate the labeling with the drawing. Explanations on graphics help the viewer and should be incorporated as much as possible. Words are data, and they can occupy space freed up by nondata or redundant data. Integrating words and captions with the graphic eliminates the need for a legend and the eye movements back and forth required to read it. Also, incorporate messages to explain the data and label interesting or important points. Never curve letters to match the shape of curved lines. This is terribly distracting. Run all text horizontally.

Use only one typeface, font, and weight. Using the same type style for graphics and text aids the visual integration of the two. If text needs to be emphasized, use different type sizes.

Do not separate labeling from the data through ruled lines. Again, this creates visual noise and impairs proper associations.

Provide information about the source of the data. This information can be placed, in small type, below the X- axis label or in a caption. It can also be made available through online help (Marcus, 1992).

Title

- Create a short, simple, clear, and distinctive title describing the purpose of the graphic.
- Position the title above, centered, or left-aligned to the rectangle formed by the extended axes.
- Spell-out fully using a mixed-case or upper-case font.

A title should be brief and descriptive of the graphic. A title may be centered or flush left to the rectangle formed by the extended axes. Marcus (1992) feels aligned left yields a stronger composition. Titles should be spelled out fully, and may be displayed larger, bolder, and in mixed- or upper-case font.

Aiding Interpretation of Numbers

- Display a grid on request.
- Permit the viewer to click on a data point to display actual values.
- Show numeric values automatically for each point or bar.
- Permit the viewer to zoom in on an area of the graphic.
- Permit the user to change the scale values.
- Permit toggling between a graphic and a table.

Computer graphics, unlike paper graphics, can be easily manipulated. Fowler and Stanwick (1995) suggest that the interpretation of numbers in graphical displays can be aided by permitting the above actions.

Types of Statistical Graphics Statistical graphics take many forms. There are curves and line graphs, surface charts, scatterplots, bar graphs, histograms, segmented or stacked bars, and pie charts.

Curve and Line Graphs Curves and line graphs can be used to show relationships between sets of data defined by two continuous variables. They are especially useful showing data changes over time, being superior to other graphic methods for speed and accuracy in determining data trends. With a curve, the data relations are summarized by a smoothed line. With a line, the data plots are connected by straight line segments. A line graph is illustrated in Figure 3.46. This kind of graph implies a

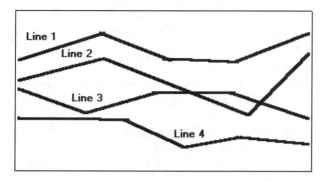

Figure 3.46   A line graph.

continuous function. If the data point elements are discrete, it is better to use a bar graph.

- Display data curves or lines that must be compared in a single graph.
- Display no more than four or five curves in a single graph.
- Identify each curve or line with an adjacent label whenever possible.
- If a legend must be included, order the legend to match the spatial ordering of the lines.
- For tightly packed curves or lines, provide data differentiation with a line coding technique such as different colors or different line composition types.
- Highlight curves or lines representing important or critical data.
- When comparing actual to projected data:
  - Use solid curves or lines for actual data.
  - Use broken curves or lines for projected data.
- Display a reference index if the displayed data must be compared to a standard or critical value.
- Display differences between two data sets as a curve or line itself.

If several curves must be compared, display them in one combined graph to facilitate their comparison.

Display no more than four or five curves in a single graph. As more curves or lines are added to a graph, visual discrimination amongst them becomes more difficult. The maximum number of lines presented should be limited to four or five. If one particular curve or line must be compared to several others, consider multiple graphs where the line of interest is compared separately with each other line.

Identify each curve or line with an adjacent label whenever possible. A label is preferable to a separate legend. If direct labeling is impossible due to the tightness of the lines, a legend may be the only alternative. If a legend is used, visually differentiate the lines (colors, line types, etc.), and include the coding scheme in the legend.

If a legend must be included, order the legend to match the spatial ordering of the lines. If legends are to be used on a series of graphs, however, maintain one consistent order for the legends on all graphs.

For tightly packed curves or lines, provide data differentiation through a line coding technique. Common coding techniques include different colors and line types. Do not exceed the maximum number of alternatives for the method selected, as shown in Table 10.1 in Step 10, "Create Meaningful Icons." If color coding is used, choose colors on the basis of the considerations described in Step 9, "Choose the Proper Color." Line width and dot size coding should be avoided because of their similarity to grids and scatterpoints. If a series of related graphs are line coded, be consistent in the selection of techniques for corresponding data.

Highlight curves or lines representing important or critical data. If one curve or line in a multiple-line graph is of particular significance, highlight that curve (high intensity, different color, etc.) to call attention to it. The coding scheme selected should be different than that used for spatial differentiation. Use solid curves or lines for actual data; use broken curves or lines for projected data.

When a curve or line must be compared to a standard or critical value, display a reference curve or line reflecting that value.

If the difference between two sets of data must be determined, display the difference itself as a curve or line. This is preferable to requiring the user to visually compare the two values and calculate the difference between them. If the difference between the related curves is of interest, consider a band chart where both lines and curves are displayed and the area between them coded through use of a texture, shading, or color.

Surface Charts If the data being depicted by a curve or line represents all the parts of a whole, consider developing a surface chart, as illustrated in Figure 3.47. In this kind of graph the curves or lines are stacked above one another to indicate individual amounts and/or aggregated amounts. Each boundary height is determined by the height of the line below it, and the area between each line or curve is differently coded, usually by textures or shading. A surface chart is similar to a segmented bar chart.

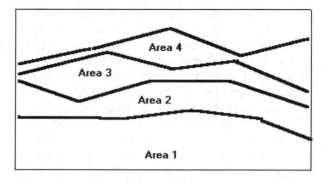

Figure 3.47   A surface chart.

- Order the data categories so that:
  - The least variable is at the bottom, and the most variable at the top.
  - The largest is at the bottom and the smallest at the top.
- Use different texture or shading coding schemes to differentiate the areas below each curve or line.
- Incorporate labels within the bands of data.

In ordering the data categories, place the least variable at the bottom and the most variable at the top. Irregularities in the bottom curve or line will affect those above it. This makes it difficult for a viewer to determine whether the irregularity in the upper curves reflect real data differences or is the result of this style of graph. Displaying the least variable data at the bottom will minimize this effect. Alternatively, place the widest area at the bottom and the narrowest at the top. Wide bands look like they belong at the bottom, narrow at the top.

If the data itself implies some logical organization must be followed, and the resulting organization creates confusing distortions in the curves, this kind of graph should not be used.

Use different texture or shading coding schemes. Ensure that the coding scheme chosen for each area is visually distinguishable from all the others. Place darker shades or colors toward the bottom.

Labels with a left-to-right reading orientation should be included within textured or shaded bands, if possible. Legends showing individual percentages, or cumulative percentages, should only be incorporated where space constraints exist within the bands.

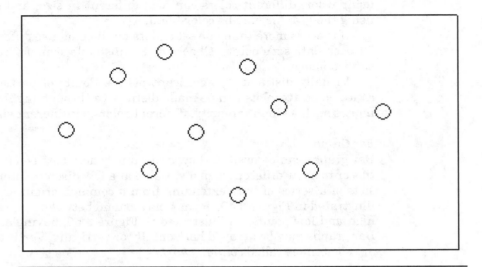

Figure 3.48 A scatterplot.

Scatterplots Scatterplots can be used to show relationships among individual data points in a two-dimensional array. A point is displayed on the plot where the X and Y axis variable intersect, as illustrated in Figure 3.48. Correlations and trends on scatterplots can be indicated by the superimposition of curves (thus combining with the scatterplot another kind of graphic display).

- Limit use to two-dimensional displays of data.
- Maintain consistent scale size intervals.
- Provide distinguishable, equal-sized plot points.
- If there is more than one set of data on the plot, use different symbols for each data set's points.
- Visually distinguish points of particular significance through a highlighting technique.

Limit to two dimensions. Three-dimensional scatterplots, while possible, do not yield clear, unambiguous displays.

Maintain consistent scale size intervals. Inconsistent spacing size between scale ticks on the two axes can distort the displayed data.

Construct the plot points of distinguishable, equal-sized circles, squares, rectangles, or diamonds. These symbols may be filled in or empty. Color may also be used to designate the points. Keep in mind when using color, different colors can look different in size, and some people using the graphic may be color-blind.

If there is more than one set of data on the plot, use different symbols for each data set's points. Choose distinguishable symbols from those described above.

Visually distinguish significant points. Points of particular significance on scatterplots can be made distinctive through highlighting techniques such as high intensity, different colors, or different shapes.

Bar Graphs

Bar graphs can be used to show a few differences between separate entities or to show differences in a variable at a few discrete intervals. It consists of a series of bars extending from a common origin or baseline, as illustrated in Figure 3.49, or they may extend between separately plotted high and low points, as illustrated in Figure 3.50, having only one axis. Bar graphs may be arrayed horizontally or vertically. Vertical bar graphs are sometimes called *column charts*.

- Orient bars consistently, either horizontally or vertically.
- Use vertical bars when the item being counted is of greatest interest.
- Use horizontal bars:
  - When the data labels are long.
  - To highlight the information rather than the count.
- Use a meaningful organizing principle.
  - If none exists, arrange so that the length of bars are in ascending or descending order.

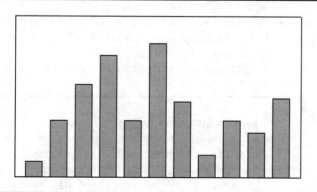

Figure 3.49   A bar graph with a common origin point.

- Make the spacing between bars equal to one-half the width of the bars, or less.
  - If groupings of bars are presented, leave space between the groupings only.
- If different kinds of bars must be easily distinguished, provide differentiation through a coding technique.
  - If possible, use a pattern or color that reinforces the data.
- Highlight bars representing important or critical data.
- Provide a consistent ordering for related groups of bars.
- Display a reference index if displayed data must be compared to a standard or critical value.
- Identify each bar with an adjacent label.
  - Place labels below, or to the left of, the baseline.
- When a great many pieces of data must be compared, consider using histograms or step charts.

While bars may be oriented either horizontally or vertically, a consistent orientation should be maintained for bars displaying similar information. In general, frequency counts are best displayed in vertical bars. Also, use vertical bars when the values or count being displayed are of greatest interest. Use horizontally arrayed bars for time durations. Also use this orientation when the data labels are long and room is needed to present them, and when the information categories must be highlighted, rather than the count.

Use a meaningful organizing principle, such as volumes, dates, or alphabetical. If no meaningful principle exists, arrange the bars so that the length of bars are in ascending or descending order. If the information is

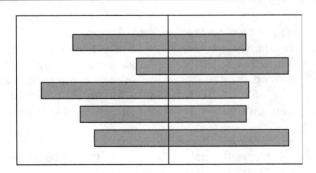

Figure 3.50   A bar graph with separately plotted high and low points.

being compared to a baseline or other comparative data, place the baseline bar to the far left or at the top.

Space bars for ease of visual comparison. Comparison of bars should be accomplishable without eye movement. Generally, the spacing between bars should be one-half or less of the bar width. If many bars are to be displayed, the alternating pattern of bright and dark bands that results can be visually disturbing to some viewers. In this case it is better to completely eliminate the spacing between bars. (The graph is then called a *histogram*.) If groupings of bars are presented, leave the space between the groupings.

If different kinds of bars must be easily distinguished, provide differentiation through a coding technique such as color, texture, or shading. If possible, use a meaningful pattern or color that reinforces the differences.

Highlight important or critical data. If one bar represents data of unusual significance, call attention to that bar through a different coding technique. Related groups of bars should be ordered in a consistent manner.

When bars must be compared to some standard or critical value, display a reference line to aid that comparison.

A label associated with each bar, in left-to-right reading orientation, is preferable to a separate legend. Place labels below, or to the left of, the baseline. If the labels on a horizontal bar chart are short, left-align them. If they are long, right-align them to the axis. If groups of bars are repeated, it is only necessary to label one group rather than all bars in all groups.

When a great many pieces of data must be compared, consider histograms or step charts. These are bar graphs without spaces between each of the bars, as illustrated in Figure 3.51. The area of a bar in a histogram reflects the amount of the value, so all bars should be of equal width.

Segmented or Stacked Bars If both the total measure of a value and its component portions are of interest, consider segmented or stacked bars. These bars are similar to bar graphs except that the bar is segmented into two or more pieces reflecting the component values, as illustrated in Figure 3.52. In this way they are similar to surface graphs and pie charts. Design guidelines are similar to stacked bars, except for the following.

- Order the data categories in the same sequence.
- Order the data categories so that:
  - The least variable is at the bottom.

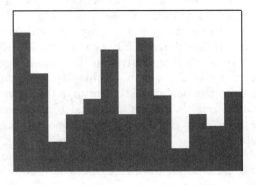

Figure 3.51   A histogram or step chart.

- The most variable is at the top.
- Limit the number of segments to those that are big enough to be seen and labeled.
- Use different texture or coding schemes to differentiate the areas within each bar.
- Clearly associate labels with bars or segments.
  - Place segment labels to the right on a vertical chart or above on a horizontal chart.

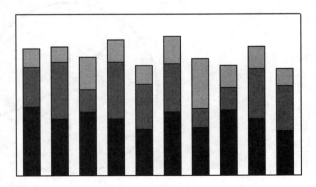

Figure 3.52   A segmented or stacked bar graph.

To provide consistency, order the data categories in the same sequence for all bars. Order data categories to show least variable at bottom and most variable at top. Irregularities in the bottom segment will affect those above it. This can make it difficult for a person to determine whether the irregularity in the upper segments reflects real data differences or is the result of this style of graph. Displaying least variable data at the bottom will minimize this effect. Also consider displaying the least variable values at the bottom, as is done with surface charts, unless the data itself dictates that some other logical organization must be followed.

Limit the number of segments to those that are big enough to be seen and labeled. If small segment components exist, group them into an "other" category.

Use different texture or shading coding schemes. Ensure that the coding scheme chosen for each segment is visually distinguishable from all others. Place darker shades or colors toward the bottom or toward the left.

Associate labels with bars and segments. Labels, with a left-to-right reading orientation, are preferable to legends. Do not place labels within segments, as they most often will not fit. Legends should only be used if space does not allow labels.

Pie Charts Pie charts, a circle broken up into pie-shaped pieces, can be used to show an apportionment of a total into its component parts, as illustrated in Figure 3.53. Bar graphs, however, usually permit more accurate estimates of proportions.

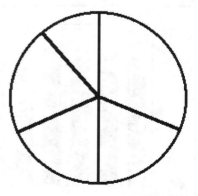

Figure 3.53   A pie chart.

- Pie charts should be used with caution.
- If pie charts are used:
  - They must add up to 100 percent.
  - Use five segments or less.
  - Place the largest wedge starting at 12:00.
  - Each segment should take up at least 5 percent (18 degrees) of the circle.
  - Directly label each segment in the normal reading orientation.
  - If leaders for labels in small segments are necessary, orient them in as few angles as possible.
  - Include numbers with segment labels to indicate percentages of absolute values.
  - Textures or colors selected for segments should not emphasize one segment over another (unless it is intended)
  - Highlight segments requiring particular emphasis through a contrasting display technique or by "exploding" it.
  - Never tilt a pie.

Experts caution against the use of pie charts because:

- They provide no means of absolute measurement.
- They cannot represent totals greater than 100 percent.
- They can only represent a fixed point in time.
- Human estimation of relationships is more accurate with linear than with angular representations.

If pie charts are used, the guidelines below should be followed.

The parts must add up to 100 percent. To convert from percentages to degrees, multiply the percentage by 3.6.

To minimize confusion, restrict pies to five segments or less. This permits adequate differentiation of its pieces and accurate labeling.

Avoid very small segments. Segments should take up at least five percent (18 degrees) of the circle in order to provide adequate segment differentiation. If small portions exist, combine the pieces into an "other" category and list them in a caption or note.

Start with the largest wedge at 12:00 (or a quarter hour) and order from largest to smallest in a clockwise order.

To provide maximum association of label with data and for reading clarity, use a left-to-right reading orientation. If it is impossible to include the label within the segment, it may be placed outside and tied to the segment with a leader line. Place the labels in one or two columns (one on each side). If multiple outside labels and leader lines are necessary, orient the lines in as few angles as possible.

Include numbers with the segment labels to indicate percentages or absolute values. Only by including numbers with segment labels can numeric values be accurately established. Alternatively, make actual percentages available when requested.

The kinds of textures or colors selected for segments should not emphasize one segment over another, unless this emphasis is intended.

Highlight segments requiring emphasis. Use a contrasting display technique or *explode* segments requiring emphasis. Exploding is accomplished by slightly displacing a segment from the remainder of the pie.

Never tilt a pie. Distortion will occur with tilting. Small wedges at the front will look larger than they actually are.

Choosing a Graph Type

- Determine what kind of information is most important for the viewer to extract.
- Choose the type of graph best suited for presenting that kind of information.

The types of graphics just described have rarely been experimentally studied to determine their most effective use. Some studies addressing this issue, however, are those of Hollands & Spence (1992) and Simkin & Hastie (1987). These researchers collected data on three tasks: (1) determining a proportion of a whole where the proportion *was* a part of the whole (proportion); (2) determining a proportion of a whole where the proportion *was not* a part of the whole (comparison); and (3) determining a change over time (change). The results are summarized in Table 3.1. In estimating proportion, if a scale is not included on the graph, pie charts and segmented bars were found to be best. If a scale is included, line graphs and bar graphs are also usable, both actually having a slight edge in speed over pie charts and bar graphs. In the comparison task, bar graphs and segmented bars were superior to pie charts. In estimating change over time, line graphs and bar graphs were both very effective, and pie charts and segmented bars the poorest.

In choosing a graph to display information, the kind of information important to the viewer must always be determined first. This will point to the kind of graphic most effective for the task.

Table 3.1   Tasks and Best Types of Graphs

| | Proportion | | | |
	With Scale	Without Scale	Comparison	Change
Best	Line Graphs	Segmented Bars	Bar Graphs	Line Graphs
	Bar Graphs	Pie Charts	Segmented Bars	Bar Graphs
	Segmented Bars			
	Pie Charts			
Poorest	—	Bar Graphs	Pie Charts	Segmented Bars
		Line Graphs		Pie Charts

From Hollands & Spence (1992) and Simkin & Hastie (1987).

Flow Charts

- Displayed steps should be designed to:
  - Follow some logical order.
  - Minimize path link.
- Orient following common flowchart reading conventions such as left-to-right and top-to-bottom.
- Follow common flowchart coding conventions to distinguish elements.
- Use arrows in conventional ways to indicate directional relationships.
- Highlight elements requiring particular attention through a contrasting display technique.
- Require only one decision at each step.
- Be consistent in all option ordering and wording.

If the data to be displayed flows in a complex, yet sequential, process, consider using a flowchart to schematically represent it. Flowcharts can also be used to aid problem solving in which a solution can be reached by answering a series of questions. They are not useful when trade-offs must be made.

Order of Steps One logical ordering scheme is to follow a sequence of operations or processes from start to finish. Other potential ordering schemes include placing the most important decisions first or the decisions that can be made with the most certainty. If no logical order is apparent, order the flowchart to minimize the length of the path through it. If some decision paths are more likely to occur than others, minimize the length of the most likely path.

Orientation Follow a left-to-right and top-to-bottom orientation.

Coding Conventions Follow existing shape coding conventions for the kinds of boxes being displayed. Adhere to standards and people's expectations.

Arrows Use arrows to indicate directional relations and sequential links.

Highlighting Contrasting display techniques, such as high intensity or color, should be used to call attention to relevant paths or elements. Color is particularly effective in this regard.

Only One Decision at Each Step Multiple decisions reduce flowchart size. However, requiring multiple decisions such as "Is A true and B false?" can be confusing. Require that only single decisions be made.

Consistently Order and Word All Choices Consistency always aids learning.

HARDWARE CONSIDERATIONS IN SCREEN DESIGN

- Screen design must be compatible with the hardware capabilities of the system, including the following:
  - System power.
  - Screen size.
  - Screen resolution and graphics capability.
  - Displayable colors.

Screen design is also affected by the physical characteristics of the display device itself. The design must be compatible with the following hardware capabilities: system power, screen size, screen resolution and graphics capability, and displayable colors.

System Power

A slow processing speed and small memory may inhibit effective use of windows. Feedback and animation capabilities may be limited, reducing the system's usability. Slow responses can be error-prone, grossly inefficient, and very aggravating. A slow screen refresh rate will increase the user's chances of perceiving screen flicker, which can be visually fatiguing. A system must be powerful enough to perform all necessary actions promptly, responsively, and meaningfully.

Screen Size

Many of today's screens are not large enough in size to take full advantage of windowing capabilities. As a result, many windows are still of "post-it" dimensions. There is some evidence (Cooper, 1985; Johnson-Laird, 1985, and personal observations) that many users of windowing systems expand their windows to cover a full screen. Either seeing all the contents of one window is preferable to seeing small parts of many windows, the operational complexity of multiple windows is not wanted, or visual noise is being eliminated. Whatever the case, these actions indicate a shortcoming in windowing systems as they exist today.

Expanding screen size, though, may create other problems. A large display area will require longer control movements to reach all locations on the screen, and more head and eye movements. Even with today's small desk top screens many activities in the peripheries of vision still go unnoticed. Larger screens will compound this problem. The effect on user physical comfort, and the possibility of needing an expanded working area, must be considered. A larger screen also creates more opportunities for a more cluttered screen. Clearly, the screen size-usability trade-off must be studied further.

Screen Resolution and Graphics Capability

Poor screen resolution and graphics capability may deter effective use of a graphical system by not permitting sharp and realistic drawings and shapes. Window structure and icon design may be severely affected. Adequate screen resolution and graphics capability is a necessity to achieve meaningful representations.

Colors

The color palette must be of a variety large enough to permit establishment of a family of discriminable colors. The colors used must be accurately and clearly presented in all situations. The contextual effect of colors must also be considered, as hues may change based on factors such as size and location in relation to other colors. Color is further discussed in Step 9.

SOFTWARE CONSIDERATIONS IN SCREEN DESIGN

- Provide compatibility with the system platform being used.
- Provide compatibility with the development and implementation tool being used.
- Provide compatibility with the platform style guide being used.
- Effectively use the various display features or attributes.

Design must be compatible with the system platform and any development and implementation tools being used. Design may also consider any available platform style guide. Finally, design must effectively utilize the various available display features or attributes.

Platform Compatibility

Design must be compatible with the windowing platform being used, Apple Computer's Macintosh, Microsoft Windows 3.1 or Windows 95, OSF Motif, or any other being used.

Development and Implementation Tool Compatibility

Myers & Rosson (1992) report that about 50 percent of software code is now devoted to user interface design. To use a very old cliché, the tail is now beginning to wag the dog. Available tools, as defined by Myers and Rosson, include toolkits, interface builders, and user interface management systems.

A *toolkit* is a library of controls or widgets such as menus, buttons, and scroll bars. Toolkits have a programmatic interface and must be used by programmers. They are usually for a specific windowing platform. Examples of toolkits include those for Motif, OpenLook, and the Macintosh.

An *interface builder* is a graphical tool that helps a programmer create dialog boxes, menus, and other controls. It provides a palette to select and position controls, and the setting of properties. Interface builders are limited to laying out the static parts of the interface. They cannot handle the parts of the interface that involve graphical objects moving around. Examples include DevGuide and Windows Maker.

A *user interface management system* (UIMS) extends the features of a builder by also providing assistance with creating and managing the insides of windows. Examples include HyperCard and Visual Basic.

Style Guide Compatibility

A thrust for commonality in graphical system application design has emerged as providers have finally come to realize that design consistency is a virtue that has been ignored too long. To achieve this consistency in interface design, most providers have developed style guidelines for system developers. These guidelines specify the appearance and behavior of the user interface. They describe the windows, menus, and various controls available, including what they look like and how they work. They also provide some guidance on when to use the various components.

Examples of industry-produced guidelines include Apple's *Macintosh Human Interface Guidelines* (1992b), Digital Equipment Corporation's *XUI Style Guide* (1988), IBM's *System Application Architecture Common User Access (SAA CUA)* (1987, 1989a, 1989b, 1991) and *Object-oriented Interface Design: IBM Common User Access Guidelines* (1992), *NeXT Publications' NeXTStep User Interface Guidelines,* for release 3 (1992), Sun Microsystems' *OPEN LOOK Graphical User Interface Application Style Guidelines* (1990), Open Software Foundation's *OSF/MOTIF Style Guide* (1993) Revision 1.2, and Microsoft's *The Windows Interface* (1992) for Windows 3.1 and *The Windows Interface Guidelines for Software Design* (1995) for Windows 95.

Product style guides vary in their ability to control compliance with the guidelines they present. Some present strict requirements leading to excellent consistency across applications; others provide little guideline compliance control.

The style guides are also suffering growing pains because of their newness and the rapid pace of technology. Terminology changes between versions can cause user confusion and learning problems (IBM 1989b, 1991; Microsoft, 1992, 1995). Terminology differences between product guides lead to the same result. The screen background area in CUA is called the "desktop." In OPEN LOOK it is referred to as the "workspace." Window names in CUA are called "primary and secondary." In Microsoft Windows 3.1, "application and document." Windows 95 has now reverted to "primary and secondary."

Display Attributes

A wide range of attributes or properties are available to aid the screen design process. Before beginning design, the designer must be aware of what capabilities exist, how they may be most effectively used, and what their limitations are.

Often these features will be used to call attention to various items on the display. The attraction capability of a mechanism is directly related to how well it stands out from its surroundings. Its maximum value is achieved when it is used in moderation. Overuse is self-defeating, as contrast with the surroundings is reduced and distraction may even begin to occur. Use of too many features at one time may also lead to increased visual clutter. The design goal: Use only the features necessary to get the message effectively communicated to the user. As in many aspects of design, too little or too much is not desirable. Not all display features are ideal for all situations. The proper usage of many of the attributes or properties described in the pages of this book are summarized in Table 3.2 and briefly summarized in the following paragraphs.

Table 3.2   Display Attributes Summary

Brightness

- Good attention-getting capability.
- Few disturbing features.
- Provide two levels only.
- Use brighter intensity for more important elements like screen data.

Fonts

- Moderate attention-getting capability.
- Use no more than two styles or weights.
- Use no more than three sizes.

Upper-Case or Capitalization
- Use for headings and title.

Mixed-Case
- Use for textual information and other screen components.

Reverse Polarity

- Good attention-getting capability used in moderation.
- Can reduce legibility with screens of poor resolution.
- Suggested uses:
  - Items selected.
  - Items in error.
  - Information being acted upon.
  - Information of current relevance.

Underlining

- Poor attention-getting capability.
- May reduce legibility.
- Use for keyboard equivalents (mnemonics).

Blinking

- Excellent attention-getting capability.
- Reduces legibility.
- Can be distracting.
- Provide two levels only (on and off).
- Suggested uses:
  - Urgent situations.
  - Situations where quick response required.
- Turn off when person has responded.

Table 3.2 *(Continued)*

Line Rulings and Borders

- Provide no more than:
  - Three line thicknesses.
  - Two line styles.
- Suggested uses:
  - Surround radio button and check box controls.
  - Break screen into groupings of controls.
  - Guide eye through screen.

Dimming or Graying

- Use to designate not applicable or not active.

Color

- Use to assist in screen component identification.
- Use no more than:
  - Four colors at one time on an alphanumeric screen.
  - Six colors at one time on a statistical graphics screen.

Brightness or Intensity A brighter element has a good attention-getting quality and no disturbing features. It may be used to indicate items in error and is the best vehicle for calling attention to data on inquiry screens. Do not use more than two brightness levels on a screen. If brightness has a fault, it is that displays with improperly set manual screen contrast controls can diminish its effectiveness, even causing it to disappear. This can be a major problem for displays placed in exceptionally bright viewing conditions.

Fonts Differences in fonts have a moderate attention-getting capability. Their varying sizes and shapes can be used to differentiate screen components. Larger, bolder letters can be used to designate higher-level screen pieces, such as different levels of headings, if the headings are used to search for something. Do not use larger fonts, however, for entry/modification (conversational) and display/read-only screens as this will place too much emphasis in the headings themselves. Emphasis should go to the screen data. If using multiple fonts, never use more than two styles or weights, and three sizes, on a screen.

Capitalization is recommended for screen headings, both section and subsection. It sets headings apart from all other screen body elements being presented in mixed-case. A screen title may also be capitalized. Mixed-case should be used for screen textual information since it is read faster than upper-case. Mixed-case may also be used for all other screen elements.

Reverse Polarity Reverse video is a display feature that permits a screen to resemble the normal printed page, dark letters on a light background.

For *entire* screens, several studies comparing reverse polarity light background screens to light character on dark background screens were conducted during the 1980s and found no performance differences between the two (Cushman, 1986; Kühne, Krueger, Graf, & Merz, 1986; and Zwahlen & Kothari, 1986) and no differences in eye-scanning behavior and feelings of visual fatigue (Zwahlen & Kothari, 1986). One study did find reverse polarity more visually fatiguing (Cushman, 1986), while another (Wichansky, 1986) found green and orange phosphor reverse polarity screens easier to read but found no differences in white phosphor readability. In general, it has also been found that people prefer dark background screens to light background screens (see Step 9 for a full discussion). There is a benefit to light background screens, however. Dark background screens can create a viewing problem, their mirrorlike surfaces reflecting light from other outside sources back into the screen viewer's eyes. Light background screens absorb most of this light, instead of reflecting back to the screen viewer.

For *elements* of screens—pieces of data, messages, and so on—reverse polarity has a very high attention-getting quality. It can be effectively used for items selected, items in error, information being acted upon, or information of current relevance.

Some cautions should be taken with reverse polarity. If reverse polarity is used to identify one kind of element such as a text box or other boxed control, avoid what can best be described as the crossword puzzle effect—the haphazard arrangement of elements on the screen creating an image that somewhat resembles a typical crossword puzzle. An arrangement of elements might be created that tries to lead the eye in directions that the designer has not intended or causes elements to compete for the viewer's attention. The cause of this problem is using reverse polarity for too many purposes or by poor alignment and columnization of boxes selected for this emphasis. Conservative use and alignment and columnization rules will minimize this effect.

If reverse polarity is used to highlight information such as messages or actions to be taken, allow an extra reversed character position on each side of the information. This will leave a margin around the information, improving legibility and giving it a more pleasing look.

Lastly, reverse polarity can make text harder to read if the screen resolution and character sizes are not sufficient. A light screen background can actually bleed into its dark characters, reducing their legibility. This is a phenomenon called *iridescence*.

Underlining Underlining is a moderate attention-getting mechanism but it can reduce legibility, so it should be used with caution. In graphical systems it is commonly used to designate keyboard equivalents or mnemonics.

Blinking Blinking has a very high attention-getting capability, but it reduces character legibility and is disturbing to most people. It often causes visual fatigue if used excessively. Therefore, it should be reserved for urgent situations and when quick response is necessary. A user should be able to turn off the blinking once his attention has been captured. The recommended blink rate is 2–5 Hz with a minimum "on" time of 50 percent. An alternative to consider is creating an "on" cycle considerably longer than the "off," a wink rather than a blink.

Line Rulings and Line Borders Use lines to guide one's eye through the screen. Use horizontal rulings as a substitute for spaces in breaking a screen into pieces. Use vertical rulings to convey to the screen viewer that a screen should be scanned from top to bottom. Use rules to surround radio button and check box controls. While many groupings are obvious without borders, borders certainly reinforce their existence. Use no more than three line thicknesses or two line styles on a screen.

Dimming or Graying Use to designate an element conditionally not applicable or not active.

Colors Use color to assist in the identification of screen components. Display no more than four colors at one time on a screen essentially alphanumeric in nature, six on a statistical graphics screen. Color considerations will be extensively reviewed in Step 9.

EXAMPLES OF SCREENS

What follows are examples of poor and proper design. The problems on the poorly designed screens will be described in the discussion to follow. Redesigned versions of these poorly designed screens will be presented at the end of Step 8. Examples of other properly designed screens will also be presented as models of good design.

Example 1

Here are three information entry/modification dialog boxes from a popular drawing program, PRINT MERGE, PAGE SETUP, and EXPORT. Analyze them for problems, including inconsistencies between them.

Screen 1.1

The controls on the PRINT MERGE screen are very poorly aligned. The File text box is located quite far from its associated list box. What does the Up button do? It is actually related to the Directories list box. This is certainly not clear. Look at the required sequence of eye movements through this screen, as illustrated by the line drawn between successive controls. This is very inefficient.

Print Merge

Path: `D:\WINDOWS\PM4\*.txt`

Files

mgximp.txt
readme1.txt
readme2.txt
tabledit.txt
typemgr.txt

File: tabledit.txt

Directories

[..]
[tutorial]
[usenglsh]
[-a-]
[-b-]
[-c-]
[-d-]

Up

Cancel

Merge

Screen 1.1 A

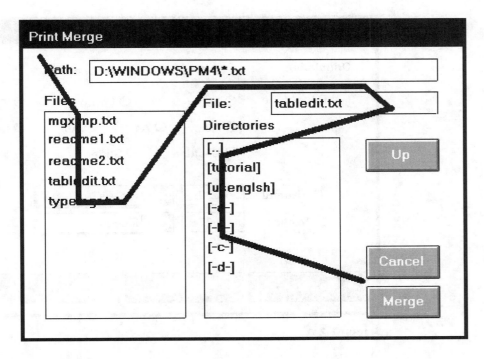

Screen 1.1 B

Screen 1.2

The controls on the PAGE SETUP screen are very poorly grouped. Are the nine radio buttons beginning at the Page Size caption one or three groupings? The horizontal orientation of the radio buttons necessitates a less efficient horizontal scanning and makes visual comparison of the alternatives more difficult. Why is the Orientation caption not right-aligned with the other captions? What are the controls inscribed with Inches? They are actually nonstandard controls but this is not clear until one discovers how to operate them (clicking on the rectangular bar changes the value, inches, now displayed). Nonstandard controls increase learning requirements and add to the complexity of the interface. Again, look at the required sequence of eye movements through this screen, as illustrated by the line drawn between successive controls. This is very inefficient.

Screen 1.2 A

Screen 1.2 B

Screen 1.3

The check boxes and radio buttons on the EXPORT screen are again very poorly grouped. Their horizontal orientation necessitates a less efficient horizontal scanning and makes visual comparison of the alternatives more difficult. Can the check boxes be grouped? The list box has no caption with it. Screen balance is also poor with the large open area in the upper-right part of the screen. Again, look at the required eye scan through this screen.

Screen 1.3 A

Screen 1.3 B

Now, look at the inconsistencies between these three screens. The PRINT MERGE title is in mixed-case; PAGE SETUP and EXPORT are capitalized. The PRINT MERGE command buttons are on the right side, PAGE SETUP and EXPORT on the bottom. PRINT MERGE uses the action being accomplished as the button label (Merge), the others use the standard OK. This will certainly cause user confusion. PRINT MERGE and EXPORT appear to use left-aligned captions, PAGE SETUP right alignment.

Example 2

Two information entry/modification dialog boxes from a popular word processing program, FOOTNOTE OPTIONS and LOCATION OF FILES. Some design enhancements are immediately obvious. The command buttons are consistently positioned in the lower-right corner and group boxes or borders are included to visually strengthen information groupings.

Screen 2.1

This screen's main problem is poor alignment of controls. The stand-alone check boxes tend to get lost. The centered headings in the group boxes are not a severe problem but they do somewhat compete with the control captions for the screen viewer's attention. The Position and Separator control borders are around single elements. This is not recommended but it does

Screen 2.1 A

help to provide screen balance, which is quite good. The sequentiality of this screen, as illustrated by one's required eye scan, is quite poor, as illustrated.

Screen 2.1 B

Screen 2.2

Note the improved alignment of this screen's controls. It is excellent, except for the single check box in the lower-left corner. Again, this check box can get lost here. This screen does have two problems. First, the headings, in mixed-case and centered in the group boxes, visually compete with the information within the boxes for the viewer's attention. It would be much better if they were positioned away from the important screen information and capitalized to set them off visually from the captions and data. Second, for completeness and closure, a group box around the top five controls should also be included.

Screen 2.2 A

Screen 2.2 B

Example 3

This is an information entry/modification screen from a banking system. The major problem is very poor alignment of the controls, as illustrated by the eye scan requirements. There are some other problems. There are no groupings. Does the name control have a caption? Are the labels above the Name text box intended as captions? Are they intended as prompts? This

Screen 3.1 A

Screen 3.1 B

is not clear. Is the prompt (dd/mm/yyyy) in the proper location? In its current position it is set up as an aid to a novice or casual user of the system. For an expert user of the system, who does not need the prompt, it is positioned where it is visual noise. For the expert it should be to the right side of the text box.

Example 4

This is a properly designed information entry/modification screen. It contains groupings reinforced by group boxes, alignment of controls, right-alignment of all captions (in this case) located consistently to the left of each control, capitalized section headings aligned to the upper-right of the group boxes, and command buttons centered at the bottom. Scanning of the columns of information is simplified by the control alignment. Headings do not compete with control captions for the viewer's attention. The screen also possesses balance.

Screen 4.1 A

Screen 4.1 B

Example 5

This is a read-only/display screen from the drawing program. It possesses good balance and nice groupings reinforced through use of group boxes. The problems are these: There are no colons with the captions. Other screens from this system have colons included with captions, violating the viewer's mental model of a caption possessing a colon. Which caption style is used, headline (all significant word initial caps) or sentence (capitalization of the first word only)? If you examine the screen you'll find many instances of both styles. The section headings are mixed-case just like the control captions, competing with each other visually for the viewer's attention. The numeric data fields are not properly right-aligned although fairly good top-to-bottom scanning does exist. Units in the Image Size/Resolution groupings are at the bottom of listing. They would more appropriately be placed at the top because they appear to be column headings. In the Image Resolution grouping the use of "res" is redundant, already appearing in the section heading.

Screen 5.1

Example 6

Here is a pair of similar read-only/display screens from another system. Both are poorly aligned, the data getting buried among the captions. See the illustration of how TEXTBLOCK INFO will be scanned. Why abbreviate INFO; there is plenty of room to spell it out. The groupings are not very strong, either. Notice the inconsistencies in captions, Character count versus Char count, Area versus Total area, and Depth versus Total depth. Again, there is room to spell them out fully. Otherwise, the viewer has to establish two mental models for the same element. Why establish this learning requirement?

Story info [OK]

File link:

Textblocks: 1   First page: 4

Char count: 1400   Last page: 4

Overset chars: 0

Total area: 23.413 sq inches

Total depth: 7.400 inches

Screen 6.1 A

Textblock info [OK]

File link:

Textblock 1 of 1 in story

Character count: 1400

Area: 23.413 sq inches

Depth: 7.400 inches

Previous textblock on page: 4

Next textblock on page:

Screen 6.1 B

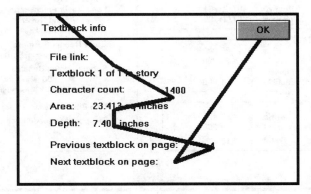

Textblock info [OK]

File link:

Textblock 1 of 1 in story

Character count: 1400

Area: 23.413 sq inches

Depth: 7.400 inches

Previous textblock on page: 4

Next textblock on page:

Screen 6.1 C

Example 7

Here are two properly designed read-only/inquiry screens, both possessing alignment, grouping, and balance. The data is displayed on the screen background for ease of identification and comprehension.

Screen 7.1

From an insurance system, this screen summarizes some of the most important kinds of information a policyholder would want to know about an insurance policy. Captions are omitted in the POLICY NUMBER/INSURED section at the top. Contextually, this information is self-explanatory. The information presented in the ENDORSEMENTS section reflects the principle of displaying something only if it is present or applicable. If one or more of these endorsements were not included with another similar policy, they would not be displayed at all. In that case, the applicable endorsements would fill this section beginning at its top. The descriptive information included with the top three endorsements reflects the conversion of the more customary caption: data format into simple data statements. The data statements are self-explanatory, captions are not required.

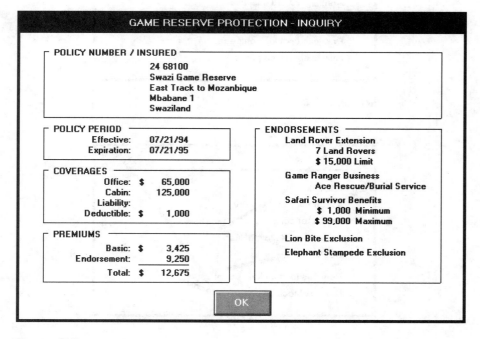

Screen 7.1

Screen 7.2

From a shoe manufacturer, this screen is similar to the insurance screen in structure.

PRODUCT STYLE INQUIRY

STYLE
Number: 4470
Name: High Jumping

DESCRIPTION
Identifying Color: Blue
Dimension Code: 00
General Prod Class: Footwear
Short Name: HJ

Gender Age: Men
Gender: Male
Family: N/A
Body Type: Shoe
Brand: Airbourne
Warehouse Codes:

Sport Activity: Track
Silhouette: 3/4 High

UNITS
Unit/Measure: 01 Each
Weight: 3.16
Units/Case: 12

FLAGS
Technical Switch: Yes
Price by Flag: Style
Finish Good Flag: Finished

SPECIAL FEATURES
1:   Air Bags
2:   Prime Tanning Leather

OK

Screen 7.2

S T E P 4

Select the Proper Kinds of Windows

A window is an area of the screen, usually rectangular in shape, defined by a border that contains a particular view of some area of the computer or some portion of a person's dialogue with the computer. It can be moved, sized, and rendered independently on the screen. A window may be small, containing a short message or a single field, or it may be large, consuming most or all of the available display space. A display may contain one, two, or more windows within its boundaries.

- Understand a window's characteristics.
- Understand a window's components.
- Understand a window's presentation styles.
- Understand the types of windows available.
- Organize window system functions.
- Provide simple window operations.

WINDOW CHARACTERISTICS

A window is seen to possess the following characteristics:

- A name or *title,* allowing it to be identified.
- A *size* in height and width (which can vary).
- A *state,* whether it is accessible or active or not accessible. (Only active windows can have their contents altered.)
- *Visibility*—the portion that can be seen. (A window may be partially or fully hidden behind another window, or the information within a window may extend beyond the window's display area.)
- A *location,* relative to the display boundary.

- *Presentation,* that is, its arrangement in relation to other windows. It may be tiled, overlapping, or cascading.
- *Management capabilities,* methods for manipulation of the window on the screen.
- Its *highlight,* that is, the part that is selected.
- The *function, task,* or *application* to which it is dedicated.

The Attraction of Windows

The value of windowing is best seen in the context of the typical office job. An office worker performs a variety of tasks, often in a fairly unstructured manner. The worker is asked to monitor and manipulate data from a variety of sources, synthesize information, summarize information, and reorganize information. Things are seldom completed in a continuous time frame. Outside events such as telephone calls, supervisor requests, and deadlines force shifts in emphasis and focus. Tasks start, stop, and start again. Materials used in dealing with the tasks are usually scattered about one's desk, being positioned in the workspace to make handling the task as efficient as possible. This spatial mapping of tools helps people organize their work and provides reminders of uncompleted tasks. As work progresses and priorities change, materials are reorganized to reflect the changes.

Single-screen technology supports this work structure very poorly. Since only one screen of information can be viewed at one time, comparing or integrating information from different sources and on different screens often requires extensive use of one's memory. To support memory, the worker is often forced to make handwritten notes or obtain printed copies of screens. Switching between tasks is difficult and interruptive, and later returning to a task requires an extensive and costly restructuring of the work environment.

The appeal of windowing is that it allows the display workspace to mirror the desk workspace much more closely. This dramatically reduces one's short-term memory loads. One's ability to do mental calculations is limited by how well one keeps track of one's place, one's interim conclusions and products, and, finally, the results. Windows act as external memories that are an extension of one's internal memory. Windows also make it much easier to switch between tasks and to maintain one's context, since one does not have to reestablish one's place continually. Windows also provide access to more information than would normally be available on a single display of the same size. This is done by overwriting or placing more important information on top of that of less importance at that moment.

While all the advantages and disadvantages of windows are still not completely understood, they do seem to be useful in the following ways.

Presentation of Different Levels of Information Information can be examined in increasing levels of detail. A document table of contents can be presented in a window. A chapter, or topic, selected from this window can be simultaneously displayed in more detail in an adjoining window. Deeper levels are also possible on additional windows.

Presentation of Multiple Kinds of Information Variable information needed to complete a task can be displayed simultaneously in adjacent windows. An order-processing system window could collect a customer account number in one window and retrieve the customer's name and shipping address in another window. A third window could collect details of the order after which another window presents factory availability and shipping dates of the desired items. Significant windows remain displayed so that details may be modified as needed prior to order completion. Low stocks or delayed shipping dates might require changing the order.

Sequential Presentation of Levels or Kinds of Information Steps to accomplish a task can be sequentially presented through windows. Successive windows are presented until all the required details are collected. Key windows may remain displayed, but others appear and disappear as necessary. This sequential preparation is especially useful if the information-collection process leads down different paths. An insurance application, for example, will include different coverages. A requested coverage might necessitate the collection of specific details about that coverage. This information can be entered into a window presented to collect the unique data. The windows disappear after data entry, and additional windows appear when needed.

Access to Different Sources of Information Independent sources of information may have to be accessed at the same time. This information may reside in different host computers, operating systems, applications, files, or areas of the same file. It may be presented on the screen alongside the problem, greatly facilitating its solution. For instance, a writer may have to refer to several parts of text being written at the same time. Or, a travel agent may have to compare several travel destinations for a particularly demanding client.

Combining Multiple Sources of Information Text from several documents may have to be reviewed and combined into one. Pertinent information is selected from one window and copied into another.

Performing More than One Task More than one task can be performed at one time. While waiting for a long, complex procedure to finish, another can be performed. Tasks of higher priority can interrupt less important ones. The interrupted task can then be resumed with no "close down" and "restart" necessary.

Reminding Windows can be used to remind the viewer of things likely to be of use in the near future. Examples might be menus of choices available, a history of the path followed or command choices to that point, or the time of an important meeting.

Monitoring Changes, both internal and external, can be monitored. Data in one window can be modified and its effect on data in another window can be studied. External events, such as stock prices, out of normal range conditions, or system messages can be watched while another major activity is carried out.

Multiple Representations of the Same Task The same thing can be looked at in several ways—for example, alternative drafts of a speech, different versions of a screen, or different graphical representations of the same data. A maintenance procedure may be presented in the form of textual steps and illustrated graphically at the same time.

Constraints in Window System Design

Windowing systems, in spite of their appeal and obvious benefits, have failed to completely live up to their expectations. Benest & Dukic (1989) describe the overall user interface as "chaotic" because of the great amount of time users must spend doing such things as pointing at tiny boxes in window borders, resizing windows, moving windows, closing windows, and so forth. Billingsley (1988) attributes the problems with windowing systems to three factors: historical considerations, hardware limitations, and human limitations.

Historical Considerations Historically, system developers have been much more interested in solving hardware problems than in user considerations. Since technical issues abound, they have received the strong focus of attention. There has been very little research addressing design issues and their impact on the usability of window systems. Therefore, there are few concrete window design guidelines to aid designers.

This lack of guidelines makes it difficult to develop acceptable and agreeable window standards. While many companies are developing style guides, they are very general and limited in scope to their products. Standardization is also made more difficult by the complexity and range of alternatives available to the designer. Without user performance data, it is difficult to compare realistically the different alternatives, and design choices become a matter of preference.

Standardization of the interface is also inhibited by other factors. Some software developers, who are proud of their originality, see standards as a threat to creativity and its perceived monetary rewards. Some companies are wary of standards because they fear other companies are promoting standards that reflect their own approach. Finally, some companies have threatened, or brought, legal action against anyone who adopts an approach similar to their own.

The result is that developers of new systems create another new variation each time they design a product, and users must cope with a new interface each time they encounter a new windowing system.

Hardware Limitations Many of today's screens are not large enough to take full advantage of windowing capabilities. As a result, many windows are still of "post-it" dimensions. As already mentioned there is some evidence that many users of personal computers expand their windows to cover a full screen. Either seeing all the contents of one window is preferable to seeing small parts of many windows or the operational and visual complexity of multiple windows is not wanted.

Also, the slower processing speeds and smaller memory sizes of some computers may also inhibit use of windows. A drain on the computer's resources may limit feedback and animation capabilities, thereby reducing the system's usability. Poor screen resolution and graphics capability may also deter effective use of windows by not permitting sharp and realistic drawings and shapes.

Human Limitations A windowing system, because it is more complex, requires the learning and using of more operations. Much practice is needed to master them. These window management operations are placed on top of other system operations, and window management can become an end in itself. This can severely detract from the task at hand. In a study comparing full screens with screens containing overlapping windows (Davies, Bury, & Darnell, 1985), task completion times were longer with the window screens, but the nonwindow screens generated more user errors. After eliminating screen arrangement time, however, task solution times were shorter with windows. The results suggest that advantages for windows do exist, but they can be negated by excessive window manipulation requirements.

Benest & Dukic (1989) suggest that to be truly effective, window manipulation must occur implicitly as a result of user task actions, not as a result of explicit window management actions by the user.

Other Limitations Other possible window problems include the necessity for window borders to consume valuable screen space, and small windows providing access to large amounts of information can lead to excessive, bothersome scrolling.

Where To? In spite of their problems, windows do have enormous benefits and are here to stay. So, we must cope with their constraints for now and, in the meantime, enjoy the benefits they possess.

COMPONENTS OF A WINDOW

A typical window may be comprised of up to a dozen or so elements. Some appear on all windows; others only on certain kinds of windows, or conditionally. For consistency purposes, these elements should always be located in the same position within a window. Most windowing systems provide consistent locations for elements in their own windows. Some inconsistencies do exist in element locations between different systems, however, as do some differences in what elements are named, or what graphic images or icons are chosen to identify them. What follows is a description of typical window components and their purposes. Also included are some new Windows 95 components. Illustrations of Microsoft 3.1 and Microsoft 95 windows are found in Figures 4.1 and 4.2. A summary of window components for Windows 95 is found in Table 4.1.

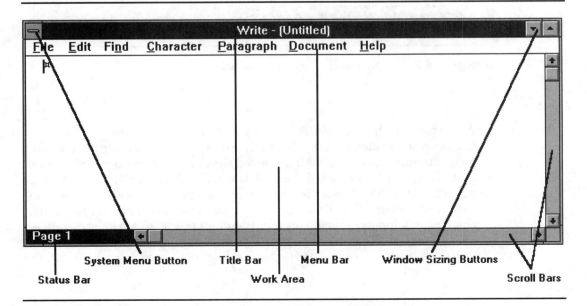

Figure 4.1   Microsoft Windows 3.1 application window.

Figure 4.2   Microsoft Windows 95 primary window.

Border

A window will have a border, usually rectangular in shape, to define its boundaries and distinguish it from other windows. While a border need not be rectangular, this shape is a preferred shape for most people, and textual materials, which are usually read left-to-right, fit most efficiently within this structure. The border is comprised of a line that may be variable in thickness and/or color. This variation can be used as an aid in identifying the type of window being displayed. Windows filling an entire screen may use the screen edge as the border. If a window is sizable, it may contain control points for sizing. Another term commonly used for border is *frame*.

Title Bar

The title bar is the top line of the window. Standard on all primary and secondary windows, it contains a descriptive title to identify the window's

Table 4.1   Microsoft Windows 95 Window Components

Component	Windows Containing Component		
	Primary	*Secondary*	*Dialog Box*
Frame or Border	X	X	X
• Boundary to define shape.			
• If sizable, contains control points for resizing.			
Title Bar Text	X	X	X
• Name of object being viewed in window.			
Title Bar Icon	X		
• Small version of icon for object being viewed.			
• Access point for commands that apply to the object.			
Title Bar Buttons	X	X	X
• Shortcuts to specific commands.			
Close	X	X	X
Minimize/Maximize/Restore	X		
What's This?		X	X
– *Displays context-sensitive help about any object displayed on window.*			
Menu Bar	X		
• Provides basic and common application commands.			
Status Bar	X		
• An area to display status information about what is displayed in window.			
Scroll Bar	X		
• Standard control to support scrolling.			
Size Grip	X		
• Control to size window located at right side of status bar.			

purpose and may possess, at the extreme left and right ends, control buttons (described below) for retrieving the system menu and performing window sizing. The area of the title bar used for displaying the title may be called the *title area* in some systems. The title bar serves as a control point for moving the window. In Windows 95 the title bar serves as the access point for commands that apply to a window. These commands are displayed in a pop-up menu.

Work Area

The work area is the portion of the screen where the user performs tasks. It is the open area inside the window's border and other relevant peripheral screen components such as the menu bar, scroll bars, or message bars. The work area may consist of an open area for typing, or it may contain controls (such as text boxes and list boxes) or customized forms (such as spreadsheets). The work area may also be referred to as the *client area*.

System Menu Button

Located at the left corner of the title bar, this button is used to retrieve a pull-down menu of commands for manipulating a window. This menu is primarily an aid to keyboard users of a system, there being other ways, such as using a mouse, to directly access to all these actions. The menu also serves as an aid to casual system users, reminding them of actions available.

The symbol most commonly inscribed on the button is a horizontal bar, as used in Windows 3.1, although versions using a form of inverted rectangle are also seen (OS/2 Workplace Shell, OPEN LOOK), as well as a downward-pointing arrow. The system menu may also be called the *window menu* or *control menu*. Windows 95 has eliminated the system menu button and replaced it with a small version of the icon of the object being viewed. This is called the *title bar icon* and is described next. In Windows 95, the access point for commands that apply to the window is the title bar itself. These commands are displayed in a pop-up menu.

Title Bar Icon (Windows 95)

Located at the left corner of the title bar, this button is used in Windows 95 to retrieve a pull-down menu of commands that apply to the object in the window. Windows 95 has eliminated the system menu button and replaced it with this button picturing a small version of the icon of the object being viewed. When clicked with mouse button 2, the commands applying to the object are presented. Window commands are now accessed through the title bar pop-up menu described above. For backward compatibility to Windows 3.1, if mouse button 1 is clicked on this title bar icon button, the commands applying to the window will be presented, instead. Windows 95 intends, however, that the title bar pop-up menu be the standard way to retrieve these window manipulation commands.

Window Sizing Buttons

These buttons are used to manipulate the size of a window. The minimize button—typically inscribed with a downward-pointing arrow—is used to reduce a window to its minimum size, usually an icon. It also hides all associated windows. The maximize button—typically inscribed with an upward-pointing arrow—enlarges a window to its maximum size, usually the entire screen. When a screen is maximized, the restore button replaces the maximize button, since the window can no longer be increased in size. The restore button—typically inscribed with a pair of arrows, one pointing up and the other down—returns a window to the size it had before a minimize or maximize action was performed. These buttons are located in the upper-right corner of the title bar and take various forms depending upon the product. These buttons are graphical equivalents to the actions available through the system menu button.

Menu Bar

A menu bar is used to organize and provide access to actions. It is located horizontally at the top of the window, just below the title bar. A menu bar contains a list of topics or items that, when selected, are displayed on a pull-down menu beneath the choice. A system will typically provide a default set of menu actions that can be augmented by an application. *IBM's SAA CUA* in its early editions called the menu bar an *action bar*. Menu bar design guidelines are presented in Step 5, "Develop System Menus."

Status Bar / Message Bar

Information of use to the user can be displayed in a designated screen area, or areas. They may be located at the top of the screen just below the title bar (SAA CUA *status area*), or at the screen's bottom (SAA CUA *information area,* Windows 95 *status bar*). The kinds of messages displayed include statuses, explanations, or helps. Messages longer than the message area should be displayed in a window. A message area may also be referred to as a *message bar*.

IBM's SAA CUA recommends that the information area be used to display a brief explanation or description about the state of an object. The status area, it recommends, should be used to display information about the view of an object rather than the object itself.

Microsoft Windows 3.1 suggests that the message bar be used to request information from the user or display status information about a selection, a command, or a process. It may also be used to explain menu and control bar items as the items are highlighted by the user. It suggests the status bar be used to display information about the current state of an application.

Microsoft Windows 95 suggests using the status bar to display information about the current state of what is being viewed in the window, descriptive messages about a selected menu or toolbar button, or other noninteractive information.

Scroll Bars

When all display information cannot be presented in a window, it must be found and made visible. This is accomplished by scrolling the display's contents through use of a scroll bar. A scroll bar is an elongated rectangular container consisting of a scroll area or shaft, a slider box or elevator, and arrows or anchors at each end. For vertical scrolling, the scroll bar is positioned at the far right side of the work area, extending its entire length. Horizontal scrolling is accomplished through a scroll bar located at the bottom of the work area.

Split Box and Split Bar

A window can be split into two or more pieces or panes by manipulating a split box located above a vertical scroll bar or to the left of a horizontal scroll bar. The separate panes or viewing areas are often delineated by a double-line separator called a *split bar*. Splitting a window permits multiple views of an object.

Control Bar

Control bars, illustrated in Figure 4.3, are permanently displayed arrays of choices or commands that must be accessed quickly. Such choices and commands include button bars, color/pattern palettes, toolbars, rulers, and ribbons. They may occupy a fixed position or be movable. The design of button bars and toolbars are discussed in Step 7, "Choose the Proper Screen-Based Controls."

Command Area

In situations where it is useful for a command to be typed into a screen, a command area can be provided. The desired location of the command area is at the bottom of the window. If a horizontal scroll bar is included in the window, position the command area just below it. If a message area is included on the screen, locate the command area just above it.

Size Grip (Windows 95)

A size grip is a Windows 95 special handle included in a window to permit it to be resized. When the grip is dragged the window resizes following the same conventions as the sizing border. It is designated by three angled

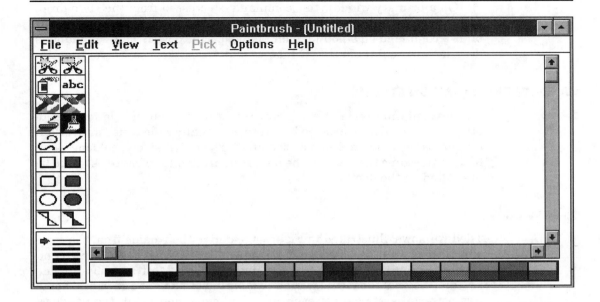

Figure 4.3   Control bars.

parallel lines in the lower-right corner of a window. If the window possesses a status bar, the grip is positioned at the bar's right end. Otherwise, it is located at the bottom of a vertical scroll bar, the right side of a horizontal scroll bar, or the junction point of the two bars. A size grip is shown in Figure 4.2.

What's This? Button (Windows 95)

The What's This? button is used to invoke the What's This? Windows 95 command to provide contextual help about objects displayed within a secondary window. When provided, it is located in the upper-right corner of the title bar, just to the left of the close button. It is inscribed with a question mark, as illustrated in Figure 4.4.

Figure 4.4   What's This? button (Microsoft Windows 95).

On a primary window this command is accessed from the Help drop-down menu. This command may also be included as a button on a toolbar or as a command on a pop-up menu for a specific object. This command is described more fully in the "Guidance and Assistance" section of Step 11.

WINDOW PRESENTATION STYLES

The presentation style of a window refers to its spatial relationship to other windows. There are two basic styles, usually called tiled or overlapping. Most systems use one or the other style exclusively, seldom using both at the same time. Often the user is permitted to select the style to be presented on the display.

Tiled Windows

Tiled windows, illustrated in Figure 4.5, derive their name from the common floor or wall tile. Tiled windows appear in one plane on the screen and expand or contract to fill up the display surface. Most systems provide two-dimensional tiled windows, adjustable in both height and width. Some less powerful systems, however, are only one-dimensional, the windows being adjustable in only one manner (typically the height). Tiled windows, the first and oldest kind of window, are felt to have these advantages:

- The system usually allocates and positions windows for the user, eliminating the necessity to make positioning decisions.
- Open windows are always visible, eliminating the possibility of them being lost and forgotten.
- Every window is always completely visible, eliminating the possibility of information being hidden.

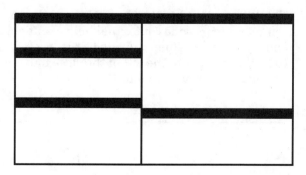

Figure 4.5   Tiled windows.

- They are perceived as less complex than overlapping windows, possibly because there are fewer management operations or they seem less "magical."
- They are easier for novice or inexperienced people to learn and use (Bly & Rosenberg, 1986).
- They yield better user performance for tasks where the data requires little window manipulation to complete the task (Bly & Rosenberg, 1986).

Perceived disadvantages include the following:

- Only a limited number can be displayed in the screen area available.
- As windows are opened or closed, existing windows change in size. This can be annoying.
- As windows change in size or position, the movement can be disconcerting.
- As the number of displayed windows increases, each window can get very tiny.
- The changes in sizes and locations made by the system are difficult to predict.
- The configuration of windows provided by the system may not meet the user's needs.
- They are perceived as crowded and more visually complex because window borders are flush against one another and they fill up the whole screen. Crowding is accentuated if borders contain scroll bars and/or control icons. Viewer attention may be drawn to the border, not the data.
- They permit less user control because the system actively manages the windows.

Overlapping Windows

Overlapping windows, illustrated in Figure 4.6, may be placed on top of one another like papers on a desk. They possess a three-dimensional quality, appearing to lie on different planes. Users can control the location of these windows, as well as the plane in which they appear. The sizes of some types of windows may also be changed. Most systems normally use this style of window. They have the following advantages:

- Visually, their look is three-dimensional, resembling the desktop that is familiar to the person.
- Greater control allows the user to organize the window to meet his or her needs.
- Windows can maintain larger sizes.

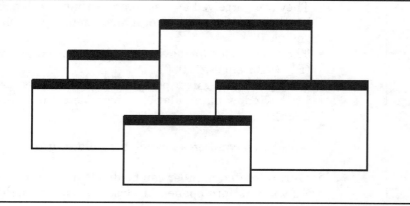

Figure 4.6   Overlapping windows.

- Windows can maintain consistent sizes.
- Windows can maintain consistent positions.
- Screen space conservation is not a problem, as windows can be placed on top of one another.
- There is less pressure to close or delete windows no longer needed.
- The possibility exists for less visual crowding and complexity. Larger borders can be maintained around window information, and the window is more clearly set off against its background. Windows can also be expanded to fill the entire display.
- They yield better user performance for tasks where the data requires much window manipulation to complete the task (Bly & Rosenberg, 1986).

Disadvantages include the following:

- They are operationally more complex than tiled windows. More control functions require greater user attention and manipulation.
- Information in windows can be obscured behind other windows.
- Windows themselves can be lost behind other windows and be presumed not to exist (Microsoft, 1995).
- That overlapping windows represent a three-dimensional space is not always realized (Microsoft, 1995).
- Control freedom increases the possibility for greater visual complexity and crowding. Too many windows, or improper set-off, can be visually overwhelming.

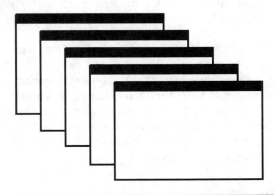

Figure 4.7   Cascading windows.

Cascading Windows

A special type of overlapping window has the windows automatically arranged in a regular progression. Each window is slightly offset from others, as illustrated in Figure 4.7. Advantages of this approach include the following:

- No window is ever completely hidden.
- Bringing any window to the front is easier.
- Simplicity in visual presentation and cleanness.

Picking a Presentation Style

- Use tiled windows for:
  - Single-task activities.
  - Tasks requiring little window manipulation.
  - Novice or inexperienced users.
- Use overlapping windows for:
  - Switching between tasks.
  - Tasks necessitating a greater amount of window manipulation.
  - Expert or experienced users.
  - Nonpredictable display contents.

Use of Tiled Windows Tiled windows seem to be better for single-task activities. Bly & Rosenberg (1986) found that tasks requiring little window manipulation can be carried out faster using tiled windows. They also found that novice users performed better with tiled windows, regardless of the task.

Use of Overlapping Windows Overlapping windows seem to be better for situations that necessitate switching between tasks. Bly and Rosenberg concluded that tasks requiring much window manipulation could be performed faster with overlapping windows but only if user window expertise existed. For novice users, tasks requiring much window manipulation were found to be carried out faster with tiled windows. Therefore, the advantage to overlapping windows comes only after a certain level of expertise is achieved.

TYPES OF WINDOWS

People's tasks must be structured into a series of windows. The type of window used will depend on the nature and flow of the task. Defining standard window types is difficult because of the varying terminology and definitions used by different windowing systems, or changes in terminology for new versions of systems. In general, however, the different types exhibit the following characteristics. Summarized are a description of the window, its purpose, and its proper usage. Any single system's windows may not behave exactly as presented, and some windows may exhibit characteristics common to more than one of those described window types.

Primary or Application Window

This type of window is the first that appears on a screen when an activity or action is started. It is required for every function or application, possessing a menu bar and some basic action controls (Windows 3.1—system menu button, sizing buttons; Windows 95—title bar icon, sizing buttons, close button). It should present the framework for the functions commands and data, and provide top-level context for dependent windows. It is variously referred to as the *primary* window (IBM's SAA CUA, Microsoft Windows 95), *application* window (Microsoft Windows 3.1), or the *main* window. It may also be referred to as the *parent* window if one or more *child* windows exist. A Microsoft Windows 3.1 application window is shown in Figure 4.8, and a Windows 95 primary window is shown in Figure 4.9.

- Should represent an independent function or application.
- Use to present constantly used window components and controls.
  - Menu bar items that are:
    - Used frequently.
    - Used by most, or all, primary or secondary windows.
  - Controls used by dependent windows.

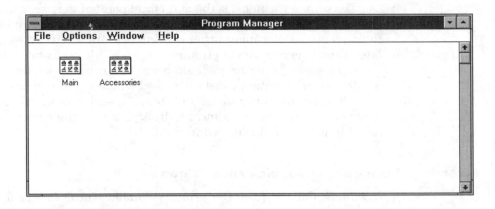

Figure 4.8   Microsoft Windows 3.1 application window.

- Use for presenting information that is continually updated.
  - For example, date and time.
- Use for providing context for dependent windows to be created.
- Do not:
  - Divide an independent function into two or more primary windows.
  - Present non-related functions in one primary window.

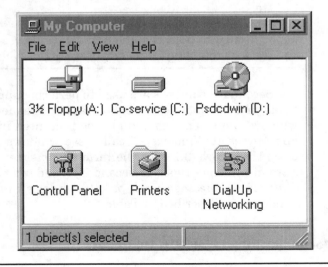

Figure 4.9   Windows 95 primary window.

The primary window is the main focal point of the user's activities and should represent an independent function. Avoid dividing an independent function into two or more primary windows, and avoid presenting nonrelated functions in a single primary window. This tends to confuse people.

Independent functions should begin in a primary window. A primary window should contain constantly used window components such as frequently used menu bar items and controls, such as control bars, used by dependent windows. Also include in a primary window continually updated information like date and time.

Secondary, Document, or Supplemental Window

A window derived from the primary window, these "offspring" windows often contain the actual data being processed. They are typically associated with a single data object, and appear on top of the active window when requested. They are sizable, movable, and scrollable. They structurally resemble a primary window, possessing some of the same action controls (Windows 3.1—system menu button and sizing buttons; Windows 95—close button and possibly a What's This? button), but they use the primary window's menu bar. Most systems permit the use of multiple secondary windows to complete a task. A Microsoft Windows 3.1 document window is shown in Figure 4.10, and a Windows 95 secondary window is shown in Figure 4.11.

- Use for performing subordinate, supplemental, or ancillary actions that are:
  - Extended or more complex in nature.
  - Related to objects in the primary window.
- Use for presenting frequently or occasionally used window components.

Secondary windows are used to perform supplemental or subordinate tasks, or tasks more extended in nature. Frequently or occasionally used window components should also be presented in them. IBM's SAA CUA and Microsoft Windows 95 call these windows *secondary* windows, Microsoft Windows 3.1 uses the term *document* window. Windows 95 consists of multiple types of secondary windows called *property windows, dialog boxes, message boxes, palette windows,* and *pop-up* windows. These windows are described in Table 4.2.

Multiple Document Interface(MDI) Windows

Microsoft Windows 3.1 and Windows 95 provide *multiple document interface* or MDI windows. These may be used when multiple views of an ob-

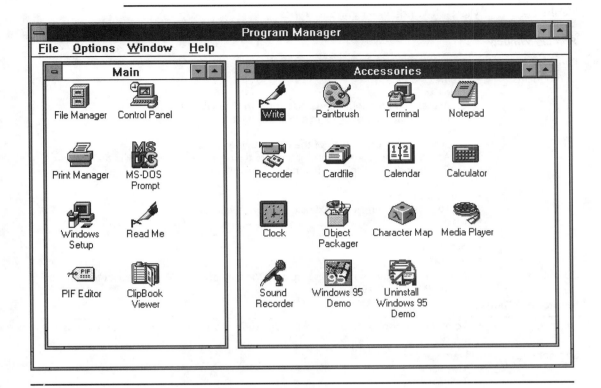

Figure 4.10 Microsoft Windows 3.1 document windows with primary window.

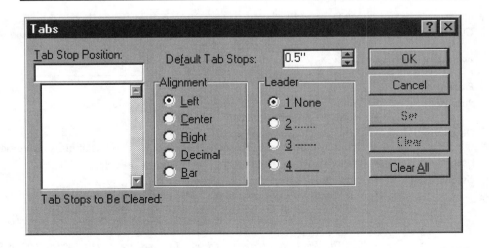

Figure 4.11 Windows 95 secondary window.

Table 4.2   Microsoft Windows 95 Window Types

Primary Window

Purpose:	• To perform a major interaction.
Components:	• Frame or Border
	• Title Bar
	– Access point for commands that apply to the window.
	– Commands are displayed in a pop-up menu.
	• Title Bar Icon
	– Small version of the icon of the object being viewed.
	– Access point for commands that apply to the object being displayed in the window.
	– Commands are displayed in a pop-up menu.
	• Title Bar Text
	• Title Bar Buttons
	– To Close / minimize / maximize / restore a window.
	• Menu Bar
	• Status Bar
	• Scroll Bar
	• Size Grip
Guidelines:	• See "Primary Windows" in this step and *The Windows Interface Guidelines for Software Design* (Microsoft, 1995).

Secondary Windows

Purpose:	• To obtain or display supplemental information related to the objects in the primary window.
Components:	• Frame or Border
	• Title Bar
	• Title Bar Text
	• Close Button
	• What's This? Button
	– Displays context-sensitive help about components displayed in the window.
	– Optional.
Kinds:	• Modal and Modeless.
Guidelines:	• See "Secondary Windows" in this step and *The Windows Interface Guidelines for Software Design* (Microsoft, 1995).

PROPERTY WINDOWS

Property Sheets

Purpose:	• To display the accessible properties of an object.
	• Viewable, but not necessarily editable.
Description:	• A modeless secondary window.
	• Typically modal with respect to the object for which it displays properties.
Usage:	• Displayed when the Properties command for an object is selected.
Guidelines:	• Title: object name plus "properties."
	• If properties must be categorized and grouped as sets in the property window:
	– For peer-related property sets—use tabbed pages.
	– If contextually or hierarchically related—use drop-down list to switch between tabbed pages.
	• See *The Windows Interface Guidelines for Software Design* (Microsoft, 1995).

Table 4.2 *(Continued)*

Property Inspector

Purpose:
- To display the most common or frequently accessed properties of a current selection, usually of a particular type of object.

Description:
- A modeless secondary window.
- Typically modal with respect to the object for which it displays properties.

Usage:
- Displayed when requested from selected object.

Guidelines:
- Title: object name plus "properties."
- Apply change immediately when made in window.
- See *The Windows Interface Guidelines for Software Design* (Microsoft, 1995).

DIALOG BOXES

Purpose:
- To obtain additional information needed to carry out a particular command or task.

Description:
- Secondary window.
- Contains the following common dialog box interfaces:
  - Open / Replace / Find.
  - Save As / Print / Print Setup
  - Page Setup / Font / Color

Guidelines:
- See "Dialog Boxes" in this step and *The Windows Interface Guidelines for Software Design* (Microsoft, 1995).

MESSAGE BOXES

Purpose:
- To provide information about a particular situation or condition.

Description:
- Secondary window.
- Types of message boxes:
  - Information / Warning / Critical

Guidelines:
- See "Messages" in Step 11 and *The Windows Interface Guidelines for Software Design* (Microsoft, 1995).

PALETTE WINDOWS

Purpose:
- To present a set of controls such as palettes or toolbars.

Description:
- Modeless secondary window.

Guidelines:
- See "Toolbars and Palettes" in Step 7 and *The Windows Interface Guidelines for Software Design* (Microsoft, 1995).

POP-UP WINDOWS

Purpose:
- To display additional information when an abbreviated form of the information is the main presentation.

Description:
- Secondary window.
- Does not contain standard secondary window components such as title bar and close button.
- Example: tooltip.

Guidelines:
- See "Tooltips" in Step 7 and *The Windows Interface Guidelines for Software Design* (Microsoft, 1995).

Table 4.3 Microsoft Windows 95 Window Organization Schemes

Single Document Interface

Description:	• A single primary window with a set of secondary windows.
Advantages:	• Most common usage • Window manipulation easier and less confusing • Data-centered approach
Disadvantage:	• Information is displayed or edited in separate windows.
Proper Usage:	• Where object and window have a simple, one-to-one relationship. • Where the object's primary presentation or use is as a single unit. • Alternative views can be supported with a control that allows the view to be changed. • Simultaneous views can be supported by splitting the window into panes.
Guidelines:	• See *The Windows Interface Guidelines for Software Design* (Microsoft, 1995).

Multiple Document Interface

Description:	• A technique for managing a set of windows where documents are opened into windows.
	• Contains:
	  – A single primary window, called the parent.
	  – A set of related document or child windows, each also essentially being a primary window.
	• Each child window constrained to appear only within the parent window.
	• The parent window's operational elements are shared by the child windows.
	• The parent window's elements can be dynamically changed to reflect the requirements of the active child window.

Advantages:	• Useful for managing a set of objects. • Provide a grouping and focus for a set of activities within the larger environment of the desktop.
Disadvantages:	• Reinforces an application as the primary focus. • Containment for secondary windows within child windows does not exist, obscuring window relationships and possibly creating confusion. • Because the parent window does not actually contain objects, context cannot always be maintained on closing and opening • Confining child windows to parent window may be inconvenient or inappropriate.
Proper Usage:	• To present multiple views of the same objects. • To present views of multiple objects. • Best suited for viewing homogeneous object types. • To clearly segregate the objects and their windows used in a task.
Guidelines:	• See *The Windows Interface Guidelines for Software Design* (Microsoft, 1995).

Workspaces

Description:	• A window or task management technique that consists of a container holding a set of objects. • Based upon the metaphor of a work area, such as a table or desktop. • The workspace (parent window) is an object. • The windows displayed within the workspace (child windows) are objects also residing in the workspace. • Otherwise, the characteristics and behavior are similar to the multiple document interface.
Advantages:	• Provides a grouping and focus for a set of activities within the larger environment of the desktop.

Table 4.3 *(Continued)*

	• Provides greater simplicity of single document window interface. • Preserves some management capabilities of multiple document interface.
Proper Usage:	• To present multiple views of the same objects. • To present views of multiple objects. • To manage a set of contained objects. • To clearly segregate the objects and their windows used in a task.
Guidelines:	• See *The Windows Interface Guidelines for Software Design,* (Microsoft, 1995).

Workbooks

Description:	• A window or task management technique that consists of a set of views organized like a tabbed notebook. • It is based upon the metaphor of a book or notebook. • Views of objects are presented as sections within the workbook's primary windows; child windows do not exist. • Each section represents a view of data. • Tabs can be included and used to navigate between sections. • Otherwise, its characteristics and behavior are similar to the multiple document interface with all child windows maximized.
Advantages:	• Provides a grouping and focus for a set of activities within the larger environment of the desktop. • Greater simplicity of the single document window interface. • Greater simplicity by eliminating child window management. • Preserves some management capabilities of multiple document interface.
Proper Usage:	• To manage a set of views of an object. • To optimize quick navigation of multiple views.
Guidelines:	• See *The Windows Interface Guidelines for Software Design* (Microsoft, 1995).

Projects

Description:	• A window or task management technique that consists of a container holding a set of objects, and their windows, but visual containment of the windows is not necessary. • The icons contained within it can be opened into windows that are peer with the parent window. • Each child window can have its own entry on the task bar. • When a project window is closed, all the child windows of objects also close. • When the project window is opened, the child windows of the contained objects are restored to their former positions. • Child windows of a project may be restored without the project window itself being restored. • Child windows of objects stored in a project do not share the operational elements of other project windows and must include their own elements.
Advantages:	• Provides a grouping and focus for a set of activities within the larger environment of the desktop. • Greater simplicity of single document window interface. • Preserves some management capabilities of the multiple document interface. • Greatest flexibility in placement and arrangement of windows.
Disadvantage:	• Increased complexity due to difficulty in differentiating child windows of the project from windows of other applications.
Proper Usage:	• To manage a set of objects that do not necessarily need to be contained. • When child windows are not to be constrained.
Guidelines:	• See *The Windows Interface Guidelines for Software Design* (Microsoft, 1995).

ject, or multiple documents, must be looked at simultaneously. Contrasting with the MDI is the *single document interface*, or SDI. Both interface styles for Windows 95 are described more fully in Table 4.3 on Windows 95 window organization schemes.

An MDI interface consists of easily moved between multiple document windows. These windows may be referred to by a name that describes their contents, such as "Main" in Windows Program Manager. When minimized, they are displayed at the bottom of the application window in iconic form. They are also sizable, movable, and scrollable. MDI windows use the application or primary window's menu bar. The application or primary window menu bar content may change dynamically, depending on the MDI window with the focus.

- Use to present multiple occurrences of an object.
- Use to compare data within two or more windows.
- Use to present multiple parts of an application.

The purpose of this scheme of windows is to provide multiple views of the same object, to permit comparisons among related objects, and to present multiple parts of an application.

Dialog Boxes

Dialog boxes are used to extend and complete an interaction within a limited context. Dialog boxes are always displayed from another window, either primary or secondary, or another dialog box. They may appear as a result of a command button being activated, a menu choice being selected, or they may be presented automatically by the system when a condition exists requiring user attention or additional input. They may possess some basic action controls (Windows 3.1—system menu button; Windows 95—close button and possibly a What's This? button), but do not have a menu bar. A Microsoft Windows 3.1 dialog box is illustrated in Figure 4.12.

Most windowing systems provide standard dialog boxes for common functions, some examples being Open, Save As, and Print. Many platforms also recommend a set of standard command buttons for use in the various kinds of dialog boxes, such as OK, Cancel, and so on. Dialog boxes are of two kinds, modal and modeless.

- Use for presenting brief messages.
- Use for requesting specific, transient actions.
- Use for performing actions that:
  - Take a short time to complete.
  - Are not frequently changed.

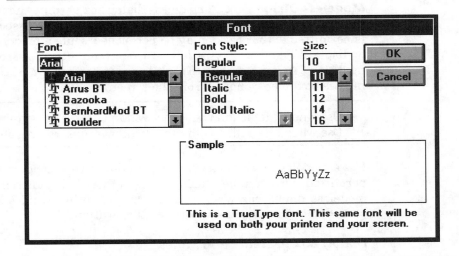

Figure 4.12   Microsoft Windows 3.1 dialog box.

Dialog boxes are used for presenting brief amounts of information or to request specific transient actions. Dialog box actions will usually be those that do not occur frequently.

Modal Dialog Boxes Most dialog boxes will be modal. A modal dialog box will not permit interaction with another window until the current dialog is completed. It remains displayed until the appropriate action is taken, after which it is removed from the screen.

- Use when interaction with any other window must not be permitted.
- Use for:
  - Presenting information.
    - For example, messages (sometimes called a message box)
  - Receiving user input.
    - For example, data or information (sometimes called a prompt box).
  - Asking questions.
    - For example, data, information, or directions (sometimes called a question box).
- Use carefully because it constrains what the user can do.

Modal dialog boxes typically request critical information or actions that must be reacted to before the dialog can continue. Since modal dialog boxes constrain what the user can do, they should be used carefully.

Modeless Dialog Box A modeless dialog box permits the user to engage in parallel dialogs. Switching between the box and its associated window is permitted. Other tasks may be performed while a modeless dialog box is displayed, and it may be left on the screen after a response has been made to it. Actions leading to a modeless dialog box can be canceled, causing the box to be removed from the screen.

- Use when interaction with other windows must be permitted.
- Use when interaction with other windows must be repeated.

Use a modeless dialog box when interaction with another window must be permitted; for example, during access of the help function. Also, use a modeless dialog box when interaction with other windows must be repeated; for example, in a word search operation.

Dialog Box Presentation Styles

Cascading

  Purpose
- To provide advanced options at a lower level in a complex dialog.

  Guidelines
- Provide a command button leading to the next dialog box with a "To a Window" indicator, an ellipsis (. . .).
- Present the additional dialog box in cascaded form.
- Provide no more than two cascades in a given path.
- Do not cover previous critical information.
  - Title Bar.
  - Relevant displayed information.

Expanding

  Purpose
- To provide advanced options at the same level in a complex dialog.

  Guidelines
- Provide a command button with an expanding dialog symbol (>>).
- Expand to right or downward.

Multiple dialog boxes needed to complete a task may be presented in two forms, *cascading* or *expanding*. A cascade, illustrated in Figures 4.13 and 4.14, is generally used when advanced options at a lower level in a complex dialog must be presented. An indication that the dialog will be cas-

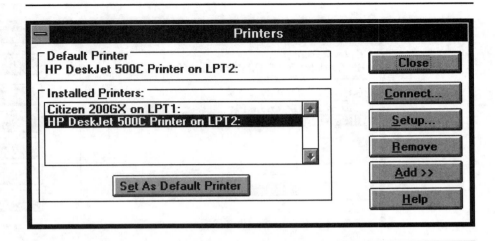

Figure 4.13   Printers dialog box with *Connect...* cascade button.

cading is signaled by an ellipsis placed in the command button used to display the additional dialog box. Because of the confusions that can develop with too many cascades, restrict the number of cascades to no more than two in a given path. Do not cover information on the upper-level dialog boxes that may have to be referred to, such as box title bars and other critical or relevant information.

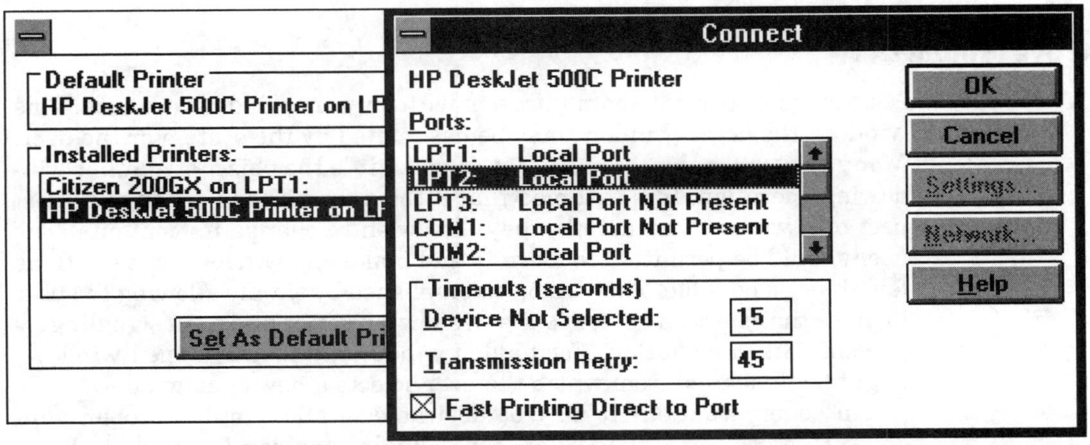

Figure 4.14   Cascading Connect dialog box.

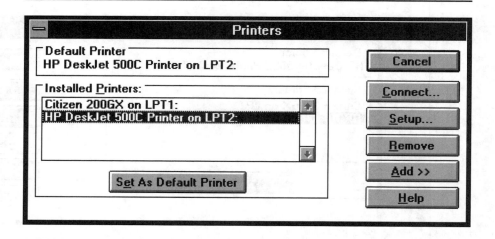

Figure 4.15   Printers dialog box with *Add* >> expanding button.

Expanding dialog boxes are generally used to provide advanced options at the same level in a complex dialog. An expansion box is illustrated in Figures 4.15 and 4.16. An indication that the dialog will be expanding is signaled by a double arrow (>>) placed in the command button used to display the additional dialog box. Expand the box to right, preferably, or downward if screen space constraints exist. IBM's SAA CUA does not recommend using expanding dialog boxes. Their suggestion: use a *notebook* control instead.

Active Window

Most systems permit communication with only one window at a time. This window, the *active* window, may be designated by the system or the user. Many systems make a window active when it is the object of another windowing operation. It is assumed that if the user wishes to change one aspect of a window's structure, they also wish to change its contents. The user should be permitted to move to and make any window active with as few steps as possible. This can be accomplished by simply allowing the user to move the selection cursor to the window's interior and then signaling by pressing a key or button. For hidden windows, a menu of open windows might be presented from which the user selects a new open window.

In some situations it may be desirable to allow multiple open windows. Hendrickson (1989) compared a single open window with multiple open windows in performing queries and found multiple open windows were related by people as more "natural." Performance was slower with

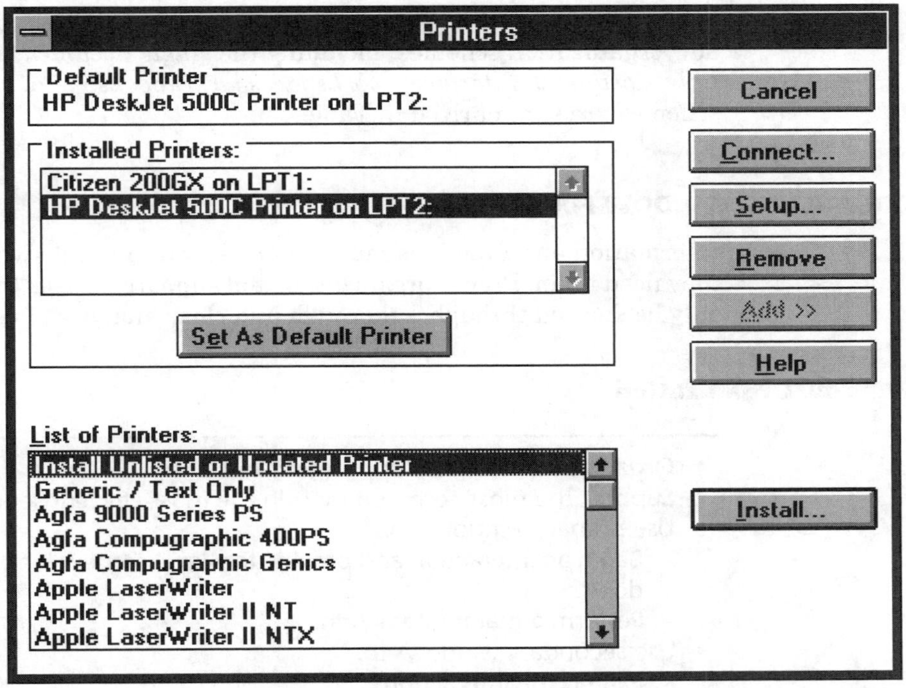

Figure 4.16   Expanded Printers dialog box.

multiple open windows, however. He concludes that if user acceptance is important, multiple open windows may be the better alternative. If speed of task handling is critical, a single active window is more desirable.

Visually differentiate the active window from other windows. It is important that the user be able to quickly identify the active window. Methods to do this include a contrasting window title bar, border, or background color. An "active" indicator in the window border, which is turned on or off, may also be used. A combination of two or more of these visual cues may also be used. The visual cue selected should be of moderate intensity, not too powerful or too subtle. Powerful cues will be distracting; subtle cues will be easily overlooked.

Microsoft Windows 95 Windows and Window Organization Schemes

Windows 95 consists of primary windows, multiple types of secondary windows called *property windows, dialog boxes, message boxes, palette windows,* and *pop-up* windows. The characteristics of these windows are briefly summarized in Table 4.2. Windows 95 also provides several window organization schemes, including the *single document interface, multiple document interface, workspaces, workbooks,* and *projects*. These schemes are summarized in Table 4.3.

ORGANIZING WINDOW FUNCTIONS

Information and functions must be presented to people when and where they need them. Proper organization and support of tasks by windows will only be derived through a thorough and clear analysis of user tasks.

Window Organization

- Organize windows to support user tasks.
- Support the most common tasks in the most efficient sequence of steps.
- Use primary windows to:
  - Begin an interaction and provide top-level context for dependent windows.
  - Perform a major interaction.
- Use secondary windows to:
  - Extend the interaction.
  - Obtain or display supplemental information related to the primary window.
- Use dialog boxes for:
  - Infrequently used or needed information.
  - "Nice-to-know" information.

People most often think in terms of tasks, not functions or applications. Windows must be organized to support this thinking. The design goal is to support the most common user tasks in the most efficient manner or fewest steps. Less frequently performed tasks are candidates for less efficiency or more steps.

Mayhew (1992) suggests that poor functional organization usually occurs because of one of, or a combination of, these factors:

- Emphasis on technical ease of implementation, rather than proper analysis of user tasks.
- Focus on applications, features, functions, or data types instead of tasks.
- Organization of the design team into applications, with little cross-team communication.

- Blindly mimicking the manual world and carrying over manual inefficiencies into the computer system.

Emphasis on implementation ease puts the needs of the designer before the needs of the customer. Focusing on tasks conforms to the model of how people think. Application orientation imposes an unnatural boundary between functions, and lack of cross-team communication seldom yields consistent task procedures. Mimicking "what is" will never permit the capabilities of the computer system to be properly exploited.

The recommended usages for the various window types are summarized in the above guidelines. These recommendations were discussed more fully earlier in this chapter.

Number of Windows

- Minimize the number of windows needed to accomplish an objective.

A person does not work with windows simply for the joy of working with windows. Windows are a means to an end, a method of accomplishing something. Multiple windows on a display, as discussed elsewhere in this text, can be confusing (Microsoft, 1995), can increase the load on the human visual system (Mori & Hayashi, 1993), or may be too small to effectively present what needs to be contained within them.

Guidelines that appeared in early stages of window evolution concerning the maximum number of windows that a person could deal with were quite generous, a limit of seven or eight being suggested. As experience with windows has increased, these numbers have gradually fallen. One study (Gaylin, 1986) found the mean number of windows maintained for experienced users was 3.7. Today, based on expressions of window users, a recommendation of no more than two or three at one time seems most realistic. The guidelines on limitations for items like cascades (1–2) reflect today's feelings. The exact number of windows a person can effectively deal with at one time will ultimately depend on both the capabilities of the user and the characteristics of the task. Some users and situations may permit handling of more than three windows; for other users and situations, three windows may be two too many.

The general rule: Minimize the number of windows to accomplish an objective. Use a single window whenever it is possible to do so. Consider, however, the user's task. Don't clutter up a single window with rarely used information when it can be placed on a second, and infrequently used, window.

Sizing Windows

- Provide large-enough windows to:
  - Present all relevant and expected information for the task.
  - Avoid hiding important information.
  - Avoid crowding or visual confusion.
  - Minimize the need for scrolling.
    - But less than the full size of the entire screen.
- If a window is too large, determine:
  - Is all the information needed?
  - Is all the information related?
- Otherwise, make the window as small as possible.
  - Optimum window sizes:
  - For text, about 12 lines.
  - For alphanumeric information, about 7 lines.

Larger windows seem to have these advantages:

- They permit display of more information.
- They facilitate learning: Data relationships and groupings are more obvious.
- Less window manipulation requirements exist.
- Breadth is preferred to depth (based on menu research).
- More efficient data validation and data correction can be performed.

Disadvantages include:

- Longer pointer movements are required.
- Windows are more crowded.
- More visual scanning is required.
- Parts are more easily obscured by other windows.
- It is not as easy to hide inappropriate data.

Always provide large enough windows to present all the relevant and expected information for the task. Never hide important or critical information, and minimize the need for scrolling. Very small windows with a significant amount of scrolling appears to increase decision-making time (Hendrickson, 1989) and scrolling is also a cumbersome operation. To avoid scrolling, consider expanding dialog boxes, cascading windows, or a notebook control. Avoid, however, making a window's default size the full size of the display. This prevents any underlying windows from being fully hidden from the user's view. The option to maximize primary and secondary windows always exists.

If, through analysis and design, a window appears to be too large, determine:

- Is all the information needed?
- Is all the information related?

Important, critical, or frequently used information must be maintained on a screen, but perhaps information exists that is needed or used infrequently, such as only 10–20 percent of the time. This kind of information is a good candidate for placing on another window or dialog box. Perhaps information is included on a screen that is not related to the task being performed. This kind of information should be located with information to which it is related. As a last resort, consider shortening some window control captions or other included window text to achieve a proper fit.

At least two studies have looked at optimum window sizes. Procedural text in window sizes of 6, 12, and 24 lines were evaluated by Desaulniers & Gillan (1988). Fastest and most accurate completion occurred with the 12-line window. The retrieval of alphanumeric information was compared in 7-, 13-, and 19-line windows by Elkerton & Williges (1984). A 7-line window was found to be more than adequate.

Microsoft Windows 95 has provided some recommended secondary window sizes; these sizes are summarized in Table 4.4. Microsoft states that the recommended sizes keep windows from becoming too large to display at some resolutions and still provide a reasonable amount of layout space.

Table 4.4   Microsoft Windows 95 Recommended Window Sizes

Secondary Windows

- No larger than 263 × 263 dialog base units*

Property Sheets

- 252w × 218h dialog base units
- 227w × 215h dialog base units
- 212w × 188h dialog base units

*The system defines size and location of user-interface elements not in pixels but in *dialog base units* (DBUs), a device-independent unit of measure.

- One horizontal DBU is equal to one-fourth of the average character width for the current system font.
- One vertical DBU is equal to one-eighth of the average character height for the current system font.

WINDOW OPERATIONS

Guidelines for windows operations are still evolving. Because of the paucity of published research data, many of the guidelines are still more anecdotal and intuitive than scientific. Guidelines will continue to develop and change as our understanding of, and experiences with, the windows interface continue to increase. Today, the following operational guidelines seem appropriate.

General Guidelines

- Design easy to use and learn windowing operations.
  - Direct manipulation seems to be a faster and more intuitive interaction style than indirect manipulation for many windowing operations.
- Minimize the number of window operations necessary to achieve a desired effect.
- Make navigating between windows particularly easy and efficient to do.
- Make setting up windows particularly easy to remember.
- In overlapping systems, provide powerful commands for arranging windows on the screen in user-tailorable configurations.

Mayhew (1992), in a review of window system research (Bly & Rosenberg, 1986; Davies et al., 1985; Gaylin, 1986), presents the following guidelines.

Design easy to use and learn window operations. The complexity of a windowing system should not cancel out its potential advantages. Operations must be carefully designed to achieve simplicity. As Benest and Dukic (1989) have suggested, the ideal is that window manipulations should occur *implicitly* as a result of the user's task actions, not as a result of explicit, conscious, window management actions.

Minimize the number of window operations needed to achieve a desired effect. Establish the kinds of window operations that people are likely to want and minimize the number of operations that must be performed to attain these configurations.

Make navigating between windows easy and efficient. Gaylin (1986) found that navigation between windows was the most frequent manipulation activity performed. High-frequency operations should always be easy to do.

Make setting up windows easy to remember. Gaylin (1986) also found that window arrangement (opening, resizing, moving, etc.) was a less frequent activity. Low-frequency operations should always be easy to learn.

In overlapping systems, provide powerful commands for arranging windows in user-tailorable configurations. When an overlapping window system is used, provide easy operations to achieve desired windowing configurations. Specific configurations should be capable of being created, named, and recalled.

Opening a Window

- Provide an iconic representation or textual list of available windows.
  - If opening with an expansion of an icon, animate the icon expansion.
- When opening a window:
  - Position in the most forward plane of the screen.
  - Designate it as the active window.
  - Set it off against a neutral background.
- When a primary window is opened or restored, position it to the top.
  - Restore all secondary windows to the states that existed when the primary window was closed.
- When a dependent secondary window is opened, position it on top of its associated primary window.
  - Position a secondary window with peer windows on top of its peers.
    - Present layered or cascaded with any related peer secondary windows.
- When a dependent secondary window is activated, its primary window and related peer windows should also be positioned at the top.
- If more than one object is selected and opened, display each object in a separate window. Designate the last window selected as the active window.
- Display a window in the same state as when it was last accessed.
  - If the task, however, requires a particular sequence of windows, use a fixed or consistent presentation sequence.
- With tiled windows, provide an easy way to resize and move newly opened windows.

Typically, when windows are opened, they are designated as active and positioned in the most forward plane of the screen so that they can be used immediately. To focus attention on the newly opened window, display the screen background behind the window in a neutral or subdued manner. When opening windows from an iconic representation, gradually expand the window so that the movement is visible. This will aid association of the icon with the window in the mind of the viewer.

When a primary window is opened or restored, position it at the top. Restore all secondary windows to the states that existed when the primary window was closed. When a dependent secondary window is opened, position it on top of its associated primary window. If a secondary windows has peers, position it on top of its peers. Present layered or cascaded windows with any related peer secondary windows.

When a dependent secondary window is activated, its primary window and related peer windows should also be positioned at the top. If more than one object is selected and opened, display each object in a separate window. Designate the last window selected as the active window. Always display a window in the same state as when it was last accessed. If the task, however, requires a particular sequence of windows, use a fixed or consistent presentation sequence.

The first opened tiled window will consume the entire screen. Subsequent windows are usually positioned by defaults in the system. The system positioning of these subsequent windows may not always be consistent with the user's needs. The system should allow the user to change the default positions, or provide a way for the user to move and resize the system-provided windows easily.

Window Placement

Considerations

- In placing a window on the display, consider:
  - The use of the window.
  - The overall display dimensions.
  - The reason for the window's appearance.

General

- Position the window so it is entirely visible.
- If the window is being restored, place the window where it last appeared.
- If the window is new, and a location has not yet been established, place it:
  - At the point of the viewer's attention, usually the pointer or cursor.
  - In a position convenient to navigate onto.
  - So that it is not obscuring important or related underlying window information.
- For multiple windows, give each additional window its own unique and discernible location.
  - A cascading presentation is recommended.
- If none apply, then:
  - Horizontally center a secondary window within its primary window just below the title bar, menu bar, and any button bars.
- Do not let the user move a window to a position where it cannot be easily repositioned.

Dialog Boxes

- If the dialog box relates to the entire system, center it on screen.
- Keep key information on underlying screen visible.

- If one dialog box calls another, make the new one movable whenever possible.

In placing a window on the display, what must be considered is how the window is used in relation to other windows, the overall dimensions of the display, and the reason the window is being presented.

First, locate the window so it is fully visible. If the window is being restored, locate it where it last appeared. If the window is new and the location has not yet been established, place it at the point of the viewer's attention. This will usually be the pointer or cursor location. Also place the window in a position where it will be convenient to navigate onto, and where it will not obscure important underlying screen information. Preferred positions are essentially below and right. The suggested order of placement is below-right, below, right, top-right, below-left, top, left, top-left.

If none of these situations applies, horizontally center a secondary window within the primary window, just below the title bar, menu bar, and any button bars. Give each additional window its own unique location. A cascading presentation, from upper-left to lower-right is recommended. Do not let the user move a window to a position where it cannot be easily repositioned.

If a dialog box relates to the entire system, center it on display, keeping key information on an underlying window visible. If one dialog box calls another, make the new one movable whenever possible.

Window Separation

- Crisply, clearly, and pleasingly demarcate a window from the background of the screen on which it appears.
  - Provide a surrounding solid line border for the window.
  - Provide a window background that sets off well against the overall screen background.
  - Consider incorporating a drop shadow beneath the window.

Component separation is especially critical in a graphics environment because of the spatial layering that can occur. All windows must be clearly set off from the underlying screen or windows. The demarcation must be crisp and visually pleasing. A solid single-line border is recommended for this purpose. Also provide a window background that sets off well against the overall screen background. If color is used, exercise caution and choose compatible colors (See Step 9). Another alternative is to use for the window a lighter shade of the color used for the screen background. Changes in the density of shades are often more visually pleasing. To emphasize the three-dimensional aspects of graphic windows, incorporate a drop shadow beneath each window

Moving a Window

- Permit the user to change the position of all windows.
- Change pointer shape to indicate the move selection is successful.
- Move the entire window as the pointer moves.
  - If it is impossible to move the entire window, move the window outline while leaving the window displayed in its original position.
- Permit moving a window without making it active.

An indication that the move operation has been successfully selected, and that the move may begin, should be indicated to the user by changing the pointer's shape. This will provide the necessary feedback that it is safe to begin the move operation and avoid false starts. Ideally, the entire window should move along with the pointer. If the entire window cannot be moved, move the window outline while leaving the full window displayed on the screen. Displaying only the window's outline during the move operation, and not the window itself, may make it harder for the user to decide when the window has been repositioned correctly (Billingsley, 1988). It may sometimes be necessary for a window to be moved without being active. This should be possible.

Resizing a Window

- Permit the user to change the size of primary and secondary windows.
- Change the pointer shape to indicate that the resizing selection is successful.
- The simplest operation is to anchor the upper-left corner and resize from the lower-right corner.
  - Also permit resizing from any point on the window.
- Show the changing window as the pointer moves.
  - If it is impossible to show the entire window being resized, show the window outline while leaving the window displayed in its original position.
- When window size changes and content remains the same:
  - Change image size proportionally as window size changes.
- If resizing creates a window or image too small for easy use, do one of the following:
  - Clip (truncate) information arranged in some logical structure or layout when minimum size is attained, or

- Format (restructure) information when no layout considerations exist as size is reduced, or
- Remove less useful information (if it can be determined), or
- When minimum size is attained, replace information with a message that indicates the minimum size has been reached and that the window must be enlarged to continue working.

An indication that the resize operation has been successfully selected, and that the move may begin, should be indicated to the user by changing the pointer's shape. This will provide the necessary feedback that it is safe to begin the resizing and avoid false starts. The simplest operation for the user, conceptually, is always to resize from the lower-right corner and anchor the window in the upper-left corner. Resizing flexibility can be provided by permitting it to occur from any point on the border (the anchor is always opposite the pulling point), but conceptually this is more complex. Some people may have difficulty predicting which window sides or corners will be resized from specific pulling points.

Ideally, the entire window should move along with the pointer. If the entire window cannot be moved, move the window outline while leaving the full window displayed on the screen. Displaying only the window's outline during the move operation, and not the window itself, may make it harder for the user to decide when the window has been repositioned correctly.

The effect of a resizing operation on the window's contents usually depends on the application. In enlarging, more data may be displayed, a larger image may be created, or blank space may be added around the image. In reducing, less data may be displayed, the image made smaller, blank space eliminated, or the data may be reformatted.

If resizing creates a window or image too small for easy use, clip or truncate information arranged in some logical structure, format, or layout. When no layout considerations exist, such as for text, format or restructure the displayed information.

Also consider removing less useful information, if it can be determined. When the minimum size is attained, for any additional attempts to reduce window size, replace the information with a message that indicates the minimum size has been reached and that the window must be enlarged to continue working.

Window Shuffling

- Window shuffling must be easy to accomplish.

Window shuffling should be easy to perform in as few steps as possible. OPEN LOOK, for example, permits toggling the two most recent windows displayed. Microsoft Windows and Presentation Manager permit rapid window shuffling and swapping of the front window and the second or back window.

Keyboard Control/Mouseless Operation

- Window actions should be capable of being performed through the keyboard as well as with a mouse.
- Keyboard alternatives should be designated through use of mnemonic codes, as much as possible.
- Keyboard designations should be capable of being modified by the user.

All window actions should be capable of being performed using the keyboard as well as the mouse. This will provide a more efficient alternative for applications that contain tasks that are primarily keyboard-oriented, for users skilled in touch typing, and for any other situations in which frequent movement between keyboard and mouse may be required. The use of mnemonic codes to reflect window mouse actions will greatly aid user learning of the keyboard alternatives. To provide the user flexibility, all keyboard designations should be capable of being user modified.

Closing a Window

- Close a window when:
  - The user requests it to be closed.
  - The user performs the action required in the window.
  - The window has no further relevance.
- If a primary window is closed, also close all of its secondary windows.
- When a window is closed, save its current state, including size and position, for use when the window is opened again.

Close a window when the user requests it to be closed, the action required in the window is performed, or the window has no further relevance to the task being performed. If the closed window is a primary window, also close its associated secondary windows. When a window is closed, it is important that its current state, including size and position, be saved for use when the window is again opened.

S T E P 5

Develop System Menus

A system contains large amounts of information and performs a variety of functions. Regardless of its purpose, the system must provide some means to tell people about the information it possesses or the things it can do. This is accomplished by displaying listings of the choices or alternatives the user has at appropriate points while using the system, or creating a string of listings that lead a person from a series of general descriptors through increasingly specific categories on following listings until the lowest level listing is reached. This lowest level listing provides the desired choices. The common name for these kinds of listings are menus.

- Understand the principles of menu design.
- Establish kinds of menus needed to perform the tasks.
- Determine what system-provided default menu items are available and use them, if applicable.
- Determine what critical functions are not represented by the default items and add new menu items.
  - Add any new required menu items.
  - Design new commands as necessary.
- Design menus using established design guidelines.

Menus are effective because they utilize the more powerful human capability of recognition rather than the weaker recall. Working with menus reminds people of available options and information that they may not be aware of or have forgotten.

Menus are not without problems, however. New system users might find learning large systems difficult because information often must be remembered and integrated across a series of displays. If each menu is viewed in isolation, relationships between menus are also difficult to grasp. Words and phrases with multiple meanings may also be interpreted incorrectly because of the inability to see relationships. Ambiguities may be improperly resolved on the basis of incorrect assumptions about menu structure. The frequent result is that people make mistakes and get lost in the hierarchical structure.

Experienced system users, while finding menus helpful at first, may find them tedious as they learn the system. Continually having to step through a series of menus to achieve the desired objective can be time consuming and frustrating. Therefore, the design of menu systems must consider the conflicting needs of both inexperienced and experienced users.

Graphical systems are heavily menu-oriented. They are used to designate commands, properties that apply to an object, documents, and windows. When selected, a graphical menu item may lead to another menu, cause a window to be displayed, or directly cause an action to be performed. To accomplish these goals, a graphical system presents a variety of menu styles to choose from. Included are entities commonly called menu bars, and menus called pull-downs, pop-ups, cascades, tearoffs, and iconic. In this chapter graphical system menus will be addressed. The various styles will be described, their purpose presented, recommendations for their proper usage given, and relevant specific design guidelines summarized.

MENU DESIGN GUIDELINES

The human-computer interface has a rich history of experimental studies with menus, the results of which can and have been applied to graphical menu design and presentation. The following summary is mostly derived from Galitz (1992).

Display

- If continual or frequent reference to menu options are necessary, permanently display the menu in an area of the screen that will not obscure other screen data.
- If only occasional references to menu options are necessary, the menu may be presented on demand.
  - Critical options should be continuously displayed, however.

Whether to display a menu continually, or on demand, is determined by the menu's frequency of use. Always permanently display menus that are frequently referenced. This will provide memory support and immediate access to what is needed most. Occasionally needed menus may be presented on request via pop-ups or pull-downs. Critical options should always be continuously displayed. Wright, Lickorish, & Milroy (1994) found superior performance for permanently displayed menus as opposed to menus which had to be retrieved through mouse clicks. They speculate that because retrieving a menu for display requires more actions, this may also impair people's memory for other tasks being performed.

Organization

- Provide a general or main menu.
- Display:
  - All relevant alternatives.
  - Only relevant alternatives.
    - Delete or gray-out inactive choices.
- Match the menu structure to the structure of the task.
  - Organization should reflect the most efficient sequence of steps to accomplish a person's most frequent or most likely goals.
- Minimize number of levels within limits of clarity.
  - Without logical groupings of elements, limit choices to four to eight.
  - With logical groupings, nine or more choices may be displayed.
- Provide decreasing direction menus, if sensible.
- Provide users an easy way to restructure a menu according to how work is accomplished

In organizing a menu, the goal is to simply and effectively reveal its structure while also reducing the number of actions needed to locate the target item.

General Menu The top-level menu in a hierarchical menu scheme should be a general or main menu consisting of basic system options. This will provide a consistent starting point for all system activities and a "home-base" to which the user may always return.

Relevant Alternatives A menu should provide all relevant alternatives, and only relevant alternatives, at the point at which it is displayed. Including nonrelevant choices on a menu screen increases learning requirements and has been found to interfere with performance. There are two exceptions to this rule, however. Alternatives that are conditionally nonactive may be displayed along with the conditionally active choices, if the active choices can be visually highlighted in some manner (such as through high intensity or reverse video), or the inactive choices can be visually subdued (perhaps as through graying out). One study (Francik & Kane, 1987), however, found that completely eliminating nonactive alternatives on a menu resulted in faster choice access time, when compared to leaving nonactive alternatives on a menu but displayed in a subdued manner. This study concludes that eliminating conditionally nonactive choices from a menu appears to be the best approach. Mayhew (1992) suggests that while deletion does provide an advantage to expert users of keyboard-driven menus, graying out seems to be advantageous to novices in systems using pointer-driven selection devices. She concludes that since menus are geared toward novices, graying appears to be the best overall choice. In general, today's graphical systems follow the gray-out approach for inactive menu choices. Whatever method is chosen should be consistently followed throughout a system.

Options to be implemented in the future may also be displayed if they can be visually marked in some way (through a display technique or some other annotation).

Matching Menu Structure to the Tasks Menus should be organized according to how people structure their tasks. They should reflect the most efficient sequence of steps to accomplish a person's most frequent or likely goals.

Minimizing Number of Levels The issue that must be addressed in creating a multilevel menu structure is determining how many items will be placed on one menu (its breadth) and how many levels it will consume (its depth). In general, the more choices contained on a menu (greater breadth), the less will be its depth; the fewer choices on a menu (less breadth), the greater will be its depth.

The advantages of a menu system with greater breadth and less depth are:

- Fewer steps and shorter time to reach one's objective.
- Fewer opportunities to wander down wrong paths.
- Easier learning by allowing the user to see relationships of menu items.

A broad menu's disadvantages are:

- A more crowded menu that may reduce the clarity of the wording of choices.
- Increased likelihood of confusing similar choices because they are seen together.

The advantages of greater depth are:

- Less crowding on the menu.
- Fewer choices to be scanned.
- Easier hiding of inappropriate choices.
- Less likelihood of confusing similar choices since there is less likelihood that they will be seen together.

Greater depth disadvantages are:

- More steps and longer time to reach one's objective.
- More difficulties in learning since relationships between elements cannot always be seen.
- More difficulties in predicting what lies below, resulting in increased likelihood of going down wrong paths or getting lost.
- Higher error rates.

A good number of studies have looked at the breadth-depth issue in recent years. Some have concluded that breadth is preferable to depth in terms of either greater speed or fewer errors (Landauer & Nachbar, 1985; Tullis, 1985; Wallace, 1987), that a low number of levels (two to three) and an intermediate number of choices (four to eight) results in faster, more accurate performance as opposed to fewer or greater numbers of levels and choices (Miller, 1981; Kiger, 1984), and that four to eight choices per menu screen is best (Lee & MacGregor, 1985). Another study found that one level was easiest to learn (Dray, Ogden & Vestewig, 1981), and a couple of studies have concluded that a menu could contain up to 64 items if it were organized into logical groups (Paap & Roske-Hofstrand, 1986; Snowberry, Parkinson, & Sisson, 1983). The least desirable alternative in almost all cases was deep-level menus that simply presented the user with a binary choice (select one of two alternatives) on each menu.

The conclusion that one might derive from these studies is this: Fewer levels of menus aid the decision-making process, but trying to put too many choices on a single menu also has a negative impact. The final solution is a compromise: Minimize the number of levels within limits of clarity. What is clarity? The studies seem to indicate that if the choices to be displayed cannot be segmented into logical categories, then confine the number of alternatives displayed to four to eight per menu. If logical categorization is possible, and meaningful, logical category names can be established, then a larger number of choices can be presented. The maximum number of alternatives will, however, be dependent upon the size of the words needed to describe the alternatives to the user. Wordy captions will greatly restrict the number of alternatives capable of being displayed. There is one exception to these basic principles. Large linearly ordered, well-learned listings, such as months of the year, or numbers, would be better presented in a one-level menu, rather than breaking them into multiple levels.

Mayhew (1992) suggests that if the menu choices are complex and/or there are no groupings of items, choices presented should be restricted to *10 or fewer*. This recommendation is similar to the eight or fewer recommendations above. If the menu choices are not complex, items on the menu can be grouped, and the users are infrequent or casual, she recommends *20 or fewer* choices. If the menu choices are not complex, items on the menu can be grouped, and the users are frequent or expert, she suggests *21 or more* choices can be provided.

Provide Decreasing Direction Menus In addition to breadth and depth, direction has been found to impact menu choice selection performance. In a multilevel menu, a *decreasing* direction structure presents successively fewer choices as each lower level is traversed. An *increasing* direction structure presents successively more choices as each lower level is traversed. Bishu & Zhan (1992) in a study of 16 and 32 item iconic menus found that decreasing direction menus were significantly faster and more accurate than increasing menus.

Easy to Restructure Menus Menus should be capable of being restructured by a user. Not everyone works the same way.

Groupings

- Create hierarchical groupings of items that are logical, distinctive, meaningful, and mutually exclusive.
- Categorize in such a way as to:
  - Maximize the similarity of items within a category.
  - Minimize the similarity of items across categories.
- If meaningful categories cannot be developed and more than eight options must be displayed on a screen, create arbitrary visual groupings that:
  - Consist of about four or five but never more than seven options.
  - Are of equal size.
- Separate groupings created through either:
  - Wider spacing, or
  - A thin ruled line.
- Provide immediate access to critical or frequently chosen items.

Items displayed on menus should be logically grouped to aid learning and speed up the visual search process. Studies have demonstrated that logically categorized menus are easier to learn and result in faster and more accurate performance. Categorical organization may facilitate the transition from novice to expert user because information is visually represented in the way people think about it.

Groupings should also cover all the possibilities and contain items that are nonoverlapping. While some collections of information will be easily partitioned into logical groups, others may be very difficult to partition. Some users may not understand the designer's organizational framework, and there may be differences among users based on experience. Thus, no perfect solution may exist for all, and extensive testing and refinement may be necessary to create the most natural and comprehensible solution.

Noncategorized menus should be broken in arbitrary visual groupings through the use of space or lines. Groups should be as equal in size as possible and consist of about four or five options. Groupings should never exceed more than seven options.

Finally, choices that are critical or frequently chosen should be accessible as quickly and through as few steps as possible.

Complexity

- Provide both simple and complex menus.
  - Simple: A minimal set of actions and menus.
  - Complex: A complete set of actions and menus.

Two sets of menus will more effectively satisfy the differing needs of the novice and expert user. The novice or casual user often only requires a minimal set of actions and menus to accomplish tasks. The expert may prefer a full set of options. Make selection, and changing, between simple and complex easy to accomplish, preferably through a menu bar choice. IBM's SAA CUA refers to these menus as *short* and *full*.

Ordering

- Order lists of choices by their natural order, or
- For lists with a small number of options (seven or less), order by:
  - Sequence of occurrence.
  - Frequency of occurrence.
  - Importance.
- Use alphabetic order for:
  - Long lists (eight or more options).
  - Short lists with no obvious pattern or frequency.

- Separate potentially destructive actions from frequently chosen items.
- If option usage changes, do not reorder menus.
- Maintain a consistent ordering of options on all related menus.
  - For variable-length menus, maintain consistent relative positions.
  - For fixed-length menus, maintain consistent absolute positions.

Within categories included on a menu, or in menus in which categories are not possible, options must be ordered in meaningful ways. When a menu contains categories of information, the ordering of categories will follow these same principles.

Natural Ordering If items have a natural sequence, such as chapters in a book, months in the year, or physical properties such as increasing or decreasing sizes or weights, the ordering scheme should follow this natural sequence. These ordering schemes will have already been well learned by the screen viewer.

Small Number of Options For groupings with a small number of options (about seven or less), sequence of use, frequency of use, or importance of the item is the best ordering scheme.

Alphabetic Order For a large number of options, alphabetic ordering of alternatives is desirable. Alphabetic ordering is also recommended for small lists where no frequency or sequence pattern is obvious.

It has been found that alphabetically ordered menus can be searched much faster than randomly ordered menus. One study, for example, found that an 18-item alphabetic menu was visually searched four times faster than a randomly organized menu. Search time was a function of saccadic eye movements through the display. Search patterns were random, but fewer eye movements were required with the alphabetic arrangement. After twenty trials, however, only one eye movement was required for all conditions and search time was the same. Learning does take place, but it will be greatly aided by the ordering scheme.

Do Not Reorder Menus Adaptivity is thought to be a desirable quality of a computer system. This may not be so for menu option ordering. Mitchell & Shneiderman (1989) compared static or fixed menus with dynamic menus whose options were continually reordered based upon the frequency in which they were chosen. Dynamic menus were slower to use and less preferred than static menus. The continual reordering interfered with menu order learning, which occurred quickly.

Consistency Between Menus Options found on more than one menu should be consistently positioned on all menus. If menus are of variable length, maintain relative positioning of all item options (for example, place EXIT at the bottom or end of the list). If menus are of fixed length, place options in the same physical position within the list.

Initial Cursor Positioning

- If one option has a significantly higher probability of selection, position the cursor at that option.
- If repeating the previously selected option has the highest probability of occurrence, position the cursor at this option.
- If no option has a significantly higher probability of selection, position the cursor at the first option.

When a menu is first displayed, position the cursor at the most likely option to be chosen, or the first option in the list if no option has a significantly higher probability of selection. If repeating the previously selected option has the highest probability of occurrence, position the cursor at this option.

Control

- Permit only one selection per menu.
- When levels of menu are used, provide one simple action to:
  - Return to the next higher level menu.
  - Return to the main menu.
- Where access of a lower-level menu is possible through multiple pathways, provide those pathways.

Requiring more than one choice per displayed menu can be confusing to the novice user. Limit the required choice to one selection per menu.

Navigation through menu levels should be accomplished through simple key actions. It should always be very easy to return to the next higher level menu and the main or general menu. If it is logical to access levels within a menu structure by meaningful and relevant multiple pathways, provide for access through such pathways.

Menu Navigation Aids

- To aid menu navigation and learning, provide:
  - A "look-ahead" at the next level of choices, alternatives that will be presented when a currently viewed choice is selected.
  - Menu maps or overviews of the menu hierarchy.

Menu navigation and learning will be assisted if a person is able to browse the next level of choices before the currently displayed choice is selected. As the cursor moves across a menu bar, for example, the pull-down menu may be automatically dropped, permitting review of the choices available if that menu bar item is selected. Such look-aheads are useful if ambiguity exists at high-level choice points. They have been found to decrease errors and improve satisfaction. Menu search time may be longer, however.

It is often difficult to maintain a sense of position or orientation as one wanders deeper into a multilevel menu system. The result is that getting lost in the menu maze is quite easy to do. The value of a menu map in reducing disorientation has been demonstrated in some studies In all cases, providing a graphic representation of the menu in map form, either in hard copy or online, resulted in fewer errors or wrong choices, faster navigation, and/or greater user satisfaction when compared to no guides or simply providing indexes or narrative descriptions of the menu structure. It was also found that being able to view on the screen the path one was following improved performance and learning.

Paap and Roske-Hofstrand (1988) suggest that the display of a list of choices selected is especially valuable if the system has many levels and the user frequently has to navigate down new pathways. Maps of the menu structure, they say, are very useful when there is high ambiguity at high-level choice points.

So, menu maps or graphic representations of the menu structure are desirable. These maps should be included in the system documentation and also should be available through a Help function.

Menu Title

- Create a short, simple, clear, and distinctive title representing the purpose of the entire series of choices.
- Locate it at the top of the listing of choices.
- Spell out fully using an upper-case font.

The menu title should immediately orient the viewer to the menu's content and purpose. It should be a short, clear, and distinctive title representing the entire series of choices. It's an important navigation component. Position it in the title bar and display in upper-case letters for emphasis.

Menu Item Descriptions

- Can be names of actions, properties, documents, or windows.
- Provide familiar, fully spelled-out descriptions of choices available.

- Item descriptions may be single words, compound words, or multiple words.
  - Exception: Menu bar items should be a single word (if possible).
- Place key word first, usually a verb.
- The first letter of each item description word should be capitalized.
- Use task-oriented not data-oriented wording.
- Use parallel construction.
- A menu item must never have the same wording as the menu title.
- Item descriptions should be unique within a menu.
- Identical items on different menus should be named identically.
- Items should not be numbered.
  - Exception: If the listing is numeric in nature, graphic, or a list of varying items, it may be numbered.
- If menu options will be used in conjunction with a command language, the capitalization and syntax of the choices should be consistent with the command language.
- Word it as a command to the computer.

Menu item descriptions should comprise familiar, fully spelled-out words. While abbreviations may occasionally be necessary, they should be kept to a minimum. Descriptions should also be concise, containing as few words as possible, and distinctive, constructed of words that make their intent as clear as possible.

Use high-imagery key words, words that elicit a mental image of the object or action. Avoid low-imagery words, those more general in connotation. For example, when obtaining a printout of a screen, the term "print" is much more descriptive than "list."

In creating menu item descriptions, never assume the description chosen by the designer will have the same meaning to the user. Furnas, Gomez, Landaver, & Dumais (1982) found that the probability of two people choosing the same name or description for something ranged from 8 to 18 percent. Names chosen by experts were no better than nonexperts. Therefore, iteratively test and refine the choices to achieve as much agreement as possible.

Size Item descriptions may be single words, compound words, or multiple words. Menu bar items should be a single word, if possible. If a menu bar item must be a multiple word, visually tie the two words together by incorporating a hyphen between them.

Key Word First Arrange multi-item descriptions so that the descriptive and unique words appear at its beginning. This optimizes scanning and recognition while the user is learning the menu. Description phrasing and wording should also be consistent across all menus to aid learning further.

Capitalization Use the headline style of presentation. Capitalize the first letter of each significant item description word.

Task-Oriented Wording Task-oriented wording is preferable to data-oriented. An example of task-oriented wording is *Manage Customer Information*. An example of data-oriented wording is *Customers*.

Parallel Construction Use a parallel word construction in creating descriptions for related choices. Parallel construction would be: *Print* a File, *Execute* a Program, and *Eject* a Disk. An example of nonparallel construction is: *Print*, *Execute* a Program, and Disk *Eject*.

Relationship to Title A menu item must never have the same wording as the menu title.

Uniqueness Item descriptions should also be unique within a menu.

Consistency Identical items on different menus should be named identically.

Numbering Items should not be numbered unless the listing is numeric in nature, graphic, or a list of varying items.

Command Language If menu options will be used in conjunction with a command language, the capitalization and syntax of the captions should be consistent with the command language.

Word as Command to Computer Phrase all menu choices as commands to the computer whenever possible. For example, say:

    Choose one:
        Save and exit
        Exit without saving

rather than:

    Do you want to save and exit?
        Yes
        No

Wording as a command to the computer provides choice phrasing consistent with other system commands, for example the standard commands Save and Exit. It also enhances learning of command mnemonics. Finally, this wording implies the initiative is with the user, not the computer.

Item Arrangement

- Align alternatives or choices into columns whenever possible.
  - Orient for top-to-bottom reading.
  - Left-justify descriptions.
- If a horizontal orientation of descriptions must be maintained:
  - Organize for left-to-right reading.

For scanning ease, options should be left-justified and aligned into columns. Research has found that columnar menus are searched significantly faster than horizontally oriented menus.

When menus are included on other screens, space constraints often exist, and the menu must be arrayed horizontally. In this case, always present the menu in the same location and use distinctive display techniques to contrast the menu with the remainder of the screen. Display techniques must, of course, be compatible with those used for other purposes on the remainder of the screen. A good way to set a menu off from the remainder of the screen is to enclose it in a box or, if it is at the screen's top or bottom, separate it with a horizontal line. Techniques chosen should be consistent throughout the system.

If a single-row (horizontal) orientation is necessary, organize for left-to-right reading based on one of the ordering principles described earlier. If two or more rows are available for displaying choices, organize for top-to-bottom, left-to-right reading to facilitate visual scanning.

Intent Indicators

Cascade Indicator

- To indicate that selection of an item will lead to a sub-menu, place a triangle or right-pointing solid arrow following the choice.
- Every cascaded menu must be indicated by a cascade indicator.

To a Window Indicator

- For choices that result in displaying a window, place an ellipsis (. . .) immediately following the choice.

- Every menu item that is followed by a window must have an ellipsis following it.
  - Exceptions—do not use when an action:
    - Causes a warning window to be displayed.
    - May or may not lead to a window.

Direct Action Items

- For choices that directly perform an action, no special indicator should be placed on the menu.

Predictability and exploration of a graphical system can be enhanced by providing an indication of what will happen when the menu item is selected. If an item leads to another lower-level menu, include a cascade indicator, a right-pointed arrow following the item description. If an item leads to a window, include an ellipsis following the item description. Items causing a direct action will have no indicator. These intent indicators are illustrated in Figure 5.1.

IBM's SAA CUA calls choices leading to submenus or windows *routing* choices, and items causing direct actions as *action* choices. A Microsoft Windows 95 intent indicator simply implies additional information is needed. This additional information request is usually presented in a window, but it need not necessarily be restricted to a window.

Line Separators

- Separate vertically arrayed groupings with subtle solid lines.
- Separate vertically arrayed sub-groupings with subtle dotted or dashed lines.
- Left-justify the lines under the first letter of the columnized item descriptions.
- Right-justify the lines under the last character of the longest item description.

Indicate groupings and subgroupings of vertically arrayed related choices by inscribing subtle solid or dashed lines between each group. The line or lines should only extend from the first character of the descriptions to the end of the longest description, as shown in Figure 5.2. Many systems extend the line from border to border, as illustrated in Figure 5.3. This extended line results in too strong a visual separation between menu parts. Visual separation should exist, but it should not be too overpowering. Reserve a full line for independent groups of choices, a partial line for separating related choices.

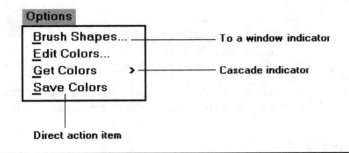

Figure 5.1 Intent indicators.

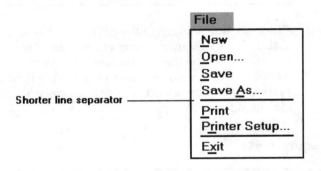

Figure 5.2 Recommended line separators.

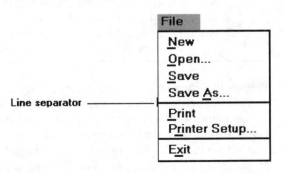

Figure 5.3 Extended line separators.

Defaults

- Provide a default whenever possible.
- Display as bold text.

Defaults aid system learning and enhance efficiency. Provide them whenever possible. Indicate a default by displaying it in bolder text.

Unavailable Choices

- Unavailable choices should be dimmed or "grayed out."
- Do not add or remove items from a menu unless the user takes explicit action to add or remove them through the application.

Choices conditionally not available to the user should be made visually distinctive by dimming or graying them. They must not compete with active items for the user's attention. Items should not be added or removed from a menu unless the user takes explicit action to do so. Allowing the system to change menu items takes control away from the user and can also lead to confusion.

Keyboard Equivalents

- Each menu item should be assigned a keyboard equivalent mnemonic to facilitate keyboard selection.
- The mnemonic should be the first character of the menu item's description.
  - If duplication exists in first characters, for duplicate items use another character in the item description.
  - Preferably choose the first succeeding consonant.
- Designate the mnemonic character by underlining it.

The ability to select a menu alternative through the keyboard should always be provided. This is accomplished by providing a keyed equivalent for each menu alternative. Keyboard equivalents that have meaningful associations with their corresponding choices will be more easily learned and remembered. Studies have found that simple truncation is a good method for creating mnemonics. Therefore, the first letter of the item description is the recommended mnemonic. Unfortunately, in following this method, duplications easily occur, so an alternative principle must also be

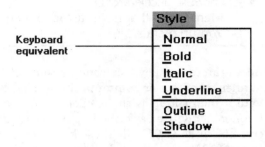

Figure 5.4   Keyboard equivalents.

provided. A simple scheme is to use the second consonant for duplicate items. This duplication-breaking scheme need not always be faithfully followed, however. Occasionally another letter in the menu item may be more meaningful to the user. In these cases, it should be selected.

Mnemonic codes can be visually indicated in a number of ways. The recommended method is an underline beneath the proper character within the choice. Other methods, a different character color, a different character intensity, or a contrasting color bar through the relevant character are visually more complex and should be avoided. See Figure 5.4.

Microsoft Windows 95 calls keyboard equivalents *access keys*.

Keyboard Accelerators

- For frequently used items, provide a keyboard accelerator to facilitate keyboard selection.
- The accelerator may be one function key or a combination of keys.
  - Function key shortcuts are easier to learn than modifier plus letter shortcuts.
- Pressing no more than two keys simultaneously is preferred.
  - Do not exceed three simultaneous keystrokes.
- Use a plus (+) sign to indicate that two or more keys must be pressed at the same time.
- Accelerators should have some associative value to the item.
- Identify the keys by their actual keytop engraving.
- If keyboard terminology differences exist, use:
  - The most common keyboard terminology.
  - Terminology contained on the newest PCs.
- Separate the accelerator from the item description by three spaces.
- Right-align the key descriptions.

- Do not use accelerators for:
  - Menu items that have cascaded menus.
  - Pop-up menus.

Accelerators are keys, or combinations of keys, that invoke an action regardless of cursor or pointer position. They are most commonly used to activate a menu item without opening the menu. They are most useful for frequent activities performed by experienced users. IBM's SAA CUA and Microsoft Windows 95 calls these keys *shortcut* keys. They may also be called *hot keys*. Many products have within their guidelines standard accelerator key recommendations as well as rules for creating new accelerator keys.

For frequently used items, assign a key, or combination of keys, to accomplish an action. Function key shortcuts are usually easier to learn than modifier plus letter shortcuts. Pressing no more than two keys simultaneously is preferred; three keystrokes is the maximum. Use a plus (+) sign to indicate that two or more keys must be pressed at the same time.

Accelerators should have some associative value to the item and be identified by their actual keytop engraving. In situations where multiple kinds of keyboards exist, and there are keyboard terminology differences, use the term most commonly found on the keyboards or use the term contained on the newest PC, if evolution to the new PCs is expected.

Display the accelerator right-aligned and enclosed in parentheses to the right of the choice. Incorporating these key names within parentheses indicates that they are prompts (which they actually are) and that they may easily be ignored when not being used. Most graphic systems do not place them within parentheses, giving them much too strong a visual emphasis. See Figure 5.5.

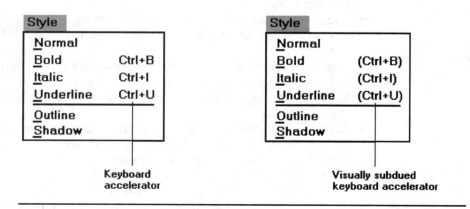

Figure 5.5   Keyboard accelerators.

Do not use accelerators for menu items that lead to cascaded menus. Also, do not use accelerators on pop-up menus as they are mouse driven.

Item Selection

Pointers

- Select the choice by pointing at it with a pointing mechanism such as the cursor, light pen, or finger.
- Indicate:
  - Which options are selectable.
  - When the option is under the pointer and can be selected.
- Visually distinguish single- and multiple-choice menus.
- If cursor pointing is the selection method used,
  - The selectable target area should be at least twice the size of the active area of the pointing device, or displayed pointer. In no case should it be less than six millimeters square.
  - Adequate separation must be provided between adjacent target areas.
- If finger pointing is the selection method used:
  - The touch area must be a minimum of 20 to 30 millimeters square.
  - The touch area must encompass the entire caption plus one character around it.

Keyboard

- The up and down arrow keys should move the cursor up or down vertically oriented menu options.
- The left and right cursor keys should move the cursor left or right between horizontally oriented menu options.
- Either upper- or lower-case typed entries should be acceptable.

Selection/Execution

- Provide separate actions for selecting and executing menu options.
- Indicate the selected choice through either:
  - Highlighting it with a distinctive display technique,
  - Modifying the shape of the cursor.
- Permit unselecting choice before execution.
  - If a multiple-choice menu, permit all options to be selected before execution.

Combining Techniques

- Permit alternative selection techniques to provide flexibility.

Items can be selected by being pointed at with a cursor, light pen, or finger. The pointer is moved to the designated item through use of a mouse, or the user's finger is used to make the selection (if the screen is touch sensitive). Depressing a key, such as Transmit or Enter, or a mouse button signals the choice to the computer. Indicate which options are selectable and when the option is under the pointer and can be selected. Visually distinguish single- and multiple-choice menus.

If cursor pointing is the selection method used, an adequate target area should be provided. This area should be at least twice the size of the active area of the pointing device or the displayed pointer. In no case should it be less than six millimeters square. To avoid unintended activation of the wrong option, provide adequate separation between selectable areas. Highlighting of the selected choice will also provide indication of an incorrect choice.

If finger pointing is the selection method used, an even larger touch area must be provided, a minimum of 20–30 millimeters. Single-character positions on a screen make poor targets for most fingers. Also, keep in mind that using a finger to signify a choice can be taxing on arm muscles, so this approach should only be used in casual or infrequent use situations.

Keyboard Selection The up and down arrow keys should move the cursor up and down a vertical column of menu options. The left and right arrow keys should move the cursor left and right across a horizontal array of options. In typing, the mnemonics should be acceptable in any case (upper and lower mixed).

Selection/Execution Provide separate actions for selecting and executing menu options. For example, require typing the mnemonic to select and then pressing the enter or return key to execute. Or, with a mouse, require moving the pointer to the option to select, and then clicking to execute. Always permit erroneous selections to be unselected and, in a multiple-choice menu, all options to be selected before execution.

The item selected should be highlighted in some way through a distinctive display technique such as reverse polarity. An alternative is to change the shape of the pointer itself. These methods provide direct visual feedback that the proper choice has been selected, reducing the probability of errors in choice selection.

Combining Techniques Permit alternative selection techniques to provide flexibility. If a pointing method is used, also provide a keyboard alternative to accomplish the same task. Pointing will probably be easier for the novice, but many experts prefer the keyboard alternative.

Regular	F5
√ Bold	Ctrl+B
√ Italic	Ctrl+I
Underline	Ctrl+U
Superscript	
Subscript	
Reduce Font	
Enlarge Font	
Fonts...	

Figure 5.6   Mark toggles.

Mark Toggles or Settings

Mark toggles or settings, illustrated in Figure 5.6, are menu items that toggle between active and not active. When it is active, an indicator is displayed adjacent to the item description. For nonexclusive choices, a check mark is displayed; for mutually exclusive choices, another distinctive symbol such as a diamond or circle is displayed. When the item is not active, no mark or symbol will appear.

Examples of items using mark toggles are: having a specific application automatically loaded after the system is loaded, having windows automatically reduced to icons when they are made inactive, or making a setting without requiring a dialog box. The purpose of mark toggles is to activate or deactivate an attribute by setting one menu item.

Advantages/Disadvantages Mark toggles provide a visual indication of the state of an item. They are accessed quickly but may not always be visible.

- Use to designate that an item or feature is active or inactive over a relatively long period of time.
- Use to provide a reminder that an item or feature is active or inactive.
- Position the indicator directly to the left of the option.
- For situations where several non-exclusive choices may be selected, consider including one alternative that deselects all the items and reverts the state to the "normal" condition.

Mark toggles are best suited to items or features that remain active or inactive over relatively long periods of time. They provide good reminders of the state that exists.

Position the mark toggle indicator directly to the left of the menu option. In situations where several nonexclusive choices may be selected on one menu, consider including one alternative that deselects all the items and reverts the state to the normal condition, as illustrated by Regular in Figure 5.6.

Toggled Menu Items

Toggled menu items are one menu item command that toggles back and forth between the current state and its alternative state. When the menu item is first displayed, it reflects the alternative state to the condition that currently exists. For example, in Figure 5.7, if a background grid is currently being displayed, the menu item reads Hide Grid. When Hide Grid is selected, the grid is removed and the menu item dynamically changes to reflect the opposite action. It will now read Show Grid. When a grid is again requested, it will change back to Hide Grid. The purpose of toggled menu items is to use a single menu item to designate and activate the one, opposite, alternative of a two-state command setting.

Advantages/Disadvantages Toggled menu items shorten menus, decrease visual clutter, provide quicker access, and foster faster comprehension of the command action. Because they are on a menu, however, the actions themselves are not always visible. The opposite action reflecting the current state of the attribute, since it too is not visible, can cause uncertainty for novice users concerning what the state actually is. Toggled menu items are also limited in use to commands only.

TOGGLED MENU ITEM GUIDELINES

- Use to designate two opposite commands that are accessed frequently.
- Use when the menu item displayed will clearly indicate that the opposite condition currently exists.
- Provide a meaningful, fully spelled-out description of the action.

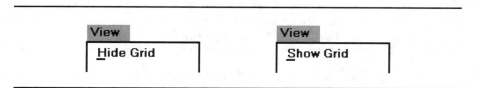

Figure 5.7   Toggled menu item.

- Begin with a verb that unambiguously represents the outcome of the command.
- Use mixed-case letters with the first letter of each word capitalized.

Use toggled menu items to designate two opposite commands that are accessed frequently. The menu item displayed must be one that clearly indicates that the opposite condition currently exists. The menu captions should clearly state what will happen when the menu item action is requested. It is most meaningful to begin the command with a verb.

KINDS OF MENUS

Providing the proper kinds of menus to perform system tasks is critical to system success. The best kind of menu to use in each situation depends on several factors. The following must be considered:

- The number of items to be presented in the menu.
- How often the menu is used.
- How often the menu contents may change.

Each kind of graphical menu will be described in terms of purpose, advantages, disadvantages, and suggested proper usage. Design guidelines for each kind are also presented. A proper usage summary for the various kinds of menus will be found in Table 5.1 at the end of the menu discussion.

Menu Bar

Proper Usage

- To identify and provide access to common and frequently used application actions that take place in a wide variety of different windows.

The highest-level graphical system menu is commonly called the menu bar. A menu bar consists of a collection of action descriptions typically arrayed in a horizontal row at the top of a window. Occasionally a menu bar is referred to as a *collection* of menu titles. In reality it is a menu in itself and it is appropriate to simply refer to it as a *menu*. A menu bar is the starting point for many dialogs. Consistency in menu bar design and use will present to the user a stable, familiar, and comfortable starting point for all interactions. Menu bars are most effectively used for presenting common or frequent actions to be used on many windows in a variety of circumstances.

Menu bars often consist of a series of textual words as represented in

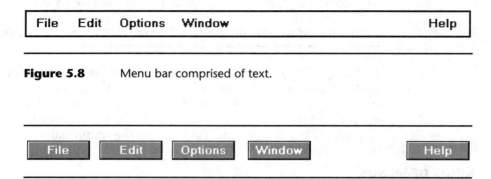

| File | Edit | Options | Window | | Help |

Figure 5.8   Menu bar comprised of text.

| File | Edit | Options | Window | | Help |

Figure 5.9   Menu bar comprised of buttons.

Figure 5.8. Examples of this textual approach are illustrated by Macintosh, Presentation Manager, Microsoft Windows 3.1, and Microsoft Windows 95. Some products have placed the choices within buttons as represented in Figure 5.9. An example of this approach is Sun Microsystems' Open Look, which calls them *menu buttons*. There are also combinations of both. OSF/Motif presents a list of textual choices, but when one is selected, it resembles a button. Motif refers to these as *cascade buttons*.

Each menu bar item will have a pull-down menu associated with it detailing the specific actions that may be performed. Some products have tried to circumvent this pull-down rule and have included items in menu bars that are direct actions themselves. These direct action items have frequently been designated by an exclamation point (!) following the menu bar description. The inclusion of direct items in a menu bar should be avoided. It creates inconsistency in menu bar use and may easily cause an action to be erroneously selected. Menu bars should always possess an associated pull-down menu.

Menu bars are used to present application alternatives or choices to the screen user. Typically, each system provides a default set of menu bar commands (e.g., File, Edit, View, Window, Help).

The advantages of menu bars are that they are:

- Always visible, reminding the user of existence.
- Easy to browse through.
- Easy to locate consistently on the screen.
- Usually do not obscure the screen working area.
- Usually are not obscured by windows and dialog boxes.
- Allow for use of keyboard equivalents.

The disadvantage of menu bars are that:

- They consume a full row of screen space.
- They require looking away from main working area to find.
- They require moving pointer from main working area to select.
- Menu options are smaller than full-size buttons, slowing selection time.
- Horizontal orientation less efficient for scanning.
- Horizontal orientation limits number of choices that can be displayed.

Display

- All primary windows must have a window bar.
- Do not allow the user to turn off the display of the menu bar.
- If all the items in its associated pull-down menu are disabled, then disable the menu bar item.
  - Display the disabled item in a visually subdued manner.
  - However, the disabled pull-down menu must always be capable of being pulled-down so that the choices may be seen.

All primary windows must have a menu bar. Secondary windows may use their primary window bar. Never permit the menu bar to be turned off, as reminders of system actions will be eliminated and possibly forgotten by inexperienced users.

If all the items in its associated pull-down menu are disabled, then disable the menu bar item but continue to display it in a visually subdued manner. The disabled pull-down menu must always be capable of being pulled down so that the choices may be seen. This will facilitate system exploration and learning.

Location

- Position choices horizontally over the entire row at the top of the screen, just below the screen title.
  - A large number of choices may necessitate display over two rows.

Choices should be positioned horizontally across the top of the screen below the screen title. A typical bar is comprised of no more than about seven or eight choices. Due to screen space constraints, and human information processing capabilities, a maximum of seven or eight is reasonable. In the event more are needed, a second line of choices may be added. Try to avoid a second line, however.

Title

- The window title will be the menu bar title.

The window title will serve as the menu bar title.

Item Descriptions

- The menu item descriptions must clearly reflect the kinds of choices available in the associated pull-down menus.
  - Menu item descriptions will be the "titles" for pull-down menus associated with them.
- Use mixed-case letters to describe choices.
- Use single-word choices whenever possible.
- Do not display choices that are never available to the user.

The menu item descriptions must clearly reflect alternatives available in the associated pull-down menus. Choices should be composed of mixed-case single words. Typically, only the first letter of the choice is capitalized. Acronyms, abbreviations, or proper nouns that are normally capitalized may be capitalized. Choices should never be numbered.

If a multiple-word item must be used for clarity, consider including a hyphen between the multiple words to associate the words and differentiate them from other items. Never display choices that are not available to the user.

Organization

- Order choices left-to-right with:
  - Most frequent choices to the left.
  - Related information grouped together.
- Choices found on more than one menu bar should be consistently positioned.
- Left-justify choices within the line.
- When choices can be logically grouped, provide visual logical groupings, if possible.
- Help, when included, should be located to the right side of the bar.

| File   Edit   Options   Window | Help |

Order all choices left-to-right, with most frequently elected choices to the left and related information grouped together. Choices found on more than one menu bar should be consistently positioned.

Left-justify all choices within the line (as opposed to centering when there are not enough choices to completely fill the line). However, always locate Help, when included, to the far right side. Right-side positioning will always keep Help in a consistent location within the bar. Also, provide visual groupings of all related choices, if space permits on the bar.

Layout

- Indent the first choice one space from the left margin.
- Leave at least three spaces between each of the succeeding choices (except Help which will be right-justified).
- Leave one space between the final choice and the right margin.

```
| xFilexxxEdit    Options    Window                              Helpx |
```

The spacing recommendations above are intended to provide clear delineation of choices, leave ample room for the selection cursor, provide a legible selected choice, and provide efficiency in bar design.

Separation

- Separate the bar from the remainder of the screen by:
  - A different background, or
  - Solid lines above and below.

In addition to being identified by its location at the top, the bar should be identifiable by a contrasting display technique. The most effective way to do this is through use of a different background, either reversed polarity (black on white for the bar, contrasted with white on black for the screen body), or a color different from the adjacent title and screen body. When a color is used, it must be chosen in conjunction with good color principles in Step 9. Affecting the background color choice will be the foreground or choice description color, the selection indicator to be described next, and the screen body background color. The contrast of the bar to the remainder of the screen should be moderate, neither too vivid nor too subtle.

Other Components

- Keyboard equivalent mnemonics should be included on menu bars.
- Keyboard accelerators, to a window, and cascade indicators need not be included.

While keyboard mnemonics should be included on menu bars, keyboard accelerators and other intent indicators should not because a menu bar selection will always lead to a pull-down menu.

Selection Indication

Keyboard Cursor

- Use a reverse video, or reverse color, selection cursor to surround the choice.
- Cover the entire choice, including one blank space before and after the choice word.

Pointer

- Use reverse video, or reverse color, to highlight the selected choice.

When using the keyboard, the selection cursor should be indicated by a contrasting reverse video or reverse color bar surrounding the choice. The cursor should extend at least one space to each side of the choice word. When using a pointer, use a reverse video or reverse color to highlight the choice when it is selected.

The recommended reverse color combination is simply to reverse the foreground and background colors of the nonselected choices. Colors chosen must be those that are completely legible in either polarity. Some good combinations would include: black-white, blue-white, and black-cyan. Other contrasting color combinations may, of course, also be used. Since limitations exist in the number of colors that may be used on a screen, however, the colors chosen for menu bars must be performed in conjunction with the colors of other screen components. Since a menu bar can be identified by its location, the use of a completely different color to identify it can be redundant and unnecessary. It is more practical to reserve the use of color for other less identifiable screen components.

Pull-Down Menu

Proper Usage

- Frequently used application actions that take place on a wide variety of different windows.
- A small number of items.
- Items best represented textually.
- Items whose content rarely changes.

Selection of an alternative from the menu bar results in the display of the exact actions available to the user. These choices are displayed in a vertically arrayed listing that appears to pull down from the bar. Hence, these listings, as illustrated in Figure 5.10 are typically referred to as *pull-downs*. Other identification terms may be used, OSF/Motif, for example, calling them *drop-downs*.

Pull-down menus are used to provide access to common and frequently used application actions that take place on a wide variety of different windows. They are most useful for a small number of rarely changing items, usually about five to ten. Larger numbers of choices become awkward to use, being best handled by incorporating cascade menus (see discussion that follows). Pull-downs are best suited for items represented textually, but graphical presentations, such as colors, patterns, and shades, may also be used.

The advantages of pull-down menus are:

- Reminder of existence cued by menu bar.
- May be located relatively consistently on the screen.
- No window space consumed when not used.
- Easy to browse through.
- Vertical orientation most efficient for scanning.
- Vertical orientation most efficient for grouping.
- Vertical orientation permits more choices to be displayed.
- Allows for display of both keyboard equivalents and accelerators.

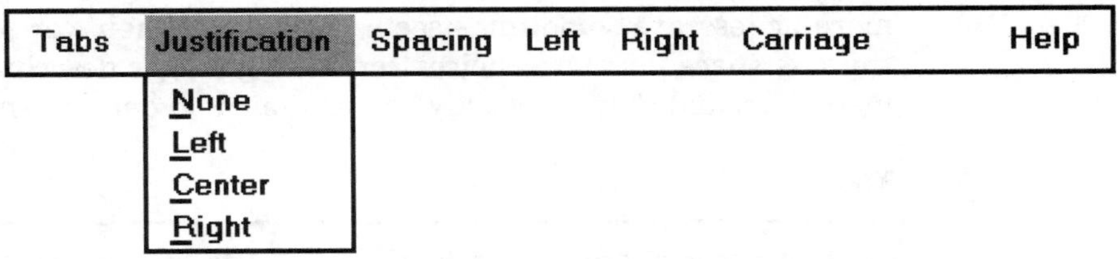

Tabs	Justification	Spacing	Left	Right	Carriage	Help
	None					
	Left					
	Center					
	Right					

Figure 5.10   Menu bar pull-down.

The disadvantages of pull-down menus are:

- Requires searching and selecting from another menu before seeing options.
- Requires looking away from main working area to read.
- Requires moving pointer out of working area to select (unless using keyboard equivalents).
- Items are smaller than full-size buttons, slowing selection time.
- May obscure screen working area.

Display

- Display all possible alternatives.
- Items that cannot be chosen due to the current state of an application must be indicated by graying out or dimming.

Display all possible alternatives on a pull-down. Items that cannot be chosen due to the current state of an application must be indicated by graying out or dimming. If all items are, at any one point, conditionally not applicable, they must still be capable of being retrieved for perusal through the menu bar.

Location

- Position the pull-down directly below the selected menu bar choice.

The pull-down will be located directly below the menu bar choice by which it is selected.

Size

- Restrict to no more than five to ten choices, preferably eight or less.

A typical pull-down is comprised of about five to ten choices, although more or less are sometimes seen. Because of their vertical orientation, there is space for more choices containing longer descriptions than on a menu bar, and they can easily be positioned on one screen.

Title

- Not necessary on a pull-down menu. The title will be the name of the menu bar item chosen.

The name of the item chosen on the menu bar serves as the title of a pull-down menu.

Item Descriptions

- Use mixed-case letters to describe choices.
  - If the choices can be displayed graphically, such as fill-in patterns, shades, or colors, textual descriptions are not necessary.
- Do not:
  - Identify a menu item by the same wording as its menu title.
  - Change the meaning of menu items through use of the shift key.
  - Use scrolling in pull-downs.
  - Place instructions in pull-downs.

Choices should be composed of mixed-case letters. Typically, only the first letter of the choice is capitalized. For multiword choice descriptions, capitalize the first letter of each significant word. Acronyms, abbreviations, or proper nouns that are normally capitalized may be capitalized. If the choices can be displayed graphically, such as fill-in patterns, shades, or colors, textual descriptions are not necessary.

Never identify a pull-down menu item by the same wording as its menu bar title. The menu bar title must reflect *all* the items within the pull-down. Never change the meaning of items through use of the shift key. Shift key activations are extremely error-prone, and their use should be reserved for key accelerators. Also, do not use scrolling in, or place instructions within, a pull-down.

Organization

- Align choices into columns, with:
  - Most frequent choices toward the top.
  - Related choices grouped together.
  - Choices found on more than one pull-down consistently positioned.
- Left-align choice descriptions.
- Multi-column menus are not desirable. If necessary, organize top-to-bottom, then left-to-right.

Align all pull-down choices into columns with their descriptions left-aligned. Locate most frequently chosen alternatives toward the top, and group related choices together. Choices found on more than one pull-down should be consistently positioned. Multicolumn menus are not desirable; if necessary, organize top-to-bottom, then left-to-right.

Layout

- Leave the menu bar choice leading to the pull-down highlighted in the selected manner (reverse video or reverse color).
- Physically, the pull-down menu must be wide enough to accommodate the longest menu item description and its cascade or accelerator indicator.
- Align the first character of the pull-down descriptions under the second character of the applicable menu bar choice.
- Horizontally, separate the pull-down choice descriptions from the pull-down borders by two (2) spaces on the left side and at least two spaces on the right side.
  - The left-side border will align with the left side of the menu bar highlighted choice.
  - The right-side border should extend, minimally, to the right side of its highlighted menu bar choice.

Tabs	Justification	Spacing	Left	Right	Carriage	Help
	None					
	Left					
	Center					
	Right					

  - Pull-downs for choices on the far-right side of the menu bar, or long pull-down descriptions, may require alignment to the left of their menu bar choice to maintain visibility and clarity.

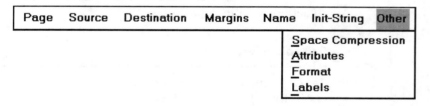

The menu bar choice leading to the pull-down should remain highlighted in the selected manner. Pull-down columnized descriptions should be aligned beginning under the second character position of the applicable bar choice. Pull-down borders should be positioned for balance and for maximum legibility and clarity of the choice descriptions. Leave two spaces to the left of the descriptions to align the left pull-down border with the left border of the selected menu bar choice. Leave a minimum of two spaces after the longest description and the right pull-down border. Minimally, the right pull-down border should extend to the right border of the highlighted menu bar choice. Menu bar choices located at the far right, or long pull-down choice descriptions, may require alignment to the left of the applicable choice, however.

Groupings

- Provide groupings of related pull-down choices:
  - Incorporate a solid line between major groupings.
  - Incorporate a dotted or dashed line between sub-groups.
  - Left-justify the lines under the first letter of the columnized choice descriptions.
  - Right-justify the lines under the last character of the longest choice description.
  - Display the solid line in the same color as the choice descriptions.

Indicate groupings of related choices by inscribing a line between each group. The line, or lines, should only extend from the first character of the descriptions to the end of the longest description, as shown above.

SAA CUA and Microsoft Windows recommend that the line extend from pull-down border to border. Many other system pull-downs also follow this border-to-border approach. This extended line, however, results in too strong a visual separation between pull-down parts. The parts should be separated but not too strongly.

Mark Toggles or Settings

- If a menu item establishes or changes the attributes of data or properties of the interface, mark the pull-down choice or choices whose state is current or active "on."
  - For nonexclusive items, display a check mark to the left of the item description.

> – If the two states of a setting are not obvious opposites, a pair of alternating menu item descriptions should be used to indicate the two states.
> – For exclusive choices, precede the choice with a contrasting symbol such as a diamond or circle.

If a menu item is made permanently active or "on" when selected, this can be made clear to the user by providing a mark by the item. For nonexclusive or independent items, display a check mark to the left of the item description. For exclusive or interdependent choices, precede the choice with a different and contrasting symbol such as a diamond or circle. Microsoft windows indicates active choices of this nature with an *option button mark.*

If a setting containing two states is not clear and obvious opposites, a pair of alternating menu item descriptions should be used to indicate the two states.

Pull-Downs Leading to Another Pull-Down

- If a pull-down choice leads to another pull-down, provide a cascade indicator as follows:
  - Place an arrow or right-pointing triangle after the choice description.
  - Align the triangles to the right side of the pull-down.
  - Display the triangle in the same color as the choice descriptions.

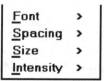

Occasionally a secondary or second level pull-down (or cascading pull-down as it is frequently called) may be desirable if the first pull-down leads to another short series of choices. Or, it may be desirable if the first pull-down has a large number of choices that are capable of being logically grouped. The existence of this second level, and hidden, pull-down should be indicated to the user on the first pull-down in a consistent manner. A simple way to do this is to include a right-pointing triangle to the right of the applicable choice description. These triangles should be positioned aligned to the right side of the pull-down.

Pull-Downs Leading to a Window

- For pull-down choices leading to a window:
  - Place an ellipsis (three dots) after the choice description.
  - Do not separate the dots from the description by a space.
  - Display the ellipsis in the same color as the choice descriptions.

```
Change...
Delete...
Copy...
Move...
```

When a window results from the selection of a pull-down choice, a visual indication of this fact is desirable. An ellipsis inscribed after the choice description is a good indicator that a window will appear.

Keyboard Equivalents and Accelerators

- Provide unique mnemonic codes by which choices may be selected through the typewriter keyboard.
  - Indicate the mnemonic code by underlining the proper character.
- Provide key accelerators for choice selection.
  - Identify the keys by their actual key top engravings.
  - Use a plus (+) sign to indicate two or more keys must be pressed at the same time.
  - Enclose the key names within parentheses ( ).
  - Right-align the key names, beginning at least three spaces to the right of the longest choice description.
  - Display the key alternatives in the same color as the choice descriptions.

```
Find...            (Ctrl+F)
Find Next             (F3)
Find Previous      (Shift+F3)
Replace...         (Ctrl+R)
```

Enabling the user to select pull-down choices through the keyboard provides flexibility and efficiency in the dialogue. One method of doing this is to provide single-character mnemonic codes which, when typed, will also cause the choice to be invoked. Mnemonic codes can be visually indicated in a number of ways. The recommended method is an underline beneath the proper character within the choice.

Another method is to assign accelerators, one key, or a combination of keys, to accomplish the action. Identify these keys exactly as they are engraved on the keyboard, indicate simultaneous depression through use of a plus sign, and right-align and position to the right of the choice descriptions.

Separation

- Separate the pull-down from the remainder of the screen, but visually relate it to the menu bar by:
  - Using a background color the same as the menu bar.
  - Displaying choice descriptions in the same color as the menu bar.
  - Incorporating a solid-line border completely around the pull-down in the same color as the choice descriptions.
- A drop shadow (a heavier shaded line along two borders that meet) may also be included.

In addition to being identified by its position below the menu bar, the pull-down should visually relate to the menu bar and also visually contrast with the screen body. The most effective way to do this is to use the same foreground and background colors that are used on the menu bar but ensure that these colors adequately contrast with the screen body background. Because good contrasting background colors are often limited, a solid-line border of the same color as the choice descriptions will clearly delineate the pull-down border. A drop shadow, when included, will give the pull-down a three-dimensional effect.

Selection Cursor

- Use a reverse video, or reverse color, selection cursor the same color as the menu bar to surround the choice.
- Create a consistently-sized cursor as wide as the pull-down menu.

The selection cursor should be a contrasting reverse video or reverse color bar of a consistent size encompassing the selected choice. The reverse color combination should be the same as appears within the menu bar. Create a consistently sized cursor as wide as the pull-down menu.

Cascading Menus

Proper Usage

- To reduce the number of choices that are presented together for selection (reduce menu breadth).
- When a menu specifies many alternatives and the alternatives can be grouped in meaningful related sets on a lower-level menu.
- When a choice leads to a short, fixed list of single-choice properties.
- When there are several fixed sets of related options.
- To simplify a menu.
- Avoid using for frequent, repetitive commands.

A cascading menu is a submenu derived from a higher-level menu, most typically a pull-down. Cascades may also be attached to other cascades or pop-up menus, however. Cascading menus are located to the right, the menu item on the previous menu to which they are related to as illustrated in Figure 5.11. Menu items that lead to cascading menus are typically indicated by a right-pointing triangle.

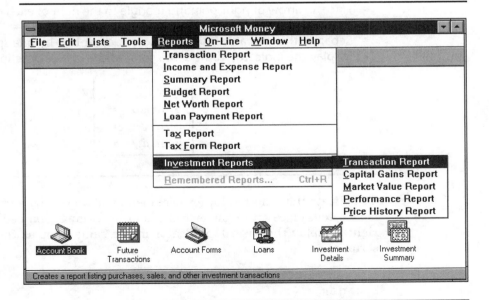

Figure 5.11   Cascading menu.

Cascading menus are developed to simplify menus by reducing the number of choices that appear together on one menu. Cascades can be used when many alternatives exist that can be grouped meaningfully. The top-level menu may contain the grouping category headings and the cascaded menu the items in each group. Any menu choices with a fixed set of related options may utilize cascades.

The advantages of cascading menus are that:

- The top-level menus are simplified because some choices are hidden.
- More first-letter mnemonics are available because menus possess fewer alternatives.
- High-level command browsing is easier because sub-topics are hidden.

The disadvantages of cascading menus are:

- Access to sub-menu items requires more steps.
- Access to sub-menu items requires a change in pointer movement direction.
- Exhaustive browsing is more difficult; some alternatives remain hidden as pull-downs become visible.

Cascade Indicator

- Place an arrow or right-pointing triangle to the right of each menu choice description leading to a cascade menu.
- Separate the indicator from the choice description by one space.
- Display the indicator in the same color as the choice descriptions.

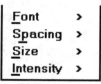

To indicate that another lower-level menu will appear when a menu item is selected, place an arrow or right-pointing triangle immediately to its right. Display the cascade indicator in the same color as the choice descriptions.

Location

- Position the first choice in the cascading menu immediately to the right of the selected choice.

- Leave the choice leading to the cascading menu highlighted.

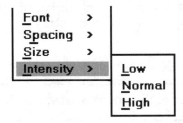

Cascading menus should be positioned so that the first choice in the cascading menu is immediately to the right of the selected choice. The choice leading to the cascade should remain highlighted in some way so that the cascade path is obvious.

Levels

- Do not exceed three menu levels (two cascades).
  - Only one cascading menu is preferred.

Each additional cascade level presented reduces ease of access and increases visual clutter. The number of cascade levels presented should represent a balance between menu simplification, ease in menu comprehension, and ease in item selection. Whenever possible, do not exceed three levels of menus (original and two cascades), as suggested by DECwindows. Try to maintain only one cascade, as recommended by Apple. If too many cascade levels are derived, create additional pull-down menus, or provide a window for some alternatives. A window is useful for establishing independent settings or the setting of multiple options. A toolbar may also be used to eliminate the necessity for traversing cascades.

Title

- Not necessary on the cascading menu.
  - The title will be the name of the higher-level menu item chosen.

The title of the cascading menu will be the choice selected on the menu from which it cascades.

Other Guidelines

- Follow the organization, content, layout, separation, and selection cursor guidelines for the kind of menu from which the menu cascades.

Design of a cascade menu should follow all relevant guidelines for the family of menus to which it belongs. Included are organization, content, layout, and selection cursor.

Pop-Up Menus

- Use to present alternatives or choices within the context of the task.

Choices may also be presented to the user on the screen through *pop-up* menus, vertically arrayed listings that only appear when specifically requested. Pop-up menus may be requested when the mouse pointer is positioned over a designated or *hot* area of the screen (a window border or text, for example) or over a designated icon. In looks, they usually resemble pull-down menus, as shown in Figure 5.12.

The kinds of choices displayed in pop-up menus are context-sensitive, depending on where the pointer is positioned when the request is made. They are most useful for presenting alternatives within the context of the user's immediate task. If positioned over text, for example, a pop-up might include text-specific commands.

Advantages of pop-up menus are that:

- It appears in working area.
- It does not use window space when not displayed.
- No pointer movement needed if selected by button.
- Vertical orientation for most efficient scanning.

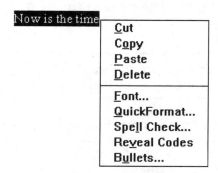

Figure 5.12   Pop-up menu.

- Vertical orientation most efficient for grouping.
- Vertical orientation allows more choices to be displayed.
- It may be able to remain showing ("pinned").
- It allows for display of both keyboard equivalents and accelerators.

Disadvantages of pop-up menus are that:

- Existence must be learned and remembered.
- Means for selecting must be learned and remembered.
- It requires a special action to see the menu (mouse click).
- Items are smaller than full-size buttons, slowing selection time.
- It may obscure screen working area.
- Display locations may not be consistent.

For experienced users, pop-up menus are an alternative to retrieve frequently used contextual choices in pull-down menus. Choices should be limited in number and stable or infrequently changing in content.

Windows 95 contains many contextual pop-up menus. They are also referred to as *context menus* or *shortcut menus*. Examples include the *window pop-up*, which replaces the system menu button pull-down, and an *icon pop-up*, which presents operations of the objects represented by icons.

Display

- Provide a pop-up menu for common, frequent, contextual actions.
  - If the pointer is positioned over an object possessing more than one quality (for example, both text and graphics), at minimum present actions common to all object qualities.
- Items that cannot be chosen due to the current state of an application should not be displayed.
- Continue to display a pop-up until:
  - A choice is selected.
  - An action outside the pop-up is initiated.
  - The pop-up is removed by the user.

Provide a pop-up menu for common, frequent, contextual actions. If, when requested, the pointer is positioned over an object possessing more than one quality (for example, both text and graphics), at minimum present actions common to all object qualities. Items that cannot be chosen due to the current state of an application should not be displayed.

Continue to display a pop-up until the user selects a choice, initiates an action outside the pop-up, or requests that the pop-up be removed.

Location

- Position the pop-up:
  - Centered and to the right of the object from which it was requested.
  - Close enough to the pointer so that the pointer can be easily moved onto the menu.
  - But not so close that the pointer is positioned on an item, possibly leading to accidental selection.
- If the pointer is positioned in such a manner that the pop-up would appear off-screen or clipped, position the menu:
  - As close as possible to the object, but not covering the object.
  - So that it appears fully on the screen.

Position a pop-up menu in a consistent location relative to the object from which it is requested. The preferable location is centered to the right. Locate the pop-up close enough to the pointer so that the pointer can be easily moved onto the menu. Positioning of the pointer on the menu itself could lead to accidental selection of an action.

If the pointer is positioned in such a manner that a right-centered position would force the pop-up partially or fully off the screen, locate the pop-up fully on the screen as close as possible to the object. Do not move the pointer to make a menu fit in the most desirable location.

Size

- Restrict to no more than five to ten choices, preferably eight or less.

Limit pop-up menus to about eight choices or fewer. If a large number of choices are needed, consider creating cascading menus. Minimize the number of levels of cascades, however, to provide ease of access and prevent visual clutter.

Title

- Not necessary on a pop-up menu.
- If included, clearly describe the menu's purpose.
- Locate in a centered position at the top.
- Display in capital letters.
- Separate from the menu items by a line extending from the left menu border to the right border.

A title is not necessary on a pop-up menu, since it is an expert feature. Typically, Motif pop-ups include titles, Microsoft Windows does not. If a title is included, it should clearly reflect the menu's purpose. This will avoid any possible confusion that may occur if the wrong menu is accidentally selected and displayed. The title should be set off from the item descriptions by capitalization and a separator line.

Other Guidelines

- Arrange logically organized and grouped choices into columns.
- If items are also contained in pull-down menus, organize pop-up menus in the same manner.
- Left-align choice descriptions.
- Use mixed-case letters to describe choices.
- Separate groups with a solid line the length of the longest choice description.
- If the choice leads to a pop-up window, place an ellipsis after the choice description.
- To separate the pop-up from the screen background:
  - Use a contrasting, but complementing, background.
  - Incorporate a solid line border around the pull-down.
- Use a reverse video, or reverse color, selection cursor slightly longer than the longest choice.

Follow the same menu guidelines as for pull-down menus regarding organization, content, layout, separation, and selection cursor.

Tear-off Menus

A tear-off menu is a pull-down menu that has been positioned on the screen for constant referral. As such it possesses all the characteristics of a pull-down. It may also be called a *push-pin* or *detachable* menu. Its purpose is to present alternatives or choices to the screen user that are needed infrequently at some times and heavily at other times.

Advantages/Disadvantages No space is consumed on the screen when the menu is not needed. When needed, it can remain continuously displayed. It does require extra steps to retrieve and it may obscure the screen working area.

Use tear-off menus in situations where the items are sometimes frequently selected and other times infrequently selected. Items should be small in number and rarely change in content. A typical use would be to detach and permanently leave displayed a pull-down menu when it must be frequently used.

- Follow all relevant guidelines for pull-down menus.

Since a tear-off menu is a pull-down style, all pull-down guidelines should be followed.

Iconic Menus

- Use to remind users of the functions, commands, attributes, or application choices available.

An iconic menu is the portrayal of menu items or objects in a graphic or pictorial form, as illustrated in Figure 5.13.

The purpose of an iconic menu is to remind users of the functions, commands, attributes, or application choices available.

Advantages/Disadvantages Pictures help facilitate memory of applications and their larger size increases speed of selection. Pictures do, however, consume considerably more screen space than text, and they are difficult to organize for scanning efficiency. To create meaningful icons requires special skills and an extended amount of time.

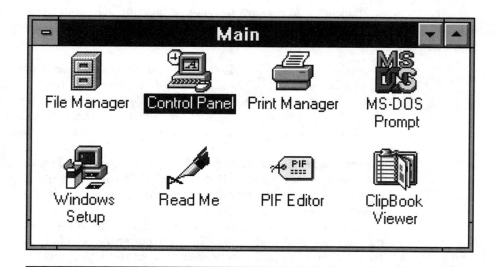

Figure 5.13 Iconic menu (from Microsoft Windows 3.1).

Iconic menus should be used to designate applications or special functions within an application. When a window is minimized it can take the form of an icon.

- Create icons that:
  - Help enhance recognition and hasten option selection.
  - Are concrete and meaningful.
  - Clearly represent choices.

Icons must be meaningful and clear. They should help enhance recognition and hasten option selection. See Step 10 for a complete review of icon design guidelines.

Pie Menus

- Consider using for:
  - Mouse-driven selections, with
  - one- or two-level hierarchies, and
  - short lists, and
  - choices conducive to the format.

A pie menu is a circular representation of menu items, as illustrated in Figure 5.14, that can be used as an alternative to a pull-down or pop-up menu. For textual menus, Callahan, Hopkins, Weiser, & Shneiderman (1988) found that this style of menu yielded a higher performance than the typical vertical array, especially when the menu tasks were unre-

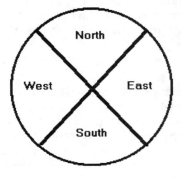

Figure 5.14   Pie menu.

lated. Zhan, Bishu, & Riley (1993) found performance advantages for pie menus containing icons. Mayhew (1992) concludes that pie menus might work well for mouse-driven selections with one- or two-level hierarchies, short choice listings, and data conducive to the format. Performance advantages for keyboard selection is doubtful, however.

Table 5.1 Menu Proper Usage Summary

MENU BAR

- To identify and provide access to:
  - Common and frequently used application actions.
  - Actions that take place in a wide variety of different windows.

PULL-DOWN MENU

- For frequently used application actions that take place in a wide variety of different windows:
  - A small number of items (5–10).
  - Items rarely changing in content.

CASCADING MENU

- To simplify a higher-level menu.
- To provide easier browsing of a higher-level menu.
- For mutually exclusive choices.
- Restrict to 1–2 cascades.

POP-UP MENU

- For:
  - Frequent users.
  - Frequently used contextual commands.
  - A small number of items (5–10).
  - Items rarely changing in content.
  - Items that require a small amount of screen space.

TEAR-OFF MENU

- For items:
  - Sometimes frequently selected.
  - Sometimes infrequently selected.
  - Small in number (5–10).
  - Rarely changing in content.

ICONIC MENU

- To designate applications available.
- To designate special functions within an application.

DEFAULT MENU ITEMS

Every system will provide a set of standard menu items. Using the default items will reduce design time and encourage interface consistency. System learning time will also be reduced. Microsoft Windows 3.1, for example, provides the following standard and optional menu bar items and pull-down actions.

File

A standard element, the file menu provides all the commands needed to open, create, and save files. The standard file functions are:

- New.
- Open.
- Save.
- Save As.
- Print.
- Print Setup.
- Exit.

Edit

A standard element, the edit menu provides commands that affect the state of selected objects. The standard edit functions are:

- Undo.
- Cut.
- Copy.
- Paste.
- Paste Links.
- Links.

View

An optional element, the view menu provides commands that affect the perspective, details, and appearance of the application. They affect the view, not the data itself. The view functions are application-specific and include the following:

- Magnify.
- Zoom In.
- Zoom Out.
- Grid Points.

Window

The window menu, an optional element, provides commands to manipulate entire windows. Included are items such as:

- New Window.
- Arrange All.
- Hide.
- Show.

Help

The Help menu, a standard element, provides Help commands, including:

- Contents.
- Search for Help On.
- How to Use Help.
- About (Application).

These standard menu items also have a prescribed order on the menu bar: File, Edit, View, Window, and Help. Items on their related pull-down menus also follow standard orders.

Standard menus and items should always be used when creating an application. Refer to a system's design documentation for exact details concerning what menu items are available and how they are used.

FUNCTIONS NOT REPRESENTED BY DEFAULT ITEMS

Having established the usability of the standard menu functions, additional system functions must be identified. Commands to accomplish these functions must be created and added to the pertinent menus. Command design guidelines include the following.

Labels

General

- Provide a label for each command.
- Use labels that indicate:
  - The purpose of the command, or
  - The result of what happens when the command is selected.
- Use familiar, short, clear, concise words.
- Use distinctive wording.

- Use mixed-case, with the first letter capitalized.
- Begin commands with verbs or adjectives, not nouns.
- Preferably, use only one word.
    - If multiple words are required for clarity, capitalize the first letter of each significant word.
    - Do not use sentences as labels.
- Provide an ellipsis (. . .) to indicate that another window will result from selection of a command.
    - Do not use the ellipsis when the following window is a confirmation or warning.

Dynamic Labels

- As contexts change, dynamically change the label wording to make its meaning clearer in the new context.
    - For example, after a cut operation, "Undo" may be changed to "Undo Cut."

Provide a clear label for each command indicating the purpose of the command, or the result of what happens when the command is selected. Preferably, use single-word commands. If multiple words are required for clarity, capitalize the first letter of each significant word. Provide an ellipsis to indicate that another window will result from selection of a command, but do not use the ellipsis when the resulting window is a confirmation or warning. As contexts change, the label wording may be dynamically changed to make its meaning clearer in the new context. For example, after a cut operation, Undo may be changed to Undo Cut. This is called a *toggled menu item* and was previously described.

Disabled Commands

- When a command is not available, indicate its disabled status by displaying it grayed or subdued.
- If selection of a disabled command is attempted, provide a message in the information area that the "Help" function will explain why it is disabled.

When a command is not available, indicate its disabled status by displaying it grayed or subdued. If selection of a disabled command is attempted, provide a message in the information area that the Help function will explain why it is disabled. Help, of course, must provide the proper explanation.

Navigation and Selection

General

- Permit multiple methods for selecting commands.

Keyboard Equivalents

- Assign a mnemonic for each command.
- A mnemonic should be as meaningful as possible. Use:
  - The first letter of the command, or if duplications exist,
  - The first letter of another word in the command, or
  - Another significant non-vowel letter in the command.
- For standard commands, use mnemonics provided by the tool set.

Keyboard Accelerators

- Assign keyboard accelerators for frequently used commands.
- For standard commands, use keyboard accelerators provided by the tool set.

Permit commands to be implemented through the keyboard as well. Provide keyboard equivalents or accelerators.

Finally, the menus needed must be designed following principles of effective menu design earlier in this chapter.

MENU EXAMPLES

What follows are examples of poor and proper menu design.

Example 1

An improperly presented menu bar and pull-down.

Menu 1.1

What are the problems in the way this menu bar and pull-down menu are presented? (1) Keyboard mnemonics are designated by capital letters. Note the uncommon shape of "foRmat," "cuT," and "clEar" when the mnemonic is not the first letter of the word. (2) Item groupings do not exist in the pull-down. The differences in basic functions are not obvious and the more destructive operations (Undo, Clear, and Delete) are positioned close to standard actions, increasing the potential for accidental selection. (3) The keyboard accelerators are adjacent to the choice descriptions and not set off in any way. Therefore, these alternative, and supplemental, actions visually compete with choice descriptions for the viewer's attention.

Menu 1.1

Menu 1.2

Keyboard mnemonics are designated by underlines, not capital letters. Choice descriptions now assume more common and recognizable shapes. Groupings through use of white space are established for choices in the pull-down. The different functions are much more obvious and separation is provided for the destructive actions. The different groupings are visually reinforced through use of separating lines. The lines are not extended to the pull-down border so as not to completely disassociate the choices. Keyboard alternatives are right-aligned to move them further from the choice descriptions. They are also enclosed in parentheses to visually de-emphasize them, thereby reducing their visual competition with the choices. Choice descriptions are now more obvious.

Menu 1.2

Example 2

An improperly organized menu bar and pull-down.

Menu 2.1

A very poor menu bar—all alternatives are presented creating a very crowded series of choices in a difficult-to-scan horizontal array. No groupings are provided and an alphabetic order causes intermixing of what appear to be different functions. While menu breadth is preferred to excessive menu depth, too many choices are presented here.

OFFICE SYSTEM				
Address Book	Calendar	Communications	Copy File	Database
Delete File	Exit	Memo Pad	Help	Move File	New File	Open File
Spreadsheet	Telephone Book	Word Processor	World Clock	

Menu 2.1

Menus 2.2 and 2.3

A better, but still poor menu bar—while File, Function, and Help are now presented separately, the cascading Function menu requires an excessive number of steps to complete selection. Note the number of levels needed to access the Address or Telephone book. Excessive levels of depth are difficult to scan and lead to one's getting lost. Some have referred to this problem as cascade confusion.

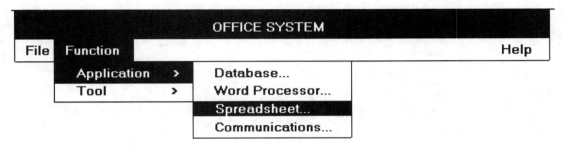

Menu 2.2

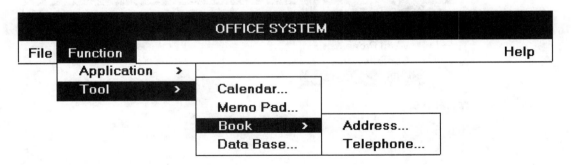

Menu 2.3

Menus 2.4, 2.5, and 2.6

A much more reasonable solution—Application and Tool menu bar items are created and all alternatives now exist on one pull-down menu. The number of steps necessary to reach any alternative is minimized and easier scanning of all items is permitted.

Menu 2.4

Menu 2.5

Menu 2.6

S T E P   6

Select the Proper Device-Based Controls

Device-based controls are the mechanisms through which people communicate their desires to the system. The evolution of graphical systems has seen a whole new family of devices provided to assist and enhance this communication. These new mechanisms are most commonly referred to as pointing devices.

- Identify the characteristics and capabilities of various device-based controls.
  - Trackball.
  - Joystick.
  - Graphic tablet.
  - Touch screen.
  - Light pen.
  - Mouse.
  - Keyboard.
- Select the proper controls for the user and tasks.

For years the device of choice in display-based systems was the standard keyboard. As graphical systems evolved, emphasis shifted to another device, the mouse. A number of other kinds of devices have also been around and have seen extended service through the years, including the joystick, trackball, light pen, and graphic tablet. Another entity, animate in nature—one's finger—has also been used in conjunction with touch-sensitive screens. The various alternatives have both strengths and weaknesses. Selecting the proper device-based control to do the required job is

303

critical to system success. A good fit between user and control will lead to fast, accurate performance. A poor fit will result in lower productivity, produce more errors, and increase user fatigue.

We'll begin by reviewing the kinds of tasks being performed using graphical systems. We'll discuss each device and identify its advantages and disadvantages. Then, we'll focus on the most popular control, the mouse, describing it in more detail and presenting a series of design guidelines for its use. The keyboard, because of its versatility and usefulness for text entry tasks, will also be examined in more detail. Finally, pertinent research will be reviewed and guidelines presented to aid in selecting the proper device.

CHARACTERISTICS OF DEVICE-BASED CONTROLS

Several specific tasks are performed using graphical systems. The first is to point at an object on the screen. Next is to select the object or identify it as the focus of attention. It is also possible to drag an object across the screen or draw something free-form on the screen. Moving objects may be tracked or followed. Objects may also be oriented or positioned. Data or information may be entered or manipulated.

The various devices vary in how well they can perform these actions. A summary of their capabilities follows. Among the considerations to be reviewed are two very important factors. First, is the mechanism a direct or indirect pointing device? *Direct* devices are operated on the screen itself. Examples include the light pen and one's finger. *Indirect* devices are operated in a location other than the screen, most often on the desktop. Examples include the mouse, trackball, and keyboard. The psychomotor skills involved in learning to use, and using, a direct device are easier than those required for an indirect device.

Second, what is the relationship between device movement in the location it is operated by hand and corresponding pointer movement on the screen in terms of *direction, distance*, and *speed*? Does the pointer movement exactly track control movement or does it not? The mouse is an entity that achieves a relationship in all three aspects. The pointer on the screen moves in the direction the mouse is pushed, at the speed the mouse is pushed, and the distance the mouse is pushed (there may be some ratios applied). A trackball does not achieve a relationship in all three aspects. The pointer moves the direction the ball is turned and the speed the ball is turned, but not the distance the ball is moved because the ball does not move forward or backwards; its socket is stationary. Devices possessing direct relationships in these aspects require less psychomotor skill learning.

Trackball

Description

- A spherical object (ball) that rotates freely in all directions in its socket.
- Direction and speed is tracked and translated into cursor movement.

Advantages/Disadvantages

+ Direct relationship between hand and pointer movement in terms of direction and speed.
+ Does not obscure vision of screen.
+ Does not require additional desk space (if mounted on keyboard).
- Movement indirect, in plane different from screen.
- No direct relationship between hand and pointer movement in terms of distance.
- Requires a degree of eye-hand coordination.
- Requires hand to be removed from keyboard keys.
- Requires different hand movements.
- Requires hand be removed from keyboard (if not mounted on keyboard).
- Requires additional desk space (if not mounted on keyboard).
- May be difficult to control.
- May be fatiguing to use over extended time.

Commonly used with portable PCs, the trackball is a ball that rotates freely in all directions in its socket. The ball is rotated with the finger tips, and its direction and speed are tracked and translated into equivalent screen cursor movement.

In terms of direction and speed, a trackball possesses a direct relationship between how it is rolled and how the cursor moves on the screen. The cursor moves in the same direction and speed ratio as the ball is rotated. Many trackballs are mounted on the keyboard itself, permitting the user's hands to remain close to the keys. Trackballs on the keyboard do not require additional desk space, although the keyboard must often be expanded to allow for their inclusion.

Trackballs share a common problem with several other controls: control movement is in a different plane from the screen, or indirect. The cursor, or pointer, is separated from the control itself—the pointer being on the screen, the control on the keyboard. To effectively use a trackball requires learning the proper psychomotor skills, fine finger movements for accurate pointing, and gross hand movements for moving longer distances. The fine finger movements necessary to use them can be difficult to do. Over longer periods of use, they can be fatiguing. When paired with keyboard tasks, they require a shift in motor activity from keystrokes to finger/hand movement.

Joystick

Description

- A stick or bat-shaped device anchored at the bottom.
- Variable in size, smaller ones being operated by fingers, larger ones requiring the whole hand.
- Variable in cursor direction movement method, force joysticks respond to pressure, movable respond to movement.
- Variable in degree of movement allowed, from horizontal-vertical only to continuous.

Advantages/Disadvantages

- + Direct relationship between hand and pointer movement in terms of direction.
- + Does not obscure vision of screen.
- + Does not require additional desk space (if mounted on keyboard).
- − Movement indirect, in plane different from screen.
- − Indirect relationship between hand and pointer in terms of speed and distance.
- − Requires a degree of eye-hand coordination.
- − Requires hand to be removed from keyboard keys.
- − Requires different hand movements to use.
- − Requires hand to be removed from keyboard (if not mounted on keyboard).
- − Requires additional desk space (if not mounted on keyboard).
- − May be fatiguing to use over extended time.
- − May be slow and inaccurate.

A joystick, like its aircraft namesake, is a stick or bat-shaped device usually anchored at the bottom. They come in variable sizes, smaller ones being operated by fingers, larger ones requiring the whole hand. The smaller joysticks require fine motor coordination, the larger ones more gross coordination. Some, called force joysticks, are immovable, responding to pressure exerted against them. The direction and amount of pressure is translated into pointer movement direction and speed. Others, called movable joysticks, can be moved within a dish-shaped area. The direction and distance of the movements create a similar pointer movement on the screen. Some kinds of joysticks permit continuous movements, others only horizontal and vertical movements. Joysticks may also be mounted on the keyboard.

Joysticks typically possess a direct relationship between hand and cursor movement in terms of direction. When mounted on the keyboard, they do not require additional desk space. Joysticks are also indirect devices, the control and its result being located in different planes. They require developing a skill to use and can be slow and inaccurate. Use over extended time may also be fatiguing. When paired with keyboard tasks, they require a shift in motor activity from keystrokes to finger/hand movement.

Graphic Tablet

Description

- Pressure-, heat-, light-, or light-blockage-sensitive horizontal surfaces that lie on the desktop.
- May be operated with fingers, light pen, or objects like a stylus or pencil.
- Pointer imitates movements on tablet.

Advantages/Disadvantages

- \+ Direct relationship between touch movements and pointer movements in terms of direction, distance, and speed.
- \+ More comfortable horizontal operating plane.
- \+ Does not obscure vision of screen.
- − Movement indirect, in plane different from screen.
- − Requires hand to be removed from keyboard.
- − Requires hand to be removed from keyboard keys.
- − Requires different hand movements to use.
- − Requires additional desk space.
- − Finger may be too large for accuracy with small objects.

A graphic tablet, also called a touch tablet, is a device with a horizontal surface sensitive to pressure, heat, light, or the blockage of light. It lies on the desk and may be operated with fingers, light pen, or objects like a pencil or stylus. The screen pointer imitates movement on the tablet.

With graphic tablets, a direct relationship exists between touch movements and pointer movements in terms of direction, distance, and speed. The screen mimics the tablet. When used with objects like styluses, light pens, or pencils, the operational angle, horizontal, is more comfortable than those vertically oriented.

Tablets are also indirect controls, creating coordination problems. To use them requires moving one's hand from the keyboard and, if using another device, picking it up. If the finger is the tablet-activation object, accuracy with small objects is difficult. Tablets also require desk space.

Touch Screen

Description

- A special surface on the screen sensitive to finger or stylus touch.

Advantages/Disadvantages

- \+ Direct relationship between hand and pointer location in terms of direction, distance, and speed.
- \+ Movement direct, in same plane as screen.
- \+ Requires no additional desk space.
- \+ Stands up well in high use environments.
- – Finger may obscure part of screen.
- – Finger may be too large for accuracy with small objects.
- – Requires moving the hand far from the keyboard to use.
- – Very fatiguing to use for extended period of time.
- – May soil or damage the screen.

Design Guidelines

- Screen objects should be at least 3/4" × 3/4" in size.
- Object separation should be at least 1/8".
- Provide visual feedback in response to activation. Auditory feedback may also be appropriate.
- When the consequences are destructive, require confirmation after selection to eliminate inadvertent selection.
- Provide an instructional invitation to begin using.

A touch screen is a screen comprised of a special surface sensitive to finger or stylus touch. Objects on the screen are pointed to and touched to select.

Touch screens possess a direct relationship between hand and pointer movement in terms of direction, distance, and speed. This relationship is direct, however, not indirect, because the control (finger or stylus) is on the same plane as the pointer. Another significant advantage of a touch screen is that it does not require any additional desk space.

A disadvantage of touch screens is that they are fatiguing to use over an extended period of time. If a finger is the touch mechanism, it may obscure part of the screen and be too large to be accurate with small objects. A stylus is usually more accurate than the finger. Fingers may also soil the screen, and a stylus may damage it. Both finger and stylus require moving of a hand from the keyboard to operate, and a stylus must also be picked up.

When using touch screens, larger screen objects should always be provided to foster accuracy in use. Minimally, objects should be 3/4" square and separated by at least 1/8". Visual, and perhaps auditory, feedback should be provided in response to activation. When the consequences of selection are destructive, require a confirmation to avoid inadvertent selection (Brown, 1988). Observational research indicates that touch screen devices placed in public places, for use by the general public, should possess an instructional invitation to begin its use.

Today, other forms of touch screen devices are being explored in research laboratories. One method involves allowing placement of a finger on the screen without item selection, selection being accomplished by lifting the finger off the screen. This may allow more accurate item selection. Another method involves placing a cross hair on the screen directly above one's finger and moving the cross hair as the finger is moved. The cross hair permits better target visibility, as well as detection of smaller targets.

Light Pen

Description

- A special surface on the screen sensitive to touch of a special stylus or pen.

Advantages/Disadvantages

- \+ Direct relationship between hand and pointer movement in terms of direction, distance, and speed.
- \+ Movement direct, in same plane as screen.
- \+ Requires minimal additional desk space.
- \+ Stands up well in high-use environments.
- \+ More accurate than finger touching.
- − Hand may obscure part of screen.
- − Requires picking up to use.
- − Requires moving the hand far from the keyboard to use.
- − Very fatiguing to use for extended period of time.

A light pen also utilizes a touch screen but is sensitive in a specific way to one kind of pen or stylus. Advantages and disadvantages are similar to those of the touch screen. Light pens possess a direct relationship between hand and pointer movement in terms of direction, distance, and speed, and are also classified as direct pointing devices because the control (pen or stylus) is on the same plane as the pointer. Another advantage of a touch screen is that it does not require any additional desk space, except for the pen to rest. A disadvantage is that they are also fatiguing to use over an extended period to time. A light pen is usually more accurate than the finger. Light pens require moving a hand from the keyboard to pick up and use.

Mouse

Description

- A rectangular or dome-shaped, movable, desktop control containing from one to three buttons used to manipulate objects and information on the screen.
- Movement of cursor mimics mouse movement.

Advantages/Disadvantages

- \+ Direct relationship between hand and pointer movement in terms of direction, distance, and speed.
- \+ Selection mechanisms included on mouse.
- \+ Does not obscure vision of screen.
- − Movement indirect, in plane different from screen.
- − Requires hand be removed from keyboard.
- − Requires additional desk space.
- − May require long movement distances.
- − Requires a degree of eye-hand coordination.

A mouse is a rectangular or dome-shaped, movable, desktop control containing from one to three buttons used to manipulate objects and information on the screen. The movement of the screen pointer mimics the mouse movement. There is a direct relationship between hand and pointer movement in terms of direction, distance, and speed. The mouse itself contains some basic controls (buttons) useful for manipulating screen objects.

Disadvantages are that they are also indirect devices, the control and its result being located in different planes. They require developing a skill to use and, when paired with keyboard tasks, they require movement away from the keyboard and a shift in motor activity from keystrokes to finger/hand movement. The mouse also requires extensive additional desk space and long positioning movements. The mouse comes in a variety of configurations, performs some basic functions, and is operated in several ways.

Configurations A mouse may possess one, two, or three buttons. Most, but not all, windowing systems permit operation using all configurations. Buttons are used to perform the three functions to be described. When three mouse buttons are not available, the pointer location or keyboard qualifiers must be used to determine the function to be performed. A multibutton mouse permits a more efficient operation, but a person must remember which button to use to perform each function. A multibutton mouse may usually be configured for left- or right-hand use.

Functions The functions performed by a mouse are Select, Menu, and Adjust. The Select function is used to manipulate controls, select alternatives and data, and select objects that will be affected by actions that follow. Select is a mouse's most important function and is the function assigned to a one-button mouse. For a multibutton mouse, it is usually assigned to the leftmost button (assuming a right-handed operation).

The Menu function is typically used to request and display a pop-up menu on a screen. A menu appears when the button is depressed within a particular defined area of the screen. This area may be, for example, the entire screen, within a window, or on a window border. This button eliminates the need for a control icon, which must be pointed at and selected. The user, however, must remember that a menu is available.

The Adjust function extends or reduces the number of items selected. It is the least used of the three functions and is usually assigned last and given the least prominent location on a mouse.

Operations Several operations can be performed with a mouse button. The first, point, is the movement and positioning of the mouse pointer over the desired screen object. It prepares for a selection or control operation. To press is to hold the button down without releasing it. It identifies the object to be selected.

To click is to press and immediately release a button without moving the mouse. This operation typically selects an item or insertion point, operates a control, or activates an inactive window or control. To double-click is to perform two clicks within a predefined time limit without moving the mouse. It is used as a shortcut for common operations such as activating an icon or opening a file.

To drag is to press and hold the button down, and then move the pointer in the appropriate direction. It identifies a range of objects or moves, or resizes items. To double-drag is to perform two clicks and hold the button down, and then move the pointer in the appropriate direction. It identifies a selection by a larger unit, such as a group of words.

Mouse Usage Guidelines

- Provide a "hot zone" around small or thin objects that might require extremely fine mouse positioning.
- Never use double-clicks or double-drags as the only means of carrying out essential operations.
- Do not use mouse plus keystroke combinations.
- Do not require a person to point at a moving target.

If an object is very small and might require fine mouse positioning, provide a "hot zone" around it. This will increase target size and speed selection. Do not require double-clicks or double-drags as the only way to carry out essential operations. Rapid double-pressing is difficult for some people. Do not use mouse plus keystroke combinations to accomplish actions. This can be awkward. One exception: multiple selection of items in a list. Do not require a person to point at a moving target, except, of course, for a game.

Keyboard

Description

- Standard typewriter keyboard and cursor movement keys.

Advantages/Disadvantages

- + Familiar.
- + Accurate.
- + Does not take up additional desk space.
- + Very useful for:
  - ++ Entering text and alphanumerics.
  - ++ Inserting in text and alphanumerics.
  - ++ Keyed shortcuts—accelerators.
  - ++ Keyboard mnemonics—equivalents.

+ Advantageous for:
  ++ Performing actions where less than three mouse buttons exist.
  ++ Using with very large screens.
  ++ Touch typists.
- Slow for non-touch typists.
- Slower than other devices in pointing.
- Requires discrete actions to operate.
- No direct relationship between finger or hand movement on the keys and cursor movement on screen in terms of speed and distance.

The standard typewriter consists of a keyboard and its associated cursor movement and function keys. The standard keyboard is familiar, accurate, and does not consume additional desk space. It is useful and efficient for entering or inserting text or alphanumeric data. For tasks requiring heavy text or data entry, shifting hands between a keyboard and an alternative control such as a mouse can be time-consuming and inefficient, especially for a touch typist. The keyboard is flexible enough to accept keyed shortcuts, either keyboard accelerators or mnemonic equivalents. Some systems also permit navigation through a screen through use of keyboard keys like the space bar, arrows, tab, and enter.

Inefficiencies in using other graphical device-based controls can occur in other ways. A mouse with a limited number of buttons will require use of the keyboard to accomplish some functions, possibly causing frequent shifting between devices. Operations that are being performed on very large screens may also find keyboard window management preferable to the long mouse movements frequently required. Therefore, to compensate for these possible inefficiencies, many windowing systems provide alternative keyboard operations for mouse tasks.

Disadvantages of a keyboard include its requiring discrete finger actions to operate instead of the more fine positioning movements. As a result, no direct relationship exists in terms of speed and distance between finger or hand movement on the keys and cursor movement on the screen. Depending on the layout of the keyboard cursor control keys, direct relationship direction problems may also exist as fingers may not move in the same direction as the cursor. Keyboards will also be slower for non-touch typists and slower than other controls in pointing tasks.

Keyboard Guidelines

- Provide keyboard accelerators.
  - Assign single keys for frequently performed, small-scale tasks.

- Assign SHIFT + key combinations for actions that extend or are complementary to the actions of the key or key combination used without the SHIFT key.
- Assign CTRL + key combinations for:
  - Infrequent actions.
  - Tasks that represent larger-scale versions of the task assigned to the unmodified key.
- Provide keyboard mnemonics.
  - Use the first letter of the item description.
  - If first letter conflicts exist, use:
    - Another distinctive consonant in the item description.
    - A vowel in the item description.
- Provide window navigation through use of keyboard keys.

Keyboard Accelerators Accelerators provide a way to access menu elements without displaying a menu. They are useful for frequent tasks performed by experienced users. Keys assigned for accelerators should foster efficient performance and be meaningful and conceptually consistent to aid learning.

Microsoft (1992) suggests that frequently performed, small-scale tasks should be assigned single keys as the keyboard alternative. Actions that extend or are complementary to the actions of a key (or key combination) should be assigned a Shift key in conjunction with the original action. Microsoft, for example, uses a single key, F6, as the key to move clockwise to the next pane of an active window. To move counterclockwise to the next pane, Shift + F6.

Infrequent actions, or tasks that represent larger-scale versions of the task assigned to the unmodified key, should be assigned CTRL + key combinations. The left arrow key in Microsoft Windows, for example, moves the cursor one character; CTRL + left arrow moves it one word.

Keyboard Mnemonics Keyboard mnemonics enable selecting a menu choice through the keyboard instead of by pointing. This enables a person's hands to remain on the keyboard during extensive keying tasks. Keyboard mnemonics should be chosen in a meaningful way to aid memorability and foster predictability of those things that may be forgotten. Mnemonics need only be unique within a menu. A simple rule is always to use the first letter of a menu item description. If the first letter of one item conflicts with that of another, choose another distinctive consonant in the item description, preferably, but not always necessarily, the second in the item word (occasionally another consonant may be more meaningful). The last choice would be a vowel in the item description.

Window Navigation Also provide ways of navigating through windows by use of keyboard keys.

SELECTING THE PROPER DEVICE-BASED CONTROLS

A number of studies have been performed comparing the various controls for assorted office tasks. Significant findings include the following.

Keyboard vs. Mouse

Why do many skilled typists prefer a keyboard to a mouse? Speed is obviously one reason. An experienced typist, through kinesthetic memory, has memorized the location of keyboard keys. The keying process becomes exceptionally fast and well-learned. The mouse is slower and it has a tendency to move about the desk. Its location cannot be memorized. The keyboard keys always remain in the same spot.

Consider the following. Using the mouse, the time to move one's hand from the keyboard, grasp the mouse, and point at a screen object ranges from 1.5 to 2 seconds. A very skilled typist can type 13 to 15 characters in that amount of time, an average typist can type 4 to 6 characters. No wonder the keyboard is often preferred.

Control Research

Which devices work better for which tasks and under what conditions has been addressed by a number of investigators. A survey of the research literature comparing and evaluating different devices was done by Greenstein & Arnaut (1988). They provide the following summarization concerning tasks involving pointing and dragging:

- The fastest tools for pointing at stationary targets on screens are the devices that permit direct pointing, the touch screen and light pen. This is most likely due to their high level of eye-hand coordination and because they use an action familiar to people.
- In positioning speed and accuracy for stationary targets, the indirect pointing devices, the mouse, trackball, and graphic tablet, do not differ greatly from one another. The joystick is the slowest, although it is as accurate as the others. Of most importance in selecting one of these devices will be its fit to the user's task and working environment.
- A separate confirmation action that must follow pointer positioning increases pointing accuracy but reduces speed. The mouse offers a very effective design configuration for tasks requiring this confirmation.

- For tracking small, slowly moving targets, the mouse, trackball, and graphic tablet are preferred to the touch screen and light pen because the latter may obscure the user's view of the target.

Another common manipulation task is dragging an object across the screen. Using a mouse, graphic tablet, and trackball for this task, as well as pointing, was studied by MacKenzie, Sellen, & Buxton (1991). They report the following:

- The graphic tablet yielded best performance during pointing.
- The mouse yielded best performance during dragging.
- The trackball was a poor performer for both pointing and dragging, and it had a very high error rate in dragging.

Guidelines for Selecting the Proper Device-based Control

- Consider the characteristics of the task.
  - Provide keyboards for tasks involving:
    - Heavy text entry and manipulation.
    - Movement through structured arrays consisting of a few discrete objects.
  - Provide an alternative pointing device for graphical or drawing tasks. The following are some suggested best uses:
    - Mouse—pointing, selecting, drawing, and dragging.
    - Joystick—selecting and tracking.
    - Trackball—pointing, selecting and tracking.
    - Touch screen—pointing and selecting.
    - Graphic tablet—pointing, selecting, drawing, and dragging.
  - Provide touch screens under the following conditions:
    - The opportunity for training is minimal.
    - Targets are large, discrete, and spread out.
    - Frequency of use is low.
    - Desk space is at a premium.
    - Little or no text input requirement exists.
- Consider user characteristics and preferences.
  - Provide keyboards for touch typists.
- Consider the characteristics of the environment.
- Consider the characteristics of the hardware.
- Consider the characteristics of the device in relation to the application.
- Provide flexibility.
- Minimize eye and hand movements between devices.

Selection of the proper device for an application, then, depends on a host of factors.

Task Characteristics Is the device suited to the task? For tasks requiring text entry and manipulation, standard typewriter keyboards are always necessary. Keyboards (cursor control keys) are usually faster when moving through structured arrays consisting of a few discrete objects.

For graphical and drawing tasks, alternative pointing devices are easier and faster. Use a mouse, joystick, trackball, or graphic tablet for pointing, selecting, drawing, dragging, or tracking. The devices best suited for each kind of task are summarized above (Mayhew, 1992).

Provide touch screens where the opportunity for training is minimal; targets are large, discrete, and spread out; frequency of use is low; desk space is at a premium; and little or no text input requirement exists (Mayhew, 1992). Touch screens also work well when the usage environment is dirty.

User Characteristics and Preferences Will the user be able to easily and comfortably operate the control? Are the fine motor movements required by some devices capable of being performed? Is the user familiar with the standard keyboard? What are the user's preferences? While preferences do not always correspond to performance, it is important that the user be comfortable with the selected device.

Environmental Characteristics Will the device fit easily into the work environment? If desk space is necessary, does it exist and is it large enough?

Hardware Characteristics Is the device itself of a quality that permits easy performance of all the necessary tasks? Joysticks, for example, are quite variable in their movement capabilities.

The Device in Relation to the Application Is the device satisfactory for the application?

Flexibility Often task and user needs will vary within an application. Providing more than one kind of device will give the user choices in how to most efficiently accomplish whatever tasks must be performed. A keyboard paired with another kind of pointing device is almost always necessary.

Minimizing Eye and Hand Movements When multiple devices are used, eye and hand movements between them must be minimized. Structure the task, if possible, to permit the user to stay in one working area. If shifts must be made, they should be as infrequent as possible.

Pointer Guidelines

- The pointer:
  - Should be visible at all times.
  - Should contrast well with its background.
  - Should maintain its size across all screen locations and during movement.
  - The hotspot should be easy to locate and see.
  - Location should not warp (change position).
    - The user should always position the pointer.
- The shape of a pointer:
  - Should clearly indicate its purpose and meaning.
  - Should be constructed of already-defined shapes.
  - Should not be used for any other purpose other than its already-defined meaning.
  - Do not create new shapes for already-defined standard functions.
- Use only as many shapes as necessary to inform the user about current location and status. Too many shapes can confuse a person.
- Be conservative in making changes as the pointer moves across the screen.
  - Provide a short "time out" before making non-critical changes on the screen.
- Animation should not:
  - Distract.
  - Restrict one's ability to interact.

The focus of the user's attention in most device operations is most often the pointer. As such, the pointer image should be used to provide feedback concerning the function being performed, the mode of operation, and the state of the system. For example, the pointer shape image can be changed when it is positioned over a selectable object, signaling to the user that a button action may be performed. When an action is being performed, the pointer can assume the shape of a progress indicator such as a sand timer, providing an indication of processing status.

A pointer should contrast well with its background and be visible at all times. The user should always be in control of its location on the screen. The shape of a pointer should clearly indicate its purpose and meaning. Always use predefined shapes provided by graphical systems. Microsoft Windows (1992), for example, provides about two dozen. To aid learning and avoid user confusion, never create new shapes for already-defined standard functions or use a shape for any purpose other than its previously defined meaning. Also, use only as many shapes as absolutely necessary to keep the user informed about current position and status. Too many shapes can also confuse a person.

Be conservative in making changes as the pointer moves across the screen. Excessive changes can be distracting to a person. To avoid frequent changes while crossing the screen, establish a short time-out before making noncritical pointer changes. Any pointer animation should not distract the viewer or restrict one's ability to interact with the system.

STEP 7

Choose the Proper Screen-Based Controls

Screen-based controls, often simply called *controls* and sometimes called *widgets*, are the elements of a screen that comprise its body. By definition, they are graphic objects that represent the properties or operations of other objects. A control may:

- Permit entry or selection of a particular value.
- Permit changing or editing of a particular value.
- Display only a particular text, value, or graphic.
- Cause a command to be performed.
- Possess a contextual pop-up window.

In recent years, some products have expanded the definition of a control to include all specifiable aspects of a screen, including screen text, headings, and group boxes (Microsoft, 1995). For purposes of this discussion, this broader definition of a screen-based control will be assumed.

- Identify the characteristics and capabilities of the various screen-based controls.
  - Buttons.
  - Text entry/read-only.
  - Selection.
  - Combination entry/selection.
  - Specialized or custom.
  - Presentation.
- Select the proper controls for the user and tasks.

320

The screen designer is presented with an array of screen-based controls to choose from. Selecting the right one for the user and the task is often difficult. But, as with device-based controls, making the right choice is critical to system success. A proper fit between user and control will lead to fast, accurate performance. A poor fit will result in lower productivity, more errors, and dissatisfaction.

We'll start by describing the types of controls and identifying their advantages, disadvantages, and proper usage. Relevant control design guidelines will also be presented. Not all toolkits or platforms will necessarily possess all the kinds of controls to be described. After describing the controls, we'll look at several research studies addressing choosing the best control, or controls, for particular situations. By the time we look at these studies, their findings will have been incorporated into the control usage and design guidelines already presented. This organization has been chosen because it is more meaningful to first clearly describe each control before discussing it in a research context. We'll finish by providing some general guidance in choosing the proper kind of control to enable the tasks to be performed quickly and efficiently by the user.

In describing the controls, we'll break them down into categories reflecting how they are used. We'll begin with operable controls, those that are manipulable, changeable, or settable. We'll then review presentation controls, those used to inscribe permanent information on a screen or used to give the screen structure.

OPERABLE CONTROLS

Classes of operable controls include buttons, text entry/read-only, selection, combination entry/selection, and other specialized controls.

BUTTONS

Description

- A square or rectangular-shaped control with a label inside that indicates action to be accomplished.
- The label may be either text, graphics, or both.

Purpose

- To start actions.
- To change properties.
- To display a pop-up menu.

Advantages/Disadvantages

+ Always visible, reminding of choices available.
+ Convenient and logically organized in the work area.
+ Can provide meaningful descriptions of the actions that will be performed.
+ Larger size generally provides faster selection target.
+ Can possess 3-D appearance:
  ++ Adds an aesthetically pleasing style to the screen.
  ++ Provides visual feedback through button movement when activated.
+ May permit use of keyboard equivalents and accelerators.
+ Faster than using a two-step menu bar/pull-down sequence.
− Consumes screen space.
− Size limits the number that may be displayed.
− Requires looking away from main working area to activate.
− Requires moving the pointer to select.

Proper Usage

• Use for frequently used actions that are specific to a window.
  − To cause something to immediately happen.
  − To display another window.
  − To display a menu of options.
  − To set a mode or property value.

A *button* comes in three styles. The first resembles the control commonly found on electrical or mechanical devices and is sometimes called a pushbutton. They are most often rectangular-shaped with text that indicates the action to be taken when they are selected. These buttons are usually placed within a window, and activating them causes the action or command described on them to be immediately performed. This kind of button may take a variety of forms, some of which are illustrated in Figure 7.1. They are often referred to as *command buttons*.

The second style is square or rectangular in shape with an icon or graphic inside. It may have an associated label. This kind of button is il-

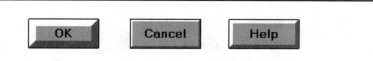

Figure 7.1   Command buttons.

Figure 7.2   Bar buttons without labels.

lustrated in Figure 7.2. The label may either be permanently affixed to the screen within the button, adjacent to it, or it may only appear when the pointer is moved to the button (called tooltip, to be discussed). These buttons may appear singly or be placed in groupings commonly called *buttonbars* or *toolbars*. We'll refer to them as buttonbars in this text. They are most frequently used to quickly access commands, many of which are normally accessed through the menu bar, or other actions or functions. These button groupings are usually placed at the screen's top or side. They are usually relocatable, and removable, by the user.

The third style is square or rectangular in shape with a symbol inscribed inside, as illustrated in Figure 7.3. The symbol, when learned, identifies the button and the action to be performed when the button is selected. These buttons, specific to a platform and provided by it, are located in the borders of windows and are used to do such things as obtaining a system menu or resizing a window. They have already been described in more detail in Step 4.

This chapter will focus on command buttons and buttonbar buttons.

Advantages/Disadvantages An advantage of a command button is that it is always visible, providing a reminder of its existence. Command buttons are conveniently and logically located in the work area and inscribed with meaningful descriptions of what they do. Their larger size speeds selection and their three-dimensional appearance is aesthetically pleasing. Buttons can also provide meaningful visual feedback through movement of the button when activated. Their activation is easier and faster than using a two-step menu bar/pull-down sequence.

Among the disadvantages of command buttons is their large size, which consumes considerable screen space and limits the number that can be displayed.

Figure 7.3   A symbol button.

Advantages of buttonbar buttons also include their continuous visibility and ease and speed of usage. They also, individually, consume a relatively small amount of space. Disadvantages include their location being away from the main work area and their small size, which slows down selection. Another disadvantage is that when a large number of buttons are grouped in a bar, they consume a great deal of screen space and they can easily create screen clutter. In circumstances where they do not possess a label, the necessity of learning and remembering what they are used for can also cause problems.

Proper Usage Buttons are best for frequently used actions in a window. They can be used to cause actions to occur immediately, such as saving a document, quitting a system, or deleting text. They can be used to display a menu of options, such as colors or fonts. Windows 95 calls a button that leads to a menu a *menu button*. Buttons can also be used to display other secondary windows or dialog boxes, and to expand the dialog or invoke dialog features. Windows 95 calls a button that expands the dialog an *unfold button*. Buttons may also be used to reflect a mode or property value setting similar to the use of radio buttons or check boxes. In some kinds of windows, command buttons may be the only command method available to the user.

Command Buttons

Command button guidelines include the following.

Usage

- For windows with a menu bar:
  - Use to provide convenient access to frequently-used commands.
- For windows without a menu bar:
  - Use to provide access to all necessary commands.

For windows having access to a menu bar, frequently used commands normally retrievable through the menu bar may also be included as command buttons. This provides much more convenient access. Buttons must also be provided for situations where a command is not available through the menu bar. For windows without menu bars, buttons must be provided to provide access to all window commands.

Structure

- Provide a rectangular shape with the label inscribed within it.
- Maintain consistency in style through an application.

The shape of a button can vary. Generally, rectangular-shaped buttons are preferred because they provide the best fit for horizontally arrayed textual captions. Square-cornered rectangles are found in Microsoft Windows and OSF/Motif, rounded-corner rectangles are found in OPEN LOOK, Presentation Manager, and suggested in IBM's SAA CUA. Drop shadows will be found in Microsoft Windows, OPEN LOOK, and in NeXTStep. OSF/Motif uses beveled edges. The button style chosen is mostly a matter of preference. It is critical, however, that the button style chosen should be consistently maintained throughout a system.

Labels

- Use standard button labels when available.
- Provide meaningful descriptions of the actions that will be performed.
- Use single-word labels whenever possible.
  - Use two-three words for clarity, if necessary.
- Use mixed-case letters with the first letter of each label word capitalized.
- Display labels:
  - In the regular system font.
  - In the same size font.
- Do not number labels.
- Center the label within the button borders leaving at least two pixels between the text and the button border.
- Provide consistency in button labeling across all screens.

Button labels should be clearly spelled out, with meaningful descriptions of the actions they will cause to be performed. Choices should be composed of mixed-case single words. Multiple words are preferred, however, to single words lacking clarity in their intent. If multiple-word labels are used, capitalize the first letter of each word. Use the same size and style of font in all buttons. The regular system font is preferred. Never change font style or size within buttons; these kinds of changes can be very distracting to the viewer. Center each label within the button borders, leaving at least two pixels between the text and the border.

Common button functions should have standard names and uses. IBM's SAA CUA, for example, provides these standard names and definitions:

OK—Any changed information in the window is accepted and the window is closed.

APPLY—Any changed information in the window is accepted and again displayed in the window.

RESET—Cancels any changed information that has not been submitted.

CANCEL—Closes window without performing nonsubmitted changes.

HELP—Displays, if available, contextual help for the item on which the cursor is positioned. If no contextual help is available, help for the entire window is displayed.

Always follow all platform presentation and usage guidelines for standard button functions.

Size

- Maintain consistent button heights and widths.
  - Exception: Buttons containing excessively long labels may be wider.

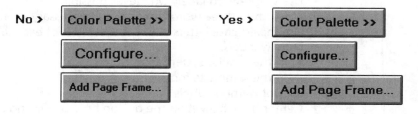

Buttons must be wide enough to accommodate the longest label. Leave at least two pixels between labels and button borders. Create standard, equal-sized buttons encompassing the majority of system functions. When a button's label will not fit within the standard size, expand the button's size to achieve a proper label fit. Never reduce the font size of some labels to create equal-sized buttons. In this case, buttons of different widths are preferable. Also, do not create an unnecessarily wide button for aesthetic balance purposes, as illustrated by the Color Palette button in Figure 7.4. The perceptual model we possess in our memory for a button will be lost.

Number

- Restrict the number of buttons on a window to six or fewer.

The maximum number of buttons on a window must reflect a balance between effectiveness, real estate efficiency, and operational simplicity. No more than six buttons on a window seems to appropriately balance these issues. If an extra button or two is necessary, and space is available, they may be included.

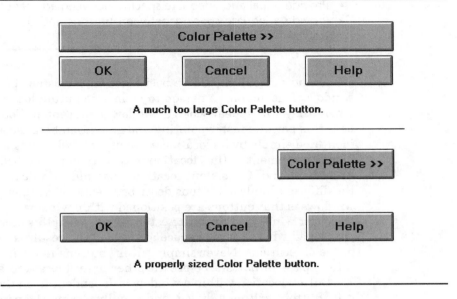

A much too large Color Palette button.

A properly sized Color Palette button.

Figure 7.4   Improper, and proper, button sizes.

Location and Layout

- Maintain consistency in button location between windows.
- Never simply "fit-in" buttons in available space.
- If buttons are for exiting the dialog:
  - Position centered and aligned horizontally at the bottom.
- If buttons are for invoking a dialog feature or expanding the dialog:
  - Position centered and aligned vertically on the right side.
- If a button has a contingent relationship to another control:
  - Position adjacent to the related control.
- If a button has a contingent relationship to a group of controls:
  - Position at the bottom or to right of related controls.
- If, due to space constraints, exiting and expanding/invoking feature buttons must be placed together:
  - If at bottom, place exiting buttons to right, separating the groupings by one button's width.
  - If along the right side, place exiting buttons to the bottom, separating the groupings by one button's height.
- For exiting and expanding/invoking feature buttons, do not:
  - Align with the other screen controls.
  - Present displayed within a line border.

- Provide equal and adequate spacing between adjacent buttons.
- Provide adequate spacing between buttons and the screen body controls.

Command buttons should be positioned in consistent positions within a window. This enables a person to memorize button locations and predict where they will appear when a window is presented. For an experienced user this permits faster pointing and activation because a button may be identified simply by its location without its label having to be read, and a mouse movement to that location may be commenced before a window is even displayed. Consistent locations also aid in quickly discriminating the different kinds of buttons described below. A common failing of many windows is that buttons are positioned within windows *after* locations for the other window controls are established. When this occurs, buttons are positioned where there is space available. The result is usually a hodgepodge of locations. Never simply "fit in" buttons in available space. Allocate a space for buttons before the other control locations are established.

Button location within a window is dependent upon the type of button it is. Buttons *exiting* a dialog, and usually closing the window, should be positioned horizontally, and centered, across the lower part of the window. If a button *invokes* a dialog feature or *expands* the dialog, position it centered and aligned vertically along the right side of the window. Maintaining these consistent locations will enable a person to quickly identify what general kind of button it is, and what kind of action will occur if the button is activated. Location of the exiting buttons across the bottom will also allow more efficient use of window real estate when invoking/expanding buttons are not included within a window. Exiting and expanding/invoking feature button locations are illustrated in Figure 7.5. If, due to screen space constraints, exiting and expanding/invoking feature buttons must be positioned together at the screen bottom, place the exiting buttons to the right, separating the groupings by one standard button's width. If they are located together along the right side, place exiting buttons to the bottom, separating the groupings by one button's height.

If a button has a *contingent* relationship to another control, position it adjacent to the related control in the order in which the controls are usually operated, as illustrated in Figure 7.6. If a button possesses a contingent relationship to a group of controls, position it to the bottom or to the right of the grouping, again in logical flow order, as illustrated in Figure 7.7.

For exiting and expanding/invoking feature buttons, do not provide alignment with the other screen controls. Maintain alignment and spacing only within the buttons themselves. Trying to align the buttons to

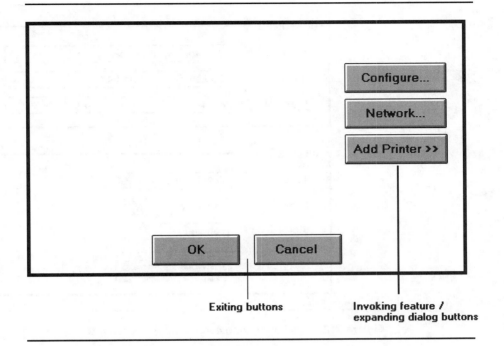

Figure 7.5   Exiting and invoking feature/expanding dialog buttons.

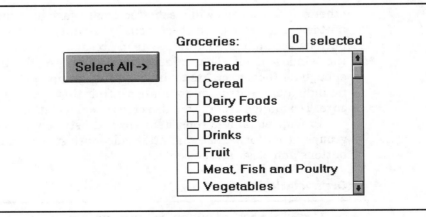

Figure 7.6   Button with contingent relationship to a control.

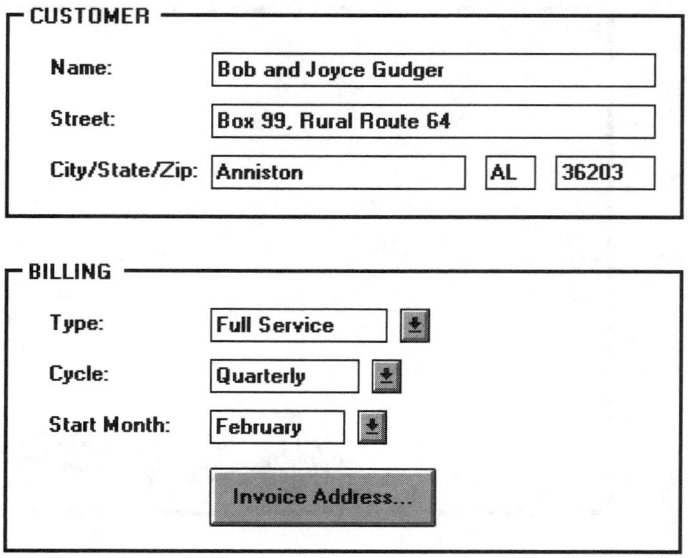

Figure 7.7   Button with contingent relationship to a grouping.

other screen controls will most often create variable spacing between the buttons themselves, which is visually distracting. Also, do not display buttons within a line border; instead present them on the background of the window itself. The unique physical look of the buttons is strong enough for them to create their own visual grouping. Reserve line borders for individual controls or groups of controls that are in greater need of closure. Too many borders can also create visual clutter.

Provide equal and consistent spacing between adjacent buttons, and groups of buttons. Also, maintain adequate separation between screen buttons and other screen controls.

Organization

- Organize standard buttons in the manner recommended by the platform being used.
- For other buttons, organize in common and customary grouping schemes.

- For buttons ordered left to right, place most frequent actions to the left.
- For buttons ordered top to bottom, place most frequent actions at the top.
- Keep related buttons grouped together.
- Separate potentially destructive buttons from frequently chosen selections.
- Buttons found on more than one window should be consistently positioned.
- The orders should never change.
- For mutually exclusive actions, use two buttons, do not dynamically change the text.

Follow the standard, consistent ordering schemes recommended by the platform being used. Windows 95 recommends the following:

- An affirmative action to left (or above).
- The default first.
- OK and Cancel next to each other.
- Help last, if supported.

IBM's SAA CUA suggests:

- Application specific buttons.
- OK.
- Apply.
- Reset.
- Cancel.
- Help.

Since platform differences sometimes exist, and people may be using more than one, some organization compromises may be necessary.

Buttons should be ordered logically, such as by frequency of use, sequence of use, or importance. For buttons arrayed left to right, start ordering from left to right. For buttons arrayed top to bottom, start ordering from top to bottom.

Keep related buttons grouped together. Separate potentially destructive buttons from frequently chosen selections to avoid inadvertent activation and potentially catastrophic results. Always locate the same buttons included on different windows in consistent positions. For mutually exclusive actions, avoid using one button that toggles changing text. This can be confusing. Use two buttons with labels that clearly describe the two actions.

Intent Indicators

- When a button causes an action to be immediately performed:
  - No intent indicator is necessary.

- When a button leads to a cascading dialog:
  - Include an ellipsis (. . .) after the label.

- When a button leads to a menu:
  - Include a triangle pointing in the direction the menu will appear after the label.

- When a button leads to an expanding dialog:
  - Include a double arrow (>>) with the label.

- When a button contingent relationship to another control must be indicated:
  - Include a single arrow (->) pointing at the control.

Button intent indicators will follow, where applicable, the same conventions used on menu items. When a button causes a command to be immediately performed, no special intent indicator on the button is necessary. When a button leads to a cascading dialog box, include an ellipsis with the label. When a button leads to a menu of choices, include a triangle after the label; point the triangle in the direction the menu will appear. If a button expands the dialog, include a double arrow with the label. When a button has a contingent relationship to another control, include a single arrow pointing at the control. Intent indicators are very useful because they enable the user to predict the consequences of an intended action.

Expansion Buttons

- Gray out after expansion.
- Provide a contraction button, if necessary.
  - Locate beneath, or to right of, expansion button.
  - Gray out when not applicable.

When a button that expands a dialog is activated, and the dialog is expanded, display the button dimmed or grayed. If the dialog can again be contracted, provide a contraction button beneath or to the right of the expansion button. Gray this button when the dialog is contracted; display at normal intensity when the dialog is expanded.

Defaults

Intent

- When a window is first displayed, provide a default action, if practical.

Selection

- A default should be the most likely action:
  - A confirmation.
  - An application of the activity being performed.
  - A positive action such as OK, unless the result is catastrophic.
- If a destructive action is performed (such as a deletion), the default should be CANCEL.

Presentation

- Indicate the default action by displaying the button with a bold or double border.

Procedures

- The default can be changed as the user interacts with the window.
- When the user navigates to a button, it can temporarily become the default.
- Use the ENTER key to activate a default button.
- If another control requires use of the ENTER key, temporarily disable the default while the focus is on the other control.
- Permit double-clicking on a single selection control on a window to also carry out the default command.

When a window with buttons is first displayed, provide a default action whenever practical. The default action should be the most likely action with the window. It may be a confirmation, an application of the activity being performed, or a positive response such as OK. If the default is irreversible or destructive (such as Delete), the default should be Cancel, requiring a person to change the selection in order to perform the destructive action. If none of the buttons is destructive in nature, the default button should be the one most frequently selected.

The default can be changed as the user interacts with a window. When the user navigates to a button, it can temporarily become the default. Return the button to its original state when the focus leaves a button. Permit use of the Enter key to activate a default button. If another control requires use of the Enter key, temporarily disable the default while the focus is on the other control. Permit double-clicking on a single selection control in a window to also carry out the default command.

Unavailable Choices

- Temporarily unavailable choices should be dimmed or "grayed out."

A button should visually indicate whether it is available for activation. Dim or gray out actions that are not available.

Keyboard Equivalents and Accelerators

Equivalents

- Assign a keyboard equivalent mnemonic to each button to facilitate keyboard selection.
- The mnemonic should be the first character of the button's label.
  - If duplication exists in first characters, for duplicate items, use another character in the label.
  - Preferably, choose the first succeeding consonant.
- Designate the mnemonic character by underlining it.
- Maintain the same mnemonic on all identical buttons on other screens.

A̲pply

Accelerators

- Assign a keyboard accelerator to each button to facilitate keyboard selection.

Enabling the user to select button actions through the typewriter keyboard provides flexibility and efficiency in the dialog. To do this, provide keyboard equivalent, single-character mnemonic codes that, when typed, will cause the action to be performed. The suggested method to indicate the accelerator is by underlining the proper character in the button label.

Keyboard accelerators, a keyboard key or combination of keys, may also be assigned to buttons to facilitate keyboard activation.

Keyboard equivalents and accelerators are more fully described in Step 5, "Develop System Menus."

Scrolling

- If a window can be scrolled, do not scroll the buttons.
- Use buttons to move between multipage forms, not scroll bars.
  - Label buttons NEXT and PREVIOUS.

If scrolling the contents of a window, never scroll the buttons. They should be available at all times. Use buttons to move between multipage forms, not scroll bars. Paging is, conceptually, easier for people to use and understand. Label the buttons Next and Previous.

Button Activation

Pointing

- Highlight the button in some visually distinctive manner when the pointer is resting on it and the button is available for selection.

Activation

- Call attention to the button in another visually distinctive manner when it has been activated or pressed.
- If a button can be pressed continuously, permit the user to hold the mouse button down and repeat the action.

Highlight the button in some visually distinctive manner when the pointer is resting on it and the button is available for selection. This will provide the user feedback that the selection process may be performed. Some systems, such as Sun's OPEN LOOK, display a brighter button.

Highlight the button in another visually distinctive manner when it has been activated or pressed to indicate that the action is successful. OPEN LOOK subdues or grays the button. OSF/Motif has raised beveled buttons that appear to sink into the screen when selected. Another alternative is to move the button slightly as if it had been depressed. If a button can be pressed continuously, permit the mouse button to be held down and the action repeated.

Buttonbar/Toolbars

Buttonbars are compilations of commands, actions, or functions grouped together for speedy access. Microsoft (1995) calls this control a *toolbar* and defines it as a panel that contains a *set* of controls. Buttonbars may also be called *control bars* or *access bars*. Specialized buttonbars may also be referred to as *ribbons*, *tool boxes*, or *palettes*.

Usage

- To provide easy access to most frequently used commands or options.
- To invoke a sub-application within an application.

Provide buttonbars to allow fast and easy access to a system's most frequently used commands, functions, or options. Also provide buttonbars for easily invoking subapplications within an application. Buttonbars are considered "fast paths" or expert aids. All buttonbar functions must also be obtainable by normal means, including through use of the menu bar.

Size

- Button.
  - 24 (w) by 22 (h) pixels including border.
  - 32 (w) by 30 (h) pixels including border.
  - Larger buttons can be used on high resolution displays.
- Label.
  - 16 (w) by 16 (h) pixels.
  - 14 (w) by 24 (h) pixels.
- Default.
  - Provide the smaller size as the default with a user option to change.
- Image.
  - Center image in button.

The above guidelines to achieve clear images are provided by Microsoft (1995). Other sizing guidelines and much more detailed image guidelines are presented in Step 10, "Create Meaningful Icons."

Organization

- Order the buttons based on common and customary grouping schemes.
  - For buttons ordered left to right, place most frequent actions to the left.
  - For buttons ordered top to bottom, place most frequent actions at the top.
- Keep related buttons grouped together.
- Separate potentially destructive buttons from frequently chosen selections.
- Permit user reconfiguration of button organization.

Buttonbar buttons should be ordered logically, such as by frequency of use, sequence of use, or importance. If the buttons reflect a quality on a continuum such as colors or shades, follow standard and expected ordering schemes. For buttons arrayed left to right, start ordering from left to right. For buttons arrayed top to bottom, start ordering from top to bottom.

Keep related buttons grouped together. Separate potentially destructive buttons from frequently chosen selections to avoid inadvertent activation and potentially catastrophic results. Permit the user to reconfigure the button organizational structure to better meet his or her unique needs.

Location

- Position main features and functions bar horizontally across top of window just below menu bar.
- Position sub-task and sub-features bars along sides of window.
- Permit the location of the bar to be changed by the user.
- Permit display of the bar to be turned on or off by the user.
  - Provide access through standard menus.

Locate the main features and functions tool bar horizontally across the top of the window just below the menu bar. Locate subtask and subfeature tool bars along sides of window. Permit the location of the buttonbar to be changed by the user. Since toolbars can create visual noise, permit its display to be turned on or off. Always provide access to the buttonbar actions through standard menus.

Structure

Images

- Provide buttons of equal size.
- Create a meaningful and unique icon.
  - Design utilizing icon design guidelines.
- Center the image within the button.

Text

- Create a meaningful label adhering to label guidelines for command buttons.

Create buttonbar buttons of equal size, following the size guidelines recently described. Create meaningful and unique images and icons utilizing the icon design guidelines in Step 10. Center the image within the button and provide an associated textual label. Create the label following the guidelines for command buttons. The label may be located within the button, positioned beneath it, or presented on demand through a tooltip control. If the label is located within the button and the system will be translated into one or more other languages, a caution: allow extra space for the label. See "International Translation" in Step 11 for further important considerations. A tooltip control is discussed later in this chapter.

For text-only toolbar buttons, create a meaningful label adhering to the label guidelines for command buttons.

Keyboard Equivalents and Accelerators

Equivalents

- Assign keyboard equivalents to facilitate keyboard selection.
- Maintain the same mnemonic on all identical buttons on other screens.

Accelerators

- Assign keyboard accelerator to facilitate keyboard selection.

Provide keyboard equivalents and accelerators to facilitate keyboard selection. Maintain the same mnemonic on all identical buttons on other screens. One caution, if a particular mnemonic is being used in the window, it may not be available for accessing the buttonbar.

Button Activation

Pointing

- Highlight the button in some visually distinctive manner when the pointer is resting on it and the button is available for selection.

Activation

- Call attention to the button in another visually distinctive manner when it has been activated or pressed.

Highlight the button in some visually distinctive manner when the pointer is resting on it and the button is available for selection. This will provide the user feedback that the selection process may be performed.

Highlight the button in another visually distinctive manner when it has been activated or pressed to indicate that the action is successful.

TEXT ENTRY/READ-ONLY CONTROLS

A Text Entry/Read-Only control contains text that is exclusively entered or modified through the keyboard. It may also contain text for reading or display purposes only.

Text Boxes

General

Description

- A control, usually rectangular in shape, in which:
  - Text may be entered or edited.
  - Text may be displayed for read-only purposes.
- Usually possesses a caption describing the kind of information contained within it.
- An outline field border:
  - Is included for enterable/editable text boxes.
  - Is not included for read-only text boxes.
- Two types exist:
  - Single line.
  - Multiple line.
- When first displayed, the box may be blank or contain an initial value.

Purpose
- To permit the display, entering, or editing of textual information.
- To display read-only information.

Advantages/Disadvantages
- + Very flexible.
- + Familiar.
- + Consumes little screen space.
- − Requires use of typewriter keyboard.
- − Requires user to remember what must be keyed.

Proper Usage
- Most useful for data that is:
  - − Unlimited in scope.
  - − Difficult to categorize.
  - − Of a variety of different lengths.
- When using a selection list is not possible.

Single Line

Description
- A control consisting of no more than one line of text.

Purpose
- To make textual entries when the information can be contained within one line of the screen.

Typical Uses
- Typing the name of a file to save.
- Typing the path of a file to copy.
- Typing variable data on a form.
- Typing a command.

Multiple Line

Description
- A control consisting of a multi-line rectangular box for multiple lines of text.

Purpose
- To type, edit, and read passages of text.

Typical Uses
- Creating or reading an electronic mail message.
- Displaying and editing text files.

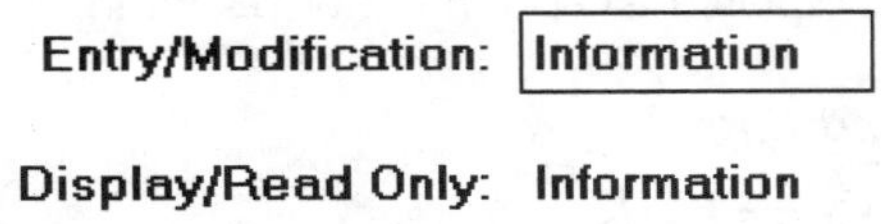

Entry/Modification: Information

Display/Read Only: Information

Figure 7.8   Text boxes.

Two kinds of *text boxes* exist. One consists of a rectangular box into which information is typed. The second is also rectangular in shape but contains text displayed purely for read-only purposes. The former have historically been referred to as *entry fields*, the latter *inquiry* or *display fields*. While display-only text boxes are not operable in the true sense of the word, the information contained within them is capable of being modified by other controls. Hence, they will be reviewed as an operable control since their characteristics, and the characteristics of an entry field, are very similar. Some platforms (e.g., Microsoft Windows 95) also classify both as text boxes. Microsoft (1995) also refers to a text box as an *edit control*.

Text boxes almost always possess a separate caption describing the kind of information to be keyed. An enterable text box is visually presented on the screen, its shape being defined by an outline border or a reversal in screen polarity. The information in a read-only text field is most effectively displayed on the screen background, not in a box. Therefore, the information contained in read-only text boxes is not surrounded by a box.

Text boxes exist in two forms: single-line and multiple-line. Single-line boxes are used when the information contained within it can be confined to one screen line. Multiple-line boxes are used when the information cannot be confined to one line. When first displayed, a text box may be blank or contain an initial value. Text boxes are illustrated in Figure 7.8.

Text boxes are familiar, flexible, and consume little screen space. They do require a typewriter keyboard, which, depending upon one's skill with a keyboard, may be an advantage or a disadvantage. A disadvantage to all is that what is keyed into an entry field must often be remembered. They are most useful for data that is difficult to categorize or unlimited in scope, or when use of a selection field is not possible. A text box's display and organizational principles are similar to those for text-based screens.

Captions

Structure and Size

- Provide a descriptive caption to identify the kind of information to be typed, or contained within, the text box.

- Use a mixed-case font.
- Display the caption in normal intensity or in a color of moderate brightness.

Formatting

- Single fields:
  - Position the field caption to the left of the text box.
    - Place a colon (:) immediately following the caption.
    - Separate the colon from the text box by one space.

  Composition: [   ]

  - Alternatively, the caption may be placed above the text box.
    - Place a colon (:) immediately following the caption.
    - Position above the upper-left corner of the box, flush with the left edge.

  Composition:
  [   ]

- Multiple occurrence fields:
  - For entry/modification text boxes:
    - Position the caption left-justified one line above the column of entry fields.

  Offices:
  [   ]
  [   ]
  [   ]

  - For display/read-only boxes:
    - If the data field is long and fixed-length, or the displayed data is about the same length, center the caption above the displayed text box data.

  Date:
  | 07/17/94 |
  | 07/21/94 |
  | 01/26/95 |
  | 08/21/95 |
  | 11/18/96 |

    - If the data displayed is alphanumeric, short, or quite variable in length, left-justify the caption above the displayed text box data.

Location:

Alice Springs
Kakadu National Park
Traralgon
Wagga Wagga
Whyalla

- If the data field is numeric and variable in length, right-justify the caption above the displayed text box data.

Balances:

12,642,123.05
53.98
355,125.44
199.13
612.01

Captions are usually added to text boxes using static text fields. Many toolsets do not include captions with text box controls. Captions must be understandable, and fully spelled out in a language meaningful to the user. In general, abbreviations and contractions should not be used. To achieve the alignment recommendations (to be discussed shortly), however, an occasional abbreviation or contraction may be necessary. If so, choose those that are common in the everyday language of the user or those that are meaningful or easily learned. Use mixed-case text in the caption, capitalizing only the first letter of each word (except for articles, conjunctions, and prepositions—a, the, and, for, etc.). Acronyms, abbreviations, or proper nouns that are normally capitalized, however, may be capitalized. If the caption is of a sentence-style nature, sentence-style capitalization should be followed. In this case, capitalize only the first letter of the first word of the caption.

In relation to the text box, the caption should be of normal intensity or consist of a moderately bright color. Visual emphasis should always be given to the information in the text box.

For single fields, it is recommended that the caption should precede the text box. Place a colon (:) directly following the caption to visually separate the caption from the data; separate the colon from the text box by one space.

For multiple-occurrence fields, the caption should be positioned above the columnized text boxes. The exact location of the caption will depend on the kind of screen and the kind of data displayed. For entry screens, the caption should be left-justified above the columnized entry fields. This will signal the starting point of the text box and assure the caption is positioned directly above the keyed data.

For display/read-only or inquiry screens where text box information already exists, positioning of the caption depends on the kind of information displayed within the box. The objective is to center the caption over the information. If the box is fixed-length, or the information to be displayed within it usually fills, or almost fills, the box, center the caption above the data. If the information is alphanumeric and can be quite variable in length, left-justify the caption. This will keep the caption directly above the data when it appears in the box. Similarly, for numeric fields, right-justify the caption to keep it above the data that will be right-justified when it appears.

Fields

Structure

- Identify entry/modification text boxes with a line border or reverse polarity rectangular box.

  Account: [Savings]

- Present display/read-only text boxes on the window background.

  Account: Savings

- Break up long text boxes through incorporation of slashes (/), dashes (–), spaces, or other common delimiters.

  Date: [ ] [ ] [ ]

  Telephone: [ ] [ ] [ ]

  Date: [/ /]

  Telephone: [( ) -]

Size

- Text boxes for fixed-length data must be large enough to contain the entire entry.
- Text boxes for variable-length data must be large enough to contain the majority of the entries.
  - Where entries may be larger than the entry field, scrolling must be provided to permit keying into, or viewing, the entire field.
  - Employ word wrapping for continuous text in multiple-line text boxes.

Highlighting

- Call attention to text box data through a highlighting technique.
  - Higher intensity.
  - If color is used, choose one that both complements the screen background and contrasts well with it.

A text box should attract attention, but not detract from the legibility of the data contained within it, be capable of allowing an indication of the structure of the data contained within it, and indicate the appropriate number of characters to be keyed into it. Savage et al. (1982) found that, in meeting these objectives, a broken underscore and an outlined box were the best delimiters for screen entry fields. The older text-based screens traditionally have used the underscore as the delimiter; graphical screens, the outlined box. Interestingly, both resemble the coding areas most frequently found on paper forms. Present display/read-only text boxes on the window background. To make text boxes more readable, it is desirable to break them up into logical pieces. Slashes, dashes, and spaces should be inserted into the entry fields as illustrated.

Text boxes for fixed-length data must be long enough to contain the entry. Variable-length text boxes should be large enough to contain the majority of the entries. The size of a variable-length text box will be dependent on field alignment, space utilization, and aesthetics. If a text box is not large enough to key, or view, the entire entry, it must be scrollable. Scrolling, however, should be avoided whenever possible.

Text box data (as opposed to captions) is the most important part of a screen. Call attention to it through highlighting techniques. With monochrome screens, display it bright or in high intensity. With color, use the brightest colors. As will be more fully described in Step 9, the brightest colors are white and yellow. If a box is the delimiter, choose a background color that complements the screen body background and provides good contrast with the color chosen for the data

SELECTION CONTROLS

A selection control presents on the screen all the possible alternatives, conditions, or choices that may exist for an entity, property, or value. From those displayed, the relevant item, or items, are selected. Some selection controls present all the alternatives together on a screen, others may require an action to retrieve the entire listing and/or scrolling to view all the alternatives. Selection controls include radio buttons, check boxes, list boxes, drop-down/pop-up list boxes, and palettes.

Radio Buttons

Description
- A two-part control consisting of the following:
  - Small circles, diamonds, or rectangles.
  - Choice descriptions.
- When a choice is selected:
  - The option is highlighted.
  - Any existing choice is automatically un-highlighted and de-selected.

Purpose
- To set one of a small set of mutually exclusive options (2-8).

Advantages/Disadvantages
- + Easy to access choices.
- + Easy to compare choices.
- + Preferred by users.
- − Consume screen space.
- − Limited number of choices.

Proper Usage
- For setting attributes, properties, or values.
- For mutually exclusive choices (i.e., only one can be selected).
- Where adequate screen space is available.
- Most useful for data and choices that are:
  - Discrete.
  - Small and fixed in number.
  - Not easily remembered.
  - In need of a textual description to meaningfully describe the alternatives.
  - Most easily understood when the alternatives may be seen together and compared to one another.
  - Never changed in content.
- Do not use:
  - For commands.
  - Singly to indicate the presence or absence of a state.

Controls of this type take several different physical forms. They are most often called *radio buttons* because of their resemblance to similar controls on radios. Microsoft Windows, however, refers to these controls as *option buttons*. One common display method consists of a circle associated with each choice description. When an alternative is selected, the center of the circle is partially or fully filled in to provide a visual indication that it is

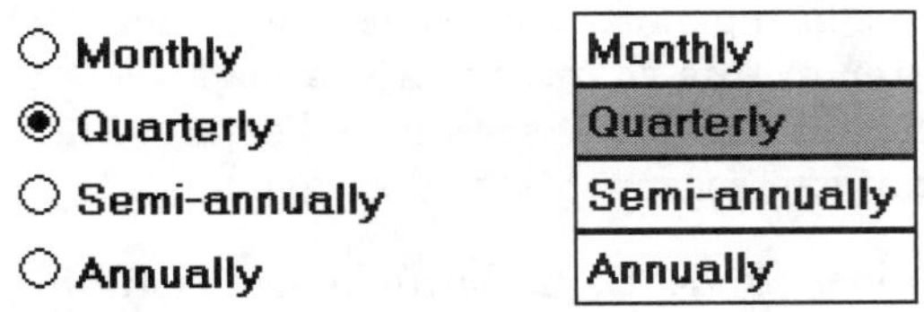

Figure 7.9   Radio buttons.

the active choice. Macintosh, OS/2 Presentation Manager, Windows 3.1, DECwindows, and IBM's SAA CUA have used this approach. Other styles of radio buttons have also been implemented. Windows 95 uses a small depressed circle that contains a small dot when selected. NeXTStep uses small circular buttons that look recessed when not selected and are raised when selected. OSF/Motif uses small diamond-shaped buttons that look raised when not selected and depressed when selected.

A different method for presenting exclusive choices is the butted box or button where the alternatives are inscribed in horizontally arrayed adjoining rectangles resembling command buttons. The selected alternative is highlighted in some way. Xerox's Star, OPEN LOOK (which calls them *two state exclusive settings*), and Silicon Graphics's SGI have used this approach.

Examples of radio buttons are illustrated in Figures 7.9 and 7.10. Deciding on which style to use seems to be more a matter of preference than performance. No published comparison studies are available for guidance.

Radio buttons are used to designate one of a small set of options, no more than about eight. Like a radio, the choices are mutually exclusive, only one *frequency* or *setting* is permitted at one time in the presented array.

Advantages/Disadvantages With radio buttons, all alternatives are always visible. Therefore, it is easy to access and compare choices. Two recent studies (Johnsgard, Page, Wilson, & Zeno, 1995; Tullis & Kodimer,

Figure 7.10   Radio buttons.

1992) have found radio buttons a preferred and very effective control for presenting mutually exclusive choices. These studies will be described later in this chapter. On the negative side, radio buttons do consume a certain amount of screen real estate, limiting the number of alternatives that can reasonably be displayed.

Proper Usage Radio buttons are useful for setting attributes, properties, or values where adequate screen space is available. The alternatives should be discrete, small in number, and in need of a textual description to identify meaningfully. Radio buttons are helpful in situations where the alternatives cannot always be easily remembered or where displaying the alternatives together facilitates understanding and selection of the proper choice. Radio button choices displayed should be stable, never changing in content.

Do not use radio buttons for implementing commands, such as causing a dialog box to immediately appear based upon a button setting. Commands to the system should result from direct user command actions, such as pressing a command button. Also, do not use one radio button by itself to indicate the presence or absence of a state. A single check box is recommended for this purpose.

Choice Descriptions

- Provide meaningful, fully spelled-out choice descriptions clearly describing the values or effects set by the radio buttons.
- Display in a single line of text.
- Display using mixed-case letters with each significant word capitalized.
- Position descriptions to the right of the button. Separate by at least one space from the button.
- When a choice is conditionally unavailable for selection, display choice description grayed or dimmed.
- Include a NONE choice if it adds clarity.

Choice descriptions must be clear, meaningful, fully spelled out, and displayed in a mixed-case text. For multiword descriptions, capitalize the first letter of each significant word. Small button-type indicators should be located to the left of the choice description; rectangular-shaped boxes will find the description within the box. Small buttons associated with text are advantageous when the choice description must be lengthy. Descriptions in boxes impose restrictions on the number of words that can be inscribed within them. When a choice is conditionally unavailable for selection, display the choice selection grayed or dimmed. Where a None alternative clarifies the alternatives presented, provide it in the listing.

Size

- Show a minimum of two choices, a maximum of eight.

Generally, selection fields of this style should not present more than eight choices. Displaying more than eight is usually not efficient, wasting screen space. If the number of choices exceeds this maximum, consider using a list box or a drop-down list box. Johnsgard et al. (1995) have found, however, that even for as many as thirty choices, radio buttons were preferred by users, and performed better, than these other controls.

Defaults

- When the control possesses a state or affect that has been predetermined to have a higher probability of selection than the others, designate it as the default and display it's button filled in.
- When the control includes choices whose states cannot be predetermined, display all the buttons without setting a dot, or in the *indeterminate* state.
- When a multiple selection includes choices whose states vary, display the buttons in another unique manner, or in the *mixed value* state.

Provide a default setting for a radio button whenever possible. In some situations, however, a default setting may be difficult to predetermine, or inappropriate to predetermine (sex: male or female?). Windows 95 provides for additional settings called the *mixed value,* or *indeterminate* states. When a default setting cannot be preestablished due to the nature of the information, leave all the buttons blank or not filled in. If a multiple selection is performed and the values in the selection differ, display the applicable radio buttons in another distinctive manner, such as a gray shadow.

Structure

- A columnar orientation is the preferred manner of presentation.
- Left-align the buttons and choice descriptions.

    ○ Red
    ◉ Yellow
    ○ Green
    ○ Blue

- If vertical space on the screen is limited, orient the buttons horizontally.
- Provide adequate separation between choices so that the buttons are associated with the proper description.
  - A distance equal to three spaces is usually sufficient.

⦿ Green   ◯ Blue   ◯ Yellow   ◯ Red

- Enclose the buttons in a border to visually strengthen the relationship they possess.

◯ Red
◯ Yellow
◯ Green
◯ Blue

◯ Green   ◯ Blue   ◯ Yellow   ◯ Red

The preferred orientation of radio buttons is columnar. This aids visual scanning and choice comparison. Controls with small button indicators usually fit best in this manner because choice descriptions do not have to be restricted in size. Left-align the buttons and choice descriptions. Provide adequate separation—about three spaces—between choices if they must be presented horizontally. Enclose the buttons in a border. Rectangular boxes should be of equal height and/or width and be butted up against one another. This will distinguish them from nonexclusive choice fields (check boxes) that will be separated from one another. Figure 7.11 illustrates the best ways to, and ways not to, present radio buttons.

Organization

- Arrange selections in expected orders or follow other patterns such as frequency of occurrence, sequence of use, or importance.
  - For selections arrayed top to bottom, begin ordering at the top.
  - For selections arrayed left to right, begin ordering at the left.
- If, under certain conditions, a choice is not available, display it subdued or less brightly than the available choices.

Selection choices should be organized logically. If the alternatives have an expected order, follow it. Other ordering schemes such as frequency of use, sequence of use, or importance may also be considered. Always begin ordering at the top or left. If, under certain conditions, a choice is not available, display the nonselectable choice subdued or less brightly than the available choices.

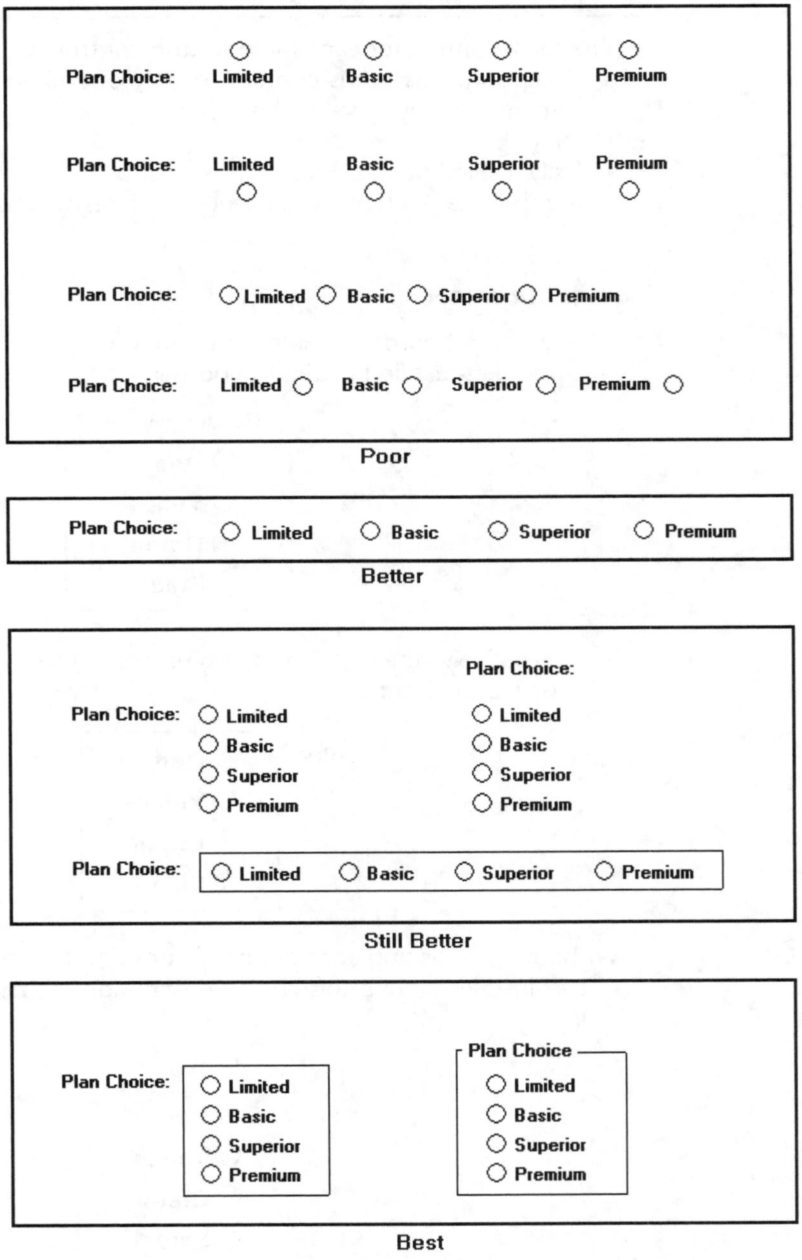

Figure 7.11 Ways to, and not to, present radio buttons.

Captions

- Provide a caption for each radio button control.
  - Exception: In screens containing only one radio button control, the screen title may serve as the caption.
- Display:
  - Fully spelled out.
  - In mixed-case letters capitalizing the first letter of all significant words.

Columnar Orientation

- With a control border, position the caption:
  - Upper-left-justified within the border.

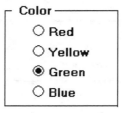

  - Alternatively, the caption may be located to the left of the topmost choice description.

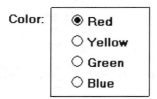

- Without an enclosing control border, position the caption:
  - Left-justified above the choice descriptions separated by one space line.

  Color:

  ◉ Red
  ○ Yellow
  ○ Green
  ○ Blue

  - Alternatively, the caption may be located to the left of the topmost choice description.

Color: ○ Red
○ Yellow
◉ Green
○ Blue

Horizontal Orientation

- Position the caption to the left of the choice descriptions.

Color: ○ Green   ○ Blue   ○ Yellow   ○ Red

  − Alternatively, with an enclosing control border, left-justified within the border.

┌ Color ───────────────────────────────────────┐
│ ○ Green   ○ Blue   ○ Yellow   ◉ Red │
└───┘

- Be consistent in caption style and orientation within a screen.

Display the caption fully spelled out using mixed-case letters. Some occasional common abbreviations may be used, however, to achieve the alignment goals to be specified. The preferred location of a radio button control caption within a screen can vary. Ideally, the caption is placed upper-left-justified within a line border, or group box, surrounding columnar-oriented radio buttons as shown in the example in the above guideline summary. If other controls on a screen possess captions positioned to the left, and the radio button control is aligned with these controls, position the caption to the left of the control. This will help achieve screen efficiency, minimize viewer eye movements, and provide caption and choice distinctiveness. Without an enclosing control border, position the caption left-justified above the choice descriptions, or to the left of the topmost choice description. In a horizontal orientation, position the caption to the left of the choice descriptions, or left-justified within an enclosing control border. If the screen contains only one radio button control, the screen title may serve as the control caption. Be consistent in caption style and orientation within a screen.

Keyboard Equivalents

- Assign a keyboard mnemonic to each choice description.
- Designate the mnemonic by underlining the applicable letter in the choice description.

◉ Red

Assign unique keyboard mnemonics for each alternative in the standard way, choosing the first letter (or another) and designating it by character underlining.

Selection Method and Indication

Pointing

- The selection target area should be as large as possible.
  - Include the button and the choice description text.
- Highlight the selection choice in some visually distinctive way when the cursor's resting on it and the choice is available for selection.
  - This cursor should be as long as the longest choice description plus one space at each end. Do not place the cursor over the small button.

   ○ Red
   ○ Yellow
   ○ Green
   ○ Blue

Activation

- When a choice is selected, distinguish it visually from the nonselected choices.
  - A radio button should be filled in with a solid dark dot, or made to look depressed, or higher, through use of a shadow.
- When a choice is selected, any other selected choice must be deselected.

Defaults

- If a radio button control is displayed which contains a choice previously selected or default choice, display the selected choice as set in the control.

The selection target area should be as large as possible in order to make it easy to move to. If a small button is the selection indication method used, the target area should include the button and the choice description text. If the rectangular box selection method is used, the entire box should be the target.

Highlight the selection choice in some visually distinctive way when the pointer is resting on it and the choice is available for selection. If a small button is the selection indication method used, a distinctive reverse video, reverse color, or dotted or dashed box selection cursor or bar may be used to surround the selected choice description. This cursor should be as long as the longest description plus one space at each end. The cursor should not cover the small button.

When a choice is selected, distinguish it visually from the nonselected choices. A radio button should be filled in with a solid dark dot or other similar marking, such as making the button look depressed or higher than the others through the use of drop shadows. A rectangular box can be highlighted in a manner different from when it is pointed at, or a bolder border can be drawn around it. When a choice is selected, any other selected choice must be deselected or made inactive.

If a selection field is displayed with a choice previously selected or a default choice, display the currently active choice in the same manner shown when it is selected.

Check Boxes

Description
- A two-part control consisting of:
  - A square box.
  - Choice text.
- Each option acts as a switch and can be either "on" or "off."
  - When an option is selected (on), a mark such as an "X" or "check" appears within the square box, or the box is highlighted in some other manner.
  - Otherwise the square box is unselected or empty (off).
- Each box can be:
  - Switched on or off independently.
  - Used alone or grouped in sets.

Purpose
- To set one or more options as either on or off.

Advantages/Disadvantages
- + Easy to access choices.
- + Easy to compare choices.
- + Preferred by users.
- + Consume screen space.
- − Limited number of choices.
- − Single check boxes difficult to align with other screen controls.

Proper Usage
- For setting attributes, properties, or values.
- For nonexclusive choices (i.e., more than one can be selected).
- Where adequate screen space is available.
- Most useful for data and choices that are:
  - Discrete.
  - Small and fixed in number.

- Not easily remembered.
- In need of a textual description to describe meaningfully.
- Most easily understood when the alternatives may be seen together and compared to one another.
- Never changed in content.
• Can be used to affect other controls.
• Use only when both states of a choice are clearly opposite and unambiguous.

Check box controls differ from radio buttons in that they permit selection of more than one alternative. Each option acts as a switch and can be either "on" or "off." When an option is selected (on), an X or check appears within the square box or it is highlighted in some other manner. When not selected, the square box is unselected or empty (off). Each box can be switched on or off independently. Check boxes may be used alone or grouped in sets.

Check boxes, too, may take different physical forms and be called by different names. The most common name is *check boxes*, used, for example, by Macintosh, OS/2 Presentation Manager, Microsoft Windows, and IBM's SAA CUA. Others include: *toggle buttons* (OSF/Motif and DECwindows), *switches* (NeXTStep), and *two state nonexclusive settings* (OPEN LOOK). As their names differ, differences also exist in the way these fields are presented on screens. One very common display method is the check box, which, resembling its namesake, consists of a square placed adjacent to each alternative. When the choice is selected, some systems place an X in the square to provide a visual indication that it is active. Macintosh, OS/2 Presentation Manager, and Microsoft Windows 3.1 have followed this approach. Others place a check mark in the square (IBM SAA CUA, NeXTStep, Windows 95), fill in the selected square (DECwindows), or make it look depressed when selected (OSF/Motif).

Interestingly, in the past several years both IBM (SAA CUA) and Microsoft (Windows 95) have switched from Xs to checks as the "on" mark in a check box. This has occurred because of possible confusions concerning Xs that have existed in some using communities. In an engineering environment, for example, an X marked in a box means not applicable, or not set, while a check mark customarily means active or set. Internationally, also, an X is not universally recognized. (This control is called a check box, isn't it?)

Another style for this type of field is a button or box with the choice description inscribed inside. When selected, the alternative is highlighted in some way. To distinguish these fields visually from similarly constructed fields presenting mutually exclusive choices, the buttons are not

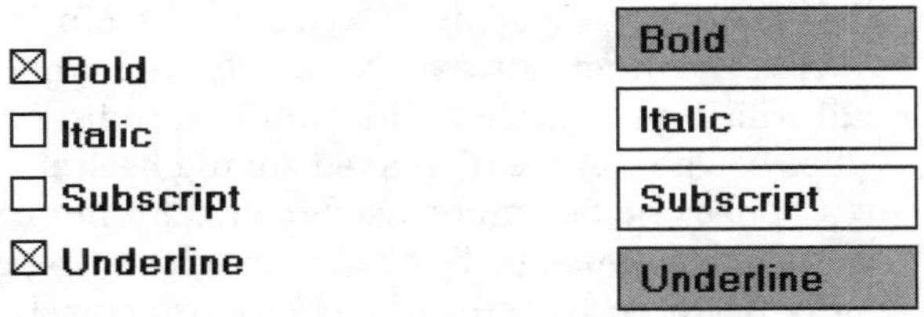

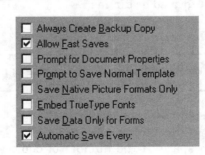

☒ Bold
☐ Italic
☐ Subscript
☒ Underline

Figure 7.12 Check boxes.

adjacent to, or butted up against, one another. OPEN LOOK also has used this approach. Check boxes are illustrated in Figures 7.12 and 7.13. Again, deciding on which style to use seems to be more a matter of preference than performance (other than for the possible confusion of Xs and checks). No published comparison studies are available for guidance.

Advantages/Disadvantages With check boxes, all alternatives are always visible. Therefore, it is easy to access and compare choices. Like radio buttons, check boxes were the preferred, and fastest to use, controls in the Johnsgard et al. (1995) study. One disadvantage is the large amount of screen real estate they consume, limiting the number of alternatives that can be efficiently displayed. Another potential disadvantage is that it can be difficult to align a single check box with other arrayed screen controls because they often possess long descriptions for clarity purposes.

Proper Usage Check boxes are useful for setting attributes, properties, or values where adequate screen space is available. The alternatives should

Figure 7.13 Check boxes.

be discrete, small in number, and in need of a textual description to identify meaningfully. Check boxes are helpful in situations where the alternatives cannot always be easily remembered, and if displaying the alternatives together aids understanding and selection of the proper choice. The choices displayed should be stable, never changing in content.

Check boxes can be used to affect other controls. The contents of a list can, for example, be filtered through setting check boxes. Use a check box only when both states of a choice are clearly opposite and unambiguous. If opposite states are not clear, use two radio buttons each clearly stating the opposite states.

Choice Descriptions

- Provide meaningful, fully spelled-out choice descriptions clearly describing the values or effects set by the check boxes.
- Display in a single line of text.
- Display using mixed-case letters with each significant word capitalized.
- Position descriptions to the right of the check box. Separate by at least one space from the box.
- When a choice is conditionally unavailable for selection, display choice description visually dimmed.

Choice descriptions must be clear, meaningful, fully spelled out, and displayed in a mixed-case text. For multiword descriptions, capitalize the first letter of each significant word. Small box-type indicators should be located to the left of the choice description, rectangular-shaped boxes will find the description within the box. Small boxes associated with text are advantageous when the choice description must be lengthy. Descriptions in boxes impose restrictions on the number of words that can be inscribed within them. When a choice is conditionally unavailable for selection, display it grayed or dimmed.

Size

- Show a minimum of one choice, a maximum of eight in a grouping.

Generally, selection fields of this style should not offer more than eight choices. Displaying more than eight is usually not efficient as it wastes screen space. If the number of choices exceeds this maximum, consider using a multiple selection list box. Johnsgard et al. (1995) have found, however, that even for as many as 30 choices, check boxes were preferred by users, and performed better, than other nonexclusive controls.

Defaults

- When the control possesses a state or affect that has been preset, designate it as the default and display it's check box marked.
- When a multiple selection includes choices whose states vary, display the buttons in another unique manner, or the *mixed value* state.

Provide a default setting for a check box whenever possible. If a multiple selection is performed and the values in the selection differ, display the applicable check boxes in the *mixed value* state, another distinctive manner such as a gray shadow.

Structure

- Provide groupings of related check boxes.
- A columnar orientation is the preferred manner of presentation for multiple related check boxes.
- Left-align the check boxes and choice descriptions.

☒ Bold

☐ Italic

☐ Underline

- If vertical space on the screen is limited, orient the boxes horizontally.
- Provide adequate separation between boxes so that the buttons are associated with the proper description.
  - A distance equal to three spaces is usually sufficient.

☒ Bold   ☐ Italic   ☐ Underline

- Enclose the boxes in a border to visually strengthen the relationship they possess.

☒ Bold
☐ Italic
☐ Underline

☒ Bold   ☐ Italic   ☐ Underline

Provide groupings of related check boxes. The preferred check box orientation is columnar. This aids scanning and choice comparison. Controls with small box indicators usually fit best in this manner because choice descriptions are not restricted in size. Left-align the check boxes and choice descriptions. Rectangular boxes should be of equal width and separated from one another by small and equidistant spaces. This will distinguish them from mutually exclusive choices that will be butted up against one another. If the boxes must be horizontally oriented, provide adequate separation between them. Enclose the boxes in a border to emphasize their relationship. Figure 7.14 illustrates ways to, and ways not to, present groupings of check boxes.

Organization

- Arrange selections in logical order or follow other patterns such as frequency of occurrence, sequence of use, or importance.
  - For selections arrayed top to bottom, begin ordering at the top.
  - For selections arrayed left to right, begin ordering at the left.
- If, under certain conditions, a choice is not available, display it subdued or less brightly than the available choices.

Selection choices should be organized logically. If the alternatives have an expected order, follow it. Other ordering schemes such as frequency of use, sequence of use, or importance may also be considered. Always begin ordering at the top or left. If, under certain conditions, a choice is not available, display the unavailable choice subdued or less brightly than the available choices.

Captions

- Provide a caption for each grouping of related check boxes.
  - Exception: In screens containing only one check box grouping, the screen title may serve as the caption.
- Display:
  - Fully spelled out.
  - In mixed-case letters capitalizing the first letter of all significant words.

Columnar Orientation

- With a control border, position the caption:
  - Upper-left-justified within the border.

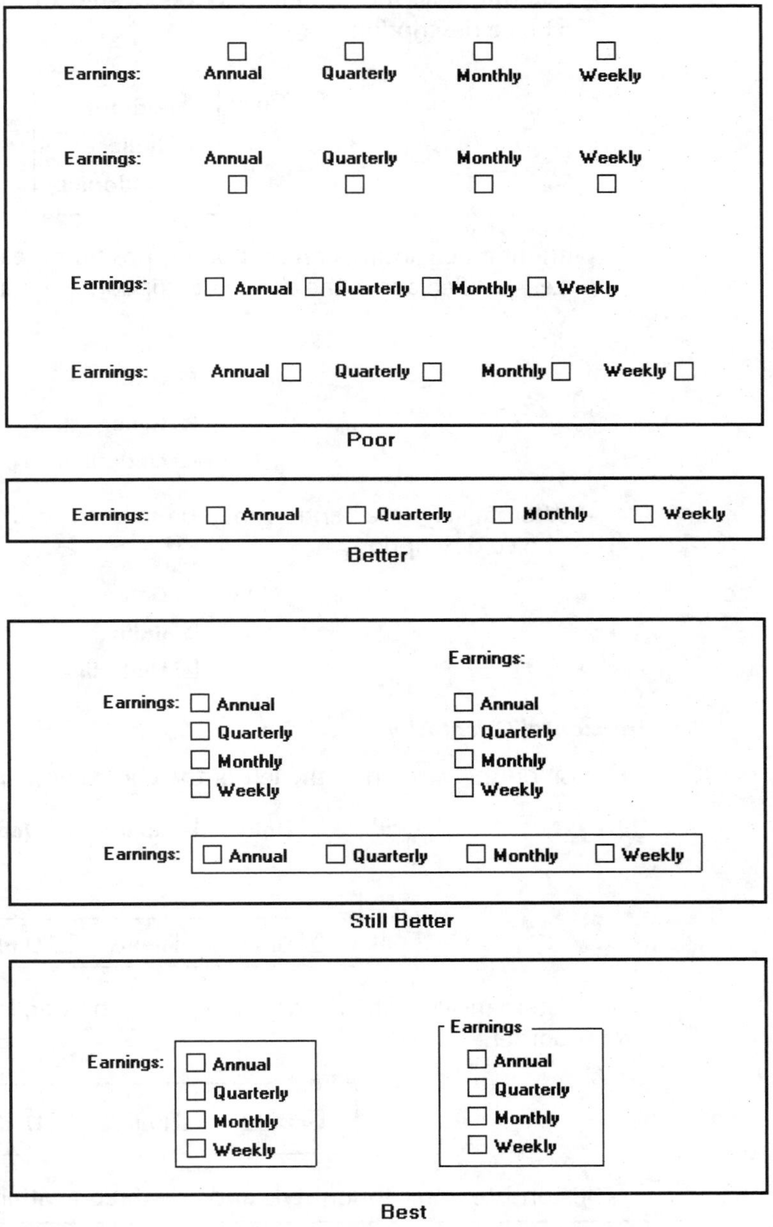

Figure 7.14 Ways to, and not to, present check boxes.

- Alternatively, the caption may be located to the left of the topmost choice description.

- Without an enclosing control border, position the caption:
  - Left-justified above the choice descriptions separated by one space line.

- Alternatively, the caption may be located to the left of the topmost choice description.

Horizontal Orientation

- Position the caption to the left of the choice descriptions.

- Alternatively, with an enclosing control border, left-justified within the border.

- Be consistent in caption style and orientation within a screen.

Provide a caption for each grouping of related check boxes. Display the caption fully spelled out using mixed-case letters. Some occasional common abbreviations may be used, however, to achieve the alignment goals to be specified. The preferred location of a check box control caption within a screen can vary. Ideally, the caption is placed upper-left-justified within a line border, or group box, surrounding columnar-oriented check boxes as shown in the first example in the above guideline summary. If other controls on a screen possess captions positioned to the left, and the check box control is aligned with these controls, position the caption to the left of the control. This is the second example illustrated above. This will help achieve screen efficiency, minimize viewer eye movements, and provide caption and choice distinctiveness. Without an enclosing border, position the caption left-justified above the choice descriptions, or to the left of the topmost choice. If horizontal orientation is necessary, position the caption to the left of the choice descriptions, or left-justified within an enclosing control border. If the screen contains only one related grouping of check boxes, the screen title may serve as the control caption. Be consistent in caption style and orientation within a screen.

Keyboard Equivalents

- Assign a keyboard mnemonic to each check box.
- Designate the mnemonic by underlining the applicable letter in the choice description.

☐ <u>U</u>nderline

Assign unique keyboard mnemonics for each check box in the standard way, choosing the first letter (or another) and designating it by character underlining.

Selection Method and Indication

Pointing

- The selection target area should be as large as possible.
  - Include the check box and the choice description text.
- Highlight the selection choice in some visually distinctive way when the cursor's resting on it and the choice is available for selection.
  - This cursor should be as long as the longest choice description plus one space at each end. Do not place the cursor over the check box.

☐ Bold

☐ Italic

☒ Underline

Activation

- When a choice is selected, distinguish it visually from the nonselected choices.
  - A check box should be filled in, or made to look depressed, or higher, through use of a shadow.

Defaults

- If a check box is displayed which contains a choice previously selected or default choice, display the selected choice as set in the control.

Mixed-value State

- When a check box represents a value, and a multiple selection encompasses multiple value occurrences set in both the on and off state, display the check box in a *mixed value* state.
  - Fill the check box with another easily differentiable symbol or pattern.

  ▓ **Bold**

  ☐ **Italic**

  ☐ **Underline**

- Toggle the check box as follows:
  - Selection 1: Set the associated value for all elements. Fill the check box with an "X" or "check."
  - Selection 2: Unset the value for all associated elements. Blank the check box.
  - Selection 3: Return all elements to their original state. Fill the check box with the mixed value symbol or pattern.

The selection target area should be as large as possible in order to make it easy to move to. If a small check box is the selection indication method used, the target area should include the box and the choice description text. If the rectangular box selection method is used, the entire box should be the target. Highlight the selection choice in some visually distinctive way when the pointer is resting on it and the choice is available for selection. If a check box is the selection indication method used, a distinctive reverse video, reverse color, or dotted or dashed box selection cursor or bar may be used to surround the selected choice description. This cursor should be as long as the longest description plus one space at each end. The cursor should not cover the check box.

When a choice is selected, distinguish it visually from the nonselected choices. A check box may be marked with an X or check or filled in. Other methods include making the button look depressed or raised through appropriate use of drop shadows. A rectangular box can be highlighted in a manner different from when it is pointed at, or a bolder border can be drawn around it. The style chosen must be consistently applied throughout an application or system.

If a selection field is displayed with a choice previously selected or a default choice, display the currently active choice in the same manner shown when it is selected.

When a check box represents a value, and a multiple selection encompasses multiple value occurrences set in both the on and off state, display the check box in a *mixed value* state. Fill the check box with another easily differentiable symbol or pattern. Toggle the check box as described in the above guidelines.

Palettes

Description

- A control consisting of a series of graphical alternatives. The choices themselves are descriptive, being comprised of colors, patterns, or images.
- In addition to being a standard screen control, a palette may also be presented on a pull-down or pop-up menu, or a buttonbar.

Purpose

- To set one of a series of mutually exclusive options that are presented graphically or pictorially.

Advantages/Disadvantages

- + Pictures aid comprehension.
- + Easy to compare choices.
- + Usually consume less screen space than textual equivalents.
- − Limited number of choices can be displayed.
- − Difficult to organize for scanning efficiency.
- − Requires skill and time to design meaningful and attractive graphical representations.

Proper Usage

- For setting attributes, properties, or values.
- For mutually exclusive choices (i.e., only one can be selected).
- Where adequate screen space is available.
- Most useful for data and choices that are:
  - Discrete.
  - Frequently selected.

  - Limited in number.
  - Variable in number.
  - Not easily remembered.
  - Most easily understood when the alternatives may be seen together and compared to one another.
  - Most meaningfully represented pictorially or by example.
  - Can be clearly represented pictorially.
  - Rarely changed in content.
- Do not use:
  - Where the alternatives cannot be meaningfully and clearly represented pictorially.
  - Where words are clearer than images.
  - Where the choices are going to change.

Like radio buttons, *palettes* can also be used to present two or more mutually exclusive alternatives. The choices presented, however, are visually descriptive within themselves. No choice descriptions are needed to identify them. Examples of palettes might be fill-in colors, patterns, or different shades of a color. A palette may also be referred to as a *value set*. Windows 95 refers to them as *wells*. A palette is illustrated in Figure 7.15. In addition to being a standard screen control, a palette may also be presented on a pull-down or pop-up menu, or be included in a buttonbar.

Advantages/Disadvantages Palettes are preferable to radio buttons in that they take up less space and allow the viewer to focus on the visual characteristics of the choice itself, instead of having to read the choice text and cross-referencing it to a radio button. Some qualities, such as colors, pat-

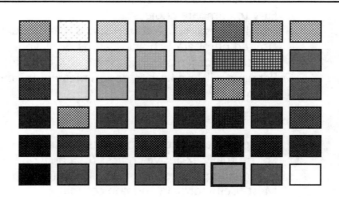

Figure 7.15   Palette.

terns, and shades, are much more easily comprehended when they are actually seen.

While a larger number of choices can be presented than with radio buttons, there is still a limit to how many can be practically displayed. Because of their larger size, palettes are also more difficult to organize for scanning efficiency. Palettes also require skill and time to design meaningful and attractive graphical representations.

Proper Usage

Palettes are used for setting attributes, properties, or values of mutually exclusive choices where adequate screen space is available. Consider using a palette when the choices have qualities that can be best described by actual illustration. They are useful for data and choices that are discrete and limited in number. They are most useful when the choices, being seen together and compared to one another, aid identification and selection of the proper alternative. They are also most useful when the alternatives can be meaningfully and clearly represented pictorially or by example. Palettes should rarely change in content.

Palettes should be displayed in the proper manner. If the attributes on a palette must be available at all times, place them on a standard control or fixed palette. If the attributes on the palette are sometimes used frequently and other times used infrequently, place them on a pop-up or tear-off menu. Do not place frequently used palettes on pull-down menus.

Also, from a presentation perspective, do not use a palette if the alternatives cannot be meaningfully and clearly represented pictorially. In addition, do not use one where words are clearer than images, or in situations where the choices are going to change.

Graphical Representations

- Provide meaningful, accurate, and clear illustrations or representations of choices.
- Create images large enough to:
  - Clearly illustrate the available alternatives.
  - Permit ease in pointing and selecting.
- Create images of equal size.
- Always test illustrations before implementing.

Provide meaningful, accurate, and clear illustrations or representations of alternative choices. Create equal size images large enough to illustrate clearly the available alternatives and permit ease in pointing and selecting. Always test illustrations with users before implementing to assure they will work satisfactorily.

While most palettes will not possess textual choice descriptions, under certain circumstances textual descriptions may be needed. For example, a choice might require selection of a style of font. The palette may contain the names of the available styles (like Roman) with the text displayed as the font style would actually appear.

Size

- Present all available alternatives within limits imposed by:
  - The size of the graphical representations.
  - The screen display capabilities.

Since palettes will consume less screen space, more are capable of being displayed in the same area of a screen than can be displayed using textual choice descriptions. Present all available alternatives within limits imposed by how big the graphical representations must be and the capabilities of the display hardware in creating clear illustrations. Human limitations in ability to differentiate accurately the kinds of graphical representations being presented must also be considered.

Layout

- Create boxes large enough to:
  - Effectively illustrate the available alternatives.
  - Permit ease in pointing and selecting.
- Create boxes of equal size.
- Position the boxes adjacent to, or butted up against, one another.
- A columnar orientation is the preferred manner.
- If vertical space on the screen is limited, orient the choices horizontally.

Palette boxes must be large enough to illustrate effectively the available alternatives and to maximize ease in selecting. Created boxes should be of equal size and positioned adjacent to, or butted up against one another, since they are mutually exclusive choices. Columns are preferred, but horizontal rows can be used if space constraints exist on the screen.

Organization

- Arrange palettes in expected or normal orders.
  - For palettes arrayed top to bottom, begin ordering at the top.

- For palettes arrayed left to right, begin ordering at the left.
- If an expected or normal order does not exist, arrange choices by frequency of occurrence, sequence of use, importance, or alphabetically (if textual).
- If, under certain conditions, a choice is not available, display it subdued or less brightly than the other choices.

Palettes should be organized logically. If the alternatives have an expected order, follow it. Colors, for example, should be ordered from the right or top by their spectral position: red, orange, yellow, green, blue, indigo, and violet. If an expected or normal order does not exist, arrange choices by frequency of occurrence, sequence of use, or importance. Palettes with text may be arranged alphabetically. If, under certain conditions, a choice is not available, display the unavailable choice subdued or less brightly than the available choices.

Captions

- Provide a caption for each palette.
  - In screens containing only one palette, the screen title may serve as the caption.
- Display the caption fully spelled out using mixed-case letters.

Columnar Orientation

- The field caption may be positioned left-aligned above the palette.

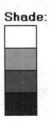

- Alternatively, the caption may be positioned to the left of the topmost alternative.

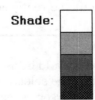

Horizontal Orientation

- The field caption may be positioned above the palette.

- Alternatively, the caption may be positioned to the left of the alternatives.

Provide a caption for each palette. In screens containing only one palette, the screen title may serve as the caption. Display the caption fully spelled out using mixed-case letters, although some abbreviations may be used to achieve the alignment goals to be specified. Captions may be located above, or to the left of, the palette, as shown above. With a horizontal orientation, the captioned may be positioned above the palette, or to the left of the alternatives. Positioning on any one screen will be dependent on other caption-control relationships within the screen.

Selection Method and Indication

Pointing

- Highlight the choice in some visually distinctive way when the pointer or cursor is resting on it and the choice is available for selection.

Activation

- When a choice is selected, distinguish it visually from the nonselected choices by highlighting it in a manner different from when it is pointed at, or by placing a bold border around it.

Defaults

- If a palette is displayed with a choice previously selected or a default choice, display the currently active choice in the manner used when selected.

The selection target should be as large as possible in order to make it easy to move to. Highlight the selection choice in some visually distinctive way when the pointer or cursor is resting on it and the choice is available for selection.

When a choice is selected, distinguish it visually from the nonselected choices by highlighting it in a manner different from when it is pointed at, or by placing a bolder border around it.

If a palette is displayed with a choice previously selected or a default choice, display the currently active choice in the manner used when selected.

List Boxes

Description

- A permanently displayed box-shaped control containing a list of attributes or objects from which:
  - A single selection is made (mutually exclusive), or
  - Multiple selections are made (non-mutually exclusive).
- The choice may be text, pictorial representations, or graphics.
- Selections are made by using a mouse to point and click.
- Capable of being scrolled to view large lists of choices.
- No text entry field exists in which to type text.
- A list box may be may be associated with a text box control where the selected choice may be displayed or an item added to the list.

Purpose

- To select from a large set of choices that may be:
  - Mutually exclusive options.
  - Non-mutually exclusive options.

Advantages/Disadvantages

- \+ Unlimited number of choices.
- \+ Reminds users of available options.
- \+ Box always visible.
- − Consumes screen space.
- − Often requires an action (scrolling) to see all list choices.
- − The list content may change, making it hard to find items.
- − The list may be ordered in an unpredictable way, making it hard to find items.

Proper Usage

- For selecting values or setting attributes.
- For choices that are:
  - Mutually exclusive (e.g., only one can be selected).
  - Non-mutually exclusive (i.e., one or more may be selected).
- Where screen space is available.

- For data and choices that are:
  - Best represented textually.
  - Not frequently selected.
  - Not well known, easily learned, or remembered.
  - Ordered in a non-predictable fashion.
  - Frequently changed.
  - Large in number.
  - Fixed or variable in list length.
- When screen space or layout considerations make radio buttons or check boxes impractical.

A *list box* is a permanently displayed rectangular-shaped box containing a list of values or attributes from which single or multiple selections are made. It can also be referred to as a *fixed* list box because it is fixed on the screen. The choices are usually text, but they may be pictorial representations or graphics as well. A list box may be scrollable to view large lists, and selections are made by using a mouse to point and click. No text entry field exists in which to type text, but a single-selection list box may be associated with a text box where the selected choice is displayed, or an item may be added to the list. Examples of single-selection list boxes are illustrated in Figure 7.16. The purpose of a list box is to select from a large set of alternatives. The choices may be mutually exclusive (single-selection) or not mutually exclusive (multiple-selection).

Advantages/Disadvantages List boxes are always visible, reminding users of the choices available. They permit an unlimited number of options to be displayed. Among their disadvantages are the excessive screen space they consume and the possible necessity for time-consuming scrolling to see all items. Since the list content can change, and items can be ordered in an unpredictable way, it can be hard to find items.

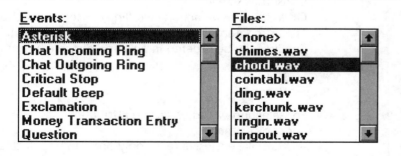

Figure 7.16   List boxes.

Proper Usage List boxes are used for selecting objects or values or setting attributes, either mutually exclusive or not, where sufficient screen space is available to display six-eight choices. Their best use is for data and choices that are textual, large in number, fixed or variable in list length, not well known, easily learned or remembered, and ordered in an unpredictable fashion. List box items should not have to be selected or changed frequently. List boxes may be used when screen space, list size, and data volatility considerations make use of radio buttons and check boxes impractical.

List Box General Guidelines First, general list box guidelines will be presented. Then, specific guidelines for single- and multiple-selection lists will be reviewed.

Selection Descriptions

- Clearly and meaningfully describe the choices available. Spell out as fully as possible.
  - Graphical representations must clearly represent the options.
- Left-align into columns.
- Use mixed-case letters.

Selection descriptions will reflect the selection alternatives available. They should be meaningful, fully spelled out, and organized in columns. Meaningful ordering schemes include logical order, frequency of use, sequence of use, or importance. If no such pattern exists, arrange the list alphabetically. Display the list of choices using mixed-case letters.

List Size

- Not limited in size.
- Present all available alternatives.
- Require no more than 40 pagedowns to search a list.
  - If more, provide method for using search criteria or scoping the options.

A list being displayed in a fixed list box has no actual size limit. All available alternatives should be capable of being displayed. Searching a very long list, however, can be very time-consuming. A list should not require more than 40 pagedowns to completely search it. If more are necessary, provide a method for using search criteria or scoping the options, perhaps through a first-letter search.

Box Size

- Must be long enough to display six to eight choices without requiring scrolling.
  - Exceptions:
    - If screen space constraints exist, the box may be reduced in size to display at least three items.
    - If it is the major control within a window, the box may be larger.
  - If more items are available than are visible in the box, provide vertical scrolling to display all items.
- Must be wide enough to display the longest possible choice.

  - When box cannot be made wide enough to display the longest entry:
    - Make it wide enough to permit entries to be distinguishable, or,
    - Break the long entries with an ellipsis (. . .) in the middle, or,
    - Provide horizontal scrolling.

The exact size of a fixed list box will depend on its function and screen space constraints. Generally, boxes should be restricted to displaying no more than eight choices at one time. Slightly larger boxes that eliminate the need for scrolling, however, are preferable to list boxes that require a little scrolling. If screen space constraints exist, the box may be reduced in size to display at least three items. If scrolling is necessary, include a scroll bar on the right side of the box.

The list box should be wide enough to display fully all selection choice wording. When a box cannot be made wide enough to display the longest entry, make it wide enough to permit entries to be distinguishable, or, break the long entries with an ellipsis in the middle. As a last resort, provide horizontal scrolling and a scroll bar at the bottom of the list box. Horizontal scrolling is disliked by many people.

Organization

- Order in a logical and meaningful way to permit easy browsing.

- If a particular choice is not available in the current context, omit it from the list.
  - Exception: If it is important that the existence and non-availability of a particular list item be communicated, display the choice dimmed or grayed instead of deleting it.

Choices should be organized logically to permit easy browsing. If the alternatives have an expected order, follow it. Other ordering schemes such as frequency of use, sequence of use, or importance may also be considered. When no obvious scheme exists, use alphabetic order. If a particular choice is not available in the current context, it should be omitted from the list. If it is important that the existence and nonavailability of a list item be communicated, however, display the choice dimmed or grayed instead of deleting it.

Layout and Separation

- Enclose the choices in a box with a solid border.
  - The border should be the same color as the choice descriptions.
- Leave one blank character position between the choice descriptions and the left border.
- Leave one blank character position between the longest choice description in the list and the right border, if possible.

Enclose the box in a solid border in the color of the choice descriptions. To provide adequate legibility, leave one space between the choice descriptions and the left border, and one space between the longest choice description and the right border. Also incorporate a solid line border around the list box in the same color as the choice descriptions.

Captions

- Use mixed-case letters.
- The preferred position of the control caption is above the upper-left corner of the list box.

- Alternatively, the caption may be located to the left of the topmost choice description.

- Be consistent in caption style and orientation within a screen, and related screens.

To identify the list box, a field caption in mixed-case letters with each significant word capitalized is necessary. Place this caption either above the upper-left corner of the box or to the left of the first choice description. The caption style chosen will again be dependent upon caption-control relationships in other controls included within the screen. It should be consistently oriented with the other control captions.

Disabling

- When a list box is disabled, display its caption and entries as grayed or dimmed.

Display a list box's caption and entries as dimmed or grayed when the list box is entirely disabled.

Selection Method and Indication

Pointing

- Highlight the selection choice in some visually distinctive way when the pointer or cursor is resting on it and the choice is available for selection.

Activation and Selection

- Use a reverse video or reverse color bar to surround the choice description when it is selected.
- The cursor should be as wide as the box itself.

- Mark the selected choice in a distinguishing way.

Highlight the selection choice in some visually distinctive way when the pointer or cursor is resting on it and the choice is available for selection. One method for this is a bold border around the choice.

Indicate the selected choice through use of a reverse video or reverse color bar, as wide as the box itself. Visually differentiate multiple (non-exclusive) from single (mutually exclusive) choice fixed list boxes, as described in the following sections.

Single-Selection List Boxes

Purpose

- To permit selection of only one item in a list.

Design Guidelines

Related Text Box

- If presented with an associated text box control:
  - Position the list box below, and as close as possible to, the text box.
  - The list box caption should be worded similarly to the text box caption.

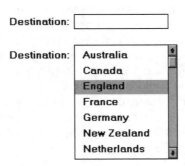

– If the related text box and the list box are very in close proximity, the caption may be omitted from the list box.

– Use the same background color for the text box as is used in the list box.

Defaults

- When the list box is first displayed:
  – Present the currently active choice highlighted or mark with a circle or diamond to the left of the entry.
  – If a choice has not been previously selected, provide a default choice and display it in the same manner that is used in selecting it.
  – If the list represents mixed values for a multiple selection, do not highlight an entry.

Other

- Follow other relevant list box guidelines.

Single-selection list boxes permit selection of only one item from the list box choices.

If the list box is associated with a text field, position the list box below and as close as possible to the related text box. If this cannot be accomplished, position the text box to the left. Captions of related text boxes and list boxes must be worded similarly. If, however, the text box and the list box are located in close physical proximity, the caption may be omitted from the list box. Visually relate a list box to a text box by using the same background color for both boxes.

For single-selection fixed list boxes, indicate an active choice by highlighting it or marking it with a circle or diamond to the left of the choice description. If the list represents mixed values for a multiple selection, do not highlight any entry.

Multiple-Selection List Boxes

Purpose

- To permit selection of more than one item in a list.

Design Guidelines

Selection Indication

- Mark the selected choice with an "X" or "check" box mark to the left of the entry.

Groceries:
☒ Bread
☐ Cereal
☒ Dairy Foods
☐ Desserts
☐ Drinks
☐ Fruit
☒ Meat, Fish and Poultry
☐ Vegetables

- Also consider providing:
  - A summary list box.
    - Position it to the right of the list box.
    - Use the same colors for the summary list box as are used in the list box.

Groceries:
☒ Bread
☐ Cereal
☒ Dairy Foods
☐ Desserts
☐ Drinks
☐ Fruit
☒ Meat, Fish and Poultry
☐ Vegetables

Groceries Selected:
Bread
Dairy Foods
Meat, Fish and Poultry

  - A display-only text control indicating how many choices have been selected.
    - Position it justified upper-right above the list box.

Groceries: [4] selected

☒ Bread
☐ Cereal
☒ Dairy Foods
☐ Desserts
☐ Drinks
☐ Fruit
☒ Meat, Fish and Poultry
☐ Vegetables

Select All / Deselect Buttons

- Provide command buttons to accomplish fast "select all" and "deselect" actions, when these actions must be frequently or quickly performed.

Defaults

- When the list box is first displayed:
  - Display the currently active choices highlighted.
  - Mark with an "X" or "check" box or mark to the left of the entry.
  - If the list represents mixed values for a multiple selection, do not highlight an entry.

Other

- Follow other relevant list box guidelines.

Multiple-selection list boxes permit selection of one, or more, items from the box choices.

For choice selections, mark with an X or check to the left of the entry. Also consider providing a summary list box, another list box containing a compilation of the active selections from the multiple-selection list box. This will permit quick scanning and comparison of these active choices and greatly reduce the need for scrolling if the selectable list is lengthy. The summary list box can be made scrollable, if necessary. Position the summary list adjacent to, and to the right of, the multiple-selection list box. Use the same colors for the summary list box and the multiple-selection list box.

Also consider providing a read-only text box control indicating how many choices have been selected in the multiple-selection list box. This text box can be associated with either the multiple-selection or summary list box. It is useful in situations where the multiple selections may be numerous and all the choices cannot be seen without scrolling. It is also useful when the user must know exactly how many choices have been selected. Position this text box justified upper-right above the list box.

Provide command buttons to accomplish fast "select all" and "deselect" actions, when these actions must be frequently or quickly performed.

When the list box is first displayed, the active selection will depend on previous activities. If a choice has been previously selected, display the currently active choice in the same manner used when it was selected. If the list represents mixed values for a multiple selection, do not highlight any list entries.

Drop-Down/Pop-Up List Boxes

Description

- A single rectangular-shaped control with a small button to the side and an associated hidden list of options.
    - The button provides a visual cue that an associated selection box is available but hidden.
- When the button is selected, a larger associated box appears containing a list of choices from which one may be selected.
- Selections are made by using the mouse to point and click.
- Text may not be typed into the control.

Purpose

- To select one item from a large list of mutually exclusive options when screen space is limited.

Advantages/Disadvantages

- + Unlimited number of choices.
- + Reminds users of available options.
- + Conserves screen space.
- − Requires an extra action to display the list of choices.
- − When displayed, all choices may not always be visible, requiring scrolling.
- − The list may be ordered in an unpredictable way, making it hard to find items.

Proper Usage

- For selecting values, or setting attributes.
- For choices that are mutually exclusive (i.e., only one can be selected).
- Where screen space is limited.
- For data and choices that are:
    - Best represented textually.
    - Infrequently selected.
    - Not well known, easily learned, or remembered.
    - Ordered in a non-predictable fashion.

  – Large in number.
  – Variable or fixed in list length.
- When screen space or layout considerations make radio buttons or fixed list boxes impractical.

A *drop-down/pop-up list box* is a single rectangular field with a small button to the side and an associated hidden list of options. The button provides a visual cue to the user that an associated selection box of choices is available but hidden. When requested, a larger associated rectangular box appears containing a scrollable list of choices from which one is selected. Selections are made by using the mouse to point and click. No text field exists in which to type text.

Fields of this nature go by many different names. IBM's SAA CUA refers to them as *drop-down lists* because they appear to drop down from the single-selection field. Windows 95 calls them *drop-down list boxes*. Xerox's Viewpoint calls them *pull-down lists*. Other list boxes of this type seem to pop up on the screen, either next to or over the selection field. OSF/Motif calls list boxes of this style *option menus*, and DECwindows uses the term *list boxes*. NeXTStep refers to them as *pop-up lists*. In this discussion these controls will be given the generic name of *drop-down/pop-up list boxes*.

A drop-down list is illustrated in Figures 7.17 and 7.18. Figure 7.19 shows a pop-up list. The purpose of these list boxes is to permit selection from a large set of mutually exclusive choices when screen space is scarce.

Advantages/Disadvantages Drop-down/pop-up list boxes are useful in that they conserve screen space. They may be retrieved on demand, reminding users of the choices available. They permit an unlimited number of options to be displayed.

A significant disadvantage is that they necessitate an extra step to display the available options. Scrolling may also be necessary to see all

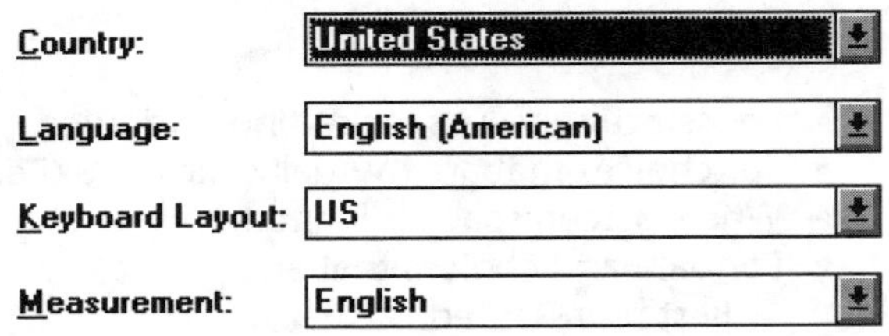

Figure 7.17 Drop-down list boxes. There are four unopened boxes, Country, Language, Keyboard, and Measurement.

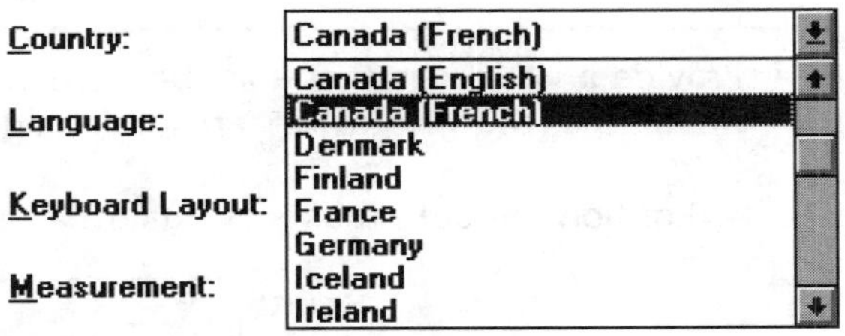

Figure 7.18 Drop-down list box opened for Country

items. Since items can be ordered in an unpredictable way, they can be hard to find occasionally. Generally, drop-down/pop-up list boxes require more work on the part of the user than many other screen-based controls because of the activation step and the possible need for scrolling.

Proper Usage Drop-down/pop-up list boxes are used much like fixed list boxes, except the choices are not visible at all times. They are used for selecting values or setting attributes when sufficient screen space is not available to display the choices permanently.

Their best use is for data and choices that are textual, large in number, fixed or variable in list length, not well known, easily learned or remembered, and ordered in a nonpredictable fashion. Items should not have to be selected frequently.

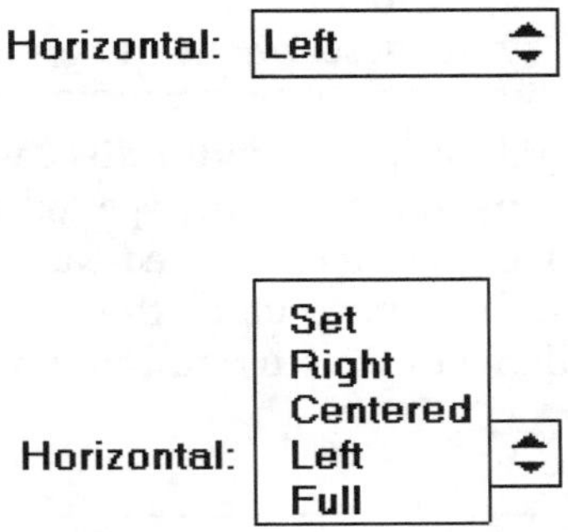

Figure 7.19 Pop-up list box, closed and opened.

Prompt Button

- Provide a visual cue that a list box is hidden by including a downward pointing arrow, or other meaningful image, to the right of the selection field.
  - Position the button directly against, or within, the selection field.

Sport: [   ] V

Most systems indicate the presence of a drop-down or pop-up list by associating a meaningful icon with the applicable field. This icon can be seen positioned to the left of the selection field (OPEN LOOK), within the selection field (NeXTStep, Windows 95), or to the right of the selection field (IBM's SAA CUA, Windows 3.1). Others do not provide any visual indication that a hidden list is available (OSF/Motif and DECwindows). An indication to the user that a drop-down or pop-up list is available should be indicated on the screen. This is especially critical if not all fields have associated hidden lists. The best location is to the right of the selection field where it is out of the way until needed. To visually differentiate it from another control, the drop-down/pop-up combination box, position the button abutting or within the selection field. (A drop-down/pop-up combination box button will be separated by a space.) The indicator should be large enough to provide a good pointing target.

Selection Descriptions

- Clearly and meaningfully describe the choices available. Spell out as fully as possible.
  - Graphical representations must clearly represent the options.
- Left align into columns.
- Display the descriptions using mixed-case letters.

Selection descriptions will reflect what choices exist in the control. They should be meaningful, fully spelled out, and organized in columns. Display the list of choices using mixed-case letters. Box descriptions should be displayed in the same color as the selection field text. If a particular choice is not available in the current context, it should be omitted from the list.

List Size

- Not limited in size.
- Present all available alternatives.

A list being displayed in a drop-down/pop-up list box has no size limit. All available alternatives should be capable of being displayed. It would seem practical that for large scrollable lists, the same rules as presented for list boxes should be applied. Restrict pagedowns to no more than 40 and provide a method to scope actions.

Box Size

- Long enough to display six to eight choices without scrolling.
  - If more than eight choices are available, provide vertical scrolling to display all items.
- Wide enough to display the longest possible choice.
  - When a box cannot be made wide enough to display the longest entry:
    - Make wide enough to permit entries to be distinguishable, or,
    - Break long entries with ellipses (. . .) in the middle, or,
    - Provide horizontal scrolling.

Drop-down/pop-up list boxes should be restricted to eight or less choices. If more must be displayed, permit scrolling and include a scroll bar on the right side of the box. The list box should be wide enough to display fully all selection choice wording. When a box cannot be made wide enough to display the longest entry, make it wide enough to permit entries to be distinguishable, or, break the long entries with an ellipsis in the middle. As a last resort, provide horizontal scrolling and a scroll bar at the bottom of the list box.

Organization

- Order in a logical and meaningful way to permit easy browsing.
- If a particular choice is not available in the current context, omit it from the list.
  - Exception: If it is important that the existence and non-availability of a particular list item be communicated, display the choice dimmed or grayed instead of deleting it.

Selection choices should be organized logically. If the alternatives have an expected order, follow it. Other ordering schemes such as frequency of use, sequence of use, or importance may also be considered. Always begin ordering at the top or left. If, under certain conditions, a choice is not available, display the unavailable choice subdued or less brightly than the available choices.

Layout and Separation

- Enclose the choices in a box composed of a solid line border.
  - The border should be the same color as the choice descriptions.
- Leave one blank character position between the choices and the left border.
- Leave one blank character position between the longest choice description in the list and the right border, if possible.

To provide adequate legibility, leave one space between the choice descriptions and the left border, and one space between the longest choice description and the right border. Extending the listing box to the right edge of the prompt button allows the user to move easily from the button to the list. To set off the box from the screen body background, use the same color background for the box as is used in the entry field. Also incorporate a solid line border around the box in the same color as the choice descriptions.

Captions

- Display using mixed-case letters.
- Position the caption to the left of the box.
  - Alternatively, it may be positioned left-justified above the box.

To identify the drop-down/pop-up list box, a field caption in mixed-case letters with each significant word capitalized is necessary. The recommended position is to the box's left. Select a positioning consistent with other controls presented on the window.

Disabling

- When a drop-down/pop-up list box is disabled, display its caption and entries as disabled or dimmed.

Display a drop-down/pop-up list box's caption and entries as dimmed or grayed when the list box is entirely disabled.

Selection Method and Indication

Pointing

- Highlight the selection choice in some visually distinctive way when the pointer or cursor is resting on it and the choice is available for selection.

Activation
- Use a reverse video or reverse color bar to surround the choice description when it is selected.
- The bar should be as wide as the box itself.

Defaults
- When the drop-down/pop-up box is first displayed:
  - Present the currently active choice highlighted.
  - If a choice has not been previously selected, provide a default choice and display it highlighted.

Highlight the selection choice in some visually distinctive way when the pointer or cursor is resting on it and the choice is available for selection.

Highlight a selected choice by using a reverse video or reverse color bar to surround the selected item. The bar should be as wide as the box itself.

When the drop-down/pop-up list box is first displayed, the active selection will depend on previous activities. If a choice has been previously selected, display the currently active choice in the same manner used when it was selected. If a choice has not been previously selected, provide a default choice and display it in the same manner that is used in selecting it.

COMBINATION ENTRY/SELECTION CONTROLS

It is possible for a control to possess the characteristics of both a text field and a selection field. In this kind of control, information may either be typed into the field or selected and placed within it. The types of combination entry/selection fields are spin boxes, attached combination boxes, and drop-down/pop-up combination boxes.

Spin Boxes

Description
- A single-line field followed by two small, vertically-arranged buttons.
  - The top button has an arrow pointing up.
  - The bottom button has an arrow pointing down.
- Selection/entry is made by:
  - Using the mouse to point at one of the directional buttons and clicking. Items will change by one unit or step with each click.
  - Keying a value directly into the field itself.

Purpose
- To make a selection by either scrolling through a small set of meaningful predefined choices or typing text.

Advantages/Disadvantages

+ Consumes little screen space.
+ Flexible, permitting selection or typed entry.
− Difficult to compare choices.
− Can be awkward to operate.
− Useful only for certain kinds of data.

Proper Usage

- For setting attributes, properties, or values.
- For mutually exclusive choices (i.e., only one can be selected).
- When the task requires the option of either key entry or selection from a list.
- When the user prefers the option of either key entry or selection from a list.
- Where screen space is limited.
- Most useful for data and choices that are:
  − Discrete.
  − Infrequently selected.
  − Well known, easily learned or remembered, and meaningful.
  − Ordered in a predictable, customary, or consecutive fashion.
  − Infrequently changed.
  − Small in number.
  − Fixed or variable in list length.

A *spin box,* also called a *spin button,* is a single-line field followed by two small, vertically arranged buttons inscribed with up and down arrows. Selection of an item is accomplished using the mouse to point at one of the buttons and clicking. Items in a listing in the display field will change by one unit or step in the direction selected with each click. The list is searched as the ring or circle of alternatives "spins" by. A spin box may also be completed by keying a value directly into the field itself. A spin box is illustrated in Figure 7.20.

A spin box is used to make a selection by scrolling through a meaningful and predictable small set of predefined choices, or by keying through typing text.

Advantages/Disadvantages Spin boxes are flexible, permitting either selection or typed entry. They also consume little screen space. On the other hand, spin boxes are useful only for certain kinds of data, that which is predictable or consecutive. Because only one item is displayed at a time, it is difficult to compare choices. Spin boxes may also be awkward to operate, often requiring several back and forth iterations to bring the desired value into view.

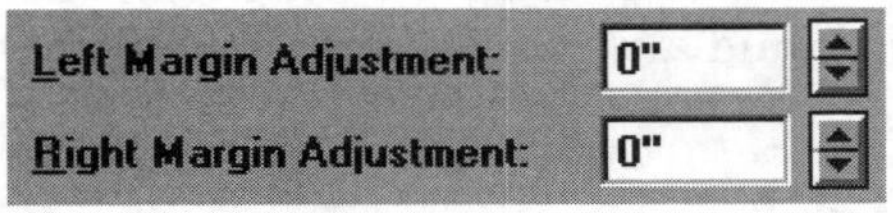

Figure 7.20   Spin boxes.

Proper Usage Spin boxes are used for setting attributes, properties, or values that are mutually exclusive. They are useful when the task requires, or user prefers, the option of either key entry or selection from a list.

Spin boxes are useful for data and choices that are discrete and small in number. The choices themselves should be well known, easily learned or remembered, and meaningful. Choices should be ordered in a predictable, customary, or consecutive fashion so people can anticipate the next not-yet-visible choice. Items in spin boxes should not require frequent selection, and the array of items listed should be stable.

List Size

- Keep the list of items relatively short.
- To reduce the size of potentially long lists, break the listing into subcomponents, if possible.

Since the list must be manipulated to display its contents, it should be as short as feasible. To reduce the size of potentially long lists, break the listing into subcomponents whenever possible. A date, for example, may be broken into its components of month, day, and year.

List Organization

- Order the list in the customary, consecutive, or expected order of the information contained within it.
  - Assure that the user can always anticipate the next (not-yet-visible) choice.
- When first displayed, present a default choice in the box.

Spin boxes are most effective when the values they contain have a customary or consecutive order that is predictable. Information can be letters or numbers with a customary or expected order. Examples would be days of the week, months of the year, shoe sizes, and so on. The user must always be able to anticipate the next choice before it is displayed. The control should always contain a default value when first displayed.

Box Size

- The spin box should be wide enough to display the longest entry or choice.

Fully display all alternatives within the spin box. The box should be wide enough to display the longest entry or choice.

Spin Indicator

- Provide an indication that a spin button is available by placing up and down arrows immediately to the right of the text box entry field.

Month: September

The clue to the user that the field is a spin button is the up and down arrows adjacent to the field. Locate the arrows to the right of the field.

Captions

- Display using mixed-case letters.
- Position the caption to the left of the box.
  - Alternatively, it may be positioned left-justified above the box.

To identify the spin box, a field caption in mixed-case letters with each significant word capitalized is necessary. The recommended position is to the box's left. Select a positioning consistent with other controls presented on the window.

Entry and Selection Methods

- Permit completion by:
  - Typing directly into the box.
  - Scrolling and selecting with a mouse.
  - Scrolling and selecting with the up/down arrow keys.
- For alphabetical values:

- Move down the order using the down arrow.
- Move up the order using the up arrow.
- For numeric values or magnitudes:
  - Show a larger value using the up arrow.
  - Show a smaller value using the down arrow.

Field completion should be possible by typing directly into the field or by scrolling and selecting with a mouse or keyboard keys. When spinning alphabetical values, move down the order using the down arrow and up the order using the up arrow. For numeric values or magnitudes, display a larger value using the up arrow and a smaller value using the down arrow.

Attached Combination Boxes

Description

- A single rectangular text box entry field, beneath which is a larger rectangular box (resembling a drop-down list box) displaying a list of options.
- The text box permits a choice to be keyed within it.
- The larger box contains a list of mutually exclusive choices from which one may be selected for placement in the entry field.
  - Selections are made by using a mouse to point and click.
- Combines the capabilities of both a text box and a list box.
- Information keyed does not necessarily have to match the list items.

Purpose

- To allow either typed entry in a text box or selection from a list of options in a permanently displayed list box attached to the text box.

Advantages/Disadvantages

- + Unlimited number of entries and choices.
- + Reminds users of available options.
- + Flexible, permitting selection or typed entry.
- + Entries not necessarily restricted to items selectable from list box.
- + List box always visible.
- − Consumes some screen space.
- − All list box choices not always visible, requiring scrolling.
- − Users may have difficulty recalling sufficient information to type entry, making text box unusable.
- − The list may be ordered in an unpredictable way, making it hard to find items.

Proper Usage

- For entering or selecting objects or values or setting attributes.
- For information that is mutually exclusive (i.e., only one can be entered or selected).
- When users may find it practical to, or prefer to, type information rather than selecting from a list.
- When users can recall and type information faster than selecting from a list.
- When it is useful to provide the users a reminder of the choices available.
- Where data must be entered that is not contained in the selection list.
- Where screen space is available.
- For data and choices that are:
  - Best represented textually.
  - Somewhat familiar or known.
  - Ordered in a non-predictable fashion.
  - Frequently changed.
  - Large in number.
  - Variable or fixed in list length.

An *attached combination box* is a single rectangular entry field, beneath which is a larger rectangular box (resembling a drop-down list box) displaying a list of options. The entry field permits a choice to be keyed within it while the larger box contains a list of mutually exclusive choices from which one may be selected for placement in the entry field. An attached combination box combines the capabilities of both an entry field and a fixed list box. It visually resembles a drop-down list box or drop-down combination box (to be described). When keying into the field, the information keyed does not have to match the list items.

Attached combination boxes are sometimes simply referred to as combination boxes. Windows 95 calls this control a *combo box*. Two are illustrated in Figure 7.21.

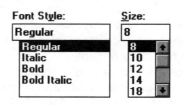

Figure 7.21   Attached combination boxes.

Advantages/Disadvantages Attached combination boxes are flexible, permitting selection or typed entry. Alternatives are always visible, or retrievable, reminding people of the available options. An unlimited variety of entries and choices are possible. Entries are not necessarily restricted to items selectable from a box.

Attached combination boxes do consume quite a bit of screen space. Because all box choices may not be visible, some scrolling may be required. It is always possible that people may have difficulty recalling sufficient information to type, making the text box unusable. The list may also be ordered in an unpredictable way, making it hard to find items. Additional work is required of the user if selection scrolling must be performed.

Proper Usage Attached combination boxes are useful for entering or selecting objects or values or setting attributes that are mutually exclusive. They are most valuable when users may find it practical to, or prefer to, type information rather than selecting from a list but where reminders of alternatives available must occasionally be provided. They are also useful when the listings are dynamic and changeable, permitting the user to key items not contained on the list in the box. They do require that screen space be available to display them, but they eliminate the extra steps involved in retrieving drop-down lists.

Attached combination boxes are useful for textual data and choices that are frequently changed and somewhat familiar or known, fostering keyed entry. The lists may be long, variable, and ordered in a nonpredictable fashion.

Attached Combination Box Guidelines For the text box entry field, see "Text Box/Single Line" guidelines. For the list box, see "Drop-Down/Pop-Up List Box" guidelines.

Drop-Down/Pop-Up Combination Boxes

Description

- A single rectangular text box with a small button to the side and an associated hidden list of options.
  - The button provides a visual cue that an associated selection box is available but hidden.
- When requested, a larger associated rectangular box appears containing a scrollable list of choices from which one is selected.
- Selections are made by using the mouse to point and click.

- Information may also be keyed into the field.
- The information keyed does not necessarily have to match list items.
- Combines the capabilities of both a text box and a drop-down/pop-up list box.

Purpose

- To allow either typed entry or selection from a list of options in a list box that may be closed and retrieved as needed.

Advantages/Disadvantages

+ Unlimited number of entries and choices.
+ Reminds users of available options.
+ Flexible, permitting selection or typed entry.
+ Entries not restricted to items selectable from list box.
− Conserves screen space.
− Requires extra step to display list of choices.
− When displayed, all box choices may not always be visible, requiring scrolling.
− User may have difficulty in recalling what to type.
− The list content may change, making it hard to find items.
− The list may be ordered in an unpredictable way, making it hard to find items.

Proper Usage

- For entering or selecting objects or values or setting attributes.
- For information that is mutually exclusive (i.e., only one can be entered or selected).
- When users may find it practical to, or prefer to, type information rather than selecting from a list.
- When users can recall and type information faster than selecting from a list.
- When it is useful to provide the users an occasional reminder of the choices available.
- Where data must be entered that is not contained in the selection list.
- Where screen space is limited.
- For data and choices that are:
  - Best represented textually.
  - Somewhat familiar or known.
  - Ordered in a non-predictable fashion.
  - Frequently changed.
  - Large in number.
  - Variable or fixed in list length.

Baud Rate: [9600] [▼]

Figure 7.22   Drop-down combination box, closed.

A *drop-down/pop-up combination box* is a single rectangular field with a small button to the side and an associated hidden list of options. The button provides a visual cue to the user that an associated selection box of choices is available but hidden. When requested, a larger associated rectangular box appears containing a scrollable list of choices from which one is selected. Selections are made by using the mouse to point and click. It closely resembles a drop-down/pop-up list box.

Information, however, may also be keyed into the field. The information keyed does not necessarily have to match items in the list. A drop-down/pop-up combination box, therefore, combines the capabilities of both a text box and a selection field. Windows 95 calls this control a *drop-down combo box*. A drop-down combination box is illustrated in Figures 7.22 and 7.23.

A drop-down/pop-up combination box allows either typed entry or selection from a list of options in a list box that may be retrieved as needed.

Advantages/Disadvantages Drop-down/pop-up combination boxes are flexible, permitting selection or typed entry. They conserve screen space, but alternatives are always retrievable, reminding people of the available options. An unlimited variety of entries and choices are possible. Entries are not restricted to items selectable from a box.

In terms of disadvantages, they necessitate an extra step to display the available options. Scrolling may also be necessary to see all items. Since the list content can change, and items can be ordered in an unpredictable way, it can be hard to find items. It is always possible also that people may have difficulty recalling sufficient information to type, making

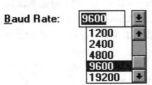

Figure 7.23   Drop-down combination box, opened.

the entry field unusable. Generally drop-down/pop-up combination boxes require more work on the part of the user than many other screen-based controls.

Proper Usage Drop-down/pop-up combination boxes are useful for entering or selecting objects or values or setting attributes that are mutually exclusive. They are most valuable when users may find it practical to, or prefer to, type information rather than selecting from a list but where reminders of alternatives available must occasionally be provided. The box may only be retrieved as needed, thereby conserving screen space. They are also useful when the listings are dynamic and changeable, permitting the user to key items not contained on the list in the box.

Drop-down/pop-up combination boxes are useful for textual data and choices that are frequently changed and somewhat familiar or known, fostering keyed entry. The list may be long, variable, and ordered in a nonpredictable fashion.

Prompt Button

- Provide a visual cue that a list box is hidden by including a downward-pointing arrow to the right of the text box.
  - Separate the button from the text box by a small space.

Sport: [   ] [↓]

Provide a visual cue that a list box is hidden by including a downward-pointing arrow to the right of the entry field. Position the button separated by a space from the entry field, differentiating it from a similar drop-down/pop-up list box whose button will be directly adjacent to its selection field. It is important that these two types of drop-down controls be visually discernible so they can each be identified without first having to be tried. Windows 3.1 provides this button separation for distinctiveness. In Windows 95 the button is separated but it is not as obvious, visually.

Other Guidelines For the text box entry field, see the "Text Box/Single Line" guidelines. For the box and selection components, see the "Drop-Down/Pop-Up List Box" guidelines.

OTHER OPERABLE CONTROLS

Other screen-based operable controls include sliders, tabs, and scroll bars.

Slider

Description

- A scale exhibiting more or less of a quality on a continuum.
- Includes the following:
  - A shaft or bar.
  - A range of values with appropriate labels.
  - An arm indicating relative setting through its location on the shaft.
  - Optionally, a pair of buttons to permit incremental movement of the slider arm.
  - Optionally, a text box for typing and/or displaying an exact value.
  - Optionally, a detent position for special values.
- Selected by using the mouse to:
  - Drag a slider across the scale until the desired value is reached.
  - Point at the buttons at one end of the scale and clicking to change the value.
  - Keying a value in the associated text box.

Purpose

- To make a setting when a continuous qualitative adjustment is acceptable, it is useful to see the current value relative to the range of possible values.

Advantages/Disadvantages

- \+ Spatial representation of relative setting.
- \+ Visually distinctive.
- − Not as precise as an alphanumeric indication.
- − Consumes screen space.
- − Usually more complex than other controls.

Proper Usage

- To set an attribute.
- For mutually exclusive choices.
- When an object has a limited range of possible settings.
- When the range of values is continuous.
- When graduations are relatively fine.
- When the choices can increase or decrease in some well-known, predictable, and easily understood way.
- When a spatial representation enhances comprehension and interpretation.
- When using a slider provides sufficient accuracy.

A *slider* is a scale exhibiting more or less of a quantity or quality on a continuum. A slider incorporates the range of possible values and includes a shaft or bar representing the range, the values themselves with appropriate labels, and a visual indication of the relative setting through the location of a sliding arm. Optionally, sliders also may include a pair of buttons to permit incremental movement of the slider arm, an entry/display text box for typing and displaying an exact value, and a detent position for special values.

Slider values can be set by using the mouse to drag a slider across the scale until the desired value is reached. A visual indication of the relative setting is seen as the setting movement is made. In addition, some sliders may also be set by pointing at slider buttons located at one end of the scale and incrementally moving the arm through button clicks. Finally, some sliders may also be set by keying a value in an associated text box.

Examples of how sliders may be used are for adjusting the volume of a beep or the speed of the mouse cursor, or setting the saturation level of a particular color. A slider is illustrated in Figure 7.24.

A slider is used to make a setting when a continuous qualitative adjustment is acceptable, and it is advantageous to see the current value relative to all possible values.

Advantages/Disadvantages A slider displays a spatial representation of a relative setting, providing an excellent indication of where a value exists within a range of values. They are also visually distinctive and very recognizable.

Sliders, however, are not as precise as an alphanumeric indication, unless a display field is provided. They also consume more screen space than other kinds of fields, and they can be more complex to operate.

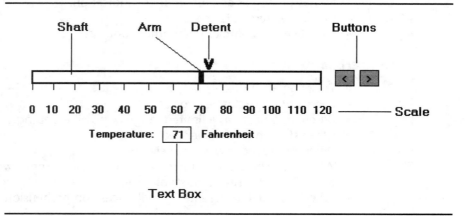

Figure 7.24 Slider.

Proper Usage Sliders are used to set an attribute when a limited range of continuous, relatively fine, possible settings exist. The choices must increase or decrease in some well-known, predictable, and easily understood way. Spatial representation of the attribute should enhance comprehension and interpretation and be sufficiently accurate.

General

- Use standard sliders whenever available.

Use of standard system sliders will speed learning

Labels

- Provide meaningful, clear, and consistent labels.

Labels must clearly reflect the quality being displayed.

Scale

- Show a complete range of choices.
- Mark the low, intermediate, and high ends of the scale.
- Provide scale interval markings, where possible.
- Provide consistent increments.
- Permit the user to change the units of measure.
- If the precise value of a quantity represented is important, display the value set in an adjacent text box.

Provide a complete range of choices on the scale. Mark the low, intermediate, and high ends of the scale. For example, volumes may be indicated by low, normal, and high. Provide scale interval markings at consistent increments. Allow the user to change the units of measure, for example, a temperature from Fahrenheit to centigrade. If the precise value of a quantity represented is critical, display the set value in an adjacent entry/display text box control. This will also permit typed entry of the desired value.

Slider Arm

- If the user cannot change the value shown in a slider, do not display a slider arm.

Do not display a slider arm if the user cannot change the value shown in a slider. Fill in the shaft in a distinctive way to indicate relative setting, as illustrated in the guideline for proportions.

Slider Buttons

- Provide slider buttons to permit movement by the smallest increment.
- If the user cannot change the value shown in a slider, do not display slider buttons.

Provide slider buttons to permit movement by the smallest increment. Movement is achieved by pointing and clicking. If the user cannot change the value shown in a slider, do not display slider buttons.

Detents

- Provide detents to set values that have special meaning.
- Permit the user to change the detent value.

For values that have special meaning, provide detents that can be changed by the user.

Proportions

- To indicate the proportion of a value being displayed, fill the slider shaft in some visually distinctive way.
  - For horizontal sliders, fill from left to right.
  - For vertical sliders, fill from bottom to top.

When the proportion of a value is also important, provide proportional indicators by filling in the slider shaft in a distinctive way. Fill from left to right and bottom to top.

Notebooks

Description

- A series of windows resembling a bound notebook.
- May contain tabbed divider pages creating sections.
- Navigation is permitted between pages or sections.

Purpose

- To present information that can be logically organized into pages or sections within the same window.

Advantages/Disadvantages

+ Resembles its paper-based cousin.
+ Visually distinctive.
+ Effectively organizes repetitive, related information.
− More visually complex.

Proper Usage

- To present logically structured, related, information.
- To present the settings choices that can be applied to an object.

A *notebook control* is a series of windows resembling a bound notebook. It may contain tabbed divider pages creating sections. Navigation is permitted between notebook pages or sections. A notebook is a standard SAA CUA control (IBM, 1991). Windows 95 has a window organization scheme called a *workbook* (see Table 4.3 in Step 4) that is similar to the notebook control, and a *tab* control described in Table 7.1. Tabs from Windows 95 are illustrated in Figure 7.25.

A notebook is used to present information that can be logically organized into pages or sections within the same window.

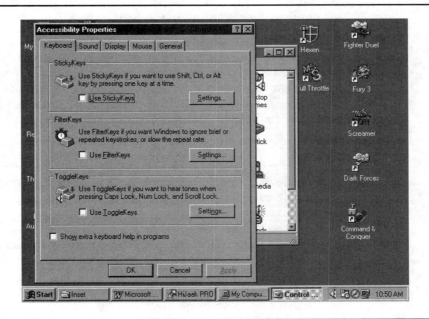

Figure 7.25   Tabs from Windows 95.

Advantages/Disadvantages Notebooks resemble their paper-based cousins, entities that are familiar to almost everyone. They are very meaningful electronic metaphors. Notebooks are visually distinctive and they permit effective organization of repetitive and related information. One drawback: They may result in a visually more complex screen.

Proper usage Notebooks can be used to present data that can be logically structured into meaningful orders or groupings. They are also useful for presenting the choices that can be applied to an object. Never place a notebook within a notebook.

Sections and Pages

Sections

- Place related information within a section.

Pages

- Order meaningfully.
- Arrange pages so they appear to go deeper, left-to-right and top-to-bottom.
- Provide pages of equal size.
- If there is more than one page in a section, provide page numbers in a consistent location within the page.

Place related information within a notebook section. Order the pages in a meaningful way based upon the notebook's content. Arrange the pages so they appear to go deeper, left-to-right and top-to-bottom. Provide pages of equal size. If there is more than one page in a section, provide page numbers in a consistent location within each page.

Tabs

- Provide fixed-width tabs for sections of related information.
- Provide either text or graphic labels.
  - If text:
    - Use system fonts.
    - Use mixed-case, capitalizing each significant word.
    - Assign a mnenomic for keyboard access.
  - If graphics, provide tooltip controls.
- Center the labels within the tabs.
- Restrict tabs to only one row.
- Arrange tabs so that they appear to go deeper, left-to-right and top-to-bottom.

Provide tabs for sections of related information. Fixed-width tabs are preferred but variable-width tabs may be used if screen space constraints exist. If textual tabs are created, use the standard system fonts in mixed case, capitalizing each significant word. Assign each tab a mnenomic for keyboard access. If the tab labels are graphics, provide tooltip controls to identify them, if available. Create meaningful graphics using the guidelines in Step 10, "Create Meaningful Icons." Center the labels within the tabs.

Provide only one row of tabs. Avoid multiple rows of tab or scrolling, which can be confusing. As an alternative, consider separating the tabbed pages into sets and using another control to move between sets. Arrange tabs so that they appear to go deeper, left-to-right and top-to-bottom.

Command Buttons

- If they affect only a page, locate the buttons on the page.
- If they affect the entire notebook, locate the buttons outside the notebook.

For command buttons that affect only the page being displayed, locate the buttons on that page. If they affect the entire notebook, position the buttons outside the notebook.

Scroll Bars

Description

- An elongated rectangular container consisting of:
  - A scroll area.
  - A slider box or elevator inside.
  - Arrows or anchors at either end.
- Available, if needed, in primary and secondary windows, and some controls.
- May be oriented vertically or horizontally at the window's edge.

Purpose

- To find and view information that takes more space than the allotted display space.

Advantages/Disadvantages

+ Permits viewing data of unlimited size.
- Consumes screen space.
- Can be cumbersome to operate.

Proper Use

- When more information is available than the window space for displaying it.
- Do not use to set values.

A *scroll bar* is an elongated rectangular container consisting of a scroll area, a slider box, or elevator inside the scroll bar, and arrows or anchors at either end. They may be placed, if needed, in primary and secondary windows and some controls. They may be oriented vertically or horizontally at the right or bottom of a window. Scroll bars come in a variety of styles, a typical one is illustrated in Figure 7.26. Scroll bars are used to find and view information that occupies more space than the allotted display space.

Advantages/Disadvantages While they permit viewing data of unlimited size, they do consume screen space and can be cumbersome to operate.

Proper Usage Use a scroll bar, or bars, when more information is available than the window space for displaying it.

Scroll Bar Guidelines

General

- Provide a scroll bar when nonvisible information must be seen.

Scroll Area or Container

- To indicate that scrolling is available, a scroll area or container should be provided.
  - Construct of a filled-in bar displayed in a technique that visually contrasts with the window and screen body background.

Figure 7.26   Scroll bar.

Scroll Slider Box or Handle

- To indicate the location and amount of information being viewed, provide a slider box or handle.
  - Constructed of a movable and sizable open area of the scroll area displayed in a technique that contrasts with the scroll area.
  - Indicate by its position, spatially, the relative location in the file of the information being viewed.
  - Indicate by its size, proportionately, the percentage of the available information in the file being viewed.

Scroll Directional Arrows

- To indicate the direction that scrolling may be performed, directional arrows should be provided.
  - Construct of arrows in small boxes with backgrounds contrasting with the scroll area.

Selection

- When the slider box/handle has been selected, highlight it in some visually distinctive way.

Location

- Position a vertical (top-to-bottom) scroll bar to the right of the window.
- Position a horizontal (left-to-right) scroll bar at the bottom of the window.

Size

- A vertical scroll bar should be the height of the scrollable portion of the window body.
- A horizontal scroll bar should be at least one-half the width of the scrollable portion of the window body.

Current State Indication

- Whenever the window size or information position changes, the scroll bar components must also change, reflecting the current state.
- Include scroll bars in all sizable windows.
  - If no information is currently available through scrolling in a particular direction, the relevant directional arrow should be subdued or grayed.

Directional Preference

- Where the choice exists, vertical (top-to-bottom) scrolling is preferred to horizontal (left-to-right) scrolling.

A scroll bar provides a method to permit display of information that may not always fit within a window displayed on a screen. One should only be included when scrolling may be necessary.

Components In today's systems, scroll bars come in a variety of styles. Scroll bars consist of three elements: a scroll area or container, a slider box or handle that moves within a track made by the scroll area/container, and directional or scroll arrows.

Scroll Area or Container The scroll area or, as it is sometimes called, the scroll container, is an elongated rectangular-shaped bar. Its presence indicates scrolling is available. It usually is constructed of a filled-in area displayed in a technique that visually contrasts with the window and screen body background. The chosen display technique should be of moderate intensity, not too powerful or too subtle. A powerful technique will be distracting; a subtle technique may be overlooked.

Slider Box or Handle To indicate the location and amount of information being viewed, a slider box or, as it is sometimes called, a scroll handle, is included within the scroll area/container. It is constructed of a movable and sizable portion of the scroll area displayed in a technique that contrasts with the scroll area. It should indicate by its position, spatially, the relative location in the file of the information being viewed. It should indicate by its size, proportionately, the percentage of the available information in the file being viewed. The usability of the slider box or handle can be further enhanced by displaying within it the page number of page-organized material being viewed.

Directional or Scroll Arrows To indicate the direction that scrolling may be performed, directional or scroll arrows are also included. They are constructed of variously shaped arrows in small boxes with backgrounds contrasting with the scroll area/container. They are most often located at each end of the scroll bar, but some systems locate them adjacent to one another within the scroll area/container itself.

Placing directional arrows at opposite ends of the scroll bar, as is done by Macintosh, OSF/Motif, Microsoft Windows, and OS/2 Presentation Manager, is conceptually the clearest. The mouse pointer is moved in the same direction, away from the current position, when either the scroll arrow or scroll handle is manipulated. The distance the directional arrows are separated, however, causes increased effort when a window's contents must be adjusted by scrolling in opposite directions.

NeXTStep solved the direction-switching problem by positioning the directional arrows adjacent to one another at one end of the scroll bar. While the forward-backward scrolling is made more efficient, the spatial correspondence between the beginning, middle, and end of the data is lost.

OPEN LOOK takes another approach, placing the directional arrows at opposite ends of the slider box/handle to maintain the desirable spatial correspondence while at the same time minimizing their separation. Since during a continuous scrolling operation the directional arrows move as the slider box/handle moves, OPEN LOOK automatically moves the mouse pointer to keep it aligned with the scroll arrow. This eliminates the need for the user to move the pointer during the continuous scrolling operation, but it requires that the user relinquish control of the mouse operation, and may be disorienting.

All of the advantages and disadvantages of these different approaches to scrolling are still not well understood and can only be experimentally resolved.

Scrolling Operation The scrolling movement can be performed in several ways. The most common actions involve grabbing the slider box/handle and moving it in the desired direction, or selecting the proper directional arrow. Clicking a mouse button while selecting a directional arrow moves the contents of a window one line. Pressing the mouse button scrolls the window's contents continuously until the button is released. NeXTStep also provides another more efficient process. A region of the scroll area/container can also be selected, automatically moving the slider box/handle to that point and displaying the proper window contents.

Based upon early scrolling research (Bury, Boyle, Evey, & Neal, 1982), movement of the window data usually follows the window-up or telescope approach, whereby the window moves around over data that appears fixed in location. This causes the data in a window to move in the direction opposite the one indicated by the directional arrow or the direction of movement of the scroll container/handle. Scrolling using window systems, however, seems to be especially mistake-prone, users often assuming the arrows will move the data in the same direction as the directional arrow or scroll container/handle. In other words, it is sensed that the data moves under the window, not the window over the data (Billingsley, 1988). Why this happens is open to conjecture. Billingsley speculates that because windows seem to move on screens, when data scrolls or moves in a window, people may conclude the data must be moving because the window remains still during the scrolling operation. Or, because of the close physical proximity of the directional arrows in scroll bars to the data, people may feel the arrows are acting on the data, not the window. The implication is that the scrolling procedure should be rethought and restudied. Some recent applications have devised scrolling methods through actually pointing at the window data.

Selection When the slider box/handle has been selected, highlight it in some visually distinctive way. Most systems do provide some visual feedback of this kind.

Location While again no universal agreement exists, the majority of systems locate the vertical (top-to-bottom) scroll bar to the right of the window and the horizontal (left-to-right) scroll bar at the bottom of the window.

Size A vertical scroll bar should be the height of the scrollable portion of the window body. A horizontal scroll bar should be at least one-half the width of the scrollable portion of the window body.

Current State Indication Whenever the window size or information position changes, the scroll bar components must also change, reflecting the current state of the scrolling process. Providing accurate information about the scrolling location facilitates user navigation and makes it easier to reposition the slider box/container. Include scroll bars in all sizable windows.

If scrolling cannot be performed in a particular direction, the relevant arrow box should be reduced in contrast or grayed. If all the information in a window is displayed and no information is available for scrolling, both directional arrows should be reduced in contrast or grayed.

Directional Preferences Where the choice exists, people prefer and deal better with vertical (top-to-bottom) scrolling rather than horizontal (left-to-right) scrolling. Avoid horizontal scrolling whenever possible.

CUSTOM CONTROLS

- Implement custom controls with caution.
- If used, make the look and behavior of custom controls unlike standard controls.

Many toolkits and interface builders provide the capability of creating custom controls; implement them with caution. The user is now presented with a multitude of controls whose usage and operation must be learned and remembered. The addition of custom controls adds to this learning and increases system complexity. If custom controls are developed and implemented, make their look and behavior as different as possible from the standard controls. This will avoid confusion between the various controls.

Toggle Switch

An example of an effective development process for a custom control is provided by Plaisant and Wallace (1992). For a touch screen application, a two-state control was needed to designate an entity as either on or off. The users of the control were classified as novice or occasional.

Design Alternatives Six different on/off controls, derived from those found on mechanical devices, were developed and tested. These were:

- One button, one word labeled ON that toggled between on and off.
- One button, two words labeled ON and OFF that toggled between on and off.
- Two adjacent buttons labeled ON and OFF.
- A rocker switch labeled ON and OFF.
- A slider with an arm moved side-to-side, labeled ON and OFF on each side.
- A lever with a handle moved side-to-side, ON/OFF labels on handle base, only one label visible at a time.

Results The various alternatives were used by study participant with no instructions, although participants did know they were dealing with on/off controls. Control preferences were obtained with the following results.

- A consistent rank order of preference as follows: one button-one word, rocker, two-button, one button-two words, slider, and lever.
- Toggles that were pushed were preferred to those that slide.
- Only the one-button and the rocker received no negative comments.
- Best overall choice for this particular application: the rocker.

While the results of this study should not be considered universal, the preference for pushing rather than sliding reinforces the complexity problem of slider controls in general. The researchers do point out one significant advantage of sliders: they are less prone to inadvertent activation, making it a more secure control. The study's final and most important message: always test selected, or designed, controls for effectiveness.

PRESENTATION CONTROLS

Presentation controls are purely informational. They provide details about screen elements or assist in giving the screen structure. Common presentation controls are tooltips, static text fields, and group boxes.

Tooltips

Description

- A small pop-up window containing descriptive text appearing when a pointer is moved over a control not possessing a label.

Purpose

- To provide descriptive information about a control.

Advantages/Disadvantages

+ Identifies an otherwise unidentified control.
+ Reduces possible screen clutter caused by control captions.
+ Enables control size to be reduced.
− Not obvious, must be discovered.
− Inadvertent appearance can be distracting.

Proper Usage

- To identify a control that has no caption.

Tooltips are a standard Windows 95 control. They have also appeared in some Windows 3.1 products. A tooltip is a small pop-up window that displays descriptive text when the pointer is moved over a control that does not possess a caption. A tooltip is illustrated in Figure 7.27. The purpose of a tooltip is to simply provide descriptive information about a control when its function must be quickly identified. It identifies a control that has no caption.

Advantages/Disadvantages A tooltip provides an easy way to identify an otherwise unidentifiable control. It reduces possible screen clutter caused by control captions, enabling the control size to be reduced. A tooltip, however, is not obvious and must be discovered. Its appearance

Figure 7.27 Tooltip.

when the pointer is positioned incorrectly, or is slowly passing over it, can be distracting to the screen viewer.

Tooltip Guidelines

- Display after a short time out.
- Present at the lower-right edge of the pointer.
  - Display fully on the screen.
  - For text boxes, display centered under the control.
- Display in the standard system tooltip colors.
- Remove the tooltip when the control is activated, or the pointer is moved away.

Display the tooltip on the screen after a short pause. This avoids its brief appearance as the pointer is just being moved over a control that possesses one. Position the tooltip to the lower-right of the pointer, but fully on the screen. Always adjust the location for a full fit, whenever necessary. For text boxes, present the tooltip centered under the control. Display it in the system's standard tooltip colors so it will be immediately recognized as a tooltip. Remove the tooltip when the control is clicked or the pointer is moved away.

Static Text Fields

Description

- Read-only textual information.

Purpose

- To identify a control by displaying a control caption.
- To clarify a screen by providing prompting or instructional information.
- To present descriptive information.

Proper Usage

- To display a control caption.
- To display prompting or instructional information.
- To display descriptive information.

A *static text field*, as illustrated in Figure 7.28, provides read-only textual information. It is a standard Windows 95 control.

Caption:

HEADING

This message is very important!

Figure 7.28 Static text.

Purpose/Proper Usage Use static text fields to create and present control captions, where necessary. Also use to clarify screen usage through providing prompting or instructional information. Other descriptive screen information can also be provided through static text fields. Examples are headings, subheadings, slider scales, progress indicator text, and so on.

Static Text Field Guidelines

- For captions:
  - Include a colon (:) as part of the caption.
  - Include a mnemonic for keyboard access.
  - When the associated control is disabled, display dimmed.
  - Follow all other presented guidelines for caption presentation and layout.
- For prompting or instructional information:
  - Display in a unique and consistent font style for easy recognition and differentiation.
  - Follow all other presented guidelines for prompting and instructional information.
- For descriptive information:
  - Follow all other guidelines for necessary screen or control descriptive information.

Captions Always include a colon as part of the caption. The colon immediately identifies the element as a caption. In Windows 95 the colon is also used by screen review utilities. Include a keyboard equivalent (mnemonic) for all captions to provide keyboard access to its associated control. Captions may also provide a means of indicating that their associated controls are disabled. Follow all the rules for caption display presented throughout these guidelines.

Other Screen Information Also, follow all the rules for other screen information presented throughout these guidelines.

Group Boxes

Description

- A rectangular frame that surrounds a control, or group of controls.
- An optional caption may be included in the frame's upper-left corner.

Purpose

- To visually relate the elements of a control.
- To visually relate a group of related controls.

Proper Usage

- To provide a border around radio button or check box controls.
- To provide a border around two or more functionally related controls.

A standardized rectangular frame that surrounds a control, or group of controls, is a group box. An optional caption may be included in the frame's upper-left corner. It is also a standard Windows 95 control. Group boxes are illustrated in Figure 7.29.

The purpose of a group box is to visually relate the elements of a single control, or a grouping of related controls.

Proper Usage Group boxes should be used to provide a border around a radio button control, a grouping of related check boxes, or two or more functionally related controls.

- Follow all presented guidelines for control and section borders.

Refer to all presented guidelines for control and section borders in designing group boxes.

Figure 7.29   Group boxes.

Progress Indicators

Description

- A rectangular bar that fills as a process is being performed.
  - Indicates the percentage of process completion.

Purpose

- To provide feedback concerning the completion progress of a lengthy operation.

Proper Usage

- To provide an indication of the proportion of a process completed.

A *progress indicator* is a rectangular bar that fills as a process is being performed. The filled-in area indicates the percentage of a process that has been completed. A progress indicator is illustrated in Figure 7.30.

Progress Indicator Guidelines

- When filling the indicator:
  - If horizontally-arrayed, fill left-to-right.
  - If vertically-arrayed, fill bottom-to-top.
- Fill with a color or a shade of gray.
- Include descriptive text for the process, as necessary.
- Place text outside of the control.

Fill horizontally arrayed progress indicators left-to-right, vertically arrayed, fill bottom-to-top. Fill with a color or a shade of gray. Create nec-

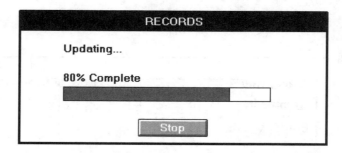

Figure 7.30   Progress indicator.

essary descriptive text using a static text control. Position the text outside of the control. Progress indicators are also discussed in the "Providing the Proper Feedback" section of Step 11.

WINDOWS 95 CONTROLS

Windows 95 controls are described in *The Windows Interface Guidelines for Software Design* (Microsoft, 1995). Many of these controls, those more generic in nature, have been referenced in the above control descriptions. A complete listing of Windows 95 controls, including several not discussed above, is found in Table 7.1.

Table 7.1   Microsoft Windows 95 Controls

Buttons

Command Buttons

Description:	• A control, commonly rectangular in shape. • Includes a label, either text, graphics, or both. • Activation immediately carries out action.
Purpose:	• To start actions. • To change properties. • To set tool modes.
Guidelines:	• See "Command Buttons" in text.

Option Buttons

Description:	• A control appearing as a set of small circles. • When set, a dot appears in the middle of the circle.
Purpose:	• Permits a single choice within a limited set (2–7) of mutually exclusive choices.
Guidelines:	• See "Radio Buttons" in text.

Check Boxes

Description:	• A control appearing as a square box. • When set, a check mark appears in the box.
Purpose:	• To designate an option either on or off.
Guidelines:	• See "Check Boxes" in text.

List Boxes

Description:	• A preconstructed box-shaped control for displaying a large list of choices. • The box may be always open and affixed to the screen, or it may appear on request. • Choices can be text, color, icons, or other graphics.
Purpose:	• To display a collection of items.

Continues

Table 7.1   *(Continued)*

Guidelines: • See "List Boxes and Drop-Down/Pop-Up List Boxes" in text.

Single-Selection List Boxes

Description: • A list box always open and displayed.

Purpose: • To permit selection of only one item in a list.

Guidelines: • See "List Boxes" and "Single-Selection List Boxes" in text.

Drop-down List Boxes

Description: • A control containing a display field, a button (called menu button), and a hidden list box.
                • The list is opened when the control or button is selected.
                • Choosing an item closes the list and displays the item in the display field.

Purpose: • To permit selection of only one item in a list.
                • To conserve screen space by hiding the list when it is not needed.

Guidelines: • See "Drop-Down/Pop-Up List Boxes" in text.

Extended and Multiple-Selection List Boxes

Description: • A list box always open and displayed.

Purpose: • To permit selection of more than one item in a list.
                • Extended List Box: Optimized for individual item or range selection.
                • Multiple-Selection List Box: Optimized for independent selection.

Guidelines: • See "List Boxes" and "Multiple-Selection List Boxes" in text.

List View Controls

Description: • Special extended-selection list box that displays a collection of items, consisting of an icon and a label.
                • Contents can be displayed in four different views:
                  – Icon: Items appear as a full-sized icon with label below.
                  – Small Icon: Items appear as a small icon with label to the right.
                  – List: Items appear as a small icon with label to the right. Arrayed in a columnar, sorted layout.
                  – Report: Items appear as a line in a multicolumn format. Leftmost column includes icon and its label. Subsequent columns include application specific information.

Purpose: • Where the representation of objects as icons is appropriate.

Guidelines: • See *The Windows Interface Guidelines for Software Design*, Microsoft (1995).

Tree View Control

Description: • A special list box control that displays a set of objects as an indented outline based upon their logical hierarchical relationship.
                • Includes buttons that allow the outline to be expanded and contracted.

Purpose: • To display the relationship between a set of containers or other hierarchical elements.

Guidelines: • See *The Windows Interface Guidelines for Software Design*, Microsoft (1995).

Table 7.1 *(Continued)*

Text Fields

Description:	• Fields for text entry. • Controls that combine a basic text-entry field with other kinds of controls.
Purpose:	• To facilitate the display, entry, or editing of text.
Guidelines:	• Add labels by using static text fields.

Text Boxes

Description:	• A rectangular control into which text is entered or edited. • Can be single line or multiple lines. • Also called "edit control." • Displaying field outline border is optional.
Purpose:	• To allow the display, entry, or editing of text. • To display read-only text.
Guidelines:	• Number of characters accepted can be limited. • Auto-exit (auto skip) can be supported; use sparingly. • Does not support individual font or paragraph properties. • For read-only text, the background color is automatically changed for differentiation. • Also, see "Text Boxes" in the text.

Rich-Text Boxes

Description:	• Same as *text boxes* except it also supports:
	  – Font properties; typeface, bold, size, color, etc.
	  – Paragraph properties; tabs, indents, etc.

Purpose:	• Same as "Text Boxes."
Guidelines:	• Same as "Text Boxes."

Combo Boxes

Description:	• A text box with an attached list box. • Text may be entered in the text field. • As text is typed, the list scrolls to the nearest match. • An item may be selected from the list. • When selected, the item appears in the text box.
Purpose:	• To allow entry or selection. • To minimize user interaction to display the list.
Guidelines:	• See "Attached Combination Box" in text.

Drop-down Combo Boxes

Description:	• A text box with a drop-down list box. • Text may be entered in the text field. • An item may be selected from the list.
Purpose:	• To allow entry or selection. • To maximize screen space efficiency.

Continues

Table 7.1 *(Continued)*

Guidelines:	• See "Drop-Down/Pop-Up Combination Box" in text.

Spin Boxes

Description:	• A text box with an associated up-down button control. • Text may be entered in the text field. • The value in the text field may be incremented or decremented using the up-down buttons.
Purpose:	• To allow entry or selection. • To maximize screen space efficiency.
Guidelines:	• See "Spin Boxes" in text.

Static Text Fields

Description:	• Read-only text information.
Purpose:	• To display control labels. • To display read-only information. • To display status information.
Guidelines:	• See "Static Text Fields" in text.

Shortcut Key Input Controls

Description:	• A special purpose text box control. • Also known as "hot key" control.
Purpose:	• To permit the user to customize shortcut keys supported by the application. • To define invalid keys or key combinations to ensure valid user input. – Only valid keys can be accessed by the control.
Guidelines:	• See *The Windows Interface Guidelines for Software Design*, Microsoft (1995).

Other General Controls

Group Boxes

Description:	• A rectangular frame with an optional label that surrounds a set of controls. • Does not directly process any input.
Purpose:	• To organize a set of controls.
Guidelines:	• See "Group Boxes" in text.

Column Headings

Description:	• A heading above a column of text or numbers. • Also known as "Header Control." • Can be divided into two or more parts for multiple columns. • Each part can be configured like a command button to support a specific function.
Purpose:	• To display headings above columns of text or numbers.

Guidelines:	• Labels:
	   – Can consist of text and graphics.
	   – Alignment can be left, centered, or right.

Table 7.1 *(Continued)*

	• Column widths can be set by dragging divisions between headings. • Also see *The Windows Interface Guidelines for Software Design*, Microsoft (1995).

Tabs

Description: • Dividers, to indicate logical pages or sections.

Purpose: • To define multiple logical pages or sections of information in a window.

Guidelines: • See "Notebook" in text.
• See *The Windows Interface Guidelines for Software Design*, Microsoft (1995).

Property Sheet Controls

Description: • A control to define property sheets.

Purpose: • To provide the basic framework for defining property sheets.
• To provide common property sheet controls.
• To provide support for creating wizards.

Guidelines: • See *The Windows Interface Guidelines for Software Design*, Microsoft (1995).

Scroll Bars

Description: • An elongated rectangular control for scrolling of data or information.

Purpose: • To create scrollable areas, other than on the window frame or in list boxes. Automatically included on window frame or in list boxes.

Guidelines: • See "Scroll Bars" in text.

Sliders

Description: • A control that consists of:
  – a bar that defines the extent or range of an adjustment.
  – An indicator that:
   – Shows the current value for the control.
   – Provides the means for changing the value.
• Sometimes called "trackbar" control.

Purpose: • For setting or adjusting values in a continuous range.

Guidelines: • See "Sliders" in text.

Progress Indicators

Description: • A display-only control that consists of a rectangular bar that fills from left to right.
• Shows percentage of completion of a process.
• Sometimes called "progress bar."

Purpose: • To provide visual feedback concerning completion of a lengthy operation.

Guidelines: • See "Progress Indicators" in text.

Tooltip Controls

Description: • A small pop-up window that displays descriptive text when the pointer is moved over a control.

Purpose: • To provide descriptive information about a control.

Continues

Table 7.1 *(Continued)*

Guidelines:	• See "Tooltips" in text.
Wells	
Description:	• Similar to a group of option buttons but presents graphic values. – Colors, patterns, images, etc.
Purpose:	• To present graphic values for selection.
Guidelines:	• Not currently provided by Windows 95. • See "Palettes" in text.

Windows 95 also defines menu bars, toolbars, and status bars as special interface constructs for managing a set of controls. Toolbars and status bars as constructs are summarized in Table 7.2.

Table 7.2 Microsoft Windows 95 Constructs for Managing a Set of Controls

Toolbars	
Description:	• A panel that contains a set of controls. • Specialized toolbars are sometimes called ribbons, tool boxes, and palettes.
Purpose:	• To provide quick access to specific commands or options.
Guidelines:	• Provide tooltips for toolbar controls that do not have a text label. • Define to be user configurable. • Allow location to be adjustable/moveable. • Provide keyboard access through shortcut keys. • Provide keyboard access through mnemonics (access keys). • Common toolbar buttons are provided. • Also, see guidelines for "Buttonbars" and "Palettes."
Status Bars	
Description:	• A special area within a window, typically at the bottom, that displays information. • It can contain controls, typically only read-only or noninteractive.

Purpose:	• To present:
	  – Information about the current state of what is being viewed in the window.
	  – Any other contextual information, such as keyboard state.
	  – Descriptive messages about a selected menu or toolbar button.

Guidelines:	• Provide tooltips for status bar controls that do not have a text label. • Define to be user configurable. • Provide keyboard access through shortcut keys. • Provide keyboard access through mnemonics (access keys).

SELECTING THE PROPER CONTROLS

Providing the proper control, or mix of controls, is critical to system success. The proper control will enable a person to make needed selections, entries, and changes quickly, efficiently, and with fewer mistakes. Improper selection most often leads to the opposite result.

This section will begin with a survey of several research studies addressing control selection. Studies such as these, while few in number, are now beginning to appear in the research literature. The results of these studies have already been incorporated within the control usage guidelines just discussed. Next, the criteria that must be considered in control selection will be summarized. Finally, some selection guidelines will be presented.

Entry Versus Selection—A Comparison

The first studies to be described are a series performed by IBM. These studies (Gould, Boies, Meluson, Rasamny, & Vosburgh, 1988; Greene, Gould, Boies, Meluson, & Rasamny, 1988; Greene, Gould, Boies, Rasamny, & Meluson, 1992) looked at the advantages and disadvantages of using either entry fields or selection fields for data collection. Entry involved keying text; selection was performed by pointing at a choice through the keyboard using the cursor control keys (not a mouse). The information compared was of three kinds: dates, text, and data. The first conclusion:

Choosing a Type of Control

- For familiar, meaningful data, choose the technique that, in theory, requires the fewest number of keystrokes to complete.
- If the data is unfamiliar, or prone to typing errors, choose a selection technique.

The studies found that if the data to be entered was familiar, the technique that required the minimum theoretical number of keystrokes to complete the task was the fastest. Theoretical keystrokes are the minimum number possible, excluding miskeys and erroneous cursor or selection movements. However, as the information became less familiar or became subject to spelling or typing errors, the minimum keystroke principle broke down. Selection techniques, and the reminders and structure they provide for unfamiliar items, hard to spell words, and items prone to typing errors becomes advantageous. The point at which the change-over occurs is not known. It would be influenced by the nature of the task and the nature of the user.

These studies point out the advantages of the techniques that permit both typed entry and selection to enter the data (spin box, drop-down/pop-up combination box, and attached combination box).

Aided Versus Unaided Entry

- Provide aided entry whenever possible.
  - Absorb any extra and unnecessary keystrokes.
  - Provide an auditory signal that autocompletion has been performed.

The studies also compared unaided typed entry (the entire field had to be keyed) with aided entry (the system automatically and immediately completed the field when enough characters were keyed to make the desired data known). They found that aided entry, also known as autocompletion, was preferred over unaided entry methods, and it was also the fastest. Autocompletion was also preferable to, and faster than, many selection methods. Greene et al. (1992) found that for keying of difficult to spell words, aided entry was much faster, and significantly reduced errors, when compared to unaided entry.

The result is that, where possible, autocompletion of text entry fields should be provided. Autocompletion will minimize the user's effort by reducing input time and keystrokes. It should also enhance the user's opinion of the system. If aided entry is provided, extra keystrokes must be absorbed by the system. The software will finish spelling a word much faster than a person's fingers are capable of stopping movement. Also, provide some kind of auditory signal that autocompletion has begun. A person may not be looking directly at the control when the completion is performed.

Comparison of GUI Controls

Tullis & Kodimer (1992) compared seven controls comprising direct manipulation, selection, and data entry. The task was to reorder four items in a table (Filename, Number, Size, and Date). The controls studied were the following. Complete descriptions of control usage methods are summarized in Table 7.3.

- Direct Manipulation.
  1. Drag and Drop On.
  2. Drag and Drop Between.
- Selection.
  3. Icons.
  4. Radio Buttons.
  5. Menus (Drop-down list boxes).

- Entry.
  6. One entry area.
  7. Four entry areas.

The direct manipulation methods reflected the perceived strength of graphical systems, namely manipulation of objects on the screen. The se-

Table 7.3 Controls Evaluated by Tullis & Kodimer (1992)

Direct Manipulation

1) Drag and Drop On
   - The items are arrayed horizontally. An item is dragged to a new location above another item and released. The item in that position moves to the old location of the arriving item.
2) Drag and Drop Between
   - The items are arrayed horizontally. An item is dragged to a new location between two other items and released. The items are readjusted into new positions, including, when necessary, automatic wrap-around for items located at the end of the line.

Selection

3) Icons
   - The items are arrayed horizontally. Icons are positioned between each pair of items. Selecting an icon switches the positions of each adjacent item.
4) Radio Buttons
   - The items are presented in a matrix, item name along the left side, item position numbers across the top. Radio buttons in the matrix are selected to represent each item's position.
5) Menus (Drop-down list boxes)
   - Items are positioned horizontally. A drop-down listing is activated and the item for that location selected.

Entry

6) One Entry Area
   - A single text entry field is provided. A one-character mnemonic (F,N,S,D) is provided for each choice. The mnemonics are keyed in the order in which the items are to be arrayed.
7) Four Entry Areas
   - Four text-entry fields, arrayed vertically, are provided. A number (1–4) is keyed into each field, indicating the order in which the items are to be arrayed.

lection methods utilized indirect manipulation and illustrated the new types of controls now available in graphical screen design. The entry methods are a carryover from text-based screens, the only way the task could be accomplished for many years.

Study participants were experienced Microsoft Windows users. No instructions were provided on how to carry out the item reorganization tasks, the experience of the participants being relied upon.

The two fastest methods were radio buttons and one entry field. The methods most preferred by participants were radio buttons, drop-down list boxes, and one entry field. The direct manipulation methods fared rather poorly, ending mid-list in the speed and preference rankings. The surprise, perhaps, was the good showing of an old control: one entry field.

Tullis (1993) performed a follow-up to this study by asking a group of programmers to predict the study results (without, of course, being privy to its results). For both reordering speeds and subjective preferences their predictions were way off the mark. They anticipated that the direct manipulation methods would be the fastest and most preferred. This, of course, was not at all the case. They predicted that radio buttons would be midway in the speed and preference ordering and that one entry field would be near the bottom. Again, they were quite mistaken. The correlation between their predictions and actual reordering speed was a dismal .07. They did slightly better on predicting preferences, the correlation being .31.

Based on these studies, Tullis concludes that control selection decisions made on convention and intuition may not necessarily yield the best results. We might modify that conclusion to say, with a great deal of justification, that such decisions made using *common sense* may not even yield *good* results. Just because a control or process is new does not necessarily make it better. Just because the control has been around a long time does not necessarily make it poorer. Controls should be selected based upon the objectives it is to achieve, and they should be subjected to the same rigorous testing as all other parts of the system.

Another control comparison study has recently been conducted by Johnsgard et al. (1995). They evaluated a variety of controls including check boxes, drop-down list boxes, drop-down combination boxes, text boxes, list boxes, radio buttons, sliders, and spin boxes. Speeds, errors, and preferences were obtained for the various controls under various conditions.

Mutually Exclusive Choice Controls For a small set of options (5), a medium set (12), and a large set (30), radio buttons were significantly faster than the other mutually exclusive controls. They were also the most accurate and most preferred by the study participants. This result is consistent with the results of the Tullis and Kodimer (1992) study. Among other findings: as control set sizes increased, control activation speeds significantly increased (took longer), and sets organized in a meaningful way were searched significantly faster than those in random orders.

The medium and large set sizes (12 and 30) are larger than generally recommended for radio buttons (8 or less). The results indicate that radio buttons may effectively be used for these larger quantities, if sufficient screen space exists for their presentation. Controls requiring scrolling to see all the choices, or require an action to display a listing of choices (drop-downs), seem to significantly impede selection speeds.

Nonexclusive Choice Controls For a small set of options (5) with two selected choices, a medium set (12) with three selected choices, and a large set (30) with eight selected choices, check boxes were significantly faster than the other nonexclusive controls. Check boxes were also the most preferred by the study participants. Among other findings: like radio buttons, as control set sizes increased, control activation speeds increased (took longer), and sets organized in a meaningful way were searched significantly faster than those in random orders.

The medium and large set sizes (12 and 30) are also larger than generally recommended for check boxes (8 or less). The results also seem to indicate that check boxes may effectively be used for these larger quantities, if sufficient screen space exists for their presentation. Again scrolling and retrieving lists slow one down.

Combination Selection and Entry Controls Two controls were compared, a drop-down combination box and an array of radio buttons including an "other" choice with an associated text entry field for keying the "other" value. The fastest, most accurate, and preferred: radio buttons with the text entry field.

Controls for Selecting a Value Within a Range Setting range values included indicating a time, a percentage, or the transmission frequency of a radio station. Controls evaluated were the spin button, text entry field, the slider. The spin button was the most accurate and the text entry field fastest and most preferred. The slider finished last in all three measurement categories.

The study's general conclusions are:

- Making all options always visible will enhance performance.
- Requiring additional actions to make further options visible slows performance.
- For longer lists, scrolling tends to degrade performance more than the action associated with retrieving a hidden list.

As set size increases, performance times increase more for controls that require scrolling than for those that do not. For a large set size (30 options) scrolling slowed performance more than the action to retrieve a list.

Control Selection Criteria

Selection of the proper control, then, depends on several factors. First is the structure and characteristics of the property or data itself. Other considerations include the nature of the task, the nature of the user, and the limitations of the display screen itself.

Property or data considerations reflect the characteristics of the data itself. Some kinds of controls are very restrictive in that they permit only specific kinds of information with specific qualities to be presented within them. Other kinds of controls may not be as restrictive concerning a data's qualities, but they are not well suited to the kind of data being used. Data considerations include the following:

- Is the property or data *mutually exclusive* or *nonexclusive*? Does entry/selection require single or multiple items?
- Is the property or data *discrete* or *continuous*? Discrete data can be meaningfully specified and categorized, while continuous cannot.
- Is the property or data *limited* or *unlimited* in scope? If limited, how many items will the data normally not exceed?
- Is the property or data *fixed* or *variable* in list length? Is there always a fixed number of items, or will it vary?
- Is the property or data ordered in a *predictable* or *nonpredictable* fashion? If predictable, will the user be able to anticipate the next, nonvisible, item?
- Can the property or data be *represented pictorially*? Will a picture or graphic be as meaningful as a textual description?

Task considerations reflect the nature of the job. Considerations include the following:

- *How often* is an item *entered* or *selected*?
- *How often* is an item *changed*?
- How *precise* must the item be entered or selected?

User considerations reflect the characteristics of the user. Important considerations:

- How much *training* in control operation will be provided?
- How *meaningful* or *known* is the property or data for the user?
- How *rememberable* or *learnable* is the property or data for the user?
- How *frequently used* will the system be?
- Is the user an *experienced typist*?

Display considerations reflect the characteristics of the screen and hardware.

- How much *screen space* is available to display the various controls?

Choosing a Control Form

In light of the above research and considerations, and the known characteristics of the various controls, some guidance in control selection can be presented.

When to Permit Text Entry?

- Permit text entry if any of the following questions can be answered YES:
  - Is the data unlimited in size and scope?
  - Is the data familiar?
  - Is the data *not* conducive to typing errors?
  - Will typing be faster than choice selection?
  - Is the user an experienced typist?

Permit text entry when any of the above conditions exist. Use of combination controls is almost always the best alternative, permitting the user to *choose* when to type or point and select.

What Kind of Control to Choose? Next is a chart and a table for providing some control recommendations based upon a control's known advantages, disadvantages, and proper usage characteristics. The chart is a simple decision chart for small listings based upon Johnsgard et al. (1995). Table 7.4 is more thorough and is based upon the known characteristics of the controls described in this chapter.

Task	*Best Control*	*If Screen Space Constraints Exist*
• Mutually Exclusive	– Radio Buttons	– Drop-down List Box
• Non-mutually Exclusive	– Check Boxes	– Multiple-selection List Box
• Select or Type a Value	– Radio Buttons with "Other" Text Entry Field	– Drop-down Combination Box
• Setting a Value Within a Range	– Spin Button	– Text Entry Field

The above recommendation presented by Johnsgard et al. is based upon their research study. The names of some controls have been modified to reflect the control classification scheme found in this text. It would seem

Table 7.4 Suggested Uses for Graphical Controls

1. IF:	USE:
• *Mutually exclusive* alternatives. • Discrete data. • Best represented verbally. • Very limited in number (2–8). *AND:* • Typed entry is never necessary. • Content can never change. • Adequate screen space is available. *OR:* • Typed entry is never necessary. • Content can never change. • Adequate screen space is not available. *OR:* • Typed entry may be necessary. • Content can change. • Adequate screen space is available. *OR:* • Typed entry may be necessary. • Content can change. • Adequate screen space is not available.	 Radio buttons Drop-down/pop-up list box Attached combination box Drop-down/pop-up combination box.

2. IF:	USE:
• *Mutually exclusive* alternatives. • Discrete data. • Best represented verbally. • Potentially large in number (9 or more). *AND:* • Typed entry is never necessary. • Content can never change. • Adequate screen space is available. *OR:* • Typed entry is never necessary. • Content can never change. • Adequate screen space is not available. *OR:* • Typed entry may be necessary. • Content can change. • Adequate screen space is available.	 Fixed list box Drop-down/pop-up list box Attached combination box

Table 7.4   *(Continued)*

OR:
- Typed entry may be necessary.
- Content can change.
- Adequate screen space is not available.   Drop-down/pop-up combination box.

3. *IF:*   *USE:*

- *Mutually exclusive* alternatives.
- Discrete data.
- Best represented graphically.
- Content rarely changes.
- Small or large number of items.   Palette

4. *IF:*   *USE:*

- *Mutually exclusive* alternatives.
- Not frequently selected.
- Content does not change.
- Well-known, easily remembered data.
- Predictable, consecutive data.
- Typed entry sometimes desirable.

AND:
- Adequate screen space is not available.   Spin Box

OR:
- Adequate screen space is available.   Attached Combination Box

5. *IF:*   *USE:*

- *Mutually exclusive* alternatives.
- Continuous data with a limited range of settings.
- Value increases/decreases in a well-known, predictable way.
- Spatial representation enhances comprehension.   Slider

6. *IF:*   *USE:*

- *Nonexclusive* alternatives.
- Discrete data.
- Best represented verbally.
- Typed entry is never necessary
- Content can never change.
- Adequate screen space is available

AND:
- Very limited in number (2–8).   Check Boxes

OR:
- Potentially large in number (9 or more).   Fixed list box (nonexclusive).

worth considering for controls containing a small number of choices. All controls in their study, except *setting a value within a range*, were limited to 30 options. For more than 30 choices, the use of radio buttons or check boxes still seems inappropriate at this time. More research is needed in this area.

Choosing Between Buttons or Menus for Commands Determining the proper way to present a command also depends on several factors. The following considerations are involved in choosing the correct command form:

- Is the command part of a *standard tool set*?
- The total *number* of commands in the application.
- The *complexity* of the commands.
- The *frequency* with which commands are used.
- Whether or not the command is used in association *with another control*.

Guidelines for choosing the proper command form are presented in Table 7.5.

Table 7.5   Choosing a Command Form

If the commands:	Use:
• Are standard commands provided by a tool set.	Commands provided by the tool set
• Total seven or more, and can be arranged hierarchically into groups.	Menu bar and pull-downs
• Total six or fewer, are selected frequently, and affect an entire window.	Buttons in a window
• Total seven or more, are selected frequently, and affect an entire window.	Buttons in a buttonbar
• Are used with other controls, or are complicated commands and need to be simplified.	Buttons in a dialog box
• Are sometimes used frequently, and are sometimes used infrequently.	Buttons in a dialog box
• Are frequently accessed, and have only two conditions.	Toggled menu item

EXAMPLES

Improper and proper usage of several controls are illustrated and discussed.

Example 1

This is an instance of improper and proper presentation of command buttons.

Screen 1.1

Here the design and display of buttons is poor. Problems include: (1) The buttons are split between the left and right side of the screen, causing a wide separation. Positioning to the left, from a screen usage and flow standpoint, is illogical. (2) Differences in sizes exist between buttons. OK, a very frequently used button, is the smallest, slowing down selection speed if a pointer is used. (3) Different size labels also exist (OK and Search). (4) There appears to be redundancy in button use and purpose. How does OK differ from Save? What does Edit do? (5) From an organization standpoint, standard and application buttons appear to be intermixed. (6) The Back and Next actions are widely separated, making fast reversal of actions more difficult.

Screen 1.2

This shows a much better button design and presentation. Enhancements include: (1) The buttons are located at the bottom of the screen, in a position following the screen usage flow. (2) Button size is standardized, presenting generally larger targets. (3) Button label size is standardized. (4) The seemingly redundant buttons are eliminated. (5) Function-specific buttons are grouped separately from standard buttons and button group-

Screen 1.1

Screen 1.2

ings are created through a larger spacing between Print and OK. (6) Back, now called Previous, and Next are positioned together for fast paging reversal.

Example 2.

Here we are dealing with inconsistent location of command buttons.

Screens 2.1 to 2.4

These are the button locations found on four windows within a graphical system. Positions range from spread out across the window's bottom (Screen 2.1), left-justified at the bottom (Screen 2.2), centered along the

Screen 2.1

Screen 2.2

Screen 2.3

right side (Screen 2.3), and top-justified along the right side (Screen 2.4). Memorization and prediction of button location will be very difficult, slowing down the experienced user.

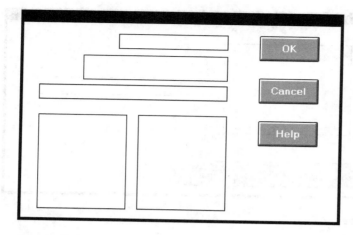

Screen 2.4

Screen 2.5

Proper positioning would have found *all* the command buttons consistently positioned, such as at the bottom center as illustrated in Screen 2.5

Screen 2.5

Control 3.1

Example 3

This is an example of improper and proper use of a control.

Control 3.1

The names of states must be selected using radio buttons. Problems include: (1) The large number of choices presented makes scanning very difficult. (2) Are all the state abbreviations familiar to you, and all users? (3) The organization of states must have been established by a lottery. The name of the state I want is Mississippi. How do I find it in the array?

Control 3.2

This shows a much better alternative, a drop-down/pop-up combination box. If the state name is known, it can be typed in the field. Ideally, typing the state code, if known, will also be acceptable. If the name of a particular state is unknown, or its spelling unclear, the drop-down/pop-up can be retrieved and the state name selected from the list presented. Ideally, also, a misspelled keyed state name will still be correctly identified by the system and displayed properly.

Control 3.2

Example 4

Here is another instance of improper and proper use of a control.

Screen 4.1

A listing of names is being collected. Courtesy title is selected through list box; last name, first name, and middle initial are typed. The problem: The task is heavily keyboard intensive. To select a title requires shifting to an alternative device control such as a mouse or tabbing through the list box listing to find the proper title. This slows down the keying process and may be awkward. The list box also consumes a great deal of space on the screen.

Screen 4.2

A solution: Collect courtesy title using a pop-up/drop-down combination box. Familiar titles may be quickly typed, along with the remainder of the name data. Rare or unusual titles may be identified by selecting, displaying, and searching the listing of all alternatives. The title may then be entered in the field by selecting from the list or keying it into the field.

Screen 4.1

Screen 4.2

Example 5

Again, improper and proper use of controls.

Screen 5.1

A collection of seashells is being cataloged by class and order. Text boxes are provided for the task. The catalog process includes typing words like "Cephalopoda" and "Eulamellibranchia." The process is slow and conducive to spelling errors.

Screen 5.1

Screen 5.2

Screen 5.2

A solution: Present Class and Order in list boxes from which the proper varieties are selected. This will speed up the cataloguing process and eliminate the possibility of spelling errors. To make the entire procedure a selection task, also make Item Number a selective and incrementable spin box.

Example 6

Again, improper and proper use of a control.

Screen 6.1

An international corporation is setting up a worldwide account database. Names from dozens of different countries are added each day. Country is collected though using a spin box. Is this proper usage for a spin box?

Screen 6.1

Screen 6.2 and 6.3

With a spin box, the following nonvisible choice must be capable of being anticipated. If not, tedious clicking and searching to find the correct choice might have to be performed. (What country follows Greece in the world-wide alphabetical listing of countries today? Guatemala—at least at this writing.) The data in spin boxes should be stable, not often changing. This quality does not accurately reflect the state of world countries today.

The best choice would really depend on the variability of the information being collected. If the account information being collected tended to be quite variable in flow, that is, successive account entries were usually from different countries, a better choice would be an attached combination box (Screen 6.2). Well-known country names can be typed and less well-known found in the listing. Due to the dynamic nature of country names, frequent reference to the list can be expected. Permanently displaying the list avoids the step of retrieving it when needed. The attached listing also permits scanning several names at one time, alleviating the predictability problem. Names can also be easily added or changed as needed. The attached combination box is also at the bottom of the window where it tends to be out of the way .

If successive account entries tended to be from the same country, that is, the information is batched, a pop-up/drop-down combination would be more appropriate (Screen 6.3). The box can remain closed through successive same country entries and only need be opened occasionally when actually needed.

Screen 6.2

Screen 6.3

Organize and Lay Out Windows

Having determined what screen controls are needed and when they are needed, the controls must be presented clearly and meaningfully in the work area of the window. Proper presentation and organization will encourage quick and correct information comprehension and the fastest possible execution of tasks and functions.

- Identify all other necessary window components to be included on the screen.
  - Title
  - Prompting Messages
- Organize and lay out screens to encourage quick and accurate information comprehension and control execution.
  - Organize for meaningfulness and efficiency.
  - Create groupings.
  - Provide alignment and balance.

A screen may, however, also contain a number of additional elements to aid in its use. Components like title and prompting messages must be incorporated in the clearest and most effective manner possible.

IDENTIFYING OTHER WINDOW COMPONENTS

Other window components include its title and prompting messages.

Window Title

- All windows must have a title located in a centered position at the top.
  - Exception: Windows containing messages.
- Clearly and concisely describe the purpose of the window.
- Spell out fully using an upper-case font.
- If title truncation is necessary, truncate from right to left.
- If presented above a menu bar, display with a background that contrasts with the bar.

The window title should be positioned at the top center and fully spelled out using upper-case letters. Using an upper-case font will give it the needed moderate emphasis, aiding setting it off from the screen body (IBM's SAA CUA and Microsoft's Windows 95 guidelines display the title, like all screen components, in mixed-case letters). Windows containing messages, however, need not have a title. The title should clearly and concisely describe the screen's purpose. If the window appears as a result of a previous selection, the title should clearly reflect the wording of the selection made to retrieve it. For small windows where title truncation is necessary, truncate from right to left.

If the title appears above the menu bar, the title's background should contrast with that of the bar. A recommendation is to use the same background color and caption color as the screen body. A title can always be identified by its topmost location on the screen, so using a color different from other screen components may add to visual confusion.

Prompting Messages

- Incorporate prompting on a screen, as necessary:
  - In a position just preceding the part, or parts, of a screen to which they apply.
  - In a manner that visually distinguishes them, such as:
    - Displaying them in a unique type style.
    - Displaying them in a unique color.
  - In a position that visually distinguishes them by:
    - Left-justifying the prompt and indenting the related field captions (or headings) a minimum of about three spaces to the right.
  - Leaving a space line between the prompt and the controls to which they refer, if possible.

Type for changes only.

Kind: [   ]

Model: [   ]

Number: [   ]

– Using a mixed-case font.

Prompting messages are instructions to the screen user on what to do with, or how to work with, the screen being presented. They are analogous to instructions for filling out a paper form. Before placing them on a screen, remember that they can quickly become visual noise. Other prompting methods, such as using Help or the message area should also be considered.

When it is necessary to place them on a screen, they must be immediately recognized as prompts. This will permit them to be easily ignored when they are not needed. Therefore, some visual aspect of the prompt must indicate that it *is* a prompt.

Displaying them in a unique color or in a unique font on all screens is one way to do this. If one of these methods is used, the cautions concerning the excessive use of color and different font styles must be heeded. Another, but less stronger visually, method is to identify the prompt simply by its location. Begin the prompt to the left of the field captions (or headings) to which it applies. This left-justification will identify it as a prompt.

Try to leave a space line between the prompting message and the controls to which it relates, whenever possible. Screen space constraints may not always permit the space line, however. The prompt should be displayed in normal sentence-style capitalization. Guidelines for writing messages will be found in Step 11.

ORGANIZING AND LAYING OUT SCREENS

Screen organizational and layout principles will now be summarized.

A Summary of Key Design Principles

How a screen is organized, and how its information is actually presented, is crucial to achieving the design goals of fast and accurate comprehension and control execution. Following is a summary of numerous design principles toward these ends. They have all been fully addressed in earlier chapters but are restated here as a reminder of their importance.

General Guidelines

Amount of Information

- Present the proper amount of information on each screen.
  - Too little is inefficient.
  - Too much is confusing.

Organization

- Provide an ordering that:
  - Is logical and sequential.
  - Is rhythmic, guiding a person's eye through the display.
  - Encourages natural movement sequences.
  - Minimizes pointer and eye movement distances.

Control Placement

- Position the most important and frequently used controls to the top left.
- Maintain a top-to-bottom, left-to-right flow.
- If one control enables or affects another, the enabling control should be above or to the left of the enabled control.
- Place the command buttons that affect the entire window horizontally, and centered, at the window bottom.

Navigation

- The flow of interaction should:
  - Require as little cursor and pointer travel as possible.
  - Minimize the number of times a person's hand has to travel between the keyboard and the mouse.

Aesthetics

- Provide a visually pleasing composition through:
  - Adequate use of white space.
  - Balance.
  - Groupings.
  - Alignment of elements.

Visual Clutter

- Avoid visual clutter by:
  - Maintaining low screen density levels. Do not exceed 30 to 40 percent.
  - Maintaining distinctiveness of elements.
    - Controls should not touch the window border.
    - Controls should not touch each other.

    – A button label should not touch the button border.
- Leaving at least two blank spaces between the left and right borders and the widest element within the window.

Focus and Emphasis

- Provide visual emphasis to the most important screen elements, its data or information.

Consistency

- Provide consistency.
  - With a person's experiences and cultural conventions.
  - Internally within a system.
  - Externally across systems.

These guidelines, along with many others, were fully addressed in Step 3. In brief, present the proper amount of information on each window, never cram information into it. Keep the proportion of the window devoted to information or "ink" to no more than 30 to 40 percent of the window's entire area. Always leave a sufficient margin around all screen elements and between elements and the screen border. The window will look much more appealing to the viewer. Provide an ordering that is logical, sequential, and rhythmic to guide a person's eye through the display. Other important factors include maintaining a top-to-bottom, left-to-right flow; efficiency in navigation; visually pleasing composition through balance, groupings and alignment; emphasizing the screen's data; and being consistent.

The following window principles are also important.

Window Guidelines

Organization

- Organize windows to support user tasks.
- Present related information in a single window whenever possible.
- Support the most common tasks in the most efficient sequence of steps.
- Use:
  - Primary windows to:
    - Begin an interaction and provide top-level context for dependent windows.
    - Perform a major interaction.
  - Secondary windows to:
    - Extend the interaction.
    - Obtain or display supplemental information related to the primary window.

- Dialog boxes for:
  - Infrequently used or needed information.
  - "Nice-to-know" information.

Number

- Minimize the number of windows needed to accomplish an objective.

Size

- Provide large enough windows to:
  - Present all relevant and expected information for the task.
  - Not hide important information.
  - Not cause crowding or visual confusion.
  - Minimize the need for scrolling.
  - But less than the full size of the entire screen.
- If a window is too large, determine:
  - Is all the information needed?
  - Is all the information related?

These guidelines, and many others, were presented and fully discussed, in Step 4. In summary, always organize windows to support user tasks. Support the most common tasks in the most efficient sequence of steps. Minimize the number of windows needed to accomplish an objective. In general, present all related information in a single window whenever it is possible to do so. A window should be large enough to accommodate the amount of data a person would typically expect to see. The needed information can only be determined through thorough task analysis.

The necessity for window scrolling should also be avoided whenever possible. If all the relevant controls or data cannot be placed within the confines of a single window, place that which is less frequently needed on another window. Do not make the default size of a window the full screen. The option to maximize a window always exists.

Finally, use primary windows, secondary windows, and dialog boxes consistently and in the manner they are intended to be used.

Organization Guidelines

Organizational guidelines to be addressed include groupings, borders, dependent controls, alignment, and balance.

Creating Groupings

General

- Provide groupings of associated elements.
  - Elements of a radio button or check box control.

- Two or more related fields or controls.
- Create groupings as close as possible to 5 degrees of visual angle.

White Space

- Provide adequate separation of groupings through liberal use of white space.
- Leave adequate space:
  - Around groups of related controls.
  - Between groupings and window borders.
- The space between groupings should be sufficiently greater than the space between fields within a grouping.

Headings

- Provide section headings and subsection headings for multiple control groupings.
- Provide headings that meaningfully and concisely describe the nature of the group of related fields.

Borders

- Enhance groupings through incorporation of borders around:
  - Elements of a single control.
  - Groups of related controls or fields.
- Individual control borders should be visually differentiable from borders delineating groupings of fields or controls.
  - Provide a border consisting of a thin line around *single* controls.
  - Provide a border consisting of a slightly thicker line around *groups* of fields or controls.
- Do not place individual field or control borders around:
  - Single entry fields.
  - Single list boxes.
  - Single combination boxes.
  - Single spin boxes.
  - Single sliders.
- Do not place borders around command buttons.

Individual controls with multiple parts, such as radio buttons or check boxes, should be identifiable as a single entity. A series of related controls should also be presented as related. Create groupings to do this as often as possible. Groupings aid learning and provide visual appeal. The optimum group size is five degrees of visual angle. At the normal viewing distance of a screen this is a circle 1.67 inches in diameter. On a text-based screen this is equivalent to about six to seven lines at a width of 12 to 14 characters. Examples of groupings are shown in Figure 8.1.

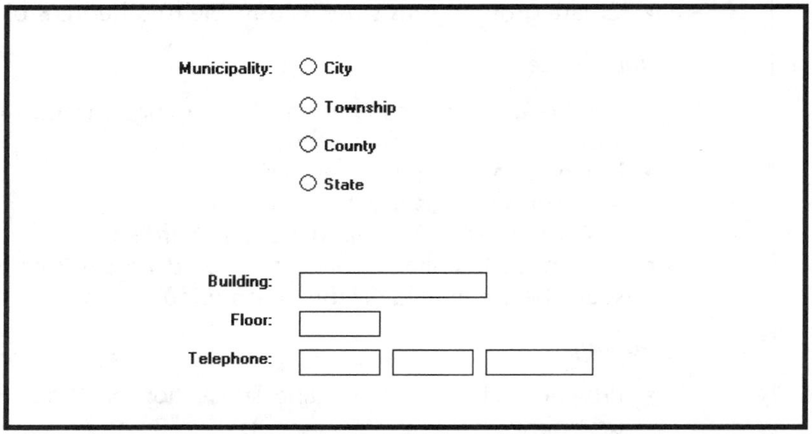

Figure 8.1   Groupings.

Groupings can be made visually obvious through liberal use of white space. Sufficient space should be left between all groupings of controls, and groupings and the window borders, as illustrated in Figure 8.2.

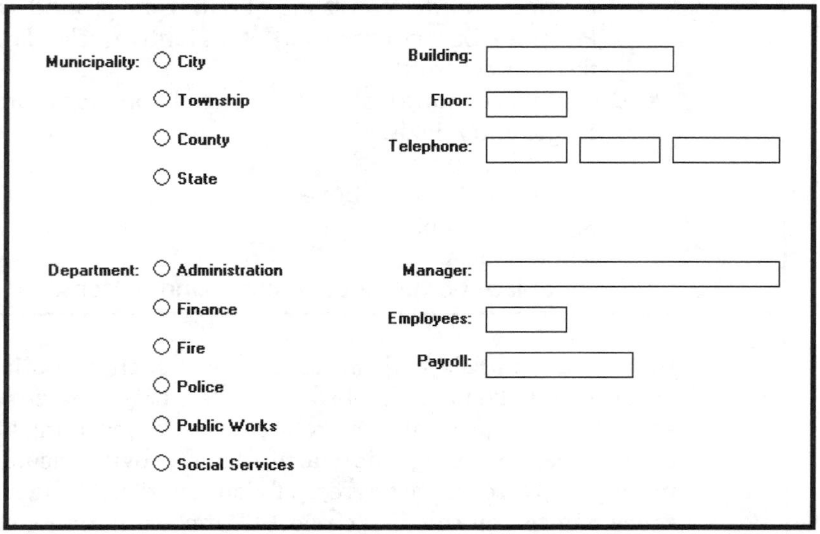

Figure 8.2   Groupings using white space.

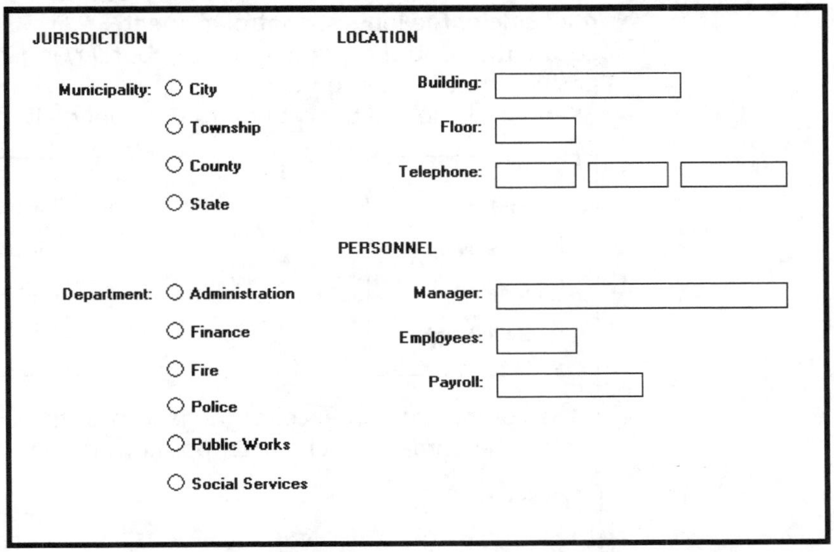

Figure 8.3 Groupings with section headings.

Headings should also be used to give groupings of controls or information an identity. This aids comprehension and learning of what is presented. See Figure 8.3.

Borders

Groupings can be further enhanced through the use of borders. Inscribe line borders around elements of a single control such as a radio button or check box and/or groups of related controls or fields. Individual control borders should be visually differentiable from borders delineating groupings of fields or controls. Provide a border consisting of a thin line around single controls and a slightly thicker line around groups of fields or controls.

Control Borders

- Incorporate a thin single-line border around the elements of a selection control.
- For spacing:
  - Vertically, leave one line space above and below the control elements.
  - Horizontally:
  - Leave at least two character positions between the border and the left side of the control elements.

- Leave at least two character positions between the border and the right side of the longest control element.
- Locate the control caption in the top border, indented one character position from the left border.
- Alternatively, locate the caption to the upper-left of the box.

- If the control caption exceeds the length of the choice descriptions, extend the border two character positions to the right of the caption.

Thin line borders may be used to surround some boxed-in controls, particularly radio buttons and check boxes. Control captions should be located upper left within the border itself, or to the left of the box. The spacing guidelines are to avoid cramping the text within the border. Some examples of control borders are illustrated in Figures 8.4 and 8.5.

Section Borders

- Incorporate a thicker single-line border around groups of related entry or selection controls.
- For spacing:
  - Vertically, leave one line space between the top and bottom row of the entry or selection control elements.
  - Horizontally, leave at least four character positions to the left and right of the longest caption and/or entry field.
- Locate the section heading in the top border, indented two character positions from the left border.

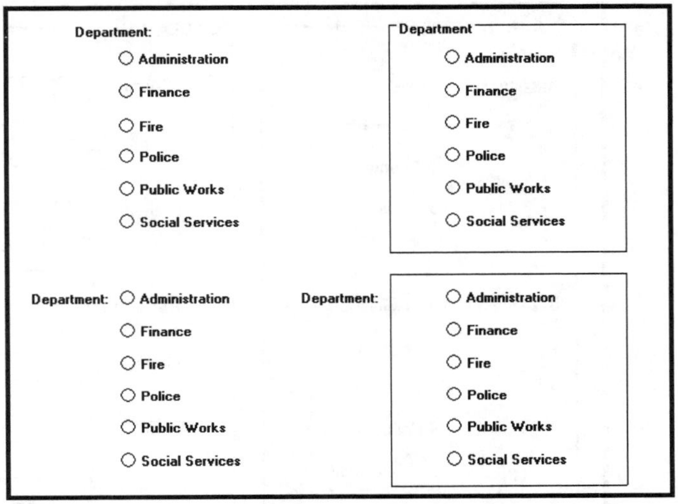

Figure 8.4   Examples of vertically arrayed controls without and with borders.

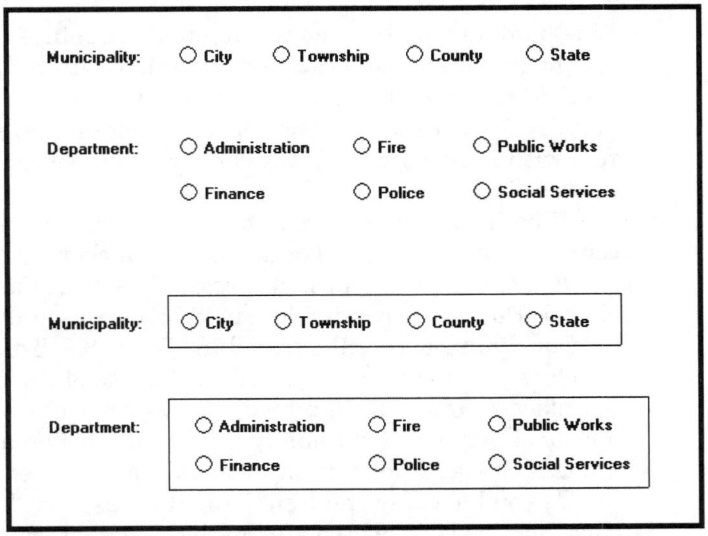

Figure 8.5   Examples of horizontally arrayed controls without and with borders.

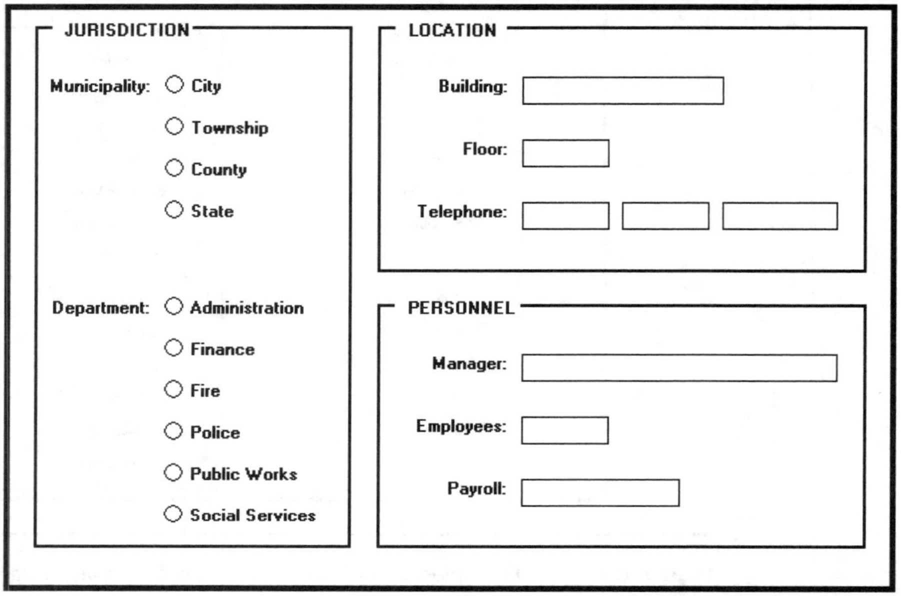

Figure 8.6 Grouping of sections using borders.

Line borders may be used to surround groupings of related controls. Section headings should be located upper left within the border itself. Display section headings in capital letters to differentiate them easily from individual control captions. The spacing guidelines are to avoid cramping the text within the border. Examples of section borders are illustrated in Figure 8.6.

If both control borders and section borders are included on the same screen, make the section border slightly thicker, as illustrated in Figure 8.7.

Be conservative in the use of borders as too many can lead to screen clutter. Do not place individual field borders around the individual controls previously listed and illustrated in Figure 8.8. The nature of their design provides them with a border. Also, because of the potential for clutter, do not place a border around groups of pushbuttons. In some circumstances, a control may be conditionally active. Only when a particular response is made is this additional information needed. For example, a question such as "Do you have any children?" might necessitate knowing their names. If this question is answered affirmatively, a field requesting their names can be displayed at that point on the screen. A "No" response and tab will cause the cursor to move to the next field, and the children names field will not appear.

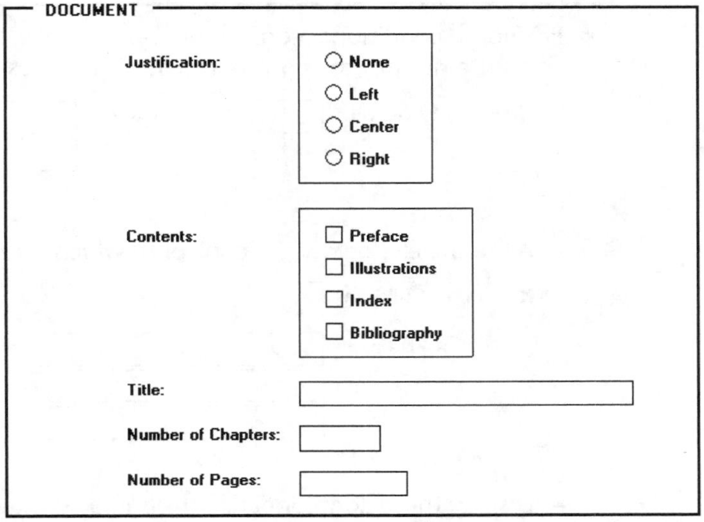

Figure 8.7 Differentiable control and section borders.

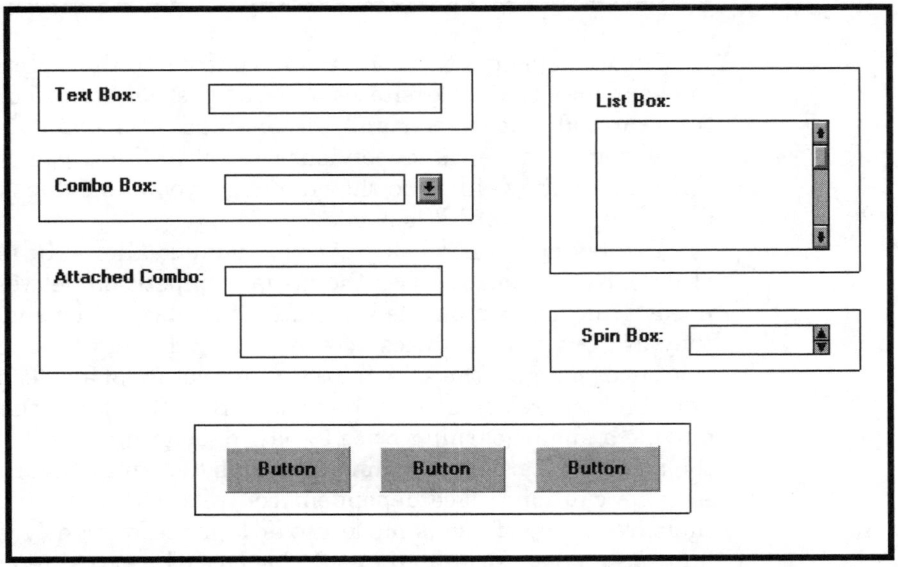

Figure 8.8 Kinds of borders to avoid using.

Dependent Controls

- Position a conditional control, or controls:
  - To the right of the control to which it relates

Number of Children: [   ] > **Names:** [   ]
[   ]
[   ]

  - Alternatively, below the control to which it relates.

Number of Children: [   ]

> **Names:** [   ]
[   ]
[   ]

- Either:
  - Display these conditional controls in a subdued or grayed manner.
    - When it is relevant, return it to a normal intensity.
  - Do not display these conditional controls until the information to which it relates is set.
- Inscribe a filled-in arrow between the selected control and its dependent controls to visually relate them to each other.

Locate dependent or conditional controls to the right of or below the field or choice that necessitates it. Exact positioning will depend upon eye flow through the screen and screen space constraints. The displayed arrow serves to tie the dependent control to the triggering control. The control field may either be shown in a grayed or subdued manner, or not displayed at all until it is needed.

Displaying a control as grayed or subdued allows the user to be aware of its existence but reduces the visual competition between it and other needed information on the screen. Not displaying dependent fields until they are triggered reduces screen clutter. Hiding their existence, however, does not give the screen user a full picture of all the possible needed data and the relationships that may exist. By hiding them, then, there may be a slight learning price to pay, depending upon the complexity of the needed data. The recommendation is to display them grayed.

One caution: Place dependent controls within a window only when their frequency of use is moderate or high. Infrequently used dependent information is best located in a dialog box. The extra step needed to occasionally obtain the dialog box is more then compensated by the additional screen space available, or reduced screen clutter.

Aligning Screen Elements

- Minimize alignment points on a window.
  - Vertically.
  - Horizontally.

Fewer screen alignment points reduce a screen's complexity and make it more visually appealing. Aligning elements will also make eye and pointer movement through the screen much more obvious and reduce the distance both must travel. Screen organization will also be more consistent and predictable. Alignment is achieved by creating vertical columns of screen fields and controls and also horizontally aligning the tops of screen elements.

Fields or controls vertically columnized may be oriented in two directions, vertically or horizontally. Vertical orientation, a top-to-bottom flow through controls and control components, is the recommended structure.

Vertical Orientation and Vertical Alignment

Radio Buttons/Check Boxes

- Left-align both choice descriptions, selection indicators, and borders.
- Captions:
  - Inscribed within borders must be left-aligned.

```
┌ Contents ──────────┐
│  ☐ Preface         │
│  ☒ Illustrations   │
│  ☒ Index           │
│  ☐ Bibliography    │
└────────────────────┘
```

```
┌ Justification ──────┐
│  ○ None             │
│  ◉ Left             │
│  ○ Center           │
│  ○ Right            │
└─────────────────────┘
```

– Located to the left may be left- or right-aligned.

Text Boxes

- Left-align the boxes. If the screen will be used for inquiry or display purposes, numeric fields should be right-aligned.
- Captions may be left- or right-aligned.

Title:

Number of Chapters:

Number of Pages:

Title:

Number of Chapters:

Number of Pages:

List Boxes

- Left-align fixed list boxes.
- Captions:
  – Located above the boxes must be left-aligned.

Location:

Bristol
Buckhead
Canton
Edison Park

Model:

Chevrolet
Edsel
Ford
GMC
Honda

– Located to the left may be left- or right-aligned.

Drop-down/Pop-up Boxes, Spin Boxes, Combination Boxes

- Left-align control boxes.
- Field captions may be left- or right-aligned.

Spin Box:

Attached Combination Box:

Drop-down/pop-up Box:

Mixed Controls

- Left-align vertically arrayed:
  - Text boxes.
  - Radio button buttons.
  - Check box boxes.
  - Drop-down/pop-up list boxes.
  - Spin boxes.
  - Combination control boxes.
  - List boxes.
- Captions may be left- or right-aligned.

Text Box:

Radio Buttons:

○ Option1
○ Option2
◉ Option3

List Box:

Attached Combination Box:

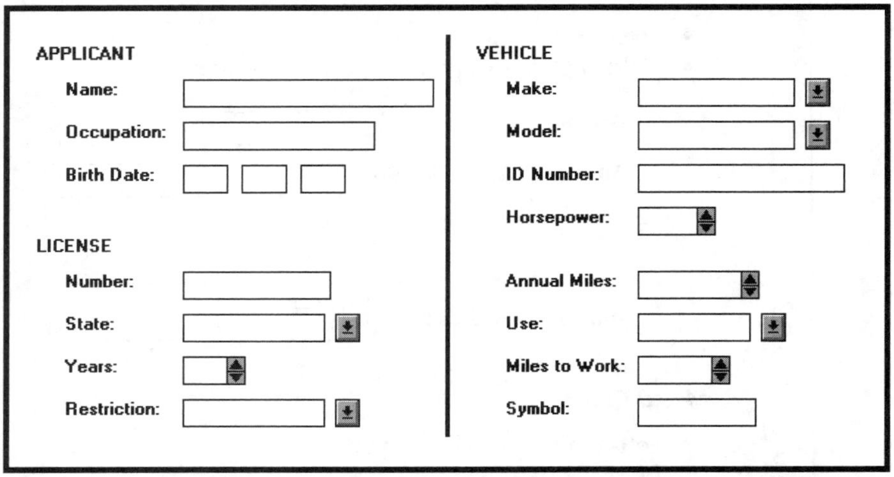

APPLICANT

Name:

Occupation:

Birth Date:

LICENSE

Number:

State:

Years:

Restriction:

VEHICLE

Make:

Model:

ID Number:

Horsepower:

Annual Miles:

Use:

Miles to Work:

Symbol:

Figure 8.9   Multicolumn controls with a separation border.

Elements and information should be organized vertically (top to bottom) as well. Two, and sometimes three, columns of controls and fields may occasionally be created. When multiple columns are presented and no section borders are used, column separation and downward flow may be emphasized through line borders, as illustrated in Figure 8.9.

In some cases, window space constraints may dictate a horizontal orientation of controls, most noticeably radio buttons and check boxes. Again the pattern created must be consistent, predictable, and distinct.

Horizontal Orientation and Vertical Alignment

Radio Buttons/Check Boxes Selection Controls

- Align leftmost radio buttons and/or check boxes.
- Field captions may be left- or right-aligned.

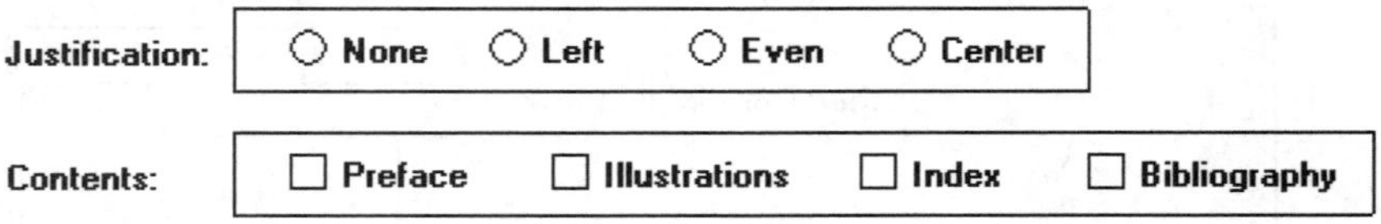

Justification: ○ None   ○ Left   ○ Even   ○ Center

Contents: ☐ Preface   ☐ Illustrations   ☐ Index   ☐ Bibliography

Text Boxes

- Left-align text boxes into columns.

- Captions may be left- or right-aligned.

  - Numeric data should be right-aligned.

Mixed Text Boxes and Selection Controls

- Align leftmost radio buttons and/or check boxes.
- Align leftmost text box under the leftmost choice description button or box.
- Captions may be left- or right-aligned.

For horizontally oriented controls, indistinctiveness can be caused if the item descriptions are positioned as close to a following button or box as they are to the button or box they relate to, as illustrated in Figure 8.10. While the objective is to create as few vertical alignment points as possible, this is usually not practical. For check boxes and radio buttons, most often the result will be inconsistently spaced item descriptions, as illustrated in Figure 8.11. Vertical alignment of items in several adjacent controls can also create a false vertical orientation perception, as also illustrated in Figure 8.11. Final positioning will be a compromise between alignment and providing clear item distinctiveness as illustrated in Figure 8.12. With vertical orientation of radio buttons and check boxes, all these problems are avoided. With horizontal orientation, borders aid discrimination and separation, as illustrated in Figure 8.13. Although the examples in the previous guidelines illustrate text boxes structured left to

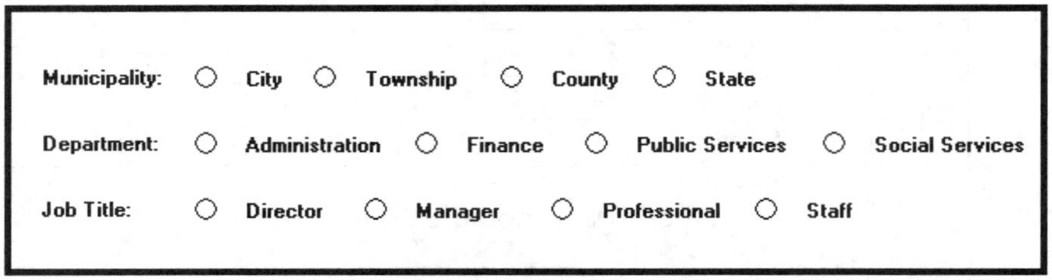

Figure 8.10   Horizontally arrayed radio buttons with poor item differentiation.

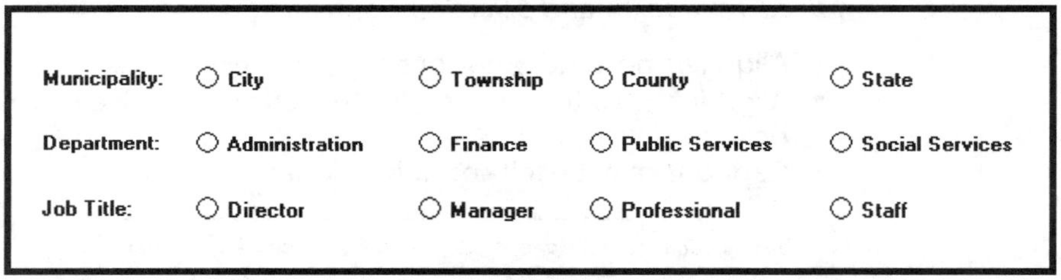

Figure 8.11   Horizontally arrayed control items with inconsistent spacing and a false vertical orientation.

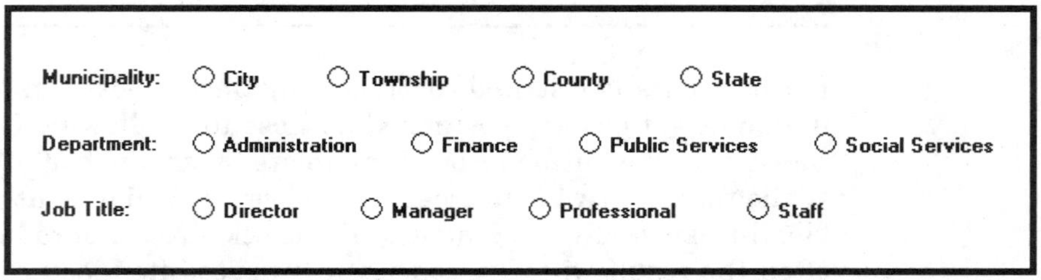

Figure 8.12   Horizontally arrayed control items comprising alignment and distinctiveness.

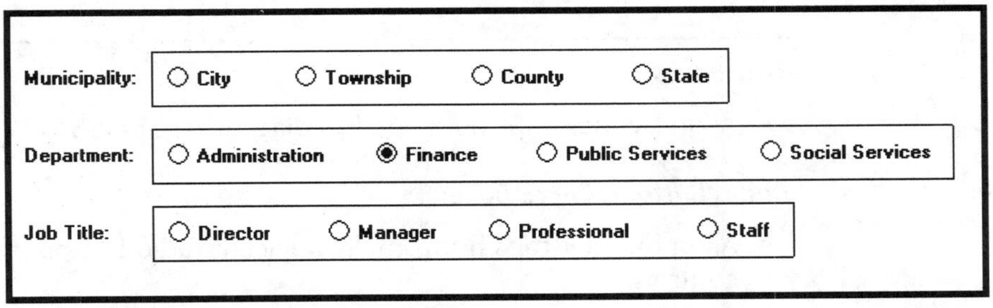

Figure 8.13   Horizontally arrayed control items with borders to improve readability.

right, every attempt should be made to maintain a top-to-bottom orientation of single entry and selection fields. The fields in the example will be more effectively structured as illustrated in Figure 8.14.

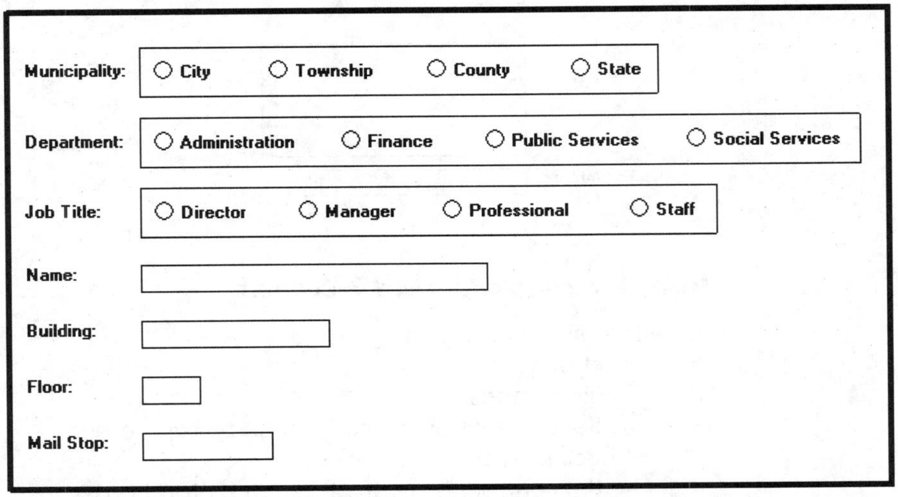

Figure 8.14   Vertical orientation of text boxes.

Horizontal Alignment

Text Boxes

- Align by their tops horizontally adjacent text boxes.

Radio Buttons/Check Boxes

- Align by their tops horizontally adjacent radio button and/or check box controls.

Fixed List Boxes

- Align by their tops horizontally adjacent fixed list boxes.

Drop-down/Pop-up List Box, Spin Box, Combination Boxes

- Align by their tops horizontally adjacent entry/selection fields.

Mixed Text Boxes and Selection Controls

- Align by their tops:
  - Text boxes.
  - Radio buttons.
    - If a control border exists, align by top border.
  - Check boxes.
    - If a control border exists, align by top border.
  - Drop-down/pop-up list boxes.
  - Spin boxes.
  - Combination boxes.
  - List boxes.

Arrangement of controls horizontally always consists of aligning by their tops. Since controls may be of different heights, screen efficiency occasionally dictates that a control must be positioned in an area where it does not align horizontally with another control. When this occurs, attempt to align it horizontally with the bottom of an adjacent control, as illustrated by the list box and adjacent combo box in the above example. Do not cramp a control, however, to achieve bottom alignment.

Section Alignment

- Align by their left side vertically arrayed groupings containing section borders.
- Align by their top horizontally arrayed groupings containing section borders.

Groupings with borders should also be aligned vertically by their left border and horizontally by their top border. Controls within a grouping will, of course, be aligned following the alignment principles previously discussed.

Balancing Elements

General

- Create balance by:
  - Equally distributing controls, spatially, within a window.
  - Aligning borders whenever possible.

Individual Control Borders

- If more than one control with borders is incorporated within a column on a screen:

- Align the controls following the guidelines for multiple-control alignment.
- Align the left and right borders of all groups.
- Establish the left and right border positions by the spacing required for the widest element within the groups.

```
┌ Contents ──────────────────┐
│  ☐ Preface                 │
│  ☐ Illustrations           │
│  ☐ Index                   │
│  ☒ Bibliography            │
└────────────────────────────┘

┌ Justification ─────────────┐
│  ○ None                    │
│  ○ Left                    │
│  ○ Center                  │
│  ⦿ Right                   │
└────────────────────────────┘
```

- With multigroupings and multicolumns, create a balanced screen by:
  - Maintaining equal column widths as much as practical.
  - Maintaining equal column heights as much as practical.

```
┌ Frame1 ────────────┐     ┌ Frame3 ────────────┐
│                    │     │                    │
│                    │     └────────────────────┘
│                    │     ┌ Frame4 ────────────┐
└────────────────────┘     │                    │
┌ Frame2 ────────────┐     └────────────────────┘
│                    │     ┌ Frame5 ────────────┐
│                    │     │                    │
│                    │     └────────────────────┘
└────────────────────┘
```

Section Borders

- If more than one section with borders is incorporated within a column on a screen:
  - Align the left and right borders of all groups.
  - Establish the left and right border positions by the spacing required by the widest element within the groups.

- With multigroupings and multicolumns, create a balanced screen by:
  - Maintaining equal column widths as much as practical.
  - Maintaining equal column heights as much as practical.

Screen balance should be attained as much as possible. Do not sacrifice screen functionality to achieve balance, however. Never rearrange controls to simply make the screen "look nice." A meaningful order of elements is most important. The "look" will be the best that can be achieved within the limits imposed by functionality.

One additional point about alignment. While these guidelines suggest aligning section, radio button, and check box borders on the right side as well as the left, a glance back at Figure 8.7 will reveal an instance where this was not done. The Justification and Contents borders were not right-aligned because the text boxes within that grouping created a ragged right edge. Aligning just these two controls would have served no purpose. So, all alignment and balancing must occur within the context of the *whole* screen.

Control Navigation

Tab / Arrow Keys

- Use the tab key to move between operable window controls, in the logical order of the controls.
  - Do not tab to field captions/labels.
- Radio Buttons:
  - Use arrow keys to move through radio buttons within a single control.
- Check Boxes:
  - Use the Tab key to move between, when they are independent controls.
  - Within a border or group box, use arrow keys to move between the check boxes since they appear as a logical group.
- List Boxes:
  - Use arrow keys to navigate within list box choices.

Command Buttons

- For exiting or expanding/feature dialog command buttons:
  - Tab to them at the end of the screen control tabbing sequence.
- For a command button with a contingent relationship to a control in the window body:
  - Tab to it at the logical point in the tabbing sequence within the window.

Keyboard Equivalents

- Use keyboard equivalents (mnemonics) for direct access to each control, whenever possible.
  - Mnemonic designations must be unique within a window.

Use the tab key to move between operable window controls, in the logical order that the controls are organized. Do not tab to control captions but the control itself. For a grouping of radio buttons, use the arrow keys to move through an array of buttons. For check boxes, use the tab key to move between them when they are arrayed as independent controls. When check boxes are located within a border or group box, use the arrow keys to move between the boxes since they appear as a logical group. Always use arrow keys to navigate within a listing of choices.

Tab to exiting or expanding/feature dialog buttons at the end of the screen control tabbing sequence. If a button has a contingent relationship to a control in the window body, tab to it at the logical point in the tabbing sequence within the window.

Use keyboard equivalents (mnemonics) for direct access to each window control, whenever possible. Mnemonic designations must be unique within a window. The command buttons OK and Cancel are not typically assigned mnemonics, the Enter and Esc keys being used instead.

SCREEN EXAMPLES

Following are more examples of good and poor design. Included are redesigns of the screens critiqued in Step 3.

Example 1

Here is a poorly designed screen and its redesigned version.

Screen 1.1

A very poor screen: Captions are not discernible from choice descriptions and the initial choice descriptions are not left-aligned. The radio buttons and check boxes are not strongly associated with, and also *follow*, their respective descriptions, certainly causing selection confusions. The horizontal orientation of choices is not efficient for human scanning. No perception of groupings exists. The ordering schemes of Family, Style, and Color is questionable. Alphabetic ordering would seem to be more appropriate.

Screen 1.2

A much better screen. The title is capitalized to set it off from the remainder of the screen. The radio buttons and check boxes are arrayed vertically to facilitate scanning and comparison of alternatives. All controls are enclosed in borders to focus the viewer's attention to them. While the overall organization does not assist the viewer in establishing a scanning

Screen 1.1

Screen 1.2

direction (horizontal or vertical), the kind of information presented does not make this critical. The screen can be effectively used left-to-right or top-to-bottom. Family, Style, and Color are alphabetized. Using the complexity measure discussed in Step 3, this redesigned screen is 42 percent less complex than the original.

Example 2

This is a representation of an actual screen from Microsoft Windows 3.1. Two alternative designs are presented.

Screen 2.1

Chapter Example 8.3 shows a screen with several faults. On a positive note, the captions on the left side are nicely aligned, as are the top four text boxes. The box alignment, however, breaks down in the middle of the screen. Also, what appear to be captions (because they possess an ending colon) are really headings, communicating a false message to the viewer (Memory Requirements, EMS Memory, and XMS Memory). The word "memory" repeated four times in succession seems redundant, indicating the potential for a heading. One radio button field (Video Memory) is arrayed horizontally; the others, vertically (Display Usage and Execution). The control "Close Window on Exit" seems lost.

Screen 2.1

Screen 2.2

This is a much improved alternative. Groupings of elements are provided. Section borders, with titles, are included in the upper part of the screen to strengthen the perception of groupings. Control borders in the lower part of the screen serve the same purpose. Proper alignment of data fields is achieved in the top two sections of the screen. The redundant word "memory" is incorporated as a section heading. Section headings are displayed capitalized to distinguish them from control captions. Subsection headings are created in the Memory section where the heading-caption confusion previously existed. Subsection headings are set off by capitalization and arrows.

The radio buttons/check boxes at the bottom of the screen are arrayed horizontally to provide screen balance. The "Close Window on Exit" control field is given an (admittedly redundant) caption to allow a control border consistent with its neighbors and to create screen balance. The Video (Memory) control remains, as a trade-off, arrayed horizontally. It would have been desirable to organize its choices vertically, but the best overall fit within the screen is achieved by horizontal orientation. This redesigned version of the screen is actually four percent *more* complex than the original. The addition of headings and subheadings added to its com-

Screen 2.2

plexity measure. In spite of this, it is a better screen. Additional information added to a screen to aid understanding can sometimes increase its complexity. So, use the complexity measure as a guide, not as an absolute and final measure of a screen's effectiveness.

Screen 2.3

Here is another redesigned version of this screen. The Memory section has been restructured to maintain a top-to-bottom flow. The trade-off is that it now requires two columns to present the information. This version is eight percent more complex than the original, again because of the added information. Which version do you prefer, 2.2 or 2.3?

Screen 2.3

Screen 3.1

Example 3

These are redesigned versions of the banking screen presented in Step 3.

Screen 3.1

The original screen.

Screen 3.2

The Name field is given a caption and a single alignment point is established for both captions and data. Captions and data are now much more readable. Name format instructions (1st, 2nd, etc.) are established as prompts. This prompt designation is signaled by placing them in italics to subdue them visually. The prompt for Date of Birth is placed to the right of its text box, out of the way but still easily viewable. This also permits the alignment point for the text boxes to be moved closer to the captions. Date is also segmented into its component pieces. The command buttons are positioned at the bottom. No groupings are established, however. This screen is nine percent less complex than the original.

Screen 3.3

This screen is identical to the above version except Sex and Marital Status are arrayed vertically. This screen is 17 percent less complex than the original.

Screen 3.2

Screen 3.3

Screen 3.4

Screen 3.4

The elements are now grouped with group boxes and section headings. Name is segmented into its three components. Address details are moved closer to the customer's name. Sex and Marital Status must be arrayed horizontally because of space constraints caused by the groupings. This screen is four percent less complex than the original. Which of these do you prefer, 3.2, 3.3, or 3.4?

Example 4

These are redesigned versions of the drawing program screens presented in Step 3.

Screen 4.1

The original PRINT MERGE screen.

Screen 4.1

Screen 4.2

The redesigned PRINT MERGE screen. Elements are aligned and the File text box is positioned by its related list box. The Up command is placed in the proper contingent relationship to the Directories list box. The command buttons are moved to the bottom of the screen and Merge is changed to OK for consistency with the other screens. The title is capitalized for consistency with the other screens. This redesigned screen is 29 percent less complex than the original.

PRINT MERGE

Path: D:\WINDOWS\PM4*.txt

File: tabledit.txt

mgximp.txt
readme1.txt
readme2.txt
tabledit.txt
typemgr.txt

Directories:

Up - >

[..]
[tutorial]
[usenglsh]
[-a-]
[-b-]
[-c-]
[-d-]

OK   Cancel

Screen 4.2

Screen 4.3

The original PAGE SETUP screen.

Screen 4.4

The redesigned PAGE SETUP screen. The radio buttons are aligned for vertical scanning and placed within borders. The "inches" control is changed to a standard drop-down/pop-up list box. This redesigned screen is 19 percent less complex than the original.

Screen 4.3

Screen 4.4

Screen 4.5

Screen 4.5

The original EXPORT screen.

Screen 4.6

The redesigned EXPORT screen. The radio buttons and check boxes are aligned for vertical scanning and placed within borders. The check boxes are given a caption, as is the list box. For balance purposes, the controls are arrayed in two columns. This redesigned screen is five percent less complex than the original.

Screen 4.6

Example 5

Here are redesigned versions of the word processing screens presented in Step 3.

Screen 5.1

The original FOOTNOTE OPTIONS screen.

Screen 5.2

The redesigned FOOTNOTE OPTIONS screen. Elements are aligned, including the single check boxes. Headings are capitalized and left-justified within the borders. "Position" and "Separator" are combined into one grouping called "LOCATION." This redesigned screen is 13 percent less complex than the original.

Screen 5.1

Screen 5.2

Screen 5.3

The original LOCATION OF FILES screen.

Screen 5.4

The redesigned LOCATION OF FILES screen. The section headings are capitalized and left-justified in the borders. Visual competition with the text box information is now minimized. A grouping called FILES is created at the screen's top for consistency and balance. The single check box is aligned under the text boxes. This redesigned screen is two percent more complex than the original, again due to the added heading.

Screen 5.3

Screen 5.4

Example 6

Here is a redesigned version of the drawing program read-only/display screen presented in Step 3.

Screen 6.1

The original screen.

Screen 6.2

The redesigned screen. Headings are capitalized to set them off from the control captions. The headline style of presentation is consistently applied to all captions. The data fields are aligned and the Units in the IMAGE sections are moved to the top. This redesigned screen is 12 percent less complex than the original.

walogo.tif Header Info.

TIFF File format
Version # 42
Byte order I I
NewSubFile Type 1

Image size
Horizontal 1888 6.3
Vertical 1656 5.5
Units Pixel Inch

Spatial Configuration
Samples per pixel 1
Bits per sample 1
Planar config. 1

Image resolution
Horizontal res. 300
Vertical res. 300
Units dpi

Photometric data
Photo Interpretation 1
Resolution Unit Inch
Compression Type PkBit

Palette: Red, Green, Blue

OK   Display image

Screen 6.1

walogo.tif Header Info.

TIFF FILE FORMAT
Version #: 42
Byte Order: I I
New Subfile Type: 1

IMAGE SIZE
Units: Pixel Inch
Horizontal: 1888 6.3
Vertical: 1656 5.5

SPATIAL CONFIGURATION
Samples Per Pixel: 1
Bits Per Sample: 1
Planar Configuration: 1

IMAGE RESOLUTION
Units: dpi
Horizontal: 300
Vertical: 300

PHOTOMETRIC DATA
Photo Interpretation: 1
Resolution Unit: Inch
Compression Type: PkBit

Palette: Red, Green, Blue

OK   Cancel

Screen 6.2

Example 7

Here are redesigned versions of the other read-only/display screen presented in Step 3.

Screen 7.1

The original STORY INFO screen.

Screen 7.2

The redesigned STORY INFO screen. Elements are aligned and incorporated within borders. Note that headings are not included within the borders. The command remains positioned in the upper-right corner, as is standard for this graphical system. This redesigned screen is eight percent less complex than the original.

Screen 7.3

Another version of the redesigned STORY INFO screen. Then only difference is that the command button is positioned at the bottom rather than at the side, creating a better balanced screen. On less complex screens this is another advantage of bottom positioning of command buttons.

Story info			OK
File link:			
Textblocks:	1	First page:	4
Char count:	1400	Last page:	4
Overset chars:	0		
Total area:	23.413 sq inches		
Total depth:	7.400 inches		

Screen 7.1

Screen 7.2

Screen 7.3

Choose the Proper Colors

Color adds a new dimension to screen usability. Color draws attention because it attracts a person's eye. If used properly, it can emphasize the logical organization of information, facilitate the discrimination of screen components, accentuate differences among elements, and make displays more interesting. If used improperly, color can be distracting and possibly visually fatiguing, impairing the system's usability.

- Understand color's characteristics.
    - What color is.
    - The uses of color.
    - Possible problems and cautions with color.
    - The results of color research.
    - Color and human vision.
- Understand how to use color.
- Choose the proper colors for textual graphic screens.
- Choose the proper colors for statistical graphics screens.

Effective use of color in screen design has taken great steps forward in the last two decades. Early displays had only a few colors to present, many of the colors themselves were not very legible, and they were often overused in combinations that reminded one more of a Christmas tree than of an effective source of communication. Today, as technology has improved, as well as our understanding of what comprises good design, colors are being used more effectively. Pastels have replaced bright reds and dark blues, and the number of colors presented at one time on a screen has been reduced, dramatically in some cases. This is not to say, however, that all the problems have been solved. A tour around the office will usually uncover some questionable, or awful, uses of color. Woods, Johannesen, & Potter (1992) feel the two most common problems are screen backgrounds being more attention-grabbing than the screen data (which is the most important element of a screen) and overuse of color as a graphic language or code (the color itself meaning something to the screen viewer). This kind of use forces the user to interpret a color's meaning *before* the message it is communicating can be reacted to.

The discussion to follow begins by defining color. Next is a review of how color may be used in screen design and some critical cautions in its use. Then, the human visual system and the implications for color are discussed. Finally, guidelines are presented for choosing and using colors.

COLOR—WHAT IS IT?

Wavelengths of light themselves are not colored. What is perceived as actual color results from the stimulation by a received light wave of the proper receptor in the eye. The name that a color is given is a learned phenomenon, based on previous experiences and associations of specific visual sensations with color names. Therefore, a color can only be described in terms of a person's report of his or her perceptions. The visual spectrum of wavelengths to which the eye is sensitive ranges from about 400 to 700 millimicrons. Objects in the visual environment often emit or reflect light waves in a limited area of this visual spectrum, absorbing light waves in other areas of the spectrum. The dominant wavelength being "seen" is the one that we come to associate with a specific color name. The visible color spectrum and the names commonly associated with the various light wavelengths are shown in Table 9.1.

Table 9.1   The Visible Spectrum

Color	Approximate Wavelengths in Millimicrons
Red	700
Orange	600
Yellow	570
Yellow-green	535
Green	500
Blue-green	493
Blue	470
Violet	400

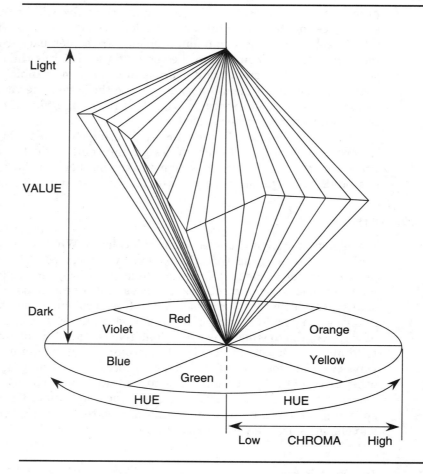

Figure 9.1 The relationship of hue, chroma, and value.

To describe a color, it is useful to refer to the three properties it possesses: hue, chroma or saturation, and value or intensity, as illustrated in Figure 9.1. *Hue* is the spectral wavelength composition of a color. It is to this we attach a meaning such as green or red. *Chroma or saturation* is the purity of a color in a scale from gray to the most vivid version of the color. The more saturated a hue is, the more visible it is at a distance. The less saturated, the less visible it is. *Value or intensity* is the relative lightness or darkness of a color in a range from black to white. Lightness differences are usually described by two-word descriptors such as light red or dark blue. Some hues are inherently lighter or darker than others, for example, yellow is very light and violet is very dark.

Primary colors of illuminated light are red, green, and blue, whose wavelengths additively combine in pairs to produce magenta, cyan, and yellow, and all the other visible colors in the spectrum. The three primary colors additively combine to produce white. The long-wavelength colors (red) are commonly referred to as warm, and short-wavelength colors (blue) as cool.

Color, then, is a combination of hue, chroma, and value. In any one instance what we call "blue" may actually be one of several hundred thousand "blues." This problem has confounded color research over the years. A "blue" may be unacceptable in one situation because it is highly saturated and dark, but perfectly acceptable in another, being less saturated and light. The exact measures are rarely reported in the literature.

RGB

Many color monitors use the three primary colors, in various combinations, to create the many colors we see on screens. By adjusting the amounts of red, green, and blue light presented in a pixel, millions of colors can be generated. Hence, color palette editors exist with labels R, G, and B (or the words spelled out).

HSV

Some palette editors use a convention based on the Munsell method of color notation called HSV, for hue, saturation, and value (or HSL for hue, saturation, and lightness). Again, combinations produce different colors.

Dithering

The eye is never steady, tremoring slightly as we see. If pixels of different colors are placed next to each other, this tremor combines the two colors into a third color. This is referred to as *dithering*, and sometimes *texture mapping*. Taking advantage of this phenomena, an optical illusion, a third color can be created on a screen. Dithering is often used to create a gray scale when only black and white pixels are available to work with. A difference of opinion exists on whether dithering should, or should not be, used on a screen. *The Macintosh Human Interface Guidelines* (Apple Computer, 1992b) discourage its use, stating it creates unnecessary visual clutter.

COLOR USES

- Use color to assist in formatting a screen:
  - Relate or tie elements into groupings.
  - Break apart separate groupings of information.

- Associate information that is widely separated on the screen.
- Highlight or call attention to important information by setting it off from the other information.
- Use color as a visual code to identify:
  - Screen components.
  - The logical structure of ideas, processes, or sequences.
  - Sources of information.
  - Status of information.
- Other color uses:
  - Realistically portray natural objects.
  - Increase screen appeal.

Color may be used as a formatting aid in structuring a screen, or it may be used as a visual code to categorize and identify information or data.

Color as a Formatting Aid

As a formatting aid, color can provide better structure and meaning to a screen. It is especially useful when large amounts of data must be included on a screen and spacing to differentiate components is problematic.

For example, differentiation of logical groupings of elements can be enhanced by displaying them in different colors. Spatially separated but related fields can also be tied together through a color scheme.

Color can also replace highlighting as a means of calling attention to information. Color is much more flexible than other techniques because of the number of colors that are available. Color as an attention-getting mechanism must, however, be chosen in light of the psychological and physiological considerations, to be described shortly.

Color as a Visual Code

A color code indicates what category the information being displayed falls into. It has meaning to the screen's user. A properly selected color-coding scheme permits a person to identify a relevant category quickly without having to read its contents first. This permits focusing on this category while the remaining information is excluded from attention.

One common color-coding scheme to differentiate screen components is to display screen captions and data in different colors. Another is to identify information from different sources—information added to a process from different locations, or text added to a message from different departments, may be colored differently. Color coding to convey status might involve displaying, in a different color, information that passed or failed system edits. Color can also be used as a prompt, guiding a person through a complex transaction.

To be effective, color as a visual code must be relevant and known. Relevance is achieved when the color enables a person to attend only to the information that is needed, and easily exclude that which is not needed. A relevant code, however, will be useless unless its meaning is also understood by the person who must use it. Not knowing a color's meaning first requires it's meaning to be interpreted. This can place burdens on a person's memory. It can also impede performance, requiring one to consult a manual or a legend in order to understand it.

Other Color Uses

Color can also be used to more realistically portray objects in the world around us that must be displayed on a screen. It is also thought that the addition of color increases a screen's appeal and makes display work more pleasant.

POSSIBLE PROBLEMS WITH COLOR

The simple addition of color to a screen will not guarantee improved performance. What may have been a poorly designed product will simply become a colorful poorly designed product. When used improperly, color may even impair performance by distracting the viewer and interfering with the handling of information. Possible problems may be caused by the perceptual system itself and/or the physiological characteristics of the human eye.

High Attention-Getting Capacity

Color has an extremely high attention-getting capacity, which causes the screen viewer to associate or tie together screen elements of the same color, whether or not such an association should be made. A person might search for relationships and differences that do not exist, or that are not valid. The result is often bewilderment, confusion, and slower reading. The effect achieved is often described as the "Christmas tree" mentioned earlier.

Interference with Use of Other Screens

Indiscriminate or poor use of color on some screens will diminish the effectiveness of color on other screens. The rationale for color will be difficult to understand and its attention-getting capacity severely restricted.

Varying Sensitivity of the Eye to Different Colors

All colors, in the eye of the viewer, are not equal. The eye is more sensitive to those in the middle of the visual spectrum (yellow and green), which appear brighter than the extremes (blue and red). Thus, text comprised of colors at the extremes is thought to be more difficult to read. Research evidence on this topic is mixed. Watanabe, Mori, Nagata, & Hiwatashi (1968), Pinkus (1982), Post (1985), and Matthews & Mertins (1987, 1988) found that acuity, contrast sensitivity, target recognition, legibility, and performance were not influenced by color. On the other hand, Haines, Dawson, Galvan, & Reid (1975), Pokorny, Graham, & Lanson (1968), and Radl (1980, 1984) found advantages for spectral center colors in reaction times, resolution, and error rates.

Also, it is thought that some combinations of screen colors can strain the eye's accommodation mechanism. The wavelengths of light producing blue are normally focused in front of the eye's retina, the red wavelengths behind it. Simultaneous or sequential viewing of red and blue cause the eye to continually refocus to bring the image directly onto the retina, thereby increasing the potential for eye fatigue. Those expressing this view include Ostberg (1982), Sivak & Woo (1983), Murch (1983), and the Human Factors Society (1988). Again the research evidence is mixed. Donohoo & Snyder (1985) found refocusing problems with a relatively saturated blue phosphor. No refocusing problems were reported in studies addressing short-term display viewing by Matthews & Mertins (1987), Walraven (1984), and Matthews, Lovasik, & Mertins (1989). Matthews does say that his test materials included relatively simple screens, and "Failure to find a large influence of display color on visual performance might be attributed to the moderate density of screen information." Thus the accommodation mechanism was not severely tested, and generalization to a more dense screen is not warranted.

What does one conclude after looking at the research addressing the above problems? The reasonable assumption is that they have neither been proved nor disproved. We have not properly defined all the terminal-based tasks being performed. The studies have used only a few of the many devices in existence, and a firm definition of "visual fatigue" remains elusive. Finally, none of the studies have addressed extended terminal viewing. The prudent course is to be cautious and avoid using colors and combinations which color theory claims could create problems. As shall be seen, the color palette to be used in screen design will be small, so avoiding potential problem areas will not be terribly restrictive.

The perceived appearance of a color is also affected by a variety of other factors, including the size of the area of color, the ambient illumination level, and other colors in the viewing area. Failure to consider the eye and how it handles color, then, can also lead to mistakes in color identification, misinterpretations, slower reading, and, perhaps, visual fatigue.

Color Viewing Deficiencies

Another disadvantage of color is that about eight percent of males and 0.4 percent of females have some form of color-perception deficiency—color blindness it is commonly called. In actuality, very few people are truly color-blind, most of those with problems simply have difficulties discriminating certain colors. Common color deficiencies and their results, and the percentage of people who experience these problems, are summarized in Table 9.2. Total color blindness affects no more than 0.005 percent of both sexes. For an individual with color-perception deficiency, all the normal colors may not be discernible, but often differences in lightness or intensity can be seen. A person experiencing any form of color blindness must not be prohibited from effectively using a screen.

Cross-Disciplinary and Cross-Cultural Differences

Colors can have different meanings in different situations to different people. A color used in an unexpected way can cause confusion. An error signaled in green would contradict the expected association of red with stop or danger. The same color may also have a different connotation, depending upon its viewer. Marcus (1986b) provides the following quite different meanings for the color blue:

- For financial managers—corporate qualities or reliability.
- For health care professionals—death.
- For nuclear reactor monitors—coolness or water.
- For American movie audiences—tenderness or pornography.

Differences in color connotations also exist between cultures. Red, for example, in the United States is associated with danger, in Egypt with death, and in India with life. Incorrect use in a different culture may

Table 9.2   Results of Color Defective Vision (From Barnett, 1993 and Fowler & Stanwick, 1995)

	Color seen with:		
Actual color	*Red-viewing deficiency (2.04%)*	*Green-viewing deficiency (6.39%)*	*Blue-viewing deficiency (0.003%)*
Red	Brown	–	–
Yellow	Greenish-Yellow	Orange	Deeper yellow
Purple	Dark Blue	Red	Deep Red
Green	–	Light Brown	–
Brown	–	Reddish-Brown	–
Blue	–	–	Green

cause severe problems. A listing of some common cultural associations with color is found in Table 11.1 in Step 11.

The proper use of color, then, requires an analysis of the expectations and experiences of the screen viewer. The use of color in design must always keep these possible problems clearly in focus. The designer must work to minimize their disruptive and destructive effects. Always keep in mind the following: *Poor use of color is worse than not using it at all.*

COLOR —WHAT THE RESEARCH SHOWS

The effectiveness of color in improving the usability of a display has yielded mixed research results. On a positive note, color has been shown to improve performance (Kopala, 1981; Nagy & Sanchez, 1992; Sidorsky, 1982), to improve visual search time (Christ, 1975; Carter, 1982), to be useful for organizing information (Engel, 1980), to aid memory (Marcus, 1986b), and to demarcate a portion of a screen (as opposed to lines or type font, Wopking, Pastoor, & Beldie 1985). Color has also created positive user reactions (Tullis, 1981), was preferred to monochromatic screens for being less monotonous and reducing eye strain and fatigue (Christ, 1975), and is more enjoyable (Marcus, 1986b).

On the other hand, it has also been shown that color does not improve performance (Tullis, 1981), does not have much of an effect on reading text (Legge and Rubin, 1986), may impair performance (Christ & Teichner, 1973; Christ, 1975), and is less important than display spacing (Haubner & Benz, 1983). It has also been demonstrated that poor character-background color combinations lead to poorer performance (McTyre & Frommer, 1985). Finally, no evidence was produced that color, as compared to black and white, can significantly improve aesthetics or legibility or reduce eye strain (Pastoor, 1990).

Research has found, moreover, that as the number of colors on a display increases, the time to respond to a single color increases, and the probability of color confusion increases (Luria, Neri, & Jacobsen 1986). Many studies have found that the maximum number of colors that a person can handle is in the range of four to ten, with emphasis on the lower numbers (for example, Brooks, 1965; Halsey & Chapanis, 1951; Luria et al., 1986).

The conclusion to be derived from these studies is that for simple displays, color may have no dramatic impact. Indeed, a monochromatic display may serve the purpose just as well. As display complexity increases, however, so does the value of color. A second conclusion is that people like using color and think it has a positive influence on their productivity, even though it may not.

To be effective, color must be properly used. Poor use of color will actually impair performance, not help it. When using color, keep in mind its value will be dependent upon the task being performed, the colors selected, how many are used, and the viewing environment.

COLOR AND HUMAN VISION

To understand how color should be used on a screen, it is helpful to know something of the physiology of the human eye. The reader requiring a detailed discussion of this subject is referred to Murch (1983, 1984).

The Lens

The lens of the eye, controlled by muscles, focuses wavelengths of light on the retina. The lens itself is not color corrected. The wavelengths of light creating different colors are focused at different distances behind the lens, the longer wavelengths (red) being focused further back than the shorter wavelengths (blue). The result is that colors of a different wavelength than the color actually being focused by the lens appear out of focus. To create a sharp image of the out-of-focus colors requires a refocusing of the eye. Excessive refocusing (such as between red and blue) can lead to eye fatigue.

The effect of this focusing for most people is that blues appear more distant and reds appear closer. It can give a three-dimensional appearance to what is being viewed. A critical problem is that the wavelength of light creating blues can never be brought into focus on the retina but is always focused in front of it. A sharp blue image is impossible to obtain. Very pure or saturated colors require more refocusing than less pure or unsaturated colors. Therefore, a color with a large white component will require less refocusing.

The lens does not transmit all light wavelengths equally. It absorbs more wavelengths in the blue region of the spectrum than those in the other regions. Additionally, as the lens ages, it tends to yellow, filtering out the shorter blue wavelengths. Thus, as people get older, their sensitivity to blue decreases. The lens also refocuses for light of different brightnesses. Sharp contrasts in differences in brightnesses in things being viewed can lead to visual fatigue as the eye continually adjusts.

The Retina

The retina is the light-sensitive surface of the eye. It comprises two kinds of receptors, rods and cones, that translate the incoming light into nervous impulses. Rods are sensitive to lower light levels and function primarily at night. Cones are stimulated by higher light levels and react to color. The sensitivity of cones to colors varies, different cones possessing maximum sensitivity to different light wavelengths. About two-thirds (64 percent) of the cones are maximally sensitive to longer light wavelengths, showing a peak response at about 575 millimicrons. These cones have traditionally been referred to as "red" sensitive cones. In actuality, however, the peak sensitivity is in the yellow portion of the visual spectrum (see Table 9.1). About one-third (32 percent) of the cones achieve maximum sensitivity at about 535 millimicrons and are commonly referred to as "green" sensitive cones. The remainder (2 percent) primarily react to short light wavelengths, achieving maximum sensitivity at about 445 millimicrons. These are known as "blue" sensitive cones. Any lightwave impinging on the retina evokes a response, to a greater or lesser degree, from most or all of these cones. A perceived "color" results from the proportion of stimulation of the various kinds.

Rods and cones vary in distribution across the retina. The center is tightly packed with cones and has no rods. Toward the periphery of the retina, rods increase and cones decrease. Thus, color sensitivity does not exist at the retina's outer edges, although yellows and blues can be detected further into the periphery than reds and greens. The very center of the retina is devoid of "blue" cones, creating a "blue-blindness" for small objects fixated upon.

The receptors in the eye also adjust, or adapt, their level of sensitivity to the overall light level and the color being viewed. Adaptation to increases in brightness improves color sensitivity. Color adaptation "softens" colors.

The brightness sensitivity of the eye to different colors also varies. It is governed by output from the "red" and "green" cones. The greater the output, the higher the brightness, which results in the eye being most sensitive to colors in the middle of the visual spectrum and less sensitive to colors at the extremes. A blue or red must be of a much greater intensity than a green or yellow even to be perceived.

The ability of the eye to detect a form is accomplished by focusing the viewed image on the body of receptors to establish edges. Distinct edges yield distinct images. Edges formed by color differences alone cannot be accurately focused and thus create fuzzy and nondistinct images. A clear, sharp image requires a difference in brightness between adjacent objects, as well as differences in color.

The components of the eye—the lens and retina—govern the choices, and combinations, of colors to be displayed on a screen. The proper colors will enhance performance; improper colors will have the opposite effect, as well as possibly increase the probability of visual fatigue.

CHOOSING COLORS

Colors chosen for display must consider these factors: the human visual system, the possible problems that its use may cause, the viewing environment in which the display is used, the task of the user, how the color will be used, and the hardware on which the color will be displayed. The primary objective in using color is communication, to aid the transfer of information from the screen to the user.

Choosing Categories of Information for Color

- Choosing categories of information for color requires a clear understanding of how the information will be used.
- Some examples:
  - If different parts of the screen are attended to separately, color code the different parts to focus selective attention on each in turn.
  - If decisions are made based on the status of certain types of information on the screen, color code the types of status the information may possess.
  - If screen searching is performed to locate information of a particular kind or quality, color code these kinds or qualities for contrast.
  - If the sequence of information use is constrained or ordered, use color to identify the sequence.
  - If the information displayed on a screen is packed or crowded, use color to provide visual groupings.

Color chosen to classify data on a screen must aid the transfer of information from the display to the user. This requires a clear understanding of how the information is selected and used. The examples above describe some common ways of classifying information for color coding purposes.

It is important to remember, however, that information on one screen may be used in more than one way. What is useful in one context may not be in another and may only cause interference. Therefore, when developing a color strategy, consider how spatial formatting, highlighting, and messages may also be useful.

Colors in Context

Colors are subject to contextual effects. The size of a colored image, the color of images adjacent to it, and the ambient illumination all exert an influence on what is actually perceived. At the normal viewing distance for a screen, maximal color sensitivity is not reached until the size of a colored area exceeds about a three-inch square. Smaller size images become desaturated (having a greater white component) and change slightly in color. Also, small differences in actual color may not be discernible. Blues and yellows are particularly susceptible to difficulties in detecting slight changes. Finally, small adjacent colored images may appear to the eye to merge or mix. Red and green, for example, might appear as yellow.

Adjacent images can influence the perceived color. A color on a dark background, for example, will look lighter and brighter than the same color on a light background. A color can be *induced* into a neutral foreground area (gray) by the presence of a colored background. A red background can change a gray into a green. Induced colors are the complement of the inducing color. Complementary afterimages can also be induced by looking at a saturated color for a period of time.

Colors change as light levels change. Higher levels of ambient light tend to desaturate colors. Saturated colors will also appear larger than desaturated colors.

Usage

- Design for monochrome first.
- Use colors conservatively.
  - Do not use color where other identification techniques such as location are available.

Design for monochrome first. A screen should be as capable of being effectively used as if it were in a monochrome environment. Spatial formatting, consistent locations, and display techniques such as highlighting, mixed- and upper-case characters should all be utilized to give it a structure independent of the color. This will permit the screen to be effectively used:

- By people with a color-viewing deficiency.
- On monochrome displays.
- In conditions where ambient lighting distorts the perceived color.
- If the color ever fails.

Use colors conservatively. Only enough colors to achieve the design objective should be used. More colors increase response times, increase the chance of errors due to color confusions, and increase the chance of the "Christmas tree" effect. If two colors serve the need, use two colors. If three colors are needed, by all means use three. A way to minimize the need for too many colors is not to use it in situations where other identification methods are available. A menu bar, for example, will always be located at the top of the screen. Its position and structure will identify it as a menu bar. To color code it would be redundant.

Discrimination and Harmony

- For best absolute discrimination, select no more than four or five colors widely spaced on the color spectrum.
  - Good colors: red, yellow, green, blue, brown.
- For best comparative discrimination, select no more than six or seven colors widely spaced on the color spectrum.
  - Other acceptable colors: orange, yellow-green, cyan, violet, or magenta.
- Choose harmonious colors.
  - One color plus two colors on either side of its complement.
  - Three colors in equidistant points around the color circle.
- For older viewers or extended viewing, use brighter colors.

The population of measurable colors is about 7.5 million. From this vast number, the eye cannot effectively distinguish many more than a handful. If color memorization and absolute discrimination is necessary (a color must be correctly identified while no other color is in the field of vision), select no more than four to five colors widely spaced along the color spectrum (Smith, 1988; Marcus, 1986b). Selecting widely spaced colors will maximize the probability of their being correctly identified. Good choices are red, yellow, green, blue, and brown (Marcus, 1986b).

Two good color opponent pairs are red/green and yellow/blue. All of these colors except blue are easy to resolve visually. Again, be cautious in using blue for data, text, or small symbols on screens because it may not always be legible. If the meaning for each of more than five colors is absolutely necessary, a legend should be provided illustrating the colors and describing their associated meanings.

If comparative discrimination will be performed (a color must be correctly identified while other colors are in the field of vision), select no more than six or seven colors widely spaced along the visual spectrum. In addition to those above, other colors could be chosen from orange, yellow-green, cyan, and violet or magenta. Again, be cautious of using blue for data, text, or small symbols.

If the intent is to portray natural objects realistically, the use of more colors might be necessary.

Choose harmonious colors. Harmonious colors are those that work well together or meet without sharp contrast. Harmony is most easily achieved with a monochromatic palette. For each background color, different lightnesses or values are established through mixing it with black and white. Marcus (1986a) suggests a minimum of three values should be obtained.

Harmonious combinations in a multicolor environment are more difficult to obtain. Marcus recommends avoiding complementary colors—those at opposite sides of the circle of hues in the Munsell color system, a standard commercial color system. He suggests using split complements, one color plus two colors on either side of its complement, or choosing three colors at equidistant points around the color circle.

For older viewers or extended viewing, use bright colors. As eye capacity diminishes with age, data, text, and symbols in the less bright colors may be harder to read. Distinguishing colors may also be more difficult. For any viewer, long viewing periods result in the eye adapting to the brightness level. Brighter colors will be needed if either of these conditions exist.

Emphasis

- To draw attention or to emphasize, use bright or highlighted colors. To de-emphasize, use less bright colors.
  - The perceived brightness of colors from most to least is white, yellow, green, blue, red.
- To emphasize separation, use contrasting colors.
  - Red and green, blue and yellow.
- To convey similarity, use similar colors.
  - Orange and yellow, blue and violet.

To draw attention or emphasize, use bright colors. The eye is drawn to brighter or highlighted colors, so use them for the more important screen components. The data or text is the most important component on most screens, so it is a good candidate for highlighting or the brightest color. Danger signals should also be brighter or highlighted. The perceived brightness of colors, from most to least, is white, yellow, green, blue, and red.

Keep in mind, however, that under levels of high ambient illumination, colors frequently appear washed out or unsaturated. If some means of light attenuation is not possible, or if colors chosen are not bright enough to counter the illumination, color should be used with caution.

Use contrasting colors to emphasize separation. The greater the contrast, the better the visibility of adjacent elements. To emphasize the separation of screen components, use contrasting colors. Possible pairs would be red/green and blue/yellow.

Use similar colors to convey similarity. Related elements can be brought together by displaying them in a similar color. Blue and green, for example, are more closely related than red and green.

Common Meanings

- To indicate that actions are necessary, use warm colors.
  - Red, orange, yellow.
- To provide status or background information, use cool colors.
  - Green, blue, violet, purple.
- Conform to human expectancies.
  - In the job.
  - In the world at large.

The warm colors, red, yellow, and orange, imply active situations or that actions are necessary. Warm colors advance, forcing attention.

The cool colors, green, blue, violet, and purple, imply background or status information. Cool colors recede or draw away.

Conform to human expectancies. Use color meanings that already exist in a person's job or the world at large. They are ingrained in behavior and difficult to unlearn. Some common color associations, as described by Marcus (1986b) are the following:

- Red—Stop, fire, hot, danger.
- Yellow—Caution, slow, test.
- Green—Go, OK, clear, vegetation, safety.
- Blue—Cold, water, calm, sky, neutrality.
- Gray—Neutrality.
- White—Neutrality.
- Warm colors—Action, response required, spatial closeness.
- Cool colors—Status, background information, spatial remoteness.

Some typical implications of color with dramatic portrayal, also by Marcus, are the following:

- High illumination—Hot, active, comic situations.
- Low illumination—Emotional, tense, tragic, melodramatic, romantic situations.
- High saturation—Emotional, tense, hot, melodramatic, comic situations.
- Warm colors—Active, leisure, recreation, comic situations.
- Cool colors—Efficiency, work, tragic and romantic situations.

Proper use of color also requires consideration of the experiences and expectations of the screen viewers.

Location

- In the center of the visual field, use red and green.
- For peripheral viewing, use blue, yellow, black, and white.
- Use adjacent colors that differ by hue and value or lightness.

The eye is most sensitive to red and green in the center of the visual field. The edges of the retina are not sensitive to these colors. If used in the viewing periphery, some other attention-getting method such as blinking must also be used.

For peripheral viewing, use blue, yellow, black, or white. The retina is most sensitive to these colors at its periphery.

Colors appearing adjacent to one another should differ in hue and lightness for a sharp edge and maximum differentiation. Also, adjacent colors differing only in their blue component should not be used so that differentiation is possible. The eye is poorly suited for dealing with blue.

Ordering

- Order colors by their spectral position.
  - Red, orange, yellow, green, blue, indigo, violet.

If an ordering of colors is needed, such as high to low, levels of depth, and so on, arrange colors by their spectral position. There is evidence that people see the spectral order as a natural one. The spectral order is red, orange, yellow, green, blue, indigo, and violet, most easily remembered as "ROY G BIV."

Foregrounds and Backgrounds

Foregrounds

- Use colors as different as possible from background colors.
- Use warmer, more active colors.
- Use colors that possess the same saturation and lightness.
- For text or data, use desaturated or spectrum center colors.
  - White, yellow, green.
- To emphasize, highlight in a light value of the foreground color, pure white, or yellow.
- To de-emphasize, lowlight in a dark value of the foreground color.

Backgrounds

- Use a background color to organize a group of elements into a unified whole.
- Use colors that do not compete with the foreground.
- Use cool, dark colors.
  - Blue, black.
- Use colors at the extreme end of the color spectrum.
  - Red, magenta.
- Use desaturated colors.

Foregrounds

Use colors as different as possible from background colors. A widely different foreground will maximize legibility. Use warmer, more active colors. Warmer colors advance, forcing attention. Use colors that possess the same saturation and lightness. Exercise caution in using more fully saturated red and orange, however, as they may be difficult to distinguish from one another.

Desaturated or spectrum center colors do not excessively stimulate the eye and appear brighter to the eye. Saturated colors excessively stimulate the eye. Marcus (1986a) recommends avoiding the use of pure white in text (except for some highlighting) because of the harsh contrast between the text and background. He suggests text should be off-white in a multicolor palette. The ISO Color Standard (Smith, 1988) suggests that for continuous reading tasks, desaturated, spectrally close colors (yellow, cyan, green) should be used to minimize disruptive eye problems.

Highlight in a light value of the foreground color, pure white, or yellow. Lowlight in a dark value of the foreground color. Marcus (1986a) suggests that to call attention to a screen element, it may be highlighted in a light value of the foreground color. If off-white is the foreground color, highlight in pure white. Yellow can also be used to highlight. To de-emphasize an element, lowlight in a darker value of the foreground color. In lowlighting, a strong enough contrast with both the background and the non-lowlighted element must be maintained so that legibility and visual differentiation is possible.

The simultaneous use of highlighting and lowlighting should be avoided. Used together they may create confusion for the viewer. Also, as with other display techniques, be conservative in using highlighting and lowlighting so that simplicity and clarity are maintained.

Backgrounds

A background color should organize a group of elements into a unified whole, isolating them from the remainder of the screen. Use colors that do not compete with the foreground. A background must be subtle and subservient to the data, text, or symbols on top of it.

Use cool, dark colors. Cool, dark colors visually recede, providing good contrast to the advancing lighter, foreground colors. Blue is especially good because of the eye's lack of sensitivity to it in the retina's central area and increased sensitivity to it in the periphery. Lalomia and Happ (1987) in a study addressing foreground and background color combinations, found the best background colors to be black and blue. In a similar study, Pastoor (1990) found that cool colors, blue and bluish cyan, were preferred for dark background screens.

Use colors at the extreme end of the color spectrum. Other spectrally extreme colors, such as red and magenta, also make better background colors. Marcus (1986a) recommends, in order of priority, the following background colors: blue, black, gray, brown, red, green, purple.

Use desaturated colors. Pastoor (1990) also found that desaturated backgrounds in almost any color work well.

Three-Dimensional Look

- Use at least five colors or color values to create a 3-D look on a screen.
  - Background: The control itself and the window on which it appears.
  - Foreground: Captions and lines for buttons, icons, and other objects.
    - Usually black or white.
  - Selected mode: The color used when the item is selected.
  - Top shadow: The bezel on the top and left of the control.
  - Bottom shadow: The bezel on the bottom and right of the control.

At least five colors or color values are needed to create a three-dimensional look on a screen (Fowler & Stanwick, 1995): the backgrounds of the control and the surface on which it is placed, the foreground (captions, lines, etc.), the selected mode, and the top and bottom shadows of the controls. These shadows assume an upper-left light source. Motif has created an algorithm to automatically calculate the top and bottom shadows, and the select color based upon the background (Kobara, 1991). Briefly, it recommends the following:

- Background: Midrange colors, 155–175 on the RGB scale.
- Foreground: Black or white, depending on the lightness or darkness of the background.

- Selected mode: About 15 percent darker than the background color, halfway between the background and bottom shadow. (Calculate by multiplying the background color's RGB value by 0.85.)
- Top Shadow: About 40–50 percent brighter than the background color. (Calculate by multiplying the background color's RGB by 1.50.)
- Bottom Shadow: About 45–60 percent darker than the background color. (Calculate by multiplying the background's RGB values by 0.50.)

One reminder: A raised look should only be used on operable controls.

Color Palette and Default

- Provide a default set of colors for all screen components.
- Provide a palette of six or seven foreground colors.
  - Provide two to five values or lightness shades for each foreground color.
- Provide a palette of six or seven background colors.

While thousands of colors may be available for display on a screen, most platform recommendations are restricted palettes. This is actually a good thing, reducing the probability of very poor color combinations and "Christmas trees." Most Macintosh colors are subdued to avoid a "circus" effect on the screen (Apple, 1992b). Microsoft offers a number of predefined schemes such as "Arizona."

While little research has been performed on color usage, Familant and Detweiler (1995) have measured the frequency of color changes for users. Compared were displayed color combinations that were judged to be "good" or "poor." They found that users with the poorer color combinations changed their screen colors more often than those with good combinations.

Provide a default set of colors. Most people do not know how to apply color to create a clear and appealing screen. Others may have the talent and skills but not the time to select a proper combination. For these users, a preselected set of colors should be developed for all screen elements. Both the Macintosh and Microsoft Windows provide standard, well thought out color schemes.

Color choices are subjective and subject to personal preference. Because of this, most systems permit users to change colors. To provide some flexibility, and to permit people the opportunity to change colors if they so desire, a palette of colors should be available. Do not provide the color spectrum; limit the number of choices available. Marcus (1986a) suggests a maximum of six or seven foreground and background colors will provide the necessary variety. He also recommends that two to five values or lightnesses for each foreground color be developed.

With these palettes, however, some sort of guidance concerning maximum number of colors to use and what are good and poor combinations should be provided. Macintosh, for example, suggests that if you create your own color schemes, that colors compatible with the ones on the Color Control Panel be used. Guidelines will make the color selection process more efficient and reduce the likelihood of visually straining conditions developing.

The basic 16 colors available in Microsoft Windows are presented in Table 9.3. Included are defaults, RGB, and HSV values. If multiple pieces of hardware are being used in a system, it is preferable to limit the choices to these.

Table 9.3   RGB and HSV Values for Microsoft Windows Basic Hues

Hue (and Default)	R	G	B	H	S	V
White (Text background)	255	255	255	240	240	240
Yellow	255	255	0	40	240	120
Dark Yellow	128	128	0	40	240	60
Red	255	0	0	0	240	120
Dark Red	128	0	0	0	240	60
Magenta	255	0	255	200	240	120
Dark Magenta	128	0	128	200	240	60
Blue	0	0	255	160	240	160
Dark Blue (Title Bar)	0	0	128	160	240	60
Cyan	0	255	255	120	240	120
Dark Cyan	0	128	128	120	240	60
Green	0	255	0	80	240	120
Dark Green	0	128	0	80	240	60
Gray (Scroll bars, buttons, other window items)	192	192	192	160	0	181
Dark Gray (Screen background)	128	128	128	160	0	120
Black (Lines, labels, cursor)	0	0	0	0	0	0

Gray Scale

- For fine discriminations use a black-gray-white scale.
  - Recommended values are white, light gray, medium gray, dark gray, black.

The perception of fine detail is poor with color. The eye resolves fine detail much better on a black-white scale. Marcus (1986b) recommends five tonal values for black and white, higher resolution screens: black, dark gray, medium gray, light gray, and white. He suggests the following general uses:

- White: — Screen background.
  Text located in any black area.
- Light Gray: — Pushbutton background area.
- Medium Gray: — Icon background area.
  Menu dropshadow.
  Window dropshadow.
  Inside area of system icons.
  Filename bar.
- Dark gray: — Window border.
- Black: — Text.
  Window title bar.
  Icon border.
  Icon elements.
  Ruled lines.

Motif presents the following scheme for designing windows in a gray scale (Kobara, 1991).

- Background: A 30 percent light gray (RGB 79, 79, 79).
- Foreground: White (RGB 0, 0, 0).
- Selected mode: A 70 percent dark gray (RGB 181, 181, 181).
- Top Shadow: White.
- Bottom Shadow: Black (RGB 255, 255, 255).

Gray scale values must differ by at least 20 to 30 percent (White, 1990).

Text in Color

- When switching text from black to color:
  - Double the width of lines.
  - Use bold or larger type:

- If originally 8-12 points, increase by 1-2 points.
- If originally 14-24 points, increase by 2-4 points.
- Check legibility by squinting at text.
  - Too-light type will recede or even disappear.

Text in color is not as visible as it is in black. Fowler and Stanwick (1995) report that the size of text has to be increased to maintain legibility when the text is switched from black to color. Lines should be doubled in width and type made larger or bolder. If the existing type ranges from eight to twelve points, increase it one or two points. If the existing type ranges from 14 to 24 points, increase it by two to four points. They suggest that the legibility of type can be checked by squinting at it. A type that is too light will recede or even disappear.

Monochromatic Screens

- At the standard viewing distance, white, orange, or green are acceptable colors.
- At a far viewing distance, white is the best choice.
- Over all viewing distances, from near to far, white is the best choice.

Monochromatic, or one-color, screens are still found in graphical systems, most frequently on notebook PCs. In a study by Hewlett-Packard (Wichansky, 1986) white, orange, and green monochrome desktop display device screens were evaluated for performance and readability at various viewing distances. At the standard screen viewing distance (18–24 inches), no performance differences were found between white, orange, and green phosphor in either polarity (light characters on a dark background, or dark characters on a light background). Subjective ratings of ease of reading were highest for green and orange light background screens as compared to dark background screens, while no differences in ease of reading were found for either polarity with white phosphor at this distance. At a far viewing distance (4–5 feet), orange and green light background screens could be seen more clearly than dark background screens, while white screens were equally legible in either polarity. More errors were found with green than the other two colors.

A green screen yielded red or pink afterimages for 35 percent of the screen viewers; orange, blue afterimages for 20 percent; white yielded afterimages for 5 percent. A 35 percent pink afterimage rate for green screen viewing was also found by Galitz (1968).

Some conclusions:

- At standard viewing distances, no significant performance differences exist for white, orange, or green. All are acceptable. Subjective preferences may vary, however, so providing the viewer a choice of any of these colors is desirable.
- At far viewing distances, white is the more legible color and therefore the best choice.
- Over all viewing distances, white is the best choice.
- White has the lowest probability for creating visual afterimages.

Consistency

- Be consistent in color use.

Consistency in color usage should exist within a screen, a set of screens, and a system. A person can sense the relatedness of color in space and over time, thereby linking elements not immediately together. An identical background color in windows on different screens, for example, will be seen as related. Changing color meanings must be avoided. It will lead to difficulties in interpretation, confusion, and errors. In general, broadly defined meanings (such as red indicating a problem) permit more scope for variations without inconsistency.

CHOOSING COLORS FOR TEXTUAL GRAPHIC SCREENS

For displaying data, text, and symbols on a textual graphical screen (as opposed to statistical graphics screens to be described shortly) colors selected should have adequate visibility, meaning, contrast, and harmony.

- Use effective foreground/background combinations.
- Use effective foreground combinations.
- Display no more than four colors at one time.
- Choose the background color first.
- Test the chosen colors.

Effective Foreground/Background Combinations

Lalomia & Happ (1987) established effective foreground/background color combinations for the IBM 5153 Color Display. From a color set of 16 different foregrounds and eight different backgrounds, 120 color combinations were evaluated for (1) response time to identify characters, and (2) subjective preferences of users. The results from each measure were

Table 9.4 Effective Foreground/Background Combinations (From Lalomia & Happ, 1987)

	Background							
Foreground	Black	Blue	Green	Cyan	Red	Magenta	Brown	White
BLACK	x			Good		Good		Good
BLUE		x			Poor			Good
H.I. BLUE			Poor	Poor			Poor	Poor
CYAN	Good		Poor	x			Poor	
H.I. CYAN	Good	Good		Good	Good	Good		
GREEN	Good	Good	x	Poor	Good		Poor	Poor
H.I. GREEN		Good						
YELLOW	Good	Good		Good		Good		
RED			Poor		x	Poor	Poor	
H.I. RED			Poor					
MAGENTA			Poor		Poor	x	Poor	
H.I. MAGENTA	Good		Good			Poor		
BROWN			Poor			Poor	x	
GRAY		Poor			Poor		Poor	
WHITE		Good		Poor				x
H.I. WHITE	Good		Good	Good				

(H.I. = High Intensity)

ranked and combined to derive an overall measure of color combination effectiveness. The best and poorest color combinations are summarized in Table 9.4. In this table "Best" means the specified combination was in the top 20 percent for overall effectiveness; "Poor" means it was in the bottom 20 percent. Those combinations comprising the "middle" 60 percent are not marked.

The results yield some interesting conclusions.

- The majority of good combinations possess a bright or high-intensity color as the foreground color.
- The majority of poor combinations are those with low contrast.
- The best overall color is black.
- The poorest overall color is brown.
- Maximum flexibility and variety in choosing a foreground color exists with black or blue backgrounds. (These backgrounds account for almost one-half of the good combinations.)
- Brown and green are the poorest background choices.

Bailey & Bailey (1989), in their screen creation utility Protoscreens, have a table summarizing research-derived good foreground/background combinations. This table, which uses the results of the Lalomia and Happ study plus some others, is shown in modified form in Table 9.5.

The studies referenced above did not control character-background luminance-contrast ratios. Because of the characteristics of the eye, some

Table 9.5   Preferred Foreground/Background Combinations from Protoscreens

Backgrounds	Acceptable Foregrounds	
Black	Dark Cyan	Light Green
	Dark Yellow	Light Cyan
	Dark White	Light Magenta
		Light Yellow
		Light White
Blue	Dark Green	Light Green
	Dark Yellow	Light Cyan
	Dark White	Light Yellow
		Light White
Green	Black	Light Yellow
	Dark Blue	Light White
Cyan	Black	Light Yellow
	Dark Blue	Light White
Red		Light Green
		Light Cyan
		Light Yellow
		Light White
Magenta	Black	Light Cyan
		Light Yellow
		Light White
Yellow	Black	
	Dark Blue	
	Dark Red	
White	Black	
	Dark Blue	

colors appear brighter to it than others. A conclusion of the Lalomia and Happ study was that good combinations usually possessed a bright or high-intensity foreground color.

Pastoor (1990) equalized luminance-contrast ratios at preoptimized levels for about 800 foreground/background color combinations. For light foregrounds and dark backgrounds, the ratio was 10:1; for light backgrounds and dark foregrounds, 1:6.5. He then had the combinations rated with the following results:

- For dark on light polarity:
  - Any foreground color is acceptable if the background color is chosen properly.
  - Increased saturation of the foreground only marginally affected ratings, implying that any dark, saturated, foreground color is satisfactory.
  - Saturated backgrounds yield unsatisfactory ratings.
  - Less saturated backgrounds generally receive high ratings with any foreground color.
- For light on dark polarity:
  - Combinations involving saturated colors tend to be unsatisfactory.
  - As foreground color saturation increases; the number of background colors yielding high ratings diminishes.
  - Generally, desaturated foreground/background color combinations yielded the best ratings.
  - Short wavelength, cool colors were preferred for backgrounds (blue, bluish cyan, cyan).

In general, Pastoor concluded that: (1) there was no evidence suggesting a differential effect of color on subjective ratings or performance (except that for light on dark polarity, blue, bluish cyan, or cyan were preferred as backgrounds), and (2) overall, desaturated color combinations yielded the best results.

Smith (1986) has recommended the two- and three-color combinations summarized at the left of Table 9.6 as being effective for dark background screens. She cautions against using the combinations described on the table's right side. She also suggests that light background screens should contain pastel colors with dark characters.

Maximum of Four Colors

While not experimentally verified, experience indicates that more than four colors displayed at one time on a screen gives rise to a feeling of "too much." Marcus (1986a) suggests an even more conservative approach, a

Table 9.6 Effective Two- and Three-Color Combinations for Dark Background Screens from Smith (1986)

Two-Color Combinations

Good	Poor
White / Green	Red / Blue
Gold / Cyan	Red / Green
Gold / Green	Red / Purple
Green / Magenta	Red / Yellow
Green / Lavender	Red / Magenta
Cyan / Red	White / Cyan
	White / Yellow
	Blue / Green
	Blue / Purple
	Green / Cyan
	Cyan / Lavender

Three-Color Combinations

Good	Poor
White / Gold / Green	Red / Yellow / Green
White / Gold / Blue	Red / Blue / Green
White / Gold / Magenta	Red / Magenta / Blue
White / Red / Cyan	White / Cyan / Yellow
Red / Cyan/ Gold	Green / Cyan / Blue
Cyan / Yellow / Lavender	
Gold / Magenta / Blue	
Gold / Magenta / Green	
Gold / Lavender / Green	

maximum of three foreground colors and, even better, only two. An application of good use of color can often be viewed in one's living room. Note the use of color by the television networks when textual or tabular information is presented (for example, sport scores, news highlights, and so on). The use of only two, or sometimes three, colors is most commonly seen.

So, while more than four colors may be displayed over a period of time or a series of screens, do not display more than four colors at one time on a single screen. For most cases, restrict the number of colors to two or three.

Choose the Background First

When choosing colors to display, it is best to select the background color first. Then choose acceptable foreground colors.

Test the Colors

Because color is such a complex phenomenon, because definitions of a color can vary, and because the hardware on which a color is used can impact its look, always test all chosen colors as part of the system testing process (See Step 12, on testing)

CHOOSING COLORS FOR STATISTICAL GRAPHICS SCREENS

The visual, spatial, or physical representation of information—as opposed to numeric, alphanumeric, textual, or symbol representation—is known as statistical or data graphics. Common kinds of statistical graphics include bar graphs, line graphs, scatterplots, and pie charts. Color can also be used to render a statistical graphic screen more legible and meaningful.

Emphasis

- Emphasize the graphic's data.

The main emphasis of color in a statistical graphics screen should be in the data area. Brighter colors and highlighting should attract the eye to the presented data so that trends and conclusions can be quickly perceived. Supporting text, numbers, and legends should receive slightly less emphasis. Aids in data interpretation such as grids should receive the least emphasis.

Number of Colors

- Use no more than:
  - Six colors at one time.
  - Five values or lightnesses of one color.

Experience indicates that displaying more than six colors at one time on statistical graphics screens is "too much." Even five or six colors, however, may be distracting or confusing if they are not properly chosen or are not harmonious. Marcus (1986a) suggests a more pleasing arrangement can often be achieved for graphics with five or less segments by using one color and displaying each segment in a different value or lightness.

Backgrounds

- Surround images:
  - In a neutral color.
  - In a color complementary to the main image.

A neutral background will help set off a full color. A background in the complementary color of the main image will minimize visual afterimages.

Size

- Provide images of an adequate size for the task.
- If the image changes in size, use colors exhibiting a minimum shift in hue or lightness.
  - White, yellow, and red on dark backgrounds.

As color areas decrease in size, they appear to change in lightness and saturation. Similar colors may look different and different colors may look similar. Interactions with the background color also increase. Thin gray images (lines or borders, for example) appear as a desaturated color complement of their background.

Provide adequate-size images. Where color identification is important, an image should be large enough to eliminate these distortions.

For images changing in size, use colors exhibiting minimum hue or lightness shifts. Marcus (1986b) recommends that white, yellow, and red be used for light text, thin lines, and small shapes on dark backgrounds (blue, green, red, light gray).

Status

- To indicate a status, use the following colors:
  - Proper, normal, or OK   - Green, white, or blue.
  - Caution   - Yellow or gold.
  - Emergency or abnormal   - Red.

To indicate a status, use green, white, or blue to indicate OK; yellow or gold for caution; and red for emergency or abnormal. The use of red, yellow, and green are well-learned color conventions.

Measurements and Area-Fill Patterns

- Display measurements in the following colors:
  - Grids   - Gray
  - Data points   - Yellow
  - Variance or error bars   - Blue
  - Out of specified range data   - Red
  - Captions and labels   - Lavender, lime green, or cyan

- Display area-fill patterns in the following colors:
  - Widely spaced dots   - Red
  - Closely spaced dots   - Green
  - Wide dashed lines   - Magenta
  - Narrow dashed lines   - Cyan
  - Wide crosshatch   - Blue
  - Narrow crosshatch   - Yellow

For measurements, Smith (1986) recommends the above. They balance emphasis considerations (gray for grids, yellow for data points, lavender, lime green, or cyan for labels) and human expectancies (red for out-of-specified range). Marcus (1986a) recommends that all text and the horizontal and vertical axis lines of a statistical graphic should be off-white. This will aid focusing main attention on the colored data.

To ensure that fill-in area patterns are identifiable, discriminable, and free from unintended brightness effects, Smith (1988) recommends the above.

Physical Impressions

Size

- To convey an impression of:
  - Larger   - Use bright or saturated colors.
  - Smaller   - Use dark or desaturated colors.
  - Similar   - Use colors of equal lightness.

Weight

- To convey an impression of:
  - Heavy   - Use dark, saturated colors.
  - Light   - Use light, desaturated colors.

Distance

- To convey an impression of:
  - Close   – Use saturated, bright, long-wavelength (red) colors.
  - Far   – Use saturated, dark, short-wavelength (blue) colors.

Height

- To convey an impression of height, use desaturated, light colors.

Depth

- To convey an impression of depth, use saturated, dark colors.

Concentration Level

- To convey an impression of concentration level, use:
  - High   – Saturated colors.
  - Low   – Desaturated colors.

Magnitude of Change

- To convey an impression of magnitude of change, use:
  - Lowest   – Short-wavelength (blue) colors.
  - Highest   – Long-wavelength (red) colors.

Actions

- To convey an impression of action, use:
  - Required   – Long-wavelength (red) colors.
  - Not required – Short-wavelength (blue) colors.

Order

- To convey an impression of order with color, use:
  - Low end of a continuum –   Short-wavelength (blue) colors.
  - High end of a continuum –   Long-wavelength (red) colors.
- When displaying an array of ordered colors, position:
  - Short-wavelength colors to the left side or at the bottom.
  - Long-wavelength colors to the right side or at the top.
- To convey an impression of order with value or lightness, use lightness order of a color (darkest to lightest or vice versa).

Neutrality

- To convey an impression of neutrality, use black, gray, and white.

Colors yield different physical impressions (Tedford, Berquist, & Flynn 1977; Smith, 1986; Smith, 1988). Bright, saturated colors convey a feeling of large and close. Dark, saturated colors mean heavy, far, and impression of depth. Desaturated, light colors indicate a light weight and height. Desaturated dark colors mean smaller. Long-wavelength (red) colors are associated with high rate of change, action required, and the high end of a continuum. Short-wavelength (blue) colors are associated with low rate of change, no actions required, and the low end of a continuum. Neutrality is best indicated by black, gray, or white.

USES OF COLOR TO AVOID

- Relying exclusively on color.
- Too many colors at one time.
- Highly saturated, spectrally extreme colors together:
  - Red and blue, yellow and purple.
- Low-brightness colors for extended viewing or older viewers.
- Colors of equal brightness.
- Colors lacking contrast:
  - For example, yellow and white, black and brown, reds, blues, and browns against a light background.
- Using colors in unexpected ways.
- Fully saturated colors for text or other frequently read screen components.
- Pure blue for text, thin lines, and small shapes.
- Colors in small areas.
- Color for fine details.
- Red and green in the periphery of large-scale displays.
- Adjacent colors only differing in the amount of blue they possess.
- Color to improve legibility of densely packed text.
- Too many colors at one time (again).

The proper use of color in screen design also suggests some things to avoid.

Relying Exclusively on Color

Consider the needs of color-blind viewers and the effects of ambient lighting on color perception. Do not underestimate the value and role of other techniques such as spatial formatting and component locations in good screen design.

Too Many Colors at one Time

Using too many colors can increase response times, cause erroneous associations, interfere with the handling of information, and create confusion. The objective is a screen that communicates; a colorful screen is not the objective. Use just enough colors to create an effective communication. Again, consider the value of other techniques like spatial formatting and consistent component locations in good design.

Highly Saturated, Spectrally Extreme Colors Together

Spectrally extreme combinations can create eye focus problems, vibrations, illusions of shadows, and afterimages. In addition to red/blue and yellow/purple, other combinations that might cause problems are yellow/blue, green/blue, and red/green (Marcus, 1986a).

Low-Brightness Colors for Extended Viewing or Older Viewers

The eye adapts to color during extended viewing. The eye's capacity also diminishes with age as the amount of light passing through the lens decreases. All colors will look less bright, and colors that are dim to begin with may not be legible. Brighter colors are needed to prevent reading problems.

Colors of Equal Brightness

Colors of equal brightness cannot be easily distinguished. A brightness difference must exist between adjacent colors.

Colors Lacking Contrast

Colors lacking contrast also cannot be easily distinguished.

Using Colors in Unexpected Ways

Colors have become associated with certain meanings. Red, for example, is always associated with stop or danger. To display a critical or error message in green would violate an ingrained association and cause confusion.

Fully Saturated Colors for Frequently Read Screen Components

Fully saturated colors excessively stimulate the eye, again possibly causing visual confusion.

Pure Blue for Text, Thin Lines, and Small Shapes

Due to its physical make-up, the eye has difficulty creating a clear and legible image for small blue shapes. They will look fuzzy.

Colors in Small Areas

Distortions in color, lightness, and saturation may occur.

Colors for Fine Details

Black, gray, and white will provide much better resolution.

Red and Green in the Periphery of Large-Scale Displays

The edges of the retina are not particularly sensitive to red and green.

Adjacent Colors only Differing in the Amount of Blue They Possess

Because of the eye's difficulty in dealing with blue, differences in color based upon varying amounts of blue in the color's mixture will not be noticed.

Color to Improve Legibility of Densely Packed Text

Space lines between paragraphs of text or after about every five lines of data will work much better.

Too Many Colors at One Time (Again)

Never overuse color (again). Too many colors at one time may make a screen confusing or unpleasant to look at. Use only enough color to fulfill the system's objectives.

Create Meaningful Icons

The symbolic representation of objects, such as office tools or storage locations, and optional actions on a screen began with Xerox's Star, continued with Apple's Lisa and Macintosh, and has been building ever since. Indeed, the faces of many 1990s screens scarcely resemble their older siblings of the early 1980s.

- Understand what an icon is.
  - Kinds.
  - Characteristics.
  - Usability influences.
- Choose window icons.
  - Determine what graphic images best represent the application.
  - Determine what relevant default icons are available and use them.
  - Create icons for images not represented by defaults through following established icon design guidelines.
- Present meaningfully on the screen.

To start, a definition of *icon,* or more appropriately, *icons,* is provided. Then, an icon's characteristics are summarized. Finally, what influences the usability of an icon is described.

KINDS OF ICONS

Icons to reflect objects, ideas, and actions are not new to mankind. We've been there before. Early humans (100,000 years or so ago) used pictographs and then ideographs to communicate. Some of these early communications can be found on rock walls and in caves around the world.

Until recently, this was also a way to communicate in some cultures (Native Americans and Australian aborigines, for example). Again, traces can still be seen.

Word writing is traced back to Chinese writing from about 6000 B.C. and Egyptian hieroglyphics from about 3000 B.C. This was followed by cuneiform (Babylonia and Assyria) from about 1900 B.C., and the contemporary Chinese vocabulary (numbering about 50,000) around 1500 B.C. In 1000 B.C. the Phoenicians developed a 22-sign alphabet that the Greeks adopted about 800–600 B.C. The Greeks passed this alphabet on to the Romans about 400 B.C., who then developed a 23-character alphabet. It has been modified and embellished but has remained essentially the same for the last 2000 years.

Pictorial representations, then, have played a prominent role in mankind's history. Word writing, however, unleashed much more flexibility and richness in communication. This has caused some skeptics to wonder why, after taking 2500 years to get rid of iconic shapes, we are now reviving them on screens.

Whatever the past, today, objects or actions *are* depicted on screens by icons. The term *icon* by itself, however, is not very specific and can actually represent very different things. An attempt has been made by some to define the actual types of icons that do exist. Marcus (1984) suggests icons fall into these categories:

- Icon—Something that looks like what it means.
- Index—A sign that was caused by the thing to which it refers.
- Symbol—A sign that may be completely arbitrary in appearance.

He states that what are commonly referred to as icons may really be indexes or symbols.

A true icon is something that looks like what it means. It is representational and easy to understand. A picture of a telephone or a clock on a screen is a true icon. An index is a sign caused by the thing to which it refers. An open door with a broken window indicates the possible presence of a burglar. The meaning of an index may or may not be clear, depending upon one's past experiences. A symbol is a sign that may be completely arbitrary in appearance and whose meaning must be learned. The menu and sizing icons on screens are examples of symbols. From this perspective, strictly speaking, so-called icons on screens are probably a mixture of true icons, signs, and indexes.

Another definition is provided by Rogers (1989).

- Resemblance—An image that looks like what it means.
- Symbolic—An abstract image representing something.

- Exemplar—An image illustrating an example or characteristic of something.
- Arbitrary—An image completely arbitrary in appearance whose meaning must be learned.
- Analogy—An image physically or semantically associated with something.

She suggests that an icon is *used* in a number of different ways: for *objects* such as a document, *object attributes* such as a color or fill pattern, *actions* such as to paste, *system states* such as ready or busy, and *message types* like critical or warning.

The different ways icons are used may then be represented by different design schemes. A *resemblance* is an image that looks like what it means—a book, for example, to represent a dictionary. This is equivalent to Marcus's icon. A *symbolic* is an abstract image that represents something. Fragile, for example, can be represented by a cracked glass. Marcus's symbol would be similar. An *exemplar* represents an example or characteristic of something. A sign at a freeway exit picturing a knife and fork has come to indicate a restaurant. An *arbitrary* image is not directly related in any way and must be learned. Marcus's symbol would be an equivalent. Finally, an *analogy* is an image physically or semantically associated with something—a wheelbarrow full of bricks for the move command, for example. Marcus's symbol would also be similar.

In a study looking at various kinds of icons, Rogers found that those depicting both an action and an object were quite effective. For example, a drawing of a page and an arrow pointing up means "go to the top of the page." She also found that arbitrary icons were only meaningful in very small sets, and that icons based on analogies were relatively ineffective.

CHARACTERISTICS OF ICONS

An icon possesses the technical qualities of syntactics, semantics, and pragmatics (Marcus, 1984). *Syntactics* refers to an icon's physical structure. Is it square, round, red, green, big, small? Are the similarities and differences obvious? Similar shapes and colors can classify a group of related icons, communicating a common relationship.

Semantics is the icon's meaning. To what does it refer—a file, a wastebasket, some other object? Is this clear?

Pragmatics are how the icons are physically produced and depicted. Is the screen resolution sufficient to illustrate the icon clearly?

Syntactics, semantics, and pragmatics determine an icon's effectiveness and usability.

USABILITY INFLUENCES

Mayhew (1992) argues that simply providing an icon on a screen does the user no particular favor, unless it is carefully designed to present a natural and meaningful association between the icon itself and what it stands for. Unfortunately, a sampling of many current systems finds icons that do not achieve this objective. Icons are included because "this is the thing to do" in a graphical system today. Little concern is given to effectiveness. The result is too often a cluttered and confusing screen that is visually overwhelming. So, proper icon design is important from an acceptance, learning, and productivity perspective. The following factors influence an icon's usability:

- Familiarity
- Clarity
- Simplicity
- Consistency
- Directness of link
- Context in which used
- Complexity of task
- Expectancies of users
- Efficiency
- Discriminability

Familiarity

How familiar is the object being depicted? Familiarity will reduce learning time. How familiar are the commonly seen icons in Figure 10.1? Lack of familiarity requires learning the icons' meanings. Many unfamiliar icons require a great deal of learning.

Experience makes words and numbers often more familiar to a person than symbols. Confusion matrices have been developed through extensive research for alphanumeric data (0 versus O, 1 versus I). Graphic symbols may be more visually similar.

Clarity

Is the icon legible? Does the shape, structure, and formation technique on the screen permit a clear and unambiguous depiction of what it is? Screen resolution should be sufficiently fine to establish clear differences of form at the normal working distance. The resolution and pixel shapes for CGA, EGA, and VGA screens differ from one another. Icons must appear correctly and consistently no matter what kind of screen. If color is used, it should contrast well with the background. Poor clarity will lead to identification errors and slower performance.

Simplicity

Is the icon simple? Is the shape clean and devoid of unnecessary embellishments? Too many parts will only confuse the screen viewer.

Consistency

Are families of icons consistent in structure and shape? Are the same icons displayed in different sizes also consistent in structure and shape?

Directness of Link

How "sign-like" is the icon; how well does it convey its intended meaning? For concrete objects and actions, direct links are more easily established. Adjectives, adverbs, conjunctions, and prepositions can cause problems, however. Also, how does one easily convey concepts like bigger, smaller, wider, or narrower?

Context

The context of a symbol may change its meaning. Does the rabbit symbol illustrated in Figure 10.1, if seen on a road sign in a national park, mean "go faster"? From this contextual perspective, icons are similar to words.

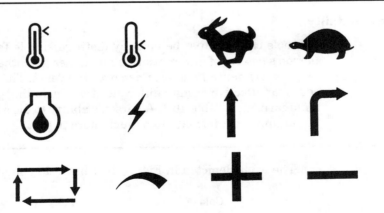

Figure 10.1   Some common icons. What do they stand for? See page 526 for the answers. (From Micro Switch, 1984.)

Complexity of Task

The more abstract or complex the symbol, the more difficult it is to extract or interpret its intended meaning. It has been found that more concrete graphic messages are easier to comprehend than the more abstract. Icons, therefore, cannot completely replace words in some more complex situations.

Expectancies

The symbol may be comprehended, but a false conclusion may be reached about the desired action because of an incorrect expectancy. Bailey (1984) reported that a study of international road signs found that eight percent of all drivers never saw the slash through the symbol on a road sign, which indicates "do not" do the pictured action. Their expectancy was that they could do it.

Efficiency

In some situations, a graphics screen may be less efficient, consuming more screen display space than a word or requiring more physical actions by the user. A telephone directory of 50 names and numbers listed on an alphanumeric screen may consume the same screen space required for, and manipulation of, 15 file cards. Raising an arm or moving a mouse may be slower than simply typing. In other situations icons can be more effective than words in communicating concepts in a smaller area of space. Their strength lies in situations where this occurs.

Discriminability

Symbols chosen must be visually distinguishable from other symbols. A person's powers of differentiation for shapes and other forms of codes have been experimentally determined over the years. The maximum number of codes for effective human differentiation, including geometric shapes, are summarized in Table 10.1. A person's ability to discriminate alphabetic or alphanumeric information is much more potent.

The icons depicted in Figure 10.1 have the following meanings:

Hot	Cold	Fast	Slow
Engine Oil	Ammeter/Generator	Straight	Turn
Automatic	Variable Regulation (Increase/Decrease)	Plus/Positive	Minus/Negative

Table 10.1   Maximum Number of Codes for Effective Human Differentiation

Encoding Method	Recommended Maximum	Comments
Alphanumerics	Unlimited	Highly versatile. Meaning usually self-evident. Location time may be longer than for graphic coding.
Geometric Shapes	10–20	High mnemonic value. Very effective if shape relates to object or operation being represented.
Size	3–5	Fair. Considerable space required. Location time longer than for colors and shapes.
Line Length	3–4	Will clutter the display if many are used.
Line Width	2–3	Good.
Line Style	5–9	Good.
Line Angle	8–11	Good in special cases (such as wind direction).
Solid and Broken Lines	3–4	Good.
Number of Dots or Marks	5	Minimize number for quick assimilation.
Brightness	2–3	Creates problems on screens with poor contrast.
Flashing/Blinking	2–3	Confusing for general encoding but the best way to attract attention. Interacts poorly with other codes. Annoying if overused. Limit to small fields.
Underlining	No data	Useful but can reduce text legibility.
Reverse Video	No data	Effective for making data stand out. Flicker easily perceived in large areas, however.
Orientation (location on display surface)	4–8	—
Color	6–8	Attractive and efficient. Short location time. Excessive use confusing. Poor for color blind.
Combinations of Codes	Unlimited	Can reinforce coding but complex combinations can be confusing.

Data derived from Martin, 1973; Barmack & Sinaiko, 1966; Mallory et al., 1980; Damodaran et al., 1980; and Maguire, 1985.

CHOOSING WINDOW ICONS

Icon design is an important process. Meaningful and recognizable icons will speed learning and yield a much more effective system. Poor design will lead to errors, delays, and confusion. While the art of icon design is still evolving, it is agreed that the usability of a system is aided by adhering to the following icon design guidelines.

A Successful Icon

- Looks different from all other icons.
- Is obvious what it does or represents.
- Is recognizable when no larger than 16 pixels square.
- Looks as good in black and white as in color.

Fowler and Stanwick (1995) provide these general guidelines. An icon must look different from all other product icons, making it discriminable and differentiable. What it does or represents must also be obvious so it is interpretable. It must be recognizable when no larger than 16 pixels square. Finally, it must look as good in black and white as in color. Color is an enhancing quality of an icon, as well.

Size

- Supply in all standard sizes.
  - 16x16 pixel (16 color).
  - 32x32 pixel (16 color).
    - Effective: 24x24 or 26x26 in 32x32 icon.
  - 48x48 pixel (256 color).
- Use an odd number of pixels along each side.
  - Provides center pixel around which to focus design.
- Minimum sizes for easy selection:
  - With stylus or pen: 15 pixels square.
  - With mouse: 20 pixels square.
  - With finger: 40 pixels square.
- Provide as large a hot zone as possible.

Typically, icons come in two standard sizes, 16 and 32 pixels square, and 16 colors. For clarity, 16 x 16 should be an icon's minimum size. An effective combination for an image is a 24 x 24 or 26 x 26 in a 32-pixel square icon. Icons may also be created in a 48 x 48, 256-color format. Microsoft (1995) suggests that while 256 colors may be used in the smaller sizes, to do so increases icon storage requirements, and they may not be displayable on all computer configurations. If 256 colors are used for icons, they suggest that the standard 16-color format should *always* be provided.

Horton (1994) recommends using an odd number of pixels along each side of the matrix. This provides a center pixel around which to focus, thus simplifying the design process. For easy selection, Horton also recommends the following minimum icon sizes: with a stylus or pen, 15 pixels square; with a mouse, 20 pixels square; with one's finger, 40 pixels square.

An icon's hot zone, the area within it that allows it to be selected, should be as large as possible, preferably the entire size of the icon. This allows easier selection.

Choosing Images

- Use existing icons when available.
- Use images for nouns, not verbs.
- Use traditional images.

Many standard icons have already been developed for graphical systems. Use these standard icons where they are available. This will promote consistency across systems, yielding all the performance benefits that consistency provides. Where standard icons are not available, determine if any applicable icons have already been developed by industries and trade or standards organizations. ISO, for example, has developed standard shapes for a variety of purposes. Always consult all relevant reference books before inventing new symbols or modifying existing ones.

An object, or noun, is much easier to represent pictorially than an action or verb. Choose nouns for icons whenever possible.

Old-fashioned, traditional images often work better than newer ones. They have been around longer, and more people recognize them.

Creating Images

The following precepts should be kept in mind when creating icons.

- Create familiar and concrete shapes.
- Create visually and conceptually distinct shapes.
  - Incorporate unique features of an object.
  - Do not display within a border.
- Clearly reflect objects represented.
- Simply reflect objects represented, avoiding excessive detail.
- Create as a set, communicating relationships to one another through common shapes.
- Provide consistency in icon type.
- Create shapes of the proper emotional tone.

Create Concrete and Familiar Shapes Ideally, an icon's meaning should be self-evident. This is enhanced when concrete shapes are provided, those that look like what they are. An icon should also be intuitive or obvious, based upon a person's preexisting knowledge. Familiar shapes are those

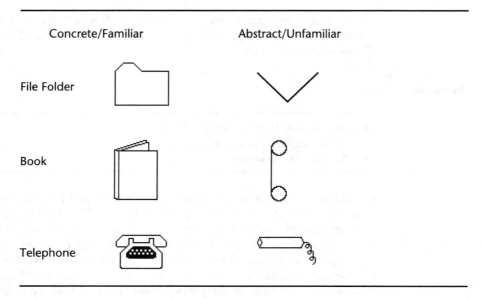

Figure 10.2   Concrete and familiar shapes.

images that are well learned. Figure 10.2 illustrates concrete and familiar icons for a file folder, book, and telephone as well as images for the same objects that are more abstract and unfamiliar. Nolan (1989) found that concrete, familiar icons were preferred to abstract, unfamiliar ones.

Keep in mind, however, that familiarity is in the eye of the viewer. The concrete images pictured may be familiar to us, readers of this book, but not to a tribal chief living in a remote area of the world where these objects do not exist. Similarly, items familiar to those working on the factory floor may not be at all familiar in the office, and vice versa. Mayhew (1992) also cautions that some abstract images should not be discounted because they have become familiar, in spite of their being abstract. On a road sign, for example, an angled red bar inscribed over an object means do not do what is pictured beneath (at least to most people). While abstract, it is a very familiar shape today. If an abstract image must be used, it should be capable of being learned quickly and easily recalled. Familiarity can only be determined through knowing one's user.

Create Visually and Conceptually Distinct Shapes   It must be easy to tell icons apart so confusions between them are minimized. Differentiation is aided when icons look visually different from one another. It is also aided when icons are conceptually different—that is, they portray specific features of an object that are relatively unique within the entire set of objects to be displayed. Figure 10.3, based upon Mayhew (1992), illustrates

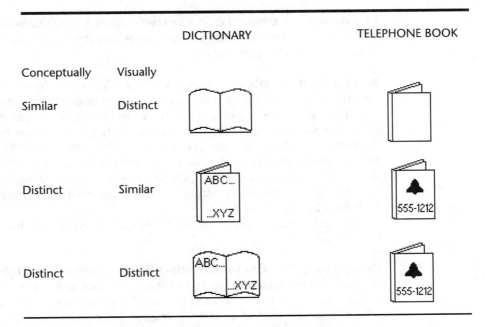

Figure 10.3 Visually and conceptually distinct shapes.

how distinctiveness may be achieved for two similar items, a dictionary and a telephone book. Visual distinctiveness is achieved by incorporating unique features of each: for the dictionary, it is its content of letters and words, for the telephone book, numbers and the telephone bell.

Visual distinctiveness is degraded when borders are placed around icons, as illustrated in Figure 10.4. Borders tend to obscure the shape of the object being displayed.

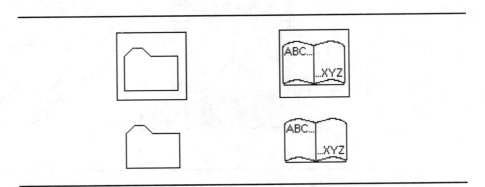

Figure 10.4 Borders degrading icon distinctiveness.

Clearly Reflect Objects Represented The characteristics of the display itself should permit drawings of adequate quality. Poorly formed or fuzzy shapes will inhibit recognition.

Simply Reflect Objects Represented Construct icons with as few graphical components as necessary, using no more than two or three, if possible. Also, use simple, clean lines, avoiding ornamentation. Byrne (1993) found that simple icons, icons containing fewer graphical elements, were found faster in a visual search task than complex icons, icons with more components. He concluded that complex icons seemed to clutter a screen with information that people were unable to employ to their advantage. Too much detail inhibits rather than facilitates perception, as illustrated in Figure 10.5.

For real-world objects, use only enough detail to permit recognition and recall.

Design as a Set, Communicating Relationships Through Common Shapes Do not design icons in isolation, but as a family considering their relationships to each other and the user's tasks. Provide a common style. When icons are part of an overall related set, create shapes that visually communicate these relationships. Objects within a class, for example, may possess the same overall shape but vary in their other design details, as illustrated in Figure 10.6. Color may also be used to achieve this design goal. In creating sets, always avoid repeating unrelated elements .

Provide Consistency in Icon Type As previously noted, there are many different kinds of design schemes for icons (resemblance, symbolic, arbi-

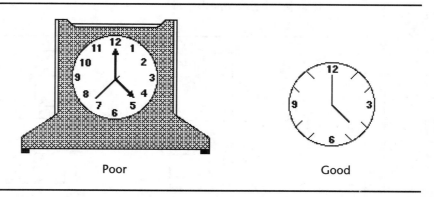

Poor   Good

Figure 10.5   Avoid excessive detail in icon design.

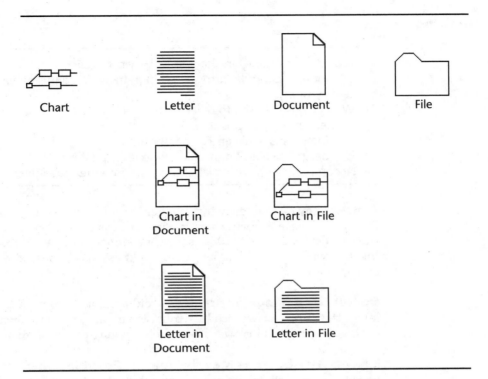

Figure 10.6   Communication relationships in icons.

trary, etc.) All these schemes might be used to create a meaningful family of icons for an application. Learning the meaning of icons and searching for the right icon, however, will be aided if the same design scheme is used for all icons within a family. In presenting a series of icons for actions such as paint, cut, etc., one could, for example, (1) depict a before-after representation of the action, (2) depict the action itself being performed, or (3) picture the tool to perform the action. While a series of meaningful icons could be developed using each scheme, the best approach would be to use only one of these schemes to develop the entire family of icons.

Create Shapes of the Proper Emotional Tone The icon should appropriately reflect the environment in which it is used. A sewage disposal system would be an inappropriate metaphor for an electronic mail system wastebasket.

Drawing Images

- Provide consistency in shape over varying sizes.
- Do not use triangular arrows in design to avoid confusion with other system symbols.
- When icons are used to reflect varying attributes, express these attributes as meaningfully as possible.
- Provide proper scale and orientation.
- Use perspective and dimension whenever possible.
- Accompany icon with a label to assure intended meaning.

Consistency When drawing images, create consistency in shapes of identical icons of differing sizing. Preserve the general shape and any distinctive detail. Marcus (1984) says consistency is achieved through limiting the variations of angles, line thicknesses, shapes, and amount of empty space.

Do Not Use Triangular Arrows Avoid using a triangular graphic similar to that used as a cascade symbol for menus, a drop-down button for controls, and scroll arrows. The similarity may cause confusion.

Express Attributes as Meaningfully as Possible When an icon is also used to express an attribute of an object, do it as meaningfully as possible. The status of a document, for example, might be represented by displaying it in a different shade, but would be more effectively illustrated by filling it in, as illustrated in Figure 10.7. Shading requires remembering what each shading stands for; the proportion is more intuitively obvious.

Provide Proper Scale and Orientation Assure that the size and orientation are consistent with other related objects. Also assure that they fit well on the screen.

Use Perspective and Dimension Use of lighting and shadow will more accurately reflect the real-world experiences of people. When a light source is used, it must be located upper-left, as is done with other screen elements.

Attach a Caption to Assure Intended Meaning The ability to comprehend and learn icons can be greatly improved by attaching textual captions or labels to the symbols. The preferred location is directly beneath the icon, not within it, for international considerations to be discussed in Step 11. Labels should always be positionally related to icons in a consistent way.

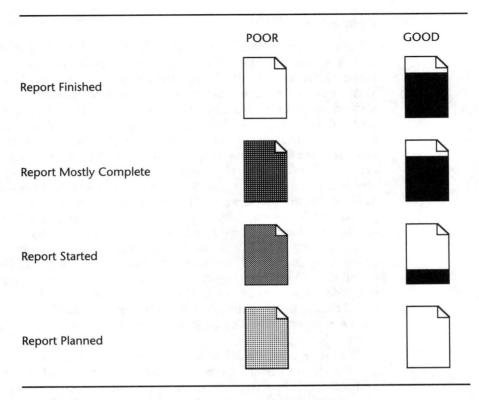

Figure 10.7   Expressing attributes in icon design.

Animation and Audition

Animation

- Use:
  - To provide feedback.
  - For visual interest.
- Make interruptible or independent of user's primary interaction.
- Do not use for decoration.
- Permit it to be turned off by the user.
- For fluid animation, present images at 16 or more frames per second.

Audition

- Consider auditory icons.

Animation

Recent research (Baecker, Small, & Mander, 1991) and others have explored the use of bringing to life on screens the icons representing objects and actions. An animated icon appears to move instead of maintaining a static position on the screen. Animation can take two forms, best described as static and dynamic. A *static* icon's appearance is unchanged over a period of time and changes only at the moment a system event occurs. An example would be the open door of a mailbox shutting when an electronic message is received. A *dynamic* icon's movement is independent of a system event, changing appearance to represent functions, processes, states, and state transitions. An example is an icon that begins movement to illustrate an action when a pointer is moved close to it.

Animation can be used to provide feedback and to create visual interest. Researchers caution, however, that there are many outstanding issues. Among them are that few animation creation rules exist, prototyping is difficult, a scheme for how they fit into a larger system is lacking, and whether they can be made useful for more complex and abstract concepts is not known. Morimoto, Kurokawa, & Nishimura, (1993) found that dynamic animation of the type in the example above did not increase comprehensibility of icon. Its only advantage was its entertainment value.

Some general guidelines, however, seem appropriate. First, do not prevent the user from interacting with the system while the animation is performed. Unless the animation is part of a process, it should be independent of what the user is doing, or interruptible. Second, be conservative in its use. Do not use simply for decoration. It can be very distracting or annoying. Finally, provide the user with the option of turning it on or off, as desired

Microsoft (1995) recommends that to achieve fluidity in movement, images should be presented at a speed of at least 16 frames per second. The reader interested in more information on animation is referred to Baecker & Small (1990).

Audition

Objects make sounds as they are touched, dragged, bumped against one another, opened, activated, and thrown away (Garver, 1993). Auditory icons are computer sounds replicating everyday sound-producing events. When a printer near one's desk begins printing, the sound of the printing mechanism is heard. This provides auditory feedback that a print operation one has just asked for has successfully started. An auditory icon would be the same sound being generated by the computer. Another example would be to convey information about an object's dimensions. If a file is large, it can sound large. If an object is dragged over a new surface, the new surface is heard. If an ongoing process starts running more quickly, it sounds quicker.

Garver suggests that sound can convey information about many events in computer systems, permitting people to listen to computers as we do the everyday world. It may be well-suited to providing information:

- About previous and possible interactions.
- Indicating ongoing processes and modes.
- Useful for navigation.
- To support collaboration.

Auditory icons are distinct from *earcons*, abstract synthetic tones used in structured combinations to create sound messages. Auditory icons may also be susceptible to the distracting influences that sounds can cause to listeners, especially others. Sound will be more fully discussed in Step 11. The reader in need of more information on auditory icons is referred to Garver.

The Design Process

- Define the icon's purpose and use.
- Collect, evaluate, and sketch ideas.
- Draw in black and white.
- Draw using an icon-editing utility or drawing package.
- Test for user:
  - Expectations.
  - Recognition.
  - Learning.
- Test for legibility.
- Register new icons in the system's registry.

Define Purpose To begin the design process, first define the icon's purpose and use. Have the design team brainstorm about possible ideas, considering real- world metaphors (Microsoft, 1995). Shneiderman (1987) suggests that simple metaphors, analogies, or models with a minimal set of concepts are the best places to start in developing icons.

Collect, Evaluate, and Sketch Ideas Start by designing on paper, not the computer (Fowler & Stanwick, 1995). Ask everyone to sketch their ideas. Do not worry about too much detail; exact pixel requirements are not necessary at this time.

Draw in Black and White Many icons will be displayed in monochrome. Color is an enhancing property; consider it as such.

Test for Expectation, Recognition, and Learning Choosing the objects and actions, and the icons to represent them, is not precise, and will not be easy. So, as in any screen design activity, adequate testing and possible refinement of developed images must be built into the design process. Icon recognition and learning should both be measured as part of the normal testing process.

Test for Legibility Verify the legibility and clarity of the icons in general. Also, verify the legibility of the icons on the screen backgrounds chosen. White or gray backgrounds may create difficulties (Microsoft, 1995). An icon mapped in color, then displayed on a monochrome screen, may not present itself satisfactorily. Be prepared to redraw it in black and white, if necessary.

Register New Icons in the System's Registry Create and maintain a registry of all system icons. Provide a detailed and distinctive description of all new icons.

SCREEN DESIGN GUIDELINES

In designing, or establishing, screen layout rules, adhere to the following presentation rules.

Screen Presentation

- Follow all relevant general guidelines for screen design.
- Limit the number of symbols to 12, if possible, and at most 20.
- Arrange icons:
  - In a meaningful way reflecting the organization of the real world.
  - To facilitate visual scanning.
  - Consistently.
- Place object and action icons in different groups.
- Permit arrangement of icons by the user.
- Permit the user to choose between iconic and text display of objects and actions.

General Guidelines Follow relevant general guidelines. All general guidelines for screen design should be followed. Icons are but one part of a larger picture.

Keep the Number of Symbols under 20 A person's ability to identify shapes is limited (see Figure 10.1). Brems and Whitten (1987), based upon a literature review, suggest using no more than eight or so functions that require icons at one time. If labels are attached to icons, however, the meaning of the icon is greatly clarified. Too many icons on a screen, however, will greatly increase screen clutter and create confusion. In general, fewer is better.

Arrange Icons in a Meaningful Way Organize icons in a way that reflects the real-world organization of the user. Place object icons and action icons in different groups.

Arrange Icons to Facilitate Visual Scanning Visual scanning studies, in a non-iconic world, universally find that a top-to-bottom scan of columnar-oriented information is fastest. Generalization of these findings to an icon screen may not necessarily be warranted if icons have attached labels. Columnar orientation icons (with labels below the icons) will separate the labels from one another by the icons themselves. The labels will be farther apart and fewer icons will fit in a column than in a horizontal or row orientation. A row orientation would seem to be more efficient in many cases, as adjacent icons will be in closer physical proximity. Until research evidence is established to the contrary, organizing icons either in a column or a row seems appropriate. In either case, a consistent straight eye movement must be maintained through the icons.

Place Object and Action Icons in Different Groups Conceptually similar items should always be arrayed together. Locating them will be easier.

Permit Arrangement of Icons by the User Allow the user to arrange the icons in a manner that is meaningful for the task. A default arrangement should be provided, however.

Permit Iconic or Text Display In some situations, and for some users, pure text labels may be more meaningful than icons. The option to display text only should always be provided.

STEP 11

Provide Effective Messages, Feedback, Guidance, and Language Translation

In addition to presenting menus and controls, screens are used for a variety of other purposes. Effective messages, feedback, and user guidance are also necessary elements of good design. If screens are to be used internationally, and must be translated into another language, additional considerations apply.

- Provide the proper words, sentences, messages, and text.
- Provide the proper feedback.
- Provide the necessary guidance and assistance.
- Translate properly for use internationally.

WORDS, MESSAGES, AND TEXT

System communications to the user should simply, clearly, and politely provide the information one must have to work effectively with a system. Words, messages, and text must adhere to established design principles.

Words

- Do not use jargon, words, or terms:
  - Unique to the computer profession.
  - With different meanings outside of the computer profession.
  - Made up to describe special functions or conditions.
- Use:

- Standard alphabetic characters to form words or captions.
- Short, familiar words.
- Complete words; avoid contractions, short forms, suffixes, and prefixes.
- Positive terms; avoid negative terms.
- Simple action words; avoid noun strings.
- The "more" dimension when comparing.
- Do not:
  - Stack words.
  - Hyphenate words.
  - Include punctuation for abbreviations, mnemonics, and acronyms.

Words displayed on screens should be easily comprehended, with minimum ambiguity and confusion. Some ways to achieve this are given below.

Do Not Use Jargon Jargon consists of several forms. It may be words or terms that are unique to the computer profession such as Filespec or Abend; words with different meaning outside of data processing such as Boot or Abort; or made-up words to describe special functions or actions such as Ungroup or Dearchive.

Use Standard Alphabetic Characters Standard alphabetic characters are most familiar to screen viewers. Never use restricted alphabetic sets. Symbols should be used only if they are familiar to all who are using the screen. Common symbols that may be considered as substitutes for alphabetic characters are # for number, % for percent, and $ for dollar. Again, all potential screen users must be familiar with a symbol if it is used as a substitute for alphabet characters.

Use Short, Familiar Words Shorter words tend to be used more often in everyday conversation, and so they are more familiar and easier to understand. The most important factor, however, is familiarization, not length. A longer but familiar word is better than a short, unfamiliar word.

Use Complete Words A complete word is better understood than a contraction or short form. Thus, "will not" is better than "won't," "not valid" is better than "invalid."

Words can also be more difficult to understand if they contain prefixes and suffixes, like "un-," or "-ness." Comprehension often involves decomposing such complex terms to establish their basic root meaning and then modifying the meaning to account for the various prefixes and suffixes (Wright, 1984). Structural complexity hinders comprehension.

Use Positive Terms It is generally easier to understand positive, affirmative information than the same information expressed in a negative way. Therefore, avoid the prefixes "ir-," "in-," "dis-," and "un-." Implicitly negative terms, such as "decrease," should be replaced with positive terms, such as "increase."

Use Simple Action Words Substitute noun strings with simple action words. Instead of saying, for example, PROJECT STATUS LISTING, say LIST PROJECT STATUS.

Use the "More" Dimension When Comparing When using comparative terms, the "more" dimension is easier to deal with. The opposite of the "more" is usually considered the "negative." So, use "longer" rather than "shorter," "bigger" rather than "smaller."

Do Not Stack Words Text is more readable if the entire statement is on one line.

Do Not Hyphenate Words Again, for better readability, never break a word between two lines. Hyphenation was created for ease in production, not ease in comprehension.

Abbreviations, Mnemonics, and Acronyms Should Not Include Punctuation This permits better readability and avoids confusion between the punctuation and other screen elements.

Messages

Messages are communications provided on the screen to the screen viewer. Several different types of messages exist and they may be displayed in different forms and places. A message should possess the proper tone and style and be consistent within itself and with other messages.

Screen messages fall into two broad categories: system and prompting. System messages are generated by the system to keep the user informed of the system's activities. They reflect the state of the system as it exists at that moment in time. Prompting messages are instructional messages provided on a screen.

System Messages System messages are of several kinds. The various platforms (e.g., IBM SAA CUA, Microsoft Windows) have developed standard dialog boxes, with standard components, for these different kinds. The components include a standard icon to assist fast recognition of message kind, and standard command buttons. Message dialog boxes from Microsoft Windows 95 are illustrated in Figures 11.1, 11.2, and 11.3.

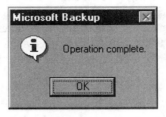

Figure 11.1   Informational message pop-up window from Microsoft Windows 95 with icon, text, and button.

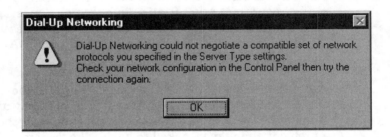

Figure 11.2   Warning pop-up window from Microsoft Windows 95 with icon, text, and button.

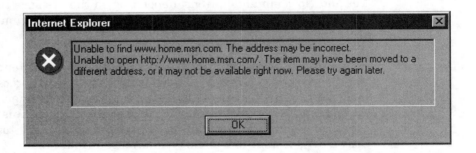

Figure 11.3   Critical pop-up window from Microsoft Windows 95 with icon, text, and button.

Status Messages A status message is used for providing information concerning the progress of a lengthy operation. It usually contains a progress indicator and a short message describing the kind of operation being performed. It typically only possesses a Cancel button to stop the operation being performed. Pause and Resume buttons may also be included, if desired.

Notification/Informational Messages Notification/informational messages provide information about the state of the system when it is not immediately obvious to the user. They may confirm that nonobvious processing is taking place or is completed. They may also be used to provide intermediate feedback when normal feedback is delayed. This kind of message is usually identified by an "I" icon to the left of the message. In Windows 95 the "I" is in a balloon. No user actions are normally necessary with these kinds of messages, although confirmation that the message has been seen can be requested. A notification/informational message window contains an OK pushbutton for confirmation that the message has been read. When OK is selected, the message is removed. SAA CUA recommends a Help button in this window.

Warning Messages Warning messages call attention to a situation that may be undesirable. They are usually identified by an "!" icon to the left of the message. The user must determine whether the situation is in fact a problem and may be asked to advise the system whether or not to proceed. A deletion request by a user is an action that commonly generates a warning message. When a user requests a deletion, a message asking for confirmation of the deletion is usually presented. A warning message can also be used for field edit error messages.

The Warning message window may contain Continue and Cancel, or Yes and No command buttons, depending on the message content. When an action is selected, the window is removed. A Help button is again also recommended.

Action/Critical Messages Action/critical messages call attention to conditions that require a user action before the system can proceed. An error message is usually presented as an action/critical message. Some inconsistency currently exists in the icons used to designate this kind of message. Some products use a "Do Not" symbol, others a "Stop" sign (IBM SAA CUA), or an X in a circle (Windows 95). Additionally, CUA provides the option of using a "?" icon if the user's attention to the problem may not be immediately needed (e.g., Printer is out of paper).

Action/critical messages require a user action to continue. Command buttons include a positive response button such as Retry. This assumes some action has been taken to correct the problem and directs the system to attempt to continue. This is usually the default. A negative response button such as Cancel is also included. This button requests the system to not take any further action, or to withdraw the request. A Help button is optional.

Question Messages Question messages are another kind of message sometimes presented. A question message asks a question and offers a choice of options for selection. It is designated by a "?" icon preceding the message text. This kind may be used when there is a question to be asked and the message does not appear to be suited to the above described types. Before using a question message keep the following in mind. SAA CUA uses the "?" icon for certain kinds of action/critical messages. Windows 95 no longer recommends the "?" icon because of possible confusion with help dialogs. If used, the question window might include OK, Cancel, and Help pushbuttons.

Prompting Messages The second category of messages, prompting messages, are instructional messages that tell the user how to work with, or complete, the screen displayed. They may be permanently affixed to a screen, or they may appear as the result of a help request. Prompting messages are of most benefit to the novice or casual system user. They will be more fully discussed in "Guidance and Assistance" to follow. Guidelines for their presentation were presented in Step 8.

Message Structure, Location, and Layout

Structure

- Use contrasting background and foreground colors for each type of message.

Location

- Use the message line for messages that must not interfere with screen information.
- Pop-up windows may be used for all kinds of messages, if available.
- Pop-up windows should always be used for action/critical messages.

Layout

- In a message area:
  - Left-justify the message.
  - Allow space for the longest message.
- In a pop-up window:
  - Include an icon to the left of the text for each message type, if feasible.
  - Center message text in window.

Messages should consist of mixed-case letters following normal sentence-style capitalization. They may be displayed either in the message line or in pop-up windows, with pop-up windows being recommended. All action/critical messages should be displayed in a window if one is available. Haubner (1992) compared locating messages in pop-up windows with messages presented in permanently displayed fixed locations, such as at the screen's bottom or top. He found pop-up windows were detected more often, and faster, than those permanently affixed on the screen.

If windows are used, and the creation of an icon is possible, also include with the message text a unique icon for each type of message, conforming to platform guidelines. This icon will immediately identify to the user the kind of message being presented.

Message Tone and Style

Sentences

- Sentences must be:
  - Brief, simple, and clear.
  - Directly and immediately usable.
  - Affirmative.
  - In an active voice.
  - Nonauthoritarian.
  - Nonthreatening.
  - Nonanthropomorphic.
  - Nonpatronizing.
  - In the temporal sequence of events.
  - Structured so that the main topic is near the beginning.
  - Cautious in the use of humor.
  - Nonpunishing.

Other Considerations

- Abbreviated, more concise versions of messages should be available.
- Something that must be remembered should be at the beginning of the text.

A message must minimize ambiguity and confusion, allowing easy, correct, and fast interpretation. It must also have the proper tone; threatening, rude, or impolite messages can evoke negative responses. The following guidelines will lead to easy, correct, and fast message interpretation and acceptance. Shneiderman (1982b), in restructuring messages along such guidelines, found higher success rates in problem resolution, lower error rates, and improved user satisfaction.

Brief, Simple Sentences A message that has to be explained does not communicate. It fails as a message. Brief, simple sentences are more readily understood than longer sentences containing multiple clauses. Break long sentences into two or more simple sentences if this can be done without changing the meaning.

Roemer & Chapanis (1982) created messages at three levels of reading ability (fifth, tenth, and fifteenth grade) and tested them on people of varying verbal abilities. The fifth-grade version was found to be best for all levels. People of high verbal ability did not perceive the fifth-grade version as insulting, as some had feared.

Directly and Immediately Usable Sentences Searching through reference material to translate a message is unacceptable, as are requirements for transposing, computing, interpolating, or mentally translating messages into other units.

Affirmative Statements Affirmative statements are easier to understand than negative statements. For example, "Complete entry before returning to menu" is easier to grasp than "Do not return to menu before completing entry."

Active Voice Active voice is usually easier to understand than passive voice. For example, "Send the message by depressing TRANSMIT" is more understandable than "The message is sent by depressing TRANSMIT."

Nonauthoritarian Imply the system is awaiting the user's direction, not that the system is directing the user. For example, phrase a message "Ready for next command", not "Enter next command."

Nonthreatening Negative tones or actions, or threats, are not very friendly. Since errors are often the result of a failure to understand, mistakes, or trial-and-error behavior, the user may feel confused, inadequate, or anxious. Blaming the user for problems can heighten anxiety, making error correction more difficult and increasing the chance of more errors. Therefore, harsh words like "illegal," "bad," or "fatal" should be avoided.

It is also suggested to avoid the word "error" in messages when it implies a user error (Paradies, 1991). "Error" tends to focus the attention on the person involved rather than on the problem. For example, instead of saying "Error—Numbers are illegal," say, "Months must be entered by name." Since the computer does not have an ego to be bruised, an excellent design approach would be to have it assume the blame for all miscommunications.

Nonanthropomorphic Having the computer "talk" like a person should be avoided for several reasons. An attribution of knowledge or intelligence will, first, imply a much higher level of computer "knowledge" than actually exists, creating shattered user expectations. Second, this attribute eliminates the distinction that actually exists between people and computers. People "control" computers; they "respect the desires" of other human beings. Third, many people express anxiety about using computers by saying things like "they make you feel dumb." The feeling of interacting with another person who is evaluating your proficiency can heighten this anxiety. There is, however, some research evidence that a nonanthropomorphic approach is best, being seen as more honest, preferred, and easier to use.

So, do not give a human personality to a machine. Imply that the system is awaiting the user's direction, not vice versa. Say, for example, "What do you need?" not "How can I help you?"

Nonpatronizing Patronizing messages can be embarrassing. "Very good; you did it right" may thrill a fourth-grader, but would be somewhat less than thrilling to an adult. Being told "You forgot again" once may be acceptable, but being told three or four times in one minute is another story. A commonly available video golf game, after a particularly bad hole, returns with the suggestion to "Try another sport." A golf professional who played this game took great offense to this advice and walked away. A person may disagree with patronizing conclusions, so why risk the offense?

Chronological Word Order If a sentence describes a temporal sequence of events, the order of words should correspond to this sequence. A prompt should say, "Complete address and page forward" rather than "Page forward after completing address.".

Messages that begin with a strange code number do not meet the user's needs. A code number, if needed at all, is only necessary after reading the message and should therefore be placed in parentheses at the end of the message.

Avoiding Humor and Punishment Until an optimal computer personality is designed, messages should remain factual and informative, and should not attempt humor or punishment. Humor is a transitory and changeable thing. What is funny today may not be funny tomorrow, and what is funny to some may not be to others. Punishment is not a desirable way to force a change in behavior, especially among adults.

Displaying Abbreviated Versions of Messages People are impatient with noninformative or redundant computer messages. A problem, however, is that the degree of computer-to-person message redundancy depends on the person's experience with the system. And it may vary with different parts of a system. So the availability of abbreviated or detailed messages allows tailoring of the system to the needs of each user. During system training and early implementation stages, detailed versions can be used. Individuals can switch to abbreviated versions as their familiarity increases, but they should always be able to receive detailed messages.

Placing Information that Must Be Remembered at the Beginning of Text One can remember something longer if it appears at the beginning of a message. Items in the middle of a message are hardest to remember.

Some Words to Forget Words should be meaningful and common to all, not just to the designers. Language perceived as "computerese" may confuse or intimidate some users. The vocabulary of the designer often finds its way into messages or system documentation. While not always bad, some words have particularly harsh or vague meanings to many users. These words, which are summarized in Table 11.1, should be avoided whenever possible. Suggested alternative words are presented.

Table 11.1   Some Words to Forget

Avoid	Use
Abend	End, Cancel, Stop
Abort	End, Cancel, Stop
Access	Get, Ready, Display
Available	Ready
Boot	Start, Run
Execute	Complete
Hit	Press, Depress
Implement	Do, Use, Put Into
Invalid	Not Correct, Not Good, Not Valid
Key	Type, Enter
Kill	End, Cancel
Output	Report, List, Display
Return Key	Enter, Transmit
Terminate	End, Exit

Text

Presentation

- Include no more than 40–60 characters on each line.
  - A double column of 30–35 characters separated by 5 spaces is also acceptable.
- Do not right-justify.
- Use headings to introduce a new topic.
- Separate paragraphs by at least one blank line.
- Start a fresh topic on a new page.
- Emphasize important things by:
  - Positioning.
  - Boxes.
  - Bold typefaces.
  - Indented margins.
- Use lists to present facts.
- Use paging (not scrolling).
- Provide a screen design philosophy consistent with other parts of the system.

The typical screen is a little too wide for comfortable reading of text. It is difficult for the eye to keep its place as it moves from the end of one line to the beginning of the next line. Rehe (1974) recommends that a text line should contain no more than 40–60 characters. Lichty (1989) suggests the line width should be even less, 1.5 lower-case alphabets or 39 characters. For greater screen efficiency, it may be desirable to consider two columns of text, each about 30–35 characters wide.

Rehe also found that non-right-justified (or ragged-right edge) text lines are just as legible as justified text lines. Large spaces in right-justified text interrupt eye movement and impede reading. Another study found that the reading speed of right-justified text was eight to ten percent slower than non-right-justified text (Trollip & Sales, 1986). Lichty states that non-right-justified text has advantages in hyphenation not being required and the visual interest it generates. It is best for very narrow columns of text. Full left and right justification, Lichty says, is familiar, predictable, and orderly. It is best for long works that require continuous reading and concentration, such as long text, newspapers, and novels.

Headings to introduce new topics provide breaks or pause points for the reader. They provide obvious closure points. Starting new topics on new pages reinforces the needed breaks. Separating paragraphs by a blank line will result in more cohesive groupings and alleviate the impression of a dense screen.

Emphasize important points by placing them in unusual places, drawing boxes around them, using bold typefaces, or providing indented left and right margins. In addition to their emphasizing capabilities, they make the screen more interesting.

Use lists to present facts. Lists are convenient, simple, and uncluttered. Designate items in a list with a "bullet," a lower-case letter *o*, or a dash (—).

Paging through screens, rather than scrolling, has been found to yield better performance and to be preferred by novice system users (Schwarz, Beldier, & Pastoor, 1983). Expert users were found to perform satisfactorily with either paging or scrolling. A severe disadvantage of scrolling for novices is loss of orientation. While experts can handle scrolling, the best choice if all users are considered is paging.

If scrolling is going to be used, the preferred approach is *telescoping*, in which the window moves around the data. This method is more natural and causes fewer errors than the *microscope* approach, in which the data appears to move under a fixed viewing window (Bury et al., 1982).

Writing Text

- Use short sentences composed of familiar, personal words.
  - Cut the excess words.
  - Try to keep the number of words in a sentence under 30.
- Cut the number of sentences.
- Keep the paragraphs short.
- Use the active writing style.
- Use the personal writing style, if appropriate.
- Write as you talk.
- Use subjective opinion.
- Use specific examples.
- Read it out loud.

Simple words and short sentences are the cornerstone of good writing. Keeping sentences under 30 words can be achieved. Long sentences often result from trying to express more than one idea in the sentence. They also result from trying to give a list of items and from the use of unnecessary words. Use separate sentences for separate ideas. Put multiple items in a list format, and delete all unnecessary words. Short paragraphs provide breaking points and make the page look less threatening.

The active writing style is easier to read and understand. It almost always uses less words and leaves no unanswered questions (contrast the passive "The customer name should be typed" with the active "Type the customer name").

The personal style, the use of "you" and "I" ("Now you must press the

Enter key"), keeps the writing active, makes writing directly relevant to the reader, and is more interesting. Materials read by a wide variety of people for informational purposes only should not use the personal style, however.

Write in the way you would say something to the reader. Also, use subjective opinion ("This screen is not used very often") to reinforce the users' understanding of what they are reading. It does not tell anything specific, but reinforces facts already read or about to be read. Do not overuse subjective opinion and make sure it is correct. Overuse makes facts harder to find, and an incorrect opinion casts suspicion on all the facts being presented.

The best way to explain a general rule is to show how it applies through examples. Examples should be short, relevant, and easy for the reader to relate to. They should also be visually different from the main text, either through indentation, boxing, or some other technique.

Finally, read what you have written out loud to yourself. If it sounds wordy, stilted, or difficult, it will to the reader, too. Rewrite it.

Conventions

- Establish conventions for referring to:
  - Individual keyboard keys.
  - Keys to be pressed at the same time.
  - Field captions.
  - Names supplied by users or defined by the system.
  - Commands and actions.

In messages and text it is often necessary to refer to keyboard keys, field captions, file names, commands, or actions. These components should be described in the same manner whenever referenced. Keyboard keys should always be referenced as they are inscribed on the keyboard. (They usually appear in a mixed-case text format.) A useful convention for referring to keys that should be pressed at the same time is a plus (+) sign between the key descriptions (Alt+F10). Names may be enclosed in quotes ("Pending").

Sequence Control Guidance

- Consider providing a guidance message telling how to continue at points in the dialogue where:
  - A decision must be made.

- A response needs to be made to continue.
- Consider indicating what control options exist at points in the dialogue where several alternatives may be available.
- Permit these prompts to be turned on or off by the user.

Consider providing prompts telling the user how to continue when a decision, and response, must be made to continue. For example, it might be indicated that:

Information is current through August 26, 1996.

Press Enter to continue.

Where several control options exist, consider providing a prompt such as:

Press S to Save, D to Delete, or P to Print.

Type C to create a new file, or E to edit a new file: _

For experienced users, these kinds of prompts can become noise. Allow users to turn them on or off as needed.

PROVIDING THE PROPER FEEDBACK

All user actions must be reacted to in some way. Feedback, as has been noted, shapes human performance. Without it, we cannot learn. To be effective, feedback to the user for an action must occur within certain time limits. Excessive delays can be annoying, interrupt concentration, cause the user concern, and impair productivity as one's memory limitations begin to be tested.

Response Time

- System responsiveness should match the speed and flow of human thought processes.
  - If continuity of thinking is required and information must be remembered throughout several responses, response time should be less than two seconds.
  - If human task closures exist, high levels of concentration are not necessary and moderate short-term memory requirements are imposed; response times of two to four seconds are acceptable.

- If major task closures exist, minimal short-term memory requirements are imposed; responses within 4 to 15 seconds are acceptable.
- When the user is free to do other things and return when convenient, response time can be greater than 15 seconds.
• Constant delays are preferable to variable delays.

What the ideal system response time is has been the subject of numerous studies. Unfortunately, there still does not exist definitive time or times that are acceptable under all conditions. What is clear is that dissatisfaction with response time is dependent on user expectations. It is also clear that expectations can vary, depending on the task as well as the situation. The ideal condition is one in which a person perceives no delays. A response time is too long when one notices that the system is taking too long. The following paragraphs summarize some study conclusions and some tentative findings.

The Optimum Response Time Is Dependent upon the Task There is an optimum work pace that depends on the task being performed. Longer or shorter response times than the optimum lead to more errors. In general, response times should be geared to the user's short-term memory load and to how he or she has grouped the activities being performed. Intense short-term memory loads necessitate short response times. While completing chunks of work at task closures, users can withstand longer response delays.

The human *now*, or psychological present, is two to three seconds. This is why continuity of thinking requires a response time within this limit. Research indicates that for creative tasks, response times in the range of four-tenths to nine-tenths of a second can yield dramatic increases in productivity, even greater in proportion to the increase in response time. The probable reason is the elimination of restrictions caused by short-term memory limitations.

As the response-time interval increases beyond 10 to 15 seconds, continuity of thought becomes increasingly difficult to maintain. It has been suggested that this happens because the sequence of actions stored in short-term memory beyond that time is badly disrupted and must be reloaded.

The response time guidelines above, then, relate to the general tasks being performed. Their applicability to every situation is not guaranteed.

Satisfaction with Response Time Is a Function of Expectations Expectations are based, in part, on past experiences. These experiences may be derived from working with a computer, or from the world in general, and they vary enormously across individuals and tasks.

Dissatisfaction with Response Time Is a Function of One's Uncertainty about Delay The degree of frustration with delay may depend on such psychological factors as a person's uncertainty concerning how long the delay will be, the extent to which the actual delay contradicts those expectations, and what the person thinks is causing the delay. Such uncertainty concerning how long a wait there will be for a computer's response may in some cases be a greater source of frustration than the delay itself.

People Will Change Work Habits to Conform to Response Time As response time increases, so does think time. People also work more carefully with longer response times. In some cases, more errors have been found with very short response times. This may not necessarily be bad if the errors are the result of trial-and-error learning that is enhanced by very fast response times.

Constant Delays Are Preferable to Variable Delays It is the variability of delays, not their length, that most frequently distresses people. From a consistency standpoint, a good rule of thumb is that response-time deviations should never exceed half the mean response time. For example, if the mean response time is four seconds, a two-second deviation is permissible. Variations should range from three to five seconds. Variation should never exceed 20 percent, however, because lower response time variability has been found to yield better performance, but small variations may be tolerated.

More Experienced People Prefer Shorter Response Times People work faster as they gain experience, a fact that leads Shneiderman (1987) to conclude that it may be useful to let people set their own pace of interaction. He also suggests that in the absence of cost or technical feasibility constraints, people will eventually force response time to well under one second.

Very Fast or Slow Response Times Can Lead to Symptoms of Stress There is a point at which a person can be overwhelmed by information presented more quickly than it can be comprehended. There is also some evidence indicating that when a system responds too quickly, there is subconscious pressure on users to respond quickly also, possibly threatening their overall comfort, increasing their blood pressure, or causing them to exhibit other signs of anxious behavior. Symptoms of job burnout have been reported after substantial reductions in response time.

Slow and variable response times have also been shown to lead to a significant build-up of mood disturbances and somatic discomfort over time, culminating in symptoms of work stress, including frustration, impatience, and irritation.

Dealing with Time Delays

General

- If an operation takes five seconds or less to complete, present a "busy" signal until the operation is complete.
  - For example, display an hourglass pointer.
- If an operation takes longer than five seconds to complete, display a progress indicator or message in addition to an hourglass pointer.
- If an operation is very time-consuming:
  - Consider breaking the operation into subtasks and providing progress indicators for each subtask.
  - Consider using a separate base window.
  - Users can close the window to an icon and start a new activity while waiting.
- When an operation not visible to the user is completed, present an acknowledgment message that it is completed.

Progress Indicators

- Provide a long rectangular bar that is initially empty but filled as the operation proceeds.
  - Dynamically fill the bar.
  - Fill with a color or shade of gray.
  - Fill from left to right or bottom to top.

Percent Complete Messages

- Provide a message that indicates the percent of the operation that is complete.
- Useful if a progress indicator takes too long to update.

Elapsed Time Messages

- Provide a message that shows the amount of elapsed time the operation is consuming.
- Useful if:
  - the length of the operation is not known in advance.
  - a particular part of the operation will take an unusually long time to complete.

The user should always be kept informed of a system's processing status through a message or graphics. A "Please wait . . ." message can be presented to indicate more complex processing has been delayed or is continuing. An indication of the percentage of processing that has been accomplished can be given through a message ("22 of 27 transactions have been processed"), or graphics such as an hourglass or rectangular processing bar, as illustrated in Figure 11.4. Processing being completed that is not visible to the user should also always be acknowledged ("Search complete, Jones not found").

Blinking for Attention

- Attract attention by flashing when an application is inactive but must display a message to the user.
  - If a window, flash the title bar.
  - If minimized, flash its icon.
- To provide an additional message indication, also provide an auditory signal (one or two beeps).
  - Very useful if:
  - The window or icon is hidden.
  - The user's attention is frequently directed away from the screen.
- When the application is activated, display the message.
- Do not display the message until requested by the user.
  - Preserves the user's control over the work environment.
  - Ensures that the message is not accidentally closed through an inadvertent key press.

A person's attention may be quickly captured by flashing an element on the screen. It is very useful if an application is inactive and a message exists for the user to read. Blinking is annoying to many people so it should not be overused on the screen.

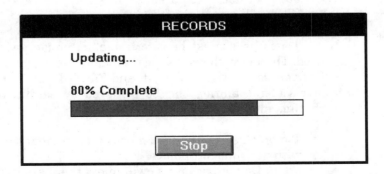

Figure 11.4   Processing progress indicator.

Use of Sound

- Always use in conjunction with a visual indication.
- Use no more than six different tones.
  - Assure that people can discriminate among them.
- Do not use:
  - Jingles or tunes.
  - Loud signals.
- Use consistently.
  - Provide unique but similar tones for similar situations.
- Provide signal frequencies between 500 and 1,000 Hz.
- Allow the user to adjust the volume or turn the sound off altogether.
- Test the sounds with users over extended trial periods.
- Use sparingly because sounds:
  - Are annoying to many people, including users and nonusers in the vicinity.
  - Can easily be overused, increasing the possibility that they will be ignored.
  - Are not reliable because:
    - Some people are hard of hearing.
    - If they are not heard, they leave no permanent record of having occurred.
    - They can be turned off by the user.

Sounds, sometimes called earcons, are useful for alerting the user:

- To minor and obvious mistakes.
- When something unexpected happens.
- Where visual attention is directed away from the screen and immediate attention is required.
- When a long process is finished.

Tones used must be discriminable, nonannoying, and consistently used. Therefore, they must be thoroughly tested for discrimination and effectiveness. Brewster, Wright, and Edwards (1993) have found that high levels of recognition can be achieved by careful use of earcon pitch, rhythm, and timbre. They recommend:

- Timbre: Use synthesized musical instrument timbres, where possible with multiple harmonics.
- Pitch: Do not use on its own unless there are very big differences between those used.

- Register: If used alone to differentiate earcons; otherwise the same, then large differences of three or more octaves, should be used.
- Rhythm: Make rhythms as different as possible. Including a different number of notes in each rhythm is very effective.
- Intensity: 10dB to 20dB above threshold. Since sound level will be under control of the user, it should be kept in a close range.
- Combinations: Leave a delay of .01 second between successively played earcons.

Since sounds can be annoying to some people, they should be capable of being turned down or off by the user. Playing jingles or tunes, or loud sounds focuses attention on the sound itself, which is distracting. Loud sounds can also be irritating, especially to those with sensitive hearing.

Never consider sounds reliable because they can be turned off, they leave no permanent record of their existence, and not all users will be able to hear all tones because of hearing defects. Sounds should always be used in conjunction with a visual indication of some kind.

GUIDANCE AND ASSISTANCE

To aid user learning and avoid frustration, it is important to provide thorough and timely guidance and assistance. We'll begin by first looking at preventing errors. Then we'll look at managing problems, providing guidance and assistance, providing prompting, and presenting help.

Preventing Errors

In spite of our high design goals, people will make mistakes using our system. When they occur, they must be properly managed. The magnitude of errors in computer systems is astounding. Shneiderman (1987) describes studies reporting error rates in commands, tasks, or transactions as high as 46 percent. In addition to stranding the user and wasting time, mistakes interrupt planning and cause deep frustrations.

Errors can be classified as slips or mistakes. A *slip* is automatic behavior gone awry. One's hands navigate the keyboard improperly and the wrong key is accidentally pressed. The wrong menu bar item is chosen because of inattentiveness. An inference error is made due to carelessness. Slips are usually easily detected and corrected by a person because they are often readily noticeable. Slips can also be reduced through proper application of human factors in design (e.g., by providing adequate separation between elements to be selected).

A *mistake* results from forming a wrong model or goal and then acting on it. A mistake may not be easily detected because the action may be proper for the perceived goal. Anticipating them is also more difficult. Mistakes can be reduced, however, by eliminating ambiguity from design. They can be detected by performing testing and watching for nonsensical (to the designer) requests and actions.

Some experts have argued that there are no errors as such; they are simply iterations toward a goal. There is much truth to that statement. It is also often said that "to err is human." The corollary to that statement, at least in computer systems, might be, ". . . to forgive, good design." Whatever we call them, errors will occur. People should be able to correct them as soon as they are detected, as simply and easily as they are made.

Problem Management

Prevention

- Disable non-applicable choices.
- Use selection instead of entry controls.
- Use aided entry.
- Accept common misspellings, whenever possible.
- Before an action is performed:
  - Permit it to be reviewed.
  - Permit it to be changed or undone.
- Provide a common action mechanism.
- Force confirmation of destructive actions.
  - Let expert users disable.

Detection

- For conversational dialogs, validate as close to point of entry as possible.
  - At character level.
  - At control level.
  - At transaction completed or window closed.
- For high speed, head down data entry.
  - At transaction completed or window closed.
- Leave window open.
- Maintain the item in error on the screen.
- Visually highlight the item in error.
- Display an error message in a window.
  - Do not obscure item in error.
- Handle as gracefully as possible.
  - The greater the error, the more dramatic the warning.
- Use auditory signals conservatively.

Correction

- At window level validation, use modeless dialog box to display an error list.
  - Highlight first error in the list.
  - Place cursor at first control with error.
  - Permit fixing one error and continuing to next error.
- Always give a person something to do when an error occurs.
  - Something to enter/save/reverse.
  - HELP button.
  - Someone to call.
- Provide a constructive correction message saying:
  - What problem was detected.
  - Which items are in error.
  - What corrective action is necessary.
- Initiate a clarification dialog if necessary.

Prevention Errors can be reduced in a number of ways. First, disable all choices that are not applicable at any one moment. Make improper alternatives impossible to select or activate. Next, after considering the task and user, then, if practical, design screens using selection instead of entry controls. Selection error rates tend to be lower than entry error rates. Use aided entry if at all possible. The computer has been found to be a better speller than most people. When entry is performed, human misspellings of commands and requests should be accepted by the system. Person-to-person communication does not require perfection. Person-to-computer communication should impose no more rigor. Use of shift keys should also be discouraged, since they are such a large cause of keying errors. Actions performed should also be reviewable and changeable by the person who made them. Human memory is poor and keying or selection errors will occasionally occur.

A common send mechanism should be provided to transmit an action to the system. Two or more keys to accomplish the same purpose, especially if their use is mandated by different conditions, can be confusing and more prone to errors. Finally, if an action causes a nonreversible change, and the change is critical, the user should be requested to confirm the change. A separate key should be used for this purpose, not the send key. Let expert users disable the confirmation request, if the action is recoverable.

Detection Errors should be detected quickly, but without disrupting a person's thought patterns and actions if this can be avoided. Generally, the longer the wait before editing is performed, the longer the delay to accomplish the editing. So, validate according to how important accuracy is to the user, and the characteristics of the task being performed. It is also preferable to wait for a closure point in the dialog. For conversational dialogs, accuracy is usually more important than speed, actions are slower paced, and more closure points usually exist. In these situations, validate as close to the point of input as possible: at the character level or at the control level, and when the transaction is completed or the window closed. High-speed, head-down data entry is generally fast-paced. Constant interruptions for errors can be a great speed detriment. In this situation, validate when the transaction is completed or the window closed. This is usually the only task closure point.

All errors should be maintained on the screen and identified to the user through a highlighting display technique (for example, high intensity or contrasting color). Display an error message in a dialog box and position it on the screen so it does not obscure the item in error. Handle all errors as gracefully as possible. Doing something wrong can be frustrating to a person. For minor problems, provide less intrusive warnings. The greater the error, the more dramatic may be the warning.

Be cautious in using auditory signals to notify of an error. Many people, especially those with status or position, do not want their inefficiencies advertised, especially to peers and subordinates.

Correction At the window level of validation, use a modeless dialog box to display a list of errors. Highlight the first error in the list and place the cursor at the first control with error. Permit fixing one error and continuing on to the next error. If multiple errors occur, and it is impossible to display messages about all of them at one time, provide an indication that there are additional messages. Say, for example, "+ 2 other problems." Also, provide with a distinct visual difference the same error message displayed more than once, if the first attempt to correct failed. Always give a person something to do when an error occurs, something to enter, save, or reverse, or someone to call. Also provide a Help button. The Help button *must* be helpful, though.

Explicit and constructive error messages should be provided. These messages should describe what error occurred, and how it should be corrected. Corrective actions will be clearer if phrased with words like "must be" or "must have." Shneiderman (1982), in restructuring messages following guidelines such as this, and others previously described, found improved success rates in fixing errors, lower error rates, and improved user satisfaction.

All error ambiguities should be resolved by having the system query the user. Errors should be corrected with minimal typing. Another important error control measure is to have the system identify and store errors. This will allow tracking of common errors so that appropriate prevention programs can be implemented.

Providing Guidance and Assistance

New users must go through a learning process that involves developing a conceptual or mental model to explain the system's behavior and the task being performed. Guidance in the form of the system's hard copy, online documentation, computer-based training, prompting messages, and system messages serve as cognitive development tools to aid this process. So does assistance provided by another form of online documentation, the Help function. Broadly speaking, online documentation is every communication provided online to help people to do their work effectively.

While it is desirable that the human-computer interface be so "self-evident" and "intelligent" that people never experience difficulties, this goal will not be achieved in the foreseeable future. So a great deal of emphasis should be placed on creating good guidance and assistance, and managing the trouble that does occur. Indeed one survey found that documentation was the second most important factor influencing the decision to purchase something. (Quality was first.)

Technical information, unlike works of fiction, is seldom read for pleasure. People turn to it only when a question has to be answered. Failure to provide the guidance and assistance needed in learning, answering questions, and problem solving makes it very difficult for the user to recover from trouble on his or her own and to avoid future trouble by learning from his or her mistakes. The result is most often more errors and great frustration.

Problems with Documentation Wright (1991) feels that poor manuals are usually not the result of stupid and careless writing. Most writers, professional or not, try to communicate their ideas as well as they can. Poor products, however, suggest that being a native speaker of the language is not a sufficient qualification to ensure communicative success. Rather, four other factors contribute to bad design.

First are organizational factors including management decisions concerning who does the writing: product developers or specialist technical authors. Product developers, by their nature, are more interested in the technical aspects and seldom have time to focus on writing. Another organizational factor is the frequency and nature of the contact between writers and developers. Successful writing requires that frequent contact be maintained between writers and developers. If not, modifications may go undocumented, and functionality may occur that is difficult to explain.

Second is the time scale allocated for the writing process. Successful writing also involves detailed early planning, drafting, testing, and considerable revising. Without adequate time being made available for the writing process, the planning, testing, and revising processes are limited, thereby increasing the potential for a mismatch between the product and its documentation.

Third, there is not yet a clear theoretical rationale about what content should be included in documentation and how this information should be presented. Until this is developed, one cannot be sure that the documentation being developed is the most effective that it can be.

Finally, Wright concludes, there are the resources. Adequate resources are needed to include people with different skills in the documentation development process. Required are people good at visual layout, writing, and test and evaluation. Rarely does the same person possess more than one of these skills. Without the proper expertise, documentation will also suffer.

Another problem with documentation is created by the need for translation in our shrinking world. The following is found in a current user guide: "The color deviation from the original is thus resulted." (KYE Systems, 1995) The product manufacturer, even today, is guilty of Wright's sins number two and four above. International considerations will be presented in detail at the end of this chapter.

How Readers Interact with Documentation   Wright (1981, 1988) has suggested that there are three broad stages through which a reader interacts with documentation: finding information that is relevant, understanding what the documentation says, and applying that understanding to the current task in order to solve the problem that prompted him to turn to the documentation.

Finding information is enhanced through use of contents pages and index lists. It is also enhanced if browsing is made easy through clearly visible page headings and subheadings. Pictures and symbols can also be used to draw the reader's attention to particular kinds of information.

Understanding information is achieved through a variety of factors. Included are following good writing principles. Understanding can also be maximized through testing and revision of materials as necessary.

Prompting

- Provide user-selectable prompting.

Prompting is instructional information placed *within the body* of a screen. It may take the form of messages or other advice, such as the values to be keyed into a field. Prompting is provided to assist a person in providing what is necessary to complete a screen.

Inexperienced users find prompting a valuable aid in learning a system. Experienced users, however, often find prompting undesirable. It slows them down, then adds "noise" to the screen, and may reduce the amount of working information that can be displayed at one time.

Since prompting can easily create screen noise, be cautious in placing it on a screen. Use it only if all screen usage will be casual or infrequent. If people with a wide range of experience, will be using a screen, it should be selectable, capable of being turned on or off as needed. As an alternative, two separate sets of screens could be made available, one with prompts, the other without. Guidelines for inscribing prompting on a screen were covered in Step 8. Another form of prompting, status bar messages, will be covered in Help to follow.

Help Facility

The most common form of online documentation is the help system. The overall objective of a Help facility is to assist people in remembering what to do. Its benefits include improving the usability of a system, providing insurance against design flaws that may develop, and accommodating user differences that may exist (novice vs. expert). Typical methods of invoking help include: through a typed command, a Help key or button, or selecting a Help option from a multiple-item menu. Helps may also automatically appear on the screen.

Some studies have found a help system can aid performance (Borenstein, 1985; Magers, 1983). Others have concluded that a help function can impair performance if it is not task-oriented, and if it makes the interface more complex (Neerincx & de Greef, 1993). One potential danger of the Help facility, as Barnard, Hammond, Maclean, & Morton (1982) found, is that a person's recall of command operations is related to frequency of Help facility access; fewer Help requests were associated with better command recall. The researchers speculate that the availability of Help may become a crutch and lead to less effective retention. People may implement a passive cognitive strategy. A Help facility may influence performance in systematic and subtle ways.

The specific design characteristics that enhance an online help are still not fully understood (Elkerton, 1988; Elkerton & Palmiter, 1991). Elkerton & Palmiter (1991) identify three broad areas of help that must be addressed in creating a help: its content, its presentation, and its access mechanisms. Of these, presentation and access are best understood. Knowledge about help content, however, is still limited.

Elkerton and Palmiter propose that the content (and structure) of an effective online help can be specified using the GOMS model (Card,

Moran, & Newell, 1983). Using GOMS, information is provided to the user on GOALS for meaningful tasks, on OPERATORS for actions required to be performed, on METHODS for accomplishing the goals, and where multiple interface methods exist, and on SELECTION RULES for choosing a specific method. Gugerty, Halgren, Gosbee, & Rudisill (1991) found this structure useful in remembering medical procedures. Elkerton (1988) presents a set of suggested principles for online assistance (which he calls Online Aiding). These principles are reproduced in Table 11.2.

Next, we'll look at some general guidelines for help. Then, we'll address some specific considerations for contextual help, task-oriented help, and reference help.

Kind

- Collect data to determine what helps are needed.

Training

- Inform users of availability and purpose of help.

Availability

- Provide availability throughout the dialogue.
- If no help is available for a specific situation, inform the user as such and provide directions to where relevant help may exist.

Structure

- Make as specific as possible.
- Provide a hierarchical framework.
  - Brief operational definitions and input rules.
  - Summary explanations in text.
  - Typical task-oriented examples.

Interaction

- Provide easy accessibility.
- Leave the Help displayed until:
  - The user exits.
  - The action eliminating the need for help is performed.
- Provide instructions for exiting.
- Return to original position in dialogue when help is completed.

Table 11.2   Suggested Design Principles for Providing Online Advice Based on the GOMS Model

Use GOALS in online aiding to do the following:

1. Describe what can be done in task-oriented terms (interface actions and objects) for improved initial skill learning.

2. Provide an adjustable level of detail on interface procedures for accommodating the information needs of a wide range of users.

3. Provide procedurally incomplete advice so that users can actively learn for improved long-term performance and understanding with the interface.

4. Provide feedback to users that may help in reminding them of appropriate procedures to use, particularly when recovering from errors.

5. Develop modular assistance and instructional dialogues that can be used to describe similar and dissimilar procedural elements of the interface.

Use OPERATORS in online aiding to do the following:

1. Describe simple actions, such as pressing specific keys or finding specific objects on the display, that are common to many interface procedures to assist the user in current task performance.

2. Provide detailed knowledge of interface procedures that inexperienced users can actively learn and that more skilled users can combine with other procedural knowledge to improve long-term performance and understanding of the interface.

3. Monitor user actions to provide context-sensitive help or to diagnose user problems actively.

Use METHODS in online aiding to do the following:

1. Present step-by-step interface procedures to assist the user with specific problems.

2. Improve user understanding and acceptance of on-line advice.

3. Decrease the cognitive load of users who are learning a new interface task by providing an explicit procedure for users to follow.

4. Provide procedural demonstrations of interface procedures so that users can quickly learn simple operations.

5. Map sequences of users' actions to a reduced set of interface goals to help provide context-sensitive advice to users.

Use SELECTION RULES in online aiding to do the following:

1. Help users select between multiple interface methods.

2. Provide users with an understanding of representative tasks to increase their knowledge of when to apply specific interface skills.

From Elkerton (1988)

Location

- Minimize obscuring screen content.
- If in a window, position priorities are: right, left, above, and below.

Content

- Minimize the help's length.
- Develop modular dialogues that can be used to describe similar and dissimilar procedural elements of the interface.
- Provide step-by-step interface procedures to assist the user with specific problems.
- Provide procedural demonstrations of interface procedures to aid quick learning of simple operations.
- Provide information to help users select between multiple interface methods.
- Provide users with an understanding of representative tasks to increase their knowledge of when to apply specific skills.

Style

- Provide easy browsing and a distinctive format.
  - Contents screens and indexes.
  - Screen headings and subheadings.
  - Location indicators.
  - Descriptive words in the margin.
  - Visual differentiation of screen components.
  - Emphasized critical information.
- Use concise, familiar, action-oriented wording.
- Refer to other materials, when necessary.

Consistency

- Provide a design philosophy consistent with other parts of the system.

Title

- Place the word "Help" in all Help screen titles.

Kind Usability problems that exist should be systematically identified through testing and evaluation. Monitoring user actions can be a useful tool in identifying user problems. Online help can then be developed to address these problems.

Training Inform users of the availability and purpose of helps. Never assume that it will be obvious.

Availability Make help available at all points in the dialogue. It is especially critical that help be available consistently in all similar situations. For example, if one particular system menu has help, assure all menus provide a help. If no help is available for a specific situation, inform the user as such and provide directions to where relevant help may exist, including hard-copy materials.

Structure The help response should be as specific as possible, tailored to the task and the user's current position. When accessed, the Help facility should be aware of the kind of difficulties a person is having and respond with relevant information. Only the information necessary to solve the immediate problem or to answer the immediate question should be presented. If the Help facility is unsure of the request, it should work with the user through prompts and questions to resolve the problem.

A Help facility should be multilevel, proceeding from very general to successively more detailed and specific explanations to accommodate a wide range of users. The first level should provide brief definitions and rules, simple reminders, and memory joggers sufficient for skilled users. The second level should incorporate more detailed explanations in a textual format. The final, and deepest, level should provide guidance in the form of task-oriented examples.

Interaction A Help facility should be retrievable simply, quickly, and consistently by either a key action, selection, or command. Leave the Help displayed until the user explicitly exits the Help, or performs the action eliminating the need for help. Instructions for exiting the Help should always be provided. These may take the form of displayed pushbuttons, function keys, or something similar.

Help should not disrupt processing. Easy return to the point of the problem should be permitted. Ideally, the problem or work should be retained on the screen when Help is accessed, but this will not always be possible unless the system provides a windowing capability.

Location When a Help is displayed, minimize relevant obscuring screen content. If Help is displayed within a window, position priorities are right, left, above, and below.

Content Minimize the Help's length, whenever possible. Carroll, Smith-Kerker, Ford, & Mazur (1986) recommend the development of help text in the form of "minimal manuals." These manuals are explicit and focus on real tasks and activities, and they have been found to be significantly better than traditional help texts (Black, Carroll, & McGuigan, 1987; Carroll et al., 1986).

Elkerton (1988) suggests that few Help users want detailed, fact-oriented knowledge such as a hierarchical list showing the syntax of a command. Instead, they want to know the methods to complete a task. Without knowledge of how to do things, users are left to browse through a wealth of information with little understanding of what may be useful. Hence, he recommends, among other things, providing the following:

- Step-by-step interface procedures to assist the user with specific problems.
- Procedural demonstrations of interface procedures to aid quick learning of simple operations.
- Information to help users select between multiple interface methods.
- Users with an understanding of representative tasks to increase their knowledge of when to apply specific skills.

Wright (1984) recommends that when procedural steps are presented, consecutive numbering will make them easy to follow.

Style Provide easy browsing and a distinctive format. Often the exact location of information needed to answer a question cannot be definitely established. Providing information in a format that can be easily skimmed aids the search process and also helps the user become familiar with the information being presented. The following techniques enhance the skimming process:

- Contents screens and indexes.
- Screen headings and subheadings.
- Location indicators.
- Descriptive words in the margin.
- Visual differentiation of screen components.
- Emphasized critical information.

Wording should also be concise, familiar, and action oriented. Reference to outside material may be included in the Help text, especially if the help information cannot be provided in a concise way.

Consistency The Help design philosophy should be consistent with the philosophy used in other parts of the system. This includes presentation techniques, style, procedures, and all other aspects.

Title For easy identification, place the word "Help" in all Help screen titles.

Contextual Help

Contextual help provides information within the context of a task being performed, or about a specific object being operated upon. Common kinds of contextual help include help command buttons, message bar/ status bar messages, and tooltips. Windows 95 has also introduced what is called the What's This? Command.

Help Command Button

Proper Usage

- To provide an overview of, summary assistance for, or explanatory information about, the purpose or contents of a window being displayed.

Design Guidelines

- Present the help in a secondary window or dialog box.

The purpose of a command button labeled Help is to provide supplemental help for a secondary window, dialog box, or message box. It should provide an overview of, summary assistance for, or explanatory information about, the purpose or contents of a window.

Present this form of help in a secondary window or dialog box. Windows 95 considers this help an optional secondary form of contextual assistance, and not a substitute for the *What's This?* command to be described shortly.

Message Bar/Status Bar Message

Proper Usage

- To provide explanatory information about the object with focus.
- Use to:
  - Describe the use of a control, menu item, button, or toolbar.
  - Provide the context of activity within a window.
  - Present a progress indicator or other forms of feedback when the view of a window must not be obscured.
- Do not use for information or access to functions essential to basic system operations unless another form of help is provided elsewhere in the help system.
- If extended help is available and must be presented, place "Press F1 for Help" in bar.

Writing Guidelines

- In writing:
  - Be constructive, not simply descriptive.
  - Begin with a verb in the present tense.
  - If a command has multiple functions, summarize.
  - If a command is disabled, explain why.

This is a contextual help message appearing in a window's message or status bar to provide abbreviated, context-sensitive help for the object with focus. Because a message displayed in the bar may not always be noticed by the user, consider it another form of secondary or supplemental assistance.

Use to provide context for the activity being performed in window, or to describe the use of toolbars, menu items, or buttons being displayed. The bar may also be used for presentation of a progress indicator, or other forms of feedback, when the view of a window must not be obscured. Never use the bar for information or access to functions essential to basic system operations, unless another form of help for this operation is provided elsewhere in the interface. If extended help must be provided, and displaying it in the bar is not possible, place "Press F1 for Help" in the bar.

Begin all messages with a verb in the present tense. Do not simply describe something but explain it in a constructive manner. If a command with multiple functions has focus, summarize its uses. If a command is disabled, explain why. Also, refer to all message and text guidelines earlier in this chapter.

Tooltip

Proper Usage

- Use to display the name of a control when the control has no text label.

Design Guidelines

- Present when the pointer remains over a control a short period of time.
- Make application-specific tooltips consistent with system-supplied tooltips.
- Use system color setting for tooltips to distinguish them.

A tooltip is a small pop-up window with a label that appears adjacent to a control without a label (such as a toolbar) when the pointer is positioned over the control. It is used to display the name of a control when the control has no text label. A tooltip is presented after the pointer remains over a button for a short period of time.

A tooltip should only be presented after the pointer sits on the control for a short period of time. This avoids the distracting effect of a tooltip appearing when a pointer is simply being moved past a control. Make application-specific tooltips consistent in size and structure with system-supplied tooltips, including using the system's color setting to distinguish them. Tooltips are also described in Step 7, on screen-based Controls.

What's This? Command (Windows 95)

Proper Usage

- Use to provide contextual information about any screen object.

Design Guidelines

- Phrase to answer the question "What is this?."
- Indicate the action associated with the item.
- Begin description with a verb.
- Include "why," if helpful.
- Include "how to" if task requires multiple steps.
- For command buttons, use an imperative form.
  "Click this to . . ."

This is a Windows 95 command or button with the label "What's This?" inscribed on it, as also described in Table 11.3. It may take the form of a command on the Help drop-down menu on a primary window, a button on a toolbar, a button on the title bar of a secondary window, or a command on a pop-up menu for a specific object.

Table 11.3   Microsoft Windows 95 User Assistance

Contextual

What's This? Command

Description:	• A command on the Help drop-down menu on a primary window. • A button on the title bar of a secondary window. • A command on a pop-up menu for a specific object. • A button on a toolbar.
Purpose:	• To provide contextual information about any screen object, including controls, dialog boxes, and property sheets.

Help Command Button

Description:	• A command button presented in a secondary window.
Purpose:	• To provide an overview of, summary assistance for, or explanatory information about, a window. • Not a substitute for the What's This? Command.

Tooltip

Description:	• A small pop-up window that appears adjacent to a pointed at control.
Purpose:	• To display the name of a control when the control has no text label.

(Continues)

Table 11.3   *(Continued)*

Status Bar Message

Description: • An abbreviated, context-sensitive message for item with focus appearing in a window's message bar or status bar.

Purpose: • To provide explanatory information about the object with focus.
     • Not to be used use for information or access to functions essential to basic system operations or provided elsewhere in the help system.

Task-oriented Help

Task Topic Windows

Description: • A primary window accessed through the Help Topics Browser.
     • Includes a set of command buttons at the top, minimally:
         – A button to display the Help Topics browser dialog box.
         – A Back button to return to the previous topic.
         – Buttons that provide access to other functions such as Copy or Print.

Purpose: • To provide the procedural steps for carrying out a task.

Shortcut Buttons

Description: • A command button included within the procedural steps presented on a Help Topics Window.

Purpose: • To automatically perform a task, providing efficiency by reducing the amount of information to be presented.
         – Do not use if goal is to enable the user to perform the task.

Guideline: • Consider a balance for common tasks.
         – Provide information that explains how to perform a task.
         – Provide a shortcut button to accomplish the task, making stepping through the task easier.

Reference Help

Reference Help Window

Description: • A primary window sometimes called the "main" help window.
     • Accessed through a:
         – Command in a Help drop-down menu.
         – Toolbar button.
         – Specific file object (icon).
     • Includes a:
         – Menu bar containing File, Edit, Bookmark, Options, and Help.
         – Toolbar containing Contents, Index, Back, and Print (others can be added).

Purpose: • To present reference help information.

Help Topics Browser

Description: • A dialog box containing a set of tabbed pages labeled Contents, Index, and Find.
         – Contents: A list of topics organized by category.

Table 11.3   *(Continued)*

	– Index: A list of topics organized by keyword.
	– Find: Full-text search capability.
	• Accessed through a:
	– Command on a Help drop-down menu.
	– Toolbar button.
Purpose:	• To provide access to help information.

Wizards

Description:	• A series of presentation pages displayed in a secondary window.
	• Includes:
	– Controls to collect input.
	– Command buttons at the bottom: Back, Next, Finish, and Cancel.
	• Accessed through:
	– Toolbar buttons.
	– Icons.
Purpose:	• To assist a user through automating a task through a presented dialog.
	– Very useful for complex or infrequently occurring tasks.
	– Not suited for teaching how to do something.

The purpose of a What's This command is to provide contextual information about any screen object, including controls in secondary windows, property sheets, and dialog boxes.

Phrase the prepared text to answer the question "What is this?" Indicate the action associated with the item by beginning the description with a verb. Include "why" something is being done if it is helpful to the user. Also, include a "how to" if the task requires multiple steps to perform. For command buttons, an imperative form "Click this to . . ." may be used. For more detail, see Microsoft (1995).

Task-Oriented Help

Proper Usage

- To describe the steps for carrying out a task.

Design Guidelines

- Provide one procedure to complete a task, the simplest and most common.
- Provide an explanation of the task's goals and organizational structure at the start.

- Divide procedural instructions into small steps.
- Present each step in the order to be executed.
- Label each step.
- Explicitly state necessary information to complete each step.
- Provide visuals that accurately depict the procedural steps.
- Accompany visuals with some form of written or spoken instructions.
- Begin any spoken instructions simultaneously with or slightly after a visual is presented.
- Segment any animation to focus attention on specific parts.
- Segment instructions.
- Delay the opportunity to perform the procedure until all the procedure steps have been illustrated.

Presentation Guidelines

- The window should consume a minimum amount of screen space, but be large enough to present the information without scrolling.
- Use a different window color to distinguish them from other windows.

Writing Guidelines

- Write simply and clearly, following all previously presented guidelines.
- Focus on "how" information, rather than "what" or why."
- Do not include introductory, conceptual, or reference material.
- Limit to four or fewer steps to avoid scrolling or multiple windows.
- If a control is referred to by its label, capitalize to set it off.
- Include topic title as part of the body.

Task-oriented help details the steps for carrying out a task. People prefer task-oriented help over product-oriented help, and research evidence shows a productivity gain using it. It is not surprising that task-oriented help has such a preference and benefits, because people think in terms of tasks, not functions. Windows 95 has two forms of task-oriented help, Task Topic Windows and Shortcut Buttons as described in Table 11.3.

Task-oriented help provides a help window to present and describe the steps in carrying out a task.

Design Guidelines The following guidelines are mostly derived from Harrison (1995). First, present only one procedure to complete a task, the simplest and most common. At the beginning, provide an explanation of the task's goals and organizational structure. Divide procedural instructions into small steps and present them in the order they are to be executed. Clearly label each step. Explicitly state what information is necessary in order to complete each step, presenting the most important information first.

Provide visuals that accurately depict the procedural steps. People prefer to follow visual examples rather than instructions and they minimize orientation errors. Accompany the visuals with some form of written or, if possible, spoken instructions. Instructions provide cues as to most important aspects of the procedure. Begin any spoken instructions simultaneously with or slightly after a visual is presented. If animation is included, segment it to focus attention on specific parts.

Segment the instructions to reinforce the concept of chunks or steps. Finally, delay the opportunity to perform the procedure until all the procedure steps have been illustrated.

Presentation Guidelines A task-oriented help window should consume a minimum amount of screen space, but be large enough to cover all the necessary information without requiring cumbersome scrolling. To distinguish them from other windows, use a different window color to display them.

Writing Guidelines Write simply and clearly, following all previously presented text guidelines. Focus on "how" information, rather than "what" or why." Do not include introductory, conceptual, or reference material. Limit to four or fewer steps to avoid scrolling or multiple windows. If a control is referred to by its label, capitalize to set it off. Include topic title as part of the body.

Reference Help

Description

- To present reference help information.

Proper Usage

- Use to present reference help information, either:
  - Reference oriented
  - User guide oriented.

Design Guidelines

- Provide a consistent presentation style, following all previously presented guidelines.
- Include a combination of contextual help, and task help, as necessary.
- Include text, graphics, animation, video, and audio effects, as necessary.
- Make displayed toolbar buttons contextual to the topic being viewed.
- Provide jumps, a button or interactive area that triggers an event when it is selected, such as:
  - Moving from one topic to another.
  - Displaying a pop-up window.

– Carrying out a command.
- Visually distinguish a jump by:
  – Displaying it as a button.
  – Using a distinguishing color or font to identify it.
  – Changing the pointer image when it is over it.

Presentation Guidelines

- Provide a nonscrolling region for long topics to keep topic title and other key information visible.

Writing Guidelines

- Write simply and clearly, following all previously presented guidelines.
- Provide meaningful topic titles.

Reference help is another form of online documentation. Its purpose is to present reference help information that may be reference-oriented, documenting the features of a product, or it may serve as a user's guide to a product. Windows 95 provides reference help through a Reference Help Window, described in Table 11.3. A reference-oriented help window is usually organized by functions and features and includes more text. A user guide-oriented help window is usually organized by tasks and may include more illustrations.

Design Guidelines Provide a consistent presentation style, following all previously presented guidelines. Include a combination of contextual help, and task help, as necessary. Include text, graphics, animation, video, and audio effects, as necessary and as available. Make toolbar buttons contextual to the topic being viewed in the help window.

Provide *jumps*, button or interactive areas that trigger an event when it is selected. The action may be to move from one topic to another, to display a pop-up window, or to carry out a command. Jumps, when in button form called *shortcut buttons* in Windows 95 (see Table 11.3), automatically perform a task, thereby providing efficiency by reducing the amount of information necessary to present for reading by the viewer. Do not use a jump, however, if the goal is to enable the user to perform the task. Microsoft (1995) suggests considering a balance for common tasks. Provide information that explains how to perform a task and also provide a shortcut button to accomplish the task, making stepping through the task easier. Visually distinguish a jump by displaying it as a unique style button or using a distinguishing color or font to identify it. The system default for a textual jump in Microsoft Windows is green underlined text. Also, change the pointer image when the pointer is positioned over the jump.

Presentation Guidelines If scrolling is necessary, provide a non-scrolling region for long topics to keep the topic title and other key information visible.

Writing Guidelines Write simply and clearly, following all previously presented guidelines. Also, provide meaningful topic titles.

Wizards

Proper Usage

- Use to assist a user by automating a task through a presented dialog.
- Useful for complex or infrequently occurring tasks.
- Not suited to teaching how to do something.

Design Guidelines

- Provide a greater number of simple pages with fewer choices, rather than a smaller number of more complex pages with too many options or too much text.
- Include on the first page:
  - A graphic on the left side to establish a reference point or theme.
  - A welcoming paragraph on the right side to explain what the wizard does.
- Include on subsequent pages:
  - A graphic for consistency.
  - Instructional text.
  - Controls for user input.
- Make it visually clear the graphic is not interactive.
  - Vary from normal size or render it as an abstract representation.
- Do not require the user to leave a wizard to complete a task.
- Make sure the design alternatives offered yield positive results.
- Include a Finish button at the point where the task can be completed.
- Make certain it is obvious how to proceed when the wizard has completed its process.

Presentation Guidelines

- Display the wizard window so it is immediately recognized as the primary point of input.
- Present a single window at one time.
- Do not advance pages automatically.

Writing Guidelines

- Write simply, concisely, and clearly, following all previously presented guidelines.
- Clearly identify the wizard's purpose in title bar.
- Use a conversational, rather than instructional, style.
- Use words like "you" and your.
- Start most questions with phrases like "Which option do you want . . ." or "Would you like . . ."

A wizard's purpose is to assist a user by automating a task and walking the user through the process. It may not appear as an explicit part of the help interface. Windows 95 provides wizards, as summarized in Table 11.3. A wizard consists of a series of presentation pages displayed in a window. The pages contain controls to collect user input and command buttons at the bottom. They are useful for complex or infrequently occurring tasks that people may have difficulty learning or doing. Wizards are designed to hide many of the steps and much of the complexity in doing something. They are not suited to teaching how to do something, and should be considered a supplement to the actual performance of the task. An experienced user who knows a process will usually find a wizard inefficient or lacking access to all necessary functionality. A wizard can be accessed through toolbar buttons or icons. Microsoft (1995) suggests the following guidelines.

Design Guidelines Provide a greater number of simple pages with fewer choices, rather than a smaller number of more complex pages with too many options or too much text. Fewer pages will make it easier to understand the wizard and the process. Include on the first page a graphic on the left side to establish a reference point or theme and a welcoming paragraph on the right side to explain what the wizard does. Include on subsequent pages a graphic for consistency, instructional text, and the necessary controls for user input. Make it visually clear the graphic is not interactive by varying it from normal size or rendering it as an abstract representation. Do not require the user to leave a wizard to complete a task. The user, often a novice, may lose context. Make sure the design alternatives offered to the user yield positive results.

Include a Finish button at the point where the task can be completed. Make certain it is obvious how to proceed when the wizard has completed its process by including proper closing text on the last page.

Presentation Guidelines Display the wizard window so it is immediately recognized as the primary point of input. Present a single window at one time. Do not advance pages automatically. The viewer may be unable to read all the information and control of the dialog is then in the hands of the computer.

Writing Guidelines Write simply, concisely, and clearly, following all previously presented guidelines. Clearly identify the wizard's purpose in the title bar. Use a conversational, rather than instructional, style, and words like "you" and "your." Start most questions with phrases like "Which option do you want," or "Would you like."

INTERNATIONAL CONSIDERATIONS

Today's market for software is global. It crosses endless cultural and language boundaries, each with its own requirements, conventions, customs, and definitions of acceptability. To be accepted, and used, a screen's text and images must reflect the needs, and sensibility of each partner in the worldwide community where it is used.

To create a product for use internationally may involve two steps, *internationalization*, then *localization*. (Russo & Boor, 1993). Internationalization is the process of isolating culturally specific elements from a product. The German text of a program developed in Germany, for example, is isolated from the program itself. This occurs in the country where the product is developed. Localization is the process of infusing a specific cultural context into a previously internationalized product. Translating German screen components and messages into English for American users is an example of localization.

Creating a product that has been properly localized and speaks fluently in another culture requires addressing a number of factors. These include text; formats for number, date, and time; images; symbols; colors; flow; and functionality.

Localization

When to Do It

- When the market includes few or no English speakers.
- When translation is required, by law or by custom.
- When the widest possible market is desired.

When Not to Do It

- When the audience already reads English.
- When the cost of retrofitting or rewriting the software is prohibitive.

This discussion of when, and when not to internationalize and localize a product, is mostly based on Fowler & Stanwick (1995). Considerations include the prospective users and their English capabilities, local laws and customs, and costs associated with translating.

English is the most widely used language in the world. The current estimate for its speakers ranges from 700 million to 2 billion (Tripathi, 1992). While many speakers of English have been taught it as a second language, and may not all be facile readers and writers, nevertheless, they can communicate using it. The first consideration, then, is the English capabilities of the prospective user. This must be ascertained. Toward this end, both IBM (National Language Technical Center, 1991) and Apple (1992a) have documents listing the official language requirements of countries, and/or regions or political divisions. In addition, within some international business and scientific communities, English is the accepted language of communication. For example, the air transportation industry uses English as the language of communication between airline pilots and flight controllers worldwide. Also, scientists and engineers in Japan also prefer to communicate their research findings in English because of its greater precision (Kohl, Barclay, Pinelli, Keene, & Kennedy, 1993). If English is accepted in the using body, then concerns are only cultural.

Legal requirements may also mandate translation. For example, Canada, being composed of both English and French speakers, requires bilingual materials. The European Economic Community (ECC) will, at some point, mandate that all documentation shipped with imported products be written in all of the ECC languages. Whether the product will actually be used in all the countries will be immaterial.

Cost will also, of course, dictate whether a translation can, or will, be performed. Software translation rates can range from $40–80 dollars an hour or more, documentation translation $50–150 or more per page. These rates are presented for illustrative purposes only. Actual costs will be driven by many factors, including the local cost of living. The reader in need of a translation will be best served by getting a quote reflecting the time and locale of the translation. A translation performed in the target country often results in better quality than a translation by those who are native speakers of the producing country.

Words and Text

- Use very simple English.
  - Develop a restricted vocabulary.
  - Restrict the sentence structure using: noun-verb-object.
- Avoid:
  - Acronyms and abbreviations.

- – Stringing three nouns together.
- – Local or computer jargon.
- – A telegraphic writing style.
- – An over-friendly writing style.
- – Culturally specific examples
- – References to national, racial, religious, and sexist stereotypes
- Adhere to local user language idioms and cultural contexts.
- Keep the original term for words that do not translate.
- Allow additional screen space for translation.
  - – Horizontally using Table 11.4.
  - – Vertically.
- When translating languages, first do:
  - – European: German
  - – Middle East: Arabic
  - – Far East: Japanese
- Position icon captions outside of the graphic.
- Modify mnemonics for keyboard access.
- Adhere to local formats for date, time, money, measurements, and telephone numbers.

Text translation is simplified, and user interpretation errors reduced, if these guidelines, many of which are derived from del Galdo (1990), Russo & Boor (1993) and Fowler & Stanwick (1995) are followed.

Use Very Simple English Simple English text will be easier to translate, and less expensive to accomplish. Simple English is aided by using a restricted vocabulary. Create a dictionary of approved terms and prohibit all synonyms, and different meanings for the same word as well. A restricted sentence structure is also necessary. Sentences meaning the same can be written in many ways in English. This makes text more interesting to look at and read. In other languages, however, word order affects the meaning. Multiple structures cause translation problems and foster errors. Follow a *noun-verb-object* structure. Another benefit of simple English: translation may not always be necessary. As English is simplified, the number of nonnative English-speaking people who will be capable of understanding it will enlarge.

What to Avoid Do not use acronyms and abbreviations. They are difficult, and often confusing, to translate. A translated acronym may not be as concise, or may possess negative associations. Abbreviations may also not be as concise, and they may not be understandable.

Avoid stringing three nouns together. Relationships between nouns become very explicit in many other languages and it is difficult to determine what terms are modifying one another when three are strung together. The use of prepositions such as *at, in, by,* and *on* can help to clarify noun relationships. Avoid local or computer jargon. Jargon is not universal and probably will not be understood.

Do not use telegraphic writing, a terse style where words such as, "and," "the," and "is" are left out. Again, translation problems can easily occur. An overly friendly style in which the reader is addressed in the first person or in a childish manner should also be avoided. It can be considered as condescending and irritating to readers in non-English speaking countries. Finally, avoid references to national, racial, religious, and sexist stereotypes and do not use culturally specific examples. The latter must be re-created by the translator so it is suitable for the language and culture.

Adhere to Local Language Idioms and Cultural Contexts Some words have different meanings in other languages. This is of special concern for product names. Auto makers have been particular victims of this problem. Italy's Fiat had an auto named "Uno." They could not sell it by that name in Finland because uno in Finnish means "garbage."

England's Rolls Royce planned to name a new car "Silver Mist." Then, someone discovered mist in German means "manure" (Taylor, 1992). Proper attention to localization can avoid some embarrassing, and costly, problems.

Some languages are not read left-to-right, as is English. Arabic, for example, is read right-to-left. Chinese is read top-to-bottom, right-to-left.

Keep the Original Terms for Words that Do Not Translate Some words do not exist in other languages. "Disk drive" and "zooming" do not exist in Thai, for example. It has been found that people often prefer the original term to a created word. Do not invent words; keep the original term for non-translatable words (Sukaviriya & Moran, 1990).

Allow Additional Screen Space for Translation English is very concise. It usually takes less space to communicate the same word, phrase, or text than most other languages. Listed below are words with the same meaning from four languages. Can you translate them?

- Besturingselement (Dutch)
- Olvadaci prvek   (Czech)
- Ohjausobjekti   (Finnish)
- Steuerelement   (German)

Here is a clue. This word in English is seven characters long and has already been mentioned many, many times in this book. The Dutch version is 17 characters in length, or 143 per cent longer than the English version.

The others are composed of 13 characters and are 85 per cent longer. The answer shortly.

Objects whose sizes are affected by translation include captions, entry areas, menu options, prompting message boxes, areas of text, and icon labels. Expansion room must be allowed for translation. Generally, the shorter the text the more room is needed. Table 11.4 (National Language Technical Center, 1991) provides some additional horizontal space guidelines. Extra vertical spacing may also have to be allowed. In many languages, accents and descenders fall above and below the usual ascender and descender lines. What is the English version of the above words? Control. Were you able to translate one or more of them?

When Translating, Where to Start From a translator's point of view, the world is divided into three parts: Europe, the Middle East, and the Far East. Fowler and Stanwick (1995) report that Microsoft addresses translation in the following manner. In Europe, where problems involve changes in words caused by gender, accented letters, and text expansion, translation begins with German. This is done because German solves for accent, gender, and expansion issues. In the Middle East difficulties in translation include bidirectional and cursive letters. To address these, Microsoft recommends starting with Arabic. When this is done, localization is accomplished for Hebrew, Farsi, Dari Persian, Pashto, and the Indian languages Sindhi and Urdu. In the Far East the main difficulty is double-byte character sets. One of the most difficult Asian languages, with ten thousand ideograms divided into four character sets, is Japanese. So Microsoft starts with it.

Table 11.4   Translation Expansion Requirements

Number of Characters in Text	*Additional Space*
Field labels and menu options	
Up to 10	100–200%
11 to 20	80–100%
Messages and on–screen instructions	
21–30	60–80%
31–50	40–60%
Online help and documentation	
51–70	31–40%
over 70	30%

From National Language Technical Center, IBM (1991)

Place Icon Captions Outside of the Graphic Text placed within an icon may cause the icon to have to be redrawn when translation occurs. Text positioned outside the icon will negate the need for redrawing (Apple, 1992a).

Modify Mnemonics Used for Keyboard Access Because mnemonics are established for ease of memorizing, and because they are based upon a letter in a text object, when the text changes, so must the mnemonic. Attempting to create unique mnemonics may constrain the translation but must be addressed. Maintaining the old mnemonic will severely impact their learning. They will no longer be mnemonics.

Adhere to Local Formats for Date, Time, Money, Measurements, and Telephone Numbers An infinite variety of these various units exist worldwide. They must also be localized to the exact needs of the user.

Images and Symbols

- Adhere to local cultural and social norms.
- Use internationally-accepted symbols.
- Develop generic images.
- Be particularly careful with:
  - Religious symbols (crosses and stars).
  - The human body.
  - Women.
  - Hand gestures.
  - The cross and check for check boxes.
- Review proposed graphical images early in the design cycle.

Images are the visible language of a culture and must be recognizable, meaningful, and acceptable. Like text, improper use of images, symbols, and icons can create problems internationally. Social norms vary, so great variations exist in what is recognizable and acceptable throughout the world. What one culture recognizes may have no meaning in another. What is acceptable in one country may not be in another. The images created for graphical interfaces are particularly susceptible to these problems. To be successful internationally, images must be carefully selected and designed. The following guidelines are also derived from del Galdo (1990), Russo & Boor (1993), and Fowler & Stanwick (1995).

Adhere to Local Cultural and Social Norms Few world travelers have not suffered embarrassment caused by failure to understand, and adhere to, local customs and mores. On an early trip to Australia I pulled in to a service station to replenish my auto's "petrol." I communicated my need to the attendant through a "thumbs-up" sign, an American convention (when there were still attendants) meaning "fill-it-up." The Australian attendant's response was a stunned look and a frown. Sensing something was wrong, I hastily lowered the window and communicated my need verbally. He smiled, replying, "ah, you're American, eh, OK." It wasn't until much later I discovered I had made a gesture considered obscene in Australia.

Examples abound in the computer literature of images that have created problems internationally. The mail box and trash can are two examples of objects whose shape, and resulting recognizability, vary substantially around the world. A cocktail glass to signify an after-work appointment is a poor image for use in countries where alcohol is not associated with social activities. In the United States a black cat is usually associated with bad luck, in the United Kingdom it means good luck. In the United States, the number 13 is considered unlucky, in Japan the number 4 is.

Images that are culturally specific must be isolated during the internationalization process. Then, proper images must be developed for use in the culture where the product will be used.

Use Internationally Accepted Symbols Before developing an image, first determine if any international images have already been created by trade or standards organizations. The ISO, for example, has developed standard shapes for a variety of purposes. Always consult all relevant reference books before inventing new images or modifying existing ones.

Develop Generic Images Whenever possible, create generic images that are usable in multiple cultures. Having different images can confuse people who may use more than one language version of a product.

Where to Be Extremely Cautious Some topics are more susceptible to acceptability problems than others. Inappropriate presentation can result in the viewer being offended or insulted. Be particularly careful when using religious symbols such as crosses or stars. Also be wary of images depicting a human body, particularly the female. In some cultures simply revealing a woman's arms and legs is unacceptable. During the World Cup soccer tournament in the United States in 1994 one Middle East country televised the soccer games using a several-second tape delay. This was done so that stadium crowd pictures potentially containing pictures of women dressed to accommodate the United States's Summer heat would not be shown on local television. What was substituted instead: crowd pictures of people attending an American football game in December in a northern city (like Green Bay, Wisconsin) when the temperature hovered around zero degrees Fahrenheit. Needless to say, *all* the fans were well-covered from toes to top of head. The soccer players on television, meanwhile, cavorted in shorts and jerseys.

Also, be wary of hand gestures, as my Australian experience illustrates. Actually, I'm in pretty good company in committing this kind of faux pas. A former American president departed Air Force One on a visit to Germany exhibiting his customary hand wave to the welcoming people. Unfortunately, his Protocol Officer neglected to inform him that his wave had a vulgar connotation in Germany. We can only hope that German viewers of this action interpreted what he felt in is heart, not what he indicated with his hands. Lastly, the X and check mark for check boxes do not have meaning universally. It has also been found that they do not have universal meaning in the United States. In recent years various graphical systems have moved away from X to the check mark as the symbol to indicate an active or set check box control. Why? In an engineering environment an X in a check box means the choice is not applicable or not set, a check means it is applicable, or it is set. Thus, an "X" was found to be confusing to some people when it meant active or set. Research has also indicated that when people complete a form with check boxes, the symbol most often used is the check mark.

Review Proposed Graphical Images Early in the Design Cycle Creating acceptable images can be a time-consuming process. Start developing them early in the design process so ample time exists for extensive testing and modification.

Color, Sequence, and Functionality

- Adhere to local color connotations and conventions.
- Provide the proper information sequence.
- Provide the proper functionality.
- Remove all references to features not supported.

Other international considerations include the following.

Adhere to Local Color Connotations and Conventions Color associations also differ among cultures. In the United States mail boxes are blue, in England they are red, in Greece they are yellow. In the United States red is associated with danger or stop, green with OK or go. This red-green association does not exist everywhere in the world. Table 11.5, derived from Russo and Boor (1993), lists some common cultural color associations. Colors used on screens must also reflect the color expectancies of its viewers.

Table 11.5   Some Cultural Color Associations

	Red	Yellow	Green	Blue	White
China	Happiness	Birth Wealth Power	Ming Dynasty Heavens Clouds	Heavens Clouds	Death Purity
Egypt	Death	Happiness Prosperity	Fertility Strength	Virtue Faith Truth	Joy
France	Aristocracy	Temporary	Criminality	Freedom Peace	Neutrality
India	Life Creativity	Success	Prosperity Fertility		Death Purity
Japan	Anger Danger	Grace Nobility	Future Youth Energy	Villainy	Death
United States	Danger Stop	Cowardice Caution	Safety Go	Masculinity	Purity

Provide the Proper Information Sequence Information within a screen will be arranged to reflect the logical flow of information. In many cultures, including those we are most familiar with, it will be left-to-right for text and top-to-bottom, left-to-right for ease of scanning. Some cultures, however, read right-to-left. For these, information sequence must be reorganized to reflect this right-to-left sequence. Similarly, cascaded windows for left-to-right readers are usually presented in an upper-left to lower-right structure. These will have to be reorganized to reflect the existing different reading patterns

Provide the Proper Functionality Product features developed for one culture may not be appropriate for all cultures. Nielsen (1990), for example, describes a school hypertext product developed in France. During requirements determination it was established that only the school teacher should be able to add comments and viewpoints to the screens, not the students. This was a socially acceptable practice in France. Later, when the product was marketed in Sweden this aspect created problems. In Sweden independent discovery is greatly valued and the inability of the students to add comments and viewpoints was unacceptable. All international products have to be reviewed for functionality, as well, and may require multiple versions to reflect the individual needs of cultures.

Remove All References to Features Not Supported Any aspects of a product not supported internationally should be removed from the system. Any references to features not supported should also be eliminated from all documentation. To leave it in creates visual noise and will be confusing.

Requirements Determination and Testing

- Establish international requirements at the beginning of product development.
- Establish a relationship within the target culture.
- Test the product as if it were new.

When a product is translated for a new culture, it becomes a new product. Russo and Boor (1993) suggest the following should be accomplished.

Establish International Requirements at the Beginning of Product Development Developers must establish what cultures the product will be used in at the start of the development cycle. Then, differing product requirements must be established reflecting the differing needs of the various users. This permits localization issues to be addressed throughout the development process.

Establish a Relationship Within the Target Culture A close working relationship with *natives* from all using cultures during requirements and development will permit local, cultural specific, feedback to be obtained in a timely manner. A close working relationship will also educate the designers about the culture where their product will be used.

Test the Product as if It Were New When a product is translated for a new culture, it is a new product and it should be subjected to a normal testing during the development cycle. If international testing is delayed until after the product is released to the domestic market, identified problems may be difficult, if not impossible, to address.

S T E P 1 2

Test, Test, and Retest

The design of a graphical system and its screens is a complicated process. A host of factors must be considered, among them the types of windows used, how the windows are organized, what controls are selected to collect and present information, and how the controls are organized within one window and between several windows. In the design process numerous design tradeoffs will be made. Also, some design decisions may be based on skimpy data and reflect the most educated guess possible at the moment. Finally, the implications for some design decisions may not be fully appreciated until the results can be seen.

To wait until after a system has been implemented to uncover and correct any system usability deficiencies can be aggravating, costly, and time-consuming for both users and developers. Indeed, after implementation many problems may never be corrected because of time constraints and costs. To minimize these kinds of problems, and assure usability, interfaces must be tested and refined before they are implemented.

What follows is a brief overview of the testing process and the role it plays in design. Its purpose is to provide an awareness of the testing procedures and methods, and to summarize some basic testing guidelines.

- Identify the purpose of testing and scope.
- Understand the importance of testing.
- Develop a prototype.
- Develop the right kind of test plan.
- Design a test to yield relevant data.
- Solicit, select, and schedule users to participate.
- Provide the proper test facility.
- Conduct test and collect data.

- Analyze the data and generate design recommendations.
- Modify the prototype as necessary.
- Test the system again.
- Evaluate the working system.

PURPOSE OF TESTING

Testing serves a two-fold purpose. First, it establishes a communication bridge between developers and users. Through testing, the developer learns about the user's goals, perceptions, questions, and problems. Through testing, the user is exposed to the capabilities of the system early on, before design is solidified.

Second, testing is used to evaluate a product. It can identify potential problems in design at a point in the development process where they can be more easily addressed. Testing also enables comparison of alternative versions of a design element, when a clear direction is not immediately evident. How well the interface and screens meets user needs and expectations can also be assessed.

IMPORTANCE OF TESTING

A thorough testing process is important for many reasons, including all of the following.

Developers and Users Possess Different Models

As discussed earlier, developers and users have different expectations and levels of knowledge. Specialized knowledge possessed by the developers enables them to deal with complex or ambiguous situations on the basis of context cues not visible to the users. Developers also frequently use terminology that does not always match that of the users.

Developer's Intuitions Are Not Always Correct

The intuition of designers, or anyone for that matter, no matter how good or bad they may be at what they do, is error-prone. This is illustrated by the previously reported Tullis & Kodimer (1992) study evaluating several screen-based controls. They found that programmer predictions of control usage speed correlated only .07 with actual measured speeds. They also found that programmer predictions of user control preferences correlated only .31 with actuality. Intuition is too shallow a foundation on which to base design decisions.

There Is No Average User

We all differ—in looks, feelings, motor abilities, intellectual abilities, learning abilities and speeds, device-based control preferences, and so forth. In a keyboard data entry task, for example, the best operators will probably be twice as fast as the poorest and make 10 times fewer errors. Design must permit people with widely varying characteristics to satisfactorily and comfortably learn and perform the task or job.

It's Impossible to Predict Usability from Appearance

Just as it is impossible to judge a person's personality from one's looks.

Design Standards and Guidelines Are Not Sufficient

Design standards and guidelines are an important component of good design, laying the foundation for consistency. But design standards and guidelines often fall victim to tradeoffs. They also cannot address the myrid of interactions occurring within a system.

Informal Feedback Is Inadequate

Informal feedback is a hit-and-miss proposition. Parts of the system may be completely overlooked, significant problems in other parts may never be documented.

Products Built in Pieces Almost Always Have System-Level Inconsistencies

A normal and expected result when different developers work on different aspects of a system. We might also say that developers differ—there is no average developer.

Problems Found Late Are More Difficult and Expensive to Fix

Unless it's really severe, it may never be fixed.

Problems Fixed During Development Mean Reduced Support Costs Later

Support costs are directly proportional to usability problems remaining after development.

Advantages over a Competitive Product Can Be Achieved

Many products can do something. The most successful products are those that permit doing something easily.

SCOPE OF TESTING

Testing should begin in the earliest stages of product development and continue throughout the development process. It should include as many of the user's tasks, and as many of the product's components, as reasonably possible. Always involve all members of the design team in the testing to insure a common reference point for all. Involving all also permits multiple insights into the test results from the different perspectives of team members.

PROTOTYPES

A prototype is primarily a vehicle for exploration, communication, and evaluation. Its purpose is to obtain user input in design, and to provide feedback to designers. Its key role is the communicative role it plays, not its accuracy or thoroughness. A prototype enables a design to be better visualized and provides insights into how the software will look and work. It also aids in defining tasks, their flow, the interface itself, and its screens.

A prototype is a simulation of an actual system that can be quickly created. A prototype may be a rough approximation, such as a simple hand-drawn sketch, or it may be interactive, allowing the user to key or select data using controls, navigate through menus, retrieve displays of data, and perform basic system functions. A prototype need not be perfectly realistic, but it must be reasonably accurate and legible. A prototype also need not be functionally complete, possessing actual files or processing data. Today, many software support tools for prototyping are available that permit the prototype to be integrated directly into the application code.

A prototype may have great breadth, including as many features as possible to present concepts and overall organization, or it might have more depth, including more detail on a given feature or task to focus on individual design aspects. By nature, a prototype cannot be used to exercise all of a system's functions, just those notable in one manner or another.

Particularly useful early in design, a prototype should be capable of being rapidly changed as testing is performed. Prototypes range in fidelity from rough hand sketches to fully functioning software (Microsoft, 1995; Weinschenk, 1995; Winograd, 1995).

Hand Sketches and Scenarios

The first, and simplest, prototype is a rough hand sketch of the screens. These should start early in the design process and before any attempt is made to create a prototype using an available toolkit or interface builder. A rough approximation often yields more substantive suggestions or critical comments than an actual screen-drawn version. The hand sketch should be an entity that has enough of a general look to suggest the functionality, interaction, and layout of screens. The goal is a rough vision, not a polished work of art. This sketch will be useful in defining and refining task organization, conceptual ideas, and the general layout of screens. Weinschenk (1995) suggests the process should include the following:

- Sketch (storyboard) the screens while determining:
  - The source of the screen's information.
  - The content and structure of individual screens.
  - The overall order of screens and windows.
- Use an erasable medium.
- Sketch the screens needed to complete each work flow task.
- Try out selected metaphors and change as necessary.
- First, storyboard common / critical / frequent scenarios.
  - Follow them from beginning to end.
  - Then, go back and build in exceptions.
- Don't get too detailed; exact control positioning is not important, just overall order and flow.
- Storyboard as a team, include at least one user.
- Only develop online prototypes when everyone agrees a complete set of screens have been satisfactorily sketched.

Sketch the screens while determining the source of the screen's information, the content and structure of the individual screens, and the overall flow of the screens. Use an erasable medium so that as ideas are explored and changed, the modifications will be easy to make. Sketch the screens needed to complete each task in the workflow. First, sketch the most common, critical, or frequent activities, following them from beginning to end. Then, go back and build in the exceptions. Try out all selected metaphors and modify them as necessary. Make sure the major user objects are very obvious. Avoid getting too detailed. Most important is the overall screen flow, order, and structure. Approximate the positioning of controls simply to verify fit. Exact positioning will come later. Sketch the screens as a team, including at least one user. To avoid solidifying the product too soon, develop online prototypes only when everyone agrees a complete set of screens have been satisfactorily sketched.

Low-Fidelity Prototypes

Another simple prototype involves use of common paper technologies such as post-its and transparencies. Menu bars, pull-down menus, pop-up windows, screen bodies, and so on reflecting system tasks are created using these media. Then, the components are manually manipulated to illustrate the dynamics of the software. The purpose of this kind of prototype is to provide a sense of the dynamics of a program without actually having to build a functional version of it. The objective, again, is to create a rough vision, not a polished piece of art in order to elicit substantive suggestions and critical comments.

Programmed Facades

To provide a realistic surface view of a real program, and to illustrate some of the program's functioning, a programmed facade can be created. Using prototyping tools such as Hypercard, Supercard, and Toolbook, examples of finished dialogs and screens for some important aspects of the system are constructed and viewed. A facade is very shallow, duplicating only a small portion of what is ultimately intended in both depth and breadth. While much is missing underneath, what is visible can provide a good impression of finished design. If a programmed facade has dangers, it is these. First, a highly polished product can foster a sense of finality because of its appearance. Significant reorganization or restructuring suggestions may be inhibited, the focus simply being on screen cosmetics. Second, the false expectation that the real thing is only a short time away may easily be created, even though much work still remains to be done.

Prototype-Oriented Languages

To present an example of completed dialogs and screens for some parts of the system, prototypes can be constructed using programming languages that support the actual programming process. Examples include Power Builder, Visual Basic, and so on. Using these tools, a real program can be created to illustrate some of the program's functioning and the mechanics of the interface. Like a programmed facade, a danger is that the highly polished product can foster a sense of finality because of its appearance, inhibiting reorganization or restructuring suggestions, the focus simply being on screen cosmetics. One consideration to be decided up-front: Will the prototype software be a "throwaway," or the actual system software? This will have implications concerning the amount of programming effort expended on the prototype.

A development effort will probably use combinations of these prototyping techniques to visualize design, solicit user input, and obtain needed developer feedback as design progresses.

A TEST PLAN

First, define the purpose of the test in simple statements, including performance goals, what the test is expected to accomplish in system learning, use of screens, system navigation, and efficiency of operation. Learning issues will center around effectiveness in starting to use the system, recognizing system features, and exploring system features. Screen issues will be directed toward general screen layout, including efficiency and aesthetics, and recognition and understanding of screen-based controls, icons, and messages. Navigation issues involve use of system navigation methods, including menus, buttons, and icons. Operational issues include how many steps are needed to accomplish a task, system responsiveness, and forms of system feedback provided.

Then, tasks to adequately satisfy the test's purpose must be identified. Ideally, the entire system will be tested, but time and costs often limit what can actually be done. When time or cost constraints exist, good candidates for testing include the user's most important tasks or the most representative tasks. Always test the functions or features whose design foundation is not as solid as desired. These are features where the trade-off issues were not clear-cut, not strongly pointing to one design alternative over other possible alternatives.

KINDS OF TESTS

Several testing techniques, at varying levels of sophistication and cost are available to exercise the system.

Guidelines Review

A checklist summarizing navigation, screen design and layout, and other interface requirements imposed by a system's standard or guideline document may be prepared. Individual screens and workflow are then evaluated for compliance with this guideline. Failure to comply indicates a design modification is necessary. This kind of test can be performed by software developers. Its advantages include its low cost and its ability to identify recurring and general problems. It is particularly useful in identifying screen design and layout problems. Because this review tends to be static in nature, as a disadvantage it may miss severe conceptual, navigation, and operational problems.

Heuristic Evaluation

In this kind of evaluation, interface specialists study a system in depth and look for properties they know, from experience, will lead to problems. Advantages of this approach include its ability to identify many problems (Bailey, Allan, & Raiello, 1992) and its relatively low cost. Its disadvantages include the necessity for the evaluators to possess user interface expertise, the method's difficulty in finding missing clearly marked exits and missing interface elements or features, and its inability to identify the most important problems from those identified (Bailey et al., 1992). The optimum expert group size to satisfactorily perform an evaluation is three to five (Nielsen, 1992).

Cognitive Walkthroughs

The developer walks through an interface in the context of the user's tasks. Actions and feedback are compared to the user's goals and knowledge, and discrepancies noted. Advantages of this approach are that the walkthrough can be performed by software developers, and that the user's goals and assumptions must be clearly defined before the walkthrough, aiding the earlier design process. Thus, the task definition methodology must have been properly accomplished in the system requirements stage. Among its disadvantages are: A cognitive walkthrough is tedious to perform and it may miss inconsistencies and general and recurring problems.

Usability Test

A usability test evaluates an interface under real-world or controlled conditions. Specific tasks are performed by users, measures of performance taken, and the results compared with the previously defined performance goals. Evaluators also gather data on problems that arise. Errors, confusion, frustrations, and complaints can be noted and discussed with the user. It is also useful to have the user talk aloud about what he or she is doing. Failure to meet these usability design objectives will indicate redesign is necessary. A usability test identifies serious or recurring problems, avoiding low priority items (Bailey et al., 1992). Its most serious problem is the high cost associated with establishing a facility to perform the testing. To effectively perform a usability test also requires a test conductor with user interface expertise. A usability test is also poorly suited to detecting problems with consistency.

Classic Experiments

Where two or more design alternatives exist, either of which may appear possible, a classic experiment may be developed to compare them directly. Two or more prototypes may be constructed, identical in all aspects except for the design issue (type of control, wording of an instruction, etc.). Speed and accuracy measures can be collected and user preferences solicited. The result will be objective measures of performance and subjective measures of user satisfaction, thereby permitting a more well-informed selection of the best alternative.

Focus Groups

A useful method for obtaining initial thoughts or trying out ideas is a focus group. An experienced moderator directs a discussion about a design or particular tasks and knowledgeable participants express their thoughts and concerns.

Demonstrations or Walkthroughs

In this test, a set of sample scenarios are illustrated and impressions obtained along the way. An experienced moderator to direct the discussion about design or tasks is also necessary.

Some studies evaluating the effectiveness of different testing methods have been performed. Jeffries, Miller & Wharton, & Uyeda (1991) compared a heuristic evaluation (four human factors experts studying a product for two weeks), a usability test (a user interface tester observing six product users and writing a report), a guidelines review (three programmers applying a set of guidelines to the product), and finally a cognitive walkthrough (by three programmers). The heuristic evaluation uncovered four times as many overall problems as each of the other methods. This method also identified three times as many problems already pre-identified by other experts. Desurvire, Kondziela, & Atwood (1992) concluded in another study, however, that usability testing is more powerful than the several other testing methods.

Each testing method, then, has its strengths and weaknesses. A well-rounded testing program will use a combination of some, or all, of these methods to guarantee the usability of its created product.

TEST PARTICIPANTS

Assembling the proper people to participate in the test is critical to its success. Always recruit participants with the proper qualifications, those currently performing the job where the product will ultimately be used. While the "boss" may profess to be knowledgeable, he or she is too far removed from the grind of daily activities and seldom knows exactly what is going on. Also, recruit participants covering the spectrum of user characteristics, including age, sex, and experience, in order to allow general conclusions based on the test results. Recruit strangers, not friends. A stranger is less likely to withhold comments possibly hurting the tester's feelings. There will also be less embarrassment if problems are uncovered.

Advise test participants of what to expect in the test. They will approach the test with less apprehension. Finally, never refer to test participants as "subjects." While many of us, including myself, have been conditioned to use this term, and have used it for very many years, the correct term today is "evaluator" or "participant."

TEST FACILITY

Always provide a proper location for a test, away from distractions and disturbances. If the test is being held in a usability laboratory, the test facility should resemble the location where the system will be used. It may be an actual office designated to the purpose of testing, or it may be a laboratory specially designed and fitted for conducting tests. The advantage of a laboratory from a data collection perspective is that it can be designed with one-way mirrors for observers and easily equipped with recording devices such as video cameras. The physical environment—lighting, temperature, and so on—can also be more precisely controlled.

TEST CONDUCT AND DATA COLLECTION

To collect usable data, the test can begin only after the proper preparation. Then, the data must be properly and accurately recorded. Finally, the test must be concluded and followed up properly. Following are guidelines for conducting a usability test. Many are from Schrier (1992).

Usability Test Guidelines

Before starting the test:

- Explain that the objective is to test the software, not the participants.
- Explain how the test materials and records will be used.
- If a consent agreement is to be signed, explain all information on it.
- If verbal protocols will be collected, let participants practice thinking aloud.
- Insure all participant questions are answered and the participant is comfortable with all procedures.

During the test:

- Minimize the number of people who will interact with the participants.
- If observers will be in the room, limit to two or three.
- Provide a checklist for recording:
  - Times to perform tasks.
  - Errors made in performing tasks.
  - Unexpected user actions.
  - System features used/not used.

- Difficult/easy to use features.
- System bugs or failures.
- Record techniques and search patterns participants employ when attempting to work through a difficulty.
- If participants are thinking aloud, record assumptions and inferences being made.
- Record with a tape recorder or video camera.
- Do not interrupt participants unless absolutely necessary.
- If participants need help, provide some response.
  - Provide encouragement or hints.
  - Give general hints before specific hints.
  - Record the number of hints given.
- Watch carefully for signs of stress in participants:
  - Sitting for long times doing nothing.
  - Blaming themselves for problems.
  - Flipping through documentation without really reading it.
- Provide short breaks when needed.
- Maintain a positive attitude, no matter what happens.

After the test:

- Hold a final interview with participants; tell participants what has been learned in the test.
- Provide a follow-up questionnaire that asks participants to evaluate the product or tasks performed.
- If videotaped, use only in proper ways.
  - Respect participants' privacy.
  - Get written permission to use tape.

Before Starting the Test Most people participating in a test will approach it with some anxiety. Fears may exist that they themselves are being judged, or apprehension may be caused by a general fear of the unknown, a common human trait. These fears must be put to rest. Before the test begins, all participants must be told exactly what will happen in the test. Explain that the test objective is to evaluate the software, not the participants themselves. Also explain how the test materials and records will be used. If participants will be signing a consent agreement, review and explain all information on it before it is signed. If verbal protocols will be collected, that is, the participants are going to be asked to think aloud, let participants practice this process. For most people this is not a common experience and it may require getting used to. Finally, do not start the test session until all participant questions are answered and people are comfortable with all of the test procedures. Providing this kind of information, and preparation, will enable participants to relax faster at the start of the test.

During the Test Minimize the number of people who will interact with participants. Many and strange voices must be avoided as they can be very distracting and disturbing. If observers will be in the room during the test, limit their number to two or three. Observers must *never* talk during the test.

For data recording, provide observers a checklist for reminding what to record and actually recording data. Useful information to collect includes times needed to perform each of the test tasks, errors made, any unexpected actions taken by the participants, how often system features are used, those features that are not used, difficulties in using features, features that are particularly easy to use, and system bugs or system failures. When participants encounter a difficulty, record the techniques and search patterns they employ when attempting to work through the difficulty. If participants are thinking aloud, record the assumptions and inferences they make as they proceed. If practical, record the test with a tape recorder and/or video camera. This will permit more leisurely review of the test session later. Details missed during the session will be uncovered and comparisons can be made between the approaches and activities of the different participants. The entire design team will also be allowed to later review and evaluate the test results.

Never interrupt a test participant unless it is absolutely necessary. If, however, it is sensed that participants need help, provide a response of some kind, first through encouragement and then hints. Provide general hints before specific hints, and record the number of hints given. Watch carefully for signs of stress. If it is detected, again give encouragement or provide hints, or provide a break. Signs of stress include a participant sitting for a long time doing nothing, blaming him or herself for problems, and flipping through documentation without really reading it. Provide short breaks when they are needed, and maintain a positive attitude no matter what happens (it probably will). A tester with a negative attitude will influence the participants in the same way and the data collected will be contaminated.

After the Test At the test's conclusion, hold a closing interview with the participants. During this interview, questions occurring to the tester during the actual test can be asked, the participants can also ask questions, and the tester can tell the participants some of what has been learned. This will make the participants feel that their effort was worthwhile. Also provide follow-up questionnaires that ask participants to evaluate the product or tasks performed. Finally, if videotaping is performed, respect the participant's privacy when the tape is later shown. If necessary, obtain the participant's written permission to later use the tape.

ANALYZE, MODIFY, RETEST, AND EVALUATE

Analyze the Data and Generate Design Recommendations

Analyze the data from the test, paying particular attention to problem areas uncovered. Make the results available to the entire design team for analysis, again to provide multiple insights into problem solutions.

Modify the Prototype as Necessary

Prototypes must, of course, be modified based on the design recommendations made during testing. The testing process continues in an iterative manner until all problems are satisfactorily solved and all criteria are met.

Test the System Again

After the prototyping is complete and all code written, a final system test must be performed to assure no software bugs exist and performance meets all specifications. The screens and interface must also be again tested to assure all established usability criteria are being met. The design steps and methods are identical to those for prototype testing.

Evaluate the Working System

Testing never stops with system implementation. Screens, like any part of a system, must be continually evaluated to assure that they are achieving their design objectives. Problems detected can be corrected in system enhancements and new releases. Many of the testing techniques used in prototype evaluation can also be applied in this design phase.

A FINAL WORD

Enjoy your journey through the wonderful world of graphical interface development. Application of these principles in design will aid greatly in creating a product that satisfies all your client's needs. A happy client, of course, also means a happy developer. Good luck!

References

Andre, A.D. & C.D. Wickens. (1995). "When users want what's NOT best for them." *Ergonomics in Design*. October.

Apple Computer, Inc. (1992a). *Guide to Macintosh Software Localization*. Reading, MA: Addison-Wesley.

Apple Computer, Inc. (1992b). *Macintosh Human Interface Guidelines*. Reading, MA: Addison-Wesley.

Baecker, R., & I. Small. (1990). "Animation at the interface." *The Art of Human-Computer Interface Design*, edited by B. Laurel. Reading, MA: Addison-Wesley.

Baecker, R., I. Small, & R. Mander. (1991). "Bringing icons to life." *Proceedings: CHI '91*.

Bailey & Bailey Software Corporation. (1989). *Protoscreens*. Ogden, UT: Bailey & Bailey Software Corporation.

Bailey, R.W., Ph.D. (1984). "Is ergonomics worth the investment?" *Proceedings: World Conference on Ergonomics in Computer Systems*. New York: Ericsson Information Systems.

Bailey, R.W., R.W. Allan, & P. Raiello. (1992). "Usability testing vs. heuristic evaluation: A head-to-head comparison." *Proceedings of the Human Factors Society 36th Annual Meeting*, Santa Monica, CA: Human Factors Society.

Barmack, J.E., & H.W. Sinaiko. (1966). *Human Factors Problems in Computer-Generated Graphic Displays*. Institute for Defense Analysis (AD-636170).

Barnard, P., N. Hammond, A. MacLean, & J. Morton. (1982). "Learning and remembering interactive commands." *Proceedings: Human Factors in Computer Systems*. March 15–17, Gaithersburg, MD.

Barnett, R. (1993). *Forms Analysis and Design*. Belconnen ACT, Australia: Robert Barnett and Associates Pty. Ltd.

Benest, I.D., & D. Dukic. (1989). "High-level user-interface objects." *Designing and Using Human-Computer Interfaces and Knowledge Based Systems*, G. Salvendy & M.J. Smith, eds. Amsterdam: Elsevier Science Publishers.

Bennett, J.L. (1979). "The commercial impact of usability in interactive systems." *Man-Computer Communication, Infotech State-of-the-Art*, Vol. 2. B. Schackel, ed. Maidenhead: Infotech International.

Bennett, J.L. (1984). "Managing to meet usability requirements." *Visual Display Terminals: Usability Issues and Health Concerns*. J.L. Bennett, D. Case, J. Sandelin, & M. Smith, eds. Englewood Cliffs, NJ: Prentice Hall.

Billingsley, P. (1988). "Taking panes: Issues in the design of windowing systems." *Handbook of Human-Computer Interactions*, M. Helander, ed. Amsterdam: Elsevier Science Publishers.

Billingsley, P. (1996). "Standards: Simplifying conformance." *SIGCHI Bulletin*. 28: 36–38.

Bishu, Ram R., & P. Zhan. (1992). "Increasing or decreasing? The menu direction effect on user performance." *Proceedings of the Human Factors Society 36th Annual Meeting,* Santa Monica, CA: Human Factors Society.

Black, J.B., J.M. Carroll, & S.M. McGuigan. (1987). "What kind of minimal instruction manual is most effective?" *Proceedings of CHI+GI*. 1987. New York.

Bly, S.A., & J.K. Rosenberg. (1986). "A comparison of tiled and overlapping windows." *Proceedings: CHI '86*. New York.

Bonsiepe, G. (1968). "A method of quantifying order in typographic design." *Journal of Typographic Research*, 2, 203–220.

Borenstein, N.S. (1985). "The design and evaluation of on-line help systems." Ph.D. diss., Carnegie-Mellon University, Pittsburgh, PA.

Bouma, H. (1970). "Interaction effects in parafoveal letter recognition." *Nature*. 226: 177–178.

Brems, D.J., & W.B. Whitten, II. (1987). "Learning and preference for icon-based interface." *Proceedings of the Human Factors Society 31st Annual Meeting,* Santa Monica, CA: Human Factors Society.

Brewster, S.A., P.C. Wright, & A.D.N. Edwards. (1993). "An evaluation of earcons for use in auditory human-computer interfaces." *INTERCHI '93*. Amsterdam.

Brooks, R. (1965). "Search time and color coding." *Psychonomic Science*. 2: 281–282.

Brown, C.M. (1988). *Human-Computer Interface Design Guidelines*. Norwood, NJ: Ablex Publishing Co.

Burns, M.J., & D.L. Warren. (1986). "Formatting space-related displays to optimize expert and nonexpert user performance." *Proceedings: CHI '86*. New York.

Bury, K.F., J.M. Boyle, R.J. Evey, & A.S. Neal. (1982). "Windowing versus scrolling on a visual display terminal." *Human Factors* 24: 385–394.

Byrne, M.D. (1993). "Using icons to find documents: simplicity is critical." *INTERCHI '93*. Amsterdam, April 24–29.

Cairney, P. & D. Sless. (1982). "Communication effectiveness of symbolic safety signs with different user groups." *Applied Ergonomics* 13: 91–97.

Callahan, J., D. Hopkins, M. Weiser, & B. Shneiderman. (1988). "An empirical comparison of pie vs. linear menus." *Conference Proceedings—Human Factors in Computing Systems*. May 15–18, Washington, DC.

Callan, J.R., L.E. Curran, & J.L. Lane. (1977). "Visual search times for navy tactical information displays (Report #NPRDC-TR-77-32)." San Diego, CA: Navy Personnel Research and Development Center (NTIS No. AD A040543).

Card, S.K. (1982). "User perceptual mechanisms in the search of computer command menus." *Proceedings: Human Factors in Computer Systems*. March 15–17, Gaithersburg, MD.

Card, S.K., T.P. Moran, & A. Newell. (1983). *The Psychology of Human-Computer Interaction*. Hillsdale, NJ: Lawrence Erlbaum.

Carroll, J.M., J.C. Thomas, & A. Malhotra. (1980). "Presentation and representation in design problem-solving." *British Journal of Psychology* 71: 143–153.

Carroll, J.M., and C. Carrithers. (1984). "Blocking learner error states in a training-wheels system." *Human Factors* 26: (4)377–389.

Carroll, J.M., P.L. Smith-Kerker, J.R. Ford, & S.A. Mazur. (1986). *The Minimal Manual* (Research Report RC 11637). Yorktown Heights, NY: IBM T.J. Watson Research Center.

Carter, R.L. (1982). "Visual search with color." *Journal of Experimental Psychology: Human Perception and Performance*. 8: 127–136.

Christ, R.E., & W.H. Teichner. (1973). "Color research for visual displays." *JANAIR* (Report No. 730703), New Mexico: New Mexico State University.

Christ, R.E. (1975). "Review and analysis of color coding research for visual displays." *Human Factors* 17: (6)542–570.

Coll, R.A., J.H. Coll, & G. Thakur. (1994). "Graphs and tables: A four-factor experiment." *Communications of the ACM*. 177–85.

Cooper, A. (1985). "Remark: Window viper." *PC World*. 25–37.

Cope, M.E., & K.C. Uliano. (1995). "Cost-justifying usability engineering: A real world example." *Proceedings of the Human Factors Society 39th Annual Meeting,* Santa Monica, CA: Human Factors Society.

Cushman, W.H. (1986). "Reading for microfiche, a VDT, and the printed page: Subjective fatigue and performance." *Human Factors* 28: (1)63–73.

Damodaran, L., A. Simpson, & P. Wilson. (1980). "Designing systems for people." *NCC*. Manchester and Loughborough University of Technology.

Danchak, M.M. (1976). "CRT displays for power plants." *Instrumentation Technology*. 23: (10)29–36.

Davies, S.E., K.F. Bury, & M.J. Darnell. (1985). "An experimental comparison of a windowed vs. a non-windowed operating system environment." *Proceedings of the Human Factors Society 29th Annual Meeting,* Santa Monica, CA: Human Factors Society.

del Galdo, E. (1990). "Internationalization and translation: Some guidelines for the design of human-computer interfaces." *Designing User Interfaces for International Use*, J. Nielsen, ed. Amsterdam: Elsevier Science Publishers.

Desaulniers, D.R., & D.J. Gillan. (1988). "The effects of format in computer-based procedure displays." *Proceedings of the Human Factors Society 32nd Annual Meeting*, Santa Monica, CA: Human Factors Society.

de Souza, F., & N. Bevan. (1990). "The use of guidelines in menu interface design." *Proceedings: IFIP Interact '90*. August 27–31, Cambridge, U.K.

Desurvire, H., J. Kondziela, & M. Atwood. (1992). "What is gained and lost when using evaluation methods other than empirical testing." *Proceedings of HCI 1992*, A. Monk, D. Diaper, & M.D. Harrison, eds. U.K.: September 15–18, University of York.

Dickey, G.L., & M.H. Schneider. (1971). "Multichannel communication of an industrial task." *International Journal of Production Research*. 9: 487–489.

Digital Equipment Corp. (1988). *XUI Style Guide* (Order No. AA-MG20A-TE). Maynard, MA.

Dodson, D.W., & N.J. Shields, Jr. (1978). "Development of user guidelines for ECAS display design (Vol. 1)." (Report No. NASA-CR-150877). Huntsville, AL: Essex Corp.

Donohoo, D.T., & H.L. Snyder. (1985). "Accommodation during color contrast." *Society for Information Display Digest of Technical Papers*. New York: New York Palisades Institute for Research Sciences.

Dray, S.M., W.G. Ogden, & R.E. Vestewig. (1981). "Measuring performance with a menu selection human-computer interface." *Proceedings of the Human Factors Society 25th Annual Meeting,* Santa Monica, CA: Human Factors Society.

Dunsmore, H.E. (1982). "Using formal grammars to predict the most useful characteristics of interactive systems." *Office Automation Conference Digest*, April 5–7, San Francisco.

Elkerton, J., & R.C. Willeges. (1984). "The effectiveness of a performance-based assistant in an information retrieval environment." *Proceedings of the Human Factors Society 28th Annual Meeting,* Santa Monica, CA: Human Factors Society. 634–638.

Elkerton, J. (1988). "Online aiding for human-computer interfaces." *Handbook of Human-Computer Interaction*. M. Helander, ed. Amsterdam: Elsevier Science Publishers.

Elkerton, J., & S.L. Palmiter. (1991). "Designing help using a GOMS model: An information retrieval evaluation." *Human Factors* 33: (2)185–204.

Ells, J.G., & R.E. Dewar. (1979). "Rapid comprehension of verbal and symbolic traffic sign messages." *Human Factors* 21: 161–168.

Engel, F.L. (1980). "Information selection from visual displays." *Ergonomic Aspects of Visual Display Terminals*. E. Grandjean, & E. Vigliani, eds. London: Taylor & Francis Ltd.

Familant, M.E., & M.C. Detweiler. (1995). "Do human factors color recommendations have any practical value?" *Proceedings of the Human Factors and Ergonomics Society 39th Annual Meeting*, Santa Monica, CA: Human Factors Society.

Fowler, S.L., & V.R. Stanwick. (1995). *The GUI Style Guide*, Cambridge, MA: Academic Press.

Francik, E.P., & R.M. Kane. (1987). "Optimizing visual search and cursor movement in pull-down menus." *Proceedings of the Human Factors Society 31st Annual Meeting*, Santa Monica, CA: Human Factors Society.

Frese, M., H. Schulte-Gocking, & A. Altmann. (1987). "Lernprozesse in Abhangigkeit von der Trainingsmethode, von Personenmerkmalen und von der Benutzeroberflache (Direkte Manipulation vs. konventionelle interaktion)." *Software-Ergonomie '87*. W. Schonpflu and M. Wittstock, eds. Tagung 11/1987 des German Chapter of the ACM. Berlin: Teubner.

Furnas, G.W., L.M. Gomez, T.K. Landauer, & S.T. Dumais. (1982). "Statistical semantics: how can a computer use what people name things to guess what things people mean when they name things?" *Proceedings: Human Factors in*

Computer Systems. March 15–17, Gaithersburg, MD.

Galitz, W.O. (1968). "CRT viewing and visual aftereffects." *UNIVAC Internal Report.* Roseville, MN.

Galitz, W.O. (1972). "IBM 3270 on-line evaluation." *INA Technical Report* (E5320-A02/M72-0001).

Galitz, W.O., & A. DiMatteo. (1974). "EIS forms and screens design manual." *International Report.* Philadelphia, PA: INA Corporation.

Galitz, W.O. (1980). *Human Factors in Office Automation.* Atlanta, GA: Life Office Management Association.

Galitz, W.O. (1981). *Handbook of Screen Format Design.* Wellesley, MA: QED Publishing Group.

Galitz, W.O. (1992). *User-Interface Screen Design.* Wellesley, MA: QED Publishing Group.

Garver, W.W. (1993). "Synthesizing auditory icons." *INTERCHI '93.* April 24–29, Amsterdam.

Gaylin, K.B. (1986). "How are windows used? Some notes on creating an empirically-based windowing benchmark task." *Proceedings: CHI '86 Human Factors in Computing Systems.* New York.

Gittens, D. (1986). "Icon-based human-computer interaction." *International Journal of Man-Machine Studies.* 24: 519–543.

Gould, J.D. (1988). "How to design usable systems." *Handbook of Human-Computer Interaction,* M. Helander, ed. Amsterdam: Elsevier Science Publishers.

Gould, J.D., S.J. Boies, M. Meluson, M. Rasamny, & A.M. Vosburgh. (1988). "Empirical evaluation of entry and selection methods for specifying dates." *Proceedings of the Human Factors Society 32nd Annual Meeting,* Santa Monica, CA: Human Factors Society.

Greene, S.L., J.D. Gould, S.J. Boies, A. Meluson, & M. Rasamny. (1988). "Entry-based versus selection-based interaction methods." *Proceedings of the Human Factors Society 32nd Annual Meeting,* Santa Monica, CA: Human Factors Society.

Greene, S.L., J.D. Gould, M.R. Boies, M. Rasamny, & A. Meluson. (1992). "Entry and selection based methods of human-computer interaction." *Human Factors* 34: (1)97–113.

Greenstein, J.S., & L.Y. Arnaut. (1988). "Input devices." *Handbook of Human-Computer Interaction,* M. Helander, ed. Amsterdam: Elsevier Science Publishers.

Guastello, S.J., M. Traut, & G. Korienek. (1989). "Verbal versus pictorial representation of objects in a human-computer interface." *International Journal of Man-Machine Studies.* 31: 99–120.

Gugerty, L., S. Halgren, J. Gosbee, & M. Rudisill. (1991). "Using GOMS models and hypertext to create representations of medical procedures for online display." *Proceedings of the Human Factors Society 35th Annual Meeting,* Santa Monica, CA: Human Factors Society.

Haines, R.M., L.M. Dawson, T. Galvan, & L.M. Reid. (1975). "Response time to colored stimuli in the full visual field." (NASA TN D-7927). Moffett Field, CA: NASA.

Hair, D.C. (1991). "Legalese: A legal argumentation tool." *SIGCHI Bulletin.* 23: (1)71–74.

Halsey, R.M., & A. Chapanis. (1951). "On the number absolutely identifiable spectral hues." *Journal of Optical Society of America*. 41: 1057–1058.

Harrison, S.M. (1995). "A comparison of still, animated, or nonillustrated on-line help with written or spoken instructions in a graphical user interface." *Proceedings of CHI '95*. May 7–11, Denver, CO.

Hatfield, D. (1981). *Conference on Easier and More Productive Use of Computer Systems*. Ann Arbor, MI. (In Shneiderman, 1986).

Haubner, P., & C. Benz. (1983). "Information display on monochrome and colour screens." *Abstracts: International Scientific Conference on Ergonomic and Health Aspects in Modern Offices*. November 7–9, Turin, Italy.

Haubner, P., & F. Neumann. (1986). "Structuring alphanumerically coded information on visual display units." *Proceedings: International Scientific Conference: Work with Display Units*. May 12–15, Stockholm, Sweden.

Haubner, P.J. (1992). "Window design and location for messages in interactive systems." *Work with Display Units*. H. Luczak, A.E. Cakir, & G. Cakir, eds.

Heckel, P. (1984). *The Elements of Friendly Software Design*. New York, NY: Warner Books.

Hendrickson, J.J. (1989). "Performance, preference, and visual scan patterns on a menu-based system: implications for interface design." *Proceedings: Human Factors in Computing Systems*, May, *CHI '89*.

Hollands, J.G., & I. Spence. (1992). "Judgments of Change and Proportion in Graphical Perception." *Human Factors*, 34: (3)313–334.

Horton, W. (1994). *The Icon Book*. New York: John Wiley & Sons.

Howlett, V. (1995). *Visual Interface Design for Windows*. John Wiley & Sons.

Human Factors Society, American National Standard for Human Factors Engineering of Visual Display Terminal Workstations. Santa Monica, CA: Human Factors Society.

Hutchins, E.L., J.D. Hollan, & D.A. Norman. (1980). "Direct manipulation interfaces." User Centered System Design: *New Perspectives on Human-Computer Interaction*. Hillsdale, NJ: Lawrence Erlbaum Associates.

International Business Machines Corporation (IBM). (1987). *Systems Application Architecture Common User Access, Panel Design and User Interaction* (SC26-4351-0). Boca Raton, FL: IBM.

International Business Machines Corporation (IBM). (1989a). *System Application Architecture Common User Access, Advanced Interface Design Guide* (SC26-4582). Cary, NC: IBM.

International Business Machines Corporation (IBM). (1989b). *Systems Application Architecture Common User Access, Basic Interface Design Guide* (SC26-4583). Cary, NC: IBM.

International Business Machines Corporation (IBM). (1991). *Systems Application Architecture Common User Access Advanced Interface Design Reference* (SC34-4289).

International Business Machines Corporation (IBM). (1992). *Object-Oriented Interface Design: IBM Common User Access Guidelines*. Carmel, IN: Que Corporation.

Jeffries, R., J.R. Miller, C. Wharton, & K.M. Uyeda. (1991). "User interface evaluation in the real world: A comparison of four techniques." *Proceedings of CHI '91.* New York: ACM Press. 119–124

Johnsgard, T.J., S.R. Page, R.D. Wilson, & R.J. Zeno. (1995). "A comparison of graphical user interface widgets for various tasks." *Proceedings of the Human Factors and Ergonomics Society 39th Annual Meeting,* Santa Monica, CA: Human Factors Society.

Johnson-Laird, A. (1985). "They look good in demos, but windows are a real pain." *Software News.* 42: 36–37.

Karat, J. (1986). "Transfer between word processing systems." *Proceedings: International Scientific Conference: Work with Display Units.* May 12–15, Stockholm, Sweden.

Karat, J. (1987). "Evaluating user interface complexity." *Proceedings of the Human Factors Society 31st Annual Meeting,* Santa Monica, CA: Human Factors Society. 566–570.

Keil, M., & E. Carmel. (1995). "Customer-developer links." *Communications of the ACM.* 38: (5)33–34.

Keister, R.S., & G.R. Gallaway. (1983). "Making software user friendly: An assessment of data entry performance." *Proceedings of the Human Factors Society 27th Annual Meeting,* Santa Monica, CA: Human Factors Society.

Kiger, J.I. (1984). "The depth/breadth tradeoff in the design of menu driven user interfaces." *International Journal of Man-Machine Studies.* 20: 201–213.

Kobara, S. (1991). *Visual Design with OSF/Motif.* Reading, MA: Hewlett-Packard/Addison-Wesley.

Kohl, J.R., R.O. Barclay, T.E. Pinelli, M.L. Keene, & J.M. Kennedy. (1993). "The impact of language and culture on technical communication in Japan." *Technical Communication.*

Kolers, P. (1969). "Some formal characteristics of pictograms." *American Scientist.* 57: (3)348–363.

Kopala, C.J. (1981). "The use of color coded symbols in a highly dense situation display." *Proceedings of the Human Factors Society 23rd Annual Meeting,* Santa Monica, CA: Human Factors Society.

Kühne, A., H. Krueger, W. Graf, & L. Merz. (1986). "Positive versus negative image polarity." *Proceedings: International Scientific Conference: Work with Display Units.* May 12–15, Stockholm, Sweden.

KYE Systems Corp. (1995). *Genius EasyScan/Color PRO User's Guide.*

Lalomia, M.J., & A.J. Happ. (1987). "The effective use of color for text on the IBM 5153 color display. *Proceedings of the Human Factors Society 31st Annual Meeting,* Santa Monica, CA: Human Factors Society.

Landauer, T.K., & D.W. Nachbar. (1985). "Selection from alphabetic and numeric menu trees using a touch screen: breadth, depth, and width." *Proceedings: CHI '85 Human Factors in Computing Systems.* New York.

Lee, E., & J. MacGregor. (1985). "Minimizing user search time in menu retrieval systems." *Human Factors.* 27: (2)157–162.

Legge, G.E., & G.S. Rubin. (1986). "Psychophysics of reading IV. Wavelengths effects in normal and low vision." *Journal of the Optical Society of America.* 3: 40–51.

Lichty, T. (1989). *Design Principles for Desktop Publishers*. Glenview, IL: Scott, Foresman & Company.

Lind, N.E., M. Johnson, & B. Sandblad. (1992). "The art of the obvious." *CHI '95*. May 3–7, Monterey, CA.

Lodding, K. (1983). "Iconic interfacing." *IEEE Computer Graphics and Applications*. 3: (2)11–20.

Luria, S.M., D.F. Neri, & A.R. Jacobsen. (1986). "The effects of set size on color matching using CRT displays." *Proceedings of the Human Factors Society 30th Annual Meeting*, Santa Monica, CA: Human Factors Society.

MacKenzie, J.S., A. Sellen, & W. Buxton. (1991). "A comparison of input devices in elemental pointing and dragging tasks." *CHI '91*.

Magers, C.S. (1983). "An experimental evaluation on on-line HELP for non-programmers." *Proceedings: CHI '83 Human Factors in Computing Systems*. New York.

Maguire, M.C. (1985). "A review of human factors guidelines and techniques for the design of graphical human-computer interfaces." *Comput & Graphics* 9: (3)25.

Mallory, K., *et al.* (1980). "Human engineering guide to control room evaluation. Essex Corporation." *Technical Report NUREG/CR-1580*. Alexandria, VA.

Mandel, T. (1994). *The GUI-OOUI War: Windows vs. OS/2, the Designer's Guide to Human-Computer Interfaces*. New York: Van Nostrand Reinhold.

Mann, T.L., & L.A. Schnetzler. (1986). "Evaluation of formats for aircraft control/display units." *Applied Ergonomics* 17.4: 265–270.

Marcus, A. (1984). "Icon design requires clarity, consistency." *Computer Graphics Today*.

Marcus, A. (1986a). "Proper color, type use improve instruction." *Computer Graphics Today*.

Marcus, A. (1986b). "Ten commandments of color." *Computer Graphics Today*.

Marcus, A. (1992). *Graphic Design for Electronic Documents and User Interfaces*. New York: ACM Press.

Martin, J. (1973). *Design of Man-Computer Dialogues*. Englewood Cliffs, NJ: Prentice Hall.

Matthews, M.L., & K. Mertins. (1987). "The influence of color on visual search and subjective discomfort using CRT displays." *Proceedings of the Human Factors Society 31st Annual Meeting*, Santa Monica, CA: Human Factors Society.

Matthews, M.L., & K. Mertins. (1988). "Working with color CRTs: Pink eye, yellow fever, and feeling blue." *Proceedings of the Ergonomics Society's 1988 Annual Conference,* E.D. Megaw, ed. London: Taylor & Francis.

Matthews, M.L., J.V. Lovasik, & K. Mertins. (1989). "Visual performance and subjective discomfort in prolonged viewing of chromatic displays." *Human Factors* 31: (3)259–271.

Mayer, R.E. (1988). "From novice to expert." *Handbook of Human-Computer Interaction*, M. Helander, ed. Amsterdam: Elsevier Science Publishers.

Mayhew, D.J. (1992). *Principles and Guidelines in Software User Interface Design*. Englewood Cliffs, NJ: Prentice Hall.

McTyre, J.H., & W.D. Frommer. (1985). "Effects of character/background color combinations on CRT character legibility." *Proceedings of the Human Factors Society 29th Annual Meeting*, Santa Monica, CA: Human Factors Society.

Microsoft Corporation. (1992). *The Windows Interface: An Application Design Guide*. Redmond, WA: Microsoft Press.

Microsoft Corporation. (1995). *The Windows Interface Guidelines for Software Design*. Redmond, WA: Microsoft Press.

Microswitch (A Honeywell Division). (1984). *Applying Manual Controls and Displays: A Practical Guide to Panel Design*. Freeport, IL: Microswitch.

Miller, D.P. (1981). "The depth/breadth tradeoff in hierarchical computer menus." *Proceedings of the Human Factors Society 25th Annual Meeting*. Santa Monica, CA: Human Factors Society.

Miller, G.A. (1956). "The magical number seven, plus or minus two: Some limits on our capability for processing information." *Psychological Science*. 63: 87–97.

Mitchell, J., & B. Shneiderman. (1989). "Dynamic versus static menus: An exploratory comparison." *SIGCHI Bulletin* 20: (4)33–37.

Mori, H., & Y. Hayashi. (1993). "Visual interference with user's tasks on multi-window system." *Proceedings of the Fifth International Conference on Human-Computer Interaction*. 80–85.

Morimoto, K., T. Kurokawa, & T. Nishimura. (1993). "Dynamic representation of icons in human-computer interaction." *Proceedings of the Fifth International Conference on Human-Computer Interaction*.

Mosier, J.N., & S.L. Smith. (1986). "Application of guidelines for designing user interface software." *Behaviour and Information Technology* 5: (1)39–46.

Moskel, S., J. Erno, & B. Shneiderman. (1984). "Proofreading and comprehension of text on screens and paper." *University of Maryland Computer Science Technical Report*.

Murch, G. (1983). "The effective use of color: physiological principles." Beaverton, OR: Tektronix, Inc.

Murch, G. (1984). "The effective use of color: Perceptual principles." Beaverton, OR: Tektronix, Inc.

Myers, B.A., & M.B. Rosson. (1992). "Survey on user interface programming." *Proceedings: CHI '92*. May 3–7, Monterey, CA.

Nagy, A.L., & R.R. Sanchez. (1992). "Chromaticity and luminance as coding dimensions in visual search." *Human Factors* 34: 601–614.

National Language Technical Center. (1991). *National Language Design Guide: Designing Enabled Products*. Vol. 1. Canada: National Language Technical Center.

Neerincx, M., & P. de Greef. (1993). "How to aid non-experts." *INTERCHI '93*, April 24–29, Amsterdam.

Nelson, T. (1980). "Interactive systems and the design of virtuality." *Creative Computing*. 16 (11)56 ff., & 6 (12)94 ff.

NeXT Publications. (1992). *NeXTStep User Interface Guidelines*. Reading, MA: Addison-Wesley.

Nielsen, J. (1990). "Usability testing of international interfaces." *Designing User Interfaces for International Use*, J. Nielson, ed. New York: Elsevier.

Nielsen, J. (1992). "Finding usability problems through heuristic evaluation." *Proceedings: CHI '95*. May 3–7, Monterey, CA.

Nolan, P.R. (1989). "Designing screen icons: Ranking and matching studies." *Pro-

ceedings of the Human Factors Society 33rd Annual Meeting, Santa Monica, CA: Human Factors Society.

Nugent, W.A., & J.W. Broyles. (1992). "Assessment of graphics and text formats for system displays." *Proceedings of the Human Factors Society 36th Annual Meeting*, Santa Monica, CA: Human Factors Society.

Open Software Foundation. (1993). *OSF/Motif Style Guide*. Englewood Cliffs, NJ: Prentice Hall.

Ortega, K.A. (1989). "Problem-solving: Expert/novice differences." *Human Factors Society Bulletin*. 32 (3).

Ostberg, O. (1982). "Accommodation and visual fatigue in display work." *Ergonomics Aspects of Video Display Terminals*. E. Grandjean, & E. Vigliana, eds. London: Taylor & Francis.

Paap, K.R., & R.J. Roske-Hofstrand. (1986). "The optimal number of menu options per panel." *Human Factors* 28: (4)377–385.

Paap, K.R., & R.J. Roske-Hofstrand. (1988). "Design of menus." *Handbook of Human-Computer Interaction*. M. Helander, ed. Amsterdam: Elsevier Science Publishers.

Paradies, M. (1991). "Root cause analysis and human factors." *Human Factors* 34: (8)1–4.

Pastoor, S. (1990). "Legibility and subjective preference for color combinations in text." *Human Factors* 32: (2)157–171.

Pinkus, A.R. (1982). "The effects of color and contrast on target recognition performance using monochromatic television displays" (Report AFAMRL-TR-82-9). Wright-Patterson AFB, OH: AFAMRL.

Plaisant, C., & D. Wallace. (1992). "Touchscreen toggle design." *Proceedings: CHI '92*, May 3–7, Monterey, CA.

Pokorny, J., C.H. Graham, & R.N. Lanson. (1968). "Effects of wavelength on foveal grating acuity." *Journal of the Optical Society of America*. 58: 1410.

Polya, G. (1957). *How to Solve It*. New York: Doubleday.

Popowicz, A. (1995). "Collecting user information on a limited budget." *SIGCHI Bulletin*. 27: (4)23–28.

Post, D.I. (1985). "Effects of color on CRT symbol legibility." *SID Digest*.

Pulat, B.M., & H.H. Nwankwo. (1987). "Formatting alphanumeric CRT displays." *INT. J. Man-Machine Studies*. 26: 567–580.

Quinn, L., & D.M. Russell. (1986). "Intelligent interfaces: User models and planners." *Proceedings: CHI '86*. 314–318.

Radl, G.W. (1980). "Experimental investigations for optimal presentation mode and colors of symbols on the CRT screen." *Ergonomics Aspects of Video Display Terminals*, E. Grandjean & E. Vigliana, eds. London: Taylor & Francis.

Radl, G.W. (1984). "Optimal presentation mode and colors of symbols on VDU's." *Health Hazards of VDT's?*, B.G. Pearce, ed. Chichester, England: John Wiley & Sons.

Rehe, R.F. (1974). *Typography: How to Make It More Legible*. Carmel, IN: Design Research International.

Remington, R., & D. Williams. (1986). "On the selection and evaluation of visual display symbology: Factors influencing search and identification times." *Human Factors*. 28: (4)407–420.

Roemer, J., & A. Chapanis. (1982). "Learning performance and attitudes as a function of the reading grade level of a computer-presented tutorial." *Proceedings: Human Factors in Computer Systems*. March 15–17, Gaithersburg, MD.

Rogers, Y. (1989). "Icons at the interface: Their usefulness." *Interacting with Computers: The Interdisciplinary Journal of Human-Computer Interaction*. 1: (1)105–117.

Russo, P., & S. Boor. (1993). "How fluent is your interface? Designing for international users." *INTERCHI '93*. April 24–29, Amsterdam.

Rutkowski,. C. (1982). "An introduction to the human applications standard computer interface, part 1: Theory and principles," *BYTE 7*. 11: 291–310.

Savage, R.E., J.K. Habinek, & N.J. Blackstad. (1982). "An experimental evaluation of input field and cursor combinations." *Proceedings of the Human Factors Society 26th Annual Meeting*, Santa Monica, CA: Human Factors Society.

Schrier, J.R. (1992). "Reducing stress associated with participating in a usability test." *Proceedings of the Human Factors Society 36th Annual Meeting*, Santa Monica, CA: Human Factors Society.

Schwarz, E., I.P. Beldie, & S. Pastoor. (1983). "A comparison of paging and scrolling for changing screen contents by inexperienced users." *Human Factors*. 25: (3)279–282.

Shackel, B. (1981). "The concept of usability." *Proceedings of IBM Software and Information Usability Symposium*. September 15–18, Poughkeepsie, NY.

Shackel, B. (1991). "Usability—context, framework, definition, design and evaluation." *Human Factors for Informatics Usability*, B. Schackel & S.J. Richardson, eds. Cambridge, U.K.: Cambridge University Press.

Shannon, C.E., & W. Weaver. (1949). *The Mathematical Theory of Communication*. Urbana, IL: The University of Illinois Press.

Shneiderman, B. (1982). "The future of interactive systems and the emergence of direct manipulation." *Behaviour and Information Technology, I*. 237–256.

Shneiderman, B. (1982a). "Control flow and data structure documentation: Two experiments." *Communications of the ACM*. 25: (1)55–63.

Shneiderman, B. (1982b). "System message design: guidelines and experimental results." *Directions in Human / Computer Interaction*. A. Badre and B. Shneiderman, eds. Norwood, NJ: Ablex Publishers. 55–78.

Shneiderman, B. (1986). "Human-computer interaction research at the University of Maryland." *SIGCHI Bulletin*. 17: 27–32.

Shneiderman, B., & S. Margono. (1987). "A study of file manipulation by novices using commands vs. direct manipulation." *Proceedings of 26th Annual Technical Symposium of the Washington, DC, Chapter of the ACM*. Gaithersburg, MD: National Bureau of Standards.

Shneiderman, B. (1987). *Designing the User Interface: Strategies for Effective Human-Computer Interaction*. Reading, MA: Addison-Wesley.

Shurtleff, M. (1993). "Say cheese! Guidelines for the use of photorealism in graphical user interfaces." *CSTG Bulletin*. 15–17.

Sidorsky, R.C. (1982). "Color coding in tactical displays: Help or hindrance." *Army Research Institute Research Report*.

Simkin, D., & R. Hastie. (1987). "An information-processing analysis of graph perception." *Journal of the American Statistical Association*. 82: 454–465.

Sivak, J.G., & G.C. Woo. (1983). "Color of visual display terminals and the eye: Green VDT's provoke the optimal stimulus to accommodation." *American Journal of Optometry and Physiological Optics*. 60: 640–642.

Smith, D.C., E.F. Harslem, C.H. Irby, R.B. Kimball, & W.L. Verplank. (1982). "Designing the star user interface." *Byte*.

Smith, S.L., & J.N. Mosier. (1986). *Guidelines for Designing User-Interface Software* (Mitre ESD-TR-86-278 MTR 10090). Hanscom AFB, MA.

Smith, W. (1986). "Computer color: Psychophysics, task application, and aesthetics." *Proceedings: International Scientific Conference: Work with Display Units*. May 12–15, Stockholm, Sweden.

Smith, W. (1988). "Standardizing colors for computer screens." *Proceedings of the Human Factors Society 32nd Annual Meeting*, Santa Monica, CA: Human Factors Society.

Snowberry, K., S.R. Parkinson, & N. Sisson. (1983). "Computer display menus." *Ergonomics* 26: 699–712.

Springer, C.J., & J.F. Sorce. (1984). "Accessing large data bases: The relationship between data entry time and output evaluation time." *Human Computer Interaction-INTERACT '95*. England. 263–267.

Stern, K.R. (1984). "An evaluation of written, graphics, and voice messages in procedural instructions. *Proceedings of the Human Factor Society 28th Annual Meeting*. Santa Monica, CA: Human Factor Society. 314–318.

Streveler, D.J., & A.I. Wasserman. (1984). "Quantitative measures of the spatial properties of screen designs." *INTERACT '95. Human-Computer Interaction*. England.

Stromoski, R. (1993). "Fighting the futz factor." *Information Week*. Feb 15: 55.

Sukaviriya, P., & L. Moran. (1990). "User interfaces for Asia." *Designing User Interfaces for International Use*, J. Nielsen, ed. New York: Elsevier.

Sun Microsystems, Inc. (1990). *Open Look Graphical User Interface Application Style Guidelines*. Reading, MA: Addison-Wesley.

Taylor, D. (1982). *Global Software*. New York: Springer Verlag.

Tedford, W.H., S.L. Berquist, & W.E. Flynn. (1977). "The size-color illusion." *Journal of General Psychology*. 17: (1)145–149.

Teitelbaum, R.D., & R. Granda. (1983). "The effects of positional constancy on searching menus for information." *Proceedings: CHI '83*. 150–153.

Temple, B., *et al.* (1990). "The benefits of the graphical user interface." *Microsoft Report*.

Tetzlaff, L., & D.R. Schwartz. (1991). "The use of guidelines in interface design." *Proceedings: CHI '91*. 329–334.

Thacker, P. (Paul). (1987). "Tabular displays: A human factors study." *CSTG Bulletin*. 14: (1)13.

Thovtrup, H., & J. Nielsen. (1991). "Assessing the usability of a user interface standard." *Proceedings: CHI '91*. 335–342.

Tinker, M.A. (1955). "Prolonged reading tasks in visual research." *Journal of Applied Psychology*. 39: 444–446.

Tombaugh, J.W., B. Paynter, & R.F. Dillon. (1989). "Command and graphic interfaces: user performance and satisfaction." *Designing and Using Human-Computer Interfaces and Knowledge Based Systems*, G. Salvendy & M.J. Smith, eds. Amsterdam: Elsevier Science Publishers.

Treisman, A. (1982). "Perceptual grouping and attention in visual search for features and for objects." *Journal of Experimental Psychology: Human Perception and Performance*. 8: 194–214.

Tripathi, P.D. (1992). "English: 'The Chosen Tongue,'" *English Today*. 8 (4):3–11.

Trollip, S., & G. Sales. (1986). "Readability of computer-generated fill-justified text." *Human Factors* 28: (2)159–163.

Tufte, E.R. (1983). *The Visual Display of Quantitative Information*. Cheshire, CT: Graphics Press.

Tullis, T. (1981). "An evaluation of alphanumeric, graphic, and color information displays." *Human Factors* 23: 541–550.

Tullis, T. (1983). "Predicting the usability of alphanumeric displays." Ph.D. diss., Rice University.

Tullis, T. (1985). "Designing a menu-based interface to an operating system." *Proceedings: CHI '85*. New York.

Tullis, T., & M.L. Kodimer. (1992). "A comparison of direct-manipulation, selection, and data-entry techniques for reordering fields in a table." *Proceedings of the Human Factors Society 36th Annual Meeting*, Santa Monica, CA: Human Factors Society.

Tullis, T. (1993). "Is user interface design just common sense?" *Proceedings of the Fifth International Conference on Human-Computer Interaction*. 9–14.

Vartabedian, A.G. (1971). "The effects of letter size, case and generation method on CRT display search time." *Human Factors*. 13: (4)363–368.

Verplank, B. (1988). "Designing graphical user interfaces." *Proceedings: CHI '88*. May 15.

Vitz, P.C. (1966). "Preference for different amounts of visual complexity." *Behavioral Science*. 2: 105–114.

Walker, M.A. (1989). "Natural language in a desktop environment." *Designing and Using Human-Computer Interfaces and Knowledge Based Systems*, G. Salvendy & M.J. Smith, eds. Amsterdam: Elsevier Science Publishers.

Walker, R.E., R.C. Nicolay, & C.R. Stearns. (1965). "Comparative accuracy of recognizing american and international road signs." *Journal of Applied Psychology* 49: 322–325.

Wallace, D. (1987). "Time stress effects on two menu selection systems." *Proceedings of the Human Factors Society 31st Annual Meeting*, Santa Monica, CA: Human Factors Society.

Walraven, J. (1984). "Perceptual artifacts that may interfere with color coding on visual displays." *Proceedings of NATO Workshop: Color Coded vs. Monochrome Electronic Displays*, C.P. Gibson, ed. Farnborough, England: Royal Aircraft Establishment.

Watanabe, A., T. Mori, S. Nagata, & K. Hiwatashi. (1968). "Spatial sine wave response of the human visual system." *Vision Research*. 8: 1245–1263.

Weinschenk, S. (1995). "Storyboarding the information process." *Session Proceedings, BFMA The 26th International Symposium on Forms and Information Systems*. May 7–11, St. Louis, MO.

Wertheimer, M. (1959). *Productive Thinking*. New York: Harper and Row.

White, J.V. (1990). *Color for the Electronic Age*. New York: Watson-Guptill Publications.

Whiteside, J., S. Jones, P.S. Levy, & D. Wixon. (1985). "User performance with command, menu, and iconic interfaces." *Proceedings CHI '85*.

Wichansky, A.M. (1986). "Legibility and user acceptance of monochrome display phospher colors." *Proceedings: International Scientific Conference: Work with Display Units*. May 12–15, Stockholm, Sweden.

Williams, J.R. (1988). "The effects of case and spacing on menu option search time." *Proceedings of the Human Factors Society 32nd Annual Meeting*, Santa Monica, CA: Human Factors Society.

Winograd, T. (1995). "From programming environments to environments for designing." *Communications of the ACM*. 38: (10)65–74.

Woods, D.D., L. Johannesen, & S.S. Potter. (1992). "The sophistry of guidelines: Revisiting recipes for color use in human-computer interface design." *Proceedings of the Human Factors Society 36th Annual Meeting*, Santa Monica, CA: Human Factors Society.

Wopking, M., S. Pastoor, & I.O. Beldie. (1985). "Design of user guidance in videotex systems." *Proceedings of the 11th International Symposium on Human Factors in Telecommunications*. Boston: Information Gatekeepers.

Wright, P. (1981). "Problems to be solved when creating usable documents." *IBM Symposium on Software and Information Usability* (HF077). Winchester, UK: IBM Hursley.

Wright, P. (1984). "User documentation." *Proceedings: World Conference on Ergonomics in Computer Systems*. Sept. 24–Oct. 4. New York: Ericsson Information Systems. 110–126.

Wright, P. (1988). "Issues of content and presentation in document design." *Handbook of Human-Computer Interaction*. M. Helander, ed. Amsterdam: Elsevier Science Publishers.

Wright, P. (1991). "Designing and evaluating documentation for I.T. users." *Human Factors for Informatics Usability*, B. Shackel, & S.J. Richardson, eds. Cambridge U.K.: Cambridge University Press.

Wright, P., A. Lickorish, & R. Milroy. (1994). "Remember while mousing: The cognitive cost of mouse clicks." *SIGCHI Bulletin*. 26: (1)41–45.

Zahn, C.T. (1971). "Graph-theoretical methods for detecting and describing gestalt clusters." *IEEE Transactions on Computers, X-20*. 68–86.

Zhan, P., R.R. Bishu, & M.W. Riley. (1993). "Screen layout and semantic structure in iconic menu design." *Proceedings of the Fifth International Conference on Human-Computer Interaction*.

Zwaga, H.J., & T. Boersema. (1983). "Evaluation of a set of graphics symbols." *Applied Ergonomics*. 14: 43–54.

Zwahlen, H.T., & N. Kothari. (1986). "The effects of dark and light character CRT displays upon VDT operator performance, eye scanning behavior, pupil diameter and subjective comfort/discomfort." *Proceedings: International Scientific Conference: Work with Display Units*. May 12–15, Stockholm, Sweden.

Index